Machine Learning Algorithms Using Scikit and TensorFlow Environments

Puvvadi Baby Maruthi
Dayananda Sagar University, India

Smrity Prasad
Dayananda Sagar University, India

Amit Kumar Tyagi
Vellore Institute of Technology, Chennai, India

A volume in the Advances in Systems Analysis,
Software Engineering, and High Performance
Computing (ASASEHPC) Book Series

Published in the United States of America by
IGI Global
Engineering Science Reference (an imprint of IGI Global)
701 E. Chocolate Avenue
Hershey PA, USA 17033
Tel: 717-533-8845
Fax: 717-533-8661
E-mail: cust@igi-global.com
Web site: http://www.igi-global.com

Copyright © 2024 by IGI Global. All rights reserved. No part of this publication may be reproduced, stored or distributed in any form or by any means, electronic or mechanical, including photocopying, without written permission from the publisher. Product or company names used in this set are for identification purposes only. Inclusion of the names of the products or companies does not indicate a claim of ownership by IGI Global of the trademark or registered trademark.

Library of Congress Cataloging-in-Publication Data

Names: Maruthi, Puvvadi Baby, 1986- editor. | Prasad, Smrity, 1978- editor.

Title: Machine learning algorithms using Scikit and TensorFlow environments
 / edited by Puvvadi Baby Maruthi, Smrity Prasad, Amit Kumar Tyagi.
Description: Hershey, PA : Engineering Science Reference, [2024] | Includes
 bibliographical references and index. | Summary: "Machine Learning
 Algorithms Using Scikit and TensorFlow Environments assists researchers
 in learning and implementing these critical algorithms. Covering key
 topics such as classification, artificial neural networks, prediction,
 random forest, and regression analysis, this premier reference source is
 ideal for industry professionals, computer scientists, researchers,
 academicians, scholars, practitioners, instructors, and students"--
 Provided by publisher.
Identifiers: LCCN 2023011165 (print) | LCCN 2023011166 (ebook) | ISBN
 9781668485316 (hardcover) | ISBN 9781668485323 (paperback) | ISBN
 9781668485330 (ebook)
Subjects: LCSH: Machine learning. | Neural networks (Computer science) |
 Computer algorithms. | TensorFlow.
Classification: LCC Q325.5 .M32132 2023 (print) | LCC Q325.5 (ebook) |
 DDC 006.3/1--dc23/eng20230626
LC record available at https://lccn.loc.gov/2023011165
LC ebook record available at https://lccn.loc.gov/2023011166

This book is published in the IGI Global book series Advances in Systems Analysis, Software Engineering, and High Performance Computing (ASASEHPC) (ISSN: 2327-3453; eISSN: 2327-3461)

British Cataloguing in Publication Data
A Cataloguing in Publication record for this book is available from the British Library.

All work contributed to this book is new, previously-unpublished material. The views expressed in this book are those of the authors, but not necessarily of the publisher.

For electronic access to this publication, please contact: eresources@igi-global.com.

Advances in Systems Analysis, Software Engineering, and High Performance Computing (ASASEHPC) Book Series

Vijayan Sugumaran
Oakland University, USA

ISSN:2327-3453
EISSN:2327-3461

MISSION

The theory and practice of computing applications and distributed systems has emerged as one of the key areas of research driving innovations in business, engineering, and science. The fields of software engineering, systems analysis, and high performance computing offer a wide range of applications and solutions in solving computational problems for any modern organization.

The **Advances in Systems Analysis, Software Engineering, and High Performance Computing (ASASEHPC) Book Series** brings together research in the areas of distributed computing, systems and software engineering, high performance computing, and service science. This collection of publications is useful for academics, researchers, and practitioners seeking the latest practices and knowledge in this field.

COVERAGE

- Engineering Environments
- Computer Graphics
- Storage Systems
- Software Engineering
- Enterprise Information Systems
- Computer Networking
- Distributed Cloud Computing
- Metadata and Semantic Web
- Performance Modelling
- Virtual Data Systems

IGI Global is currently accepting manuscripts for publication within this series. To submit a proposal for a volume in this series, please contact our Acquisition Editors at Acquisitions@igi-global.com or visit: http://www.igi-global.com/publish/.

The Advances in Systems Analysis, Software Engineering, and High Performance Computing (ASASEHPC) Book Series (ISSN 2327-3453) is published by IGI Global, 701 E. Chocolate Avenue, Hershey, PA 17033-1240, USA, www.igi-global.com. This series is composed of titles available for purchase individually; each title is edited to be contextually exclusive from any other title within the series. For pricing and ordering information please visit http://www.igi-global.com/book-series/advances-systems-analysis-software-engineering/73689. Postmaster: Send all address changes to above address. Copyright © 2024 IGI Global. All rights, including translation in other languages reserved by the publisher. No part of this series may be reproduced or used in any form or by any means – graphics, electronic, or mechanical, including photocopying, recording, taping, or information and retrieval systems – without written permission from the publisher, except for non commercial, educational use, including classroom teaching purposes. The views expressed in this series are those of the authors, but not necessarily of IGI Global.

Titles in this Series

For a list of additional titles in this series, please visit: http://www.igi-global.com/book-series/advances-systems-analysis-software-engineering/73689

ODE, BVP, and 1D PDE Solvers for Scientific and Engineering Problems With MATLAB Basics
Leonid Burstein (ORT Braude College of Engineering, Israel (Retired))
Engineering Science Reference • copyright 2024 • 300pp • H/C (ISBN: 9781668468500) • US $245.00 (our price)

Digital Technologies in Modeling and Management Insights in Education and Industry
GS Prakasha (Christ University, India) Maria Lapina (North-Caucasus Federal University, Russia) and Deepanraj Balakrishnan (Prince Mohammad Bin Fahd University, Saudi Arabia)
Information Science Reference • copyright 2024 • 320pp • H/C (ISBN: 9781668495766) • US $250.00 (our price)

The Software Principles of Design for Data Modeling
Debabrata Samanta (Rochester Institute of Technology, Kosovo)
Engineering Science Reference • copyright 2023 • 318pp • H/C (ISBN: 9781668498095) • US $270.00 (our price)

Investigations in Pattern Recognition and Computer Vision for Industry 4.0
Chiranji Lal Chowdhary (Vellore Institute of Technology, Vellore, India) Basanta Kumar Swain (Government College of Engineering, Bhawanipatna, India) and Vijay Kumar (Dr B R Ambedkar National Institute of Technology Jalandhar, India)
Engineering Science Reference • copyright 2023 • 276pp • H/C (ISBN: 9781668486023) • US $270.00 (our price)

Cyber-Physical System Solutions for Smart Cities
Vanamoorthy Muthumanikandan (Vellore Institute of Technology, Chennai, India) Anbalagan Bhuvaneswari (Vellore Institute of Technology, Chennai, India) Balamurugan Easwaran (University of Africa, Toru-Orua, Nigeria) and T. Sudarson Rama Perumal (Rohini College of Engineering and Technology, India)
Engineering Science Reference • copyright 2023 • 182pp • H/C (ISBN: 9781668477564) • US $270.00 (our price)

Cyber-Physical Systems and Supporting Technologies for Industrial Automation
R. Thanigaivelan (A.K.T. Memorial College of Engineering and Technology, India) S. Kaliappan (Velammal Institute of Technology, India) and C. Jegadheesan (Kongu Engineering College, India)
Engineering Science Reference • copyright 2023 • 444pp • H/C (ISBN: 9781668492673) • US $270.00 (our price)

Perspectives and Considerations on the Evolution of Smart Systems
Maki K. Habib (American University in Cairo, Egypt)
Engineering Science Reference • copyright 2023 • 419pp • H/C (ISBN: 9781668476840) • US $325.00 (our price)

701 East Chocolate Avenue, Hershey, PA 17033, USA
Tel: 717-533-8845 x100 • Fax: 717-533-8661
E-Mail: cust@igi-global.com • www.igi-global.com

Editorial Advisory Board

Abdullah, *College of Engineering and Technology, Adigrat University, Ethiopia*

G. Aghila, *National Institute of Technology, Trichy, India*

Shakeel Ahmed, *College of Computer Sciences and Information Technology, King Faisal University, Saudi Arabia*

Hamid Ali Abed Al-Asadi, *Communications Engineering Department, Iraq University College, Iraq*

Samaher Al-Janabi, *Faculty of Science for Women, University of Babylon, Iraq*

Jani Anabarsi, *School of Computer Science and Engineering, Vellore Institute of Technology, Chennai, India*

Micheal Olaolu Arowolo, *Department of Computer Science, Landmark University, Omu-Aran, Nigeria*

Nebojša Bačanin-Džakula, *Singidunum University, Serbia*

Aswani Kumar Cherukuri, *School of Information Technology and Engineering, Vellore Institute of Technology, India*

Govindarajan, *BACI Pvt. Ltd., India*

Vijayalakshmi Kakulapati, *Sreenidhi Institute of Science and Technology, India*

Kiran Kumar, *BACI Pvt. Ltd ., India*

Magdy Mahmoud, *Computer Science and Information System, Ismailia, Egypt*

Yassine Maleh, *SMIEEE, Sultan Moulay Slimane University, Morocco*

Saad Motahhir, *Mohamed Ben Abdellah University, Morocco*

Tuan Anh Nguyen, *Vietnam Academy of Science and Technology, Hanoi, Vietnam*

Awujoola Olalekan, *Nigerian Defence Academy, Kaduna, Nigeria*

C. Prabhu, *Financial Software and Systems Ltd., India*

Pachhaiammal Alias Priya, *Computer Science and Engineering, Sri Sairam Institute of Technology, India*

Mahmoud Ragab, *Information Technology Department, Faculty of Computing and Information Technology, King Abdulaziz University, Saudi Arabia*

G. Rekha, *Koneru Lakshmaiah Education Foundation University, India*

T. Ruso, *Wipro Ltd., India*

Yakub Kayode Saheed, *School of IT and Computing, American University of Nigeria, Nigeria*

Thamari Selvam, *Zoho, India*

Abdelhakim Senhaji Hafid, *Université de Montréal, Canada*

Alan D. Smith, *Department of Marketing, Robert Morris University, USA*

N. Sreenath, *Puducherry Technological University, India*

Rehena Sulthana, *Independent Researcher, India*
Loai Tawalbeh, *SMIEEE, Texas A&M University, San Antonio, USA*

Table of Contents

Detailed Table of Contents

Chapter 1

Amit Majumder, National Institute of Technology, Jamshedpur, India

Classification is the process of identifying, understanding, and grouping objects and ideas into specified categories. These pre-categorized training datasets are used by machine learning techniques to classify datasets into relevant and acceptable categories. Using the incoming training data, machine learning classifiers assess the chance or probability that the incoming data will fall into one of the established categories. One of categorization's most prominent applications is used by the largest email service providers of today: classifying emails as "spam" or "non-spam." In essence, classification is a form of "pattern recognition." Following the application of classification algorithms to the training data, the same pattern (similar number sequences, words, or attitudes, etc.) is found in future data sets. Classification falls within the category of supervised learning in the context of machine learning.

Chapter 2

Aryan Chopra, Vellore Institute of Technology, India
Aditya Modi, Vellore Institute of Technology, India
Brijendra Singh, Vellore Institute of Technology, India

Machine learning plays a vital role in all major sectors like healthcare, banking, finance, and marketing. There is a need to understand the role and working of ML algorithms in a better way. Google also uses a learning algorithm to rank the web pages whenever we try to browse the internet to get the desired information. Understanding the platform and working of these algorithms is crucial for researchers. In this chapter, the authors have presented an overview of machine learning fundamentals and the working of these algorithms with suitable examples. They have also highlighted the importance of major machine learning libraries like TensorFlow and SciKit in developing and deploying vast applications. Finally, a case study of ML application is presented to better understand the concept. Future prospects of ML applications are also depicted in detail.

    Aswathy Ravikumar, Vellore Institute of Technology, Chennai, India
    Harini Sriraman, Vellore Institute of Technology, Chennai, India

In academia and business, deep-learning-based models have exhibited extraordinary performance over the last decade. The learning potential of Convolutional Neural Networks (CNNs) derives from a combination of several feature extraction levels that completely use a vast quantity of input. CNN is an important technique for tackling computer vision issues, although the theories behind its processing efficacy are not yet completely understood. CNN has achieved cutting-edge performance on a variety of datasets in computer vision applications like remote sensing, medical image categorization, facial detection, and object identification. This is due to the efficiency with which they process visual features. This chapter presents the most significant advancements in CNN for efficient processing in computer vision, including convolutional layer configurations, pooling layer approaches, network activation functions, loss functions, normalization approaches, and CNN optimization techniques.

    Aswathy Ravikumar, Vellore Institute of Technology, Chennai, India
    Harini Sriraman, Vellore Institute of Technology, Chennai, India

Long Short-Term Memory (LSTM) is a specific kind of recurrent neural network (RNN) structure that addresses the constraints of conventional RNNs in effectively capturing and learning long-term relationships in sequential input. In this chapter, the authors examine the LSTM cell and its modifications to investigate the LSTM cell's capability for learning. Furthermore, future study prospects for LSTM networks are outlined. LSTM networks have gotten extensive attention in scientific papers, technical websites, and deployment manuals because of their efficacy in a variety of practical situations. Gradient-based learning techniques used in RNNs are too slow because as the error is transmitted back, it disappears, resulting in a much more extended learning period. LSTMs handle the issue with a novel additive gradient design that incorporates direct access towards the forget gate's activations, allowing the network to promote desirable behavior from the error gradient by updating the gates often at each time step of learning.

    Sudhir Kumar Mohapatra, Sri Sri University, India
    Anbesaw Belete, Werabe University, Ethiopia
    Ali Hussen, Werabe University, Ethiopia
    Abdelah Behari, Werabe University, Ethiopia
    Seid Huseen, Werabe University, Ethiopia
    Srinivas Prasad, GITAM University, India

Agricultural production is among the key techniques for alleviating extreme poverty, boosting economic stability, and feeding the 9.7 billion people expected to live by 2050. However, crop diseases are major obstacles to agriculture production. The most prevalent diseases that reduce production are late diseases which attack the leaves, which are particularly prevalent in coffee crops. To solve the issue, a suitable approach for identifying and categorizing these illnesses in this crop's leaf is required. Particularly in coffee crops, rust, coffee wilt, and brown spot are the most common diseases. Therefore, automatic identifying of these diseases through the system is critical. Thus, the main objective of this study is to design an automated system that can recognize and classify coffee leaf diseases' severity levels. Design science research methodology will follow. Accordingly, the required images have been collected from the SNNP.

COVID-19 is the contagious ailment caused by Sars-Cov-2. This causative 2019-nCoV is a communication to the lines of millions of people. This study employs ML and DL epitomes to determine sickness along with predicting if a person is afflicted with the virus as the previous reports can examine the data pre-processing, feature extraction, classification, evaluation of experimental results to find advanced fact-finding directions around COVID-19 classification employing machine-deep approaches. The comparison shows that chest x-rays and CT are the most frequently used data in the diagnosis of COVID-19 rather than RT-PCR, and that the most-used test techniques were found to be insensitive and less beneficial after changing the limited number of datasets. This study suggests image preprocessing, exploratory data analysis, feature extraction (LBP), and other ML as well as DL classification methods. It attempts to minimise some of the issues that have been addressed for early identification for future work and studies.

Machine learning (ML) models have made significant strides in disease prediction, providing new avenues for early detection and intervention. These models have demonstrated remarkable capabilities in analysing vast and complex datasets to identify patterns and trends that can aid in early diagnosis and treatment. However, opacity of these models often leaves healthcare practitioners and patients in the dark about the reasoning behind their predictions, raising concerns about trust, fairness, and practical adoption of AI-based disease prediction. This review delves into the critical topic of interpretability in ML models for disease prediction, its importance, techniques to achieve it, impact on clinical decision-making, challenges, and implications in healthcare. Urgent issues and moral dilemmas pertaining to model interpretability in healthcare, areas for further research to enhance interpretability of predictive models, and applications are also highlighted. Thus, the chapter provides insights into the applicability of AI-driven models to improve healthcare decision-making and patient outcomes.

The integration of deep learning in healthcare holds tremendous promise for improving patient care and medical research. However, this transformation comes with ethical considerations and privacy challenges that demand careful examination. An effort is made to explore fundamental ethical principles, data privacy issues, and the impact of bias and fairness on healthcare AI. It scrutinizes the critical need for informed consent, patient rights, and adherence to regulatory frameworks. The work established in this chapter highlights transparency and explainability as essential aspects of responsible AI deployment in healthcare services. Furthermore, the chapter also offers additional information on ethical decision-making frameworks, mechanisms for accountability, and auditing in deep learning projects. Case studies and real-world examples illustrate these concepts, guiding practitioners and researchers in their quest to navigate the intricate intersection of ethics and privacy in healthcare deep learning.

Chapter 9

A. Sivasangari, Sathyabama Institute of Science and Technology, India
V. J. K. Kishor Sonti, Sathyabama Institute of Science and Technology, India
L. Suji Helen, Sathyabama Institute of Science and Technology, India
D. Deepa, Sathyabama Institute of Science and Technology, India
T. Samraj Lawrence, College of Engineering and Technology, Ethiopia

The prominence of technological progress is evident only when its fruits reaching the society. Any disruptive technology has such a profound effect; artificial intelligence is not an exception. This chapter highlights one such technological impact for the benefit of mankind. Alzheimer's is a known neurological illness, sometimes leading to terminal stage of human life. The treatment becomes complicated when diagnosis takes place at a later stage of the disease. The prognosis and diagnosis, if supported by a technology such as artificial intelligence, will be made better by delaying the disease progression. In this chapter, machine learning algorithms such as random forest, cross validation method is used to analyze, train, and predict Alzheimer's disease and its progression. This in turn helps in improving the emotional support system to the patients. Several research groups are working on this domain, and here the insights provided are going to be more significant and useful for further investigations.

Chapter 10

Swadeep Swadeep, Vellore Institute of Technology, Chennai, India
Karmel Arockiasamy, Vellore Institute of Technology, Chennai, India
Karthika Perumal, Vellore Institute of Technology, Chennai, India

In modern times, it has become common practice for major corporations to utilize computers for storing data. Unfortunately, the frequency of malware attacks has increased, which facilitates unauthorized individuals' access to private information. Analyzing malware has become a critical task in safeguarding information systems against malicious attacks. Therefore, machine learning techniques have become an effective tool for automating investigations using static and dynamic analysis, combining malware with similar behavior into separate families based on proximity. Deep learning techniques improve the accuracy of malware variant detection and classification by building neural networks with more potentially different layers. This research aims to address this issue by training machine learning models using various algorithms on a dataset obtained by performing static and dynamic analysis on both malicious and benign samples. The resulting models were then combined to produce superior results compared to those obtained from a single model, which can be seen in the results.

Chapter 11

Improved Breast Cancer Detection in Mammography Images: Integration of Convolutional Neural Network and Local Binary Pattern Approach 221

Olalekan Joel Awujoola, Nigerian Defence Academy, Nigeria
Theophilus Enem Aniemeka, Nigerian Airforce Institute of Technology, Nigeria
Francisca N. Ogwueleka, University of Abuja, Nigeria
Oluwasegun Abiodun Abioye, Nigerian Defence Academy, Nigeria
Abidemi Elizabeth Awujoola, Nigerian Defence Academy, Nigeria
Celestine Ozoemenam Uwa, Nigerian Defence Academy, Nigeria

Cancer, characterized by uncontrolled cell division, is an incurable ailment, with breast cancer being the most prevalent form globally. Early detection remains critical in reducing mortality rates. Medical imaging is vital for localizing and diagnosing breast cancer, providing key insights for identification. This study introduces an automatic hybrid feature recognition method for breast cancer diagnosis using images from two mammography datasets. The method employs a convolutional neural network (CNN) and local binary pattern (LBP) for feature extraction. Correlation-based feature selection techniques reduce dimensionality, enabling faster computation and improved accuracy. The proposed model's superiority is established through comparative analysis with cutting-edge deep models, achieving 96% accuracy across the MIAS and INbreast datasets. The hybrid method demonstrates high accuracy with minimal computational tasks.

Chapter 12

Predicting Depression From Social Media Users by Using Lexicons and Machine Learning Algorithms 249

Santhi Selvaraj, Mepco Schlenk Engineering College, India
S. Selva Nidhyananthan, Mepco Schlenk Engineering College, India

Depression is one of the most common health issues among individuals. The rate of psychotic treatments is increasing day by day. Depression is created in many ways among the people, especially through work stress, financial burden, unemployment among the adults. Today, the emergence of social media into people's lives makes them expose their feelings and emotions on the social media platforms. The aim of this work is to predict the depressive features from social media users' comments by using machine learning techniques. Multinomial naïve bayes, non-linear support vector machine, and artificial neural network methods are used for classifying the features and comparing it using performance evaluation metrics and get the best classifier. This system includes data pre-processing, feature extraction, data splitting, classification, and performance evaluation. The results show that the proposed system has gradually improved performance accuracy. According to the results, ANN gives 99.19%, the best accuracy compared to other machine learning classifiers.

Chapter 13

Mental Stress Detection Using Bidirectional Encoder Representations From Transformers 266

A. Vennila, Kongu Engineering College, India
S. Balambigai, Kongu Engineering College, India
A. S. Renugadevi, Kongu Engineering College, India
J. Charanya, Kongu Engineering College, India

It seems as if people start losing control as they become easily upset, frustrated, and overwhelmed, having problems in resting and quieting their mind, and also feeling bad about themselves, lonely, worthless, and depressed, and avoiding others. If they have experienced the above symptoms, then there is a chance that they are suffering from mental stress. They have to take proper care of their mental health. Stress can be taken care of if it is properly handled and for that detection of stress or the mental state is necessary to provide proper care. The first step in stress detection is sentiment analysis of the users' daily conversations. The authors have proposed an NLP model and have trained it to produce a score for the input ranging between 0 and 1 where 0 is the negative end and 1 is the positive end. The trained model can predict the scores with an accuracy of above 92% on Twitter.

Chapter 14

K. G. Suma, VIT-AP University, India

Gurram Sunitha, Mohan Babu University, India

Mohammad Gouse Galety, Samarkand International University of Technology, Uzbekistan

Colorectal cancer holds a prominent place on the global health landscape. Its early detection is crucial for successful patient outcomes. Histological analysis of tissue samples plays an indispensable role in diagnosing and classifying colorectal cancer. Accurate classification is paramount, as it influences the choice of treatment and patient prognosis. This chapter investigates the statistics surrounding colorectal cancer, its vital role in the healthcare sector, and the transformative potential of artificial intelligence in automating its diagnosis. This chapter proposes a ShuffleNetV2-CRNN (SCRNN), a novel deep learning architecture designed for colorectal cancer classification from histological images. SCRNN combines the efficiency of ShuffleNetV2 for feature extraction with the context-awareness of a convolutional-recurrent neural network for precise classification. SCRNN is evaluated against chosen deep models – Simple CNN, vGG16, ResNet-18, and MobileNet. Experimental results demonstrate appreciable performance of SCRNN across a diverse range of tissue types.

Chapter 15

M. Parvathi, BVRIT HYDERABAD College of Engineering for Women, India

In the scenario of growing technologies towards single digit nanometer range, the existing algorithmic contemporary test methods have become inadequate in detecting all the faults within the static random access memory. To address the issues related to contemporary test methods, machine learning-based test analysis is proposed, which elevates the method of dataset preparation using various process parameters that are drawn from functional fault models (FFMs). The outcome of this proposed work is modeling of FFMs using ML regression, classification, and further prediction with accuracy analysis. The experiments resulted that logistic regression is best suited model that resulting with high accuracy in the range of 95% to 97%, compared to the linear regression model that results in accuracy levels in the range of 26.58% to 63%.

Chapter 16

Richa Singh, BIT Mesra, India
Amit Kumar Tyagi, National Institute of Fashion Technology, New Delhi, India
Senthil Kumar Arumugam, Christ University, Bangalore, India

Industry is defined as the production of goods and services through the transformation of raw materials and resources into valuable products. It involves the creation of finished products or services through various stages of production that may include manufacturing, processing, assembly, packaging, and distribution. Industries have played a significant role in the economic growth and development of nations throughout history. They have contributed to the creation of employment opportunities, the development of new technologies, and the improvement of living standards. Over the years, the industrial sector has gone through numerous changes, and each of these changes has been termed as an "Industry Revolution."

Chapter 17

Amit Kumar Tyagi, National Institute of Fashion Technology, New Delhi, India

Dew computing is an emerging paradigm that extends the edge computing concept by leveraging the resources available in the surrounding environment. This chapter presents a state-of-the-art review of dew computing, including its definition, characteristics, and architecture. The authors also discuss the opportunities and challenges of dew computing and provide a comprehensive survey of recent research efforts in this area. Specifically, they highlight the potential of dew computing to address the challenges of resource-constrained devices, increase data privacy and security, and improve network efficiency. However, several research challenges need to be addressed, including resource management, security, privacy, and interoperability. They discuss the future research directions and potential applications of dew computing in various domains, such as healthcare, smart cities, and the internet of things (IoT). In summary, dew computing has the potential to revolutionize the way we perceive and utilize computing resources and opens up a new research frontier for computer science and engineering.

Chapter 18

Amit Kumar Tyagi, National Institute of Fashion Technology, New Delhi, India
Shrikant Tiwari, Galgotias University, Greater Noida, India

The integration of artificial intelligence (AI) and blockchain technologies represents a powerful synergy with the potential to revolutionize various industries. This chapter explores the promising future of AI in blockchain applications, shedding light on the significant impacts, challenges, and opportunities it offers. AI's capabilities in data analysis, pattern recognition, and automation find natural alignment with blockchain's immutable, transparent, and decentralized ledger technology. The chapter examines several key use cases where AI and blockchain intersect, including supply chain management, healthcare, finance, and smart contracts. It also discusses the challenges of scalability, data privacy, and regulatory compliance, and how AI can address or mitigate these issues. Furthermore, the chapter highlights the opportunities for innovation and disruption in emerging AI-powered blockchain applications, such as self-executing smart contracts, fraud detection, and identity verification.

The transformative effects of ChatGPT, an advanced AI language model, on the modern era of education and society are profound. This work explores these effects from the perspectives of both society and industry, shedding light on the far-reaching implications of this technology. ChatGPT, an AI tool which is developed by OpenAI, represents a significant leap in natural language understanding and generation, making it a valuable tool in education, communication, and problem-solving. Its applications spread from personalized learning support to enhancing customer service, streamlining administrative tasks, and facilitating innovative approaches to knowledge dissemination. However, alongside the benefits, this work also discusses/addresses the ethical and privacy issues and potential challenges associated with the global adoption of ChatGPT in educational and societal contexts.

The branch of computer science and artificial intelligence known as machine learning is used to program machines to learn. Algorithms for machine learning are software programs or methods used to find hidden patterns in data, predict outcomes, and improve performance based on past performance. A technique used in machine learning called ensemble learning combines several models, such as classifiers or experts that have been carefully constructed to solve a particular computational intelligence problem. Ensemble refers to a collaborative effort to create a single impact. An ensemble can predict events more accurately and perform better in general than a single contributor. A random forest is a technique for ensemble learning in which many decision trees are combined to create the forest. This chapter covers the fundamentals of ensemble learning using random forest, implementation with real-world examples, and developing a model.

Preface

The intersection of machine learning and practical applications has reshaped the landscape of technology, ushering in an era where intelligent systems are not only conceivable but integral to solving complex problems. This book discusses about the realm of Machine Learning Algorithms, utilizing the powerful capabilities of the Scikit-learn and TensorFlow environments. Machine learning algorithms are at the forefront of innovation, driving advancements in diverse fields such as healthcare, finance, and information technology. This book explains the potential of these algorithms, offering a comprehensive exploration of their principles, applications, and implementation. Scikit-learn, a versatile and user-friendly machine learning library, provides an accessible entry point for enthusiasts and professionals alike. With a rich array of tools for data preprocessing, model selection, and evaluation, Scikit-learn is a cornerstone in the journey toward mastering machine learning techniques. Complementing this, we discuss about the sophisticated capabilities of TensorFlow, an open-source machine learning framework developed by the Google Brain team. TensorFlow's flexibility and scalability make it an indispensable tool for building and deploying machine learning models, particularly in scenarios demanding deep neural networks and complex data structures. Further few works on Industry 6.0, Dew computing, etc., have been included for in this book for future readers/ researchers.

We assure that our book will be more helpful to beginners and practitioners through the intricacies of machine learning, starting with fundamental concepts and gradually progressing to advanced algorithms. Hands-on examples and practical implementations (of various sectors like education, healthcare, etc.) using Scikit-learn and TensorFlow are woven throughout, ensuring a pragmatic understanding of the material.

Hence, whether we are a student aspiring to enter the realm of machine learning, or a researcher pushing the boundaries of artificial intelligence/ blockchain Technology, or a academicians/professional who is seeking to enhance our skill set, this book aims to be a reliable companion on our journey to all.

Thanks

Puvvadi Baby Maruthi
Dayananda Sagar University, India

Smrity Prasad
Dayananda Sagar University, India

Amit Kumar Tyagi
National Institute of Fashion Technology, New Delhi, India

Acknowledgment

First of all, we would to extend our gratitude to my Family Members, Friends, and Supervisors, which stood with us as an advisor in completing this book. Also, we would like to thanks our almighty "God" who makes us to write this book.

We would like to extend our heartfelt gratitude to the management and leadership team of our University/ Institute and for their unwavering support and encouragement throughout our research activities. Their commitment to fostering a conducive research environment and providing essential technical support has been instrumental in the successful completion of this book project on Machine Learning/ Tensor Flow.

We also thank IGI Global Publishers (who has provided their continuous support during this COVID 19 Pandemic) and my friends/ colleagues with whom we have work together inside the college/ university and others outside of the college/ university who have provided their continuous support towards completing this book on Machine Learning Algorithms Using Scikit and TensorFlow Environments.

Chapter 1
Classification Models in Machine Learning Techniques

Amit Majumder

National Institute of Technology, Jamshedpur, India

ABSTRACT

Classification is the process of identifying, understanding, and grouping objects and ideas into specified categories. These pre-categorized training datasets are used by machine learning techniques to classify datasets into relevant and acceptable categories. Using the incoming training data, machine learning classifiers assess the chance or probability that the incoming data will fall into one of the established categories. One of categorization's most prominent applications is used by the largest email service providers of today: classifying emails as "spam" or "non-spam." In essence, classification is a form of "pattern recognition." Following the application of classification algorithms to the training data, the same pattern (similar number sequences, words, or attitudes, etc.) is found in future data sets. Classification falls within the category of supervised learning in the context of machine learning.

1. WHAT IS CLASSIFICATION?

Classification is the process of identifying, understanding, and grouping objects and ideas into specified categories. These pre-categorized training datasets are used by machine learning techniques to classify datasets into relevant and acceptable categories.

Using the incoming training data, machine learning classifiers assess the chance or probability that the incoming data will fall into one of the established categories. One of categorization's most prominent applications is used by the largest email service providers of today: classifying emails as "spam" or "non-spam" (Dada et al., 2019). In essence, classification is a form of "pattern recognition." Following the application of classification algorithms to the training data, the same pattern (similar number sequences, words, or attitudes, etc.) is found in future data sets.

Classification falls within the category of supervised learning in the context of machine learning. While learning is being done under supervision, the data being fed to an algorithm or network for clas-

DOI: 10.4018/978-1-6684-8531-6.ch001

Copyright © 2024, IGI Global. Copying or distributing in print or electronic forms without written permission of IGI Global is prohibited.

sification has already been labelled, with the key characteristics/attributes having already been divided into distinct groups.

The act of sending data into a neural network or any machine learning algorithms and allowing it to recognise patterns in the data is known as "training" a model. To build a model for classification task it needs input data or input example in the format of features and the tag or the class label of the example. The data in feature format is processed during the training phase to generate predicted output. Both the features and the labels of the training data are provided to the network or machine learning algorithm as input during training for a supervised classification type work, but only the features are fed as input to the network during testing.

During training it needs data from a number of examples. For example, to classify a person as male or female it needs to consider data (feature data or attribute data e.g., hair length, height etc. of a person) of some male persons and some female persons. Here each person is considered as an example. The set of example's data which is also called a dataset is split into training and testing sets, which are two distinct sets of inputs. Since the model has already discovered the patterns in this collection of data, testing the classifier on the same dataset that it was trained on would be extremely biased. Instead, the dataset is divided into two sets: a training set that the classifier uses to refine its predictions, and a testing set that the classifier has never seen before. The primary objective of a classification algorithm is to determine the category of a given dataset, and these algorithms are frequently applied to forecast the results for categorical data.

An illustration of supervised categorization is shown in Figure 1. Breast cancer patients' benign and malignant tumours are identified in the dataset. By fitting a straight line through the data, the supervised classification algorithm will try to divide tumours into two groups. Based on the straight-line categorization, subsequent data can subsequently be categorised as benign or malignant. Only two discrete outputs

Figure 1. Classification example

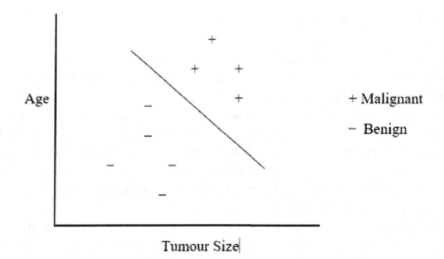

are shown in Figure 1, although there might be many more categories (benign, Type 1 malignant, Type 2 malignant, etc.).

An algorithm that performs classification on a dataset is called a classifier. There are mainly two types of classification. One is binary classification and the other type is multi-class classification:

Binary Classifier: The term "Binary Classifier" refers to a classification problem where there are only two possible outputs like *YES* or *NO*, *PLAY* or *NOT TO PLAY*, *MALE* or FEMALE etc.

Multi-class Classifier: A classification problem is referred to be a Multi-class Classifier if there are more than two possible outputs. Classifying images into different categories like dog, cat, horse etc., classifying words into different parts-of-speech (POS) tag, emotion detection etc. are some examples of multi-class classification.

2. CLASSIFICATION ALGORITHMS

Scikit-Learn makes a wide range of classification algorithms (Dada et al., 2019; Mukhamediev et al., 2015) accessible. These classifiers include:

- Naive Bayes
- K-Nearest Neighbour
- Decision Trees
- Logistic Regression
- Support Vector Machine (SVM)

2.1 Naive Bayes

The Bayes theorem, which makes use of prior information and naive assumptions that the input features exhibit substantial independence from one another, calculates probabilistic categorization.

As an illustration, the classifier may assign an apple to the categories of fruit, red colour, and round form, but each of these labels will be assigned separately. The most popular, quick, and straightforward machine learning classification algorithm, it performs well even with modest amounts of training data.

Mathematically, the Bayes theorem is stated as:

$$P(A|B) = P(B|A) * P(A) / P(B)$$

where,

- $P(A|B)$ represents the probability of happening event A, given that event B has occurred
- $P(B|A)$ represents the probability of happening event B, given that event A has occurred
- $P(A)$ is the probability of the event A
- $P(B)$ is the probability of the event B

2.2 K-Nearest Neighbour

K-Nearest Neighbour is a straightforward machine learning algorithm that relies on the supervised learning technique. When using the K-NN algorithm, it is assumed that the new case and the existing cases can be compared and categorized into the most similar category. When all the existing data is stored, the K-NN algorithm uses similarity to determine the classification of a new data point. The utilization of the K-NN method enables speedy and precise sorting of fresh data into a suitable category. The K-NN algorithm is mainly used to solve classification problems, but it can also be used to solve regression type problems.

Machine learning used in K-Nearest Neighbour classification models is instance-based and functions as a lazy learner. It doesn't create an internal model because it is a lazy learner. Instead, the n characteristics defined in this categorization are used to represent the data points in n-dimensional space.

The algorithm chooses the class that is most prevalent among the data point's k nearest neighbours. The labelled points are used to label the closest unobserved data points. The k closest neighbours' votes are tallied, and the label with the most support from those neighbours is allocated to a new location.

2.3 Decision Tree

Decision Tree algorithm is a machine learning algorithm for classification that tries to create a tree structure for visualising a decision-making model. The classification is based on the "if-then-else" scenario, which is equally comprehensive and mutually exclusive. By segmenting the dataset into subsets and selecting the most crucial features for classification, the model's branches are constructed.

Divide and conquer from the top-down is used to construct the tree. The training set eventually becomes associated with an incremental decision tree as we descend. The final classification structure has nodes and leaves that resemble a tree.

To learn and create rules, singular training data units are employed consecutively. The rows that cover a rule are removed once it has been learned. Until the termination point is reached, the same procedure is carried out on the training set.

2.4 Logistic Regression

Logistic Regression algorithm is a machine learning algorithm to classify data. A sigmoid function is used in the logistic regression model to identify the dependencies between the input and output variables and to produce class-label predictions. In order to predict a result, it makes use of numerous independent variables.

A probability output from the sigmoid function is then evaluated with a predetermined threshold in order to assign the label to the object in the appropriate way. For binary classification techniques, it works well.

Logistic regression's primary flaw is that it makes the assumption that the predictors are independent of one another and that the data are free of missing values. The logistic regression algorithm can be classified as binary, multinomial, or ordinal depending on the kind of output variable.

2.5 Random Forest

An ensemble learning technique called random forest categorization is essentially a collection of decision trees. The data from various predictors are combined through ensemble learning. It is a meta-estimator that takes into account the number of trees on various training data subsamples. Subsequently, the predictive model's accuracy is enhanced using their average. In the training phase, the classification creates a large number of decision trees, which produce output as a class, which is the mode of regression prediction of the individual trees.

2.6 Support Vector Machine (SVM)

Support Vector Machine (SVM) algorithm is very popular algorithm to classify data. A gap between the two classes and the training data points are represented by the support vector machine in the space. In N-dimensional space (where N is the number of features), the classifier seeks to locate a hyperplane that clearly assigns the data points to either of the classes. The margin is the set of data points from each class that are closest to the chosen hyperplane. The prediction is made to determine the data point category upon the entry of a new point. A non-probabilistic binary classifier is the SVM. By overfitting the data, the regularisation parameter utilised in SVMs facilitates optimization procedures. The classifier uses memory effectively and performs well in high-dimensional domains.

3. EXAMPLES OF CLASSIFICATION TASKS

Any work that requires you to group instances into two or more classes is a classification task. Identifying a cat or puppy in a photograph or a wine's quality based on characteristics like acidity and alcohol concentration are examples of categorization tasks. There many examples of classification type task. Few examples of classification task are mentioned below.

- Handwritten Digit Recognition
- Speech Recognition
- Sentiment analysis
- Email classification (Spam or Not Spam)
- Image classification
- Text classification

You should employ several classifiers depending on the categorization task that you are dealing with. Even while multiple variable logistic regression models exist, a logistic regression model, for instance, works well for binary classification tasks.

You will get a better understanding of when to utilise each classifier as you use them more frequently. Nonetheless, it is usual practise to instantiate several classifiers, compare them to one another in terms of performance, and then choose the classifier that performs the best.

4. IMPLEMENTING A CLASSIFIER IN SCIKIT-LEARN

After talking about the many classifiers that Scikit-Learn makes available, let's look at how to put a classifier into practise.

Importing the required classifier into Python is the initial step in developing a classifier. Let's examine the logistic regression import statement (Pedregosa et al., 2011):

```
from sklearn.linear_model import LogisticRegression
```

The import statements for the additional classifiers are as follows:

```
from sklearn.naive_bayes import GaussianNB
from sklearn.neighbors import KNeighborsClassifier
from sklearn.svm import LinearSVC
from sklearn.tree import DecisionTreeClassifier
```

To construct an instance of the classifier or object within your Python programme, you must first instantiate the classifier.

Usually, all that is required to accomplish this is to create a variable and call the classifier's related function:

```
clf = LogisticRegression()
```

It is now necessary to train the classifier. In order to accomplish this, the classifier must be fit with the training data.

The classifier receives the training features and training labels via the fit command:

```
clf.fit(features, labels)
```

The classifier model can make predictions on the testing data once it has been trained on the training data.

This is done by using the predict command on the classifier and giving it the features from your testing dataset as the parameters it needs to make predictions about:

```
predictions=clf.predict(test_features)
```

The fundamental workflow for classifiers in Scikit-Learn consists of these steps: instantiation, fitting/training and prediction.

Example using Logistic Regression algorithm:

```
import numpy as np
from sklearn.linear_model import LogisticRegression
X = np.array([
[-2, 4],
```

```
[4, 1],
[1, 6],
[2, 4],
[6, 2]
])
y = np.array([-1,-1,1,1,1])
clf = LogisticRegression(random_state=0).fit(X, y)
pred=clf.predict([ [4,1],[1,6] ]) # predict 2 examples with feature values [4,1] and [1,6]
print('Prediction=',pred)
Output:
Prediction= [-1 1]
```

Example using Decision Tree algorithm:

```
import numpy as np
from sklearn.tree import DecisionTreeClassifier
X = np.array([
[-2, 4],
[4, 1],
[1, 6],
[2, 4],
[6, 2]
])
y = np.array([-1,-1,1,1,1])
clf = DecisionTreeClassifier(random_state=0)
clf.fit(X, y)
pred=clf.predict([ [-2,4],[4,1], [1,6] ]) # predict 3 examples with feature values [-2,4], [4,1] and [1,6]
print('Prediction=',pred)
Output:
Prediction= [-1 -1 1]
```

Example using Support Vector Machine algorithm:

```
from sklearn.svm import SVC
import numpy as np
X = np.array([
[-2, 4],
[4, 1],
[1, 6],
[2, 4],
[6, 2]
])
y = np.array([-1,-1,1,1,1])
clf = SVC(random_state=56)
```

```
clf.fit(X, y)
pred=clf.predict([ [-2,4],[2,4], [1,6] ]) # predict 3 exaples with feature values [-2,4], [2,4] and [1,6]
print('Prediction=',pred)
Output:
Prediction= [-1 1 1]
```

Example using K-Nearest Neighbour algorithm:

```
from sklearn.neighbors import KNeighborsClassifier
import numpy as np
X = np.array([
[-2, 4],
[4, 1],
[1, 6],
[2, 4],
[6, 2]
])
y = np.array([-1,-1,1,1,1])
clf = KNeighborsClassifier(n_neighbors=3)
clf.fit(X, y)
pred=clf.predict([ [2,4], [1,6] ]) # predict 2 examples with feature values [2,4] and [1,6]
print('Prediction=',pred)
Output:
Prediction= [1 1]
```

5. EVALUATING A CLASSIFIER

There are a variety of methods you can measure the performance of a classifier (Vujovic, Z. (2021) while evaluating it.

5.1 Classification Accuracy

The most popular and straightforward technique of assessing accuracy is classification accuracy. The number of accurate predictions divided by all forecasts, or a ratio of accurate predictions to total predictions, is how classification accuracy is calculated.

Although it can offer you a fast indication of how your classifier is doing, it works best when there are nearly equal numbers of observations and examples in each class. You're generally better off using another statistic because this doesn't happen very frequently.

Table 1. Metrics to assess performance on classification and its function

Metrics to Assess Performance on Classification	Function
precision_recall_curve(y_actual, probas_pred, *)	For various probability thresholds, compute precision-recall pairings.
confusion_matrix(y_actual, y_predicted, *[, ...])	To assess a classification's accuracy, compute a confusion matrix.
classification_report(y_actual, y_predicted, *[, ...])	Create a text report that displays the key classification metrics.
precision_score(y_actual, y_predicted, *[, labels, ...])	Calculate the accuracy.
recall_score(y_actual, y_predicted, *[, labels, ...])	Determine the recall.

5.2 Loss Logarithmic

In essence, the logarithmic loss, or LogLoss, measures how certain the classifier is of its predictions. LogLoss returns probabilities for an example's membership in a specific class, adding these probabilities to indicate the classifier's overall confidence.

Prediction values range from 1 to 0, with 1 representing total confidence and 0 representing no confidence. Smaller values are preferable since the loss, or overall lack of confidence, is represented as a negative integer with 0 denoting a perfect classifier.

This measure is only applied to binary classification issues. The model's capacity to accurately distinguish between one class or another, between negative and positive examples, is shown by the area under the curve.

5.3 Confusion Matrix

An accurate model with reference to two or more classes is represented by a confusion matrix, which is a table or chart. The model's predictions will be plotted along the X-axis, while the results and accuracy will be on the y-axis.

The number of predictions the model makes is represented in the cells. In a diagonal line running from the top left to the bottom right, correct predictions can be discovered. Further information on analysing a confusion matrix can be found here.

5.4 Classification Report

A built-in statistic for classification problems in Scikit-Learn is called the classification report. The classification report can help you quickly gain an understanding of how well your model is working. Recall compares the number of cases your model classified as Class A (or another class) to the overall number of Class A examples, and this comparison is shown in the report.

Prediction and f1-score are also returned in the report. The proportion of examples that your model correctly identified as belonging to Class A (true positives against false positives) is known as precision, and the f1-score is calculated by averaging recall and precision.

6. CLASSIFICATION METRICS

The sklearn.metrics (Dada et al., 2019) module offers a variety of loss, score, and utility methods to measure classification performance. Confidence intervals, binary decision values, or probability estimates of the positive class may be required by some metrics. Most implementations allow each sample to contribute to the final score in a weighted manner using the sample weight parameter. Few metrics to assess performance on classification are mentioned in Table 1.

6.1 Precision_recall_curve

For various probability thresholds, compute precision-recall pairings. Only the binary classification task is supported by this implementation. The ratio of the number of true positives to the number of false positives, or tp/(tp + fp), is used to measure precision. Intuitively, the classifier's precision is its capacity not to classify a negative sample as positive. The ratio of the number of true positives to the number of false negatives, tp/(tp + fn), is known as the recall. The classifier's capacity to locate all the positive samples is known as recall.

Example:

```
import numpy as np
import matplotlib.pyplot as plt
from sklearn.metrics import precision_recall_curve
y_actual = np.array([0, 0, 1, 1, 1, 0, 0, 1, 1, 1 ])
y_scores = np.array([0.1, 0.4, 0.35, 0.8, 0.9, .3, 0.47, 0.35, 0.8, 0.9])
#print(sorted(list(set(y_scores.tolist()))))
precision, recall, thresholds = precision_recall_curve(y_actual, y_scores)
print(list(precision))
print(list(recall))
print(list(thresholds))
plt.plot(recall, precision, marker='.', label='Curve')
plt.xlabel('Recall')
plt.ylabel('Precision')
plt.show()
Output:
[0.6, 0.6666666666666666, 0.75, 0.6666666666666666, 0.8, 1.0, 1.0, 1.0]
[1.0, 1.0, 1.0, 0.6666666666666666, 0.6666666666666666, 0.6666666666666666, 0.3333333333333333,
    0.0]
[0.1, 0.3, 0.35, 0.4, 0.47, 0.8, 0.9]
```

6.2 Confusion Matrix

A confusion matrix, also known as an error matrix, is a compact table used to assess the effectiveness of a classification model. The number of accurate and incorrect predictions for each class is expressed using count values.

Figure 2. Output

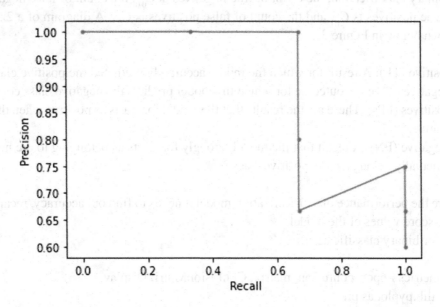

By definition, if *C* is a confusion matrix then $C_{i,j}$ is equal to the number of observations known to be in group *i* and predicted to be in group *j*

Figure 3. Confusion matrix

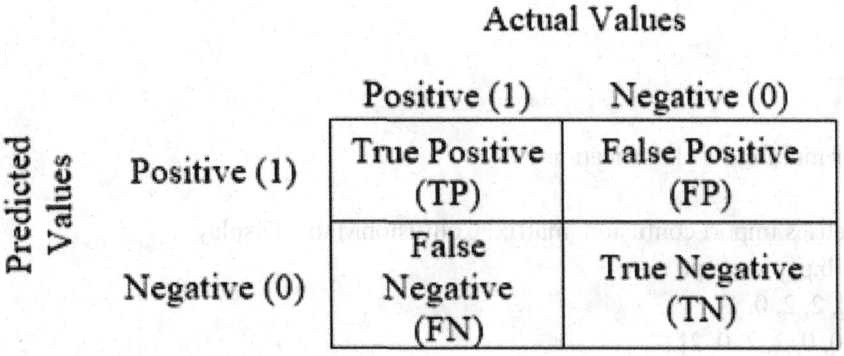

Actual Values

		Positive (1)	Negative (0)
Predicted Values	Positive (1)	True Positive (TP)	False Positive (FP)
	Negative (0)	False Negative (FN)	True Negative (TN)

Thus, in binary classification, the count of true negatives is $C_{0,0}$, the count of false negatives is $C_{1,0}$, the count of true positives is $C_{1,1}$ and the count of false positives is $C_{0,3}$. A diagram of a 2x2 confusion matrix is shown below in Figure 3.

- True Positive (TP): A result for which the model accurately predicted the positive class.
- True Negative (TN): An outcome for which the model predicts the negative class correctly.
- False Positives (FPs): These are the results that the model forecasts as positive when they are actually negative.
- False Negative (FN): A result that the model wrongly forecasts as belonging to the negative class when it actually belongs to the positive class.

To measure the performance of a classification model it needs to find out accuracy, recall, precision, specificity, f1-score values of the model.

Example (for binary classification):

```
from sklearn.metrics import confusion_matrix, ConfusionMatrixDisplay
import matplotlib.pyplot as plt
y_actual = [1, 0, 1, 0, 0, 1]
y_predicted = [1, 1, 1, 0, 1, 1]
conf_mat=confusion_matrix(y_actual, y_predicted)
print(conf_mat)
disp=ConfusionMatrixDisplay(confusion_matrix=conf_mat, display_labels=[0,1])
disp.plot()
plt.show()
```

Output:

```
[[1 2]
 [0 3]]
```

Example (for multi-class classification):

```
from sklearn.metrics import confusion_matrix, ConfusionMatrixDisplay
import matplotlib.pyplot as plt
y_actual = [2, 0, 2, 2, 0, 1]
y_predicted = [0, 0, 2, 2, 0, 2]
conf_mat =confusion_matrix(y_actual, y_predicted)
print(conf_mat)
disp = ConfusionMatrixDisplay(confusion_matrix= conf_mat, display_labels=[0,1,2])
disp.plot()
plt.show()
```

Output:

Figure 4. Output

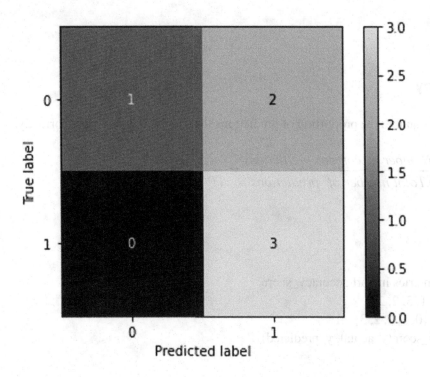

Figure 5. Output

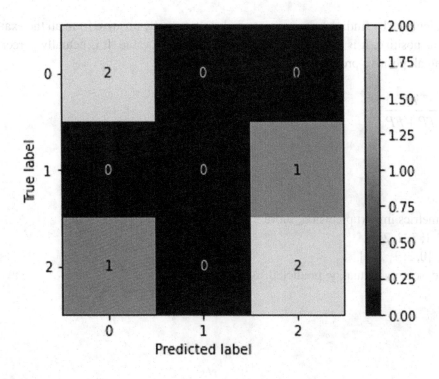

[[2 0 0]
[0 0 1]
[1 0 2]]

6.3 Accuracy

This is simply equal to the proportion of predictions that the model classified correctly.

$$Accuracy = \frac{Number\ of\ correct\ predictions}{Total\ number\ of\ predictions} = \frac{TP+TN}{TP+TN+FP+FN}$$

Example:

```
# Accuracy
from sklearn.metrics import accuracy_score
y_actual = [0, 1, 3, 2, 2]
y_predicted = [0, 3, 1, 2, 3]
print(accuracy_score(y_actual, y_predicted))
Output:
0.4
```

6.4 Precision

Precision is calculated by finding how many examples are actually positive from all the examples which are predicted as positive. It is also known as positive predictive value. It is actually percentage of true positive among all positive predictions.

$$Precision = \frac{TP}{TP+FP}$$

Example:

```
# Precision
from sklearn.metrics import precision_score
y_actual = [0, 1, 3, 2, 2]
y_predicted = [0, 3, 1, 2, 3]
print(precision_score(y_actual, y_predicted, average=None))
Output:
[1. 0. 1. 0.]
```

6.5 Recall

Recall, also known as the sensitivity, hit rate, or the true positive rate (TPR), is calculated by finding how many examples are predicted correctly from all the given positive examples. It answers the question "What proportion of actual positives was identified correctly?"

$$Recall = \frac{TP}{TP + FN}$$

Example:

```
# Recall
from sklearn.metrics import recall_score
y_actual = [0, 1, 3, 2, 2]
y_predicted = [0, 3, 1, 2, 3]
print(recall_score(y_actual, y_predicted, average=None))
Output:
[1. 0. 0.5 0. ]
```

6.6 Specificity

Specificity measures the proportion of actual negatives that are correctly identified as such. It is also known as the true negative rate (TNR). It is the opposite of recall.

$$Specificity = \frac{TN}{TN + FP}$$

6.7 F1 Score

The F1 score is the harmonic mean of precision and recall. It can have a maximum score of 1 which indicates perfect precision and recall.

$$F1\ Score = \frac{2*(precision*recall)}{precision + recall}$$

Example:

```
# f1_score
from sklearn.metrics import f1_score
y_actual = [0, 1, 3, 2, 2]
y_predicted = [0, 3, 1, 2, 3]
```

```
print(f1_score(y_actual, y_predicted, average='macro'))
print(f1_score(y_actual, y_predicted, average='micro'))
print(f1_score(y_actual, y_predicted, average='weighted'))
Output:
0.41666666666666663
0.4000000000000001
0.4666666666666666
```

REFERENCES

Dada, E. G., Bassi, J. S., Chiroma, H., Shafi'i, M. A., Adetunmbi, A. O., & Ajibuwa, O. E. (2019). Machine learning for email spam filtering: Review, approaches and open research problems. *Heliyon, 5*(6). doi:10.1016/j.heliyon.2019.e01802

Mukhamediev, R., Yakunin, K., Iskakov, S., Sainova, S., Abdilmanova, A., & Kuchin, Y. (2015). *Comparative analysis of classification algorithms.* . doi:10.1109/ICAICT.2015.7338525

Pedregosa, Varoquaux, Gramfort, Michel, Thirion, & Grisel. (2011). Scikit-learn: Machine learning in Python. *Journal of Machine Learning Research, 12*(Oct), 2825–2830.

Vujovic, Z. (2021). Classification Model Evaluation Metrics. *International Journal of Advanced Computer Science and Applications, 12*(6), 599–606. doi:10.14569/IJACSA.2021.0120670

Chapter 2
Machine Learning Algorithm With TensorFlow and SciKit for Next Generation Systems

Aryan Chopra
Vellore Institute of Technology, India

Aditya Modi
Vellore Institute of Technology, India

Brijendra Singh
iD https://orcid.org/0000-0003-2608-3388
Vellore Institute of Technology, India

ABSTRACT

Machine learning plays a vital role in all major sectors like healthcare, banking, finance, and marketing. There is a need to understand the role and working of ML algorithms in a better way. Google also uses a learning algorithm to rank the web pages whenever we try to browse the internet to get the desired information. Understanding the platform and working of these algorithms is crucial for researchers. In this chapter, the authors have presented an overview of machine learning fundamentals and the working of these algorithms with suitable examples. They have also highlighted the importance of major machine learning libraries like TensorFlow and SciKit in developing and deploying vast applications. Finally, a case study of ML application is presented to better understand the concept. Future prospects of ML applications are also depicted in detail.

1. INTRODUCTION

Since the Stone Age, humanity has used different types of tools to make life easier. The ingenuity of the human brain has in turn made many different machines possible. Machine learning is one such invention. According to Arthur Samuel Machine learning is defined as "the field of study that gives computers the

DOI: 10.4018/978-1-6684-8531-6.ch002

Copyright © 2024, IGI Global. Copying or distributing in print or electronic forms without written permission of IGI Global is prohibited.

Figure 1. Rise in popularity of ML algorithms (Sarker, 2021)

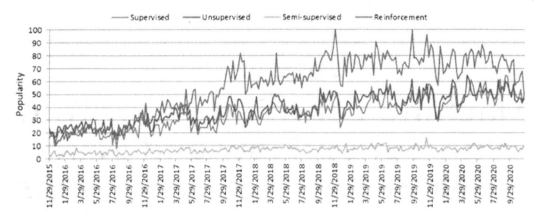

ability to learn without being explicitly programmed" (Mahesh, 2020). A quick overview of different types of Machine Learning (ML) algorithms is presented in Figure-1.

Machine learning has emerged as a crucial branch of artificial intelligence (AI) that focuses on data manipulation and modeling to make predictions and analyze complex patterns. This literature review aims to provide an overview of machine learning fundamentals, explore various machine learning algorithms, emphasize the importance of popular machine learning libraries such as TensorFlow and SciKit, and highlight the practical applications through a case study.

"The worldwide popularity score of various types of ML algorithms (supervised, unsupervised, semi-Supervised, and reinforcement) in a range of 0 (min) to 100 (max) over time where x-axis represents the timestamp information and y-axis represents the corresponding score" (Sarker, 2021).

Machine learning is a branch of AI that deals with data manipulation and model which in turn help in making predictions and graphs from the data to collectively analyze it. Through use of statistical methods algorithms make predictions ranging from cost of a stock price in a week to level of global warming increase in the next decade. With the advancement of technology, machine learning is prevalent in every facet of our life and is often use by big companies to help do behavioral analysis of the consumers and then suggest them products and services which they would be inclined to purchase, thus in turn boosting their revenue. The manipulation of data to make models which aid in prediction of next data sets is called machine learning algorithm.

Now we will discuss various types of learning methods:

1.1 Supervised Learning

Supervised learning takes place in the supervision of the teacher. For a given set of inputs we know the output or we can say the class levels are known. We can train the models based on supervised data. When we present the new data to the model, it will predict the class level which is not known to us. Classification is one of the supervised learning techniques which have lot of real world applications. For example in medical field we can classify if the cancer is benign or malignant. Figure-2 depicts the working of supervised machine learning algorithms. The goal of supervised learning is to build a predictive model that can accurately predict the output for new, unseen input data.

Figure 2. Supervised learning

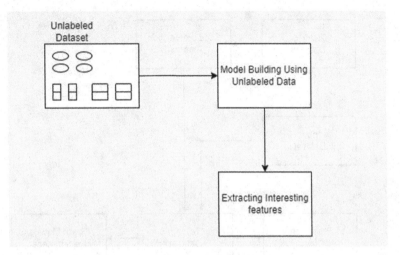

One of the key advantages of supervised learning is that it allows for accurate predictions to be made for new, unseen input data. This is because the algorithm has learned a mapping between the input data and the output labels, and can use this mapping to make predictions. However, supervised learning requires labeled data, which can be difficult and time-consuming to obtain.

Another potential disadvantage of supervised learning is that it can suffer from overfitting. Overfitting occurs when the model is too complex and captures noise or random fluctuations in the training data, rather than the underlying patterns. This can lead to poor performance on new, unseen input data. Regularization techniques can be used to prevent overfitting by adding a penalty term to the objective function that encourages simpler models.

1.2 Unsupervised Learning

In this learning data learn by itself to find the interesting patterns in the dataset without the any guidance. We can also say that class levels are unknown for the given data. It identifies interesting patterns in the data from the features learned in the past. Feature reduction and clustering are some of the popular applications of unsupervised learning algorithms (Mahesh, 2020). Clustering is used to group similar data which helps in its identification. For example it is used to segment bank customers based on type of account like savings account. We have illustrated the working of unsupervised learning in figure-3, where dataset is divided into training and testing dataset and performance of developed model is evaluated in terms of various matrices.

The primary objective of unsupervised learning is to extract meaningful patterns from the data and group similar data points together based on their inherent similarities or shared characteristics. By doing so, it helps in uncovering underlying structures and gaining a deeper understanding of the data, which can be invaluable in various applications.

Unsupervised learning has several advantages and applications. It enables the discovery of previously unknown patterns and relationships in the data, facilitating data exploration and generating insights. It can be used for exploratory analysis, data preprocessing, feature engineering, and anomaly detection.

Figure 3. Unsupervised learning

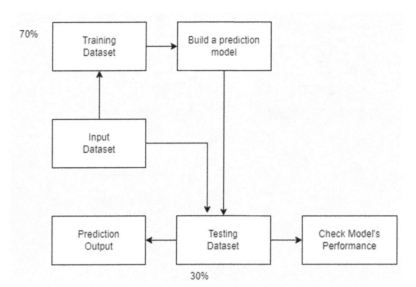

Unsupervised learning is especially valuable in scenarios where labeled data is scarce, expensive to obtain, or simply not available.

However, unsupervised learning also comes with challenges. Without labeled data, it can be difficult to objectively evaluate the performance and quality of the learned models. Interpreting the results can also be challenging, as the patterns and clusters identified by the algorithm may not have explicit meanings or be immediately understandable. Additionally, unsupervised learning algorithms may be sensitive to outliers or noise in the data, requiring careful preprocessing and parameter tuning.

1.3 Reinforcement Learning

Reinforcement learning is a decision making based approach where smart decisions are made by an intelligent agent by communicating with an learning environment. In RL, an agent learns by receiving feedback in the form of rewards or punishments for the actions it takes in the environment. RL may be broken down into three primary parts: The agent's operating and interacting context is referred to as the environment. The entity that decides and acts in the environment is known as the agent. The feedback an agent receives from its surroundings as a result of its activities is known as the reward signal. The agent chooses an action based on its present state in the RL process, receives feedback in the form of a reward signal, and then modifies its policy or strategy for choosing actions depending on the observed results. This iterative process keeps on until the agent discovers how to operate in way that maximizes its long-term cumulative benefit.

The agent's learning process involves optimizing its policy to maximize the expected cumulative reward. Here the agent learns by itself through trial and error from its actions, experiences and feedback to secure more reward points. It learns through rewards and punishments. Agent is trained in such a way that it has tendency to gain more reward points and minimize the punishment. It has capability to interact with an environment and learn from the actions from the environment. Favorable behavior can be rewarded while unfavorable can be punished. One fundamental goal here is to increase total reward points gain by an agent. Reinforcement learning is divided into two different categories i.e positive and negative reinforcement. Positive reinforcement described by the favorable behavior of an agent by supporting it through reward points by enhancing the performance of the system. On the other hand negative reinforcement discourage the behavior or action to not repeat in the future events. Mainly used models for reinforcement learning are Markov Decision Process and Q-learning. Majority of applications are found in automation industry, automated cars, gaming, image processing, traffic control systems, natural language processing and marketing.

1.4 Semi-Supervised Learning

Semi supervised learning uses both supervised and unsupervised learning. It uses large amount of unlabelled data and small labeled data which helps skip the need of finding a large amount of labeled data. It uses semi labeling to train the model. In this label first we train with fewer amounts of labeled data similar to supervised learning till we obtain accurate results. Then we train the model with unlabelled data with pseudo labels and now the data may not be as accurate. We then link both the data tables together. It is used in speech analysis and to classify text documents. While considered similar to reinforcement learning it is different as in reinforcement learning there is a reward and punishment logic followed and in semi supervised learning what is followed is training of model with less labeled data.

1.5 Deep Learning

Compared to machine learning, deep learning involves more hidden layers. Deep learning is a subset of artificial intelligence. It makes use of the back propagation technique, which reveals how the network's internal parameters evolve by identifying intriguing patterns. It is suggested to use deep learning techniques when data size is huge and required to develop automated applications.

Deep learning is preferred over machine learning for a multitude of reasons, some of them being, feature extraction is automated in DL, it can handle complex data and large volume of information, DL models have higher performance and accuracy and are also much easier to scale. The most terrifying benefit of deep learning is that the model continuously trains and improves itself on its own making them well suited for applications that require adaptation and evolution over time.

1.6 Natural Language Processing

Natural Language Processing gives machine the ability to understand and interpret human language. With NLP, machines can understand written and spoken text; it is further applied for speed recognition and automatic text summarization. It is used in catboats, for language translation, sentiment analysis like for recognizing and identifying emotions as positive, negative etc. The quality of NLP models depends on the quality and quantity of training data used to build them. Challenges faced by NLP are also numerous ranging from ambiguity, context-dependency to need to understand different languages and dialects. NLP has practical applications in customer service, healthcare, e-commerce as well.

1.7 Computer Vision

Computer vision is a field dealing with images and videos to extract interesting patterns from them by processing and analyzing it for intelligent decision making. Machine learning is a vital part of this as it enables computers to learn from examples and improve themselves over time. Some further applications of ML algorithms for computer vision are in object detection, where ML algorithms are used to detect and recognize images and videos, these in turn are used in image and video classification and then in image and video segmentation. Some of the practical applications of CV and ML are autonomous vehicles, medical imaging and industrial inspection. They can also be used in gaming, augmented reality and digital cameras.

The book chapter is articulated as follows. Section 2 talks about applications of machine learning and how different professionals have used in the field have used it for their work through an literature review. Following section 2, various machine learning algorithms are discussed in detail in section 3, including their scikit implementation. In section 4 we talk about what is tensorflow followed by scikit in section 5. The limitations of AI and ML are discussed in section 6. There is a case study of an online e-commerce website in section 7 and the article being concluded in section 8.

2. LITERATURE REVIEW

Artificial Neural Network (ANN) models to analyse the impact of groundwater pollution on healthcare risk management in Nigeria. Their study found that the groundwater was heavily contaminated and geodetically influenced. The newer proposed models proved more reliable and provided better and accurate results (Akakuru et al., 2023). A new approach is proposed which found better accuracy for time series analysis up to the point of divergence. The novelty of this approach is that it is able to use entire time series data with any bias. They suggested using of this model in healthcare outcomes (Valsamis et al., 2019) evaluation. Mendarissian Aritonang applied Backpropagation Neural Network and Linear regression for sales forecasting in rice milling unit. Their research aimed to forecast the rice sales so that prediction of raw material can be done so as to reduce idle time. The results found helped increase the productivity as compared to older models (Aritonang & Sihombing, 2019). Neda Khanmohammadi applied multiple linear regression method in reference evapotranspiration trend calculation. The paper analyzed evapotranspiration as a key factor in irrigation programming and trends between it and its effective parameters using MLR models (Khanmohammadi et al., 2018). Nathawat used multiple linear regression techniques to find correlation between distance of health centers and malaria hotspots as a whole map to predict the disease in India. There model proposed to map the malaria prone zones into 5 classes based on severity from low to high. The findings show that as a distance to health facilities increases, malaria incidences are also likely to increase (Ra et al., 2012). Brijendra Singh used computational intelligent techniques to predict use of information technology in private Hospitals of Tamil Nadu (Singh B & D.P Acharjya, 2020). Another application of IT uses by school students of Tamil Nadu is analyzed using intelligence techniques (Magesh G et al., 2015).

Jong Woo Kim applied decision tree approaches in order to develop advertisements which can be personalized according to the need of business applications. The paper proposed a rule generation approach on marketing data and personalized recommendation system using machine learning and decision tree technique (2001). Muh Cherng Wu applied decision tree to stock trading by combining filter rule and decision tree technique. Compared to previous literature which tried a similar method, this work is different in terms of adding futuristic information into the criteria. Decision tree is used to modify existing filtering techniques for more accurate prediction of Taiwan stock market data (2006). Mohammad M Ghiasi applied decision tree to classify breast cancer. Random forest techniques are used to modify classical techniques for detection of breast cancer and classification into malignant and benign lumps. Their model vastly outperformed classical techniques in terms of its performance and it is easy to deploy as well for other healthcare applications (2021). Jun Wu applied a decision tree to modernize the classification of agriculture data. A decision tree classifier is utilized for classification and prediction of agriculture information. The main advantage of this approach is that it works for complete as well an incomplete datasets, therefore more generalized approach for all kinds of agricultural data with enhanced performance by the model (U. et al., 2009).

Shujun Huang used support vector machine classifier to extract meaningful information from cancer genomics datasets. It resulted in the discovery of advanced biomarkers, advanced drug targets and provide more insights on genes of cancer disease (Huang et al., 2018). Byvatov E developed SVM and neural models in medical field with improved outcomes in classification and prediction task (Byvatov & Schneider, 2003). Artificial intelligence based approach is used to build an electrical forecasting model with improved outcomes with better accuracy (Ahmad et al., 2014; Deka, 2014). Mathias M. Adankon proposed an approach for model selection using an advanced approach for handwritten character recognition. LS-SVM method is used for the classification task and shows best performance and generalized approach or other applications as well (Adankon & Cheriet, 2009).

Mucahid Mustafa Saritas purposed an approach for breast cancer analysis based on various parameters of blood routine dataset. ANN and Naïve Bayes classification algorithms were used for analysis and classification of the data and performance of the approaches are evaluated based on different metrics (Saritas & Yasar, 2019). M. Wiggins analyzes ECG data using Bayesian classification technique. Patients were classified based on age and ECG. Findings show improved performance when compared to the existing classifiers (Wiggins et al., 2008). Joanna Kazmierska analyzes risk of cancer disease after radiotherapy using naïve bayes classifier approach (Kazmierska & Malicki, 2008). Naive Bayes algorithms are widely used various applications including recommendation systems as they are easy to implement. However, some challenges are still remain same such a requirements of the predictor. They have used large training dataset to eliminate the above said problem, leads to higher accuracy (Rrmoku et al., 2022).

3. MACHINE LEARNING ALGORITHMS

The fundamental of any machine learning model is lies in the algorithm part of it. Now we will describe major ML algorithms in detail.

3.1 Linear Regression

Linear regression is one of the fundamental algorithm in ML which is used to predict continuous variable. It is commonly used for predictive analysis and modeling. It is mainly used in finding out relationship between variables and forecasting variable. Regression models are based on number of dependent and independent variables. It predicts a continuous value, for e.g. CO2 emission from a car.

Figure 4. Linear regression

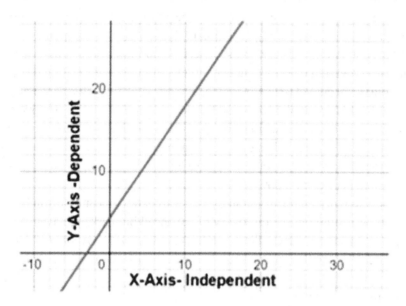

Here, continuous data is used to learn a function for predicting a dependent variable. Say an example, we want to establish a relationship between some variables x and related y variables. A relationship between these variables is learned through an hypothesis. Hypothesis is a straight line in case of a linear regression problem. Linear model uses parameters called weight and bias which are adjusted based on the trained data points. Further an error is used to assess the performance of the developed model is known a mean square error. Predicting a house price based on various factors is a linear regression problem.

Linear regression is a regression model whose value is predicted by an integer number, and doesn't require an activation function or any threshold value. Logistic regression is a classification model where we predict values by 0 or 1, it also requires both an activation function and a threshold value. In linear regression we use root mean square energy method for prediction of next value, whereas in logistic regression we use precision to predict or we predict based on maximum likelihood estimation. The graph of a logistic regression is S shaped for positive and Z shaped for negative.

The cost function is given by:

$$j(w,b) = \frac{1}{2m} \sum_{i=1}^{m} (yi - h(xi))^2$$

where w=weight and b=bias.

Here's an example of how to implement linear regression using scikit-learn in Python (Simplilearn, n.d.)

In this example the necessary modules from scikit learn are first imported. Next, we define our sample data. We have an array X that represents the input features and an array y that represents the target variable. We then create a Linear Regression object called regression. This will be our linear regression model. To train the model, we call the fit() method on the regression object, passing in the input features X and the target variable y.

Figure 5. How to implement linear regression using scikit-learn in Python (Simplilearn, n.d.)

```python
import numpy as np
from sklearn.linear_model import LinearRegression
from sklearn.metrics import mean_squared_error
import matplotlib.pyplot as plt


# Sample data
X = np.array([[1], [2], [3], [4], [5]])  # Input features
y = np.array([2, 4, 5, 4, 5])  # Target variable


# Create a linear regression model
regression = LinearRegression()


# Train the model
regression.fit(X, y)


# Make predictions on the training data
y_pred = regression.predict(X)


# Calculate the mean squared error
mse = mean_squared_error(y, y_pred)
print("Mean Squared Error:", mse)


# Plot the data points and the regression line
plt.scatter(X, y, color='blue', label='Actual')
plt.plot(X, y_pred, color='red', label='Predicted')
plt.xlabel('X')
plt.ylabel('y')
plt.legend()
plt.show()
```

Once the model is trained, we can make predictions on the training data by calling the predict() method on the regression object and passing in X. The predicted values are stored in the y_pred array. To evaluate the performance of our model, we calculate the mean squared error (MSE) between the actual target variable y and the predicted values y_pred. The MSE is a common metric used to measure the quality of regression models.

Finally, we visualize the data points and the regression line using matplotlib. The scatter() function is used to plot the actual data points, and the plot() function is used to plot the predicted regression line. We also add labels to the x-axis and y-axis and include a legend for clarity. The resulting plot will show the data points as blue dots and the regression line as a red line. Running the code will output the mean squared error and display the scatter plot with the actual data points and the predicted regression line.

3.2 Logistic Regression

A binary dependent variable—one with just two potential outcomes, like yes or no—and one or more independent variables are analysed using the statistical technique known as logistic regression. Data is frequently divided into two or more groups using machine learning and data science techniques. A probability between 0 and 1 that represents the chance of the dependent variable falling into a certain category is the output of a logistic regression model. Binary classification issues (where the dependent variable has two potential outcomes) and multiclass classification problems may both be solved using logistic regression models (where the dependent variable has more than two possible outcomes). The logistic function, which converts any input with a real value to a number between 0 and 1, serves as the foundation for the logistic regression model. Given the values of the independent variables, the logistic function is used to model the likelihood of the dependent variable. The maximum likelihood estimation method is used to estimate the parameters of a logistic regression model. The model may be used to forecast the likelihood that a fresh set of data points will fall within a specific category of the dependent variable once the parameters have been calculated. For a variety of prediction problems, the machine learning and data science sectors of finance, healthcare, and marketing frequently employ the popular and effective method of logistic regression.

Here's an example of how to implement logistic regression using scikit-learn in Python (Towardsdatascience, n.d.-a):

In this example the necessary modules from scikit learn are first imported. Next, we define our sample data. We have an array X that represents the input features and an array y that represents the target variable. The target variable is binary, with values of 0 or 1. Next, we create a LogisticRegression object called logreg. This will be our logistic regression model. To train the model, we call the fit() method on the logreg object, passing in the input features X and the target variable y.

Once the model is trained, we can make predictions on the training data by calling the predict() method on the logreg object and passing in X. The predicted values are stored in the y_pred array.b. To evaluate the performance of our model, we calculate the accuracy by comparing the actual target variable y with the predicted values y_pred. The accuracy is a common metric used to measure the performance of classification models.

Finally, we visualize the data points and the decision boundary using matplotlib. The scatter() function is used to plot the actual data points, and the plot() function is used to plot the predicted probabilities of the positive class. The predicted probabilities are obtained using the predict_proba() method of the logreg object. We also add labels to the x-axis and y-axis and include a legend for clarity. The resulting plot will show the data points as blue dots and the decision boundary as a red curve. Running the code will output the accuracy and display the scatter plot with the actual data points and the decision boundary.

Figure 6. How to implement logistic regression using scikit-learn in Python (Towardsdatascience, n.d.-a)

```python
import numpy as np
from sklearn.linear_model import LogisticRegression
from sklearn.metrics import accuracy_score
import matplotlib.pyplot as plt

# Sample data
X = np.array([[1], [2], [3], [4], [5]])  # Input features
y = np.array([0, 0, 1, 1, 1])  # Target variable

# Create a logistic regression model
logreg = LogisticRegression()

# Train the model
logreg.fit(X, y)

# Make predictions on the training data
y_pred = logreg.predict(X)

# Calculate the accuracy
accuracy = accuracy_score(y, y_pred)
print("Accuracy:", accuracy)

# Plot the data points and the decision boundary
plt.scatter(X, y, color='blue', label='Actual')
plt.plot(X, logreg.predict_proba(X)[:, 1], color='red', label='Predicted')
plt.xlabel('X')
plt.ylabel('y')
plt.legend()
plt.show()
```

3.3 Decision Tree

A supervised learning approach used for classification or regression analysis is known as a decision tree. In decision tree, input data is recursively divided into subsets and build a machine learning model which looks like a tree data structure, used for outcomes and prediction. Entire dataset of the given application is represented by root node of the decision tree. Later on it will be decided that which characteristic of the dataset will be used to find the threshold value to further produce subsets of data with respect to the target variable. The splitting criterion is determined by the feature and threshold that results in the most homogenous subgroups.

Step by step working of Decision Tree is described below:

Figure 7. Decision tree

1. The first step is to load the dataset you intend to utilize for regression or classification. There should be labelled instances in the dataset (i.e., the class or target value should be known for each example).
2. Choose the target variable: The decision tree's target variable must be selected in the next step. For classification and regression tasks, this variable ought to be categorical.
3. Decide on the splitting criterion: A split's quality is measured by the splitting criterion. Entropy and Gini impurity are the most often used splitting criteria for classification tasks, whereas mean squared error or mean absolute error is utilised for regression tasks.
4. Create the decision tree: To create the decision tree, use the dataset and the splitting criteria. Recursively split the data starting at the root node using the input feature values that maximise the splitting criterion. Continue splitting until either a halting requirement is satisfied or the leaf nodes are pure (all instances in the leaf nodes belong to the same class) (e.g., a maximum depth is reached or a minimum number of examples per leaf node is required).
5. Pruning is a strategy used to lessen the complexity of the decision tree and avoid overfitting. It is optional. This entails pruning tree branches that don't raise the tree's accuracy on a validation set.
    6.A test set can be used to gauge the decision tree's effectiveness. Determine performance measures for the model, such as accuracy, precision, recall, and F1 score.
    7. Adjust the hyperparameters (optional): If the decision tree's performance isn't up to standard, consider adjusting the hyperparameters. This entails modifying the splitting criterion, the minimum number of cases per leaf node, and the maximum depth of the tree.
    8. Create predictions: Use the decision tree to make predictions on fresh, new cases once it has been trained and its hyperparameters have been adjusted.

Figure 8. How to implement a decision tree classifier using scikit-learn in Python (Datacamp, n.d.-a)

```python
from sklearn.model_selection import train_test_split
from sklearn.tree import DecisionTreeClassifier
from sklearn.metrics import accuracy_score
from sklearn import tree
import matplotlib.pyplot as plt
# Load the iris dataset
iris = load_iris()
X = iris.data  # Features
y = iris.target  # Target variable
# Split the data into training and testing sets
X_train, X_test, y_train, y_test = train_test_split(X, y, test_size=0.2, random_state=42)
# Create a decision tree classifier
clf = DecisionTreeClassifier()
# Train the classifier
clf.fit(X_train, y_train)
# Make predictions on the test data
y_pred = clf.predict(X_test)
# Calculate the accuracy
accuracy = accuracy_score(y_test, y_pred)
print("Accuracy:", accuracy)
# Plot the decision tree
fig, ax = plt.subplots(figsize=(10, 10))
tree.plot_tree(clf, filled=True, ax=ax, feature_names=iris.feature_names, class_names=iris.target_names)
plt.show()
```

The Decision Tree algorithm is a straightforward yet effective method that may be applied to both regression and classification challenges. Up until pure leaf nodes are reached, the data is separated recursively depending on the values of the input characteristics. Decision trees are excellent for illustrating how a model generates its predictions since they are recognized to be interpretable and comprehensible. Nevertheless, they are susceptible to overfitting, particularly when the data is noisy or the tree is deep.

Here's an example of how to implement a decision tree classifier using scikit-learn in Python (Datacamp, n.d.-a):

In this example the necessary modules from scikit learn are first imported. Next, we load the iris dataset using the load_iris() function and store the features in X and the target variable in y. We then split the data into training and testing sets using train_test_split(). In this case, we allocate 20% of the data for testing, and set the random state to ensure reproducibility. We create a DecisionTreeClassifier object called clf. This will be our decision tree classifier. To train the classifier, we call the fit() method on the clf object, passing in the training data X_train and the corresponding target variable y_train.

Once the classifier is trained, we can make predictions on the test data by calling the predict() method on the clf object and passing in X_test. The predicted values are stored in the y_pred array. To evaluate the performance of our model, we calculate the accuracy by comparing the predicted labels y_pred with the actual labels y_test using the accuracy_score() function from scikit-learn.

Finally, we visualize the decision tree using matplotlib. We create a figure and axes using subplots(), specify the size of the plot, and then use tree.plot_tree() to visualize the decision tree. We also pass in the feature names and class names to label the tree accordingly. The resulting plot will display the decision tree structure. Running the code will output the accuracy and display the decision tree plot..

3.4 Random Forest (RF)

Random forest is the combination of various decision tress, processed in parallel fashion, on different samples of the dataset and generate the desired outcome based on the majority voting concept.

Figure 9. Random forest

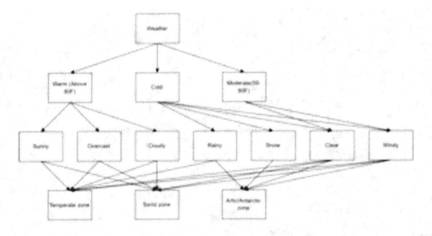

Step by step working of Random Forest

1. The first step is to load the dataset you intend to utilize for regression or classification. There should be labelled instances in the dataset (i.e., the class or target value should be known for each example).
2. Choose the number of trees: The number of trees to be employed in the random forest is the next stage. It is possible to fine-tune this hyperparameter via cross-validation or experimentation.
3. Choose the features: At each node of a decision tree, random forests randomly choose a subset of the features. This is done to broaden the variety of the trees and lessen overfitting. Another hyperparameter that may be modified is the amount of features to choose at each node.
4. Create the decision trees: Create the decision trees using the dataset and the chosen characteristics. A randomly chosen subset of the cases and the randomly chosen subset of the characteristics are used to train each decision tree. The Decision Tree algorithm's splitting criteria are used to build the trees (i.e., entropy or Gini impurity for classification tasks and mean squared error or mean absolute error for regression tasks).
5. Once all of the decision trees have been constructed, combine their forecasts to arrive at the ultimate conclusion. This is accomplished for classification jobs by casting a vote on the anticipated classes of the different trees. This is accomplished for regression tasks by averaging the predicted values of the different trees.
6. Make use of a test set to gauge the random forest's effectiveness. Determine performance measures for the model, such as accuracy, precision, recall, and F1 score.
7. Adjust the hyperparameters: If the random forest's performance isn't up to standard, consider adjusting the hyperparameters. The number of trees, the number of attributes to choose at each node, and the maximum depth of the trees may all be altered.
8. Create predictions: When the hyperparameters have been adjusted and the random forest has been trained, use it to make predictions on brand-new cases.

Figure 10. How to implement a random forest classifier using scikit-learn in Python (Datacamp, n.d.-b)

```
from sklearn.datasets import load_iris
from sklearn.model_selection import train_test_split
from sklearn.ensemble import RandomForestClassifier
from sklearn.metrics import accuracy_score
import matplotlib.pyplot as plt
# Load the iris dataset
iris = load_iris()
X = iris.data  # Features
y = iris.target  # Target variable
# Split the data into training and testing sets
X_train, X_test, y_train, y_test = train_test_split(X, y, test_size=0.2, random_state=42)
# Create a random forest classifier
clf = RandomForestClassifier(n_estimators=100)
# Train the classifier
clf.fit(X_train, y_train)
# Make predictions on the test data
y_pred = clf.predict(X_test)
# Calculate the accuracy
accuracy = accuracy_score(y_test, y_pred)
print("Accuracy:", accuracy)
# Feature importance
importance = clf.feature_importances_
plt.bar(range(len(importance)), importance)
plt.xticks(range(len(importance)), iris.feature_names, rotation='vertical')
plt.xlabel('Features')
plt.ylabel('Importance')
plt.show()
```

The Random Forest algorithm is an ensemble learning method that blends different decision trees to increase the predictability and accuracy. It functions by creating numerous decision trees using arbitrary subsets of the data and characteristics, then combining the predictions made by each tree. It is well known that random forests are efficient at managing high-dimensional data, missing values, and noisy data. In contrast to single decision trees, they can be computationally costly and challenging to comprehend.

Here's an example of how to implement a random forest classifier using scikit-learn in Python (Datacamp, n.d.-b):

In this example the necessary modules from scikit learn are first imported. Then we load the iris dataset using the load_iris() function and store the features in X and the target variable in y. Next, we split the data into training and testing sets using train_test_split(). In this case, we allocate 20% of the data for testing, and set the random state to ensure reproducibility. We create a RandomForestClassifier object called clf. This will be our random forest classifier. In this example, we set the number of estimators (decision trees) to 100. To train the classifier, we call the fit() method on the clf object, passing in the training data X_train and the corresponding target variable y_train.

Once the classifier is trained, we can make predictions on the test data by calling the predict() method on the clf object and passing in X_test. The predicted values are stored in the y_pred array. To evaluate the performance of our model, we calculate the accuracy by comparing the predicted labels y_pred with the actual labels y_test using the accuracy_score() function from scikit-learn.

Additionally, we can analyze the feature importance in the random forest classifier. We can obtain the importance scores using the feature_importances_ attribute of the clf object. In this example, we visualize the feature importance using a bar plot, where the x-axis represents the features and the yaxis represents the importance scores. Running the code will output the accuracy and display the feature importance plot.

3.5 KNN: K Nearest Neighbors

Here, test sample is allocated to the class which is most frequently represented in the training data samples. In the case of more than two different classes, the test data sample will be allocated to the class based on the minimum average distance from the test sample (Kataria & Singh, 2013).

It classifies points based on their position in the graph. For eg if the output cluster is closer to a blue group than a red group then it would be called a member of the blue group. This approach indicates that KNN can be used to either group known data or predict where unknown data should lie.

Step by step working of KNN is described below:

1. The first step is to load the dataset you intend to utilise for regression or classification. There should be labelled instances in the dataset (i.e., the class or target value should be known for each example).
2. The next step is to determine the value of K, which represents the number of closest neighbours that will be taken into account for prediction. Often, cross-validation or experimentation are used to select this value.
3. Compute distance: Using a distance measure like the Euclidean distance, determine the distance between each example in the dataset and the test example. The distance metric computes the separation in feature space between two locations.
4. Depending on the distance measure determined in the previous phase, choose the K closest neighbours to the test case. The examples closest to the test example are those that are its neighbours.
5. Predict the class or value: In classification problems, choose the test example's class by getting a majority of the K closest neighbours' class labels. By averaging the goal values of the K closest neighbours, you may forecast the value of the test example in regression tasks.
6. Output prediction for the sample

For running the KNN we just run steps 3-6 each time. KNN is a powerful algorithm which can be used both in classification and regression tasks.

Here's an example of how to implement the K-nearest neighbors (KNN) algorithm using scikit-learn in Python (Towardsdatascience, n.d.-b):

In this example the necessary modules from scikit learn are first imported. Then we load the iris dataset using the load_iris() function and store the features in X and the target variable in y. Next, we split the data into training and testing sets using train_test_split(). In this case, we allocate 20% of the data for testing, and set the random state to ensure reproducibility.

We create a KNeighborsClassifier object called clf. This will be our KNN classifier. In this example, we set the number of neighbors (k) to 3. To train the classifier, we call the fit() method on the clf object, passing in the training data X_train and the corresponding target variable y_train.

Once the classifier is trained, we can make predictions on the test data by calling the predict() method on the clf object and passing in X_test. The predicted values are stored in the y_pred array. To evaluate the performance of our model, we calculate the accuracy by comparing the predicted labels y_pred with

Figure 11. How to implement the k-nearest neighbors (KNN) algorithm using scikit-learn in Python (Towardsdatascience, n.d.-b)

```python
from sklearn.datasets import load_iris
from sklearn.model_selection import train_test_split
from sklearn.neighbors import KNeighborsClassifier
from sklearn.metrics import accuracy_score

# Load the iris dataset
iris = load_iris()
X = iris.data  # Features
y = iris.target  # Target variable

# Split the data into training and testing sets
X_train, X_test, y_train, y_test = train_test_split(X, y, test_size=0.2, random_state=42)

# Create a KNN classifier
k = 3  # Number of neighbors
clf = KNeighborsClassifier(n_neighbors=k)

# Train the classifier
clf.fit(X_train, y_train)

# Make predictions on the test data
y_pred = clf.predict(X_test)

# Calculate the accuracy
accuracy = accuracy_score(y_test, y_pred)
print("Accuracy:", accuracy)
```

the actual labels y_test using the accuracy_score() function from scikit-learn. Running the code will output the accuracy of the KNN classifier on the test data.

3.6 Clustering

Clustering is an unsupervised learning technique used for grouping the data into like groups. Its use is that the clusters thus formed help in quick data analysis for example a company may use clustering to group its users as males or females then while shopping it can show them more relevant products for that group. Clustering can be done in a variety of methods, two of the most popular ones are k-means and DBSCAN.

3.6.1 K-Means

K-means is a kind of unsupervised learning algorithm used for data exploration and grouping. The technique is employed to create k clusters of comparable data points. The user selects the value of k, which denotes how many clusters the algorithm should produce. K points are chosen at random to serve as the starting centroids in the K-means algorithm. The original cluster centres are represented by these centroids. The programme then generates k clusters by allocating each data point to the closest centroid. Euclidean distance is typically employed as the distance metric to determine how far apart each data point is from the centroid. The centroids of each cluster are then recalculated by the algorithm by taking the mean of all the data points in that cluster. The procedure of computing new centroids and reassigning data points is then repeated until the centroids stop changing or a maximum number of iterations is achieved. The algorithm then reassigns each data point to the nearest centroid once again. The K-means method produces a collection of k clusters as its final output, each of which contains several related data points. The centroids of the clusters, which stand for the mean of all the data points in that cluster, serve as a defining feature of the clusters. For a variety of purposes, including picture segmentation, customer segmentation, and anomaly detection, K-means is often used in machine learning and data mining. The K-means method may lead to less-than-ideal results since it is sensitive to the starting centroids chosen. The K-means technique also makes the assumption that the clusters are spherical and have a common variance, which may not necessarily be true in datasets from real-world applications.

Here's an example of how to implement the K-means clustering algorithm using scikit-learn in Python (Datacamp, n.d.-c):

In this example the necessary modules from scikit learn are first imported. Then we generate sample data using the make_blobs() function. In this case, we create 200 samples with 4 centers using the centers parameter. We create a KMeans object called kmeans. This will be our K-means clustering model. In this example, we set the number of clusters (k) to 4.

To fit the K-means model to the data, we call the fit() method on the kmeans object, passing in the data X. After fitting the model, we can obtain the cluster labels using the labels_ attribute of the kmeans object.

We can also get the cluster centroids (representing the mean of the points in each cluster) using the cluster_centers_ attribute of the kmeans object. To visualize the clusters, we plot the data points using plt.scatter(), where the color of each point is determined by its cluster label. We also plot the cluster centroids as red 'x' markers. Finally, we label the axes and provide a title for the plot. Running the code will display a scatter plot of the data points with different colors representing different clusters, along with the cluster centroids.

3.6.2 DBSCAN

DBSCAN (Density-Based Spatial Clustering of Applications with Noise) is a machine learning algorithm used for clustering data points into groups based on their density. It is an unsupervised learning algorithm, meaning that it does not require labeled data for training.

DBSCAN works by identifying "core" points, which are points that have at least a minimum number of other points within a specified radius. It then identifies "border" points, which are points that are within the radius of a core point but do not have enough neighbors to be considered core points. Finally, it identifies "noise" points, which are points that are not core points or border points. The algorithm starts with a randomly chosen data point and identifies all other points within a specified radius. If the number of points within the radius is greater than or equal to the minimum number of points, then it is classified as a core point and a cluster is formed around it. If not, the point is labeled as noise. The process continues until all points have been classified.Some applications of DBSCAN are image processing, natural language processing, and anomaly detection.

Figure 12. How to implement the K-means clustering algorithm using scikit-learn in Python (Datacamp, n.d.-c)

```python
from sklearn.datasets import make_blobs
from sklearn.cluster import KMeans
import matplotlib.pyplot as plt

# Generate sample data
X, y = make_blobs(n_samples=200, centers=4, random_state=0)

# Create a K-means clustering object
k = 4  # Number of clusters
kmeans = KMeans(n_clusters=k)

# Fit the K-means model to the data
kmeans.fit(X)

# Get the cluster labels
labels = kmeans.labels_

# Get the cluster centroids
centroids = kmeans.cluster_centers_

# Visualize the clusters
plt.scatter(X[:, 0], X[:, 1], c=labels, cmap='viridis')
plt.scatter(centroids[:, 0], centroids[:, 1], marker='x', color='red', s=200)
plt.xlabel('Feature 1')
plt.ylabel('Feature 2')
plt.title('K-means Clustering')
plt.show()
```

Example of how to implement the DBSCAN (Density-Based Spatial Clustering of Applications with Noise) algorithm using scikit-learn in Python (Levelup, n.d.) is described below:

In this example the necessary modules from scikit learn are first imported. Then we generate sample data using the make_moons() function. In this case, we create 200 samples with added noise. We create a DBSCAN object called dbscan. This will be our DBSCAN clustering model. In this example, we set the maximum distance between samples (eps) to 0.3 and the minimum number of samples in a neighborhood (min_samples) to 5. To fit the DBSCAN model to the data, we call the fit() method on the dbscan object, passing in the data X.

After fitting the model, we can obtain the cluster labels using the labels_ attribute of the dbscan object. We can also determine the number of clusters present in the data by counting the unique labels and subtracting 1 if -1 (representing noise) is present. To visualize the clusters, we plot the data points using plt.scatter(), where the color of each point is determined by its cluster label. We use the 'viridis' colormap for better visualization. Noise points are labeled as -1. Finally, we label the axes and provide

Figure 13. Code displaying scatter plot

```
from sklearn.datasets import make_moons
from sklearn.cluster import DBSCAN
import matplotlib.pyplot as plt

# Generate sample data
X, y = make_moons(n_samples=200, noise=0.05, random_state=0)

# Create a DBSCAN clustering object
eps = 0.3  # Maximum distance between samples to be considered in the same neighborhood
min_samples = 5  # Minimum number of samples in a neighborhood for a point to be considered as a core point
dbscan = DBSCAN(eps=eps, min_samples=min_samples)

# Fit the DBSCAN model to the data
dbscan.fit(X)

# Get the cluster labels
labels = dbscan.labels_

# Number of clusters in labels, ignoring noise if present
n_clusters = len(set(labels)) - (1 if -1 in labels else 0)
n_noise = list(labels).count(-1)

# Visualize the clusters
plt.scatter(X[:, 0], X[:, 1], c=labels, cmap='viridis')
plt.xlabel('Feature 1')
plt.ylabel('Feature 2')
plt.title('DBSCAN Clustering')
plt.show()
```

a title for the plot. Running the code will display a scatter plot of the data points with different colors representing different clusters, along with noise points labeled as black.

3.7 Support Vector Machine

Support vector machine is a machine learning algorithm which has applications both in regression and classification problems. The goal in this is to segregate the data plane into parts or classes which helps us in classifying the data. This boundary is called a hyperplane. In SVM the points for the hyperplane are often called support vectors, which is what gives it its name.

Step by step working of SVM

1. The first step is to load the dataset you intend to utilise for regression or classification. There should be labelled instances in the dataset (i.e., the class or target value should be known for each example).
2. Choose the kernel function: The data will be transformed into a higher-dimensional space using a kernel function, which must be selected as the following step. The linear kernel, polynomial kernel, and radial basis function (RBF) kernel are the most often utilised kernel functions.
3. To divide the dataset: Make a training set and a test set out of the dataset. The SVM model is trained using the training set, and its performance is assessed using the test set.

4. Apply the training set to the SVM model to perform training. Finding the hyperplane that optimises the margin between the two classes is the aim of model training. A collection of weights (w) and a bias term (b), which are learnt during training, together define the hyperplane.

5. Choose a value for the hyperparameter C, which governs the trade-off between increasing the margin and reducing the classification error. A lower value of C yields a greater margin but may result in more mistakes in the training set, whereas a higher value of C yields a smaller margin but may result in more errors in the training set. The value of C is typically chosen through cross validation.

6. The SVM model will be trained using the training set. The goal of model training is to identify the hyperplane that optimises the margin between the two classes. The hyperplane is defined by a set of weights (w) and a bias term (b), both of which are learned during training.

7. The hyperparameter C, which controls the trade-off between boosting the margin and lowering the classification error, must have a value. Although a larger value of C produces a smaller margin but might produce more mistakes in the training set, a lower value of C produces a greater margin but could produce more mistakes in the training set.

SVMs are known to be effective when dealing with data of multiple dimensions as well as handling large datasets.

Here's an example of how to implement the Support Vector Machine (SVM) algorithm using scikit-learn in Python (SciKit-Learn, n.d.-b):

In this example the necessary modules from scikit learn are first imported. Then we generate sample data using the make_classification() function. In this case, we create 200 samples with random classification. We split the data into training and testing sets using train_test_split(). In this example, we allocate 20% of the data for testing, and set the random state to ensure reproducibility. We create an SVC object called svm. This will be our SVM classifier. In this example, we set the kernel to 'linear', indicating a linear SVM. To train the classifier, we call the fit() method on the svm object, passing in the training data X_train and the corresponding target variable y_train.

Once the classifier is trained, we can make predictions on the test data by calling the predict() method on the svm object and passing in X_test. The predicted values are stored in the y_pred array.

To evaluate the performance of our model, we calculate the accuracy by comparing the predicted labels y_pred with the actual labels y_test using the accuracy_score() function from scikit-learn. Running the code will output the accuracy of the SVM classifier on the test data

3.8 Naive Bayes Classifier

It is a supervised learning algorithm base on Bayes theorem used for solving classification problems. Is mainly used in text classification and operates on a high level training dataset. It predicts based on the probability of the object.

Step By Step Working Of Naive Bayes Classifier

1. Load the dataset: The dataset that you intend to utilise for classification must first be loaded. There should be labelled instances in the dataset (i.e., the class or target value should be known for each example).

Figure 14. How to implement the support vector machine (SVM) algorithm using scikit-learn in Python (SciKit-Learn, n.d.-b)

```python
from sklearn.datasets import make_classification
from sklearn.model_selection import train_test_split
from sklearn.svm import SVC
from sklearn.metrics import accuracy_score

# Generate sample data
X, y = make_classification(n_samples=200, random_state=0)

# Split the data into training and testing sets
X_train, X_test, y_train, y_test = train_test_split(X, y, test_size=0.2, random_state=42)

# Create an SVM classifier
svm = SVC(kernel='linear')

# Train the classifier
svm.fit(X_train, y_train)

# Make predictions on the test data
y_pred = svm.predict(X_test)

# Calculate the accuracy
accuracy = accuracy_score(y_test, y_pred)
print("Accuracy:", accuracy)
```

2. Preprocess the data to accommodate missing values, eliminate noise, and normalise the features. It's crucial to preprocess the data in accordance with the assumptions made by naive Bayes, which holds that the characteristics are independent and normally distributed.

3. To divide the dataset: Create training and testing sets from the dataset. The Naive Bayes model is trained using the training set, and its performance is assessed using the testing set.

4. Compute the prior probabilities for each class in the training set to determine the class probabilities. To do this, multiply the total number of examples by the number of instances in each class.

5. The conditional probabilities of each characteristic given each class should be calculated. The mean and variance of each characteristic for each class are calculated to achieve this. The probability density function of each feature may be determined using the mean and variance since Naive Bayes makes the assumption that the features are normally distributed.

6. Once the model has been trained, use it to predict outcomes on the testing set. Use the Bayes theorem to each case to determine the likelihood of each class, then choose the class with the highest probability to serve as the predicted class.

7. Review the model: To assess the model's performance, use the testing set. Determine performance measures for the model, such as accuracy, precision, recall, and F1 score.

8. Adjust the hyperparameters (optional): If the model's performance is subpar, consider adjusting the hyperparameters. Adjusting the smoothing value is part of this process since it helps to avoid zero probability and guard against overfitting.

Figure 15. How to implement the naive bayes classifier (NBC) algorithm using scikit-learninPython (SciKit-Learn, n.d.-c)

```python
from sklearn.datasets import load_iris
from sklearn.model_selection import train_test_split
from sklearn.naive_bayes import GaussianNB
from sklearn.metrics import accuracy_score

# Load the Iris dataset
iris = load_iris()

# Split the data into training and testing sets
X_train, X_test, y_train, y_test = train_test_split(iris.data, iris.target, test_size=0.2, random_state=42)

# Create a Naive Bayes classifier
nb_classifier = GaussianNB()

# Train the classifier
nb_classifier.fit(X_train, y_train)

# Make predictions on the test data
y_pred = nb_classifier.predict(X_test)

# Calculate the accuracy
accuracy = accuracy_score(y_test, y_pred)
print("Accuracy:", accuracy)
```

9. Once the model has been trained and the hyperparameters have been adjusted, use it to generate predictions on fresh, new data.

Both binary and multi-class classification jobs may be handled with the straightforward yet efficient Naive Bayes method. It operates under the presumption that the features are independent and normally distributed, and it applies Bayes' theorem to determine the probability of each class given the features. The "naive" assumption of feature independence might cause Naive Bayes to perform poorly when the features are correlated, despite the fact that it is known to be computationally efficient and capable of handling high-dimensional data.

Here's an example of how to implement the Naive Bayes Classifier (NBC) algorithm using scikit-learninPython (SciKit-Learn, n.d.-c):

In this example the necessary modules from scikit learn are first imported. Then we load the Iris dataset using the load_iris() function. The dataset consists of samples of iris flowers, and the task is to classify the flowers into three different species. We split the data into training and testing sets using train_test_split(). In this example, we allocate 20% of the data for testing, and set the random state to ensure reproducibility.

We create a GaussianNB object called nb_classifier. This will be our Naive Bayes classifier. In this example, we assume that the features follow a Gaussian (normal) distribution. To train the classifier, we call the fit() method on the nb_classifier object, passing in the training data X_train and the corresponding target variable y_train.

Once the classifier is trained, we can make predictions on the test data by calling the predict() method on the nb_classifier object and passing in X_test. The predicted labels are stored in the y_pred array.

To evaluate the performance of our model, we calculate the accuracy by comparing the predicted labels y_pred with the actual labels y_test using the accuracy_score() function from scikit-learn. Running the code will output the accuracy of the Naive Bayes classifier on the test data.

4. TENSORFLOW

Tensorflow is an open-source software library which is developed by engineers at Google. Data low graphs are used, mathematical operations are represented by nodes and graph edges acts as a multi-dimensional array of data known as tensor. It is a library which provides various APIs for developing advanced applications. Construction of computational graph and running it are some fundamentals or main components of Tensorflow Core. It consists of various nodes which will be responsible for a specific task. These nodes are used to take tensor as an input data and generate output as a tensor.

An important difference between a variable and constant is that a constant is stored in the graph and gets loaded whenever we open the graph whereas the variable exists independently and may be stored in a parameter server.

Google created the open-source machine learning framework known as TensorFlow. It offers a platform for creating and honing machine learning models, such as deep neural networks, utilising a range of data sources, including time series data, pictures, and text.

TensorFlow supports distributed computing across a number of hardware platforms, including CPUs, GPUs, and TPUs, and employ a computational graph to describe the mathematical operations in a machine learning model. Python, C++, and Java are just a few of the programming languages supported by TensorFlow.

Tensorflow is used in a variety of domains like healthcare, in companies for prediction and analysis, in the stock market etc. It is used for image detection, voice recognition, text based application etc. Tensorflow for instance could be used to aid people with motor disabilities as their devices would be controllable just via text or a simple gesture. Microsoft in 2019 used tensorflow to make an app controllable just with your gaze, hands-free.

Tensors have a type of data structure like vectors and matrices and can be used for calculating arithmetic operators. Tensors can have a variety of dimensions and are often referred to as N dimensional arrays. It can be thought of as nested array of multiple dimensions, the number of dimensions a tensor has is called rank and the length in each dimension describes its shape.

Convulational Neural Networks do processing over multiple layers. Its main features are convolution and pooling. tf.session starts the session and tf.placeholder is used to create a space to store variables which will be assigned later.

Recurrent Neural Networks are a class of neutral networks that are used in model sequencing of data such as time series or natural language. We can use tensorflow cloud to train RNN models made from keras.

Multiple layer perceptron is formed from as it says multiple layers of perceptron. It has an input layer, hidden layers and output layers. In image recognition we input into a neural network and it gets assigned a label which we get as output. We will input the sample images to the system lets say 4000, then we will do an 80:20 split and use 80% of them for training and leave the last 20% for testing purposes.

Dimensionality reduction can be used in both supervised and unsupervised learning. In unsupervised learning it is mainly used to preprocess the data by doing feature extraction on it. We do this with the

Figure 16. Sample code on how to use TensorFlow to create a simple neural network

```python
import tensorflow as tf
import numpy as np

# Create input data
X = np.array([[0, 0],[0, 1],[1, 0],[1, 1]])
# Create output data
y = np.array([[0],[1],[1],[0]])
# Define the model architecture
model = tf.keras.models.Sequential([
    tf.keras.layers.Dense(4, input_shape=(2,), activation='relu'),
    tf.keras.layers.Dense(1, activation='sigmoid')])
# Compile the model
model.compile(optimizer='adam', loss='binary_crossentropy', metrics=['accuracy'])
# Train the model
model.fit(X, y, epochs=1000)
# Test the model
test_data = np.array([[0, 0],[0, 1],[1, 0],[1, 1]])
predictions = model.predict(test_data)
# Print the predictions
print(predictions)
```

help of an Autoencoder which is comprised of an encoder part and a decoder. Autoencoders are a type of neural network used in unsupervised learning that try to optimise a set of parameters to sort the input data and improve comprehension of the data set as a whole.

Here's a sample code on how to use TensorFlow to create a simple neural network:

We first import TensorFlow and numpy libraries. Then we create the input data X and output data y. In this example, X represents the four possible combinations of boolean values, and y represents the XOR of those values.

We define the architecture of the neural network using tf.keras.models.Sequential. We have two dense layers: the first layer has 4 neurons, takes input shape of 2 (the number of features in our input data), and uses ReLU activation function. The second layer has 1 neuron, uses sigmoid activation function. We compile the model using the compile function, where we specify the optimizer as 'adam', the loss function as 'binary_crossentropy', and the metric as 'accuracy'.

We train the model by calling fit function, which takes input data X and output data y, and specifies the number of epochs. We test the model by creating a test_data array of the same shape as the input data X, and calling the predict function to get the predicted outputs. Finally, we print the predictions.

5. SCIKIT

Scikit is an open source library originally developed in 2007 for a GSOC and is used for predictive analysis. It is built on numpy, SciPy and Matplotlib. It focuses more on modelling than on data maipulation. It is used for clustering, feature extraction, dimensionality reduction, feature selection not to mention its use in Supervised and Unsupervised learning algortithms such as SVM, decision tree, PCA etc.

In classification, It can be used for image detection, spam identification; in clustering it can help segment users; in regression it could show stock prices, drug efficacy (SciKit-Learn, n.d.-a). Supervised learning which contain decision tree, random forest, etc, unsupervised learning which contain starting from unsupervised clustering extending to unsupervised neural network are all the part of sklearn .Also sklearn provides models like cross validation i.e. to check the accuracy of unknown data, dimensionality reduction which reduces the number of attributes in data which can be used further for visualization.

Typically scikit is a 2x2 matrix by dimension, where rows represent individual elements of the dataset and columns represent related quantities to the data (JakeVDP, n.d.).

In Recurrent Neural Networks, the information is cycled in a loop, i.e the output is determined by current input and previously received inputs. Some types of RNN are one to one, many to one, one to many etc.

Multiple layer perceptron is formed from as it says multiple layers of perceptron. It has an input layer, hidden layers and output layers. It learns a function by training on its dataset across multiple dimensions.

Collected dataset will split into 80-20 ratio. Then we will Histogram of Oriented Gradients method and divide the image into 8x8 pixels to make it undergo convolutions. Dimensionality reduction is one of the popular techniques to reduce the complexity of the dataset by eliminating unnecessary variables to improve the performance of the model. It is applicable for both supervised and unsupervised learning approaches. Feature extraction is mainly used for unsupervised learning to extract necessary features needed to train the ML model. Principal Component Analysis (PCA) and Singular Value Decomposition (SVD) are few popular approaches for reducing the dimensions in unsupervised approach. In SVD we simplify a matrix to make doing calculations with the matrix easier. In PCA we create new features after analysing the characteristics of the dataset.

Tensorflow is more popular and it is used in the design process to assist developers as well as for training new models. It is a low level library wheras scikit is a high level one. Neural network in tensorflow is used indirectly and it used for deep learning. It can also be called a barebones neural network implementation. A barebone neural network model cannot be implemented in scikit. Scikit is easier to use and debug as opposed to tensorflow. Scikit-learn is based on the traditional machine learning programming paradigm, where the focus is on designing and selecting appropriate features and algorithms. TensorFlow, on the other hand, is based on the more recent deep learning paradigm, where the focus is on designing and training neural networks.

Data is a collection of information. It is central to every machine learning algorithm and is used to train parameters for the algorithm. Without good quality and quantity of data we can't develop a machine learning model. AI requires a massive scale of data to learn and improve decision making process. The more data you have access to, the better will be the performance. The data input is used to generate new rules for future analysis and prediction. The sample data quality is important to prevent problems from arising.

6. LIMITATIONS OF ML

From healthcare to banking to transportation, machine learning (ML) is a formidable technology that has the potential to disrupt a wide range of sectors. To guarantee that ML is utilised responsibly and ethically, like with any technology, there are some ethical issues that need to be addressed. The following are some of the main ethical issues for ML:

6.1 Bias and prejudice: ML algorithms can reinforce biases and discrimination if they were developed by biassed individuals or if they were trained on biassed data. This has the potential to produce biassed results and maintain social inequality.

6.2 Privacy: To train, ML algorithms frequently need a lot of data, some of which may contain sensitive information about specific people.

6.3 Responsibility: As machine learning (ML) technology advances, there is a danger that humans may grow overly dependent on it and delegate responsibility for critical choices to the technology. It's crucial to keep in mind that ML should only be used as a tool in combination with human judgement and decision-making.

6.4 Accountability: It can be challenging to pinpoint blame when things go wrong using ML. The development and application of the technology may include a number of parties, and it can be challenging to identify who is accountable when anything goes wrong.

6.5 Safety: ML algorithms may be used to automate or control physical systems, including autonomous vehicles or medical equipment. It is crucial to make sure that these systems are secure, trustworthy, and do not endanger human life or health.

6.6 Fairness: By evaluating a person's eligibility for loans or jobs, for example, ML algorithms may have a big influence on their life. Making ensuring that these algorithms are just and do not unfairly disfavour particular groups of individuals is crucial.

Ultimately, it's critical to be aware of these ethical issues and make every effort to reduce them. ML has enormous potential for good, but in order to ensure that it serves everyone, it must be utilised responsibly. The absence of data is one of the main problems with machine learning (ML). Large amounts of high-quality data are essential for ML models to train efficiently and produce reliable predictions. Without enough data, ML models could perform poorly, have high error rates, and have a hard time generalising to new data.

There are a number of reasons why data in ML may be constrained. Data gathering can be difficult and time-consuming, especially for complicated jobs that call for specific knowledge or skill. Data can occasionally be sensitive or secret, which makes it difficult to collect or utilize for ML purposes. Data bias may have a big influence on how well ML models function, resulting in erroneous predictions and little generalisation. It's essential to have a wide variety of data to build solid machine learning models that can adapt to different settings. Finding varied data, however, can be difficult, especially in specialised or specialist domains. Many methods, including data augmentation, transfer learning, and synthetic data creation, can be employed to lessen the effect of data limits on ML models. With the generation of new data or the use of already trained models, these strategies can assist overcome the data shortage.

ML is an effective tool for handling complicated issues, especially those that are challenging to resolve using conventional algorithmic techniques. Yet, some issues, particularly deterministic issues, could be more resistant to machine learning. Deterministic issues are ones with a solitary, established answer. Frequently, these issues may be resolved using predetermined rules or algorithms. For instance, finding a number's square root is an example of a deterministic issue that may be resolved with the aid of a certain method.

Statistical techniques are used in ML, on the other hand, to identify patterns in data and create predictions. The majority of the times, ML algorithms are not created to identify a single, exact answer to a problem.

This implies that ML may not be the optimum strategy for all deterministic issues. Alternatively, classic algorithmic techniques that are created to discover exact answers to particular issues may be more appropriate for deterministic situations.

Yet, ML may still be helpful with deterministic issues in a variety of ways. For instance, ML may be used to find trends or outliers in data that can be important for finding a solution.

ML may also be used to optimise solutions, such as determining the approach that is most effective at solving an issue or reducing the amount of resources needed to do so. In conclusion, even if solving deterministic issues may not be the best use for machine learning, the technology may still be useful in seeing trends, improving solutions, and lowering the amount of resources needed to complete a task. The ideal strategy will ultimately rely on the particular issue at hand and the resources that are accessible.

A further drawback of machine learning (ML) is the inability of some models to be transparent or interpretable. In crucial applications where mistakes might have serious repercussions, this implies that it may be challenging to grasp how the model is coming to conclusions or generating predictions. Many issues, such as the following, can contribute to the lack of interpretability:

Complexity: Many ML models include millions of parameters that interact non-linearly, making them extremely complicated. Even for the professionals who developed the model, this might make it challenging to comprehend how it comes to judgements.

Black-box nature: Some models are created to be "black boxes," which means they are purposefully opaque and don't reveal how they make decisions. Deep Neural Networks (DNNs) and various ensemble models are examples of such models.

Data-driven design: Machine learning (ML) models are trained on data, and their output is exclusively dependent on the patterns they identify in that data. It might not be immediately clear how such patterns convert into choices or forecasts as a consequence.

Lack of standards: It might be difficult to compare or assess various models since there are presently no global standards for model interpretability.

ML models may be made more effective in real-world applications, where it is crucial to comprehend how choices are made, by enhancing interpretability.

The lack of repeatability is a key disadvantage of machine learning (ML). Reproducibility is the capacity to get the same outcomes when a research is repeated using the same information and procedures. Lack of repeatability in ML can be caused by a number of things, such as:

Data variability makes it challenging to exactly duplicate results since the quality, amount, and format of the data used for ML models might vary widely.

Model variability: ML models may be trained differently even when given the same data, leading to a range of possible predictions. Variability in the code and environment used to train and test machine learning models can potentially provide diverse outcomes.

Lack of transparency: As was already said, it may be difficult to comprehend or interpret some models, which might make it difficult to duplicate results.

Because it can provide findings that cannot be verified or trusted, the lack of repeatability in ML is a serious problem. In crucial applications like healthcare or finance, where mistakes can have serious repercussions, this can be especially troublesome.

Researchers are investigating a number of approaches to solve the lack of reproducibility, including providing thorough documentation of the data and techniques used to train a model, sharing code and data in an open manner, and utilising standardised assessment criteria. Enhancing repeatability can make ML models more dependable and trustworthy, which is essential for their widespread acceptance in practical applications.

Neural Networks in AI work by copying the working of the human brain. Like how in brain, first we receive stimulus from outside, then we process the input, then generate an output response. Similarly, in a neural network we have input layer, hidden layer and output layer.

In the input layer we take in inputs as vectors, then next comes the hidden layer, in this layer we have our activation functions. What activation functions do is filter out the noise from the data, until all we are left with is our required datasets. Some examples of activation functions are EELU, RELU, Leaky RELU etc. Output layer then gives the output like sigmoid graph etc.

7. CASE STUDY

As a Data scientist you have been asked to help increase business revenue for a cosmetic company. Help them make a model that looks at user purchases and helps recommend them similar products.

Problem Identification-First whenever tasked with doing anything we need to identify the problem. Here it is to find a product aligned to the client's needs.

Data Collection-The next step is to do data collection, the more data we have the better suggestion we can give. Data includes user data like purchase history, search history, their most viewed product, their saved products etc. It also includes data on the product like the ingredients, the inventory of it, its rating, its function.

After data collection we access it and move on to Data Preparation stage.

Data Preparation-Most of the time the data we obtain will have errors and inconsistencies; formatting errors, missing data, data redundancy etc. Thus a need to filter out irrelevant data, like extreme values, and replacement or removal of missing data is apparent. The data column needs to be in the exact format like date should be in date time format and text should be in string so we don't get any error while accessing it. We also need to create relevant new features like average cost per product, or what the of issue each product fixes etc. We will use correlation analysis next to explore and group the data.

Data Analysis: Now that we have prepared the data, we will access it and split it into 5 parts. We will keep one part of this aside for testing purposes and use the rest 80% data as sample data for model development.

Model Development- First and foremost we will try and use as many pre-existing methods as possible to make out job easier. Here for instance we can use content based filtering, like for eg someone uses a cleaner with lot of water means that they have dry skin.

After this we will use correlation analysis. Its benefit is that for eg say the user while searching uses the word organic then we will know that whatever product we are going to recommend to the user needs to be organic and must not contain any chemicals else the user would not purchase it.

Corr. and filtering also check similarities between two users and how they view products. We can group users too on the basis of age, then further filtering them based on purchases, average ratings and then recommending a product which others rated highly.

Model Evaluation- After model is prepared we will test it. This involves tuning model and checking data set. The model lifecycle is iterative, since if we find some problem during the evaluation phase then we may need to go back to say data collection step and change the process used for instance.

After the test data clears the model, we proceed to live testing. The live testing helps give us valuable feedback on the functioning of the model.

Performance Report-There is also a need to track model performance after it has been deployed and also if needed at a later date, retrain it. We do this to check whether quality of model is retained after few years have passed.

8. CONCLUSION

In this book chapter we have presented all major machine learning algorithms in detail. We have seen that there is a trend in federated learning wherein data privacy is a concern. Federated learning is a machine learning paradigm that involves training models on decentralized data. In this approach, multiple devices or clients, each with their own local data, collaborate to train a shared global model, without exchanging their data with each other or with a central server. Federated learning can be used over a wide range of machine learning algorithms. Federated learning has been successfully applied to train deep neural networks for tasks such as image classification, natural language processing, and speech recognition. Federated learning can be used to train gradient boosting models for tasks such as regression and classification. Federated learning can be used to train support vector machines for tasks such as anomaly detection and fraud detection. Federated learning can be used to train decision tree models for tasks such as recommendation systems and personalized marketing.

Over ML methods, federated learning offers a wide range of applications. Data from several hospitals and healthcare organizations may be utilized to train models using federated learning. As a result, patient data privacy may be maintained while helping to increase the accuracy of medical diagnoses, medication development, and treatment recommendations. Federated learning may be used to create models for credit rating, risk analysis, and fraud detection. Federated learning can assist increase the accuracy of these models while safeguarding the privacy of consumer data by enabling collaboration across various financial organizations. Federated learning may be used to create models on the Internet of Things (IoT) that can learn from information produced by sensors and devices dispersed throughout many areas. This can increase the effectiveness of IoT applications while protecting user data privacy. Federated learning may be used to train models for natural language processing tasks like speech recognition and language translation. Federated learning can assist increase the accuracy of these models while safeguarding the privacy of user data by enabling several devices to work together in creating them. Federated learning enables several cars to work together to develop these models, which may be used to train models for autonomous vehicles. This can enhance these models' accuracy while protecting the privacy of user data. In conclusion, federated learning offers a strong tool for developing precise models while protecting the privacy of sensitive data and has a wide variety of applications across ML methods in numerous sectors.

REFERENCES

Adankon, M. M., & Cheriet, M. (2009). Model selection for the LS-SVM. Application to handwriting recognition. *Pattern Recognition*, *42*(12), 3264–3270. doi:10.1016/j.patcog.2008.10.023

Ahmad, A. S., Hassan, M. Y., Abdullah, M. P., Rahman, H. A., Hussin, F., Abdullah, H., & Saidur, R. (2014). A review on applications of ANN and SVM for building electrical energy consumption forecasting. *Renewable & Sustainable Energy Reviews*, *33*, 102–109. doi:10.1016/j.rser.2014.01.069

Akakuru, O. C., Adakwa, C. B., Ikoro, D. O., Eyankware, M. O., Opara, A. I., Njoku, A. O., Iheme, K. O., & Usman, A. (2023). Application of artificial neural network and multi-linear regression techniques in groundwater quality and health risk assessment around Egbema, Southeastern Nigeria. *Environmental Earth Sciences*, *82*(3), 77. doi:10.100712665-023-10753-1

Aritonang, M., & Sihombing, D. J. C. (2019, November). An Application of Backpropagation Neural Network for Sales Forecasting Rice Miling Unit. In *2019 International Conference of Computer Science and Information Technology (ICoSNIKOM)* (pp. 1-4). IEEE. 10.1109/ICoSNIKOM48755.2019.9111612

Byvatov, E., & Schneider, G. (2003). Support vector machine applications in bioinformatics. *Applied Bioinformatics*, *2*(2), 67–77. PMID:15130823

Datacamp. (n.d.-a). https://www.datacamp.com/tutorial/decision-tree-classification-python

Datacamp. (n.d.-b). https://www.datacamp.com/tutorial/random-forests-classifier-python

Datacamp. (n.d.-c). https://www.datacamp.com/tutorial/k-means-clustering-python

Deka, P. C. (2014). Support vector machine applications in the field of hydrology: A review. *Applied Soft Computing*, *19*, 372–386. doi:10.1016/j.asoc.2014.02.002

Ghiasi, M. M., & Zendehboudi, S. (2021). Application of decision tree-based ensemble learning in the classification of breast cancer. *Computers in Biology and Medicine*, *128*, 104089. doi:10.1016/j.compbiomed.2020.104089 PMID:33338982

Huang, S., Cai, N., Pacheco, P. P., Narrandes, S., Wang, Y., & Xu, W. (2018). Applications of support vector machine (SVM) learning in cancer genomics. *Cancer Genomics & Proteomics*, *15*(1), 41–51. PMID:29275361

JakeVDP. (n.d.). https://jakevdp.github.io/PythonDataScienceHandbook/05.02-introducing-scikit-learn

Kataria, A., & Singh, M. D. (2013). A review of data classification using k-nearest neighbour algorithm. *International Journal of Emerging Technology and Advanced Engineering*, *3*(6), 354–360.

Kazmierska, J., & Malicki, J. (2008). Application of the Naïve Bayesian Classifier to optimize treatment decisions. *Radiotherapy and Oncology : Journal of the European Society for Therapeutic Radiology and Oncology*, *86*(2), 211–216. doi:10.1016/j.radonc.2007.10.019 PMID:18022719

Khanmohammadi, N., Rezaie, H., Montaseri, M., & Behmanesh, J. (2018). The application of multiple linear regression method in reference evapotranspiration trend calculation. *Stochastic Environmental Research and Risk Assessment*, *32*(3), 661–673. doi:10.100700477-017-1378-z

Kim, J. W., Lee, B. H., Shaw, M. J., Chang, H. L., & Nelson, M. (2001). Application of decision-tree induction techniques to personalized advertisements on internet storefronts. *International Journal of Electronic Commerce*, *5*(3), 45–62. doi:10.1080/10864415.2001.11044215

LeCun, Y., Bengio, Y., & Hinton, G. (2015). Deep learning. *Nature, 521*(7553), 436-444.

Levelup. (n.d.). https://levelup.gitconnected.com/how-to-perform-dbscan-clustering-in-python-using-scikit-learn-cef05848cbfc

Liu, R., Nageotte, F., Zanne, P., de Mathelin, M., & Dresp-Langley, B. (2021). Deep reinforcement learning for the control of robotic manipulation: A focussed mini-review. *Robotics (Basel, Switzerland)*, *10*(1), 22. doi:10.3390/robotics10010022

Mahesh, B. (2020). Machine learning algorithms-a review. *International Journal of Science and Research, 9*, 381-386.

Magesh, G., Muthuswamy, P., & Singh, B. (2015). Use of Information Technology among school students in the State of Tamil Nadu, India. *International Journal of Applied Engineering Research: IJAER*, *10*(1), 2201–2209.

Ra, P. K., Nathawat, M. S., & Onagh, M. (2012). Application of multiple linear regression model through GIS and remote sensing for malaria mapping in Varanasi District, India. *Health Science Journal*, *6*(4), 731.

Rrmoku, K., Selimi, B., & Ahmedi, L. (2022). Application of trust in recommender systems—Utilizing naive Bayes classifier. *Computation (Basel, Switzerland)*, *10*(1), 6. doi:10.3390/computation10010006

Saritas, M. M., & Yasar, A. (2019). Performance analysis of ANN and Naive Bayes classification algorithm for data classification. *International Journal of Intelligent Systems and Applications in Engineering, 7*(2), 88-91.

Sarker, I. (2021). Machine Learning: Algorithms, Real-World Applications and Research Directions. *SN Computer Science*. doi:10.1007/s42979-021-00592-x

SciKit-Learn. (n.d.-a). https://scikit-learn.org/stable/

SciKit-Learn. (n.d.-b). https://scikit-learn.org/stable/modules/svm.html

SciKit-Learn. (n.d.-c). https://scikit-learn.org/stable/modules/naive_bayes.html

Simplilearn. (n.d.). https://www.simplilearn.com/tutorials/scikit-learn-tutorial/sklearn-linear-regression-with-examples

Singh, B., & Acharjya, D. P. (2020). Computational intelligence techniques for efficient delivery of healthcare. *Health and Technology*, *10*, 167–185.

Towardsdatascience. (n.d.-a). https://towardsdatascience.com/logistic-regression-using-python-sklearn-numpy-mnist-handwriting-recognition-matplotlib-a6b31e2b166a

Towardsdatascience. (n.d.-b). https://towardsdatascience.com/building-a-k-nearest-neighbors-k-nn-model-with-scikit-learn-51209555453a

U., J., Olesnikova, A., Song, C. H., & Lee, W. D. (2009, January). The development and application of decision tree for agriculture data. In *2009 Second International Symposium on Intelligent Information Technology and Security Informatics* (pp. 16-20). IEEE.

Valsamis, E. M., Husband, H., & Chan, G. K. W. (2019). Segmented linear regression modelling of time-series of binary variables in healthcare. *Computational and Mathematical Methods in Medicine*. doi:10.1155/2019/3478598 PMID:31885678

Wiggins, M., Saad, A., Litt, B., & Vachtsevanos, G. (2008). Evolving a Bayesian classifier for ECG-based age classification in medical applications. *Applied Soft Computing*, 8(1), 599–608. doi:10.1016/j.asoc.2007.03.009 PMID:22010038

Wu, M. C., Lin, S. Y., & Lin, C. H. (2006). An effective application of decision tree to stock trading. *Expert Systems with Applications*, 31(2), 270–274. doi:10.1016/j.eswa.2005.09.026

Zhao, L., Chen, Y., & Schaffner, D. W. (2001). Comparison of logistic regression and linear regression in modeling percentage data. *Applied and Environmental Microbiology*, 67(5), 2129–2135. doi:10.1128/AEM.67.5.2129-2135.2001 PMID:11319091

Chapter 3
Understanding Convolutional Neural Network With TensorFlow:
CNN

Aswathy Ravikumar

https://orcid.org/0000-0003-0897-6991

Vellore Institute of Technology, Chennai, India

Harini Sriraman

https://orcid.org/0000-0002-2192-8153

Vellore Institute of Technology, Chennai, India

ABSTRACT

In academia and business, deep-learning-based models have exhibited extraordinary performance over the last decade. The learning potential of Convolutional Neural Networks (CNNs) derives from a combination of several feature extraction levels that completely use a vast quantity of input. CNN is an important technique for tackling computer vision issues, although the theories behind its processing efficacy are not yet completely understood. CNN has achieved cutting-edge performance on a variety of datasets in computer vision applications like remote sensing, medical image categorization, facial detection, and object identification. This is due to the efficiency with which they process visual features. This chapter presents the most significant advancements in CNN for efficient processing in computer vision, including convolutional layer configurations, pooling layer approaches, network activation functions, loss functions, normalization approaches, and CNN optimization techniques.

INTRODUCTION

The core of intelligence for computers and other electronic devices is machine learning. It use predictive models based on previous data to forecast future behaviors, outcomes, and patterns. Deep learning

DOI: 10.4018/978-1-6684-8531-6.ch003

Copyright © 2024, IGI Global. Copying or distributing in print or electronic forms without written permission of IGI Global is prohibited.

is an subfield of machine learning in which models brain - inspired are represented mathematically. Deep Neural Networks' (DNN) parameters, which may vary from a few hundred to over 1.2 billion, are dynamically learnt from the data. DNNs can describe complex nonlinear relationships between inputs and outputs. Their designs result in compositional models that depict the thing as a layered mixture of primitives. There are several variations of a few core approaches with deep structures. DNN utilizes hierarchical structures to learn high-level representations from data. It is a relatively recent technique that is commonly used in traditional applications of artificial intelligence, such as text categorization, learning techniques, natural-language processing, and machine vision. There are three key reasons for the rise in popularity of deep learning: vastly increased chip processing capabilities, decreased computer system prices, and substantial breakthroughs in machine learning techniques. As a consequence, DNNs have garnered a great deal of interest in recent years, and multiple models for diverse applications have been proposed.

Artificial Neural Networks (Guo et al., 2016) are computer processing systems that are substantially influenced by the operation of natural nervous systems. ANNs are primarily composed of many linked computational nodes (called neurons) that function dispersedly to train from inputs to maximize their output. Its input, often in the shape of multidimensional vectors, would have been loaded into the input layer and redistributed among the hidden units. This is known as the learning experience. The hidden units would then make judgments based on the last layer and evaluate how an unexpected change inside itself affects or enhances its correct outcome. Hidden layer levels built atop one another is referred to as deep learning. Supervised and unsupervised learning are the primary learning approaches in image analysis jobs. Supervised learning involves learning using inputs that have been pre-labeled and serve as objectives. Every training sample will have a set of input variables (feature vector) and one or more associated corresponding outputs. This kind of training aims to lower the overall classification error of a model by the proper computation of the actual output of training images.

In unsupervised, the trained model does not contain any labels. Typically, the success of a network is assessed by whether or not it can lower or raise an associated cost factor. However, it is essential to highlight that most image-based pattern recognition tasks rely on categorization utilizing supervised learning. Convolutional Neural Network is similar to conventional ANNs in that it consists of neurons that optimize themselves via learning. Each neuron will continue to receive inputs and execute an action (including a scalar product and then a nonlinear variable) - the fundamental building blocks of innumerable ANNs. The complete network will continue representing a single perceptual criterion (the weight) through input raw picture vectors to output class scores. The last layer will include loss functions connected with the classes, and every one of the standard techniques established for conventional ANNs will still be applicable.

CNN is one of the most essential and useful kinds of neural networks (Albawi et al., 2017) and is commonly used for categorization and object segmentation. The three major layers of a CNN are convolution, pooling, and fully connected. Each level is accountable for certain spatial tasks. CNN uses a variety of kernels in convolution layers to convolve the input image and create feature maps. The pooling layer often follows the convolution layer. This layer compresses both feature maps and system parameters. Following a layer that has been flattened and the layer that is pooling, there are a series of layers that are all interconnected. The flattened layer transforms the 2D feature maps of the previous layer into 1D feature maps suitable for the future fully connected levels. The vector that has been flattened may be used to categorize the photographs later. Pooling is a crucial step in convolutional networks since it reduces the size of the feature maps. By merging a collection of values into a lower number of values,

Figure 1. Shallow neural network structure

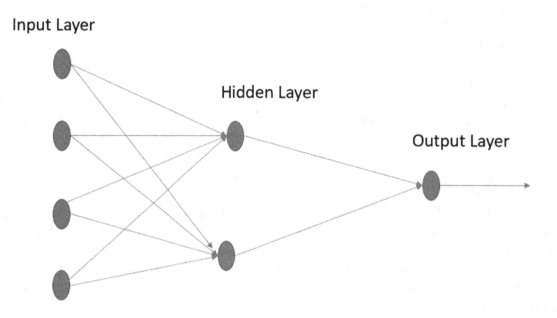

it decreases the complexity of a feature map. It turns the composite visual features into information that may be used by conserving essential data and deleting extraneous data.

By eliminating specific connections among convolutional layers, pooling operators enable spatial translation invariance while reducing the computational cost of top layers. This layer conducts downsampling on the previous layer's feature maps to generate new maps with a lower resolution. This layer has two basic functions: the first is to reduce the computational cost by minimizing the number model parameters or weights, and the second is to avoid overfitting. A smart pooling strategy should only extract relevant data and eliminate superfluous pieces.

The Dropout (N. Srivastava et al., n.d.) can be applied for the Regularization of CNN. The regularization of CNN is done by Dropout by the addition of noise to the feature map of the corresponding layer.

Overfitting (Carremans, 2019) occurs when a network cannot properly learn due to various factors. It is a crucial notion in the majority, if not all, ML algorithms, and every effort must be made to minimize its impacts. If our models exhibited symptoms of overfitting, our capacity to identify generalized characteristics for not just our training dataset but also our testing and prediction datasets might be diminished. This is the primary motivation for simplifying our ANNs. The fewer parameters are necessary to train a network, the less probable it is to overfit - and, thus, the better its predictive accuracy. A small ANN structure is shown in Figure 1.

CONVOLUTIONAL NEURAL NETWORK

CNN is a type of algorithm for deep learning for handling gridded data, such as images, that is impacted by the architectural style of the mammal visual cortex (Albawi et al., 2017; Fukushima, 1980; Hubel &

Figure 2. CNN layers

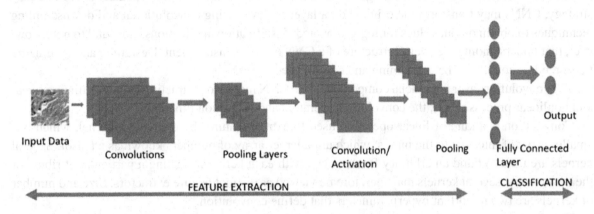

Wiesel, 1962) and designed to dynamically and adaptively learn advanced of character traits, from low- to high-level patterns. CNN typically consists of three distinct types of layers (or elements): convolution, pooling, and fully connected. The first two layers, convolution and pooling, automatically extract features, whereas the third, a fully linked layer, transfers the extracted information to the final output, including classification. CNN is composed of a stack of arithmetic calculations, including convolution, a particular kind of single output that plays a crucial role. In digital photographs, pixel values are stored in a two-dimensional grid, and a tiny grid of variables known as the kernel, feature extractor, is applied to each picture point. As a feature may appear anywhere inside the picture, CNN is very efficient for image analysis. As one level feeds its result to the succeeding layer, the gathered attributes may grow hierarchically and become increasingly complex. Training is the process of modifying parameters, such as kernels, to minimize the gap between output and regression coefficient labels by using backpropagation or gradient descent, among other other optimizers. CNN does not need a manually performed extraction of features. Second, CNN designs only sometimes need human expertise to segregate tumors or organs. CNN requires graphics processing units for model training since it is computationally more costly due to the millions of estimated able trainable parameters. The primary layers of CNN are shown in Figure 2.

Convolutional Layer

CNN is comprised of three separate levels. These layers are convolutional, pooling, and completely linked. A Framework is produced by layering these layers. CNN's core operation may be broken down into four main components. As with earlier versions of ANN, every input will contain the number of pixels in the picture. Using the scalar product of its own weight and the size of the area connected to the input, the convolutional layer produces the output for cells associated to certain portions of the input. The rectified unit (sometimes abbreviated ReLU) seeks to apply an "elementwise" activation function, such as the sigmoid, to the output of the activation created by the layer below it. Each pooling layer will then execute basic down sampling along the spatial dimension of an input, therefore reducing the number of activation parameters. All fully-connected levels will then conduct the same tasks as traditional ANNs and attempt to create class scores from the activations in order to classify the data.

In addition, ReLU is advised for usage between these layers to improve performance. Using this easy strategy, CNNs may transform the original data layer by layer using convolutional and downsampling techniques to obtain output values for regression and classification applications. It is vital to note, however, that understanding the overall structure of a CNN model is insufficient. Designing and optimizing these models could be time-consuming and complicated.

The convolution layer is a crucial component of the CNN model for extracting features utilizing linear and nonlinear processes, i.e., the convolution operators and activation functions.

Convolution is a kind of linear operation used to extract features by applying a kernel, which is a smaller array of integers, to the inputs, which are a larger array of numbers known as a tensor. Several kernels are used to build an arbitrary feature map, with each kernel reflecting a particular attribute of the raw tensors; several kernels may therefore be viewed as distinct feature extractors. Size and number of kernels are two important hyperparameters that define convolution.

The disclosed convolution approach avoids each kernel's center from overlapping the outermost component of the input vector. It minimizes the height and width of the output feature map compared to the input feature map. In order to preserve in-plane dimensions for the application of further layers, modern CNN architectures often use no padding. Without zero padding, the size of each successive feature map would decrease after the convolution operation.

A stride is the distance between two adjacent kernel points, which also influences the convolution technique. Occasionally, a stride bigger than one is utilized to complete the down sampling of the retrieved features. As shown below, pooling is an alternative approach for down sampling.

Sharing of weight is the fundamental feature of a convolution process; kernels were spread over all image locations. Weight sharing generates the following convolutional characteristics: Increasing model efficiency by decreasing truncation error.

Nonlinear Activation Function: An Afterwards, a nonlinear activation function is applied towards the conclusions of a sequential process, which includes this convolution. But although seamless nonlinear activation features, such as the sigmoid and tanh functions, were formerly employed because they represent mathematical descriptions of biological neural action, the rectified linear unit is today the most often used nonlinear activation feature (Glorot et al., 2011).

Pooling: NNs are built by stacking layers of two types: convolutional and pooling (subsampling). The pooling layer (Hutchison et al., 2010) is critical in CNNs since it is primarily responsible for data invariance and perturbation resistance. The pooling layer may be obtained using a two-step pooling procedure. Aggregation of information can improve the representation's resistance to translation and elastic distortions to a certain extent.

Furthermore, downsampling can reduce the size of feature channels, hence alleviating computational load. The two phases may be considered a feature selection technique that retains the most critical information while minimizing the feature space. The most frequently used pooling processes, such as maximum and average pooling, are entirely handcrafted. However, such an ad hoc pooling process has several drawbacks. For instance, max pooling extracts the region's most significant value, whereas average pooling extracts only the region's average value. Additionally, handcrafted pooling methods cannot ensure that classification error is minimized throughout the training stage. As a result, we propose in this study to train one pooling operator for each feature channel to aggregate data within the local region.

CNN uses pooling layers to integrate the information learnt from the conv layer feature space. Its primary function is to reduce overfitting throughout model training by reducing or summarizing the extracted features. Pooling is straightforward to create because they frequently down sample the incoming data using its maximum or mean value. Feature maps were particularly sensitive to their location within the input, while convolutional layers summarize the relevant information in the data using image features. For example, if an object changes unintentionally between images, the convolution layer must reconstruct the feature map. Due to the previously preserved one, our projections must be changed. To overcome this problem, it is important to down sample the map, which is performed via the use of CNN pooling layers that summarize all data from the feature space.

Max-Pooling A max-pooling operator (Ranzato et al., n.d.) may be used to reduce the variability of the convolutional output bands. With max-pooling, layer must operate on the significant element in the convolutional layer's feature map. In a nutshell, it chooses the element with the highest value from the area covered by the filters in any feature space. Max polling aids in extracting low-level features from data such as edges, points, etc. Alternatively, when it comes to image processing, max-pooling aids in extracting the sharpest features on the picture, which are the best lower-level representations of the image.

Min Pooling: With min pooling, this layer acts on the least significant element inside the feature map of the convolution layers. Simply said, it selects the element with the lowest value inside the region covered by the filters in any given feature space. Min pooling is used for removing the least important features from data or when extracting features with weaker values or edgeless features from an image.

Average Pooling: The notion of an average or median for pooling and gathering features was invented by (LeCun et al., 1989a) and first implemented in (LeCun et al., 1998), the very first convolution deep neural network. When employing average pooling, the layer picks the average of a components available in the feature map's patch. The entire feature map is tested to the average value of the area. Thus, max-pooling recognizes the most prominent feature of each patch, while pooling identifies the whole covered area. A level of invariance is provided through pooling. Moreover, pooling is a faster operation than convolutions. Using average pooling facilitates the extraction of smooth features. If we apply an average max - pooling to image data, we will receive a mixture of any and all colors in the feature map's coverage region. If the dispersion of data points and colors in any image is smooth, or to be more specific, if the distribution is right, then we may use average pooling to get reliable data.

Global Pooling Layer: Whenever the down sampled input is fed into the CNN's fully connected layer, the data is vectorized and delivered directly to the fully linked layer, where activation functions carry out their duties. This method provides a bridge among convolutional structures and traditional neural networks. Following the extraction of features that used a convolutional architecture, the resulting features are classified using standard methods. When finally coupled layers are susceptible to overfitting, use the dropout function. The dropout function improves generalization and prevents overfitting. During learning, the dropout function zeros out fifty percent of the activation function. In this instance, we may use a different technique referred to as the global pooling layer. They may replace CNN's layers that have been flattened. A flatten layer reduces a tensor of any dimension with a one tensor while preserving all of the original tensor's values. Adding values to a tensor of this kind raises the probability of overfitting. This eliminates the danger of overfitting.

Dropout

Deep neural systems feature several nonlinear hidden units, which makes them very descriptive models capable of discovering extremely complex correlations among their inputs and outcomes. With minimal training information, unfortunately, many of these complex interactions cannot be accurately predicted will be the consequence of sampling error. Thus, they will exist inside the training dataset and not with actual test data, despite the training set and test data being chosen from identical distributions. These include halting training when performance on a validation set begins to deteriorate, adding weight penalties of various types, including L1 and L2 regularization, and gentle weight sharing, including applying weight exchange. With infinite computing, the optimal technique to regularize' would be to "A xed-sized system would aggregate the outputs of all potential parameter values, with each setting weighted of posterior probability provided the training examples. Combining models enhances the efficacy of machine learning methods almost always. With big neural nets, though, it is cost prohibitive to average the outputs of several independently trained networks. Integrating several systems is most effective when the models are distinct. To make neural net models distinct, they must either have distinct architecture or be learned on distinct data. Finding the optimum hyperparameters for each design is challenging, and training each huge network requires a significant amount of computing. In addition, big networks often need enormous quantities of training data, and there might need to be more data to train several networks on distinct portions of the data. Even if it were possible to train several distinct big networks, it would be impractical to use all of them at test time for applications where rapid response is essential. A dropout is an approach that tackles both of these problems. It avoids overfitting and provides a technique of essentially mixing infinitely many neural network architectures. By dropping a component out, it implies temporary disconnection from the network.

The method for adding Dropout to a neuron is equivalent to sampling a "thinned" structure. The thinning network is comprised of units which escaped Dropout. A network having n units may be seen as a group of 2n potential neural networks that have been thinned. These networks exchange weights such that the overall number of variables remains at or below O(n2). A new sampling and thin training network are constructed for each training example display.

Consequently, training a neural network using Dropout resembles training a group of 2n thinned systems with considerable weight transfer, in which each thin network is trained seldom, if at all. As a result, it is not possible to explicitly aggregate the predictions of an increasingly large number of thinning models at test time. In reality, though, a simple approximation approach of averaging works well. The concept is to employ a single neural network without dropouts during testing. This network's weights are reduced copies of the learned weights. Learning a net with Dropout and employing this approximation averaging strategy at test time significantly reduces prediction error on a broad range of classification tasks relative to training with other methods. The variation in accuracy concerning Dropout is shown in Figure 3.

The dropout layer has a drawback in that, at times, the training time may be high for updating the parameters. Each training example aims to successfully train a unique random architecture. As a result, the gradients calculated are not those of the final design that will be utilized during testing. As a result, it is unsurprising that training takes so long. However, this stochasticity is likely to avoid overfitting. As a result, a barter between overfitting and training time is established. With more training time, one may employ a high rate of Dropout and have less overfitting. Accelerating Dropout is an intriguing area for further research. Dropout may be seen as the bagging of models trained on distinct data groups. The regularization impact of Dropout in convolutional layers comes mostly from their resilience to noisy inputs.

Fully Connected Neural Network Layer

All local output features of both the final convolution are generally deconstructed, i.e., transformed to a one-dimensional array of tensors and connected within one or more dense layers, often known as a

Figure 3. Accuracy vs. dropout
Source: Maklin (n.d.)

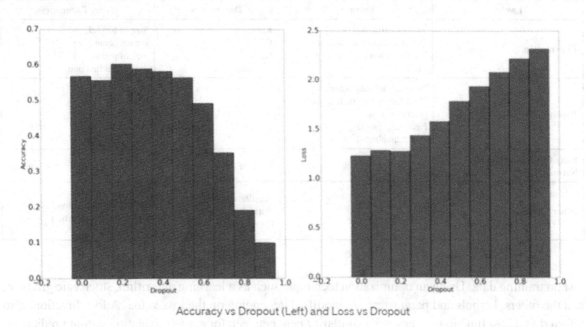

Accuracy vs Dropout (Left) and Loss vs Dropout

fully-connected layer, in which each input is coupled from each outcome by a trainable value. After the convolution recovers the characteristics, a lack of relevance is detected more by pooling layers; they were transferred by a set of something like the fully connected layer to the output of the network, which includes the probability for each class in classification. The final completely connected layer often has the same number of output links as subclasses. Following each layer that is finally connected is a function f, such as ReLU. Table 1 shows the final layer activation function. Typically, the last layer's activation function varies from that of the other layers. The suitable activation function should be established for each task.

CNN Training

The neural network training process involves identifying kernels for convolution operations and weights in fully-connected networks in order to reduce discrepancies between output predictions with ground truth labelling on a training example. Error function with stochastic gradient optimization approaches are important in backpropagation, which is frequently employed for training neural networks. A loss method computes the effectiveness of a model with specified kernels and weights with forward propagation

Table 1. Final CNN layer activations

Task	Activation
Classification - Binary	Sigmoid activation function
Classification – Multi	Softmax activation function
Regression	ReLU

Table 2. CNN layers

Layers	Features	Parameters	Hyper Parameters
Convolution	Feature extraction 2-dimensional convolution The operation performed: Dot Product	Kernels Filters Stride Padding	Size of Kernel Kernel count Size of padding bits Activation function
Pooling	Time Complexity is high Used for sensitivity, reduction of parameter count Faster processing Downsampling	NA	Filter size Padding bits Pooling technique
Fully Connected Neural Network Layer	-	Weights	Weights value Activation function
Other Layers	Feature extraction Reduce overfitting	Regularization Normalization Dropout	Learning rate Optimization function Regularization function Dropout rate

just on training data. Using an optimization technique such as a learning algorithm, stochastic gradient, and the others, kernels and parameters are modified depending on the loss value. A loss function, also referred as a cost function, assesses the similarity here between forward propagation output predictions of a system and the labeling of the underlying data. Cross entropy is a conventional loss function for classifiers, although mean squared loss is frequently employed for regression on continuous variables. The main layers of CNN are shown in Table 2.

APPLICATIONS OF CNN

CNN's are used to determine the layout of an image. Typically, a picture is an input into the system as a grid of integers; nevertheless, it is preferable to partition the image into overlapping image tiles which are then transmitted to a tiny neural network. Main applications of CNN in image processing are the following.

Image Segmentation

As a nonparametric clustering technique, mean-shift extraction was applied to divide the picture into objects with homogeneous both spectral and spatial information. As multiple input dataset sets for picture segmentation, RGB and close multispectral regions were merged with the digital surface model. To emphasize the relevance of spectral similarity, a little over-segmentation instead of under-segmentation was employed. All image classifications were converted into Geographic Information System polygons with discrete geometrical file types (Chen et al., 2018; Robin et al., 2021).

Image Classification

With the progress of CNN, among the most important jobs is anticipating meaningful representation, which contributes to good classification results (John et al., 2021; Ravikumar et al., 2022; Ravikumar & Sriraman, 2023; Robin et al., 2022).

Image Translation

CNN is not inherently translation-independent. However, CNN can acquire translation-invariant forms, provided it is trained with a suitable dataset. Learning the data with substantial amounts of change due to translating is the most critical factor in creating translation-invariant systems (Kauderer-Abrams, 2017).

Image Tagging

Image tagging represents the most fundamental sort of image categorization technique. An image tag is a descriptive word or phrase which makes photographs simpler to locate. This strategy is used by major corporations such as Instagram, Google, and Amazon. In addition, it is one of the key components of visual search. Tagging encompasses item detection and even assessment of the emotional tone of a picture.

Face Recognition

Face recognition generates a series of related issues, which are as follows: Identifying the faces in the image, Focusing on every expression, regardless of the face's quality or the positions it is exhibited in, and Recognizing distinctive traits., Comparing the identified traits to those in the database and identifying the individual's name Expressions are complex, multimodal visual stimuli that were demonstrated using a neural net hybrid consisting of a local image sample, a self-organizing mapping neural net, and a CNN.

RELATED WORKS

Since AlexNet (Deng et al., 2009; Krizhevsky et al., 2012) gained tremendous success in the ImageNet Challenge, CNNs have demonstrated superior performance on picture classification and a variety of other visual tasks. With the rapid expansion of hardware capacity, it can be used to train huge networks without difficulty. Nowadays, the primary trend for boosting networks' overall performance is to increase their depth. LeNet5 (Lecun et al., 1998), the first proposed CNNs are large and complex, gradient vanishing is a significant issue throughout the training process. ResNets (He et al., 2016) and DenseNets (R. K. Srivastava et al., 2015) explicitly use the structure of shortcuts between every two blocks. Highway Networks (R. K. Srivastava et al., 2015) inherently include nonlinear transforms and transform gates to provide shortcuts. FractalNets (Larsson et al., 2017; Yang et al., 2015) employ drop routes like ResNets. All of the solutions above are effective at resolving the gradient vanishing problem. According to research, classification accuracy degrades significantly when backpropagation (LeCun et al., 1989b) is used on deeper plain networks. The normalization approach (Ioffe & Szegedy, 2015) can assist in alleviating the difficulty. Despite their lack of depth, simple networks nevertheless provide several advantages, mainly when dealing with specific embedded vision applications. ALL Convolution Net (ALL-CNN)

(Springenberg et al., 2015) performs very well because it employs solely convolutional layers with a minimal number of parameters rather than alternating convolutional and max-pooling layers. Numerous tiny networks perform better on a few resources due to their simple network topology. They often use the similarity operator and global MEX pooling to maximize the capacity of small networks. SqueezeNet (Iandola et al., 2016) reduce the count of channels from 3x3 to 1x1 to simplify networks without impairing network capacity. MobileNets (Howard et al., 2017) construct lightweight networks that operate well on embedded devices by utilizing depth-wise separable convolutions. Additionally, important works such as ShufeNet (Zhang et al., 2017) and SEP-Nets have demonstrated that residual structure may effectively reduce computing complexity on mobile devices. Numerous studies use various types of CNNs as part of their model to analyze large amounts of data, which enhances overall performance.

TENSORFLOW

The design of TensorFlow is taught in such a manner that the reader understands why it is a necessity for learning Keras. TensorFlow, as well as its underlying Python libraries, are discussed in this context. It is necessary to comprehend the compatibility of these packages to comprehend TensorFlow. Therefore, prior to learning researching Keras, it is necessary to explore TensorFlow in depth. TensorFlow is Google's most renowned library for deep learning applications. The toolkit is designed to operate on CPU, GPUs, TPU processors, neural net devices, etc. This library first opened to the general public in 2015. In 2017, though, a stable version was made available under the Apache Open-sourced License. Libraries licensed under the Apache Open - sourced License may be used, modified, and transferred without paying a fee to Google. Tensors are indeed the multiple arrays that TensorFlow accepts as input. TensorFlow is named after the flow of multidimensional arrays. These tensors enter the system from input at one end and undergo many processes before producing output.

TensorFlow's core algorithms are developed in C and CUDA, a parallel processing language. NVIDIA created a system and API. It offers APIs in multiple languages. Python's API is among the most robust and extensive.

TensorFlow (Abadi et al., n.d., 2016) script is divided into two phases constructing a computational graph and executing the computational graph. Inside the building phase, TensorFlow functions are often used to generate a computational graph that depicts a deep learning model. This graph consists of both edges and nodes. The edges represent tensor data that will flow through graphs, which gives the framework its name, TensorFlow. Operations are indeed the nodes that describe calculations on tensors. The input of an operation is zero or more tensors, and the output is zero or more tensors. TensorFlow offers fundamental building pieces, including fully - connected layers, a convolutional layer, an RNN module, and nonlinear activation units.

These operations are the significant elements of a computational graph that perform the calculation from model input to output. In addition, TensorFlow provides a variety of loss functions, including cross-entropy and mean squared error. With a forward pass of neural networks, the model is concluded by adding loss compute operations to the output tensor. The basic modules of TensorFlow are shown in Figure 4.

Keras is a Python-based Framework for neural networks that enables the execution of TensorFlow and Theano. tf.Keras is the syntax for using Keras in Python. It operates based on the following basic concepts: Customer interaction: Modularity, easiness of expansion, and Implementation in Python.

Figure 4. TensorFlow architecture

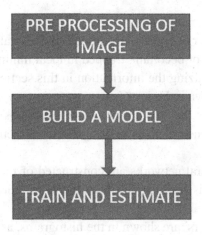

Models represent the most significant data structures inside the Keras language. For example, sequential is an often-used model.

TENSORBOARD

Models of neural nets are often extensive and complex, which may lead to misunderstanding. Tensor-Board is a graphical device that makes TensorFlow applications simpler to comprehend and debug. Users may quickly see the computation graph of a network, learning metrics, and parameter settings using TensorBoard. The TensorFlow component tf.summary generates operations to capture training metrics and store graph definition. Additionally, it stores them on disk as an event collection in a manner that TensorBoard could read. When TensorBoard is started, those files will be displayed in a web browser. Deep learning algorithms tend to outperform conventional approaches as the number of data grows. However, this increases the algorithm's complexity and, thus, its interpretability. In addition, the intricacy complicates hyperparameter adjustment. tensorboard is the answer (Fasi et al., 2021). The TensorFlow team developed this visualization module to reduce the complexities of neural nets. It may be used to build several kinds of graphs. For profiling with TensorFlow, the prerequisites must be initially satisfied, and all required plugins must be added, as shown in Figure 5.

Figure 5. TensorBoard plugins

```
!pip install -U tensorboard_plugin_profile

Looking in indexes: https://pypi.org/simple, https://us-python.pkg.dev/colab-wheels/public/simple/
Collecting tensorboard_plugin_profile
  Downloading tensorboard_plugin_profile-2.8.0-py3-none-any.whl (5.3 MB)
     |████████████████████████████████| 5.3 MB 5.4 MB/s
Collecting gviz-api>=1.9.0
  Downloading gviz_api-1.10.0-py2.py3-none-any.whl (13 kB)
Requirement already satisfied: protobuf>=3.12.0 in /usr/local/lib/python3.7/dist-packages (from tensorboard_plugin_profile) (3.19.6)
Requirement already satisfied: werkzeug>=0.11.15 in /usr/local/lib/python3.7/dist-packages (from tensorboard_plugin_profile) (1.0.1)
Requirement already satisfied: setuptools>=41.0.0 in /usr/local/lib/python3.7/dist-packages (from tensorboard_plugin_profile) (57.4.0)
Requirement already satisfied: six>=1.10.0 in /usr/local/lib/python3.7/dist-packages (from tensorboard_plugin_profile) (1.15.0)
Installing collected packages: gviz-api, tensorboard-plugin-profile
Successfully installed gviz-api-1.10.0 tensorboard-plugin-profile-2.8.0
```

Components

It includes the following elements, notably:

Scalars: Due to the high number of epochs, it is impossible to evaluate the accuracy and inaccuracy for each epoch, and there is a risk of becoming trapped in local minima rather than global ones. These two issues may be resolved by utilizing the information in this section. It provides accuracy and error graphs concerning epochs, as shown in Figure 6.

Graphs: The subsection depicts the "model.summary()" findings using graphs as shown in Figure 7. In many other words, it renders neural network design more attractive. This facilitates the process of architectural comprehension.

Distributions: In typically, neural networks are constructed of many layers, each including a large number of biases and weights. This segment describes the distribution of various hyperparameters, as shown in Figure 8.

Histograms: All hyperparameters' are shown in the histograms, as shown in Figure 9.

Time-Series: Contains the same values throughout time, as shown in Figure 10. By evaluating the trends of the hyperparameters, these parts are essential for regulating them.

Figure 6. Scalars in tensor board

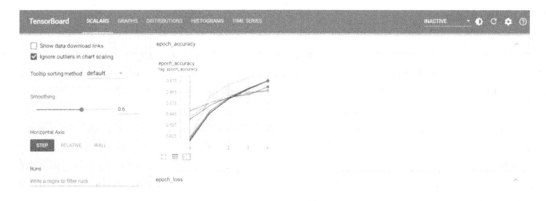

Figure 7. Graphs in tensor board

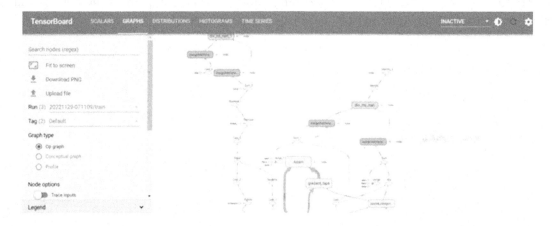

Figure 8. Distribution in tensor board

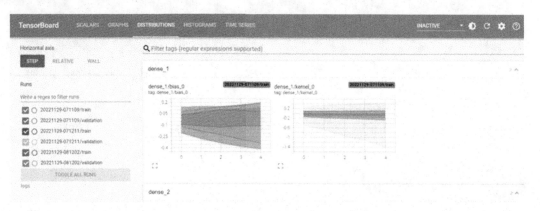

Figure 9 Histogram in tensor board

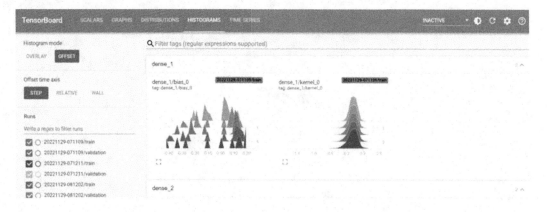

Figure 10. Time series in tensor board

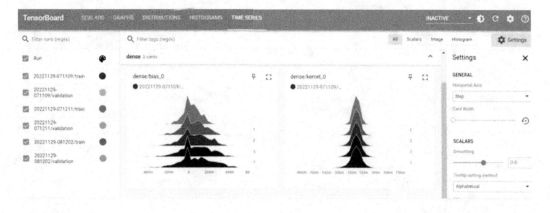

Figure 11. Tensor board CNN graph

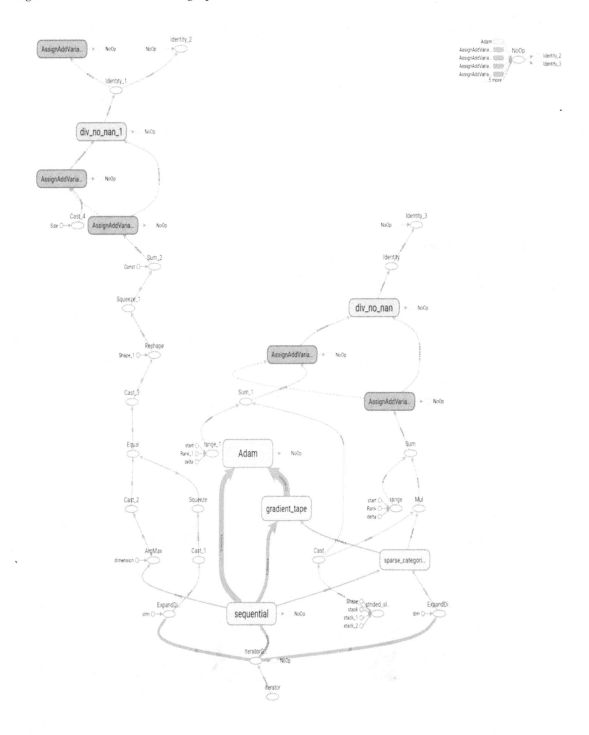

Figure 12. Hyperparameters in tensor board

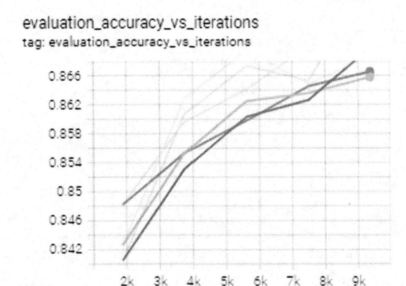

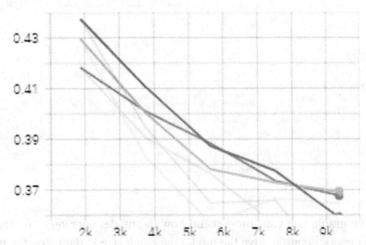

Figure 13. Dataset used for model

```
fashion_mnist = tf.keras.datasets.fashion_mnist

(x_train, y_train),(x_test, y_test) = fashion_mnist.load_data()
x_train, x_test = x_train / 255.0, x_test / 255.0
```

```
Downloading data from https://storage.googleapis.com/tensorflow/tf-keras-datasets/train-labels-idx1-ubyte.gz
29515/29515 [==============================] - 0s 0us/step
Downloading data from https://storage.googleapis.com/tensorflow/tf-keras-datasets/train-images-idx3-ubyte.gz
26421880/26421880 [==============================] - 1s 0us/step
Downloading data from https://storage.googleapis.com/tensorflow/tf-keras-datasets/t10k-labels-idx1-ubyte.gz
5148/5148 [==============================] - 0s 0us/step
Downloading data from https://storage.googleapis.com/tensorflow/tf-keras-datasets/t10k-images-idx3-ubyte.gz
4422102/4422102 [==============================] - 0s 0us/step
```

Figure 14. NN model

```
Model: "sequential_1"

_____
 Layer (type)                Output Shape              Param #
=================================================================
 flatten_1 (Flatten)         (None, 784)               0

 dense_2 (Dense)             (None, 512)               401920

 dropout_1 (Dropout)         (None, 512)               0

 dense_3 (Dense)             (None, 10)                5130

=================================================================
Total params: 407,050
Trainable params: 407,050
Non-trainable params: 0
_____
```

Figure 15. NN training

```
Train on 60000 samples, validate on 10000 samples
Epoch 1/5
60000/60000 [==============================] - 11s 184us/sample - loss: 0.4968 - accuracy: 0.8223 - val_loss: 0.4216 - val_accuracy: 0.8481
Epoch 2/5
60000/60000 [==============================] - 11s 176us/sample - loss: 0.3847 - accuracy: 0.8587 - val_loss: 0.4056 - val_accuracy: 0.8545
Epoch 3/5
60000/60000 [==============================] - 11s 176us/sample - loss: 0.3495 - accuracy: 0.8727 - val_loss: 0.3600 - val_accuracy: 0.8700
Epoch 4/5
60000/60000 [==============================] - 11s 179us/sample - loss: 0.3282 - accuracy: 0.8795 - val_loss: 0.3636 - val_accuracy: 0.8694
Epoch 5/5
60000/60000 [==============================] - 11s 176us/sample - loss: 0.3115 - accuracy: 0.8839 - val_loss: 0.3438 - val_accuracy: 0.8764
```

If you examine the graph, you can comprehend how the model operates. Add the data to that same model's queue: After every iteration, give the model the batch size in data, i.e., the number of information feeds. Load the Tensors with the data. Develop the model. Show the complete number of training sessions. Save the model to the hard drive. The underlying concept tensorboard is that a neural network may be seen as a "black box," and we require a tool to analyze the contents of this box. Tensorboard may be compared to a spotlight for beginning a dive inside a neural network. It aids in understanding the interdependencies between procedures, where weights are generated, shows the loss function, and provides a wealth of other information. You have a powerful debugging and model improvement tool whenever you combine all of these bits of information. The graph generated is shown in Figure 11.

The Figures 13, 14, and 15 represents the dataset (Fashion MNIST) with 60000 samples, the neural network model and the training phase of the model.

CONCLUSION

CNN offers well-suited multidimensional image classification and regression analysis models and has coarsely arbitrary spatial functions. It is adept at understanding spatial connections from picture data, enabling the model to recognize locations and sizes in various structures. A neural network's explanation and prediction capabilities may be enhanced by feeding it high-dimensional patterns pictures as inputs and extracting complex characteristics from the imageries. CNN's usefulness in predicting tasks may be expanded when pictures are supplied at a greater temporal rate. CNN is distinct from conventional multilayer visual neural networks in that it can learn multiresolution spatial characteristics from multisensor gridded input. CNN examines each dimension of the input picture using a convolution as a kernel. Rectified linear unit is a preferred activation function in the hidden Convolution layer as it is less costly than other nonlinear functions and has been found to accelerate CNN training considerably. Information on local fault pictures is used to establish sparse connections. Weights are exchanged by employing the same filter over an entire input picture, resulting in translation equivariance. Pooling operation leads to significant shift invariance limitation of CNN has indeed been highlighted due to the requirement of a large quantity of data. The main limitation of CNN is that it may be a waste of time to analyze the data in a particular colossal watershed region.

Nevertheless, CNN provides more precision than other standard techniques. In addition, its unique characteristics, including shared weights or local connections, enhance its efficiency. As a result, CNN has shown its supremacy in applications linked to machine vision and natural language analysis by mitigating the typical issues.

REFERENCES

AbadiM.AgarwalA.BarhamP.BrevdoE.ChenZ.CitroC.CorradoG. S.DavisA.DeanJ.DevinM.GhemawatS. GoodfellowI.HarpA.IrvingG.IsardM.JiaY.JozefowiczR.KaiserL.KudlurM.ZhengX. (2016). TensorFlow: Large-Scale Machine Learning on Heterogeneous Distributed Systems. https://arxiv.org/abs/1603.04467

Abadi, M., Barham, P., Chen, J., Chen, Z., Davis, A., Dean, J., Devin, M., Ghemawat, S., Irving, G., Isard, M., Kudlur, M., Levenberg, J., Monga, R., Moore, S., Murray, D. G., Steiner, B., Tucker, P., Vasudevan, V., Warden, P., ... Zheng, X. (n.d.). *TensorFlow: A system for large-scale machine learning*. Academic Press.

Adek, R. T., & Ula, M. (2020). A Survey on The Accuracy of Machine Learning Techniques for Intrusion and Anomaly Detection on Public Data Sets. *2020 International Conference on Data Science, Artificial Intelligence, and Business Analytics (DATABIA)*. 10.1109/DATABIA50434.2020.9190436

Aerts, H. J. W. L., Velazquez, E. R., Leijenaar, R. T. H., Parmar, C., Grossmann, P., Carvalho, S., Bussink, J., Monshouwer, R., Haibe-Kains, B., Rietveld, D., Hoebers, F., Rietbergen, M. M., Leemans, C. R., Dekker, A., Quackenbush, J., Gillies, R. J., & Lambin, P. (2014). Decoding tumour phenotype by noninvasive imaging using a quantitative radiomics approach. *Nature Communications*, *5*(1), 1. Advance online publication. doi:10.1038/ncomms5006 PMID:24892406

Ahmed, W. S., & Karim, A. A. (2020). The Impact of Filter Size and Number of Filters on Classification Accuracy in CNN. *2020 International Conference on Computer Science and Software Engineering (CSASE)*, 88–93. 10.1109/CSASE48920.2020.9142089

Albawi, S., Mohammed, T. A., & Al-Zawi, S. (2017). Understanding of a convolutional neural network. *2017 International Conference on Engineering and Technology (ICET)*, 1–6. 10.1109/ICEngTechnol.2017.8308186

Burges, C. J. C., Platt, J. C., & Jana, S. (2003). Distortion discriminant analysis for audio fingerprinting. *IEEE Transactions on Speech and Audio Processing*, *11*(3), 165–174. doi:10.1109/TSA.2003.811538

Carremans, B. (2019, January 8). *Handling overfitting in deep learning models*. Medium. https://towardsdatascience.com/handling-overfitting-in-deep-learning-models-c760ee047c6e

Chan, T.-H., Jia, K., Gao, S., Lu, J., Zeng, Z., & Ma, Y. (2015). PCANet: A Simple Deep Learning Baseline for Image Classification? *IEEE Transactions on Image Processing*, *24*(12), 5017–5032. doi:10.1109/TIP.2015.2475625 PMID:26340772

Chen, K., Fu, K., Yan, M., Gao, X., Sun, X., & Wei, X. (2018). Semantic Segmentation of Aerial Images With Shuffling Convolutional Neural Networks. *IEEE Geoscience and Remote Sensing Letters*, *15*(2), 173–177. doi:10.1109/LGRS.2017.2778181

Deng, J., Dong, W., Socher, R., Li, L.-J., Li, K., & Fei-Fei, L. (2009). ImageNet: A large-scale hierarchical image database. *2009 IEEE Conference on Computer Vision and Pattern Recognition*, 248–255. 10.1109/CVPR.2009.5206848

Dropout Neural Network Layer In Keras Explained | by Cory Maklin | Towards Data Science. (n.d.). Retrieved November 29, 2022, from https://towardsdatascience.com/machine-learning-part-20-dropout-keras-layers-explained-8c9f6dc4c9ab

Fasi, M., Higham, N. J., Mikaitis, M., & Pranesh, S. (2021). Numerical behavior of NVIDIA tensor cores. *PeerJ. Computer Science*, *7*, e330. doi:10.7717/peerj-cs.330 PMID:33816984

Fukushima, K. (1980). Neocognitron: A self-organizing neural network model for a mechanism of pattern recognition unaffected by shift in position. *Biological Cybernetics*, *36*(4), 193–202. doi:10.1007/BF00344251 PMID:7370364

Glorot, X., Bordes, A., & Bengio, Y. (2011). Deep Sparse Rectifier Neural Networks. *Proceedings of the Fourteenth International Conference on Artificial Intelligence and Statistics*, 315–323. https://proceedings.mlr.press/v15/glorot11a.html

GongY.WangL.GuoR.LazebnikS. (2014). Multi-scale Orderless Pooling of Deep Convolutional Activation Features. doi:10.1007/978-3-319-10584-0_26

Grauman, K., & Darrell, T. (2005). The pyramid match kernel: Discriminative classification with sets of image features. *Tenth IEEE International Conference on Computer Vision (ICCV'05)*, 1, 1458-1465. 10.1109/ICCV.2005.239

Guo, Y., Liu, Y., Oerlemans, A., Lao, S., Wu, S., & Lew, M. S. (2016). Deep learning for visual understanding: A review. *Neurocomputing*, *187*, 27–48. doi:10.1016/j.neucom.2015.09.116

He, K., Zhang, X., Ren, S., & Sun, J. (2015). Spatial Pyramid Pooling in Deep Convolutional Networks for Visual Recognition. *IEEE Transactions on Pattern Analysis and Machine Intelligence*, *37*(9), 1904–1916. doi:10.1109/TPAMI.2015.2389824 PMID:26353135

HeK.ZhangX.RenS.SunJ. (2016). Identity Mappings in Deep Residual Networks. doi:10.1007/978-3-319-46493-0_38

HintonG. E.SrivastavaN.KrizhevskyA.SutskeverI.SalakhutdinovR. R. (2012). Improving neural networks by preventing co-adaptation of feature detectors. https://arxiv.org/abs/1207.0580

HowardA. G.ZhuM.ChenB.KalenichenkoD.WangW.WeyandT.AndreettoM.AdamH. (2017). MobileNets: Efficient Convolutional Neural Networks for Mobile Vision Applications. https://arxiv.org/abs/1704.04861

Huang, Z., Wang, J., Fu, X., Yu, T., Guo, Y., & Wang, R. (2020). DC-SPP-YOLO: Dense connection and spatial pyramid pooling based YOLO for object detection. *Information Sciences*, *522*, 241–258. doi:10.1016/j.ins.2020.02.067

Hubel, D. H., & Wiesel, T. N. (1962). Receptive fields, binocular interaction and functional architecture in the cat's visual cortex. *The Journal of Physiology, 160*(1), 106-154.

Hutchison, D., Kanade, T., Kittler, J., Kleinberg, J. M., Mattern, F., Mitchell, J. C., Naor, M., Nierstrasz, O., Rangan, P. C., Steffen, B., Sudan, M., Terzopoulos, D., Tygar, D., Vardi, M. Y., Weikum, G., Scherer, D., Müller, A., & Behnke, S. (2010). Evaluation of Pooling Operations in Convolutional Architectures for Object Recognition. In K. Diamantaras, W. Duch, & L. S. Iliadis (Eds.), Artificial Neural Networks – ICANN 2010 (Vol. 6354, pp. 92–101). Springer Berlin Heidelberg. doi:10.1007/978-3-642-15825-4_10

IandolaF. N.HanS.MoskewiczM. W.AshrafK.DallyW. J.KeutzerK. (2016). SqueezeNet: AlexNet-level accuracy with 50x fewer parameters and <0.5MB model size. https://arxiv.org/abs/1602.07360

IoffeS.SzegedyC. (2015). Batch Normalization: Accelerating Deep Network Training by Reducing Internal Covariate Shift. https://arxiv.org/abs/1502.03167

Jégou, H., Perronnin, F., Douze, M., Sánchez, J., Pérez, P., & Schmid, C. (2012). Aggregating Local Image Descriptors into Compact Codes. *IEEE Transactions on Pattern Analysis and Machine Intelligence*, *34*(9), 1704–1716. doi:10.1109/TPAMI.2011.235 PMID:22156101

John, J., Ravikumar, A., & Abraham, B. (2021). Prostate cancer prediction from multiple pretrained computer vision model. *Health and Technology, 11*(5), 1003–1011. doi:10.100712553-021-00586-y

Kauderer-AbramsE. (2017). Quantifying Translation-Invariance in Convolutional Neural Networks. https://arxiv.org/abs/1801.01450

Keras: The Python deep learning API. (n.d.). Retrieved June 24, 2022, from https://keras.io/

Krizhevsky, A., Sutskever, I., & Hinton, G. E. (2012). ImageNet Classification with Deep Convolutional Neural Networks. *Advances in Neural Information Processing Systems, 25.* https://papers.nips.cc/paper/2012/hash/c399862d3b9d6b76c8436e924a68c45b-Abstract.html

Lambin, P., Rios-Velazquez, E., Leijenaar, R., Carvalho, S., van Stiphout, R. G. P. M., Granton, P., Zegers, C. M. L., Gillies, R., Boellard, R., Dekker, A., & Aerts, H. J. W. L. (2012). Radiomics: Extracting more information from medical images using advanced feature analysis. *European Journal of Cancer, 48*(4), 441–446. doi:10.1016/j.ejca.2011.11.036

LarssonG.MaireM.ShakhnarovichG. (2017). FractalNet: Ultra-Deep Neural Networks without Residuals. https://arxiv.org/abs/1605.07648

Lazebnik, S., Schmid, C., & Ponce, J. (2006). Beyond Bags of Features: Spatial Pyramid Matching for Recognizing Natural Scene Categories. *2006 IEEE Computer Society Conference on Computer Vision and Pattern Recognition, 2,* 2169–2178. 10.1109/CVPR.2006.68

LeCun, Y., Boser, B., Denker, J., Henderson, D., Howard, R., Hubbard, W., & Jackel, L. (1989a). Handwritten Digit Recognition with a Back-Propagation Network. *Advances in Neural Information Processing Systems, 2.* https://proceedings.neurips.cc/paper/1989/hash/53c3bce66e43be4f209556518c2fcb54-Abstract.html

LeCun, Y., Boser, B., Denker, J. S., Henderson, D., Howard, R. E., Hubbard, W., & Jackel, L. D. (1989b). Backpropagation Applied to Handwritten Zip Code Recognition. *Neural Computation, 1*(4), 541–551. doi:10.1162/neco.1989.1.4.541

Lecun, Y., Bottou, L., Bengio, Y., & Haffner, P. (1998). Gradient-Based Learning Applied to Document Recognition. *Proceedings of the IEEE, 86*(11), 2278–2324. doi:10.1109/5.726791

Mou, J., & Li, J. (2020). Effects of Number of Filters of Convolutional Layers on Speech Recognition Model Accuracy. *2020 19th IEEE International Conference on Machine Learning and Applications (ICMLA),* 971–978. 10.1109/ICMLA51294.2020.00158

PascanuR.GulcehreC.ChoK.BengioY. (2014). How to Construct Deep Recurrent Neural Networks. https://arxiv.org/abs/1312.6026

Ranzato, M., Boureau, Y.-L., & LeCun, Y. (n.d.). *Sparse Feature Learning for Deep Belief Networks.* Academic Press.

Ravikumar, A. (2021). Non-relational multi-level caching for mitigation of staleness & stragglers in distributed deep learning. *Proceedings of the 22nd International Middleware Conference: Doctoral Symposium,* 15–16. 10.1145/3491087.3493678

Ravikumar, A., & Sriraman, H. (2023). Acceleration of Image Processing and Computer Vision Algorithms. In Handbook of Research on Computer Vision and Image Processing in the Deep Learning Era. IGI Global. doi:10.4018/978-1-7998-8892-5.ch001

Ravikumar, A., Sriraman, H., Saketh, P. M. S., Lokesh, S., & Karanam, A. (2022). Effect of neural network structure in accelerating performance and accuracy of a convolutional neural network with GPU/TPU for image analytics. *PeerJ. Computer Science*, *8*, e909. doi:10.7717/peerj-cs.909 PMID:35494877

Ren & Malik. (2003). Learning a classification model for segmentation. *Proceedings Ninth IEEE International Conference on Computer Vision*, 10–17. 10.1109/ICCV.2003.1238308

Robin, M., John, J., & Ravikumar, A. (2021). Breast Tumor Segmentation using U-NET. *2021 5th International Conference on Computing Methodologies and Communication (ICCMC)*, 1164–1167. 10.1109/ICCMC51019.2021.9418447

Robin, M., Ravikumar, A., & John, J. (2022). Classification of Histopathological Breast Cancer Images using Pretrained Models and Transfer Learning. In M. Saraswat, H. Sharma, K. Balachandran, J. H. Kim, & J. C. Bansal (Eds.), *Congress on Intelligent Systems* (pp. 587–597). Springer Nature Singapore. doi:10.1007/978-981-16-9113-3_43

SimonyanK.ZissermanA. (2015). Very Deep Convolutional Networks for Large-Scale Image Recognition. https://arxiv.org/abs/1409.1556

Sivic & Zisserman. (2003). Video Google: A text retrieval approach to object matching in videos. *Proceedings Ninth IEEE International Conference on Computer Vision*, 1470–1477. 10.1109/ICCV.2003.1238663

SpringenbergJ. T.DosovitskiyA.BroxT.RiedmillerM. (2015). Striving for Simplicity: The All Convolutional Net. https://arxiv.org/abs/1412.6806

Srivastava, N., Hinton, G., Krizhevsky, A., Sutskever, I., & Salakhutdinov, R. (n.d.). *Dropout: A Simple Way to Prevent Neural Networks from Overfitting*. Academic Press.

Srivastava, R. K., Greff, K., & Schmidhuber, J. (2015). Training Very Deep Networks. *Advances in Neural Information Processing Systems, 28*. https://proceedings.neurips.cc/paper/2015/hash/215a71a12769b056c3c32e7299f1c5ed-Abstract.html

Szegedy, C., Liu, W., Jia, Y., Sermanet, P., Reed, S., Anguelov, D., Erhan, D., Vanhoucke, V., & Rabinovich, A. (2015). Going deeper with convolutions. *2015 IEEE Conference on Computer Vision and Pattern Recognition (CVPR)*, 1–9. 10.1109/CVPR.2015.7298594

Wan, L., Zeiler, M., Zhang, S., LeCun, Y., & Fergus, R. (n.d.). *Regularization of Neural Networks using DropConnect*. Academic Press.

Xu, C., Yang, J., Lai, H., Gao, J., Shen, L., & Yan, S. (2019). UP-CNN: Un-pooling augmented convolutional neural network. *Pattern Recognition Letters*, *119*, 34–40. doi:10.1016/j.patrec.2017.08.007

Xu, L., Yan, S., Chen, X., & Wang, P. (2019). Motion Recognition Algorithm Based on Deep Edge-Aware Pyramid Pooling Network in Human–Computer Interaction. *IEEE Access : Practical Innovations, Open Solutions*, *7*, 163806–163813. doi:10.1109/ACCESS.2019.2952432

Yang, Y., Li, H. T., Han, Y. S., & Gu, H. Y. (2015). High resolution remote sensing image segmentation based on graph theory and fractal net evolution approach. *The International Archives of the Photogrammetry, Remote Sensing and Spatial Information Sciences*, *XL-7*(W4), 197–201. doi:10.5194/isprsarchives-XL-7-W4-197-2015

Yu, D., Wang, H., Chen, P., & Wei, Z. (2014). Mixed Pooling for Convolutional Neural Networks. In D. Miao, W. Pedrycz, D. Ślęzak, G. Peters, Q. Hu, & R. Wang (Eds.), Rough Sets and Knowledge Technology (pp. 364–375). Springer International Publishing. doi:10.1007/978-3-319-11740-9_34

ZeilerM. D.FergusR. (2013). Stochastic Pooling for Regularization of Deep Convolutional Neural Networks. https://arxiv.org/abs/1301.3557

ZhangX.ZhouX.LinM.SunJ. (2017). ShuffleNet: An Extremely Efficient Convolutional Neural Network for Mobile Devices. https://arxiv.org/abs/1707.01083

KEY TERMS AND DEFINITIONS

Convolutional Neural Network: A Convolutional Neural Network is a Deep Learning method that can receive an image as an input, ascribe significance to different attributes in the picture, and distinguish between them. CNN requires far less pre-processing than other classification techniques. CNN can learn these characteristics with sufficient training, whereas filters in basic approaches are handcrafted.

Deep Learning: Deep Learning is a branch of artificial intelligence dealing with artificial neural network learning algorithms and brain function. These neural networks seek to imitate the activity of the human brain, though imperfectly, allowing them to "learn" from massive amounts of data.

Overfitting: An unfavorable machine learning characteristic happens when a model provides correct predictions for training examples but not for new data. Researchers first build the model on a collection of available information whenever data analysts make predictions using machine learning algorithms. Depending on this knowledge, the algorithm then attempts to predict results for additional data types. An overfit model might provide erroneous forecasts and need to function more effectively with all new data sources.

Pooling: Pooling merely refers to an image's down-sampling, in pooling layers to minimize the dimensionality of feature maps. Consequently, it decreases both the number of parameters that must be learned and the amount of computation done by the network. The pooling layer summarizes the characteristics contained in an area of the convolution layer-generated feature map.

Profiling: The objective of profiling a software program is to learn more about its behavior. By comprehending a program's behavior, engineers may carry out modifications that result in enhanced performance. Moreover, the programmer can identify the program's limitations by profiling a system.

Tensor Flow: A free, open-source artificial intelligence and machine learning software library. It may be used for various applications, but training and inference of deep neural networks are its primary emphasis.

TensorBoard: TensorBoard is the platform for visualizing the graph and other capabilities required to comprehend, troubleshoot, and improve the models. It is a program that offers a machine-learning process with metrics and visuals. In addition, it assists in tracking parameters such as loss and accuracy, graph representation, application integration in lower-dimensional environments, etc.

Underfitting: Underfitting occurs when a mathematical model or machine learning algorithm cannot reflect the fundamental patterns in data; it works well just on training examples but badly on testing data. Its recurrence merely indicates that our model or method does not adequately suit the data. It often occurs when there needs to be more data to develop an appropriate model and while attempting to construct a linear regression model with insufficient nonlinear data. In such situations, the machine learning model's rules are too simple and flexible also to be used for such little data; hence, the model will likely produce many incorrect predictions. Underfitting may be prevented by employing more data and limiting the number of characteristics via feature selection.

Chapter 4
A Deep Understanding of Long Short-Term Memory for Solving Vanishing Error Problem:
LSTM-VGP

Aswathy Ravikumar

https://orcid.org/0000-0003-0897-6991

Vellore Institute of Technology, Chennai, India

Harini Sriraman

https://orcid.org/0000-0002-2192-8153

Vellore Institute of Technology, Chennai, India

ABSTRACT

Long Short-Term Memory (LSTM) is a specific kind of recurrent neural network (RNN) structure that addresses the constraints of conventional RNNs in effectively capturing and learning long-term relationships in sequential input. In this chapter, the authors examine the LSTM cell and its modifications to investigate the LSTM cell's capability for learning. Furthermore, future study prospects for LSTM networks are outlined. LSTM networks have gotten extensive attention in scientific papers, technical websites, and deployment manuals because of their efficacy in a variety of practical situations. Gradient-based learning techniques used in RNNs are too slow because as the error is transmitted back, it disappears, resulting in a much more extended learning period. LSTMs handle the issue with a novel additive gradient design that incorporates direct access towards the forget gate's activations, allowing the network to promote desirable behavior from the error gradient by updating the gates often at each time step of learning.

INTRODUCTION

Deep Neural Networks, a subfield of machine learning that uses associations learned from data to make judgments (Nweke et al., 2018). This is a promising area of machine learning that can produce outcomes

DOI: 10.4018/978-1-6684-8531-6.ch004

Copyright © 2024, IGI Global. Copying or distributing in print or electronic forms without written permission of IGI Global is prohibited.

that are more and more agreeable as data is gathered (LeCun et al., 2015).

Among the most popular DL algorithms is CNN. LeCun et al. (1989) presented this model in 1989, and it performed well in computer vision. Businesses such as Google, Apple, and Instagram are among those conducting ongoing research and integrating CNN to their services, in addition to academic institutions (Khan et al., 2020). Convolutional layer, down - sampling layer (also known as a pooling layer), plus fully linked layer are the three layers that make up the CNN model. Regional receptive fields with weight sharing are applied by the convolution and sub-sampling levels. They can be layered in various levels, with the final stage of categorization being carried out by a completely linked layer. Regarding feature extraction and classification, CNN is fantastic. In machine vision, categorization, and video recognition, it has risen to the top (John et al., 2021; Ravikumar & Sriraman, 2023; Zhang et al., 2018).

An effective learning paradigm when handling sequential data, such as voice recognition and language understanding, is the RNN, one of the promising DL models. Through the inner representation of a neural network's recollection of prior inputs, it develops characteristics for time information. RNN can also forecast information based on historical and current data. However, due to the gradient disappearing or gradient exploding issue, it is challenging to learn stored data over an extended period of time using the RNN structure (Gelenbe, 1993; Robin et al., 2021).

The LSTM model, first presented in 1997 (Hochreiter & Schmidhuber, 1997), provides a solution to this RNN problem in its core. By utilizing numerous gate components, LSTM cells are able to extract information, remember the information, or delete information stored that is no longer be required. As previously indicated, this model has many traits with RNN while also addressing some of its shortcomings. It can be applied in areas where sequential analysis data and event forecasting utilizing current data are necessary. In other respects, LSTM is among the most sophisticated time-series handling networks.

Since the first LSTM study published in 1997 (Hochreiter & Schmidhuber, 1997), several theoretical and practical publications have been released on the topic of this sort of RNN, with many describing the remarkable results produced in a broad range of sequential data application fields. The LSTM has exerted a significant influence on language modeling and speech-to-text conversion. machine translation, and more uses. Many academic and business readers, encouraged by the remarkable benchmarks given in the literature, desire to understand LSTM network to assess its relevance to their own study or practical use-case. Numerous RNN and LSTM network designs are efficiently and production-ready implemented in all of the main open-source platforms for deep learning.

Obviously, some professionals, even if they are unfamiliar with RNN/LSTM methods, take full advantage of such an accessibility and cost-effectiveness and immediately begin research and experimenting. Others want a comprehensive understanding of the working of this beautiful and successful system. The benefit of this longer path in that it effectively gives the opportunity to develop a degree of intuition that can prove useful all during phases of the procedure of integrating an open-source component to meet the requirements of their research program or productivity applications, including data preparation, troubleshooting, and tuning.

RNN

The fact that RNNs are the sole neural net type including an internal storage makes them among the most viable algorithms currently in use. RNN is a sort of neural network in which the output of the preceding step is used as input for the current phase. In conventional neural networks, all inputs and outputs

Figure 1. Shallow neural network structure

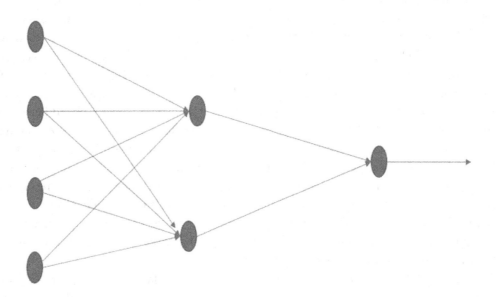

Figure 2. Neural network with loop connections

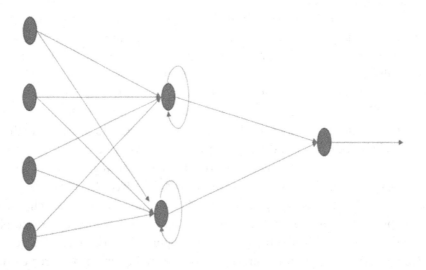

are autonomous of one another. However, when it is necessary to predict the next word in a phrase, the preceding words are needed, therefore it is necessary to remember them. As a result, RNN was created, which resolved this problem with the use of Hidden Units. Hidden state, which retains certain information about a sequence, is the primary and most crucial aspect of RNN. A RNN is a form of artificial neural network that is often used in voice recognition and NLP. RNN identifies the sequential features of input and use patterns to anticipate the most probable future event.

RNNs are used for deep learning and the creation of models that imitate neuron activation in the brain. These are unique from those other kinds of ANN because they employ feedback loops that digest a series of input that influences the final output. They are particularly effective in situations where context is crucial for forecasting a result. Such feedback loops enable for the persistence of information. This phenomenon is often referred to as memory. The normal shallow neural network is shown in Figure 1 and Figure 2 shows structure with loop.

RNN use cases are often associated with language models wherein understanding a next letter inside a word or the following word in a sentence is dependent on the preceding data. A intriguing experiment includes training an RNN on the Shakespeare works in order to generate language that effectively resembles Shakespeare's. RNN authoring is an example of computational innovation. This emulation of human creativity is made feasible by the AI's acquired knowledge of syntax and semantics out of its training set.

Working

To comprehend RNNs, you must have a solid understanding of "regular" feed-forward neural nets and sequential data. Sequential data are essentially simply sorted data wherein related items are presented in sequence. Financial data and the DNA sequence were instances. One of the most common sort in sequential data is time series, that is simply a collection of data points in chronological order. RNNs and FNNs derive its name from the way they transmit data. Inside a FNN, information flows from input nodes, via the hidden units, to the output nodes. The data flows directly across the network. FNN have little recall of the data they are given and are poor at forecasting the future. A FNN has no concept of time order since it only analyzes the current input. Other than its schooling, it simply cannot recall anything that occurred in the past. A RNN cycles data via a loop. When making a decision, it takes into account both the input signal and what it has learnt from prior inputs. The two graphics below highlight the difference in flow of information between such a FNN and RNN as shown in Figure 3.

Figure 3. FFNN vs. RNN

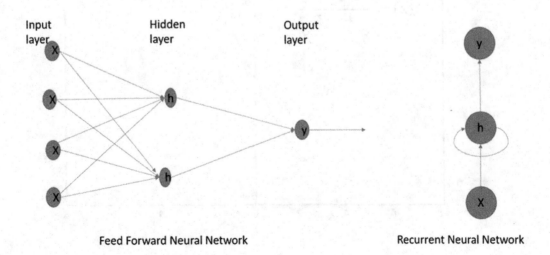

Feed Forward Neural Network   Recurrent Neural Network

A typical RNN has a limited memory capacity. In addition to an LSTM, they possess a long-term memory. Providing an example is another effective technique to teach the notion of a recurrent neural network's memory. Nevertheless, a RNN may recall these characteristics because to its internal storage. It generates output, duplicates that output, and re-enters the system. Broadly said, RNN augment the present with the recent past. Consequently, an RNN has 2 parameters: the current time and the recent history. This is significant because the data sequence carries crucial information regarding what is to come, allowing RNNs to do tasks that other algorithms cannot. Like all other learning algorithms, a FNN applies a weight matrix towards its inputs before producing an output. Notably, RNNs add weights to both the current and prior input. In addition, a recurrent neural network modifies the weights for gradient descent and optimization algorithms over time. The input layer x of a neural network collects and processes the input before delivering it to the inner layer. Hidden layers, all having its own convolution layers, weights, and bias, are present in the intermediate layer h. The RNN will standardize the various activation units, weights, including biases, guaranteeing so each layer has same features. Instead of creating several hidden layers, this will simply generate one and iterate over it as numerous times as required.

Typical Activation Operations

The activation function of a neuron determines if it should be activated or deactivated. Nonlinear functions often convert the output of a neuron to a value ranging from 0 to 1 or -1 and 1.

Sigmoid Activation function: Range from 0-1 as shown in Figure 4.

Tanh: Range from -1to+1 as shown in Figure 5.

ReLU: Range from 0 to positive value as shown in Figure 6.

Figure 4. Sigmoid activation function

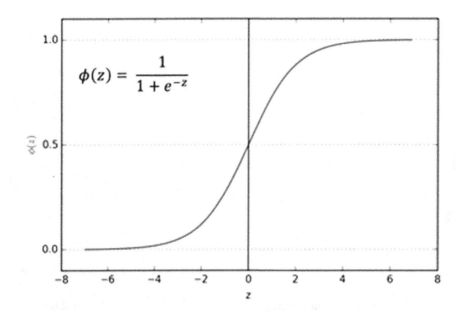

Figure 5. Tanh activation function

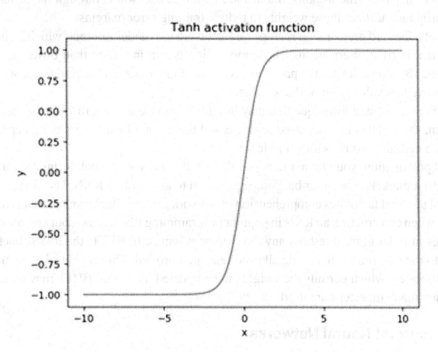

Figure 6. ReLU activation function

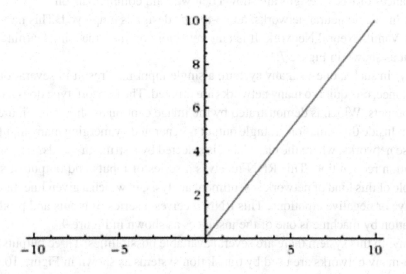

Backpropagation Through Time (BPTT)

To comprehend the notion of backpropagation through time, one must first comprehend forward and backpropagation. Backpropagation is a well-known method in deep learning. Backpropagation is employed to compute the slope of an error function in regard to the weights of a neural net. To get the partial derivative of a faults about the weights, the method traverses backwards through the different gradient stages. Backprop then utilizes these weights to reduce training error margins.

In neural nets, forward propagation is employed to obtain the model's output, which is then evaluated to determine if it is right or erroneous. Backpropagation is nothing more than traversing your neural network backwards in order to get the partial derivatives of an errors with regard to the weights, allowing you to remove this value from of the weights.

Then, gradient descent, a technique that may iteratively reduce a given function, employs these derivatives. Then, the weights are increased or decreased based on which lowers the inaccuracy. This is precisely how a neural network is taught to learn.

Using backpropagation, you attempt to adjust the weights for your model during training.

BPTT is just a marketing term for backpropagation on to an unrolled RNN. Unrolling is a graphical and conceptual tool that facilitates comprehension of network activity. Backpropagation is often handled automatically when constructing an RNN in popular programming frameworks, but you must understand how it operates in order to troubleshoot any development issues. In BPTT, the loss is backpropagated as from final to the first time - step while all timesteps are unrolled. This enables the calculation of the error at each timestep, which permits the weights to be updated. Note that BPTT may be computationally costly when many timesteps are used.

Types of Recurrent Neural Networks

RNN architecture might vary based on the issue being addressed. With those who have a single output and inputs to those with several inputs and outputs.

Various instances of RNN designs are shown below to aid comprehension.

One to One: In classic neural networks, a one-to-one design is employed. This neural network type is referred to as Vanilla Neural Network. It is employed for common machine learning tasks with sole input and output as shown in Figure 7.

One to Many: In such a one-to-many system, a single input may result in several outputs. In music creation, for instance, one quite so many networks are utilized. The network type does have a single input and numerous outputs. Which is demonstrated by the image caption as shown in Figure 8.

Many to One: Inside this situation, a single output is generated by merging many inputs from different time steps. These networks, where the class label is selected by a string of words, are used for sentiment analysis & emotion recognition. This RNN receives a series of inputs and outputs a single value. An excellent example of this kind of network is sentiment analysis, in which a given line may be categorized as having positive or negative emotions. This RNN receives a series of inputs and produces a series of outputs. Translation by machine is one of the instances as shown in Figure 9.

Many to Many: In this system there are several available possibilities. Three outputs result from two inputs. Many-to-many networks are used by translation systems as shown in Figure 10.

Problems of RNN

The two key challenges RNNs have faced, but to comprehend them, you must first grasp what is a gradient as shown in Figure 11.

The gradient is the partial derivative of an output about its input. A gradient quantifies how significantly the outcome of a functional varies when its inputs are altered slightly. Gradient may alternatively

Figure 7. One to one RNN

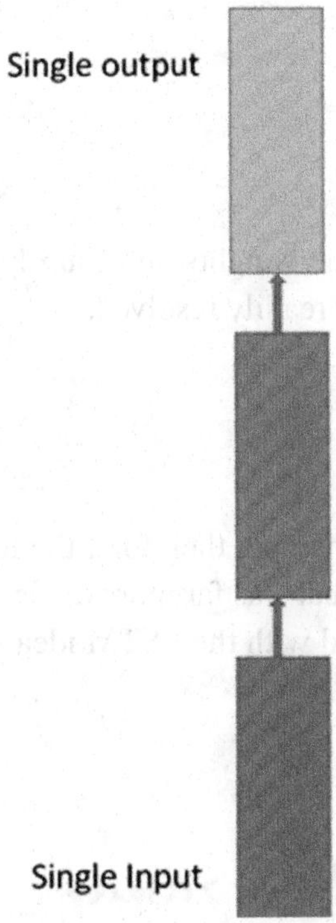

Single output

Single Input

Figure 8. One to many RNN

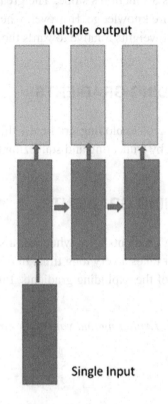

Figure 9. Many to one RNN

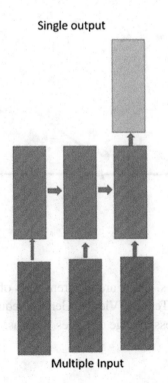

Figure 10. Many to many RNN

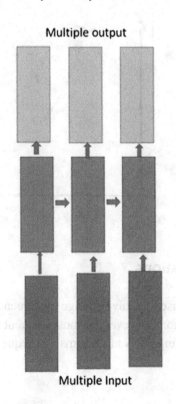

be seen as a function's slope. The greater the gradient, the sharper the slope, and the quicker a model may acquire knowledge. However, when the gradient is zero, learning ceases. A gradient quantifies the shift in all weights relative towards the error shift.

EXPLODING GRADIENTS

In the case of exploding gradients, this method arbitrarily gives the weights an absurdly high value. However, by truncating and squeezing the slopes, this issue may be readily resolved.

VANISHING GRADIENTS

Vanishing gradients arise whenever a slope's values are also too tiny and, therefore, the model ceases to learn or takes a very long time. In the 90s, this was a huge issue that was far more difficult to resolve than that of the exploding gradients. Finally, the problem was solved with the LSTM idea.

Figure 11. Exploding and vanishing gradient

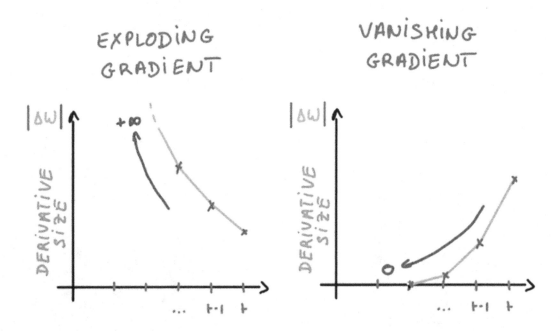

Applications

RNN is used to solve a range of sequence data-based challenges. There are different sorts of sequence information, however the most frequent are as follows: Sound, Textual, Videos, Genetic sequences.

Utilizing RNN algorithms and sequence data, we may address a range of issues, such as:

Speech recognition
Generation of popular music
Computerized translations
Evaluation of video content
Analysis of the genome with DNA's structure

Related Work

Gelenbe's (1989) invention of the randomized neural net has influenced other theoretical and empirical investigations. What differentiates the arbitrary neural net from many other neural net modeling techniques presently offered where the activity of a neuron could indeed either be a categorical data or even an independent variables is that every neurotransmitter is represented by its probability and a neuron is considered to be within its "firing state" only if probability is positive; thus, in the RNN the representation of a neuron's state is far more modular compared to other artificial neural modeling techniques Instructions are sent from one neuron to another in the RNN by means of spikes at a specific rate, which very much closely matches how signals are transmitted in a physical neural network. The neuronal system may be compared to a system of queues, where the status of each queue is reliant on the states of a queue with which it is related.

Gelenbe (1990) demonstrated that, under certain conditions, the probability that a neuron's effectiveness is positive is capable of approximating a steady state; he also demonstrated that the vector of potentials of all the connections in the brain in the RNN has, within its steady state, a probability distribution function of the an actual product, and so this steady flow probability density characteristic of all the neuron. In parallel study (Gelenbe, 1990), Gelenbe demonstrated that two types of random neural nets display well-defined consistent performance. In 1993 (Gelenbe, 1993), Gelenbe attempted to reintroduce supervised learning for recurrent RNN using a gradient descent learning experience implemented to an organized approach error function, and whose execution requires locating a fixed point by inverting a matrix that uses the same dimension as the amount of RNN neurons. This learning strategy described in Gelenbe (1993) for the recurrent RNN model is relevant to the feed forward RNN model as well. However, the learning process is much streamlined when the RNN model employs the feed-forward type rather than the recurrent type (Bakircioğlu & Koçak, 2000). The document (Bakircioğlu & Koçak, 2000) provides a complete summary of RNN applications, including those issued till the year 2000. A 2010 paper (Timotheou, 2010) on RNNs shows an assortment of RNN applications, including those launched after 2000. The design and implementation of this RNN-based protocol stack is described in Kocak et al. (2003). Several image processing difficulties, such as texture generation (Atalay et al., 1992), segmentation approaches (Gelenbe et al., 1996), picture enhancement and merging (Melo et al., 2018), and image and video compression (Cramer et al., 1998), have been addressed using the RNN model. Identifying and classifying patterns is another arena where RNN-based solutions are dominant. In Bakircioğlu et al. (1997), a target tracking system is constructed, in Abdelbaki et al. (1999), an RNN is used to discriminate land mines, in Hussain and Moussa (2005). A RNN model with several signal classes is provided in Gelenbe and Fourneau (1999) for use in applications requiring the concurrent processing of various data streams, such as color picture analysis. Gelenbe and Hussain (Gelenbe & Hussain, 2002) extended the learning strategy from a single class of RNN data to many classes of RNN signals and demonstrated its applicability to texture analysis modeling. Gelenbe and his colleagues enhanced the RNN model in 1999 (Gelenbe et al., 1999) by analyzing a bipolar RNN model with both negative and positive cells and demonstrating that this new RNN model is truly a universal function estimator (Hochreiter & Schmidhuber, 1997). Gradient descent is the dominant learning method in the vast bulk of reported RNN research, perhaps because of its usability.

LSTM

RNN contains feedback links between nodes as well as layers capable of handling input variables of variable - length. Nevertheless, training a simple RNN may be a difficult undertaking. The techniques for weight update in RNN are mostly gradient based, leading to either disappearing or inflating gradient difficulties, which have been shown to be resolved by the invention of "long short-term memory" (LSTM). LSTM is a kind of RNN with internal memory with multiplying gates. Since the debut of the LSTM in 1997 (Hochreiter & Schmidhuber, 1997), several LSTM cell configurations were developed. The default tendency of LSTMs is to be able to learn long-term relationships by memorizing information for extended durations.

All RNNs consist of a series of neural network modules that are repeated. This repeating module in ordinary RNNs will have a relatively basic architecture, like a single tanh layer.

LSTMs also possess a chain-like layout, however the structure of the recurring module is somewhat different. Instead of a single neural network layer, the four layers communicate greatly with one another.

Working

Inside an LSTM, each recurrent unit attempts to "learn" all the prior knowledge that system has encountered and "forget" irrelevant information. This one is achieved by establishing distinct "gate" nonlinear activation levels for various reasons. Every LSTM recurrent cell further retains a vector known as the Internal Cell State, that theoretically represents the information selected for retention by the preceding LSTM recurrent unit. A LSRM is comprised of four distinct gates with distinct functions, as shown below:

Forget Gate(f): Indicates the extent to which past data is forgotten.

Input Gate: It establishes the amount of information that will be recorded into the Inner Cell State.

Input Modulation Gate(g): It is typically regarded as a sub-component of the input gate, as well as the vast majority of research on LSTMs doesn't even discuss it, assuming that it is included inside the Input nodes. It is employed to modify the data that Input gate will record onto to the Internal States Cell by introducing non-linearity and Zero-mean to the data. As Zero-mean input provides quicker convergence, this one is done to minimize the learning time. It is standard practice to include this gate in the LSTM unit's construction, even though its actions are less significant than those of the other gates and are frequently seen as a notion that provides finesse.

Output Gate(o): This gate decides which output should be generated from the present Internal Cell State.

The sole difference between the fundamental workflow of a LLSTM and a Recurrent Neural Network is the fact that Internal Cell State also is transmitted along with the Hidden State. Consider as input any current input, the prior concealed state, and the prior internal cell state.

Follow the methods listed below to determine the values of both the four distinct gates:

- For each gate, compute the parameterized variables for the input signal and the prior concealed state by element-by-element multiplying the concerned vector with the corresponding weights for each gate with the vector containing the parameters.

Apply the corresponding activation function element-by-element to the parameterized vectors for each gate. The list of gates with activation function to also be applied to each gate is provided below.

Determine the current internal cell status by first computing the element-wise multiplying vector of the input nodes and the input modulating gate, followed by the component wise multiplication matrix of a forget gate and the prior internal cell status, and finally by summing the two vectors.

Determine the present hidden layer by first calculating the hyperbolic tangent element-by-element of the present internal cell vector field, followed by element-by-element combination with output gate.

Figure 12. LSTM

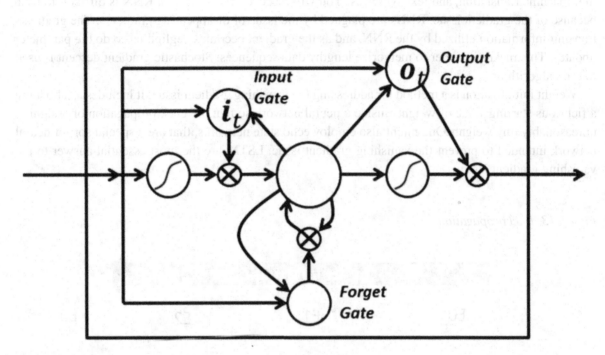

VANISHING GRADIENT PROBLEM

Training neural networks use stochastic gradient descent. This entails first evaluating overall prediction error that the model produces and then utilizing the error as compute a gradient used it to modify each weight inside the net so that future predictions will be less inaccurate. The error gradient is transported from the output layer to an input layer across the network.

It is advantageous to train algorithms with several layers since the addition of additional layers boosts the network's capacity, allowing it to learn a huge training dataset to represent more complicated mapping functions between inputs and outputs.

As the gradient is transmitted backwards via training networks with several layers, it suffers a significant decrease. Even by time the mistake reaches layers near to the model's inputs, it could be so minor that it has minimal impact. Consequently, this issue is known as "vanishing gradients" issue. Vanishing gradients are unique to RNN since updating the network necessitates unrolling its network at every input time step, resulting in a very deep network that needs weight updates. A moderate RNN could contain 200 to 400 input intervals, giving in a deep network theoretically. In MLP, vanishing gradients issue may emerge as a sluggish rate of development of a model throughout learning and perhaps fast convergence, i.e. prolonged training does not lead to additional progress. Examining the changes in weight during learning, you would observe greater change in the layers closest to the output nodes and less change in the levels closest to the input layer. There are several ways for mitigating the effect of the vanishing gradient issue in feed-forward neural nets, most prominently the use of alternative weight initialization approaches and activation functions.

RNN allows the modeling of time-dependent or sequential data issues, such as stock market forecasting, machine translation, and text synthesis. You will discover, however, that RNN is difficult to train because of the gradient issue. RNNs are plagued by the issue of disappearing gradients. The gradients transmit information utilized by the RNN, and as the gradient becomes negligible, so do the parameter updates. This makes it harder to memorize lengthy data sequences. Stochastic gradient descent is used to train algorithms.

Weight initialization is a method for addressing the vanishing gradient issue. It includes establishing a fictitious starting value of weights inside a neural network so that the back propagation of assigning unreasonably tiny weights.One might also employ echo state networks, that are a special sort of neural network intended to prevent the vanishing gradient issue. LSTM are the most essential answer to the vanishing gradient issue.

Figure 13. Backpropagation

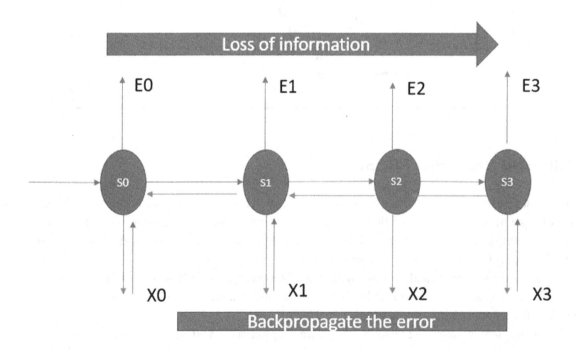

How to Find Vanishing Gradient Problem

By analyzing the kernels distribution of weight, you may discover it. The slope is diminishing if the weights were consistently approaching zero. This issue may be identified when the training speed of a neural net is exceedingly sluggish. Neural networks really aren't well-trained for the data we are utilizing, or they exhibit odd findings.

Solution for Vanishing Gradient Problem

There are a number of strategies for resolving vanishing gradient issues: Multi-level structure, LSTM, Residual neural network, Activation function – ReLU.

Multiple-Tiered Hierarchy: It is among the most fundamental and earliest remedies for the vanishing gradient issue in MLPs. It is only a technique that involves training each at a time and refining the level via backpropagation. Thus, each layer acquires a condensed observation that advances to the next level.

Residual Neural Net: Residual links in the neural net allow the model to train effectively, as well as the batch normalization characteristic ensures that gradients will not vanish. This batch normalizing functionality is available via the skip connection.

ReLU Activation: A linear activation function, which is superior to the sigmoid and tanh activation functions. The fundamental function for ReLU input conversion may be expressed as

$$f(x) = \max(0,x)$$

In which the ReLU function exists, the derivatives remain constant. If the input is negative, the function returns 0, and if it is more than 0, it returns the same number. Therefore, we may claim that the ReLU's output has varied from 0 to infinity.

While referring to the back-propagation algorithm method, gradients are adjusted by multiplying with various factors. As the input approaches the beginning of the network, a greater number of components are multiplied to increase the gradient. Numerous of these variables may be called activation functions. Derivatives of the activation function may be seen as a type of tuning factor aimed to achieve precise gradient descent.

Multiplying a number with a value larger than one will trend towards infinity in this circumstance. Therefore, if the numbers are less than one, we will have a slope that is less than one, leading to the vanishing gradient issue.

But if we can get the contributions of these derivatives of an input signal to equal 1, we can address the model's gradient-vanishing issue. Essentially, we may argue that each gradient update contributes to the models from input to output or model in this instance. Here ReLU enters the scene, which has just two 0 or 1 gradients. Gradient one if the output of the algorithm is greater than zero.

Gradient zero whenever the function's output is less than zero.

When these derivatives are multiplied together, they produce either 0 or 1. The backpropagation formula will only have two possible values, either 1 or 0. The update is either null or consists only of contributions from other weights and biases.

LSTM Mitigates Vanishing Gradient Problem

Weights as well as the activation function's derivative are the main determinants of gradient magnitude. The gradient size is kept consistent with the aid of an easy LSTM. We frequently employ an identity mapping, a derivative of 1, as the activation function inside the LSTM. Therefore, in gradient backpropagation, a gradient's size doesn't really disappear. The forget gate activating is equivalent to the practical weight of the gradient. As a result, the gradient does not disappear if the forget gate is activated (activation near to 1.0). Because of this, LSTM is among the finest solutions for handling long-distance dependencies.

Figure 14. LSTM structure

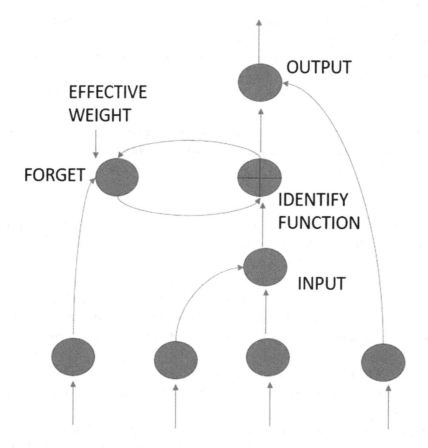

CONCLUSION

In this chapter, we summarized the most relevant material about the development of LSTM. Particularly, we emphasized the vanishing error issue, that is a significant drawback of RNNs. By injecting a continual error flow across the internal states of specialized memory cells, LSTM presents a potential solution to this issue. By bridging time periods greater than 1,000-time steps, LSTM can address lengthy time-lag concerns. Finally, we presented two LSTM modifications that allow self-resets and accurate timing to be learned by LSTM. Using self-resets, LSTM can remove irrelevant information from memory.

REFERENCES

Abdelbaki, H., Gelenbe, E., & Kocak, T. (1999). Matched neural filters for EMI based mine detection. *IJCNN'99. International Joint Conference on Neural Networks. Proceedings, 5,* 3236–3240. 10.1109/IJCNN.1999.836174

Adek, R. T., & Ula, M. (2020). A Survey on The Accuracy of Machine Learning Techniques for Intrusion and Anomaly Detection on Public Data Sets. *2020 International Conference on Data Science, Artificial Intelligence, and Business Analytics (DATABIA).* 10.1109/DATABIA50434.2020.9190436

Atalay, V., Gelenbe, E., & Yalabik, N. (1992). The random neural network model for texture generation. *International Journal of Pattern Recognition and Artificial Intelligence, 06*(01), 131–141. doi:10.1142/S0218001492000072

Bakircioğlu, H., Gelenbe, E., & Carin, L. (1997). Random neural network recognition of shaped objects in strong clutter. In W. Gerstner, A. Germond, M. Hasler, & J.-D. Nicoud (Eds.), *Artificial Neural Networks—ICANN'97* (pp. 961–966). Springer. doi:10.1007/BFb0020277

Bakırcıoğlu, H., & Koçak, T. (2000). Survey of random neural network applications. *European Journal of Operational Research, 126*(2), 319–330. doi:10.1016/S0377-2217(99)00481-6

Cramer, C., Gelenbe, E., & Gelenbe, P. (1998). Image and video compression. *IEEE Potentials, 17*(1), 29–33. doi:10.1109/45.652854

de Melo, G., Macedo, S. O., Vieira, S. L., & Leandro Oliveira, L. G. (2018). Classification of images and enhancement of performance using parallel algorithm to detection of pneumonia. *2018 IEEE International Conference on Automation/XXIII Congress of the Chilean Association of Automatic Control (ICA-ACCA),* 1–5. 10.1109/ICA-ACCA.2018.8609734

Gelenbe, E. (1989). Random Neural Networks with Negative and Positive Signals and Product Form Solution. *Neural Computation, 1*(4), 502–510. doi:10.1162/neco.1989.1.4.502

Gelenbe, E. (1990). Stability of the Random Neural Network Model. *Neural Computation, 2*(2), 239–247. doi:10.1162/neco.1990.2.2.239

Gelenbe, E. (1993). Learning in the Recurrent Random Neural Network. *Neural Computation, 5*(1), 154–164. doi:10.1162/neco.1993.5.1.154

Gelenbe, E., Feng, Y., & Krishnan, K. R. R. (1996). Neural network methods for volumetric magnetic resonance imaging of the human brain. *Proceedings of the IEEE, 84*(10), 1488–1496. doi:10.1109/5.537113

Gelenbe, E., & Fourneau, J.-M. (1999). Random Neural Networks with Multiple Classes of Signals. *Neural Computation, 11*(4), 953–963. doi:10.1162/089976699300016520 PMID:10226191

Gelenbe, E., & Hussain, K. F. (2002). Learning in the multiple class random neural network. *IEEE Transactions on Neural Networks, 13*(6), 1257–1267. doi:10.1109/TNN.2002.804228 PMID:18244525

Gelenbe, E., Mao, Z.-H., & Li, Y.-D. (1999). Function approximation with spiked random networks. *IEEE Transactions on Neural Networks, 10*(1), 3–9. doi:10.1109/72.737488 PMID:18252498

Hochreiter, S., & Schmidhuber, J. (1997). Long Short-Term Memory. *Neural Computation, 9*(8), 1735–1780. doi:10.1162/neco.1997.9.8.1735 PMID:9377276

Hussain, K. F., & Moussa, G. S. (2005). Laser Intensity Vehicle Classification System Based on Random Neural Network. *Proceedings of the 43rd Annual Southeast Regional Conference, 1*, 31–35. 10.1145/1167350.1167372

John, J., Ravikumar, A., & Abraham, B. (2021). Prostate cancer prediction from multiple pretrained computer vision model. *Health and Technology, 11*(5), 1003–1011. doi:10.100712553-021-00586-y

Khan, A., Sohail, A., Zahoora, U., & Qureshi, A. S. (2020). A survey of the recent architectures of deep convolutional neural networks. *Artificial Intelligence Review, 53*(8), 5455–5516. doi:10.100710462-020-09825-6

Kocak, T., Seeber, J., & Terzioglu, H. (2003). Design and implementation of a random neural network routing engine. *IEEE Transactions on Neural Networks, 14*(5), 1128–1143. doi:10.1109/TNN.2003.816366 PMID:18244566

LeCun, Y., Bengio, Y., & Hinton, G. (2015). Deep learning. *Nature, 521*(7553), 7553. Advance online publication. doi:10.1038/nature14539 PMID:26017442

LeCun, Y., Boser, B., Denker, J. S., Henderson, D., Howard, R. E., Hubbard, W., & Jackel, L. D. (1989). Backpropagation Applied to Handwritten Zip Code Recognition. *Neural Computation, 1*(4), 541–551. doi:10.1162/neco.1989.1.4.541

Nweke, H. F., Teh, Y. W., Al-garadi, M. A., & Alo, U. R. (2018). Deep learning algorithms for human activity recognition using mobile and wearable sensor networks: State of the art and research challenges. *Expert Systems with Applications, 105*, 233–261. doi:10.1016/j.eswa.2018.03.056

Ravikumar, A., & Sriraman, H. (2023). Acceleration of Image Processing and Computer Vision Algorithms. In Handbook of Research on Computer Vision and Image Processing in the Deep Learning Era. IGI Global. doi:10.4018/978-1-7998-8892-5.ch001

Robin, M., John, J., & Ravikumar, A. (2021). Breast Tumor Segmentation using U-NET. *2021 5th International Conference on Computing Methodologies and Communication (ICCMC)*, 1164–1167. 10.1109/ICCMC51019.2021.9418447

Timotheou, S. (2010). The Random Neural Network: A Survey. *The Computer Journal, 53*(3), 251–267. doi:10.1093/comjnl/bxp032

Zhang, Q., Yang, L. T., Chen, Z., & Li, P. (2018). A survey on deep learning for big data. *Information Fusion, 42*, 146–157. doi:10.1016/j.inffus.2017.10.006

Chapter 5
Coffee Leaf Diseases Classification Using Deep Learning Approach

Sudhir Kumar Mohapatra
https://orcid.org/0000-0003-3065-3881
Sri Sri University, India

Anbesaw Belete
Werabe University, Ethiopia

Ali Hussen
Werabe University, Ethiopia

Abdelah Behari
Werabe University, Ethiopia

Seid Huseen
Werabe University, Ethiopia

Srinivas Prasad
GITAM University, India

ABSTRACT

Agricultural production is among the key techniques for alleviating extreme poverty, boosting economic stability, and feeding the 9.7 billion people expected to live by 2050. However, crop diseases are major obstacles to agriculture production. The most prevalent diseases that reduce production are late diseases which attack the leaves, which are particularly prevalent in coffee crops. To solve the issue, a suitable approach for identifying and categorizing these illnesses in this crop's leaf is required. Particularly in coffee crops, rust, coffee wilt, and brown spot are the most common diseases. Therefore, automatic identifying of these diseases through the system is critical. Thus, the main objective of this study is to design an automated system that can recognize and classify coffee leaf diseases' severity levels. Design science research methodology will follow. Accordingly, the required images have been collected from the SNNP.

DOI: 10.4018/978-1-6684-8531-6.ch005

Copyright © 2024, IGI Global. Copying or distributing in print or electronic forms without written permission of IGI Global is prohibited.

1. INTRODUCTION

Agriculture is one of the diverse and the backbone sources of income for the national economy, and which further plays a critical role in feeding the world's population.. Hence, agricultural researchers and experts are strongly doing their research to obtain maximum yield without affecting the environment (Bashir & Sharma, 2012). Because of this, emerging nations like Ethiopia prioritize the effective execution of agriculture initiatives in order to improve the quality of life for their citizens (Varshney & Dalal, 2016).

The Ethiopian government Agricultural Development Led Industrialization (ADLI) is a central pillar of economic policy in the recently completed plan for accelerated and sustained development to end poverty (Welteji, 2018). More than one-third of the world's population currently consumes coffee as a soft drink. Coffee is additionally one of the most traded commodities nationally and internationally, making it a major commodity on the market and a source of income for millions of people involved in its production. marketing, and processing of the crop. (Pinto et al., 2017). Surprisingly, over 50 developing economies are involved in the manufacture of coffee, while the majority of its consumers are in far-off industrialized nations (Varshney & Dalal, 2016).

The agricultural sector is very important to Ethiopia's economy. The sub-sector of coffee agriculture-based production contributes significantly to the nation's economy. It is the largest source of foreign exchange earnings and significantly boosts the GDP. The usage of coffee as an ingredient in some food processing industries is growing in recent years. For example, it is used as a flavour to various pastries, ice creams, and chocolate, making it not only one of the most popular international beverages but also one of the most important trading commodities in the world after petroleum, candie (Mengistu et al., 2016).

In the cultivation of plant crops, there are many risks. Diseases are one of the risks that attack leaves. In plant science, several diseases attack a crop (Yadessa, Burkhardt, Bekele, Hundera, & Goldbach, 2020). Likewise, in the cultivation of coffee crops, several diseases include rust, brown leaf spot, leaf miner, and Cercospora. If one of the diseases once appear on one leaf, it expands to normal leaves per night and destroys the farm within a few periods (Yadessa, Burkhardt, Bekele, Hundera, & Goldbach, 2020).

Nowadays, the development of soft-computing technologies provided a platform for plant pathologists to use more intelligent tools to diagnose and give appropriate treatment for recognized diseases of plant leaves and make it possible to detect and classify plant leaf diseases (Yadessa, Burkhardt, Bekele, Hundera, & Goldbach, 2020). Nowadays, the development of soft-computing technologies provided a platform for plant pathologists to use more intelligent tools to diagnose and give appropriate treatment for recognized diseases of plant leaves and make it possible to detect and classify plant leaf diseases (Prakash et al., 2017). In contrast with the above idea, the technological advancement in this digital is incomplete if it is not combined with artificial intelligence (Prakash et al., 2017).

The Artificial Intelligence (AI) method is especially helping several sectors to increase productivity and efficiency. The obstacles in any and every sector are being addressed with the assistance of Technologies such as Artificial intelligence. Similar to how it helps other industries, AI in agribusiness is assisting farmers in increasing their productivity and reducing adverse ecological effects. In order to improve the efficiency of agricultural production, the majority of startups in this industry now use AI (Vinuesa et al., 2020).

Image processing helps computer vision to get more meaningful information from the image data. To perform computer vision tasks, machines have to learn from experience (data), so it leads to machine learning, it is a an area of artificial intelligence (AI) that enables systems to automatically learn from experience and improve without explicitly human involvement or with relatively little of it. It focuses on creating computer systems that can gather data and create models based on previous observation or records to help people make better decision (McQueen et al., 1995).

Recently, computer vision made feasible by deep learning has paved the way for computer-assisted disease classification. So, the development of a proper methodology for coffee leaf disease classification is quite useful. In general, this research paper will go to develop a coffee leaf's disease classification system using deep learning techniques. Ethiopia is among the countries in which the coffee plant blooms, and it provides approximately 40% of the country's agricultural production. Around 80–85 percent of Ethiopia's population is dependent upon agriculture. Ethiopia does indeed have a large coffee plant population where 80 to 85% of the population depends on agriculture, with coffee production accounting for approximately 40% of such industry (Sorte, Ferraz, Fambrini, dos Reis Goulart, & Saito, 2019).

Furthermore, Coffee production is constrained by many factors, including losses due to damage caused by pests and diseases, poor management practices, soil infertility (Yadessa, Burkhardt, Bekele, Hundera, & Goldbach, 2020). Hence, rust, Coffee Leaf Rust Coffee Berry Disease, and Coffee Wilt disease are particularly confirm that the most constraint to production and number one priority for farmers (Sorte, Ferraz, Fambrini, dos Reis Goulart, & Saito, 2019). Those diseases can affect any stage of crop growth and if left untreated, leads to the drying of leaves, and the disease occurs throughout the country where coffee production is common (Mengistu et al., 2016).

The most practiced approach for the classification of coffee crop diseases is naked eye observation by experts (human vision). Therefore, this approach is unfeasible due to subjective decisions, prone to error, excessive processing time, unavailability, and less number of experts at farms to identify these diseases and to give an appropriate treatment. According to an expert interview: "First of all, During in the seeding the coffee, they saw the seeds that are resistant to coffee disease." Secondly, wilt disease can harm coffee as it matures. When specialists and farmers notice Wilt disease, they chop down and burn the entire tree. Furthermore, anytime they have a doubt about the diseases that have occurred, they collect a sample from the current disease and analyze it in a laboratory to identify it. The existing illness identification technique has the disadvantage of iterating until they are certain about the type of diseases examined in the laboratory. The technique is typically time-consuming, error-prone, and inefficient, as a result of which the illness has a significant impact on coffee output. As a result of these challenges, a number of undesirable effects have taken place, including an estimated loss of 600 million Ethiopian Birr (ETB), or 73.6 million US dollars, in Ethiopian, as according to (Zeru, 2006). Hence, it needs imperative special attention to the healthy growth of coffee crops. Therefore, automatically detecting and classifying these diseases on the leaves are becomes very critical.

2. THEORETICAL LITERATURE AND RELATED WORKS

2.1 Ethiopian Coffee Production

Ethiopian coffee is primarily cultivated in the shadow of trees (shade or forest coffee),either in forests or forest-like settings or in farming systems that contain specific shade plants, typically native (native) trees, or occasionally fruit trees and other crop plants (Moat et al., 2017).Coffee was first consumed in Ethiopia, where its discovery preceded that of the rest of the globe. Over 70 different species of coffee (Coffea spp.) exist in the tropics, many of which are indigenous to Africa. With 10.3 million hectares of land being farmed globally, the Arabica (Coffea arabica, 64 percent of world production) and Robusta

(Coffea canephora, var. Robusta, 35 percent) types are currently the most economically significant. Brazil, Vietnam, Colombia, Indonesia, and Ethiopia are the major producers. One of the most valuable cash crops in the developing world, more than 60% of farmers produce and export the crop.

2.2 Coffee Leaf Diseases

According to multiple sources, coffee has been attacked by multiple diseases in recent years, and coffee products in Ethiopia can really be degraded as a result of various factors, particularly coffee plant diseases such as Brown Eye Spot (BES) and Coffee Berry Disease (CBD), Coffee Leaf Rust (CLR), Coffee Wilt Disease (CWD).

2.3 Brown Eye Spot

When plants are stressed, a fungus called brown spot disease appears on the leaves. This area On the leaves, there are tiny brown specks that are more noticeable on the upper surface. Within the leaf, the dots typically appear between the veins and also near the margins. The Brown spot diseases are depicted in the following Image.

The above mentioned Figure illustrates that the spots, which have light brown or occasionally light grey cores, wide dark brown rings, and yellow margins, can get up to 15 mm in diameter. Leaf blight develops when the dots enlarge into big patches. They typically have a more amorphous shape than on the leaves, are brown, and are mostly on the side that faces the sun. The spots on the berries may begin when they are still green (Suhartono, 2013).

Figure 1. Brown spot

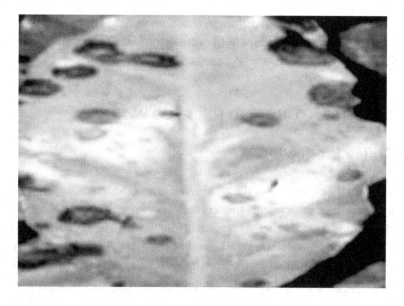

2.4 Leaf Rust

Coffee rust is distinguished by small, oily, yellowish spots on the upper leaf surface that grow into larger, rounded spots that eventually turn brilliant orange, red, and brown with a yellow border. The signs of rust infections that have affected coffee leaves are depicted in the following Figure.

The under leaf surface is powdery and orange-yellow, as shown in the figures above. The pustules eventually turn black. Rusted leaves fall to the ground, leaving damaged trees almost bare. These trees produce substantially less coffee and typically die within a few years (Suhartono, 2013).

Figure 2. Leaf rust

2.5 Coffee Berry

The fungus known as coffee berry disease affects all phases of coffee plant development, although it is most easily recognized by the small, dark, sunken, brown patches that develop on the green berry. The symptoms of this condition are shown in the following Figure.

A particularly harmful condition known as coffee berry disease (CBD), which is brought on by the bacterium Colletotrichum kahawae Waller Bridge, affects growing berries and causes them to rot and shed before the beans are developed (Alemu et al., 2016).

Figure 3. Coffee berry

2.6 Computer Vision

A great deal of emphasis has recently been placed on early modern, non-destructive approaches like image processing techniques systems. Machine vision is the analysis of visual input and it gives the machine the power to see, recognize, and process images in the same way that human vision does, then provide appropriate output to users (Al-Hiary et al., 2011).

2.7 Deep Learning

The deep learning approach is a subset of machine learning (ML) and artificial intelligence (AI), and it is utilized to train algorithms that replicate human behavior in order to make machines knowledgeable enough to think, learn, and decide things by themselves like people. This approach employs a multi-layered neural network with many hidden layers to learn how to describe information with various levels of abstraction, and it is inspired by the way the human brain works (Guo & Guo, 2017).

2.8 Convolutional Neural Network

Convolutional neural networks (CNNs) are a subset of deep learning models used to process image data. CNNs are modeled after the structure of animal visual cortexes and are created to automatically and adaptively learn spatial hierarchies of feature sets, ranging from low-level to high-level patterns. Convolutional neural networks (CNNs) have lately achieved considerable success in many fields of computer vision, particularly image recognition and classification. Its name derives from a mathematical linear operation between matrices. Contains neurons with some weights and biases in a convolution neural network (Albawi et al., 2017).

2.9 Related Work

To develop a classifier model of coffee leaf diseases, it is expected to know to what extent the problems are explored, so an extensive survey has been conducted at local and international levels on detection and classification of coffee crop diseases employing image processing, classical machine learning, and a recent advanced method referred to as deep learning.

Sorte, Ferraz, Fambrini, dos Reis Goulart, & Saito (2019) has proposed a classifier model that can be able to classify the recognized coffee leaves and classify as Cercospora and Rust. So as to develop the classifier model, the researcher tried to collect the necessary data from agricultural farm using digital camera via 300 dpi. A total of 1500 samples images are captured before the images are mirroring or rotating. The necessary texture data is extracted using gray level co-occurrence matrix. Seven attributes is extracted and it has given to the Pre-trained network model called Alex-Net, the predictive power of the developed model is measure through different performance metrics and it achieves 0.98. However, the developed model is not estimate the severity level of the recognized images.

Manso et al. (2019) have developed a smartphone application towards recognizing and identifying the given coffee leaves as miner or rust. The diseases may frequently happen therefore developing the system becomes very important. The images used in this work were captured using the ASUS Zenfone 2 smartphone (ZE551ML) with a resolution of 10 Megapixels (4096x2304 pixels). Three background colors were used: white; black and blue. So as to segment the images from the background the researcher has ygrcb color space and otsu segmentation algorithms is used. For the classification, artificial neural network trained with extreme learning machine have been used.

Marcos et al. (2019) has developed that can be able to recognized and classify Coffee Leaf Rust diseases Using Convolutional Neural Network. The major aim of the paper is recognizing and classifying the recognized coffee leaves as healthy or Rust, because if it is not early treated the diseases has an ability to minimize the production of the coffee up to 45%. The researcher has collected the necessary images from the different cultivated area. Towards developing the classifier model, the researcher has used convolutional neural network, the developed classifier model has been evaluated through different performance evaluation metrics such as precision, recall and accuracy. The result of the model shows that effective and robust classifier. However, the work has not considered other types of diseases that is highly affecting the leaves.

Sorte, Ferraz, Fambrini, dos Reis Goulart, & Saito (2019) has proposed an automatic coffee disease detection and classification using machine learning algorithms. The developed system can be able to recognize the given coffee leave diseases like rust, and brown eye spot. Towards developing the model, the researcher has collected 620 images from the farm, and the necessary image filtering techniques is implemented. Finally, k-nearest neighbor algorithm has used to separate the foreground and background of the images. Gray level co-occurrence matrix is used to extract the necessary features from the given images and machine learning algorithms such as support vector machine is used. Finally, the developed model power is evaluated via Accuracy, precision, and recall. Hence, it achieves 0.78. However, the remaining class label of the coffee leaf diseases not incorporated.

Esgario et al. (2020) the major aim of the study is estimating the severity level of the recognized coffee leaf diseases as bacterial or fungus. The major aim of the research is identifying the recognized diseases factor why it comes to the leaves. Identifying and estimating the stress severity caused by biotic agents on coffee leaves. The largest public dataset currently was from PlantVillage over than 54 thousand images of leaves and 38 classes, among them, healthy and diseased leaves of different species.

Kumar et al. (2020) has developed a classifier model that can be able to classify the recognized coffee leaves as Rust, Cercospora. Towards developing the classifier model the researcher has collect different types of images or dataset. The collected image has been pre-processed by applying different types of image filtering techniques, the preprocessed images are given to convolutional neural network. The developed classifier model performance has been evaluated through different performance evaluation metrics such as precision and accuracy. The result shows that effective and robust techniques with an accuracy of 97.61%. However, the system has a limitation like severity of the recognized coffee leaves diseases is not measured.

Lewis & Espineli (2020) have developed the a classifier model that can be able to identify the nutrients deficiency from the coffee plants using convolutional neural network. Towards developing the classifier model the researchers have collected the required images from the National Coffee Research, Development and Extension Center (NCRDEC),used digital camera so as to capture the data. However, the developed classifier model only consider the nutrient deficient not the infected diseases.

Researchers classify different plant diseases using transfer learning, and deep learning. They have also used computer vision integrated with machine learning for wheat, potato, and other plant disease detection (Mohapatra et al., 2021; Nanda et al., 2023; Sinshaw et al., 2021; Sinshaw et al., 2022).

3. METHODOLOGY OF THE STUDY

3.1 Research Design

In this study, design science research (DSR) methodology has been selected as an approach for discovering and identifying opportunities and problems of coffee production in the agricultural sector and creating new artifacts to overcome those productivity challenges. This methodology has chosen because of the following reasons.

3.2 Proposed Architecture

According to numerous academic studies, convolutional neural networks are the most widely used and recently discovered technology and from this perspective, this study has attempted to implement convolutional neural networks for improving agricultural productivity, specifically for coffee production and leaf disease classification by using their leaves as an input.

The study has employed two different methods such as a multi-layer convolutional neural network from scratch (MCNN) and transfer learning of pre-trained networks to develop the best classifier model to detect and categorize the coffee leaf problem, and then it has compared the outcomes between both.

3.3 Transfer Learning

Pre-trained deep learning models are well acknowledged for their affinity at resolving complex issues. Because the layers are frozen and loaded from a previously trained network and it doesn't need as much training data, this method is used to develop high performance classification networks for limited datasets.

Some characteristics of utilized pre-trained models are introduced in Table 1.

Table 1. Properties of the CNN models used in this study

CNN Architectures	Parameters(M)	Layers	Classification Accuracy
VGG19	138	19	92.7%
RESN50	25	50	94.11%

3.4 MCNN

For the task, a Multilayer CNN is proposed from the scratch, in this approach an architecture of the model is consists of 5 convolutional layers each followed by Relu activation and maxpooling layers, dropout layers, a Flatten, and a fully connected layer followed by softmax activation. During the training Keras reduce learning rate is used as a metric for stopping the training if it has no improving. The architecture for the model that classifies the coffee leaf diseases, and it shows all the input, process, and output of the developed model, using data collected from different place as an input. The following figure shows an architecture for coffee leaf diseases classification model.

Figure 4. CNN architecture

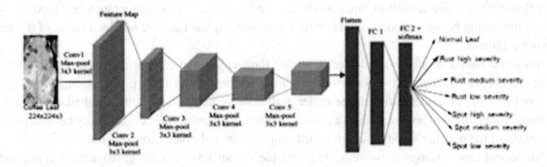

3.5 Hyper-Parameters

A hyper-parameter is a parameter that is set before the learning process begins. Furthermore, these parameters are tunable and can directly affect how well model trains. In a convolutional neural network, experiments can be conducted by various methods; mainly changing types of parameters as well as hyper-parameters the network enables us to switch the parameters to build different classification experiments. The following hyper-parameters are selected as a bench mark. Accordingly, the following hyper-parameters are incorporated. Padding: While we are going to solve a given problems using convolutional neural network, one of the problem is reduction of the output dimension is the problem in the convolutional layer, since some specific area may be lost at every convolution. So, the study has add zero layer to preserve the output as it is.

Stride: It represents how many pixels our filter matrix slides over the input matrix (i.e. when the stride is 1 then we move the filter one pixel at a time).

Table 2. CNN training hyper-parameters

Parameters	Values
Optimizer	Adam
Loss-Function	categorical cross-entropy
Epoch	100
Stride	1
Padding	0 layer
Bach Size	32
Learning rate*	Initial: 0.01
Momentum	0.09
Weight decay	0.005

*Decreases by a factor of 1/2

Epoch: In this study, 50 images are going forward and backward propagation through neural network just once is called one epoch and the researcher has decided to use 32 images at a time because the number of batch size increases, it needs high memory space utilization.

Learning Rate: The default value of the Adaptive learning rate was used initially, and then the ReduceLRonPlateau callback built-in function was utilized to reduce the learning rate when metrics have stopped improving because models often benefit from reducing the learning rate by a factor of 0.5 once learning stagnates.

Optimizer: Adam optimizer is selected to update the weights and categorical cross- entropy loss is implemented as a loss function to evaluate the training set through forward- propagation.

Loss Function: A model performance under particular kernels and weights is calculated by a loss function through forward propagation on a training dataset. It measures the compatibility between output predictions of the network through feed-forward propagation and given ground truth.

Categorical cross-entropy is implemented, and the output layer is configured with 3 class, and a "Softmax" activation in order to predict the probability for each class.

$$Loss = -\sum_{c=1}^{M} y_{o,c} \log(p_{o,c}) \tag{1}$$

where M is the number of class for this study.

3.6 Proposed System Framework

This research work was concerned with designing a coffee leaf disease classification model that has trained on the convolutional neural network using images. The trained network has used to recognize images as an input into a defined set of the output classes. The proposed system accepts a coffee leaf images in any image format collected through the digital camera. To develop the classifier model, the researcher has started a job from the first step called image acquisition.

Accordingly, the required coffee leaf images were collected and prepared. Then, pre-processing is the next step that the researcher has followed like normalization that means normalizing the pixel intensity of an image to minimize the computational difficulty during training the network or to reduce the number of representable values, removing the barrier that is occurred during image acquisition. As well as image resizing also another pre-processing task because the images were captured by a digital camera since feeding them into algorithms vary in size. Therefore, the researcher has established a base size for all images feed into our algorithms.

Finally, pre-processed and smooth datasets were obtained. On the classification stage to classify the coffee leaf image into the appropriate class, the researcher has used deep learning-based approach with convolutional neural network models for image analysis such as for feature extraction and classification because this approach doesn't require a handcrafted feature instead it can extract higher or abstract features from images automatically without human interaction. The following Figure illustrates the proposed coffee leaf disease convolutional neural network system architecture. The above Figure depicts

Figure 5. Proposed framework

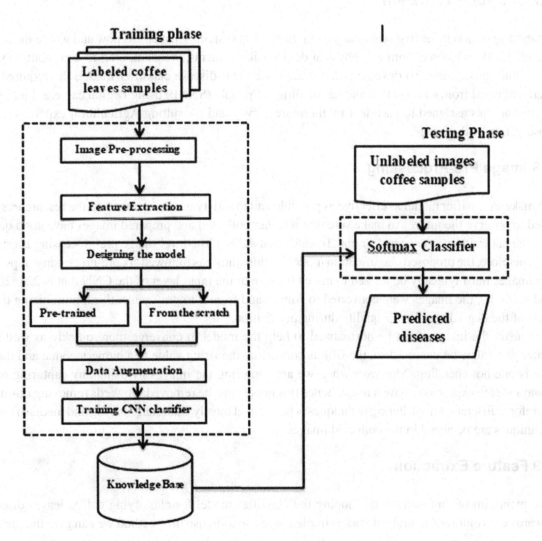

that the proposed framework towards achieving the planned aim of this research. The required images are captured with a digital camera, and then the necessary preprocessing tasks are followed using image preprocessing techniques. Based on this, the dataset had divided into training to train the classifier and testing phase to test the final predictive power of the developed model.

Hence, transfer learning convolutional neural network methods were employed to develop the coffee leaves disease classifier model. To achieve this, pre-trained convolutional neural network models are loaded, labeled images are given to it and transfer the kernel values of the models for feature extraction and the value of the weights in fully connected layers and modify the output class label corresponding with this study class label, and then abstract features are extracted from image automatically.

Besides, the necessary features of the given images are extracted manually towards gabour filtering techniques is used to extract texture features from the images, In line with this, these methods have used data augmentation techniques during training to make the system see a given image in a different dimension and to overcome model overfitting. Finally, the convolutional neural network classifier models are trained and create a model.

3.7 Dataset Preparation

Image acquisition is the first step of any computer vision system. This tells us how and where the images are obtained and stored from any physical device (like cameras, webcam, etc.) to a computer system for further processing. To develop an accurate coffee leaf disease classifier model, the required data were collected from south nation and nationalities of people (SNNP) using Digital camera. Finally, the class label has assigned to each leaf by literature survey and consulting Agricultural experts via their observation of the image.

3.8 Image Pre-Processing

To make a classifier model as effective as possible and to satisfy user requirements, the researchers have tried to observe the images to make sure that whether collected and prepared images have good quality and the naturalness as expected or not. Towards that at least low-level image pre-processing is critical.

Therefore, the proposed classification model for this study has followed six pre-processing steps, first, the images must typically be resized to match the size of the input layer of the CNN that is 224*224x3, and secondly, the images were converted to Binary and from it to gray-scale, third, minimizing the effects of the degradation image quality during acquisition.

Fourth, the images must be normalized to help the model to converge more quickly as well as to better generalize on unseen data, the fifth is converting the string value to a numeric value and the last one is one hot encoding. Moreover when we are capturing the images by using any capturing media always we are expected to have a noise, hence this noise must be removed. Towards removing this noise, therefore, different noise filtering techniques is performed mostly Gaussian filtering and median filtering techniques are occurred in the collected images.

3.9 Feature Extraction

The main aim of this study is developing the classifier model for classifying coffee leaves diseases, towards convolutional neural network is implemented so as to use this method we can give the image to the convolutional neural network or we can extract the necessary feature from the given images and given to the classifier of the convolutional neural network. In this study this two options have been used so as to extract the necessary features the researchers have used GLCM feature extraction techniques because it is one of the most popular techniques in computer vision especially for texture feature extraction or analysis and it uses different frequencies and orientations, and it is highly recommended for gray-scale images, using this the numeric features of the images such as used to extract the necessary features from the gray scale images such as Entropy, Energy, Skewness, Correlation, kurtosis, Homogeneity and contrast. Accordingly, from every individual coffee leaf, these features are extracted, the following tables shows that sample texture features that represent the images.

3.10 Training Methods

In this study, deep learning-based approaches with the convolutional neural network are selected, because it is designed for image analysis and classification. Additionally, it overcomes the difficulties in traditional machine learning algorithms that required manual feature extraction before the classification process.

It performs classification it allows us to extract features directly from raw images by using the convolutional and pooling layer of convolutional neural network. It provides the flexibility of extracting essential and discriminating features from images that are the most appropriate for classification. Accordingly, the researchers has used training from scratch (where all its parameters are tuned for the problem), and transfer learning which was already a pre-trained convolutional neural network. During training pretrained models which are visual geometry group (VGG-19)having 19 and Residual network having 50 layers is implemented, besides, up to four convolutional neural network layers as feature extraction, and 6 layers in fully connected layers in training from scratch method.

Table 3. Sample extracted texture features

Entropy	Energy	Skewness	Correlation	Kurtosis	Homogeneity	Contrast
0.060531	0.126300	2.158966	0.122762	0.014473	0.999979	5.955812
0.048359	0.119846	1.790197	0.108784	0.011800	0.999974	9.667867
0.109139	0.310662	0.591271	0.171572	0.041189	0.999988	7.309303
0.049143	0.115944	1.576878	0.084203	0.009574	0.999974	5.893919
2.109827	90.112730	0.158711	0.849868	0.688051	0.972534	0.999991
0.138084	0.222362	4.086589	0.214822	0.037851	0.999991	4.783699
1.708922	128.583792	0.070821	0.894121	0.439642	0.973956	0.310662

*GLCM techniques

3.11 Experimental Setup

In doing this study on coffee leaf disease detection and classification, the researcher used software named Python and flask framework has been used, and this experiment is executed in a desktop computer with a configuration of Intel® core TM i7 CPU @ 2.70GHz 2.90 GHz, 8.00 GB of installed memory (RAM), 64-bit Microsoft Windows 10 operating system.

4. EXPERIMENTAL RESULT AND ANALYSIS

This study, the result obtained from the experiment using different algorithms test option namely Assigning 80% for training and the remaining for testing, 70% for training and 30% for testing. Besides, an experiments are done using both extracted features and non-extracted features are given to the classifier. Gray level co-occurrence matrix (GLCM) is used to extract the necessary features from the gray scale images such as Entropy, Energy, Skewness, Correlation, kurtosis, Homogeneity and contrast. Finally, the developed classifier model performance has been evaluated through accuracy, precision, recall, and F-measure. Hence, such analysis was done with:

$$Accuracy = \frac{TP + TN}{TP + TN + FP + FN} \tag{2}$$

$$Sensitivity = Recall = \frac{TP}{TP = FN} \tag{3}$$

$$Precision = \frac{TP}{TP + FP} \tag{4}$$

$$Specificity = \frac{TN}{FP + TN} \tag{5}$$

$$F_1 = \frac{2 * Precision * Recall}{Precision + Recall} = \frac{2 * TP}{2 * TP + FP + FN} \tag{6}$$

4.1 ResNet-50 Pre-Trained Model Result

while we are using this model for this coffee classification problems, the default parameters of this state-of-art model has not been modified. However, the last layer is fully connected layers is modified into our classification problem. In this experiment, different scenarios were applied to develop a model like 80% for training and 20% testing, and 70% for training, and 30% testing, and it achieves 84% and 69% accuracy respectfully. Accordingly, the first scenario better than the second one, it selected for detail analysis.

The above confusion matrix show that to what extent the developed classifier model is correctly work, hence the developed model can predict 84.1% accuracy in real-world use. Therefore, the detailed accuracy of the residual network (ResNet50) state-of-art algorithm with the perspective of each class is presented in the following Table.

Figure 6. ResNet-50 confusion matrix

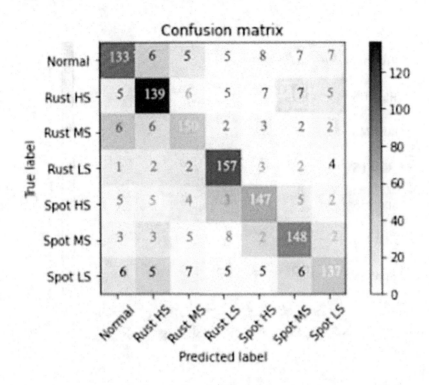

Table 4. Detail analysis for ResNet-50 model by class

Class	Performance Metrics				
	Recall	Precision	F-Measure	TPR	FPR
Normal	77.7%	83.6%	80.5%	77.7%	22.3%
Rust high severity	79.8%	83.7%	81.7%	79.8%	20.2%
Rust Medium severity	87.7%	83.7%	85.6%	87.7%	12.3%
Spot high severity	85.9%	84%	84.9%	85.9%	14.1%
Spot Medium severity	86.5%	83.6%	85%	86.5%	13.5%
Spot Low severity	80.1%	86.1%	82.9%	80.1%	19.9%
Weighted average	84.2%	84.1%	84.2%	84.2%	15.8%

4.2 VGG-19

It has 19 layers including convolutional layers, pooling layer, and three fully connected layers with three blocks and two of them with 4096 neurons and 1000 neurons which is the output of the class probabilities. Besides, this state-of-art architecture, hyper-parameters, and parameters like the number of filters,

Figure 7. VGG-19 confusion matrix

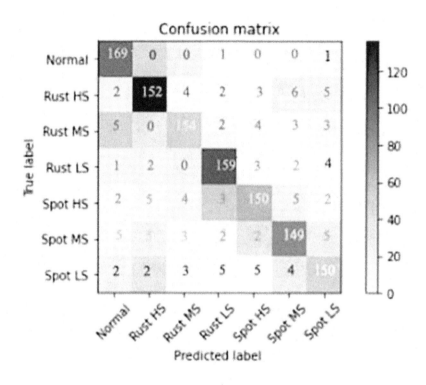

filter size, stride, and padding were taken as it is with the default value to train the network. However, the last layers of this network were modified as per the number of the class in this study.

For this experiment, two test options were tested during training the network by splitting the collected dataset into 80% of the images for training and 20% for testing, 70% of the dataset was assigned for training and 30% of the dataset for testing. hence, it achieves 90% and 87.3% respectfully, and the first test option is selected for detail analysis. so, the following confusion matrix shows the performance of the model.

The researcher has used a confusion matrix to show the experimental results of the developed classification model of coffee leaf diseases. This experiment was conducted by manually splitting the dataset into training and testing. Therefore, out of the 6000 total images, 4800 (80%) of the images were used as a training dataset and the remaining, 1200 (20%) of the images were used as a testing dataset. Therefore, this state-of-art algorithms called VGG-19 scored an accuracy out of 1200 total number of testing images 1,080 (90%) of them were classified correctly and the remaining 120 (10%) testing images were incorrectly classified. Based on all test option results, the first test option has selected for detailed analysis and is presented below in Table.

For this experiment, the researcher has tried to observe the recall, precision, and F1- measure value for better understanding and analyzing of the result. Precision indicates the ratio of properly predicted true classifications to the total predicted true classifications. Recall indicates the properly predicted true classifications of all classifications of the actual class.

Table 5. Detailed accuracy by class for VGG-19

Class	Performance Metrics				
	Recall	Precision F-Measure TPR			FPR
Normal	98.8%	90.8% 94.6% 98.8%			1.2%
Rust high severity	87.3%	91.5%	89.3%	87.3%	12.7%
Rust Medium severity	90%	91.6%	90.7%	90%	10%
Rust Low severity	92.9%	91.3%	92%	92.9%	7.1%
Spot high severity	87.7%	90%	88.8%	87.7%	12.3%
Spot Medium severity	87.1%	88%	87.5%	87.1%	12.9%
Spot Low severity	87.7%	88%	87.8%	87.7%	12.3%
Weighted average 90.2% 90.17% 90.1% 90.2% 10%					

The experimental result shows that, the developed classifier model using residual network-50 with 80% for training and 20% for testing is 86% accuracy, and the remaining 14% error which is 1,032 records correctly classified, the remaining 168 records are classified incorrectly.

Besides, this pre-trained model also tested the result by 70% for training and 30% for testing, it shows that from 1800 records 1404 records are classified correctly, and the remaining 396 records are incorrectly classified, so it perform 78% accuracy.

Moreover, the researcher have tried to developed the model by using whole extracted features in VGG-19 Pretrained model, via different test option, the first test option is assigned 80% for training and 20% for testing, the result depicts that 960 records are correctly classified, and 240 records are incorrectly classified. Furthermore, this model also applied to develop the model by assigned 70% for training and 30% for testing, and the result is 75%. Generally, the following Figure shows an experimental Analysis using pre-trained model with whole attributes.

Figure 2 shows that the comparison performance of the developed model using both residual network50 and visual geometry group(VGG-19) via different test options, accordingly, residual network Pre-trained model achieves the best accuracy than visual geometry group having 19 layers in the selected attributes.

The experiment also extended to develop the classifier model using these pre-traned model with selected attributes. Towards selecting the selects an attributes the researcher has information Gain ratio with ratio of *0.5 Energy, Skewness, Correlation, kurtosis, Homogeneity* features are selected. The following Figures are depicted that an experiment result with these selected attributes. Additionally, an experiment is done the selected attributes, and the selected attributes is implemented by the pre-trained model and from the scratch namely ResNet50 and VGG-19 by assigning 80%for Training and the remaining 20% for testing, accordingly 91%, 90%, 80% achieved from each model respectfully.

An experiment also extended without extracting the necessary features from the giving images, in this scenario's, the only thing that we have done is download the pre-tranied weight and such as ResNet50 and VGG-19, developing the network from the scratch having 6 layers and compare the performance of this classifier. Accordingly, ResNet-50 have achieved the 98%, and VGG-19 have achieved 94%, from the scratch is achieved 91%, diagrammatically, it seems like the following.

Figure 7 shows that convolutional neural network from

Figure 8. Pre-trained model with whole attributes

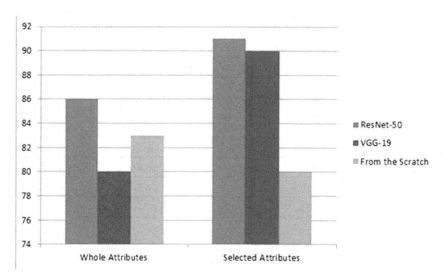

Figure 9. Pre-trained with whole attributes

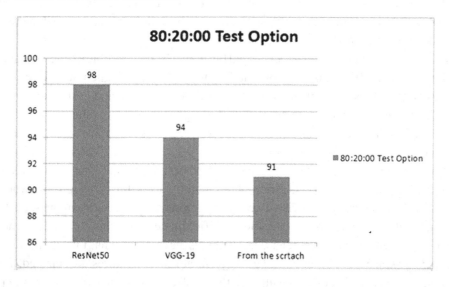

5. CONCLUSION AND FUTURE WORKS

This research is mainly focused on developing a classifier model that can be able to detect and recognize a given coffee leaf images and classify as Healthy, Rust with high severity, Middle severity, Low severity, besides, brown spot with high severity, middle Severity, low severity, towards developing this the required data is collected from the south nation and nationalities of people and different preprocessing tasks are applied on the collected images towards making the data more smooth and clean for the actual classification, Finally, convolutions neural network approach such as pre-trained model and training from the scratch are applied by default test option that means assigning 80% for training and the remaining 20% for testing purpose.

Besides, experiments are tested by by extracting the necessary features from the and given to the convolutional neural network and with extracting the necessary features from the given coffee image that means using convolutional neural network for both feature extraction and classification. finally, the developed classier model can be able classify the diseases 98% accuracy by ResNet50.

In the future, recognising a given images and classifying based on the nutrient deficiency and other class label also future research direction.

ACKNOWLEDGMENT

This research work is supported by Research and Community Service Vice President Office, Wolaita Sodo University, Ethiopia.

REFERENCES

Al-Hiary, H., Bani-Ahmad, S., Reyalat, M., Braik, M., & Alrahamneh, Z. (2011). Fast and accurate detection and classification of plant diseases. *International Journal of Computer Applications*, *17*(1), 31–38. doi:10.5120/2183-2754

Albawi, S., Mohammed, T. A., & Al-Zawi, S. (2017). Understanding of a convolutional neural network. 2017 International Conference on Engineering and Technology (ICET), 1–6. doi:10.1109/ICEngTechnol.2017.8308186

Alemu, K., Adugna, G., Lemessa, F., & Muleta, D. (2016). Current status of coffee berry disease (colletotrichum kahawae waller & bridge) in Ethiopia. *Archiv für Phytopathologie und Pflanzenschutz*, *49*(17-18), 421–433. doi:10.1080/03235408.2016.1228736

Bashir, S., & Sharma, N. (2012). Remote area plant disease detection using image processing. *IOSR Journal of Electronics and Communication Engineering*, *2*(6), 31–34. doi:10.9790/2834-0263134

Esgario, J. G., Krohling, R. A., & Ventura, J. A. (2020). Deep learning for classification and severity estimation of coffee leaf biotic stress. *Computers and Electronics in Agriculture*, *169*, 105162. doi:10.1016/j.compag.2019.105162

Guo & Guo. (2017). *Deep learning for visual understanding*. Academic Press.

Kumar, M., Gupta, P., & Madhav, P. (2020). Disease detection in coffee plants using convolutional neural network. *2020 5th International Conference on Communication and Electronics Systems (ICCES)*, 755–760. 10.1109/ICCES48766.2020.9138000

Lewis, K. P., & Espineli, J. D. (2020). Classification and detection of nutritional deficiencies in coffee plants using image processing and convolutional neural network (CNN). *International Journal of Scientific and Technology Research*, *9*(4), 2076–2081.

Manso, G. L., Knidel, H., Krohling, R. A., & Ventura, J. A. (2019). *A smartphone application to detection and classification of coffee leaf miner and coffee leaf rust*. arXiv preprint arXiv:1904.00742.

Marcos, A. P., Rodovalho, N. L. S., & Backes, A. R. (2019). Coffee leaf rust detection using convolutional neural network. *2019 XV Workshop de Visão Computacional (WVC)*, 38–42. 10.1109/WVC.2019.8876931

McQueen, R. J., Garner, S. R., Nevill-Manning, C. G., & Witten, I. H. (1995). Applying machine learning to agricultural data. *Computers and Electronics in Agriculture*, *12*(4), 275–293. doi:10.1016/0168-1699(95)98601-9

Mengistu, A. D., Mengistu, S. G., & Alemayehu, D. M. (2016). Image analysis for ethiopian coffee plant diseases identification. IJBB, 10(1).

Moat, Williams, Baena, Wilkinson, Demissew, Challa, Gole, & Davis. (2017). *Coffee farming and climate change in ethiopia: impacts, forecasts, resilience and opportunities-summary*. Academic Press.

Mohapatra, Prasad, & Nayak. (2021). Wheat Rust Disease Detection Using Deep Learning. *Data Science and Data Analytics: Opportunities and Challenges*, 191.

Nanda, Mohapatra, & Satpathy. (2023). Wheat Rust Disease Detection Using Convolutional Neural Network. *Journal of Harbin Engineering University, 44*(6), 253-259.

Pinto, C., Furukawa, J., Fukai, H., & Tamura, S. (2017). Classification of green coffee bean images basec on defect types using convolutional neural network (CNN). *2017 International Conference on Advanced Informatics, Concepts, Theory, and Applications (ICAICTA)*, 1–5. 10.1109/ICAICTA.2017.8090980

Prakash, R. M., Saraswathy, G., Ramalakshmi, G., Mangaleswari, K., & Kaviya, T. (2017). *Detection of leaf diseases and classification using digital image processing. In 2017 international conference on innovations in information, embedded and communication systems (ICIIECS)*. IEEE.

Sinshaw, N. T., Assefa, B. G., & Mohapatra, S. K. (2021). Transfer Learning and Data Augmentation Based CNN Model for Potato Late Blight Disease Detection. *2021 International Conference on Information and Communication Technology for Development for Africa (ICT4DA)*, 30-35. 10.1109/ICT4DA53266.2021.9672243

Sinshaw, N. T., Assefa, B. G., Mohapatra, S. K., & Beyene, A. M. (2022). Applications of Computer Vision on Automatic Potato Plant Disease Detection: A Systematic Literature Review. *Computational Intelligence and Neuroscience, 2022*, 7186687. doi:10.1155/2022/7186687 PMID:36419507

Sorte, L. X. B., Ferraz, C. T., Fambrini, F., dos Reis Goulart, R., & Saito, J. H. (2019). Coffee leaf disease recognition based on deep learning and texture attributes. *Procedia Computer Science*, *159*, 135–144. doi:10.1016/j.procs.2019.09.168

Suhartono. (2013). Expert system in detecting coffee plant diseases. *Int. J. Electr. Energy*, *1*(3), 156–162.

Varshney, S., & Dalal, T. (2016). Plant disease prediction using image processing techniques-a review. *International Journal of Computer Science and Mobile Computing*, *5*(5), 394–398.

Vinuesa, R., Azizpour, H., Leite, I., Balaam, M., Dignum, V., Domisch, S., Felländer, A., Langhans, S. D., Tegmark, M., & Fuso Nerini, F. (2020). The role of artificial intelligence in achieving the sustainable development goals. *Nature Communications*, *11*(1), 1–10. doi:10.103841467-019-14108-y PMID:31932590

Welteji, D. (2018). A critical review of rural development policy of ethiopia: Access, utilization and coverage. *Agriculture & Food Security*, *7*(1), 1–6. doi:10.118640066-018-0208-y

Yadessa, A., Burkhardt, J., Bekele, E., Hundera, K., & Goldbach, H. (2020). The major factors influencing coffee quality in ethiopia: The case of wild arabica coffee (coffea arabica l.) from its natural habitat of southwest and southeast afromontane rainforests. *African Journal of Plant Science*, *14*(6), 213–230. doi:10.5897/AJPS2020.1976

Zeru, A. (2006). *Diversity of arabica coffee populations in afromontane rainforests of Ethiopia in relation to colletotrichum kahawae and gibberella xylarioides* [Ph.D. dissertation]. Addis Ababa University.

Chapter 6
COVID–19 Classification With Healthcare Images Based on ML–DL Methods

Shreeharsha Dash

Odisha University of Technology and Research, India

Subhalaxmi Das

Odisha University of Technology and Research, India

ABSTRACT

COVID-19 is the contagious ailment caused by Sars-Cov-2. This causative 2019-nCoV is a communication to the lines of millions of people. This study employs ML and DL epitomes to determine sickness along with predicting if a person is afflicted with the virus as the previous reports can examine the data pre-processing, feature extraction, classification, evaluation of experimental results to find advanced fact-finding directions around COVID-19 classification employing machine-deep approaches. The comparison shows that chest x-rays and CT are the most frequently used data in the diagnosis of COVID-19 rather than RT-PCR, and that the most-used test techniques were found to be insensitive and less beneficial after changing the limited number of datasets. This study suggests image preprocessing, exploratory data analysis, feature extraction (LBP), and other ML as well as DL classification methods. It attempts to minimise some of the issues that have been addressed for early identification for future work and studies.

1. INTRODUCTION

1.1. Coronavirus

Coronavirus is a broad family of infectious agents spreading out incurable health problems to heavy-handed sickness namely MERS-CoV and SARS-CoV. On December 31, 2019, Wuhan, in the Hubei province of China, reported to the World Health Organization (WHO) that instances of pneumonia with an unknown chronic infection had been found. This slow-moving illness is characterized by a protracted incubation

DOI: 10.4018/978-1-6684-8531-6.ch006

Copyright © 2024, IGI Global. Copying or distributing in print or electronic forms without written permission of IGI Global is prohibited.

Figure 1. Comparisons of RT-PCR, CXR images, and CT scan images used for COVID-19 detection

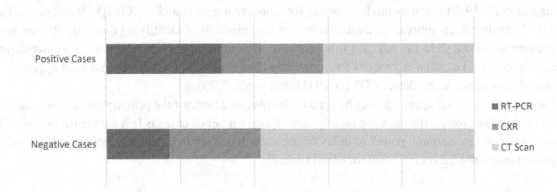

period and progressive disease. On 11 March 2020, the WHO declared the COVID as an epidemic as it spread out all over the world with a very quick manner in a very short period. This pandemic is not only a health emergency; it is also a socioeconomic emergency of unprecedented proportions. It has the potential to have devastating social, economic, and political repercussions that will leave permanent wounds, stressing every nation it touches. Under the direction of the UN Resident Coordinators, the WHO and the Global Humanitarian Response Plan lead the health response, while UNDP (United Nations Development Programme) is in charge of the technical lead for the UN's socioeconomic recovery.

As soon as possible, anyone who fear they may have COVID-19 should find out whether they are infected so they may get the right care, isolate themselves, and let those they have had close contact with known (Benmalek et al., 2021). RT-PCR (Real-Time Reverse Transcription - Polymerase Chain) is a method of collecting samples from a individual's nasal or gullet, two areas of the body where the coronavirus is presumable to cluster. The material is extracted, during which genetic information is separated from potential viruses. A specific chemical is used in conjunction with PCR (polymerase chain reaction) equipment (thermal cycler) to start a process that produces millions of facsimiles of the SARS-CoV-2 virus and its transcriptome. One of the chemicals produces a laser beam when the sample contains SARS-COV-2. The PCR machine tracks the light beam, which demonstrates a cocksure test result for the presence of COVID (Shah et al., 2021).

Although RT-PCR can clearly detect coronavirus disease, it has a significant false negative rate, which occurs when the model prognosticates a negative sequel but the result is positive (false negative). In addition, RT-PCR is not widely available in many parts of the world. As a result, medical imaging such as computed tomography (CT) and chest x-rays (CXR), which are available in most medical or hospital settings, may be the best option for detecting this infection. If RT-PCR is not available, CT scan or X-ray are readily available. In addition, RT-PCR is extravagant and tedious for diagnosis. This requires the use of special equipment and takes at least 24 hours. Chest imaging has been shown to be useful in the progression of this lung disease (Benmalek et al., 2021). In addition, healthcare workers need adequate training to collect samples for PCR, whereas CT and X-ray pictures are comparatively convenient and create (Zhao et al., 2020) shown in Figure 1.

Surprisingly, research has demonstrated that a chest X-ray and a CT can detect COVID-19-related lung abnormalities. A radiologist's services are required for this assessment. Because radiologists are in short supply and there are many COVID-19 patients, system is needed to assist radiologists and medical professionals. The expansion of ml and dl approaches using medical pictures is thought to complement existing COVID-19 detection methods, allowing for more precise and quicker COVID-19 diagnosis. The COVID-19 outbreak has spurred specialists to look at new methods of identifying the virus. Researchers are seeking to use ml-dl to prevail over this problem. This foregoing work was applied to investigate research questions, i.e., what techniques are commonly used to classify COVID-19 and what approaches are available to classify and detect COVID-19 (Daniel et al., 2023).

The machine learning approach may be used to discover and forecast the primary parameters impacting COVID-19 recovery. Although the rapidly increasing number of cases is less for the timing but still if someone with low immune power or delay of accurate diagnosis to defeat the coronavirus infection the person may infected severely and may lead to death.

2. RELATED THEORY

Image pre-processing and ml and dl techniques-based applications have rapidly grown due to their significant influence on human existence in terms of social, scientific, medical, and technical applications. This piece of study explains why studies on the Coronavirus issue are being undertaken in order to save lives. Image pre-processing for medical diagnosis systems is effective and can be used to prevent COVID-19 spread and safeguard humans.

2.1. Image Pre-Processing

The purpose of preprocessing is to improve the image resolution so that we can analyse it more efficiently. We can reduce unwanted distortion and improve certain features required by the pre-processed application we are working on. These features may change depending on the application. It is numerously used on medical images processing for different disease detection and classification.

Image pre-processing prepares data for subsequent processing. The primary purpose of medical image pre-processing is to eliminate image acquisition artefacts and standardise pictures across data sets. The precise pre-processing needs are determined by the data acquisition modality and technique, as well as the target workflow. Background removal, denoising, resampling, registration, and intensity normalisation are all standard pre-processing processes.

- **Background Removal:** The background removal entails separating the region of interest from the backdrop of an image. Improve the efficiency and precision of your target workflow by restricting the image to the region of interest.
- **Denoising:** Medical imaging techniques are vulnerable to noise, which causes unpredictable intensity changes in images. Images can be filtered in the spatial and frequency domains to decrease noise.
- **Resampling:** To adjust the pixel or voxel size of a picture without changing its spatial bounds in the patient coordinate system, use resampling. Resampling can be used to standardise picture resolution across a data collection containing images from several scanners.
- **Registration:** To standardise the spatial alignment of 2-D or 3-D medical pictures in a data set, use image registration. Registration might be beneficial for aligning pictures of various patients or

images of the same patient taken at different times, on separate scanners, or with different imaging modalities.

- **Intensity Normalization:** It standardises the intensity range of images across a data collection. This procedure is typically carried out in two phases. First, reduce the range of intensities. Second, normalise the clipped intensity range to the image data type's range. Unlike visualising image data with a display window, intensity normalisation really refreshes the picture values.

There are 4 distinct Image Pre-processing way of working i.e.

1. **Pixel brightness transformations/ Brightness corrections:** Brightness alterations alter the brightness of pixels, and the transfiguration is determined by the pixels' properties. The matched input pixel value determines the output pixel value in the PBT. Such operations include changes in brightness and contrast, in addition to colour corrections and transforms. Image processing for both human and machine power of observation relies heavily on contrast enhancement. It's often used as a preprocessing step for speech recognition, texture and various other image/video processing applications, as well as in medical image processing.

Brightness transformations are classified into two categories:

- **Brightness corrections**: We alter the value of all pixels by a constant to alter the illumination of an image. Adding a positive constant to all of the picture pixel values brightens the image. Similarly, we may darken the image by subtracting a positive constant from all of the pixel values.
- **Gray scale transformation**: Since all Image Processing Techniques functions directly on pixels, all focus on grey level transformation. During the vertical axis has an effect on the number of pixels in the image, a grayscale image is having 256 gray plumbs perfectly horizontal in 0-255 histogram.

The following are the most common pixel brightness conversion procedures:

- **Gamma correction or power law transform:** The correction of gamma values for each pixel value is a non linear adjustment. Gamma correction applies a non-linear treatment to the pixels in the original image, potentially causing image saturation, whereas picture standardization used linear operations to individual pixels, which includes scalar multiplication and addition/subtraction.
- **Histogram equalization**: Due to its versatility, histogram equalization is a widely used improvement of contrast method for a wide range of picture types. The technique of histogram compensation is a complex process to adjust the dynamic range and contrast in an image, by changing it's intensity histogram to its desired shape. In contrast to contrast stretching, histogram base operators can utilise non-linear and non-monotonic consign functions to map betwixt pixel intensity levels in the input and output images.

The normalised histogram is as follows:

$$p(n) = \frac{Number \ of \ pixels \ with \ intensity \ (n)}{Total \ number \ of \ pixel} \tag{1}$$

- **Sigmoid stretching:** Sigmoid is a nonlinear activation function which remains constant. As the function is a "S" shape, the word "sigmoid" comes from it. In the statistical world, this is known as a logistic function. fs(x,y) is the first picture, where g (x,y) is the upgraded pixel esteem, c is the difference variable, and that is the limit esteem. It is feasible to adjust the level of easing up and obscuring to direct the general difference improvement by modifying the differentiation factor 'c' and limit esteem.

    2. **Geometric transformations:** In order to avoid geometric distortion that occurs during acquisition, geometrical transformation changes the placement of pixels in an image and leaves its colour unchanged. Two main steps of the Geometric transformations are spatial transformation, where pixels in a image are adjusted to their respective dimensions and grey level interpolation, which determines gray levels for different images.

    Interpolation methods: In these cases, the brightness interpolation stumbling block can be expelled in two ways. In the output image, where x and y are on a discrete raster and different types of Interpolation methods are used, the brightness of the pixel x',y' is ;

- Nearest neighbour interpolation is the simplest technique that re samples the pixel values present in the input vector or a matrix
- Linear interpolation explores four points neighbouring the point (x, y), and assumes that the brightness function is linear in this neighbourhood.
- By approximating the brightness function locally on a bicubic polynomial surface, bicubic interpolation ameliorates the model of brightness function. For the interpolation, 16 adjacent points shall be used.
    I. **Image filtering and segmentation:** Using filters aims to modify or enhance image properties, as well as extract prized possessions information from pictures, such as edges, corners, and blobs A kernel, a small array, defines a filter that is utilized on every pixel and its surrounding neighbours within an image.
- **Low pass filtering (smoothing)**: Most smoothing methods rely on a low pass filter as their foundation. One way to enhance an image is to reduce the difference in pixel values by averaging neighbouring pixels.
- **High pass filters (edge detection, sharpening)**: A higher-pass filter has the ability to enhance the sharpness of an image. The purpose of these filters is to enhance the fine details present in the image, which is the complete opposite of what the low-pass filter does. Similar to low-pass filtering, high-pass filtering functions in a comparable manner, except that it utilizes an alternate convolution kernel.
    a. **Directional filtering:** The directional filter serves as an edge detector and is utilized for calculating the initial derivatives of an image. The most remarkable manifestation of the first derivatives, i.e., the slopes, is observed when there is a significant alteration between

the values of adjacent pixels. Filters that are directional can be created to cover any direction within a specified area.

b. **Laplacian filtering**: The Laplacian filter is a useful tool in image analysis for identifying edges. It calculates the second derivatives of an image, allowing us to gauge the speed at which the first derivatives alter. The determination is made to distinguish whether a modification in the values of adjacent pixels indicates an edge or a smooth progression. In the typical formulation, Laplacian filter kernels are structured with negative values forming a cross pattern, positioned at the centre of the array. The corners are defined as either zero or having positive values. The centre value has the potential to be negative or positive.

In the realm of digital image processing and analysis, image segmentation takes centre stage as a pivotal technique. It entails dividing an image into distinct portions or areas, a task often accomplished by leveraging the pixels present in the picture. Image segmentation may involve the separation of foreground and background components, or the clustering of pixel groups according to similarities in colour or shape.

- **Non-contextual thresholding**: Thresholding, without considering the context, is the most basic technique for segmenting. The process involves the utilization of a solitary threshold to convert a grayscale or color image into a binary image, commonly referred to as a binary region map. The binary map can be separated into two potentially separate regions: the first containing pixels with input data values below a certain threshold, while the second includes pixels with input data values that are equal to or higher than the threshold. There are three forms of thresholding: simple thresholding, adaptive thresholding, and colour thresholding.

- **Contextual segmentation**: Non-contextual thresholding categorizes pixels irrespective of their location on the image plane. Contextual segmentation achieves better results in discriminating individual items due to its consideration of the proximity of pixels associated with the same object. There are two types of contextual segmentation: signal discontinuity and similarity-based segmentation. The approaches that are based on discontinuity aim to encompass entire boundaries that consist of mostly homogeneous regions, while assuming that there are abrupt signal changes occurring across each boundary. Similarity-based strategies aim to create uniform zones by disposing interconnected pixels that meet specific alikeness criteria. When considering the division of regions by a complete border, these two strategies can be considered equivalent. Pixel connection, region similarity, region growth, and split-and-merge segmentation are instances of contextual segmentation.

- **Texture segmentation**: Many image exploration consider texture to be the most crucial attribute. The texture problem procedures can be classified into four categories: structural approach, statistical approach, model-based approach, and filter-based approach.

II. **Fourier transform and Image restauration**: The decomposing of an image into its sine and cosine constituents is done through the application of the Fourier Transform, a vital tool in image processing. The image is represented in the Fourier or frequency domain after the transformation, whereas the spatial domain equivalent is the input image. The wide range of applications in which the Fourier Transform finds utility include image analysis, image filtering, image reformation, and image compress. The DFT (Discrete Fourier Transform) lacks all frequencies that form the entirety of an image. Instead, it consists of a large enough collection of samples to effectively represent the image's spatial domain.

Image processing involves the extraction of information and enhancement of a picture through various operations. Digital image processing enables a wide range of applications such as image restoration, medical imaging, remote sensing, image segmentation, and more. Each procedure needs a distinct approach.

2.2. Phases of Image Processing

Image Acquisition: The inceptive step in image processing involves the acquisition of images. Preprocessing, which is commonly referred to as a stage in image processing, involves various techniques and methods. In order to obtain the image, it involves retrieving it from a typically hardware-based source.

Image Enhancement: Image enhancement involves the proceedings of revealing and highlighting specific elements of importance within a concealed image. One may consider modifying the brightness, contrast, and other settings as part of the process.

Image Restoration: Image restoration refers to the method used to improve the aesthetic appeal of a picture. Picture restoration differs from picture augmentation in terms of the methods used. While picture augmentation involves applying various techniques to enhance or modify an image, picture restoration focuses on employing probabilistic models.

Colour Image Processing: A multitude of digital colour modelling criterion fall under the umbrella term of colour image processing. The widespread utilization of digital images on the internet has led to the increased popularity of this procedure.

Wavelets and Multiresolution Processing: The purpose of wavelets is to portray images with different levels of detail. To achieve data compression and pyramidal representation, the images are divided into wavelets or smaller segments.

Compression: One way to decrease the amount of storage needed for a picture or the bandwidth needed to send it is through compression. This notion holds particularly true when the photograph is aimed for utilization on the Internet.

Morphological Processing: It involves employing a sequence of techniques to alter the appearance of images based on their shapes.

Segmentation: Segmentation is undeniably one of the most challenging phases in image processing. The process involves dissecting an image into its fundamental components or elements.

Representation and Description: After dividing an image into segments, each region is then expressed and detailed in a manner that is appropriate for subsequent computerized handling. Representation focuses on the elements and spatial characteristics of the image. The purpose of description is to gather numerical data that assists in differentiating one category of objects from another.

Object Recognition: Recognition of an item is attained through its description labelling.

3. LITERATURE REVIEW

When we get the information about diagnosis of any disease is like a reason to believe that a bad situation will end soon and the improvement in current situation will be getting preferably. When it comes to the COVID-19 epidemic, quick identification and detection of the disease is more important for the people. First, utilise data to develop a model that will be employed by ml and dl approach algorithms for Covid diagnosis. Due to the challenges with RT-PCR, analysers have mostly relied on CT scan and X-ray images for diagnosis. Chest X-ray images capture the concentration of calcium in our bones by using organic photographic detectors that absorb more radiation, where as a chest CT scan images is taken using computed tomography (CT) scan procedure by which the patient is positioned on a bed that navigates across the gantry, as the X-ray tube spins around the patient, it emits concentrated beams of X-rays into the body.

CT scan takes less time to demonstrate, but it is more expensive. As a result, many researchers created a COVID-19 detection model that uses X-ray images rather than CT scans. It is also cheaply priced and easy to maintain. X-ray images of COVID-19 patients, viral, bacterial and a healthy individual.

Transferring and exchanging data and information between the researcher and the information source is extremely challenging during a lockdown. Due to the rapid spreading of this disease, there was numerous data are available for the continuous changing of active cases, recoveries, death cases, kinds of rapid testing procedures and vaccination etc. Several COVID-19 data sets, however, are available and used by researchers, and they produce outstanding results in detecting COVID-19 injured lungs.

Relation between chest CT finding and clinical conditions of coronavirus disease (COVID-19) pneumonia: a multicentre study. Qizhi Yu et. al. (Zhao et al., 2020) presented imaging interpretation and statistical analysis method and got 86.1% with GGO (Ground Glass Opacity), 64.4% with GGO and consolidation, 73.3% with vascular enlargement. Osama R. Shanin et. al. (Shahin et al., 2022) described CT-lung screening and CAD system with decision tree (DT), support vector machine (SVM), K-means clustering and radial basic function. The classifier determines whether a person is affected by a disease. The classification can be divided into 4 categories, part 1 is test positive and negative, while part 2 is false positive and negative using paper machine learning method to detect and classify the COVID. A fault is that the efficacy and correctness of the proposed model can be improved by increasing the number of samples used. A deep learning system to screen novel coronavirus disease 2019 Pneumonia, Xia Owei Xu et. al. (2020) calculate using noisy or Bayesian function, the overall accuracy was 86.7% in the CT-cases taken together and better performance only in case of large amount of data. Guang Lia et. al. (2023) pertaining batch knowledge assembly-based fine-tuning using self-supervised learning, high identification accuracy when training images is greatly reduced. This method is insensitive to changes in hyper parameters.

ML and DL techniques have the potential to significantly reduce the time required to conduct electronic exams. Additionally, these methods enable skilled professionals to assist clinicians and allow artificial intelligence experts to support both clinicians and laboratory professionals.

4. PROPOSED SYSTEM

In the following subsection, we delineate an extensive experiment along with the step-by-step approach undertaken to scrutinize the efficacy of the suggested technique. The dataset which is imperturbable from Kaggle archives and methods and forecasting case techniques that are used. Experiments accomplished on the frontal view of chest x-ray images on standard PC using Jupyter Notebook. Figure 2 represents the spitting images of COVID, NORMAL and PNEUMONIA cases as well as proposed framework.

4.1. COVID-19 Dataset

The utilization of datasets holds immense significance in the identification of COVID-19 through deep learning methods based on computer vision. Let us now delve into the dataset employed for our experi-

Figure 2. Workflow of the proposed system

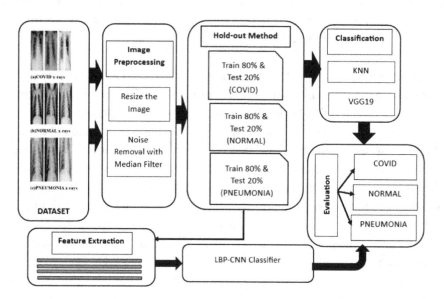

mental work in this section. There are a total of 5228 images, with 1626 confirmed as COVID-19 cases, 1802 categorized as normal, and 1800 classified as pneumonia.

4.2. Preprocessing

Participating in the process involved the development of a classifier model. The sample is isolated from the remaining dataset and sent to the preprocessing stage for additional analysis. When going through the preprocessing stage, it is crucial to consider a variety of factors. It is best to discard data samples that are scrappy or enigmatic. In order to obtain a genuine outcome, a substantial amount of data is essential. In the realm of medical image analysis, data scarcity can pose a significant challenge due to the expensive and time-consuming nature of annotating data.

Resize the Image: Resizing an image involves altering its dimensions, either increasing or decreasing them, while preserving all original content. When we resize the image, its dimensions undergo a change, leading to alterations in both its size and quality.

Median Filter: A nonlinear method for eliminating noise from photos is median filtering. Because of how well it keeps edges while minimizing noise, it is frequently utilized. It's excellent at eliminating "salt and pepper" noises. The median filter works by iteratively going over each pixel in the picture and substituting the median value of neighbouring pixels for each value. The "window" refers to the neighbor pattern that advances pixel by pixel across the whole picture. The process of calculating the median involves first sorting all of the window's pixel values into numerical order. Next, the pixel under consideration is swapped out with the pixel with the middle (median) value (Auckland, n.d.; Hasoon et al., 2021).

4.3. Feature Extraction

Once the X-ray images have been analyzed, the subsequent stage involves feature extraction. This process reduces the dimensionality of the raw data and transforms it into meaningful information for further processing. The purpose of feature extraction is to streamline the portrayal of an image by converting it into more significant data. Local Binary Pattern (LBP) is a popular image feature extraction operator that is utilised in a wide range of real-world applications. The LBP is a simple yet effective texture extraction operator. The LBP may be employed in sophisticated and real-time image processing applications due to its low computer complexity. It is a synthesis of structural and statistical models (Hasoon et al., 2021). LBP bitmaps are calculated using natural texture as the object. For each LBP bitmap, the histogram will be retrieved. Divide the data into two groups using this histogram as the sample pattern. The initial group will be employed as reference patterns, whereas the subsequent group will be utilized as testing patterns. By averaging numerous sample patterns, a reference pattern can be created. Once the reference patterns are generated, they are stored in the pattern database. In pattern classification, the role of the pattern classifier is to identify the minimum discrepancy between the testing pattern and the reference patterns stored in the database. The input pattern can be identified as belonging to that group if the minimum difference is reached.

4.4. Classification

This material is very useful for the researcher and opens up exciting and new opportunities in the field of research. A retention method is used to divide the dataset into training and test data in 80%of train set-20% test set respectively. KNN, VGG19 and CNN classifiers are selected for classification. KNN is also known as a lazy learner algorithm because it does not learn immediately from the training set; instead, it stores the dataset and performs an operation on it during classification. This algorithm considers the similarity between new instances or data and available instances and places the new instance in a class similar to the existing class, and it may be used for both regression and classification. To determine the variance between the training and test instances, the KNN method employs the Euclidean distance standard. The "K" is the number of nearest neighbours who aid in predicting the test pattern class (Hasoon et al., 2021). With 19 connection layers—16 convolution layers and 3 fully connected levels—the VGG-19 is a deep learning neural network. The fully connected layers categorize the leaf pictures based on the attributes that the convolution layers have extracted from the input photos. Convolutional neural networks, or CNNs for short, are a class of deep learning algorithms used for image processing and analysis. To extract pertinent information from a picture, it does a number of mathematical operations on it, including pooling and convolutions.

5. RESULT

A range of performance criteria can be used to evaluate the suggested COVID-19 detection and classification methods. To control the presentation of the suggested structure, a confusion matrix is constructed. Accuracy, precision, recall, and F1-score may be used as performance measures to assess the classification model's performance.

Figure 3. Comparisons among performances of implemented classifiers

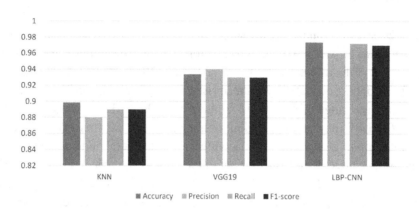

$$Accuracy = \frac{(TP+TN)}{(TP+FN+TN+FP)} \times 100 \qquad (2)$$

$$Precision = \frac{TP}{TP+FP} \qquad (3)$$

$$Recall = \frac{TP}{TP+FN} \qquad (4)$$

$$F1-score = \frac{2 \times (Precision + Recall)}{Precision + Recall} \qquad (5)$$

The TP correctly identified Xray images can be represented by a model predicting positive and also true in the above formula. TN model implies negative and it is truly predicted. FP's model projected a positive outcome, but it turned out to be false. FN predicted a negative outcome, which turned out to be incorrect. There performance measures are suggested in Figure 3, comparisons are made.

6. CONCLUSION

Machine Learning and Deep learning are the exciting technologies that are being used in a broad range of sectors, including healthcare. There are several gaps in the literature study, which gives a comprehensive evaluation of different image preprocessing and machine-deep approaches for controlling the COVID-19 outbreak. The proposed model employs a number of techniques, including image pre-processing (such as image resizing, noise removal with median filter), feature extraction (LBP), ml-dl techniques (KNN and VGG19) and hybridization of LBP with CNN for improved results using the confusion matrix and got the highest score as 97.37%(LBP-CNN).

7. FUTURE SCOPE

With the help of this research work we will be able to accurately detect disease and able analyze the effectiveness of treatment procedures if require for effective care.

REFERENCES

Auckland. (n.d.). https://www.cs.auckland.ac.nz/courss/compsci373s1c/PatricesLectures/Image%20 Filtering.pdf

Benmalek, E., Elmhamdi, J., & Jilbab, A. (2021). Comparing CT scan and chest X-ray imaging for COVID-19 diagnosis. *Biomedical Engineering Advances*, *1*, 100003. doi:10.1016/j.bea.2021.100003 PMID:34786568

Daniel, C., Cenggoro, T. W., & Pardamean, B. (2023). A systematic literature review of machine learning application in COVID-19 medical image classification. *Procedia Computer Science*, *216*, 749–756. doi:10.1016/j.procs.2022.12.192 PMID:36643182

Hasoon, J. N., Fadel, A. H., Hameed, R. S., Mostafa, S. A., Khalaf, B. A., Mohammed, M. A., & Nedoma, J. (2021). COVID-19 anomaly detection and classification method based on supervised machine learning of chest X-ray images. *Results in Physics*, *31*, 105045. doi:10.1016/j.rinp.2021.105045 PMID:34840938

Li, G., Togo, R., Ogawa, T., & Haseyama, M. (2023). Boosting automatic COVID-19 detection performance with self-supervised learning and batch knowledge ensembling. *Computers in Biology and Medicine*, *158*, 106877. doi:10.1016/j.compbiomed.2023.106877 PMID:37019015

Shah, F. M., Joy, S. K. S., Ahmed, F., Hossain, T., Humaira, M., Ami, A. S., Paul, S., Jim, M. A. R. K., & Ahmed, S. (2021). A Comprehensive Survey of COVID-19 Detection Using Medical Images. *SN Computer Science*, *2*(6), 434. doi:10.100742979-021-00823-1 PMID:34485924

Shahin, O. R., Alshammari, H. H., Taloba, A. I., & El-Aziz, R. M. A. (2022). Machine Learning Approach for Autonomous Detection and Classification of COVID-19 Virus. *Computers & Electrical Engineering: An International Journal*, *101*, 108055. doi:10.1016/j.compeleceng.2022.108055

Xu, X., Jiang, X., Ma, C., Du, P., Li, X., Lv, S., Yu, L., Ni, Q., Chen, Y., Su, J., Lang, G., Li, Y., Zhao, H., Liu, J., Xu, K., Ruan, L., Sheng, J., Qiu, Y., Wu, W., ... Li, L. (2020). A Deep Learning System to Screen Novel Coronavirus Disease 2019 Pneumonia. *Engineering (Beijing)*, *6*(10), 1122–1129. doi:10.1016/j. eng.2020.04.010 PMID:32837749

Zhao, W., Zhong, Z., Xie, X., Yu, Q., & Liu, J. (2020). Relation Between Chest CT Findings and Clinical Conditions of Coronavirus Disease (COVID-19) Pneumonia: A Multicenter Study. *AJR. American Journal of Roentgenology, 214*(5), 1072–1077. doi:10.2214/AJR.20.22976 PMID:32125873

Chapter 7
Unravelling the Enigma of Machine Learning Model Interpretability in Enhancing Disease Prediction

Rati Kailash Prasad Tripathi
Assam University, Silchar, India

Shrikant Tiwari
iD https://orcid.org/0000-0001-6947-2362
Galgotias University, Greater Noida, India

ABSTRACT

Machine learning (ML) models have made significant strides in disease prediction, providing new avenues for early detection and intervention. These models have demonstrated remarkable capabilities in analysing vast and complex datasets to identify patterns and trends that can aid in early diagnosis and treatment. However, opacity of these models often leaves healthcare practitioners and patients in the dark about the reasoning behind their predictions, raising concerns about trust, fairness, and practical adoption of AI-based disease prediction. This review delves into the critical topic of interpretability in ML models for disease prediction, its importance, techniques to achieve it, impact on clinical decision-making, challenges, and implications in healthcare. Urgent issues and moral dilemmas pertaining to model interpretability in healthcare, areas for further research to enhance interpretability of predictive models, and applications are also highlighted. Thus, the chapter provides insights into the applicability of AI-driven models to improve healthcare decision-making and patient outcomes.

1. INTRODUCTION

The integration of machine learning into the healthcare sector represents a monumental leap in the ongoing evolution of medical science and patient care. In recent years, artificial intelligence (AI), par-

DOI: 10.4018/978-1-6684-8531-6.ch007

Copyright © 2024, IGI Global. Copying or distributing in print or electronic forms without written permission of IGI Global is prohibited.

ticularly machine learning (ML), has emerged as a disruptive force with the potential to revolutionize the healthcare landscape (Davenport & Kalakota, 2019). ML, a subfield of artificial intelligence, endows computer systems with the ability to learn and adapt from data, making predictions and decisions without explicit programming. In the context of healthcare, this translates to an unprecedented capacity to analyse vast and complex medical datasets, extract meaningful insights, and make informed predictions (Bohr & Memarzadeh, 2020).

One of the primary areas where ML excels in healthcare is disease prediction and diagnosis (Marr, 2018). These models can comb through electronic health records, medical images, and genetic data to identify patterns that might elude even the most seasoned healthcare professionals (Miller & Brown, 2018). Early detection of diseases such as cancer, diabetes, neurodegenerative and cardiovascular conditions has the potential to significantly improve patient outcomes, leading to timely interventions and more effective treatments (Ekins, 2019). Additionally, ML contributes to the development of precision medicine (Konieczny & Roerman, 2019). By analysing a patient's genetic makeup and medical history, these models can recommend treatments tailored to an individual's unique characteristics, increasing the likelihood of successful outcomes and reducing adverse effects. Beyond clinical applications, machine learning assists in hospital operations, streamlining administrative processes, optimizing resource allocation, and improving patient management. It is also instrumental in epidemiology, tracking the spread of diseases, and monitoring public health trends (Johnson et al., 2021).

However, the integration of ML in healthcare is not without challenges. Ensuring data privacy, maintaining the security of sensitive medical records, addressing issues of bias and fairness in AI algorithms, and meeting regulatory compliance are critical concerns that demand attention (Murdoch, 2021; Nicholson Price & Glenn Cohen, 2019). This transformation, driven by ML, represents a paradigm shift in healthcare, enabling practitioners to move from a reactive, one-size-fits-all approach to a proactive, patient-centric, and data-driven model of care (Murdoch, 2021; Nicholson Price & Glenn Cohen, 2019). A deeper exploration of the myriad applications, challenges, and ethical considerations that underpin the integration of machine learning into healthcare, ultimately paves the way for a brighter and more data-informed future in medicine and patient well-being (Murdoch, 2021).

This chapter delves into the critical subject of interpretability in ML models for disease prediction, exploring the techniques, challenges, and implications that surround it. The pivotal role of model interpretability in healthcare and disease prediction has been examined herein, stressing the consequences of relying on black-box models in clinical decision-making. Furthermore, to unravel the enigma of ML model interpretability, a range of techniques and methodologies that have been developed to make these models more transparent and interpretable have been explored. Methods such as Local Interpretable Model-agnostic Explanations (LIME), Shapley values (SHAP), and feature importance analysis are discussed, shedding light on how these techniques can provide insights into the decision-making process of complex models.

Besides, the challenges and limitations associated with achieving model interpretability in the healthcare domain has also been confronted. Ethical considerations, particularly those related to fairness, bias, and transparency in predictive models has also been delved into. Furthermore, the tangible impact of interpretable models on clinical decision-making, from more accurate diagnoses to tailored treatment recommendations, ultimately improving patient care has also been considered. Understanding the importance of trust in healthcare, the role of model interpretability in building trust between patients and healthcare providers has been explored. Furthermore, areas of further research and development to enhance the interpretability of machine learning models in disease prediction has also been discussed.

This chapter also considers the potential for hybrid models that strike a balance between accuracy and interpretability, as well as the evolving regulatory landscape that aims to ensure the responsible and transparent use of AI in healthcare. It also presents a comparison of performance of interpretable models to traditional black-box models in disease prediction and their applications in various healthcare domains.

The present discussion serves as a gateway to understanding the transformative impact of machine learning in healthcare, offering a glimpse into the multifaceted facets of this technology and its wide-ranging implications.

2. SIGNIFICANCE OF INTERPRETABILITY

2.1. Importance of Interpretability in Healthcare and Disease Prediction

Interpretability in ML models refers to the ability to explain how a model arrives at its predictions or decisions. It is becoming increasingly important in healthcare applications of ML, where the accuracy and reliability of predictions are critical for patient outcomes (Hall & Gill, 2018; Brakto, 1997. In disease prediction, early intervention is often critical. Interpretable models can identify the key factors contributing to a prediction, allowing healthcare providers to understand the patient's risk factors and take proactive steps to prevent or manage diseases (Stiglic et al., 2020). Interpretability can help build trust in the model's predictions, providing a clearer understanding of the underlying data and factors contributing to the prediction. This can improve clinical decision-making by identifying the most relevant features or biomarkers for diagnosis, treatment, and disease progression (Stiglic et al., 2020; Linardatos et al., 2020). Furthermore, interpretability can aid in identifying potential biases or errors in the model, allowing for correction or refinement. In healthcare applications, this can be particularly important in ensuring that the model does not perpetuate existing biases or contribute to healthcare disparities. Healthcare organizations can use the insights gained from interpretability to refine their models over time, ensuring that they adapt to changing patient populations and medical practices. Moreover, interpretability is essential for regulatory compliance and ethical considerations (Murdoch, 2021). Regulatory agencies require that ML models used in healthcare are transparent and explainable to ensure patient safety and privacy. Ethically, it is crucial to ensure that the model's predictions are fair and unbiased and do not perpetuate discrimination. Finally, interpretability can facilitate the translation of ML models from research to clinical practice. Clinicians may be more likely to use a model in their practice if they can understand and interpret its predictions, leading to improved patient outcomes and more widespread adoption of ML in healthcare. Last but not the least, interpretability serves as an educational tool for both healthcare professionals and patients. It enables them to understand the rationale behind diagnoses and treatment recommendations, which can lead to more informed discussions and shared decision-making (Stiglic et al., 2020; Hall & Gill, 2018; Brakto, 1997).

Interpretability in healthcare and disease prediction is not merely a desirable feature; it is an ethical, practical and regulatory necessity. Interpretability in ML models is crucial for building trust, identifying biases, complying with regulations, ensuring ethical considerations, and translating research into clinical practice (Hall & Gill, 2018; Brakto, 1997). Figure 1 illustrates the significance of interpretability and healthcare and disease prediction (Stiglic et al., 2020; Hall & Gill, 2018; Brakto, 1997).

Notably, in contrast, relying on opaque models in medical decision-making can have significant and often detrimental outcomes.

Figure 1. Significance of interpretability in healthcare and disease prediction

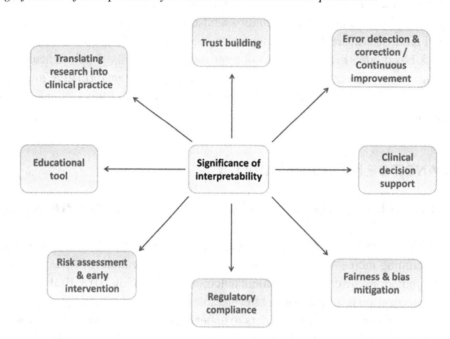

2.2. Opaque Models and Their Consequences in Medical Decision-Making

Opaque models in ML, also known as black-box models, are machine learning algorithms that are complex and difficult to interpret or understand. These models make predictions or decisions based on intricate, non-linear combinations of input data, but the reasoning behind their predictions is not readily apparent to humans. Unlike interpretable models, which provide clear and understandable explanations for their decisions, opaque models often lack transparency and can be challenging to dissect or explain (Adadi & Berrada, 2018). Some common examples of opaque models in ML include deep neural networks (DNNs), random forests, support vector machines (SVM), gradient boosting models (GBM), and deep reinforcement learning (Figure 2) (Luo et al., 2019; Park et al., 2021; Ahsan et al., 2022; Maeo et al., 2021; Zhou et al., 2021).

2.2.1. Deep Neural Networks (DNNs)

Deep learning models, particularly deep neural networks, are known for their complexity. They consist of multiple layers of interconnected neurons, and the relationship between input and output is highly non-linear. Understanding how a DNN arrives at a particular prediction can be challenging, especially in deep architectures with numerous parameters (Park et al., 2021; Ahsan et al., 2022).

2.2.2. Random Forests

Random Forest is an ensemble learning technique that combines the predictions of multiple decision trees. While it can be accurate in making predictions, understanding why it makes a particular prediction can be challenging due to the combined influence of multiple trees (Ahsan et al., 2022).

Figure 2. Opaque (black-box) models in machine learning

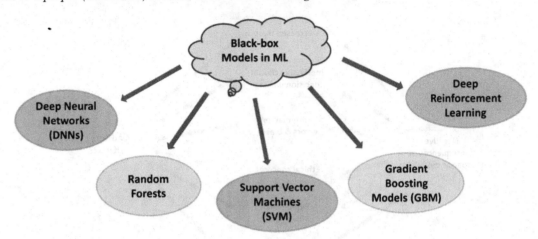

2.2.3. Support Vector Machines (SVM)

SVMs are effective for binary classification tasks, but the decision boundary in high-dimensional feature spaces can be complex. Explaining how an SVM arrives at a specific classification can be challenging (Ahsan et al., 2022).

2.2.4. Gradient Boosting Models (GBM)

Algorithms like Gradient Boosting Machines (GBM) and XGBoost are powerful, but the ensemble of decision trees they use makes it challenging to interpret the overall model's decision process (Maeo et al., 2021).

2.2.5. Deep Reinforcement Learning

In deep reinforcement learning, where agents learn to make decisions through trial and error in complex environments, it can be difficult to explain the agent's behaviour (Zhou et al., 2021).

The opacity of these models is due to their inherent complexity and the large number of parameters involved. While they are capable of achieving high accuracy in various tasks, their use in critical domains like healthcare can be problematic, as the users require transparency and interpretability in decision-making processes. As a result, there is a growing interest in developing techniques to make these opaque models more interpretable and explainable, especially in areas where the consequences of their decisions have significant real-world implications (Adadi & Berrada, 2018).

Summarily, relying on opaque models in medical decision-making can have profound negative consequences, including decreased trust, ineffective clinical decision-making, the potential for errors and biases, ethical concerns, regulatory challenges, missed opportunities for early intervention leading to adverse effects on patient care and outcomes (Adadi & Berrada, 2018) (Figure 3). Therefore, there is a growing push for transparency and interpretability in AI models used in healthcare to address these issues and ensure responsible, equitable, and effective medical decision-making.

Figure 3. Negative consequences of opaque models

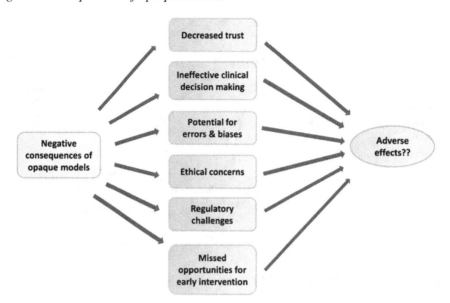

3. INTERPRETABILITY TECHNIQUES

3.1. Methods for Making Machine Learning Models Interpretable

There are various methods that provide valuable tools for improving model interpretability, with each having unique strengths. The three popular techniques that makes the ML models interpretable includes local interpretable model-agonistic explanations (LIME), Shapley additive explanations (SHAP), and feature importance analysis (Figure 4). These techniques, helps us to gain valuable insights into complex machine learning models, enabling them to make informed decisions and build trust in AI-driven systems (Du et al. 2019; Wu et al., 2023; ElShawi et al., 2021; Pudjihartono et al., 2022; Altmann et al., 2010; Jie et al., 2018).

3.1.1. Local Interpretable Model-Agnostic Explanations (LIME)

LIME is a model-agnostic method designed to explain individual model predictions. It operates by training a simple interpretable model, such as linear regression, on a local neighbourhood of data points around the prediction of interest. The interpretable model approximates the behaviour of the complex black-box model within the vicinity of the specific data point. LIME provides quantitative explanations in the form of feature weights and contributions. These values indicate how much each feature influenced the prediction for the specific instance, helping users understand which aspects of the input data were most critical in the decision. Thus, LIME bridges the gap between complex black-box models and human understanding by providing insights into individual predictions. By offering quantitative and feature-level explanations, LIME empowers individuals to trust and make use of AI-driven systems in contexts where interpretability is paramount (Wu et al., 2023; ElShawi et al., 2021).

Figure 4. Approaches of interpretability in ML

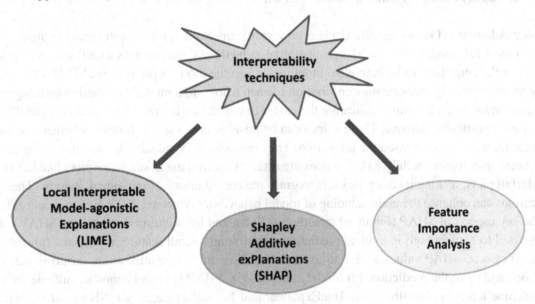

The key features (Figure 5) include (a) Local interpretability, viz. LIME focuses on explaining predictions for individual instances, offering local interpretability; (b) Model agnostic, viz. LIME can be applied to any ML model, making it highly versatile; (c) User-defined proximity, viz. it allows users to define the proximity or neighbourhood of data points to be considered when building the interpretable model.

LIME has been used in natural language processing, image classification, and healthcare, where it is important to comprehend the reasoning behind a certain prediction produced by the model (Wu et al., 2023; ElShawi et al., 2021).

Figure 5. Key aspects of LIME approach

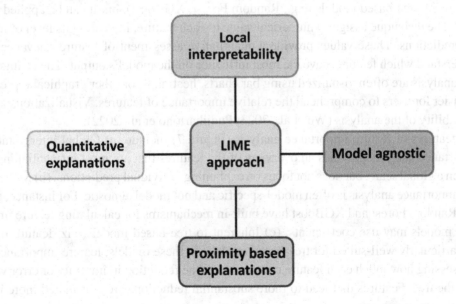

3.1.2. SHapley Additive exPlanations (SHAP)

SHapley Additive exPlanations (SHAP) is a powerful framework for interpreting and explaining the predictions of ML models. It is based on cooperative game theory and provides a unified framework for attributing the contributions of individual input features to the model's predictions. SHAP values offer a way to quantitatively measure the contribution of each feature to a model's prediction by assigning a numerical value to each feature, indicating the extent to which that feature influenced the model's prediction for a particular instance. These values can be positive or negative, showing whether a feature's presence increased or decreased the prediction. They are especially valuable for understanding feature importance in complex models. SHAP values are often visualized using summary plots like bar charts or waterfall plots, making it easier for users to grasp the contributions of individual features. These visualizations can enhance the understanding of model behaviour (Wu et al., 2023; ElShawi et al., 2021).

The key aspects of SHAP (Figure 6) include (a) Global and local interpretability, viz. SHAP values can be used to explain both individual predictions (local) and overall feature importance (global). (b) Consistency, viz. SHAP values adhere to axioms of consistent feature attribution, ensuring that contributions add up to the prediction. (c) Model agnostic, viz. SHAP is model agnostic, suitable for various machine learning algorithms. (d) TreeExplainer and KernelExplainer, viz. SHAP offers different explainer algorithms, such as TreeExplainer for tree-based models (e.g., decision trees, random forests) and KernelExplainer for more complex models. This versatility allows SHAP to be applied to a wide range of machine learning algorithms (Wu et al., 2023; ElShawi et al., 2021).

SHAP values are applied in risk assessment models, healthcare (explaining disease predictions and treatment recommendations), and natural language processing (Wu et al., 2023; ElShawi et al., 2021).

3.1.3. Feature Importance Analysis

Feature importance analysis aims to determine the contribution of input features in making model predictions. This analysis is particularly useful for gaining insights into the relative importance of different features in understanding the relationship between inputs and outputs. This method is particularly useful when using tree-based models (e.g., Random Forest, XGBoost), but it can be applied to various model types. The technique assigns a numerical value to each feature, indicating its level of importance in making predictions. These values provide a quantitative assessment of feature relevance, allowing users to understand which features have the most influence on the model's output. The results of feature importance analysis are often visualized using bar charts, heatmaps, or other graphical representations to make it easier for users to comprehend the relative importance of features. Visualization can enhance the interpretability of the analysis (Wu et al., 2023; Pudjihartono et al., 2022).

The key features of feature importance analysis (Figure 7) include (a) Global interpretability, viz. feature importance analysis provides an overview of the features that are most influential in a model's predictions on a global scale, but does not focus on explaining individual predictions. (b) Model specific, viz. feature importance analysis is often model-specific and not model agnostic. For instance, tree-based models like Random Forest and XGBoost have built-in mechanisms for calculating feature importance, while linear models may use coefficients. (c) Inherent to tree-based models, viz. feature importance analysis is particularly well-suited for tree-based models. In these models, feature importance is determined by assessing how much each feature contributes to the reduction in impurity or error when making splits in the tree. Features that lead to more substantial reductions are considered more important.

Figure 6. Key aspects of SHAP approach

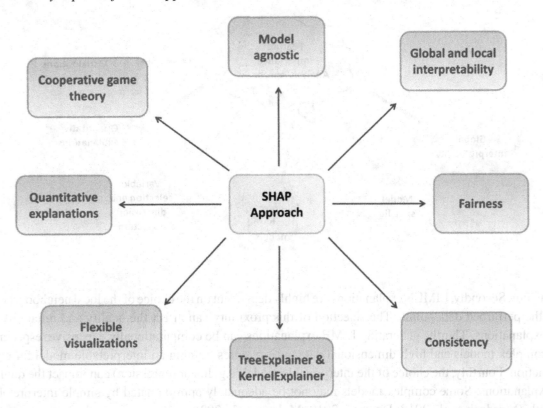

(d) Variable selection and dimension reduction, viz. The method can be used for variable selection and dimension reduction. By identifying the most important features, it is possible to focus on a subset of the most informative variables, which can lead to more efficient and interpretable models (Wu et al., 2023; Pudjihartono et al., 2022).

Feature importance analysis is widely used in various fields, primarily in healthcare for disease risk assessment, marketing for customer segmentation, and natural language processing for sentiment analysis. In these domains, understanding the factors or features that are most influential can guide decision-making processes, optimize models and improve transparency in data-driven processes (Wu et al., 2023; Pudjihartono et al., 2022; Altmann et al., 2010; Jie et al., 2018).

3.2. Limitations of Interpretability Methods

While techniques like LIME, SHAP, and feature importance analysis are valuable for improving model interpretability, they come with trade-offs and limitations that should be considered (Murdoch et al., 2018; Du et al., 2019; Molnar et al., 2022) (Figure 8).

3.2.1. LIME

Firstly, LIME provides local interpretability, explaining individual predictions, but it may not always capture the global behaviour of the model. It is essential to use other methods for assessing overall model

Figure 7. Key aspects of feature importance analysis approach

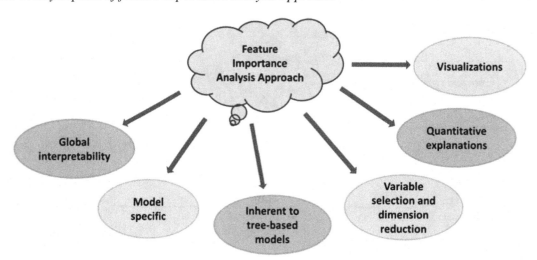

behaviour. Secondly, LIME's explanations are highly dependent on the choice of the local neighbourhood and the perturbed data points. The selection of this proximity can affect the quality and reliability of the explanations. Thirdly, generating LIME explanations can be computationally expensive, especially for complex models and high-dimensional data, as it requires training an interpretable model for each prediction. Fourthly, the choice of the interpretable model (e.g. linear regression) can impact the quality of explanations. Some complex models may not be adequately approximated by simple interpretable models (Murdoch et al., 2018; Du et al., 2019; Molnar et al., 2022).

Figure 8. Limitations of LIME, SHAP and feature importance analysis

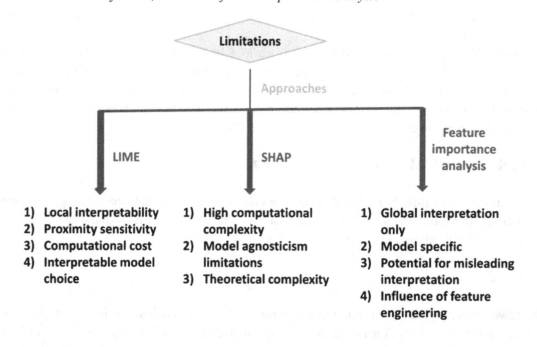

3.2.2. SHAP

Firstly, calculating SHAP values for complex models can be computationally intensive, particularly when dealing with large datasets and high-dimensional feature spaces. This can slow down the explanation process. Secondly, while SHAP is generally model-agnostic, some models may require specialized implementations or approximations of SHAP values, which could introduce inaccuracies. Thirdly, understanding the theoretical underpinnings of SHAP values can be challenging, especially for non-experts. This can limit its practical application and interpretation (Murdoch et al., 2018; Du et al., 2019; Molnar et al., 2022).

3.2.3. Feature Importance Analysis

Firstly, feature importance analysis provides global interpretability, which means it offers insights into feature importance across all predictions. It does not explain the reasoning behind specific individual predictions. Secondly, the technique is often model-specific. While it is well-suited for tree-based models, the methodology may not directly apply to other model types, requiring different techniques for model-specific feature importance analysis. Thirdly, feature importance does not necessarily imply causation. A highly important feature may not be causally related to the target variable, leading to potentially misleading interpretations. Fourthly, the results of feature importance can be influenced by the feature engineering process. The choice of feature representation can impact the perceived importance of specific variables (Murdoch et al., 2018; Du et al., 2019; Molnar et al., 2022).

Thus, summarily, although the above-mentioned techniques are valuable tools for improving interpretability of model, it is crucial to choose the most suitable technique based on the specific context and requirements of particular machine learning project, taking into account factors like computational resources, the desired level of interpretability, and the nature of the model being explained. Additionally, it will be appropriate to use a combination of these techniques to gain a more comprehensive understanding of model behaviour (Murdoch et al., 2018; Du et al., 2019; Molnar et al., 2022).

4. CHALLENGES AND ETHICAL CONSIDERATIONS

In healthcare, the benefits of model interpretability, such as improved patient care, early disease detection, and better decision-making, are substantial. Achieving model interpretability in healthcare settings is crucial for ensuring the safe and responsible deployment of machine learning models. However, this endeavour comes with several challenges and limitations. Addressing these challenges and limitations is vital to ensure that AI and machine learning contribute positively to healthcare outcomes while adhering to the highest standards of ethics, security, and transparency. Table 1 enlists various issues, the challenges associated with them and measures that can be taken to address them (Rudin et al., 2022; Moraffah et al., 2020; Watson, 2022; Kelly et al., 2019; Borrellas & Unceta, 2021).

Moreover, ethical concerns, including fairness, bias, and transparency, are critical aspects of predictive models, especially when applied in sensitive domains like healthcare. Addressing these concerns is essential for building trust in predictive models, avoiding discrimination, and ensuring equitable outcomes in decision-making processes. Table 2 illustrates the various aspects, the challenges associated

Table 1. Challenges associated with achieving model interpretability and various measures to avert them

Issue	Challenge	Mitigation
Complexity of medical data	Healthcare data is often complex, high-dimensional, and heterogeneous, making it challenging to understand the relationships between features and predictions.	Feature selection, dimensionality reduction, and data pre-processing techniques can help simplify the data while retaining important information.
Black-box models	Some of the most accurate models, such as deep learning, are inherently black-box, making it difficult to interpret their decision processes.	Techniques like LIME, SHAP, and surrogate models can be used to provide local and global interpretability for complex models in healthcare.
Data privacy and security	Protecting patient data is paramount in healthcare, and sharing data for interpretability purposes may raise privacy concerns.	Privacy-preserving techniques, such as federated learning and secure multi-party computation, can enable data sharing while preserving patient confidentiality.
Data imbalance	Healthcare datasets often exhibit class imbalance, where some diseases or conditions are rare. Imbalanced data can lead to biased models and pose challenges for interpretation.	Careful handling of class imbalance through techniques like oversampling, under-sampling, or cost-sensitive learning can help address this issue.
Clinical validation and adoption	Clinicians and healthcare providers may be skeptical of AI models, and their adoption can be slow due to a lack of trust and clinical validation.	Collaborating closely with healthcare professionals, conducting rigorous clinical studies, and transparently sharing results can help build trust and validate model interpretability.
Ethical and bias concerns	Models may inadvertently perpetuate biases present in healthcare data, leading to unfair or discriminatory outcomes.	Addressing bias through fairness-aware machine learning and continuous monitoring of model behaviour can help mitigate ethical concerns.
Regulatory compliance	Healthcare is subject to stringent regulations (e.g., HIPAA), and meeting regulatory requirements for model interpretability can be complex.	Careful compliance with regulatory standards, including transparency in data use and model decision-making, is essential.
Patient understanding	Ensuring that patients understand the explanations provided by models is crucial for informed decision-making.	Developing user-friendly and patient-oriented explanations and tools to help individuals comprehend and trust AI-driven healthcare decisions.
Interoperability with clinical workflow	Integrating AI models into existing clinical workflows and Electronic Health Record (EHR) systems can be complex, and model explanations should align with clinical processes.	Developing user interfaces and tools that seamlessly integrate with EHR systems and provide interpretable model outputs for clinicians.
Interdisciplinary collaboration	Effective communication and collaboration between data scientists, clinicians, and domain experts are essential but can be challenging due to differences in terminology and priorities.	Encouraging multidisciplinary teams and facilitating communication through regular meetings and shared understanding can bridge this gap.

with them and measures to obviate them (Rudin et al., 2022; Moraffah et al., 2020; Watson, 2022; Kelly et al., 2019; Borrellas & Unceta, 2021; Gerke et al., 2020).

Table 2. Challenges associated with ethical concerns and measures to forefend them

Ethical Concerns	Challenges	Mitigation
Fairness	Ensuring that predictive models provide equitable outcomes across different demographic groups is a significant challenge. Biased or unfair predictions can lead to disparities and discrimination.	Defining fairness criteria: Clearly defining fairness criteria, such as demographic parity, equal opportunity, or predictive parity, depending on the specific context.Data pre-processing: Identifying and mitigating biases in training data, such as through re-sampling, re-weighting, or generating synthetic data. Algorithmic fairness: Implementing fairness-aware machine learning techniques that aim to reduce bias and discrimination in model predictions.Monitoring and audits: Continuously monitoring models for fairness and conduct audits to identify and rectify discriminatory behaviour.
Bias	Predictive models can inherit biases from historical data, which can lead to biased outcomes in the present. For example, if past medical data is biased toward a particular demographic, the model may make unfair healthcare recommendations.	Data collection and curation: Collecting diverse and representative data, and carefully curate training datasets to minimize historical bias.Fair feature engineering: Selecting features that are relevant to the problem without introducing bias. Avoiding features that may be proxies for sensitive attributes (e.g., ZIP codes indicating income).Bias audits: Regularly auditing datasets and models for bias, and addressing bias at the data level and model level.Regular retraining: Periodically updating models to adapt to changing demographics and social norms.
Transparency	Many predictive models, particularly complex ones like deep learning, are often considered "black boxes." Understanding the rationale behind model predictions can be difficult.	Explainable AI (XAI): Using explainable AI techniques, such as LIME and SHAP, to provide human-interpretable explanations for model predictions.Model documentation: Maintaining comprehensive documentation of models, including their architecture, training data, and performance metrics.Transparency standards: Adhering to industry-specific transparency standards and guidelines, like the General Data Protection Regulation (GDPR) or the Equal Credit Opportunity Act (ECOA).
Algorithmic auditing	Models and algorithms are subject to changes, and their performance may degrade over time. Auditing models for ethical concerns and ensuring ongoing fairness and transparency is challenging.	Implementing regular audits: Setting up a framework for periodic model audits to ensure ongoing adherence to ethical standards. Ethical review boards: Establishing boards or committees responsible for ethical oversight of AI and predictive models in sensitive domains.Continuous learning: Encouraging a culture of continuous learning and improvement, where lessons from audits and ethical issues inform future model development and deployment.
Human oversight	Over-reliance on automated decision-making can diminish the role of human experts, which may be essential in cases requiring nuanced judgment.	Human-in-the-loop systems: Designing models that incorporate human oversight, allowing experts to intervene when necessary. Transparency interfaces: Developing user interfaces that facilitate interaction with models and provide interpretable explanations to human users.
Legal and regulatory compliance	Staying compliant with evolving legal and regulatory requirements, such as GDPR, HIPAA, or the Fair Credit Reporting Act (FCRA), is a complex and ever-changing task.	Legal expertise: Employing legal experts to ensure ongoing compliance with relevant laws and regulations.Robust data governance: Implementing robust data governance and data management practices to protect sensitive data and maintain compliance.

5. CLINICAL ADOPTION AND DECISION-MAKING

Interpretable machine learning models can positively impact clinical decision-making by enhancing diagnosis, enabling personalized treatment selection, improving patient care, advancing medical research, and ensuring regulatory compliance and accountability. Their transparency and reliability make them valuable tools in the healthcare sector, fostering trust among healthcare professionals and patients while driving better outcomes and cost-efficiency (Belenguer, 2022; Weissler et al., 2021; Javaid et al., 2022). The various benefits (Belenguer, 2022; Weissler et al., 2021; Javaid et al., 2022) have been discussed below:

5.1. Improved Diagnosis

(a) Early detection: Interpretable models can identify subtle patterns and risk factors in medical data, leading to early detection of diseases. This can be particularly critical for conditions like cancer, where early diagnosis significantly improves patient outcomes.

(b) Transparent decision-making: Clinicians can understand why a model made a specific diagnosis. This transparency enhances their confidence in the model's recommendation and allows them to validate the diagnosis.

(c) Reduced misdiagnosis: Interpretability can help reduce misdiagnoses and ensure that the correct diagnosis is made. This is especially important for complex conditions with overlapping symptoms.

(d) Assisting rare disease diagnosis: Interpretable models can assist in diagnosing rare diseases by highlighting uncommon symptoms or genetic markers that might be overlooked by human experts.

5.2. Treatment Selection

(a) Personalized treatment plans: Interpretable models can provide insights into the most effective treatments for individual patients based on their specific clinical and genetic profiles. This enables personalized medicine.

(b) Identifying adverse effects: Models can predict potential adverse effects or interactions of treatments, helping healthcare providers make informed decisions and reduce the risk of complications.

(c) Optimizing medication dosages: Models can assist in optimizing medication dosages to ensure patients receive the most effective treatment while minimizing side effects.

(d) Clinical guidelines compliance: Interpretable models can help healthcare providers adhere to clinical guidelines and best practices, ensuring evidence-based care for patients.

5.3. Patient Care

(a) Enhanced care coordination: Interpretability aids in care coordination among multidisciplinary teams. When healthcare professionals can understand and trust AI-driven recommendations, they can collaborate more effectively.

(b) Patient engagement: Transparent AI models empower patients to actively engage in their healthcare decisions. They can better comprehend and discuss treatment options, leading to shared decision-making.

(c) Reduced errors: By providing clear explanations for its recommendations, interpretable models help reduce medical errors, such as incorrect prescriptions, misinterpretation of test results, or improper surgical decisions.

(d) Efficient resource allocation: Interpretable models can help hospitals and healthcare systems allocate resources more efficiently, such as predicting patient admission rates and optimizing bed allocation.

5.4. Research and Knowledge Discovery

(a) Hypothesis generation: Interpretable models can assist researchers in generating hypotheses and identifying previously unrecognized relationships in medical data. This can lead to new discoveries and advancements in medical science.

(b) Validation of findings: AI models can validate or support research findings, providing additional evidence for the effectiveness of certain treatments or diagnostic approaches.

5.5. Regulatory Compliance and Accountability

(a) Regulatory compliance: Interpretable models are better equipped to meet regulatory requirements, such as explaining why a specific treatment or diagnosis was recommended, aligning with laws like HIPAA or GDPR.

(b) Accountability: In cases of adverse outcomes or malpractice claims, interpretable models provide a transparent record of the decision-making process, aiding in accountability and legal defense.

6. INTERPRETABILITY AND PATIENT TRUST

Model interpretability is a bridge that connects healthcare providers and patients, enhancing communication, transparency, and engagement. It empowers patients to make informed decisions, addresses fairness and bias concerns, promotes shared decision-making, and ensures ethical data handling. Ultimately, the role of model interpretability in healthcare is pivotal for building and maintaining trust between patients and healthcare providers, resulting in better patient outcomes and experiences. Trust between patients and healthcare practitioners is greatly aided by model interpretability in a number of ways as discussed below (Diprose et al., 2020; Hakkoum et al., 2022; Carvalho et al., 2019; Siala & Wang, 2022; Pfob et al., 2022):

6.1. Role of Model Interpretability in Trust Building Between Patients and Healthcare Providers

6.1.1. Transparency in Decision-Making

(a) Explainable predictions: Interpretable models provide clear and understandable explanations for their predictions and recommendations. When healthcare providers can easily grasp why a specific diagnosis or treatment plan is being suggested, they can communicate this information effectively to patients.

(b) Informed consent: Patients are more likely to trust healthcare decisions when they are informed about the rationale behind those decisions. Interpretable models contribute to the transparency needed for obtaining informed consent for treatments and procedures.

6.1.2. Shared Decision-Making

(a) Patient engagement: Interpretability empowers patients to actively participate in their healthcare decisions. When patients understand the reasons behind a recommended treatment, they are more likely to engage in shared decision-making with their healthcare providers.

(b) Respect for patient preferences: Patients have unique preferences, values, and priorities. Interpretable models help healthcare providers tailor treatment options to align with these preferences, promoting a patient-centered approach.

6.1.3. Reducing Information Asymmetry

(a) Balanced information: Interpretability addresses the information asymmetry that can exist between healthcare providers and patients. When patients can access comprehensible explanations, they are better equipped to engage in a meaningful dialogue with their providers.

(b) Empowering patients: Patients who understand the factors contributing to their diagnosis and treatment options are empowered to ask questions, seek clarifications, and actively participate in their care. This empowerment fosters trust in the provider-patient relationship.

6.1.4. Fostering Accountability and Confidence

(a) Clinical confidence: Healthcare providers are more confident in using AI-assisted tools when they can explain and justify their recommendations. This confidence is conveyed to patients, who, in turn, have greater trust in the recommendations.

(b) Accountability: Interpretable models help establish accountability. In the event of unexpected outcomes or adverse events, both healthcare providers and patients can review the decision process and understand how a particular recommendation was made, enhancing transparency and trust.

6.1.5. Mitigating Bias and Fairness Concerns

(a) Equitable care: Interpretable models can assist in identifying and mitigating biases in decision-making, ensuring that care is delivered equitably. Patients are more likely to trust a system that is designed to be fair and unbiased.

(b) Ethical use of data: Patients are concerned about the ethical use of their health data. Interpretability measures can assure patients that their data is being handled responsibly and with ethical considerations, strengthening their trust in the healthcare system.

6.1.6. Data Privacy and Security

(a) Patient confidence: Patients are concerned about data privacy and security. Interpretable models can assure patients that their data is being used responsibly and securely, fostering trust in the healthcare system's ability to protect their sensitive information.

6.2. Patient Understanding and Acceptance of AI-Driven Disease Predictions

Patient understanding and acceptance of AI-driven disease predictions depend on effective communication, transparency, trust, and a patient-centered approach. Healthcare providers have a pivotal role in facilitating these aspects to ensure that AI-driven predictions are embraced as valuable tools that enhance patient care and improve healthcare outcomes (Diprose et al., 2020; Hakkoum et al., 2022; Carvalho et al., 2019; Siala & Wang, 2022; Pfob et al., 2022).

6.2.1. Critical Factors Related to Patient Understanding

6.2.1.1. Explanation and Transparency

Patients must receive clear and transparent explanations of how AI-driven predictions are generated. These explanations should be in plain language and free of technical jargon.

6.2.1.2. Visual Aids

Visual aids, such as graphs and charts, can help patients comprehend the data and predictions. Visual representations make complex information more accessible.

6.2.1.3. Educational Materials

Providing patients with educational materials about AI and its role in healthcare can enhance understanding. These materials should be designed for various literacy levels.

6.2.1.4. Engaging Patients in Decision-Making

Healthcare providers can engage patients in shared decision-making. By involving patients in the process, providers can address their concerns and ensure they understand the implications of AI predictions.

6.2.1.5. Question and Answer Sessions

Offering question-and-answer sessions where patients can ask about AI predictions and their potential impact on their care helps clarify any doubts and fosters understanding.

6.2.2. Critical Factors Related to Patient Acceptance

6.2.2.1. Demonstrated Value

Patients are more likely to accept AI-driven predictions when they see demonstrated value. This could include better diagnosis accuracy, personalized treatment recommendations, or improved outcomes.

6.2.2.2. Transparency and Trust

Transparency in how AI predictions are generated, and trust in the technology and healthcare provider, are essential for patient acceptance. Patients must have confidence in the system's reliability.

6.2.2.3. Patient-Centered Care

AI-driven predictions should complement patient-centered care. When patients perceive that the predictions are tailored to their unique needs and preferences, they are more likely to accept them.

6.2.2.4. Involvement in Decision-Making

Patients who feel actively involved in decisions based on AI predictions are more likely to accept them. AI should be a tool that supports, rather than replaces, the patient-provider relationship.

6.2.2.5. Ethical Considerations

Patients are concerned about the ethical use of their data. They are more likely to accept AI-driven predictions when they are assured that data privacy and security are prioritized.

6.2.2.6. Clear Communication

Healthcare providers play a crucial role in patient acceptance. They should communicate clearly, empathetically, and in partnership with patients. Patients need to feel heard and understood.

6.2.2.7. Educational Initiatives

Educational initiatives that promote AI literacy and health literacy among patients can improve acceptance. When patients understand the capabilities and limitations of AI, they are more likely to accept its role in their care.

6.2.2.8. Feedback Loop

A feedback loop for patients to provide input and feedback on AI predictions can help improve acceptance. This process allows patients to actively contribute to the refinement of AI models.

6.2.2.9. Cultural Competence

Cultural competence is vital. Healthcare providers should understand and respect the cultural beliefs and values of their patients, as these factors can influence acceptance.

6.2.2.10. Demonstrated Safety

Patients need assurance of the safety of AI-driven predictions. Highlighting instances where AI has improved safety, reduced errors, and enhanced outcomes can boost acceptance.

7. FUTURE DIRECTIONS AND RESEARCH GAPS

The field of interpretability in machine learning for disease prediction is evolving, and several future directions and research gaps are worth exploring (Kline et al., 2022; Hutchinson et al., 2022; L'heureux et al., 2017; Dahlin, 2021; Manley et al., 2022).

(a)   Standardization and benchmarking

Developing standardized evaluation metrics and benchmark datasets specific to healthcare applications can help compare the performance and interpretability of different models effectively.

(b)   Explainability in deep learning

Extending interpretability techniques to deep learning models is an ongoing challenge. Research should focus on making complex neural networks more transparent and comprehensible.

(c)   Personalization of interpretations

Exploring methods to personalize model explanations based on individual patient preferences and health literacy levels is essential for improving the patient experience.

(d)   Model-data mismatch

Investigation of various ways to handle situations where the model's interpretation does not align with the expectations of healthcare providers and patients due to differences in the data distribution is crucial.

(e)   Ethical and legal aspects

Research should continue to explore the ethical and legal implications of model interpretability, particularly in the context of data privacy, informed consent, and regulatory compliance.

(f)   Multi-modal data integration

Enhancing the interpretability of models that integrate multiple types of data (e.g., medical images, genomic data, clinical notes) is vital for comprehensive disease prediction.

(g)   Bias mitigation and fairness:

Further research should address ways to detect and mitigate bias in interpretable models while maintaining fairness in healthcare predictions.

(h)   Model agnosticism

Investigating methods for achieving model-agnostic interpretability across a wide range of machine learning algorithms and architectures is necessary for practical healthcare applications.

(i)   Explainable reinforcement learning

Exploring ways to make reinforcement learning models more interpretable, as these are relevant in optimizing treatment plans and interventions.

(j)   Patient-centered interfaces

Designing patient-centered interfaces that present interpretable model outputs in an intuitive and user-friendly manner, ensuring that patients can easily comprehend and engage with the information.

(k)   Interdisciplinary collaboration

Promoting interdisciplinary collaboration between machine learning researchers, healthcare providers, ethicists, and policymakers to address the complex challenges of model interpretability in healthcare.

Thus, addressing the above-mentioned research gaps and exploring these future directions will contribute to the advancement of interpretable machine learning models in disease prediction, fostering trust and transparency in healthcare and improving patient outcomes. In this respect, development of hybrid models holds a great promise.

8. POTENTIAL OF HYBRID MODELS TOWARDS ENHANCEMENT OF INTERPRETABILITY

Research is needed to develop hybrid models that combine the strengths of interpretable models (e.g., decision trees, linear models) with complex, high-performing models (e.g., deep learning). Finding the right balance between accuracy and interpretability is crucial. Figure 9 depicts the potential of hybrid models towards interpretability enhancement (Alcala-Fdez, 2006; Linardatos et al., 2021; Hotvedt et al., 2021; Wang, 2019; Yoon et al., 2022).

Complex models, such as deep learning or ensemble methods, are known for their high predictive accuracy. Hybrid models can leverage the accuracy of these models to deliver state-of-the-art disease predictions. Hybrid models designed with a human-centric approach, helps in prioritizing the needs of healthcare providers and patients. They take into account the importance of delivering insights in a manner that aligns with human cognition and decision-making processes. Interpretable models, like decision trees or linear models, are inherently transparent and provide clear decision pathways. This transparency is essential for healthcare professionals and patients to trust and understand the model's recommendations. Hybrid models allow for varying degrees of interpretability. Healthcare providers can choose the level of detail and complexity they need in the explanations, depending on the context and the patient's understanding. Hybrid models can be seamlessly integrated into clinical decision support systems, providing real-time guidance to healthcare professionals. They offer decision aids that enhance clinical workflows while explaining the rationale behind each recommendation. Interpretable components in hybrid models can help in detecting and mitigating bias and discrimination in the model's predictions, aligning with fairness-aware machine learning techniques. Healthcare providers may customize or fine-tune the interpretable components to better align with their clinical practice and preferences, while the more complex part of the model retains its high accuracy (Alcala-Fdez, 2006; Linardatos et al., 2021; Hotvedt et al., 2021; Wang, 2019; Yoon et al., 2022).

Figure 9. Potentials of hybrid models towards interpretability enhancement

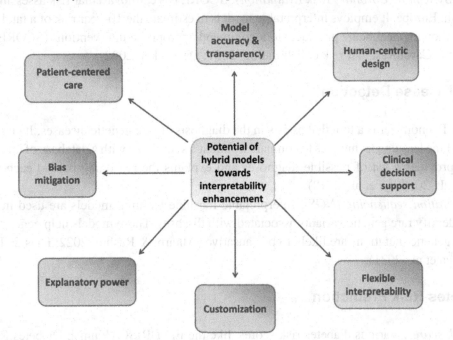

9. APPLICATIONS OF INTERPRETABLE ML MODELS IN DISEASE PREDICTION

Interpretable machine learning models have found successful applications in various disease prediction tasks, such as cancer diagnosis, cardiovascular risk assessment, rare disease prediction, and others.

9.1. Cancer Diagnosis

PathAI: PathAI is a company that uses interpretable machine learning models to assist pathologists in diagnosing cancer from histopathology slides (https://www.pathai.com/). Their models provide clear visualizations of the regions within a slide that are most indicative of cancer, helping pathologists make more accurate and informed decisions (Bera et al., 2019; Alpsoy et al., 2021).

Breast cancer risk assessment: Interpretable models have been applied to breast cancer risk assessment. For instance, the Gail model uses a combination of risk factors and provides a straightforward risk estimate for developing breast cancer, aiding in personalized screening and prevention strategies (Bener et al., 2019; Rockhill et al., 2001).

9.2. Cardiovascular Risk Assessment

Framingham heart study: The Framingham Heart Study, a long-term cardiovascular study, has incorporated interpretable models to predict the risk of cardiovascular disease. Their models provide a risk score based on a set of risk factors like age, gender, blood pressure, cholesterol levels, and smoking status (Bitton & Gaziano, 2010; Zhuang et al., 2022).

SCORE (Systematic Coronary Risk Evaluation): SCORE is a cardiovascular risk assessment system widely used in Europe. It employs interpretable models to estimate the 10-year risk of a fatal cardiovascular event, allowing healthcare providers to recommend appropriate interventions (SCORE2 working group and ESC Cardiovascular risk collaboration, 2021; De Backer, 2022).

9.3. Rare Disease Detection

Phenomizer: Phenomizer is a tool that assists in the diagnosis of rare genetic diseases. It employs interpretable machine learning techniques to compare a patient's symptoms with a database of known genetic diseases. It provides a list of possible diagnoses and explains the reasoning behind each suggestion (Fujiwara et al., 2018; Jia et al., 2018).

Next-generation sequencing (NGS): Interpretable machine learning models are used in NGS data analysis to identify rare genetic variants associated with diseases. These models help geneticists understand which genetic mutations are likely to be causative (Alharbi & Rashid, 2022; Dias & Torkamani, 2019; La Vega et al., 2021).

9.4. Diabetes Risk Prediction

Diabetes risk scores: Various diabetes risk scores, like the FINDRISC (Finnish Diabetes Risk Score) and the ADA Risk Test, use interpretable models to estimate an individual's risk of developing type 2 diabetes. These models consider factors such as age, family history, physical activity, and BMI (Bernabe-Ortiz et al., 2018; Abdallah et al., 2020).

9.5. Stroke Risk Assessment

CHA2DS2-VASc Score: This score, used for assessing the risk of stroke in patients with atrial fibrillation, employs interpretable models to assign scores based on factors like age, gender, and comorbidities. The score helps guide anticoagulant therapy decisions (Olesen et al., 2012; Gazova et al., 2019).

9.6. Alzheimer's Disease Prediction

ADNI (Alzheimer's Disease Neuroimaging Initiative): ADNI uses interpretable machine learning models to analyze neuroimaging data and clinical information to predict the progression of Alzheimer's disease. These models provide insights into the key brain regions and biomarkers associated with disease progression (Aberathne et al., 2023; Bogdanovic et al., 2022; Diogo et al., 2022).

These examples demonstrate the practical applications of interpretable machine learning models in disease prediction across various medical specialties. They aid in diagnosis, risk assessment, and treatment decisions while providing transparent and understandable explanations, which are essential for building trust among healthcare providers and patients.

10. COMPARISON OF PERFORMANCE OF INTERPRETABLE MODELS TO TRADITIONAL BLACK-BOX MODELS IN DISEASE PREDICTION

The performance of interpretable models compared to traditional black-box models in disease prediction depends on various factors, including the specific disease, the dataset, the complexity of the disease and the associated data, and the availability of labelled examples. Both types of models have their strengths and limitations, and the decision should be made based on the specific context and goals of the healthcare application. Table 3 presents the advantages and limitations of these two types of models.

The following points should be taken into consideration while working with these models to get accurate and reliable results.

(a) *Data availability:* The amount of labelled data available for a specific disease prediction task can influence the choice of model. If data is scarce, interpretable models may be more practical.

(b) *Clinical interpretability:* In cases where medical professionals need to understand and justify the model's recommendations, interpretable models are often preferred.

(c) *Complexity of disease:* The complexity of the disease and the data can impact model selection. For complex diseases or intricate genetic interactions, black-box models may offer better predictive accuracy.

Table 3. Comparison of interpretable models to traditional black-box models in disease prediction

Model Type	Interpretable Models	Traditional Black-Box Models
Advantages	Transparency: Interpretable models, such as decision trees, linear regression, and logistic regression, provide clear decision rules and feature importance rankings. This transparency makes it easier to understand why a particular prediction was made.Human-Centric: Interpretable models are designed to align with human intuition and decision-making processes. Healthcare professionals and patients can relate to the model's explanations, which can enhance trust and collaboration.Lower Data Requirements: Interpretable models often require fewer labelled examples for training and can perform well even with limited data, making them suitable for situations with data scarcity.Fewer Parameters: These models typically have fewer parameters to tune, reducing the risk of overfitting and simplifying model selection.	High Predictive Accuracy: Black-box models, like deep neural networks, gradient boosting, and random forests, can capture intricate patterns and relationships in complex data. This often results in superior predictive accuracy. Automated Feature Learning: These models can automatically learn relevant features from the data, reducing the need for extensive feature engineering.Scalability: Black-box models can handle large, high-dimensional datasets effectively, making them suitable for complex healthcare applications.
Limitations	Lower Complexity: Interpretable models may struggle to capture complex, non-linear relationships in the data, limiting their predictive accuracy.Feature Engineering: The performance of interpretable models can be highly dependent on feature engineering, which may require domain expertise to select and prepare relevant features.	Lack of Transparency: Black-box models are challenging to interpret. They provide little insight into the decision-making process, which can hinder their adoption in healthcare where transparency is crucial.Data Requirements: They typically require larger volumes of labelled data for training and may not perform well with limited samples.Overfitting: Black-box models can be prone to overfitting if not appropriately regularized, potentially leading to unreliable predictions.

(d) *Ethical and regulatory considerations:* In highly regulated environments, or when ethical and legal considerations are paramount, interpretable models may be preferred for transparency and accountability.

(e) *Hybrid approaches:* Hybrid models that combine interpretable and black-box components can provide a balance between predictive accuracy and transparency.

11. CONCLUSION

The implications of incorporating interpretable machine learning models in disease prediction are far-reaching. By striking a balance between accuracy and transparency, these models have the potential to enhance healthcare outcomes, while respecting ethical and regulatory boundaries. As research in this field continues and standards are further developed, interpretable models can play a pivotal role in shaping the future of responsible and effective healthcare AI.

In conclusion, the use of interpretable machine learning models in disease prediction offers a promising pathway to enhance transparency, understanding, and trust in healthcare AI applications. These models have the potential to revolutionize the way diseases are diagnosed, risk is assessed, and treatment decisions are made. However, their adoption is not without challenges and implications. Further research is needed to address gaps, enhance the interpretability of models, and ensure their practical utility and real-world impact in healthcare.

REFERENCES

Abdallah, M., Sharbaji, S., Sharbaji, M., Daher, Z., Faour, T., Mansour, Z., & Hneino, M. (2020). Diagnostic accuracy of the Finnish Diabetes Risk Score for the prediction of undiagnosed type 2 diabetes, prediabetes, and metabolic syndrome in the Lebanese University. *Diabetology & Metabolic Syndrome*, *12*(1), 84. doi:10.118613098-020-00590-8 PMID:33014142

Aberathne, I., Kulasiri, D., & Samarasinghe, S. (2023). Detection of Alzheimer's disease onset using MRI and PET neuroimaging: Longitudinal data analysis and machine learning. *Neural Regeneration Research*, *18*(10), 2134–2140. doi:10.4103/1673-5374.367840 PMID:37056120

Adadi, A., & Berrada, M. (2018). Peeking inside the black-box: A survey on explainable artificial intelligence (XAI). *IEEE Access : Practical Innovations, Open Solutions*, *6*, 52138–52160. doi:10.1109/ACCESS.2018.2870052

Ahmad, A. M., Eckert, C., Teredesai, A., & McKelvey, G. (2018). Interpretable Machine Learning in Healthcare. In *IEEE Intelligent Informatics Bulletin* (pp. 1–7). IEEE.

Ahsan, M. M., Luna, S. A., & Siddique, Z. (2022). Machine-learning-based disease diagnosis: A comprehensive review. *Healthcare (Basel)*, *10*(3), 541. doi:10.3390/healthcare10030541 PMID:35327018

Alcala-Fdez, J. (2006). Hybrid learning models to get the interpretability – accuracy trade-off in fuzzy modeling. *Soft Computing*, *10*(9), 717–734. doi:10.100700500-005-0002-1

Alharbi, W. S., & Rashid, M. (2022). A review of deep learning applications in human genomics using next-generation sequencing data. *Human Genomics*, *16*(1), 26. doi:10.118640246-022-00396-x PMID:35879805

Alpsoy, A., Yavuz, A., & Elpek, G. O. (2021). Artificial intelligence in pathological evaluation of gastrointestinal cancers. *Artif Intell Gastroenterol, 2*(6), 141-156.

Altmann, A., Tolosi, L., Sander, O., & Lengauer, T. (2010). Permutation importance: A corrected feature importance measure. *Bioinformatics (Oxford, England)*, *26*(10), 1340–1347. doi:10.1093/bioinformatics/btq134 PMID:20385727

Banegas-Luna, A. J., Pena-Garcia, J., Iftene, A., Guadagni, F., Ferroni, P., Scarpato, N., Zanzotto, F. M., Bueno-Crespo, A., & Perez-Sanchez, H. (2021). Towards the interpretability of machine learning predictions for medical applications targeting personalised therapies: A cancer case survey. *International Journal of Molecular Sciences*, *22*(9), 4394. doi:10.3390/ijms22094394 PMID:33922356

Belenguer, L. (2022). AI bias: Exploring discriminatory algorithmic decision-making models and the application of possible machine-centric solutions adapted from the pharmaceutical industry. *AI and Ethics*, *2*(4), 771–787. doi:10.100743681-022-00138-8 PMID:35194591

Bener, A., Barisik, C. C., Acar, A., & Ozdenkaya, Y. (2019). Assessment of the Gail Model in estimating the risk of breast cancer: Effect of cancer worry and risk in healthy women. *Asian Pacific Journal of Cancer Prevention*, *20*(6), 1765–1771. doi:10.31557/APJCP.2019.20.6.1765 PMID:31244298

Bera, K., Schalper, K. A., Rimm, D. L., Velcheti, V., & Madabhushi, A. (2019). Artificial intelligence in digital pathology – new tools for diagnosis and precision oncology. *Nature Reviews. Clinical Oncology*, *16*(11), 703–715. doi:10.103841571-019-0252-y PMID:31399699

Bernabe-Ortiz, A., Perel, P., Miranda, J. J., & Smeeth, L. (2018). Diagnostic accuracy of the Finnish Diabetes Risk Score (FINDRISC) for undiagnosed T2DM in Peruvian population. *Primary Care Diabetes*, *12*(6), 517–525. doi:10.1016/j.pcd.2018.07.015 PMID:30131300

Bitton, A., & Gaziano, T. (2010). The Framingham Heart Study's impact on global risk assessment. *Progress in Cardiovascular Diseases*, *53*(1), 68–78. doi:10.1016/j.pcad.2010.04.001 PMID:20620429

Bogdanovic, B., Eftimov, T., & Simjanoska, M. (2022). In-depth insights into Alzheimer's disease by using explainable machine learning approach. *Scientific Reports*, *12*(1), 6508. doi:10.103841598-022-10202-2 PMID:35444165

Bohr, A., & Memarzadeh, K. (2020). The rise of artificial intelligence in healthcare applications. *Artifical Intelligence in Healthcare*, 25-60.

Borrellas, P., & Unceta, I. (2021). The challenges of machine learning and their economic implications. *Entropy (Basel, Switzerland)*, *23*(3), 275. doi:10.3390/e23030275 PMID:33668772

Bratko, I. (1997). Machine Learning: Between Accuracy and Interpretability. In *Learning, networks and statistics* (pp. 163–177). Springer. doi:10.1007/978-3-7091-2668-4_10

Carvalho, D. V., Pereira, E. M., & Cardoso, J. S. (2019). Machine learning interpretability: A survey on methods and metrics. *Electronics (Basel)*, *8*(8), 832. doi:10.3390/electronics8080832

Dahlin, E. (2021). Mind the gap! On the future of AI research. *Humanities & Social Sciences Communications*, *8*(1), 71. doi:10.105741599-021-00750-9

Davenport, T., & Kalakota, R. (2019). The potential for artificial intelligence in healthcare. *Future Healthcare Journal*, *6*(2), 94–98. doi:10.7861/futurehosp.6-2-94 PMID:31363513

De Backer, G. (2022). New insights in cardiovascular risk estimation and stratification. *e-Journal of Cardiology Practice, 22*, 16.

De La Vega, F. M., Chowdhury, S., Moore, B., Frise, E., McCarthy, J., Hernandez, E. J., Wong, T., James, K., Guidugli, L., Agrawal, P. B., Genetti, C. A., Brownstein, C. A., Beggs, A. H., Löscher, B.-S., Franke, A., Boone, B., Levy, S. E., Õunap, K., Pajusalu, S., ... Kingsmore, S. F. (2021). Artificial intelligence enables comprehensive genome interpretation and nomination of candidate diagnoses for rare genetic diseases. *Genome Medicine*, *13*(1), 153. doi:10.118613073-021-00965-0 PMID:34645491

Dias, R., & Torkamani, A. (2019). Artificial intelligence in clinical and genomic diagnostics. *Genome Medicine*, *11*(1), 70. doi:10.118613073-019-0689-8 PMID:31744524

Diogo, V. S., Ferreira, H. A., & Prata, D. (2022). Early diagnosis of Alzheimer's disease using machine learning: A multi-diagnostic, generalizable approach. *Alzheimer's Research & Therapy*, *14*(1), 107. doi:10.118613195-022-01047-y PMID:35922851

Diprose, W. K., Buist, N., Hua, N., Thurier, Q., Shand, G., & Robinson, R. (2020). Physician understanding, explainability, and trust in a hypothetical machine learning risk calculator. *Journal of the American Medical Informatics Association : JAMIA*, *27*(4), 592–600. doi:10.1093/jamia/ocz229 PMID:32106285

Du, M., Liu, N., & Hu, X. (2019). Techniques for interpretable machine learning. *Communications of the ACM*, *63*(1), 68–77. doi:10.1145/3359786

Ekins, S., Puhl, A. C., Zorn, K. M., Lane, T. R., Russo, D. P., Klein, J. J., Hickey, A. J., & Clark, A. M. (2019). Exploiting machine learning for end-to-end drug discovery and development. *Nature Materials*, *18*(5), 435–441. doi:10.103841563-019-0338-z PMID:31000803

ElShawi, R., Sherif, Y., Al-Mallah, M., & Sakr, S. (2021). Interpretability in healthcare: A comparative study of local machine learning interpretability techniques. *Computational Intelligence*, *37*(4), 1633–1650. doi:10.1111/coin.12410

Fujiwara, T., Yamamoto, Y., Kim, J. D., Buske, O., & Takagi, T. (2018). PubCaseFinder: A case-report-based, phenotype-driven differential-diagnosis system for rare diseases. *Journal of Human Genetics*, *103*(3), 389–399. doi:10.1016/j.ajhg.2018.08.003 PMID:30173820

Gazova, A., Leddy, J. J., Rexova, M., Hivak, P., Hatala, R., & Kyselovic, J. (2019). Predictive value of CHA2DS2-VASc scores regarding the risk of stroke and all-cause mortality in patients with atrial fibrillation (CONSORT compliant). *Medicine*, *98*(31), e16560. doi:10.1097/MD.0000000000016560 PMID:31374021

Gerke, S., Minssen, T., & Cohen G. (2020). Ethical and legal challenges of artificial intelligence-driven healthcare. *Artificial Intelligence in Healthcare*, 295-336.

Hakkoum, H., Abnane, I., & Idri, A. (2022). Interpretability in the medical field: A systematic mapping and review study. *Applied Soft Computing*, *117*, 108391. doi:10.1016/j.asoc.2021.108391

Hall, P., & Gill, N. (2018). *An Introduction to Machine Learning Interpretability: An Applied Perspective on Fairness, Accountability, Transparency, and Explainable AI*. O'Reilly.

Hotvedt, M., Grimstad, B., & Imsland, L. (2021). Identifiabiliy and physical inerpretability of hybrid, gray-box models – a case study. *IFAC-PapersOnLine*, *54*(3), 389–394. doi:10.1016/j.ifacol.2021.08.273

Hutchinson, B., Rostamzadeh, N., Greer, C., Heller, K., & Prabhakaran, V. 2022. Evaluation Gaps in Machine Learning Practice. *ACM Conference on Fairness, Accountability, and Transparency (FAccT '22)*. 10.1145/3531146.3533233

Javaid, M., Haleem, A., Singh, R. P., Suman, R., & Rab, S. (2022). Significance of machine learning in healthcare: Features, pillars and applications. *Intelligent Networks*, *3*, 58–73. doi:10.1016/j.ijin.2022.05.002

Jia, J., Wang, R., An, Z., Guo, Y., Ni, X., & Shi, T. (2018). RDAD: A machine learning system to support phenotype-based rare disease diagnosis. *Frontiers in Genetics*, *9*, 587. doi:10.3389/fgene.2018.00587 PMID:30564269

Jie, C., Jiawei, L., Shulin, W., & Sheng, Y. (2018). Feature selection in machine learning: A new perspective. *Neurocomputing*, *300*, 70–79. doi:10.1016/j.neucom.2017.11.077

Johnson, K. B., Wei, W. Q., Weeraratne, D., Frisse, M. E., Misulis, K., Rhee, K., Zhao, J., & Snowdon, J. L. (2021). Precision medicine, AI, and the future of personalized health care. *Clinical and Translational Science*, *14*(1), 86–93. doi:10.1111/cts.12884 PMID:32961010

Kelly, C. J., Karthikesalingam, A., Suleyman, M., Corrado, G., & King, D. (2019). Key challenges for delivering clinical impact with artificial intelligence. *BMC Medicine*, *17*(1), 195. doi:10.118612916-019-1426-2 PMID:31665002

Kline, A., Wang, H., Li, Y., Dennis, S., Hutch, M., Xu, Z., Wang, F., Cheng, F., & Luo, Y. (2022). Multimodal machine learning in precision health: A scoping review. npj. *Digital Medicine*, *5*, 171. PMID:36344814

Konieczny, L., & Roterman, I. (2019). Personalized precision medicine. *Bio-Algorithms and Med-Systems*, 15.

L'heureux, A., Grolinger, K., & Capretz, M. A. M. (2017). Machine learning with big data: Challenges and approaches. *IEEE Access : Practical Innovations, Open Solutions*, *5*, 7776–7797. doi:10.1109/ACCESS.2017.2696365

Linardatos, P., Papastefanopoulos, V., & Kotsiantis, S. (2020). Explainable AI: A review of machine learning interpretability methods. *Entropy (Basel, Switzerland)*, *23*(1), 18. doi:10.3390/e23010018 PMID:33375658

Lu, S. C., Swisher, C. L., Chung, C., Jaffray, D., & Sidey-Gibbons, C. (2023). On the importance of interpretable machine learning predictions to inform clinical decision making in oncology. *Frontiers in Oncology*, *13*, 1129380. doi:10.3389/fonc.2023.1129380 PMID:36925929

Luo, Y., Tseng, H. H., Cui, S., Wei, S., Ten, R. K., & Naqa, I. E. (2019). Balancing accuracy and interpretability of machine learning approaches for radiation treatment outcomes modeling. *BJR Open*, *1*(1), 20190021. doi:10.1259/bjro.20190021 PMID:33178948

Maeo, J., Rius-Peris, J. M., Marana-Perez, A. I., Valiente-Armero, A., & Torres, A. M. (2021). Extreme gradient boosting machine learning method for predicting medical treatment in patients with acute bronchiolitis. *Biocybernetics and Biomedical Engineering*, *41*(2), 792–801. doi:10.1016/j.bbe.2021.04.015

Manley, K., Nyelele, C., & Egoh, B. N. (2022). A review of machine learning and big data applications in addressing ecosystem service research gaps. *Ecosystem Services*, *57*, 1010478. doi:10.1016/j.ecoser.2022.101478

Marr, B. (2018). How is AI used in healthcare – 5 powerful real-world examples that show the latest advances. *Forbes*.

Miller, D. D., & Brown, E. W. (2018). Artificial intelligence in medical practice: The question to the answer? *The American Journal of Medicine*, *131*(2), 129–133. doi:10.1016/j.amjmed.2017.10.035 PMID:29126825

Molnar, C., Konig, G., Herbinger, J., Freiesleben, T., Dandl, S., & Scholbeck, C. A. (2022). General pitfalls of model-agnostic interpretation methods for machine learning models. AI - Beyond Explainable AI, Science, 13200, 39-68.

Moraffah, R., Karami, M., Guo, R., Raglin, A., & Liu, H. (2020). Causal interpretability for machine learning – problems, methods and evaluation. *SIGKDD Explorations*, *22*(1), 18–33. doi:10.1145/3400051.3400058

Murdoch, B. (2021). Privacy and artificial intelligence: Challenges for protecting health information in a new era. *BMC Medical Ethics*, *22*(1), 122. doi:10.118612910-021-00687-3 PMID:34525993

Murdoch, W. J., Singh, C., Kumbier, K., Abbasi-Asl, R., & Yu, B. (2018). Interpretable machine learning: Definitions, methods, and applications. *Proceedings of the National Academy of Sciences of the United States of America*, *116*(44), 22071–22080. doi:10.1073/pnas.1900654116 PMID:31619572

Nicholson Price, W. II, & Glenn Cohen, I. (2019). Privacy in the age of medical big data. *Nature Medicine*, *25*(1), 37–43. doi:10.103841591-018-0272-7 PMID:30617331

Nieto-Martinez, R., Barengo, N. C., Restrepo, M., Grinspan, A., Assefi, A., & Mechanick, J. I. (2023). *Large scale application of the Finnish diabetes risk score in Latin American and Caribbean populations: A descriptive study*. Academic Press.

Olesen, J. B., Torp-Pedersen, C., Hansen, M. L., & Lip, G. Y. H. (2012). The value of the CHA2DS2-VASc score for refining stroke risk stratification in patients with atrial fibrillation with a CHADS2 score 0-1: A nationwide cohort study. *Thrombosis and Haemostasis*, *107*(6), 1172–1179. doi:10.1160/TH12-03-0175 PMID:22473219

Park, D. J., Park, M. W., Lee, H., Kim, Y. J., Kim, Y., & Park, Y. H. (2021). Development of machine learning model for diagnostic disease prediction based on laboratory tests. *Scientific Reports*, *11*(1), 7567. doi:10.103841598-021-87171-5 PMID:33828178

Pfob, A., Lu, S. C., & Sidey-Gibbons, C. (2022). Machine learning in medicine: A practical introduction to techniques for data pre-processing, hyperparameter tuning, and model comparison. *BMC Medical Research Methodology*, *22*(1), 1–15. doi:10.118612874-022-01758-8 PMID:36319956

Pudjihartono, N., Fadason, T., Kempa-Liehr, A. W., & O'Sullivan, J. M. (2022). A review of feature selection methods for machine learning-based disease risk prediction. *Frontiers in Bioinformatics, 2,* 927312. doi:10.3389/fbinf.2022.927312 PMID:36304293

Rockhill, B., Spiegelman, D., Byrne, C., Hunter, D. J., & Colditz, G. A. (2001). Validation of the Gail et al. Model of Breast Cancer Risk Prediction and Implications for Chemoprevention. *Journal of the National Cancer Institute, 93*(5), 353–366. doi:10.1093/jnci/93.5.358 PMID:11238697

Rudin, C., Chen, C., Chen, Z., Huang, H., Semenova, L., & Zhong, C. (2022). Interpretable machine learning: Fundamental principles and 10 grand challenges. *Statistics Surveys, 16*(none), 1–85. doi:10.1214/21-SS133

SCORE2 working group and ESC Cardiovascular risk collaboration. (2021). SCORE2 risk prediction algorithms: new models to estimate 10-year risk of cardiovascular disease in Europe. *Eur Heart J, 42*(25), 2439-2454.

Siala, H., & Wang, Y. (2022). SHIFTing artificial intelligence to be responsible in healthcare: A systematic review. *Social Science & Medicine, 296,* 114782. doi:10.1016/j.socscimed.2022.114782 PMID:35152047

Stiglic, G., Kocbek, P., Fijacko, N., Zitnik, M., Verbert, K., & Cilar, L. (2020). Interpretability of machine learning-based prediction models in healthcare. *Wiley Interdisciplinary Reviews. Data Mining and Knowledge Discovery, 10*(5), e1379. doi:10.1002/widm.1379

Wang, T. (2019). Gaining free or low-cost transparency with interpretable partial substitute. *Proceedings of the 36th International Conference on Machine Learning, Long Beach, California, PMLR 97.*

Watson, D. S. (2022). Conceptual challenges for interpretable machine learning. *Synthese, 200*(2), 65. doi:10.100711229-022-03485-5

Weissler, E. H., Naumann, T., Andersson, T., Ranganath, R., Elemento, O., Luo, Y., Freitag, D. F., Benoit, J., Hughes, M. C., Khan, F., Slater, P., Shameer, K., Roe, M., Hutchison, E., Kollins, S. H., Broedl, U., Meng, Z., Wong, J. L., Curtis, L., ... Ghassemi, M. (2021). The role of machine learning in clinical research: Transforming the future of evidence generation. *Trials, 22*(1), 537. doi:10.118613063-021-05489-x PMID:34399832

Wu, Y., Zhang, L., Bhatti, U. A., & Huang, M. (2023). Interpretable machine learning for personalized medical recommendations: A LIME-based approach. *Diagnostics (Basel), 13*(16), 2681. doi:10.3390/diagnostics13162681 PMID:37627940

Yoon, C. H., Torrance, R., & Scheinerman, N. (2022). Machine learning in medicine: Should the pursuit of enhanced interpretability be abandoned? *Journal of Medical Ethics, 48*(9), 581–585. doi:10.1136/medethics-2020-107102 PMID:34006600

Zhou, S. K., Le, H. N., Luu, K., Nguyen, H. V., & Ayache, N. (2021). Deep reinforcement learning in medical imaging: A literature review. *Medical Image Analysis, 73,* 102193. doi:10.1016/j.media.2021.102193 PMID:34371440

Zhuang, X. D., Tian, T., Liao, L. Z., Dong, Y. H., Zhou, H. J., Zhang, S. Z., Chen, W. Y., Du, Z. M., Wang, X. Q., & Liao, X. X. (2022). Deep phenotyping and prediction of long-term cardiovascular disease: Optimized by machine learning. *The Canadian Journal of Cardiology, 38*(6), 774–782. doi:10.1016/j.cjca.2022.02.008 PMID:35157988

Chapter 8
Deep Learning for the Intersection of Ethics and Privacy in Healthcare

Kanchan Naithani

Galgotias University, Greater Noida, India

Shrikant Tiwari

ⓘ https://orcid.org/0000-0001-6947-2362

Galgotias University, Greater Noida, India

ABSTRACT

The integration of deep learning in healthcare holds tremendous promise for improving patient care and medical research. However, this transformation comes with ethical considerations and privacy challenges that demand careful examination. An effort is made to explore fundamental ethical principles, data privacy issues, and the impact of bias and fairness on healthcare AI. It scrutinizes the critical need for informed consent, patient rights, and adherence to regulatory frameworks. The work established in this chapter highlights transparency and explainability as essential aspects of responsible AI deployment in healthcare services. Furthermore, the chapter also offers additional information on ethical decision-making frameworks, mechanisms for accountability, and auditing in deep learning projects. Case studies and real-world examples illustrate these concepts, guiding practitioners and researchers in their quest to navigate the intricate intersection of ethics and privacy in healthcare deep learning.

1. INTRODUCTION

In recent years, the field of healthcare has witnessed a remarkable transformation, thanks to the ever-advancing realm of deep learning and artificial intelligence. These technologies have emerged as powerful tools in disease diagnosis, personalized treatment, predictive analytics, and medical research, promising to revolutionize patient care and the healthcare industry. However, standing at the cusp of this transformative journey, it is critically important to pause and reflect on the ethical considerations and privacy

DOI: 10.4018/978-1-6684-8531-6.ch008

Copyright © 2024, IGI Global. Copying or distributing in print or electronic forms without written permission of IGI Global is prohibited.

concerns that accompany this rapid evolution. This chapter will provide a comprehensive overview of the ethical landscape within which healthcare deep learning operates. As healthcare professionals, researchers, and policymakers strive to harness the potential of deep learning, they must also grapple with the fundamental questions of autonomy, consent, transparency, and accountability. Real-world case studies are delved into along with legal frameworks, and emerging challenges to provide a holistic understanding of the multifaceted issues at the intersection of healthcare, ethics, and privacy. In This chapter readers will be equipped with the knowledge and guidance necessary to navigate these challenges responsibly and ethically, ensuring that the promises of healthcare deep learning are realized while preserving the rights, dignity, and privacy of patients and individuals.

1.1 The Importance of Ethics and Privacy in Healthcare Deep Learning

The integration of deep learning into the healthcare domain has ushered in a new era of possibilities, offering innovative solutions for diagnosing diseases, optimizing treatment plans, and streamlining medical research (Henke, N., & Jacques Bughin, L. 2016). While the potential for positive transformation is vast, the fundamental importance of ethics and privacy in healthcare deep learning cannot be overstated, the Importance of Ethics and Privacy in Healthcare Deep Learning shown in Figure 1.

In ethics and privacy are not peripheral concerns but rather fundamental pillars in the development and deployment of deep learning in healthcare. These considerations not only protect patient rights and maintain trust but also promote the responsible and equitable use of advanced technologies to enhance healthcare outcomes. Ethical practices in healthcare deep learning are not just a choice but a moral imperative.

Figure 1. The importance of ethics and privacy in healthcare deep learning

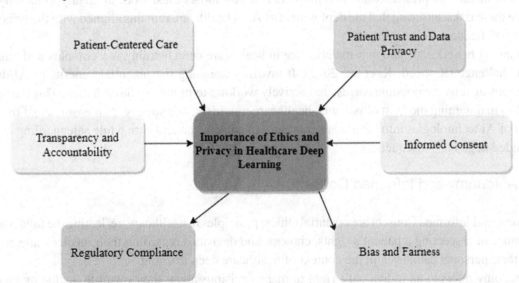

1.2 Ethical Principles in Healthcare Deep Learning

Ethical principles serve as the moral compass guiding the integration of deep learning into the healthcare sector. In this context, several fundamental ethical principles are of paramount importance.

1.2.1 Beneficence and Non-Maleficence

Beneficence and non-maleficence are two closely interrelated ethical principles that are fundamental in the field of healthcare, including the context of healthcare deep learning (Rasheed, K. et al., 2022). Beneficence is the principle that emphasizes the moral obligation to do good and promote the well-being of patients. In healthcare, this principal guide healthcare professionals and researchers to act in ways that advance the health, welfare, and best interests of patients. In the context of healthcare deep learning, beneficence is manifested by using AI and machine learning technologies to enhance patient care and improve health outcomes (Rajkomar, A. et al., 2018). This can involve developing predictive models to identify diseases at an early stage, optimizing treatment plans, or streamlining medical procedures. Deep learning algorithms, for example, can analyze medical images, detect anomalies, and assist in making accurate diagnoses, ultimately benefiting patients by improving the accuracy and speed of healthcare delivery.

Non-maleficence, on the other hand, is the principle that underscores the ethical obligation to do no harm. It is often stated as "First, do no harm," and it serves as a counterbalance to beneficence. In the healthcare deep learning context, non-maleficence means that while AI technologies aim to do good, they must not cause harm to patients (Amann, J. et al., 2020). It is crucial to recognize that the use of AI in healthcare, like any other medical intervention, carries potential risks. These risks may include data breaches, biases in algorithms that lead to health disparities, or overreliance on AI that diminishes the role of healthcare professionals. Practitioners and developers must work diligently to identify and mitigate these risks, ensuring that the deployment of AI in healthcare remains aligned with the principles of non-maleficence.

Balancing beneficence and non-maleficence in healthcare deep learning is a complex and ongoing ethical challenge (Rasheed, K. et al., 2022). It involves weighing the potential benefits of AI-driven innovations against the possible harms, and actively working to minimize those harms. This balance is crucial to maintaining the trust of patients, healthcare providers, and society, as it ensures that the integration of AI technologies into healthcare continues to enhance patient care while safeguarding against unintended negative consequences.

1.2.2 Autonomy and Informed Consent

Autonomy and Informed Consent are essential ethical principles in healthcare, reflecting the fundamental importance of respecting a patient's rights, choices, and decisions regarding their medical care and the use of their personal data, even in the context of healthcare deep learning.

Autonomy refers to an individual's right to make decisions about their own life, including medical treatment and the use of their personal information (O'neill, O., 2002). In the healthcare domain, autonomy means that patients have the right to be involved in decisions about their care, to give or withhold consent for medical procedures, and to control the use of their health-related data. Deep learning technologies, with their data-intensive nature, have made the principle of autonomy even more critical. Patients should be informed, empowered, and actively engaged in deciding how their data is used in AI applications. This can include granting explicit consent for data sharing, understanding the purposes of data usage, and having the option to withdraw consent at any time. The principle of autonomy acknowledges that patients are the ultimate decision-makers in their healthcare journey.

Informed Consent is a direct application of the autonomy principle. It involves the process of fully informing patients about the nature, risks, benefits, and alternatives of a medical procedure or the use of their data in healthcare deep learning applications. Informed consent means that patients should be given clear and comprehensible information about how their data will be used, the potential implications of this usage, and the ability to make a voluntary decision without coercion (Shultz, M. M., 1985). In the context of deep learning, this is particularly important when patient data is used to train AI models or when AI-based systems are involved in patient diagnosis or treatment planning.

Respecting autonomy and obtaining informed consent is not only an ethical requirement but is often enshrined in legal frameworks such as the Health Insurance Portability and Accountability Act (HIPAA) in the United States and the General Data Protection Regulation (GDPR) in Europe. Violating these principles can result in severe legal and ethical consequences.

In healthcare deep learning, autonomy and informed consent emphasize the patient's central role in decision-making and data sharing. Ensuring that these principles are upheld is not only ethically imperative but also essential for building and maintaining trust in the healthcare system, where patients should feel confident that their rights and choices are respected and their well-being is prioritized.

1.2.3 Justice and Fairness

Justice and Fairness are critical ethical principles in healthcare, including the context of healthcare deep learning. These principles emphasize the equitable distribution of benefits and burdens and the elimination of biases and discrimination in healthcare decision-making.

- **Equitable Distribution of Benefits**: The principle of justice requires that the benefits derived from healthcare, including the use of deep learning technologies, should be distributed fairly among all individuals, without discrimination (Guidance, 2021). In the context of healthcare deep learning, this means that AI applications and technologies should be designed and implemented in a way that does not favour one group over another. Healthcare disparities, which may exist due to socioeconomic factors, geographic location, or other variables, should be actively addressed, and reduced through the responsible use of AI.
- **Bias Mitigation**: Healthcare deep learning models should be developed and trained to minimize biases. Biases in AI models can result in unequal access to healthcare services, misdiagnoses, and disparities in treatment. The principle of justice demands that developers and practitioners actively identify and mitigate bias in AI algorithms to ensure that healthcare is delivered fairly to all patients, regardless of their demographic characteristics.
- **Fair Allocation of Resources**: In healthcare, there are often limited resources, such as medical supplies, organ transplants, or access to experimental treatments. The principle of justice calls for a fair and equitable allocation of these resources, ensuring that individuals have an equal opportunity to access them, based on need rather than factors like social status or wealth.
- **Ethical Considerations in Research**: In the realm of healthcare deep learning research, the principle of justice is especially relevant. Researchers should ensure that their studies are conducted

ethically, without exploiting vulnerable populations or conducting research that could exacerbate existing healthcare inequalities.

- **Access to Healthcare**: Healthcare should be accessible to all, irrespective of one's socio-economic status. Deep learning technologies should be used to improve healthcare access, making healthcare more affordable, efficient, and widely available. The principle of justice underscores the importance of using AI to bridge healthcare access gaps.

The healthcare industry can ensure that the benefits of deep learning technologies are not concentrated in a privileged few but are instead distributed equitably, and that biases and disparities are actively addressed and minimized. These principles are essential for building an ethical and equitable healthcare system that serves the best interests of all patients.

1.3 Privacy and Confidentiality

Privacy and Confidentiality are fundamental ethical and legal considerations in healthcare, especially when applying deep learning technologies (Rasheed, K. et al., 2022). They pertain to the protection of patients sensitive information and data.

- **Patient Privacy**: Patient privacy is a cornerstone of healthcare ethics. It entails safeguarding an individual's personal and medical information from unauthorized access, use, or disclosure. Deep learning often involves the collection, storage, and analysis of extensive healthcare data, which can range from medical records to genetic information. Respecting patient privacy means ensuring that this data remains confidential and is used only for legitimate and authorized purposes.
- **Data Security**: Protecting patient data from breaches, theft, or unauthorized access is not only an ethical obligation but also a legal requirement in many jurisdictions. Deep learning systems that process sensitive patient information must be fortified with robust data security measures, encryption, access controls, and auditing to ensure the integrity and confidentiality of patient data.
- **De-identification and Anonymization**: To balance the need for data analysis with privacy protection, healthcare data can be de-identified or anonymized. De-identification involves removing or encrypting personally identifiable information (PII), while anonymization goes further to ensure that individuals cannot be re-identified. These techniques enable the use of data in research and AI applications while preserving patient confidentiality.
- **Data Ownership and Consent Management**: Patients have a right to know who owns their healthcare data and how it will be used. Managing patient consent is a crucial aspect of privacy and confidentiality. Patients should have the ability to grant or withhold consent for the use of their data in deep learning projects, and they should be informed about the specific purposes of data usage.
- **Legal and Regulatory Frameworks**: Laws such as the Health Insurance Portability and Accountability Act (HIPAA) in the United States and the General Data Protection Regulation (GDPR) in Europe provide legal frameworks for safeguarding patient privacy and data confidentiality. Compliance with these regulations is both an ethical and legal obligation.
- **Ethical Handling of Data**: Beyond legal requirements, healthcare professionals and researchers have an ethical responsibility to handle patient data with the utmost care and respect for individual

privacy. This includes minimizing data collection to what is necessary for a specific purpose and securing it throughout its lifecycle

Ensuring privacy and confidentiality in healthcare deep learning not only upholds ethical standards but also builds trust between patients, healthcare providers, and technology developers. Patients must be confident that their personal information is secure and used responsibly in the development of AI applications, ensuring that the benefits of deep learning in healthcare are realized without compromising patient privacy.

1.4 Transparency and Accountability

Transparency and Accountability are two crucial ethical principles in the context of healthcare deep learning, emphasizing the need for clear, understandable, and responsible AI practices (Reddy, S. et al., 2020).

Transparency
- **Openness and Clarity:** Transparency requires that the operations, decision-making processes, and inner workings of deep learning models be made clear and understandable to healthcare professionals, patients, and stakeholders. This is especially important in healthcare where critical decisions may be influenced by AI algorithms.
- **Explainability:** Healthcare deep learning models should be designed to provide explanations for their decisions. This means that the rationale behind a diagnosis or treatment recommendation should be transparent to clinicians and patients, enhancing trust and aiding in clinical decision-making.
- **Model Behavior:** Transparency involves making the behavior of AI models predictable and reliable. In healthcare, it is essential that AI systems do not exhibit unpredictable behavior that could lead to unintended consequences.
- **Disclosure of Data Usage:** Patients and individuals should be informed about how their data is being used in AI applications. Transparency ensures that data usage is disclosed, and patients can make informed decisions about data sharing and consent.

Accountability
- **Responsibility for AI Outcomes:** Accountability entails that those involved in the development and deployment of healthcare deep learning models take responsibility for the outcomes and consequences of these technologies. Developers, healthcare providers, and organizations must be accountable for the decisions made by AI systems.
- **Error Correction:** In healthcare, where mistakes can have life-altering consequences, accountability is vital for addressing errors made by AI models. A mechanism for recognizing and rectifying errors is crucial to prevent harm.
- **Data Security and Privacy:** Ensuring the security and privacy of patient data is a primary ethical and legal obligation. Accountability means that individuals and organizations handling healthcare data take responsibility for its protection.
- **Ethical Decision-Making:** Accountability also involves making ethical decisions throughout the development and use of healthcare deep learning. When ethical dilemmas arise, responsible individuals should have a framework in place to make the right choices.

Transparency and accountability work in tandem to ensure that the deployment of deep learning in healthcare is responsible and ethically sound. Transparent AI systems that are accountable for their actions build trust among healthcare professionals and patients, and they help mitigate the risks associated with complex technology in a high-stakes environment. These principles underpin ethical and responsible AI deployment in healthcare.

2. PRIVACY CHALLENGES IN HEALTHCARE DATA

The healthcare industry is undergoing a digital transformation, with increasing reliance on electronic health records (EHRs), wearable devices, and telehealth solutions (Hermes, S. et al., 2020). While this technological evolution has the potential to improve patient care and medical research, it also introduces numerous privacy challenges which is shown in the Figure 2:

Figure 2. Privacy challenges in healthcare data

Navigating these privacy challenges in healthcare data is essential to maintain trust between patients and the healthcare system, ensure legal compliance, and enable the responsible and secure use of data in healthcare research and deep learning applications. Addressing these challenges requires a multi-faceted approach that includes technology, policy, and ethical considerations.

2.1 Types of Sensitive Healthcare Data

Sensitive healthcare data encompasses a wide array of information that, if exposed or mishandled, could lead to significant harm to individuals, breach their privacy, and potentially violate legal and ethical standards. These types of data are integral to medical care and research but require stringent protection measures due to their sensitivity.

Table 1. The primary types of healthcare data

Personal Identifiable Information (PII)	• Name: A person's full name or initials. • Date of Birth: Birthdate is often used as a unique identifier. • Social Security Number (SSN): In the United States, SSNs are linked to personal identity and financial data. • Address: Residential or mailing addresses.
Medical History and Diagnosis Information	• Medical Records: These include diagnoses, treatment plans, and details of healthcare encounters, often in electronic health records (EHRs). • Diagnostic Tests: Results of medical tests, such as blood tests, X-rays, and MRIs. • Prescription History: Details of prescribed medications and dosage. • Allergies: Information on allergies to medications or substances. • Mental Health Data: Data related to psychiatric conditions and therapy.
Genetic and Biometric Data	• Genomic Information: Genetic data can reveal hereditary conditions and is sensitive due to its long-term implications. • Biometric Data: Biometrics, such as fingerprints and retinal scans, are used for patient identification and access control.
Financial and Insurance Information	• Health Insurance Data: Information about insurance coverage and claims. • Billing Records: Details of healthcare services rendered and associated costs.
Demographic Information	• Race and Ethnicity: These data can be used for assessing health disparities and ensuring equitable care. • Gender and Sexual Orientation: Information that relates to medical conditions and care.
Communications and Correspondence	• Emails and Messages: Patient-provider communications via email or messaging platforms. • Telehealth Records: Records of virtual consultations and telemedicine interactions.
Location Data	• Geolocation Data: Tracking the location of patients, especially for mobile health apps or emergency services
Emerging Technologies Data	• Wearable Device Data: Health-related data collected from wearable devices, such as fitness trackers and smartwatches. • IoT Device Data: Data from Internet of Things (IoT) devices in healthcare, such as smart home health monitoring devices.
De-identified Data	• Data that, while de-identified, may still be re-identified with effort. De-identification is crucial for research, but protecting it from re-identification is a privacy challenge.

Each of these categories contains sensitive information that must be handled with care, secured against unauthorized access, and protected from data breaches to ensure patient privacy, maintain trust, and comply with relevant privacy regulations like HIPAA or GDPR. Healthcare organizations and providers are tasked with the responsibility of safeguarding these data types to uphold the ethical principles and legal requirements of patient data protection.

2.2 Data Security and Compliance

Data security and compliance are paramount in the healthcare industry due to the sensitivity of patient information and the legal and ethical obligations surrounding its protection (Mohammad Amini et al., 2023). An overview of the critical aspects of data security and compliance in healthcare shown in the Table 2:

Data security and compliance are interdependent and must be approached with a proactive and comprehensive strategy. Healthcare organizations and their technology providers must continually adapt to evolving threats and regulatory changes, invest in security infrastructure, and educate their staff to

Table 2. Critical aspects of data security and compliance in healthcare

Data Security	**Cybersecurity Measures**	Robust cybersecurity practices are essential to protect healthcare data. These measures include firewalls, intrusion detection systems, encryption, and continuous monitoring for unusual or suspicious activities.
	Access Controls	Limiting access to patient data to authorized personnel is crucial. This involves implementing role-based access controls and strong authentication methods, such as multi-factor authentication (MFA).
	Data Encryption	Data at rest and data in transit should be encrypted to prevent unauthorized access, even if a breach were to occur. Encryption ensures that data is unreadable without the necessary decryption keys.
	Regular Data Backups	Healthcare organizations should perform regular data backups to ensure data recovery in the event of system failures or data breaches.
	Security Awareness Training	Employees and staff should receive ongoing training on security best practices, recognizing social engineering attempts, and understanding their role in data security.
	Incident Response Plan	Having a well-defined incident response plan is critical. It outlines steps to take in the event of a data breach, including notifying affected parties and regulatory authorities.
Compliance	**Health Insurance Portability and Accountability Act**	HIPAA is a U.S. federal law that sets standards for the security and privacy of patient health information. Covered entities and their business associates must comply with HIPAA regulations to protect patient data.
	GDPR (General Data Protection Regulation)	GDPR, applicable in the European Union and beyond, regulates the processing of personal data. Healthcare organizations handling data of EU residents must adhere to GDPR standards.
	HITECH Act	The Health Information Technology for Economic and Clinical Health (HITECH) Act works in conjunction with HIPAA and provides further regulations related to electronic health records, breach notification, and healthcare data security.
	State and International Regulations	In addition to federal and regional laws, healthcare organizations may need to adhere to specific state-level regulations and international data protection laws if they operate across borders.
	Auditing and Compliance Checks	Regular compliance assessments and audits are conducted to ensure healthcare organizations are complying with relevant data protection regulations. This can involve external audits, self-assessments, and risk assessments.
	Consent Management	Compliance with data protection laws often requires managing patient consent effectively, ensuring patients understand how their data will be used and giving them the opportunity to provide or withdraw consent.

ensure the privacy and security of patient data, foster trust, and uphold ethical and legal responsibilities in healthcare data handling.

2.3 De-Identification and Anonymization Techniques

De-identification and anonymization are critical processes in healthcare data management to balance the need for data utility in research and analytics with the imperative of protecting patient privacy (Colonna, L. 2019). These techniques help remove or obscure personally identifiable information (PII) while preserving the data's value for legitimate purposes.

De-identification and anonymization play a crucial role in healthcare data sharing, research, and analytics, enabling healthcare organizations and researchers to use data for legitimate purposes while protecting patient privacy. However, it is essential to strike a balance between de-identification and data

Table 3. An overview of de-identification and anonymization techniques in healthcare

De-identification Techniques	**Data Aggregation**	This method groups data into broader categories, reducing the granularity of information. For example, ages might be grouped into age ranges.
	Pseudonymization	Pseudonymization involves replacing direct identifiers with pseudonyms or codes. These pseudonyms are usually reversible only by authorized parties.
	Data Masking	Data masking, also known as data obfuscation, involves partially or entirely concealing specific data values, making them unreadable or unreadable without the necessary decryption.
	Generalization	Generalization involves replacing precise values with less precise but still useful categories. For instance, specific dates might be generalized to months or years.
	Data Swapping	In this method, data records are shuffled, ensuring that specific individuals' data cannot be linked back to them while maintaining the integrity of the dataset for analysis.
	Random Noise Addition	This technique involves adding random noise to numerical values, making it challenging to identify specific individuals while preserving statistical properties.
Anonymization Techniques	**Full Anonymization**	Full anonymization is the most robust technique, rendering data completely unidentifiable. This is achieved by removing all identifiers and ensuring no residual information can be used for re-identification.
	K-Anonymity	K-anonymity ensures that each data record is indistinguishable from at least "K" other records, making it difficult to identify specific individuals.
	L-Diversity	L-diversity extends K-anonymity by ensuring that each group of indistinguishable records contains at least "L" different values for sensitive attributes, reducing the risk of attribute disclosure.
	T-Closeness	T-closeness aims to ensure that the distribution of sensitive data attributes in each group of indistinguishable records is like the overall dataset's distribution.
	Differential Privacy	This advanced technique adds noise to query results, ensuring that even with knowledge of the dataset, it is statistically difficult to determine if an individual's data is included.

utility, as overly aggressive techniques can render data less useful for research and analysis. Healthcare organizations must adopt these techniques while adhering to relevant data protection regulations, such as HIPAA in the United States and GDPR in Europe, to ensure the ethical and legal handling of patient data.

2.4 Data Ownership and Consent Management

Data ownership and consent management are integral components of ethical healthcare data practices, especially in an era of digital health and data-driven decision-making (Marelli, L. et al., 2020). These concepts address who has rights over healthcare data and how individuals data is used with their knowledge and consent shown in the Figure 3.

Data ownership and consent management intersect in healthcare. Individuals own their healthcare data and, as a result, have the right to consent to its use. Effective consent management processes not only uphold ethical standards but also ensure that healthcare data is used in a manner that respects patient autonomy and privacy. In addition, healthcare organizations must adhere to relevant data protection

Figure 3. Data ownership

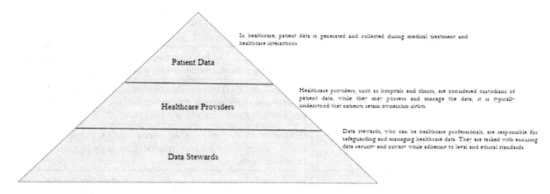

Figure 4. Consent management

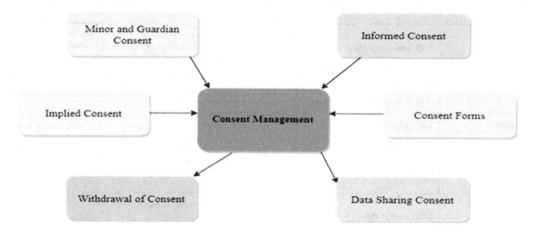

regulations, such as HIPAA or GDPR, to maintain ethical data practices and legal compliance shown in Figure 4.

3. BIAS AND FAIRNESS IN HEALTHCARE DEEP LEARNING

Bias and fairness are critical considerations in the application of deep learning technologies to healthcare (Giovanola, B., & Tiribelli, S., 2023). These concepts are essential because they impact the accuracy of diagnoses, the effectiveness of treatment recommendations, and the equitable distribution of healthcare resources. An overview of the issues related to bias and fairness in healthcare deep learning shown in the Figure 5 and Figure 6:

Ensuring bias reduction and fairness in healthcare deep learning is not only an ethical imperative but also crucial for patient safety and the equitable delivery of healthcare services. Efforts to eliminate bias and enhance fairness contribute to building trust in AI systems and ensure that they provide accurate and unbiased support to healthcare professionals in diagnosis, treatment, and decision-making.

Figure 5. Bias in healthcare deep learning

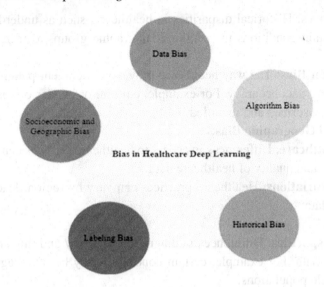

Figure 6. Fairness in healthcare deep learning

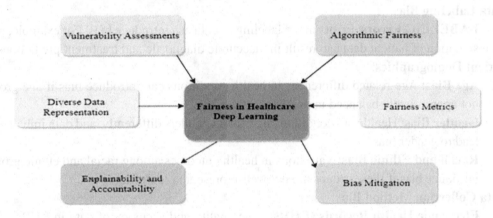

3.1 Sources of Bias in Healthcare Data

Bias in healthcare data is a critical concern, as it can lead to inaccurate diagnoses, treatment recommendations, and healthcare disparities (Hoffman et al., 2016). Understanding the sources of bias is essential for mitigating these issues and improving the quality of healthcare data. Here are some common sources of bias in healthcare data:

1. **Data Collection Bias**:
    ◦   **Selection Bias**: Occurs when data collection is not random, leading to an unrepresentative sample. For example, clinical trials may exclude certain populations, making it difficult to generalize results to those groups.
    ◦   **Volunteer Bias**: In studies where participants voluntarily enroll, those who volunteer may differ significantly from the general population, potentially skewing data.

2. **Historical Bias**:
   - **Legacy Practices**: Historical disparities in healthcare, such as underdiagnosis or underreporting of certain conditions in specific demographic groups, can introduce bias into the data.
   - **Documentation Bias**: The way healthcare providers document patient information can be biased, affecting data accuracy. For example, cultural or gender biases may influence how symptoms are described and recorded.

3. **Socioeconomic and Geographic Bias**:
   - **Access to Healthcare**: Differences in access to healthcare services can lead to disparities in the availability and quality of healthcare data.
   - **Geographic Variations**: Healthcare practices can vary by region, leading to regional bias in healthcare data.

4. **Diagnostic Bias**:
   - **Diagnostic Disparities**: Differences in diagnostic accuracy and thresholds can lead to disparities in the data. For example, certain conditions may be overdiagnosed or underdiagnosed in specific populations.
   - **Implicit Biases**: Healthcare providers' implicit biases can influence their diagnostic decisions, potentially leading to disparities in healthcare data.

5. **Data Labeling Bias**:
   - **LABELING Errors**: Errors in the labeling of data can introduce bias. For example, misclassification of patient data can result in inaccurate diagnostic and treatment predictions.

6. **Patient Demographics**:
   - **Age Bias**: Age-related differences in health conditions can introduce bias if age groups are not appropriately balanced in the data.
   - **Gender Bias**: Healthcare conditions may affect genders differently, and data imbalances can lead to gender bias.
   - **Racial and Ethnic Bias**: Variations in health outcomes among racial and ethnic groups can introduce bias if these groups are not well-represented in the data.

7. **Data Collection Method Bias**:
   - **Electronic Health Records (EHRs)**: The quality and accuracy of data in EHRs can vary, introducing bias. EHRs may also be subject to errors or misinterpretations.
   - **Surveys and Self-reporting**: Data collected through surveys or self-reporting methods can be influenced by participant bias, recall bias, and social desirability bias.

8. **Data Integration Bias**:
   - **Data from Different Sources**: When integrating data from various sources, inconsistencies and disparities in data quality and documentation practices can lead to bias.

Addressing bias in healthcare data is essential to ensure accurate, equitable healthcare delivery and the responsible development of AI and deep learning technologies. Efforts to mitigate bias should focus on improving data collection methods, enhancing data quality, promoting diversity in healthcare research, and implementing bias reduction strategies in AI algorithms and models.

Figure 7. Measuring bias

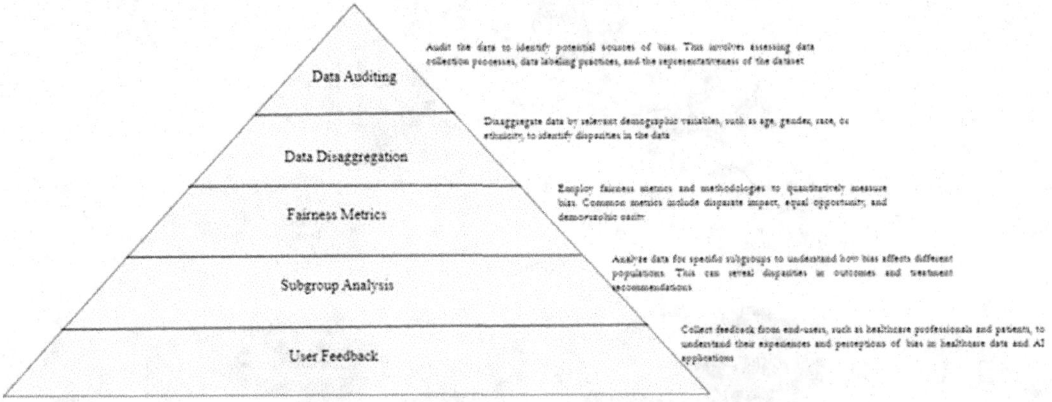

3.2 Measuring and Mitigating Bias

Bias in healthcare data can have severe consequences, affecting patient care, medical research, and the development of AI and deep learning models. Measuring and mitigating bias is crucial to ensure data quality and fairness (Santosh Kumar et al., 2017). Measuring and mitigating bias is shown in the Figure 7 and Figure 8:

Measuring and mitigating bias in healthcare data and AI applications is an ongoing process that requires a multidisciplinary approach, involving healthcare professionals, data scientists, ethicists, and diverse stakeholders. It is a critical step in ensuring that healthcare data is used ethically, that AI systems are fair and equitable, and that healthcare disparities are minimized, ultimately leading to improved patient care and health outcomes.

3.3 Fairness Metrics and Approaches

Fairness metrics and approaches are essential in healthcare deep learning to assess and improve the equitable performance of AI models and ensure that they do not discriminate against specific demographic groups (Giovanola, B., & Tiribelli, S. 2023). These metrics and approaches aim to reduce bias, promote fairness, and uphold ethical standards. An overview of key fairness metrics and approaches in healthcare deep learning is shown in Table 4 and Figure 9:

In healthcare deep learning, ensuring fairness is a complex and evolving process. It requires a combination of fairness metrics, bias reduction techniques, and ethical principles to address disparities and promote equitable healthcare practices. Striving for fairness in AI models is not only an ethical imperative but also essential for building trust and ensuring the responsible and ethical use of AI in healthcare.

3.4 Case Studies on Addressing Bias in Healthcare Models

Case Study 1: IBM's Fairness in AI for Oncology

Background: IBM Watson for Oncology is an AI-based system designed to provide treatment recommendations for cancer patients. In 2018, a report by STAT News raised concerns about the system's fair-

Figure 8. Mitigating bias

Table 4. An overview of key fairness metrics

Fairness Metrics	Definition	Application
Disparate Impact (DI)	DI measures the ratio of favorable outcomes for one group to that of another group. A DI value close to 1 indicates fairness, while values significantly different from 1 suggest disparities.	DI is commonly used to assess disparate impact in healthcare data, such as differences in diagnostic accuracy among different demographic groups.
Equal Opportunity (EO)	EO assesses the true positive rate (sensitivity) across different demographic groups. It evaluates whether all groups have an equal opportunity to benefit from an AI model.	EO is used to ensure that AI models do not favor one group over another when making predictions, such as detecting diseases or recommending treatments.
Demographic Parity (DP)	DP measures the proportion of positive outcomes (e.g., treatment recommendations) received by each group, irrespective of the group's size.	DP helps ensure that each demographic group receives a proportionate share of positive outcomes, promoting fairness in healthcare decisions.
Accuracy Disparity (AD)	AD quantifies the difference in accuracy between different groups. It assesses how accurate predictions are for various demographic categories.	AD is used to identify and rectify accuracy disparities in healthcare data and AI models to ensure equal predictive performance.

Figure 9. Fairness approaches in healthcare deep learning

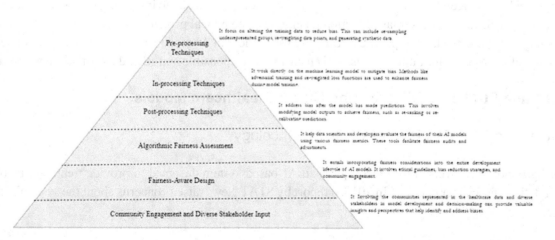

ness (Gerke, S. 2020). The report alleged that the system was biased towards recommending treatments that were more commonly prescribed in Western countries and less aligned with treatment practices in regions like India.

Addressing Bias:

- **Transparent Review**: IBM conducted a transparent review of the system's recommendations, algorithms, and training data to identify potential sources of bias.
- **Data Diversification**: The company started the process of diversifying training data to include more global sources and regional treatment guidelines.
- **Enhanced AI Explainability**: Efforts were made to improve the transparency of the system by enhancing the explainability of AI-generated recommendations for oncologists and patients.
- **Collaboration with Medical Experts**: IBM sought collaboration with medical experts to review and refine the AI's recommendations, ensuring that they align with best practices.

Outcome: The case highlights the importance of continuous monitoring, transparency, and collaboration with domain experts to address bias in healthcare AI models. IBM's commitment to rectifying the fairness issues in Watson for Oncology demonstrated the significance of fairness and ethical considerations in healthcare AI.

Case Study 2: Google Health's Cardiovascular Risk Prediction Model

Background: Google Health developed a deep learning model to predict cardiovascular risk using electronic health records (Tiwari, P. et al., 2020). An internal audit revealed that the model had racial and gender biases, as it tended to underestimate the risk of heart disease for Black patients.

Addressing Bias:

- **Bias Assessment**: Google Health conducted a thorough bias assessment to identify sources of bias in the model, including imbalances in the training data.
- **Data Rebalancing**: The company worked on rebalancing the dataset to ensure that it was more representative of the diverse patient population.
- **Model Adjustments**: The model's algorithms were adjusted to address the underestimation of risk for Black patients.
- **External Review**: Google Health sought external review by medical experts and regulators to validate the fairness and performance of the model.

Outcome: This case illustrates the importance of conducting proactive bias assessments and seeking external reviews to ensure fairness and equitable performance in healthcare models. Google Health's commitment to addressing and rectifying the bias demonstrated a dedication to responsible AI development.

These case studies demonstrate that addressing bias in healthcare AI models is an ongoing process that involves transparency, data diversification, collaboration with domain experts, and a commitment to ethical and fair AI practices. Such efforts are essential to building trust, improving model accuracy, and ensuring equitable healthcare outcomes for diverse patient populations.

4. INFORMED CONSENT AND PATIENT RIGHTS

Informed consent and patient rights are fundamental ethical and legal principles in healthcare that empower individuals to make informed decisions about their medical care and protect their autonomy and privacy (Scott, P. A. et al., 2003). These principles are based on the belief that patients have the right to participate in decisions about their healthcare and to know the potential risks and benefits of medical procedures. An overview of informed consent and patient rights in healthcare is shown in the Figure 10:

Informed Consent: Informed consent is a voluntary and informed agreement made by a competent patient to a proposed medical intervention. It involves the patient's understanding of the nature of the procedure, potential risks, expected outcomes, and available alternatives.

1. **Components of Informed Consent**:
    - **Information Disclosure**: Healthcare providers must disclose all relevant information about the procedure, including its purpose, potential risks, expected benefits, and alternative treatments.
    - **Patient Understanding**: Patients must comprehend the provided information. Healthcare professionals should use clear and simple language and may employ visual aids or interpreters as necessary.
    - **Voluntariness**: Consent should be given willingly without coercion or pressure. Patients have the right to refuse treatment without fear of retaliation.
2. **Types of Informed Consent**:
    - **General Consent**: Given for routine procedures, examinations, or common treatments.
    - **Specific Consent**: Required for more complex or invasive procedures where detailed information is essential.
    - **Implied Consent**: Often used in emergency situations when obtaining explicit consent is not possible.
3. **Capacity and Decision-Making**: Patients must have the capacity to make decisions, and when they lack this capacity, a legally authorized representative may provide consent on their behalf.
4. **Consent Documentation**: Healthcare providers typically document the informed consent process by having patients sign a consent form, but the signature is not the sole indicator of valid consent.

Informed consent and patient rights are essential in maintaining the autonomy, privacy, and dignity of individuals in the healthcare system. These principles form the basis for ethical and legal healthcare practices, fostering trust and ensuring that medical care is patient-centered and respectful of individual choices and preferences.

In the context of healthcare data usage, informed consent is a fundamental ethical and legal concept. It ensures that individuals have the right to make informed decisions about how their health information is used for purposes such as research, treatment, or sharing with third parties. Informed consent entails healthcare providers and researchers transparently presenting individuals with information about the nature of the data usage, its potential benefits, risks, and any available alternatives. Patients or research participants are empowered to comprehend this information fully before voluntarily granting or withholding their consent, safeguarding their autonomy and privacy. This principle upholds the ethical imperative that individuals have a say in how their healthcare data is utilized, contributing to responsible, respectful, and patient-centered healthcare practices.

Figure 10. Patient rights

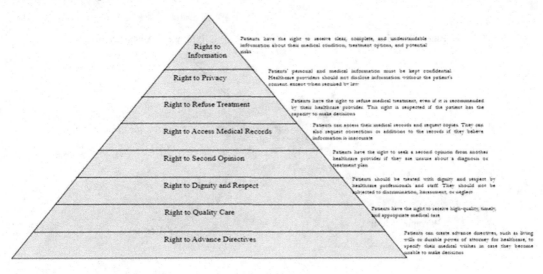

4.1 Legal and Ethical Frameworks for Patient Rights

Patient rights are protected by a combination of legal and ethical frameworks that ensure individuals receive appropriate medical care, maintain their autonomy, and safeguard their privacy (Cohen, J., & Ezer, T., 2013). These frameworks establish a foundation for patient-centered healthcare practices. An overview of the legal and ethical underpinnings of patient rights shown in the Table 5 and Figure 11:

Table 5. Legal framework of patient rights

Legal Framework of Patient Rights	Purpose	Provisions
Health Insurance Portability and Accountability Act (HIPAA)	HIPAA, enacted in the United States, safeguards patient privacy and the security of healthcare data. It provides patients with the right to control their health information and know who has access to it.	HIPAA sets rules for the use and disclosure of health information and requires healthcare providers and organizations to obtain patient consent and protect health data.
Patient Self-Determination Act (PSDA)	PSDA ensures patients' rights to make decisions about their healthcare, including the right to create advance directives, like living wills and durable power of attorney.	Healthcare providers must inform patients of their rights to make decisions and provide written information about advance directives.
Patient Bill of Rights	Many countries have established a Patient Bill of Rights, outlining patients' entitlements to informed consent, privacy, confidentiality, and high-quality medical care.	These bills emphasize respect for patients, their right to refuse treatment, and access to their medical records.
International Regulations	International agreements, such as the Universal Declaration of Human Rights and the International Covenant on Economic, Social and Cultural Rights, recognize the right to health and healthcare as a fundamental human right.	These agreements commit signatory countries to ensuring that healthcare is accessible, available, and of good quality for all.

Figure 11. Ethical frameworks for patient rights

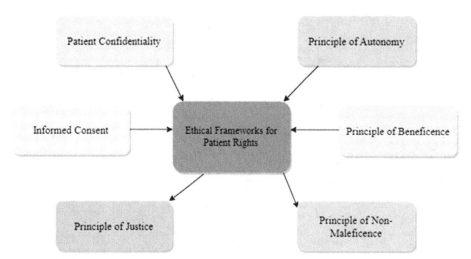

These legal and ethical frameworks collectively establish a patient's right to receive respectful, high-quality healthcare, make informed decisions about their medical care, and maintain control over their health information. They are essential in upholding the dignity and autonomy of individuals in the healthcare system and promoting patient-centered, ethical, and equitable healthcare practices.

4.2 Building Trust With Patients

Trust is the cornerstone of the patient-provider relationship and is essential for delivering high-quality healthcare. Patients must feel confident that their healthcare providers are acting in their best interests, respecting their autonomy, and maintaining their privacy (Lin, Y. P., & Tsai, Y. F., 2011). Here are key strategies for building trust with patients in the healthcare setting:

1. **Effective Communication**:
   - **Active Listening**: Healthcare providers should actively listen to patients, valuing their perspectives, concerns, and preferences.
   - **Clear and Open Communication**: Use plain language to explain medical information, diagnoses, and treatment options. Encourage questions and provide comprehensible answers.
2. **Respect for Autonomy**:
   - **Informed Consent**: Prioritize obtaining informed consent from patients before treatments, tests, or procedures. Ensure patients understand their choices and are making decisions voluntarily.
   - **Respecting Refusals**: Acknowledge and respect a patient's right to refuse treatment, as long as within the bounds of informed consent.
3. **Empathy and Compassion**:
   - **Empathetic Care**: Display empathy by recognizing and validating patients' emotions, fears, and pain. Show genuine concern for their well-being.
   - **Cultural Sensitivity**: Be culturally sensitive and respectful of diverse backgrounds and beliefs.

4. **Transparency and Honesty**:
   - **Truthfulness**: Be honest with patients about their medical condition, prognosis, and potential risks and benefits of treatment.
   - **Disclosure of Errors**: If errors occur, openly disclose them to the patient, take responsibility, and explain how the situation will be rectified.
5. **Respecting Privacy and Confidentiality**:
   - **Data Security**: Ensure that patient data is securely stored and access is limited to authorized personnel.
   - **Confidentiality**: Assure patients that their personal health information will not be shared without their consent, except when required by law.
6. **Quality Care**: Provide evidence-based, high-quality medical care, following established clinical guidelines. This ensures that patients receive the best treatment available.
7. **Shared Decision-Making**: Engage patients in shared decision-making processes by discussing treatment options, risks, and benefits. Encourage them to actively participate in their care.
8. **Continuity of Care**: Maintain continuity in care by ensuring consistent communication and collaboration among healthcare providers. This minimizes confusion and errors.
9. **Accessibility and Availability**: Be accessible and available to patients for questions, concerns, and emergencies. This fosters a sense of security and trust.
10. **Patient Education**: Provide patients with educational materials and resources to help them better understand their medical conditions and the steps to manage them.
11. **Respectful Behavior**: Ensure that all interactions with patients, including staff behavior, are respectful and professional.
12. **Responding to Feedback**: Listen to patient feedback, both positive and negative, and use it to improve healthcare services.

Building trust with patients is an ongoing process that requires healthcare providers to consistently uphold ethical standards, prioritize patient well-being, and maintain open lines of communication. Trust not only enhances the patient-provider relationship but also leads to better health outcomes and patient satisfaction, ultimately improving the overall quality of healthcare.

4.3 Real-World Examples of Informed Consent Implementation

Informed consent is a fundamental ethical and legal practice in healthcare, and it is critical for ensuring that patients understand their medical options and have the autonomy to make decisions about their care (Cocanour, C. S., 2017). Here are some real-world examples of how informed consent is implemented in healthcare:

1. **Clinical Trials and Research Studies**:
   - In the context of clinical trials and research studies, obtaining informed consent is a rigorous and standardized process. Researchers provide participants with detailed information about the study, including its purpose, procedures, potential risks, benefits, and alternatives.
   - A signed consent form is required from participants before they can enroll in the study. The process also involves ensuring that participants can withdraw their consent at any time without repercussions.

2. **Surgical Procedures**:
   - Informed consent is a crucial step before any surgical procedure. Surgeons explain the nature of the surgery, potential complications, expected outcomes, and alternative treatment options.
   - Patients are typically provided with consent forms that detail the procedure and its associated risks. They must sign the form to indicate their understanding and agreement.
3. **Medical Treatment and Interventions**:
   - Before initiating medical treatments, healthcare providers ensure that patients are fully informed about the recommended course of action. This includes discussing the diagnosis, treatment options, potential side effects, and expected outcomes.
   - Patients are encouraged to ask questions and seek clarification before providing verbal or written consent for the proposed treatment.
4. **Emergency Situations**:
   - In emergencies, obtaining formal written consent may not be feasible due to time constraints. In such cases, healthcare providers aim to secure verbal consent when possible or rely on implied consent, acting in the patient's best interests.
   - Once the patient's condition stabilizes, a more detailed discussion and written consent may be sought.
5. **End-of-Life Care and Advance Directives**:
   - Advance directives, including living wills and durable power of attorney for healthcare, provide patients with the means to outline their preferences for end-of-life care.
   - Healthcare providers are obligated to respect these directives, ensuring that patients receive care consistent with their wishes.
6. **Mental Health Treatment**:
   - In the field of mental health, informed consent is particularly critical. Healthcare providers must explain the nature of treatment, potential side effects of medications, and the purpose of therapy.
   - Patients with mental health conditions must provide consent for treatment, and they are often encouraged to participate in treatment planning.

These real-world examples illustrate the diverse applications of informed consent in healthcare. Whether in clinical research, surgical procedures, emergency care, or mental health treatment, the practice of informed consent ensures that patients are informed, actively involved in their care decisions, and their autonomy and rights are respected. It is a cornerstone of ethical medical practice and patient-centered care.

5. TRANSPARENCY AND EXPLAINABILITY

Transparency and explainability are critical principles in the development and deployment of healthcare AI systems. These principles aim to enhance trust, accountability, and ethical considerations in the use of artificial intelligence in healthcare (Kiseleva, A., 2022). An exploration of transparency and explainability in healthcare AI:

Transparency: Transparency refers to the openness and clarity with which healthcare AI systems operate (Bernal, J., & Mazo, C., 2022). It involves disclosing how algorithms function, the data they use, and the decision-making processes.

- **Patient Trust**: Transparency fosters trust among patients and healthcare professionals. Patients are more likely to accept AI-generated recommendations when they understand how the system arrived at those recommendations.
- **Algorithm Understanding**: Transparency helps healthcare providers understand how AI models reach conclusions, which is crucial for making informed decisions about patient care.
- **Ethical Compliance**: Transparent AI systems make it easier to ensure that algorithms and data usage comply with ethical and legal standards, such as patient consent and data privacy regulations like HIPAA.
- **Bias Detection**: Transparent AI systems facilitate the detection of bias and discrimination. They enable researchers and healthcare organizations to assess and address any biases that may be present in the data or algorithms.

Explainability: Explainability involves the ability to provide clear and understandable reasons for the decisions made by AI systems (Confalonieri, R. et al., 2021). It Is about making the "black box" of AI more interpretable.

- **Clinical Decision Support**: In healthcare, explainability is vital for clinical decision support systems. Healthcare providers need to understand why a particular diagnosis or treatment recommendation was made.
- **Enhancing Diagnostic Confidence**: Explainable AI systems can provide healthcare professionals with the rationale behind a specific diagnosis, increasing their confidence in the accuracy of the AI's assessment.
- **Patient Communication**: Explainability allows healthcare providers to convey complex medical information to patients in a way that they can comprehend. Patients can make more informed decisions about their care.
- **Risk Assessment**: In critical care scenarios, such as assessing patient risk or predicting outcomes, explainability is essential. Healthcare providers need to know which variables and factors influenced the AI's assessment.
Benefits:
- **Improved Patient Care**: Transparent and explainable AI leads to more accurate diagnoses, better treatment recommendations, and ultimately improved patient outcomes.
- **Legal and Ethical Compliance**: Healthcare organizations can ensure they comply with legal and ethical standards in data usage and patient care.
- **Reduced Error and Bias**: These principles contribute to error reduction and the mitigation of biases in AI algorithms, ensuring fair and equitable healthcare.
- **Enhanced Trust**: Transparent and explainable AI systems build trust among patients, healthcare providers, and regulatory bodies.
- **Patient-Centered Care**: Patients are more empowered when they understand the reasoning behind medical decisions, leading to a more patient-centered approach to healthcare.

In the evolving landscape of healthcare AI, transparency and explainability are not only ethical and legal requirements but also essential components in building trust, improving patient care, and ensuring responsible and equitable use of artificial intelligence in healthcare.

5.1 The Need for Transparent Models

The integration of artificial intelligence (AI) and machine learning in healthcare has brought about significant advancements in diagnosis, treatment, and patient care (Ahmed, Z. et al, 2020). However, alongside these benefits, there is a growing demand for transparent models in healthcare AI. Transparency is essential to ensure that AI systems are trustworthy, ethically sound, and accountable. An exploration of why transparent models is crucial in healthcare AI shown in the Figure 12:

Figure 12. The need for transparent AI models

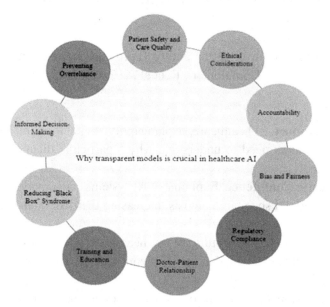

The need for transparent models in healthcare AI is paramount. Transparency ensures that AI supports, rather than undermines, the core values of healthcare, including patient safety, ethical practices, accountability, and fairness. As AI continues to transform the healthcare landscape, transparency is not only a requirement but also a catalyst for responsible and patient-centered care.

5.2 Explainability Techniques in Healthcare

Explainability in healthcare AI is crucial to ensure that healthcare professionals, patients, and regulatory bodies can trust and understand the decisions made by AI models (Amann, J. et al., 2020). Various techniques and methods have been developed to enhance the explainability of healthcare AI systems. Here are some of the key techniques:

- **Local Interpretable Model (LIM) Techniques**: This approach involves building a simple, interpretable model (e.g., linear regression or decision tree) around a specific instance or group of instances to explain the AI predictions for those cases. Local models provide context-specific explanations. Identifying the most important features for a specific prediction can help healthcare professionals understand why a particular decision was made by focusing on the features that influenced it the most.

- **Saliency Maps**: Saliency maps highlight the most influential regions or features in medical images, such as X-rays, MRIs, or CT scans. These maps help radiologists and clinicians quickly identify areas of concern within an image and understand the AI's rationale.

- **SHAP (SHapley Additive exPlanations)**: SHAP values provide a unified measure of feature importance for a particular prediction. They allocate a contribution score to each feature, indicating how much it contributed to the AI's decision, making it easier to comprehend complex models.

- **LIME (Local Interpretable Model-Agnostic Explanations)**: LIME generates locally faithful explanations by perturbing the input data and observing how the AI model's predictions change. It then fits an interpretable model to these perturbations, offering insights into the model's behavior.

- **Decision Trees and Rule-Based Models**: Using decision trees or rule-based models for AI predictions can enhance explainability. These models break down decision logic into a series of easy-to-understand rules that healthcare professionals can follow.

- **Counterfactual Explanations**: Counterfactual explanations provide an alternate scenario that could have led to a different prediction. This helps healthcare providers understand the necessary changes to obtain a different result.

- **Natural Language Generation (NLG)**: NLG techniques can transform complex AI-generated predictions or insights into natural language explanations. This simplifies the communication of AI findings to non-technical stakeholders, including patients.

- **Attention Mechanisms**: Attention mechanisms in deep learning models can highlight the regions of an image or the words in a text that had the most influence on a prediction. This is particularly valuable for medical imaging and natural language processing tasks.

- **Feature Importance Plots**: Feature importance plots, often used in ensemble methods like random forests, rank the most important features in a model. Visualizations make it easy for healthcare professionals to grasp the significance of each feature.

- **Model-Agnostic Techniques**: Many explainability techniques are model-agnostic, meaning they can be applied to a wide range of AI models, including deep learning, without needing to understand the model's internal workings.

Using these explainability techniques, healthcare AI developers and practitioners can make AI systems more transparent and interpretable. This empowers healthcare professionals to trust AI-assisted recommendations, collaborate effectively with AI systems, and provide clearer explanations to patients, ultimately leading to improved patient care and clinical decision-making.

5.3 Interpretable Deep Learning Models

Deep learning models, known for their exceptional performance in various domains, are often criticized for being considered "black boxes" due to their complexity (Guidotti, R. et al., 2018). However, there is a growing need for interpretable deep learning models, especially in critical areas like healthcare,

Figure 13. Interpretable deep learning models

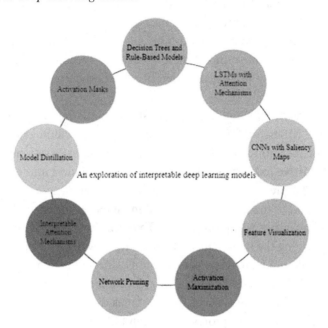

where trust, accountability, and understanding is paramount. Interpretable deep learning models aim to bridge the gap between the power of deep learning and the need for transparency and comprehension. An exploration of interpretable deep learning models shown in the Figure 13:

Interpretable deep learning models are of particular importance in healthcare, as they enable healthcare professionals to understand the AI's recommendations and share these explanations with patients. These models enhance trust, facilitate collaboration between human experts and AI systems, and improve the overall quality of care. As research in this field continues to evolve, interpretable deep learning models will play a pivotal role in making AI systems more transparent and trustworthy in healthcare and other critical domains.

5.4 Balancing Transparency With Model Complexity

One of the key challenges in the development of artificial intelligence (AI) models is striking the right balance between transparency and model complexity (Chowdhury, S. et al., 2023). While complex models often yield superior performance, they can become "black boxes" that are challenging to interpret. Balancing these aspects is essential, especially in domains like healthcare and finance, where trust, accountability, and regulatory compliance are critical. Here is an exploration of the need to balance transparency with model complexity in AI:

The Trade-Off:
1. **Transparency**: Transparency in AI refers to the model's ability to provide clear explanations for its decisions. It involves understanding the inner workings, decision criteria, and factors contributing to a prediction.

- **Advantages**: Transparent models are easier to understand, troubleshoot, and validate. They foster trust among users, including regulatory bodies and end-users. Transparency is essential for accountability and ethical compliance.
- **Challenges**: Highly transparent models might struggle to capture the intricacies of complex data, potentially leading to lower predictive accuracy.

2. **Model Complexity**: Model complexity refers to the sophistication and depth of AI models, including deep neural networks, that can capture intricate patterns in data. Complex models can achieve state-of-the-art performance in tasks like image recognition, natural language processing, and medical diagnostics.

- **Advantages**: Complex models can provide more accurate and nuanced predictions, especially when data is multifaceted and intricate. They are well-suited for tasks that demand a high level of precision.
- **Challenges**: Complex models can be challenging to interpret and explain. The inner workings of deep learning architectures are often complex, making it difficult to provide intuitive explanations for decisions.

Strategies for Balancing Transparency and Complexity:

- **Hybrid Models**: Combine transparent models (e.g., decision trees, linear models) with complex models. Use the transparent model to provide explanations for the complex model's predictions. This hybrid approach enhances interpretability without sacrificing performance.
- **Feature Engineering**: Prioritize feature engineering to select and transform relevant features, making the data more interpretable. Reducing feature dimensionality can simplify complex models.
- **Rule-Based Post-Processing**: Apply post-processing techniques to extract rules or decision logic from complex models. This allows for the creation of interpretable rule-based models that mirror the complex model's behavior.
- **Quantify Uncertainty**: When using complex models, incorporate uncertainty estimation to provide a measure of confidence in predictions. Uncertainty estimates can guide users in understanding the reliability of model outputs.
- **Regularization Techniques**: Implement regularization methods like L1 or L2 regularization to encourage simpler model architectures. This can reduce model complexity and promote interpretability.
- **Sensitivity Analysis**: Conduct sensitivity analysis to understand how model outputs change with variations in input features. This helps identify which features are most influential in predictions.

In healthcare, finance, and autonomous systems, the need for balancing transparency with model complexity is particularly critical. Complex AI models must be able to explain medical diagnoses, financial risk assessments, and self-driving car decisions to instill trust and ensure safety.

As AI research continues to advance, the challenge of striking the right balance will persist. Researchers, developers, and regulators must collaborate to define the acceptable trade-off between complexity and transparency, ensuring that AI systems are not only highly accurate but also understandable, trustworthy, and accountable in their decision-making processes.

6. ETHICAL DILEMMAS AND DECISION-MAKING

Ethical dilemmas are situations in which individuals or organizations face complex moral choices, often involving conflicting principles, values, or interests (Lefkowitz, J., 2021). The resolution of these dilemmas requires careful ethical decision-making. In various contexts, from healthcare to business, addressing ethical dilemmas is essential for maintaining trust, integrity, and responsible conduct. Here is an exploration of how ethical dilemmas arise and the principles guiding ethical decision-making:

Sources of Ethical Dilemmas:

- **Conflicting Values**: Ethical dilemmas often stem from conflicting values. For example, the value of patient autonomy in healthcare may clash with the obligation to provide the best medical care.
- **Uncertainty**: Ethical dilemmas may emerge when there is uncertainty about the right course of action, such as in the early stages of medical research with unclear potential risks and benefits.
- **Resource Allocation**: Scarcity of resources, as seen in healthcare, can lead to dilemmas when deciding who receives treatment or medical resources.
- **Legal vs. Ethical**: Legal requirements and ethical considerations do not always align. An action may be legal but ethically questionable, as seen in some business practices.
- **Conflicting Stakeholder Interests**: In organizations, ethical dilemmas can arise from conflicting interests of various stakeholders, such as shareholders, employees, and customers.

Ethical Decision-Making Principles:

- **Utilitarianism**: This principle suggests that the morally right action is the one that maximizes overall happiness or minimizes harm. Ethical decisions are based on the assessment of consequences.
- **Deontology**: Deontological ethics emphasize moral duties and principles. Decisions are based on whether an action adheres to certain ethical rules, regardless of consequences.
- **Virtue Ethics**: Virtue ethics focus on the character of individuals and organizations. Ethical decisions are based on the development of virtues like honesty, integrity, and empathy.
- **Rights-Based Ethics**: This approach centers on protecting individual rights and respecting the autonomy of individuals. Ethical decisions prioritize upholding these rights.
- **Principlism**: In healthcare ethics, principlism relies on four key principles: autonomy, beneficence, non-maleficence, and justice. Decisions are made by balancing these principles.
- **Relational Ethics**: In complex social contexts, relational ethics consider the quality of relationships and the moral responsibilities tied to those relationships. Decision-making involves understanding the impact on relationships. Different steps in ethical decision making shown in the Figure 14.

Ethical dilemmas are an inherent part of various aspects of life, from personal choices to professional responsibilities. Ethical decision-making, guided by well-established principles and careful consideration of consequences, is essential for navigating these dilemmas while upholding ethical standards, promoting trust, and ensuring responsible conduct.

Figure 14. Steps in ethical decision-making

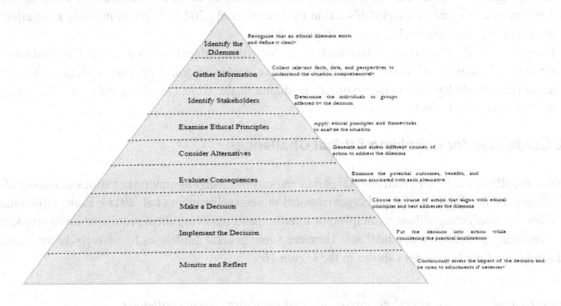

6.1 Ethical Decision-Making Frameworks

Ethical decision-making frameworks provide structured approaches to resolving moral dilemmas and making choices that align with established ethical principles and values (Schwartz, M. S., 2016). These

Figure 15. Ethical decision-making frameworks

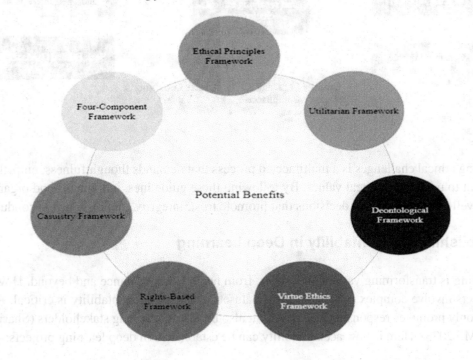

frameworks guide individuals and organizations in navigating complex ethical issues by offering step-by-step processes for analysis and deliberation (S. Kumar et al., 2023). Some commonly used ethical decision-making frameworks shown in the Figure 15:

These frameworks offer structured methodologies for making ethical decisions, providing guidance in a wide range of situations, from individual dilemmas to complex organizational and societal issues. The choice of framework depends on the nature of the dilemma, the ethical values at stake, and the context in which the decision is made.

6.2 Guidelines for Resolving Ethical Challenges

Addressing ethical challenges is an integral part of responsible decision-making in various aspects of life, including personal, professional, and organizational domains (Hartman et al. 2011). Ethical dilemmas often involve conflicting values, principles, or interests, and resolving them requires careful consideration and adherence to ethical guidelines. Here are some general guidelines for effectively navigating and resolving ethical challenges shown in the Figure 16:

Figure 16. Guidelines for effectively navigating and resolving ethical challenges

Resolving ethical challenges is a multifaceted process that demands thoughtfulness, empathy, and a commitment to upholding ethical values. By following these guidelines, individuals and organizations can make well-informed, ethical decisions that promote trust, integrity, and responsible conduct.

6.3 Establishing Accountability in Deep Learning

Deep learning is transforming various industries, from healthcare to finance and beyond. However, as these projects involve complex models and vast datasets, ensuring accountability is critical. Accountability not only promotes responsible use of AI but also builds trust among stakeholders (Sharifani, K., & Amini, M., 2023). Here is how accountability can be established in deep learning projects:

1. Data Governance
   - **Data Collection and Quality**: Establish protocols for data collection, ensuring data is accurate, relevant, and representative of the problem you are trying to solve. Transparently document data sources, cleaning processes, and transformations.
   - **Data Privacy and Security**: Implement rigorous data privacy and security measures, following applicable regulations (e.g., GDPR or HIPAA). Protect sensitive information, and grant access only to authorized personnel.
   - **Data Ownership**: Clearly define data ownership and stewardship. Establish procedures for data sharing and access permissions while respecting data contributors' rights.
2. Model Development and Validation
   - **Transparent Models**: Develop models that are as transparent as possible, using interpretable architectures where feasible. Document model architectures, hyperparameters, and training procedures.
   - **Model Validation**: Rigorously validate models with proper cross-validation, testing, and evaluation techniques. Ensure models generalize well and avoid overfitting.
   - **Bias and Fairness**: Address bias and fairness issues by analyzing model predictions across different demographic groups. Implement mitigation strategies to reduce bias.
3. Documentation
   - **Project Documentation**: Maintain thorough documentation that outlines project goals, methodologies, and results. Include a detailed record of data collection, data preprocessing, model development, and testing processes.
   - **Model Documentation**: Provide documentation for the deployed model, describing its functionality, inputs, outputs, and performance metrics. Include explanations for predictions, when possible.
   - **Ethical Considerations**: Document any ethical considerations, potential risks, and mitigation strategies employed throughout the project.
4. Governance and Oversight
   - **Ethics Committees**: In highly sensitive domains like healthcare, consider establishing ethics committees or review boards to oversee deep learning projects.
   - **Accountable Roles**: Clearly define roles and responsibilities within the project team. Assign an accountable individual who ensures ethical and responsible practices.
5. Auditing and Review
   - **Regular Auditing**: Periodically conduct audits of your deep learning systems to assess their performance, accuracy, fairness, and ethical alignment.
   - **External Review**: Encourage external reviews and audits of your models and data to ensure impartial assessments.
6. **Transparency and Explainability**: **Explainable AI (XAI)**: Utilize XAI techniques to make model decisions more interpretable. This aids in understanding and auditing model behavior.
7. **Compliance with Regulations**: **Regulatory Compliance**: Ensure your project adheres to relevant regulations, such as GDPR for data privacy or FDA guidelines for medical applications. Compliance demonstrates a commitment to ethical standards.
8. **Continuous Improvement**: Establish feedback loops to learn from past projects and improve future ones. Continuous improvement helps address challenges and maintain accountability.

9. **Ethical Frameworks and Principles**: Adhere to established ethical principles, such as those found in healthcare ethics or AI ethics guidelines. Ensure alignment with principles like autonomy, beneficence, non-maleficence, and justice.

10. **Communication and Transparency**: **Stakeholder Communication**: Maintain open lines of communication with stakeholders, including data subjects, users, and the public. Transparently communicate about your project's goals, methods, and outcomes.

By implementing these practices and emphasizing accountability in deep learning projects, you can help ensure that your AI systems are used responsibly, ethically, and in a manner that engenders trust among stakeholders and the wider community. Accountability is a fundamental aspect of AI development and deployment, fostering a responsible and ethical AI ecosystem.

6.4 Auditing Models for Ethical Compliance

Auditing models for ethical compliance is a critical step in ensuring that AI systems and machine learning models adhere to ethical principles, avoid biases, and make fair and just decisions (Landers, R. N., & Behrend, T. S., 2023). Auditing is a structured process of reviewing the development, training, and deployment of these models to identify and rectify ethical issues. Effectively audit models for ethical compliance shown in the Figure 17:

Figure 17. Effectively audit models for ethical compliance

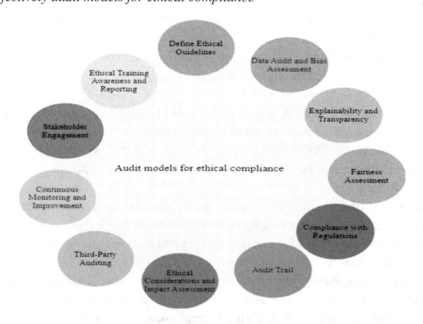

Auditing models for ethical compliance is essential for building trust, promoting responsible AI development, and ensuring that AI systems operate in an ethical and equitable manner. This process is a proactive approach to address ethical issues before they lead to negative consequences or controversies.

7. FUTURE DIRECTIONS AND EMERGING ETHICAL ISSUES

As technology continues to advance, the field of healthcare, including the application of deep learning and artificial intelligence (AI), is evolving rapidly. This evolution introduces new ethical challenges and complexities that require thoughtful consideration (Lee, D., & Yoon, S. N., 2021). Here are some future directions and emerging ethical issues in healthcare:

- **AI-Driven Diagnostics and Decision-Making**: As AI systems become more involved in diagnostic processes and treatment recommendations, concerns about the transparency, accountability, and liability of AI-driven decisions arise. Ethical dilemmas surround the balance between human expertise and algorithmic decisions.

- **Data Privacy in Genetic Testing**: Genetic testing and the use of genomic data are growing in importance. Protecting genetic information is critical, and ethical questions about data ownership, consent, and privacy emerge. Ensuring that individuals maintain control over their genetic data is a primary concern.

- **Ethical Use of Biometric Data**: The use of biometric data for patient identification and healthcare access is expanding. Ethical issues related to data security, consent, and the potential for misuse of biometric information are at the forefront.

- **AI in Resource Allocation**: AI-driven decision support systems can optimize resource allocation in healthcare, such as bed assignments, staff scheduling, and equipment allocation. Ethical dilemmas center around fairness, ensuring that vulnerable populations are not disadvantaged, and avoiding discrimination.

- **Telemedicine and Equity**: The increasing use of telemedicine raises questions about equitable access to healthcare services. Addressing issues of healthcare access, particularly for underserved or remote populations, is crucial.

- **Autonomous Medical Devices**: The use of autonomous medical devices, such as surgical robots, introduces ethical considerations related to accountability, transparency, and the potential for technical failures.

- **Ethical AI for End-of-Life Care**: The use of AI in end-of-life care, including decision support for withdrawal of life-sustaining treatments, raises complex ethical questions about patient autonomy, beneficence, and non-maleficence.

- **Data Bias and Fairness**: Ensuring that AI models are free from bias and deliver equitable results is an ongoing challenge. Addressing bias in healthcare data and AI algorithms is imperative to maintain fairness.

- **Explainability and Trustworthiness**: Ethical concerns center around the explainability of AI models, especially in cases where AI is making clinical decisions. Ensuring that AI is understandable and trustworthy is essential for responsible adoption.

- **Ethical AI Research and Development**: Ethical considerations in AI research, such as data collection, experimentation, and model development, will continue to be a focus. Responsible research practices are key to ethical AI development.

- **Combating Misinformation**: The spread of healthcare misinformation, especially online, has ethical implications. Healthcare providers and AI systems must address the dissemination of false or misleading information to the public.

- **Interoperability and Data Sharing**: Ethical issues around data sharing and interoperability in healthcare systems involve striking a balance between privacy and the potential benefits of shared data for patient care and research.
- **Autonomous Decision-Making in Psychiatry**: The use of AI for mental health diagnosis and treatment raises ethical questions about the boundaries of AI-driven interventions and their impact on human agency and privacy.
- **Ethical Challenges in Precision Medicine**: Precision medicine, which tailors medical treatment to an individual's genetic makeup, brings ethical questions about informed consent, data security, and the potential for unintended consequences.

Navigating these emerging ethical issues in healthcare requires collaboration among stakeholders, including healthcare providers, AI developers, policymakers, and ethicists. Developing clear guidelines, frameworks, and regulations is essential to ensure that advancements in healthcare technology are deployed ethically and responsibly while safeguarding patient rights and well-being.

7.1 The Evolving Landscape of Healthcare Deep Learning

The healthcare industry is undergoing a profound transformation driven by advancements in deep learning and artificial intelligence (AI). Deep learning, a subset of machine learning, has demonstrated its potential to revolutionize patient care, medical research, and healthcare operations (Ahmed et al., 2020). As the landscape of healthcare deep learning evolves, several key trends and developments are shaping its future shown in the Table 6.

The evolving landscape of healthcare deep learning presents significant opportunities to improve patient outcomes, enhance research capabilities, and streamline healthcare processes. However, addressing ethical, regulatory, and security challenges is crucial to ensure that the potential benefits are realized responsibly and ethically. The future of healthcare is being reshaped by deep learning, and its continued evolution promises innovative solutions to long-standing healthcare challenges.

7.2 Anticipating Ethical Challenges in Emerging Technologies

Emerging technologies are driving significant advancements across various fields, from artificial intelligence and biotechnology to robotics and quantum computing. These innovations hold great promise, they also bring forth ethical challenges that must be anticipated and addressed. Proactively recognizing and responding to these challenges is essential for responsible development and deployment of emerging technologies (Banerjee et al., 2020). The key ethical challenges shown in the Figure 18:

Anticipating ethical challenges in emerging technologies is a proactive step toward responsible innovation. Multidisciplinary collaboration among technology developers, ethicists, policymakers, and the public is crucial in identifying, understanding, and mitigating these ethical concerns. As technologies continue to evolve, a commitment to ethical principles and values is essential to ensure that the benefits of innovation are balanced with ethical responsibility and accountability.

Table 5. Key trends and it's developments

Key Trends	Developments
Enhanced Diagnostics and Imaging	Deep learning models are becoming increasingly adept at analyzing medical images such as X-rays, MRIs, and CT scans. They can assist in early disease detection, providing critical insights for healthcare professionals.
Personalized Treatment Plans	Deep learning enables the development of personalized treatment plans by analyzing a patient's genetic makeup and medical history. This approach tailors medical interventions to an individual's unique characteristics.
Drug Discovery and Development	Deep learning is streamlining the drug discovery process by analyzing vast datasets to identify potential candidates for new therapies. This has the potential to accelerate research and development in pharmaceuticals.
Predictive Analytics and Preventive Care	Deep learning models are predicting patient outcomes, enabling healthcare providers to take a more proactive approach to care. These models help in identifying individuals at risk of specific health conditions, allowing for early interventions.
Natural Language Processing (NLP)	NLP models are transforming unstructured medical records into structured data, making it easier for healthcare professionals to access and analyze patient information.
Robotics and Surgical Assistance	Deep learning is improving the accuracy of surgical procedures through robotic assistance. These systems enhance surgical precision and reduce the risk of errors.
Remote Patient Monitoring	The integration of deep learning with telemedicine and wearable devices allows for remote patient monitoring. This enables patients to receive continuous care, especially those with chronic conditions.
Ethical and Regulatory Challenges	The increased use of deep learning in healthcare raises ethical concerns related to data privacy, transparency, and bias in algorithms. Regulatory bodies are working to establish guidelines for responsible AI deployment.
Interoperability and Data Sharing	Achieving interoperability and efficient data sharing among healthcare systems is critical for the success of deep learning applications. Standards and protocols for data exchange are evolving to support this.
Cybersecurity	Protecting patient data from cyber threats is paramount. Healthcare organizations are investing in robust cybersecurity measures to safeguard patient information and maintain trust.
Ethical AI Development	Ethical considerations in AI development are gaining prominence. Ethical frameworks are being implemented to ensure that AI systems align with healthcare values and principles.
Public Awareness	As deep learning becomes more integral to healthcare, public awareness and health literacy regarding AI applications are increasing. Patients are becoming more informed and demanding transparency in AI-driven care.
Collaboration and Research	Collaboration between data scientists, healthcare providers, researchers, and policymakers are essential for the continued advancement of deep learning in healthcare.

8. CONCLUSION

The rapid advancement of emerging technologies is ushering in a new era of innovation and possibilities across various fields, from healthcare and artificial intelligence to robotics and biotechnology. However, with this progress comes a host of complex ethical challenges that necessitate thoughtful and proactive solutions.

As we navigate the evolving landscape of emerging technologies, ethical considerations must be at the forefront of our decision-making processes. The potential solutions and recommendations presented here underscore the importance of creating a robust ethical foundation for the development and deployment of these technologies.

Ethical frameworks, accountability structures, and regulations tailored to each domain are essential for guiding the responsible development of emerging technologies. It is imperative that interdisciplinary

Figure 18. Ethical challenges in emerging technologies

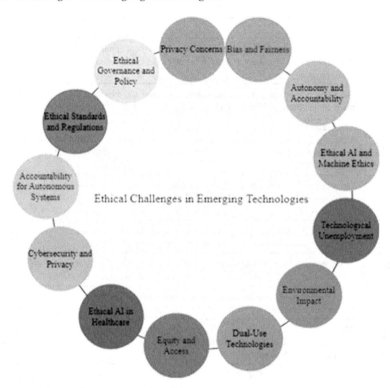

collaboration, involving technology experts, ethicists, policymakers, and the public, becomes the norm to address these challenges effectively.

Additionally, promoting digital literacy and ensuring inclusive access to technology is crucial in bridging disparities and fostering equitable use. Public engagement and education will empower individuals to make informed choices and voice their concerns about the ethical implications of emerging technologies.

The responsibility of addressing these ethical challenges does not rest solely with regulators or developers but extends to society. It calls for ethical leadership, corporate responsibility, and an unwavering commitment to the values and principles that underpin the ethical use of technology.

The ethical considerations surrounding emerging technologies are not merely obstacles to overcome but opportunities to build a better, more responsible future. By embracing these challenges and implementing the recommended solutions, we can harness the potential of emerging technologies while safeguarding the well-being, privacy, and rights of individuals and communities. Ethical technology development is not an option but a necessity as we venture into the uncharted territory of the future.

Encouraging responsible practices in healthcare is an ongoing commitment that transcends individual actions and encompasses the broader healthcare ecosystem. By embracing ethics, patient-centered care, sustainability, and continuous learning, we pave the way for a healthier and more equitable future in healthcare, where individuals and communities thrive, and trust is built upon responsible, compassionate, and sustainable practices.

REFERENCES

Ahmed, Z., Mohamed, K., Zeeshan, S., & Dong, X. (2020). Artificial intelligence with multi-functional machine learning platform development for better healthcare and precision medicine. *Database (Oxford)*, *2020*, baaa010. doi:10.1093/database/baaa010 PMID:32185396

Amann, J., Blasimme, A., Vayena, E., Frey, D., & Madai, V. I. (2020). Explainability for artificial intelligence in healthcare: A multidisciplinary perspective. *BMC Medical Informatics and Decision Making*, *20*(1), 1–9. doi:10.118612911-020-01332-6 PMID:33256715

Banerjee, A., Chakraborty, C., Kumar, A., & Biswas, D. (2020). Emerging trends in IoT and big data analytics for biomedical and health care technologies. Handbook of data science approaches for biomedical engineering, 121-152. doi:10.1016/B978-0-12-818318-2.00005-2

Bernal, J., & Mazo, C. (2022). Transparency of artificial intelligence in healthcare: Insights from professionals in computing and healthcare worldwide. *Applied Sciences (Basel, Switzerland)*, *12*(20), 10228. doi:10.3390/app122010228

Chowdhury, S., Joel-Edgar, S., Dey, P. K., Bhattacharya, S., & Kharlamov, A. (2023). Embedding transparency in artificial intelligence machine learning models: Managerial implications on predicting and explaining employee turnover. *International Journal of Human Resource Management*, *34*(14), 2732–2764. doi:10.1080/09585192.2022.2066981

Cocanour, C. S. (2017). Informed consent—It's more than a signature on a piece of paper. *American Journal of Surgery*, *214*(6), 993–997. doi:10.1016/j.amjsurg.2017.09.015 PMID:28974311

Cohen, J., & Ezer, T. (2013). Human rights in patient care: A theoretical and practice framework. *Health & Hum. Rts.*, *15*, 7. PMID:24421170

Colonna, L. (2019). Privacy, risk, anonymization, and data sharing in the internet of health things. *Pitt. J. Tech. L. & Pol'y*, *20*, 148.

Confalonieri, R., Coba, L., Wagner, B., & Besold, T. R. (2021). A historical perspective of explainable Artificial Intelligence. *Wiley Interdisciplinary Reviews. Data Mining and Knowledge Discovery*, *11*(1), e1391. doi:10.1002/widm.1391

Gerke, S., Minssen, T., & Cohen, G. (2020). Ethical and legal challenges of artificial intelligence-driven healthcare. In *Artificial intelligence in healthcare* (pp. 295–336). Academic Press. doi:10.1016/B978-0-12-818438-7.00012-5

Giovanola, B., & Tiribelli, S. (2023). Beyond bias and discrimination: Redefining the AI ethics principle of fairness in healthcare machine-learning algorithms. *AI & Society*, *38*(2), 549–563. doi:10.100700146-022-01455-6 PMID:35615443

Guidance, W. H. O. (2021). *Ethics and governance of artificial intelligence for health*. World Health Organization.

Guidotti, R., Monreale, A., Ruggieri, S., Turini, F., Giannotti, F., & Pedreschi, D. (2018). A survey of methods for explaining black box models. *ACM Computing Surveys*, *51*(5), 1–42. doi:10.1145/3236009

Hartman, L. P., DesJardins, J., & MacDonald, C. (2011). Decision making for personal integrity & social responsibility. McGraw Hill International.

Henke, N., & Jacques Bughin, L. (2016). *The age of analytics: Competing in a data-driven world.* Academic Press.

Hermes, S., Riasanow, T., Clemons, E. K., Böhm, M., & Krcmar, H. (2020). The digital transformation of the healthcare industry: Exploring the rise of emerging platform ecosystems and their influence on the role of patients. *Business Research, 13*(3), 1033–1069. doi:10.100740685-020-00125-x

Hoffman, K. M., Trawalter, S., Axt, J. R., & Oliver, M. N. (2016). Racial bias in pain assessment and treatment recommendations, and false beliefs about biological differences between blacks and whites. *Proceedings of the National Academy of Sciences of the United States of America, 113*(16), 4296–4301. doi:10.1073/pnas.1516047113 PMID:27044069

Kiseleva, A., Kotzinos, D., & De Hert, P. (2022). Transparency of AI in healthcare as a multilayered system of accountabilities: Between legal requirements and technical limitations. *Frontiers in Artificial Intelligence, 5*, 879603. doi:10.3389/frai.2022.879603 PMID:35707765

Kumar, S., Sharma, R., Singh, V., Tiwari, S., Singh, S. K., & Datta, S. (2023). Potential Impact of Data-Centric AI on Society. *IEEE Technology and Society Magazine, 42*(3), 98-107. doi:10.1109/MTS.2023.3306532

Kumar, Singh, Singh, Singh, & Tiwari. (2017). Privacy Preserving Security using Biometrics in Cloud Computing. *Multimedia Tools and Applications, 77*(9), 11017-11039.) doi:10.1007/s11042-017-4966-5

Landers, R. N., & Behrend, T. S. (2023). Auditing the AI auditors: A framework for evaluating fairness and bias in high stakes AI predictive models. *The American Psychologist, 78*(1), 36–49. doi:10.1037/amp0000972 PMID:35157476

Lee, D., & Yoon, S. N. (2021). Application of artificial intelligence-based technologies in the healthcare industry: Opportunities and challenges. *International Journal of Environmental Research and Public Health, 18*(1), 271. doi:10.3390/ijerph18010271 PMID:33401373

Lefkowitz, J. (2021). Forms of ethical dilemmas in industrial-organizational psychology. *Industrial and Organizational Psychology: Perspectives on Science and Practice, 14*(3), 297–319. doi:10.1017/iop.2021.65

Lin, Y. P., & Tsai, Y. F. (2011). Maintaining patients' dignity during clinical care: A qualitative interview study. *Journal of Advanced Nursing, 67*(2), 340–348. doi:10.1111/j.1365-2648.2010.05498.x PMID:21044135

Marelli, L., Lievevrouw, E., & Van Hoyweghen, I. (2020). Fit for purpose? The GDPR and the governance of European digital health. *Policy Studies, 41*(5), 447–467. doi:10.1080/01442872.2020.1724929

Mohammad Amini, M., Jesus, M., Fanaei Sheikholeslami, D., Alves, P., Hassanzadeh Benam, A., & Hariri, F. (2023). Artificial Intelligence Ethics and Challenges in Healthcare Applications: A Comprehensive Review in the Context of the European GDPR Mandate. *Machine Learning and Knowledge Extraction, 5*(3), 1023–1035. doi:10.3390/make5030053

O'neill, O. (2002). *Autonomy and trust in bioethics*. Cambridge University Press. doi:10.1017/CBO9780511606250

Rajkomar, A., Hardt, M., Howell, M. D., Corrado, G., & Chin, M. H. (2018). Ensuring fairness in machine learning to advance health equity. *Annals of Internal Medicine*, *169*(12), 866–872. doi:10.7326/M18-1990 PMID:30508424

Rasheed, K., Qayyum, A., Ghaly, M., Al-Fuqaha, A., Razi, A., & Qadir, J. (2022). Explainable, trustworthy, and ethical machine learning for healthcare: A survey. *Computers in Biology and Medicine*, *149*, 106043. doi:10.1016/j.compbiomed.2022.106043 PMID:36115302

Reddy, S., Allan, S., Coghlan, S., & Cooper, P. (2020). A governance model for the application of AI in health care. *Journal of the American Medical Informatics Association : JAMIA*, *27*(3), 491–497. doi:10.1093/jamia/ocz192 PMID:31682262

Schwartz, M. S. (2016). Ethical decision-making theory: An integrated approach. *Journal of Business Ethics*, *139*(4), 755–776. doi:10.100710551-015-2886-8

Scott, P. A., Vlimki, M., Leino-Kilpi, H., Dassen, T., Gasull, M., Lemonidou, C., & Arndt, M. (2003). Autonomy, privacy and informed consent 1: Concepts and definitions. *British Journal of Nursing (Mark Allen Publishing)*, *12*(1), 43–47. doi:10.12968/bjon.2003.12.1.10999 PMID:12574725

Sharifani, K., & Amini, M. (2023). Machine Learning and Deep Learning: A Review of Methods and Applications. *World Information Technology and Engineering Journal*, *10*(07), 3897–3904.

Shultz, M. M. (1985). From informed consent to patient choice: A new protected interest. *The Yale Law Journal*, *95*(2), 219. doi:10.2307/796352 PMID:11658859

Tiwari, P., Colborn, K. L., Smith, D. E., Xing, F., Ghosh, D., & Rosenberg, M. A. (2020). Assessment of a machine learning model applied to harmonized electronic health record data for the prediction of incident atrial fibrillation. *JAMA Network Open*, *3*(1), e1919396–e1919396. doi:10.1001/jamanetworkopen.2019.19396 PMID:31951272

Chapter 9
Early Detection of Alzheimer's Using Artificial Intelligence for Effective Emotional Support Systems

A. Sivasangari

Sathyabama Institute of Science and Technology, India

V. J. K. Kishor Sonti

Sathyabama Institute of Science and Technology, India

L. Suji Helen

Sathyabama Institute of Science and Technology, India

D. Deepa

Sathyabama Institute of Science and Technology, India

T. Samraj Lawrence

College of Engineering and Technology, Ethiopia

ABSTRACT

The prominence of technological progress is evident only when its fruits reaching the society. Any disruptive technology has such a profound effect; artificial intelligence is not an exception. This chapter highlights one such technological impact for the benefit of mankind. Alzheimer's is a known neurological illness, sometimes leading to terminal stage of human life. The treatment becomes complicated when diagnosis takes place at a later stage of the disease. The prognosis and diagnosis, if supported by a technology such as artificial intelligence, will be made better by delaying the disease progression. In this chapter, machine learning algorithms such as random forest, cross validation method is used to analyze, train, and predict Alzheimer's disease and its progression. This in turn helps in improving the emotional support system to the patients. Several research groups are working on this domain, and here the insights provided are going to be more significant and useful for further investigations.

DOI: 10.4018/978-1-6684-8531-6.ch009

Copyright © 2024, IGI Global. Copying or distributing in print or electronic forms without written permission of IGI Global is prohibited.

1. INTRODUCTION

"Health is Wealth "is a universal truth. A healthy mind and body can do wonders in one's life time. But life is very uncertain at times, it throws unforeseen challenges. If this challenge is a terminal illness, the fight becomes much tougher. Technology intervention in such cases is much sought to make this battle better. In this chapter of the book, one such close battle that becomes better for the mankind is discussed vividly. The real essence of human evolution shall be celebrated when the achievements related to our safe existence is promised. The nexus between healthcare and technology has become so clear and significant in the recent past.

Whenever world found a disruptive technology's arrival, the impact in various fields is becoming an interesting aspect for research circles. Artificial intelligence (AI) is one such technology that research groups across the globe is enthusiastic. The usage of in spectrum of fields is exponentially increasing year by year. In the post-pandemic scenario the urge for this surge has become more in healthcare industry. Researchers are working on a specific case of "Alzheimer's Disease" prediction using AI. In this chapter of the book, an attempt has been made to provide more insights on the research gaps, analysis, interpretations, investigations and future prospects. The reading of this topic will be more useful for early researchers, techno-groups and enthusiastic academicians.

Alzheimer's disease (AD) is a form of dementia. The share of this AD is around 70% in dementia related cases as stated by World Health Organization. This is a brain disorder that leads to malfunctioning of a person's daily activity. AD pathogenesis is believed due to the overproduction of amyloid-β and hyperphosphorylation of tau protein. There are several stages in AD's progress; cognitive normal (CN), Mild cognitive impairment (MCI), Late Mild cognitive impairment (LMCI), and Alzheimer's disease (AD).

Lifestyle for Brain Health (LIBRA) index assesses the AD's risk factors. There are few risk factors mentioned related to the development of dementia, those include, age, severe diabetic condition, smoking, higher blood pressure, alcohol abuse and physical inertia. Obesity and social isolation also mentioned as other possible reasons. Even though dementia related with age is a common phenomenon but necessarily occurring for above 65 years population, AD is a specific case.

Alzheimer's is precarious because it is often leads to termination of life, if not recognized early. Some of the symptoms include loss of recent events memory, misplacement of belongings, fuzzy walking, often losing the destinations, confusion, non-familiarity of places, misjudgment in visual distances, difficulty in performing regular tasks, inability to make decisions and searching for words in common conversations. Any early intervention in finding this disease helps in prolonging the progression of the disease.

As per a study of Centers for Disease Control and Prevention (CDC), nearly 7 million people in the USA have Alzheimer's. In other parts of the world also AD effected people number is increasing, in India dementia prevalence for adults ages above 60 is 7.4% as per a survey by Jinkook Lee and group in 2023. Aforementioned statistics insists on the early detection of AD patients that may help in strengthening the emotional support system.

Socio-economic implications of AD needs more research attention. Psychological factors, emotional balance and health of caretakers needs more focused analysis, research and thorough investigations. Alzheimer's disease early detection, prognosis-diagnosis, emotional support system reduces the progression of the disease, as there is no permanent cure found in many cases so far. In this context, a novel perspective is proposed here in terms of 3D model approach.

Figure 1. Influential factors in predicting and dealing with Alzheimer's disease

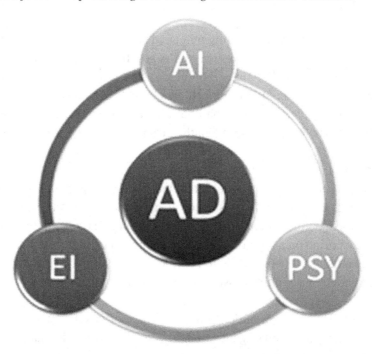

A distinct perspective of predicting and handling AD is depicted in Figure 1. We propose that dealing with AD patients has atleast 3 extended dimensions, one related to technology, whereas the other two psychological aspects, apart from the regular and efficient healthcare support (which is the basic dimension).

Here, AD refers to Alzheimer's disease, AI refers to Artificial Intelligence, EI refers to Emotional Intelligence and PSY refers to Psychological factors. AI assists in the early prediction of AD, whereas EI independently and when combined with AI as AEI (Artificial Emotional Intelligence) along with the study of Psychological factors influencing the patient's current and future state of health assists in strengthening the overall Medical and Emotional health support system. A brief understanding on these extended dimensions will help in getting clear perception about the establishment of effective emotional support system to AD patients.

Artificial intelligence emergence has paved way to the distinct methods of prediction, scaling and analysis of the data. Machine learning algorithms (ML) became vital in this process, followed by the Deep Learning (DL) methods. The applications of AI, ML and DL are wide and some of them include Medical Diagnosis, e-commerce, transport, market prediction, product recommendation and speech recognition and language translation. The mechanism is applying the algorithms on the preprocessed datasets, analyzing the data, exploring the patterns, prediction and storing the feedback for further improvement of the outcomes. The first phase is the data acquisition. The dataset has to be acquired for the diagnosis. Second Phase has the preprocessing of the data to enhance the quality of the dataset for the further classification. In the third phase, splitting of the data takes place. This is for training, testing and validation. The final phase is the feature extraction, learning from the data, updating of the parameters and the classification of the disease.

Here, the focus is on the implications of using ML and DL on the datasets of AD patients. Several researchers worked on using these algorithms for the classification, analyzing and predicting the outcomes from the MRI images. Alzheimer's Disease Neuroimaging Initiative (ADNI) dataset is a complex unit of data that is unique and collected from biospecimens. Some of the earlier include; Jain et al. work on classifying MRI images. Transfer learning approach has been used in this work. Chitradevi et al. emphasized on several optimization algorithms such as Genetic algorithm, Cuckoo Search to segment the brain into sub-regions.

Three models were proposed to high accuracy outcomes by Nawaz et al. In first model, image extraction followed by classification using Support Vector Machine (SVM), Random Forest (RF) is used. Concurrent Neural Network (CNN) based model is used in second approach on the preprocessed data. AlexNet was used in third model to extract the features profoundly in this work.

Kundaram et al. worked on ADNI dataset and images are preprocessed images by rescaling to 255. Training and classification is carried out using CNN models to decide the disease presence. Similarly, Odusami et al. used deep learning method for the early prediction of AD. ADNI datasets are used and CNN model applied for the training. An accuracy of 99.09% was claimed in their work using 18 layered fine tuned CNN model.

Automatic encoders are used by Venugopalan et al. for removing the noise from MRI images. This group concentrated on hippocampus area of the brain and proposed a 3D CNN model. An accuracy of 78% was claimed in this work.

Literature survey study suggested various better algorithms to apply on ADNI datasets. Random Forest (RF) is one machine learning algorithm, proposed by Leo Breiman and Adele Cutler. This is a supervised model, which is constructed using decision trees. This is easy to apply, versatile, robust, highly accurate, less sensitive to noise, adaptable, scalable and flexible. This can be used for classification as well as for the regression problems. RF algorithm is more accurate, effective in handling the missed data and solves the overfitting problem. The major difference between RF and Decision tree algorithm is the establishment of root and nodes in segregating the nodes (in RF this is done randomly). RF employs bagging method for the prediction.

Applications of the Random Forest are in banking sector, health care, and stock market and in e-commerce, but are not limited. This algorithm is not suitable to the data extrapolation and also not producing great results on sparse data. Usage of RF is advantageous because the prediction accuracy is high, handles data efficiently and overcoming the shortcomings of decision tree algorithm.

Literature also suggests that "Deep Learning" algorithms such as CNN, LSTM are giving results that are encouraging in the prediction of Alzheimer's disease. A research group from Massachusetts General Hospital (MGH) developed and validated a deep-learning model recently to detect AD by analyzing data from brain magnetic resonance images.

Machine learning can be applied on small to medium datasets, whereas DL is good for large amounts of data. The training time of ML is comparatively less than DL. Interpretation of the algorithms in ML is much simpler than DL. But DL offers more accuracy in most of the cases; this work actually highlights the pros and cons of the prediction of the AD using ML and DL. The main challenge is the collection of sufficient data related to AD. Data augmentation and scaling techniques helps to improve the performance.

The other significant dimensions of the 3D approach are Emotional Intelligence and Psychological factors of patient as well as the caretaker. Early prediction of AD helps to reduce the cognitive skills malfunctioning to certain extent. A balanced emotional approach towards AD affected patients resulted in ensuring the better and prolonged lifestyle for them. Technology support in mitigating this emotional conflict is evident in this chapter of the book. This proposed 3D approach is paving a new way of Artificial Emotional Intelligence's application in this kind of complex health conditions. Psychological factors assessment of caretakers using ML and DL algorithms is a future exploration that requires much attention.

2. RELATED WORK

Lee et.al suggested estimating the prevalence of dementia in India by a national research. In order to obtain nationwide and state-specific prevalence estimates, data gathering probably involved extensive questionnaires, cognitive tests, statistical analysis, and maybe restricted access to healthcare, all of which may have an impact on the precision of prevalence estimates. Furthermore, discrepancies in the methods used for gathering data and defining the diagnostic criteria could lead to inconsistent findings (Lee et al., 2023).

Similarly Chitradevi et.al discussed use deep learning techniques to assess the brain subregions that have been segmented from medical pictures in the context of Alzheimer's disease. Preprocessing of the images, feature extraction, and model training for insights relevant to diseases were probably part of this procedure. Large and high-quality imaging datasets are needed, however they might not be as readily available or of as high a quality for reliable deep learning analysis (Chitradevi & Prabha, 2020).

Jain et.al proposed a convolutional neural network (CNN) architecture, preprocessing magnetic resonance brain pictures, and training the network to categorize Alzheimer's illness. The procedure probably included data augmentation, model optimization, and performance assessment. Training a deep learning model requires a large amount of labeled data, which may not be available and could compromise the generalizability of the model (Jain et al., 2019).

Nawaz et.al it probably involved taking deep features out of clinical evaluations or brain imaging data and applying them to create a real-time Alzheimer's disease stage diagnosis system. The procedure probably involved real-time processing, optimization, and model training. Additionally, real-time processing may necessitate a large amount of computer power and resources, making it necessary to prioritize computational complexity for practical applications (Nawaz et al., 2021).

Kundaram et.al required building a deep learning architecture, preparing different data kinds (such as clinical records and medical photos), and training the system to identify Alzheimer's disease. Processes like data augmentation, fine-tuning, and model validation were probably involved. One possible disadvantage is the requirement for sizable labeled datasets, which could be scarce, especially for specific Alzheimer's disease subtypes or stages (Kundaram & Pathak, 2021).

Ding et.al proposed using 18F-FDG PET brain scans, a deep learning model was created and trained to forecast the diagnosis of Alzheimer disease. Evaluation, model optimization, and data augmentation Limitations probably played a role in the procedure. One of the challenges in this case is the significant quantity of labeled 18F-FDG PET data, which could be scarce and compromise the robustness of the model (Ding et al., 2019).

Odusami et.al finds method for identifying functional brain alterations in MRI data, honing a ResNet18 deep learning network, and teaching it to identify Alzheimer's disease in its early stages. The procedure probably included data preprocessing, model optimization, and performance assessment. One of the limitations is that efficient fine-tuning depends on the availability of high-quality and thoroughly annotated MRI data, which may not always be possible (Odusami et al., 2021).

Venugopalan et.al proposed combining various data modalities, including genetic, clinical, and imaging data, and creating deep learning models to identify Alzheimer's disease in its early stages. There was probably data fusion, feature extraction, model training, and performance evaluation involved. One of the drawbacks is that integrating different data modalities can be complicated, necessitating a lot of preprocessing and raising the possibility of model overfitting (Venugopalan et al., 2021).

Kumari et.al suggested methods for training models and extracting features using machine learning. It's possible that performance assessment and cross-validation were employed to create a trustworthy Alzheimer's disease detection model. Acquiring large and varied datasets that accurately reflect the early stages of Alzheimer's disease can be challenging and may affect the accuracy of the model (Kumari et al., 2020).

Fisher et.al analyzed a variety of data sources, including patient demographics, genetics, and cognitive evaluations, using machine learning algorithms to predict the course of Alzheimer's disease in a comprehensive manner. One of the challenges in forecasting the progression of Alzheimer's disease is obtaining large and high-quality datasets, which can be difficult to come by. Furthermore, complicated machine learning models may not be very interpretable, which makes it challenging to comprehend the underlying principles guiding predictions (Fisher et al., 2019).

Bron et.al to evaluate the generalizability of MRI-based methods for diagnosing and predicting Alzheimer's disease across different cohorts, a wide range of MRI data were gathered. In order to test the performance and robustness of deep learning and traditional machine learning algorithms across various datasets and gauge their suitability for diagnosis and prediction across various populations, the algorithms were trained on one cohort and tested on other cohorts. A few drawbacks include the possibility of variability in data quality between cohorts, which can affect the generalizability of the model, and MRI acquisition protocols. The possibility of cohort-specific biases, which could impair machine learning models' performance and prevent them from generalizing to a variety of populations, is another difficulty (Bron et al., 2021).

Franzmeier et.al to develop a predictive tool for sporadic Alzheimer's disease, this article takes a different approach that includes data integration, feature engineering, model training, and evaluation. Furthermore, the difficulty in acquiring thorough hereditary Alzheimer's data may limit the model's ability to forecast the sporadic progression of Alzheimer's disease (Franzmeier et al., 2020).

Kavitha et.al suggested a machine learning model to predict early-stage Alzheimer's disease by identifying patterns and characteristics linked to the illness using clinical, genetic, and neuroimaging data. Obtaining large and diverse datasets for early-stage Alzheimer's prediction has a drawback that could restrict the generalizability of the model (Kavitha et al., 2022).

Leong et.al employed a process for utilizing machine learning tools, such as the Boruta feature selection algorithm, to evaluate the significance of different features and build Alzheimer's disease (AD) prediction models using pertinent data. The accuracy of AD prediction models may be impacted by the Boruta algorithm's inability to consistently identify the most clinically relevant features, despite its effectiveness in feature selection (Leong & Abdullah, 2019).

YİĞİT et.al entailed utilizing structural MRI data to train deep learning models for the purpose of predicting the stage of Alzheimer's disease. This process probably involved data preprocessing, model architecture design, and performance evaluation. The requirement for sizable, high-quality MRI datasets poses a possible disadvantage because it can be resource-intensive and restrict the applicability of the model (Yiğit & Işik, 2020).

Bari Antor et.al suggested a variety of datasets related to Alzheimer's disease and used a variety of machine learning techniques, including neural networks, decision trees, and support vector machines. The predictive accuracy of the algorithms was compared, and their applicability for Alzheimer's disease prediction was evaluated, using performance evaluation metrics. The need is that the models' ability to predict outcomes may be limited if the algorithms used fail to take into consideration the intricate and multifaceted nature of Alzheimer's disease (Bari Antor et al., 2021).

Neelaveni et.al with the help of this data, suggested machine learning algorithms—like decision trees and support vector machines—were trained to create predictive models for Alzheimer's disease. The effectiveness of the models was evaluated using cross-validation validation methods. Additionally, the difficulty in deciphering some machine learning algorithms' "black-box" nature restricts our ability to comprehend the variables influencing the prediction of Alzheimer's disease (Neelaveni & Devasana, 2020).

Yang et.al proposed deep learning model that was developed to estimate the likelihood of developing Alzheimer's disease. Preparing the data, designing the model architecture, and utilizing the right metrics to assess performance were probably all part of the process.Large amounts of labeled 18F-FDG PET data present a challenge because they can be hard to come by and may have an impact on the generalizability of the model (Yang & Liu, 2020).

Park et.al proposed combining DNA methylation and gene expression datasets, preprocessing the data, extracting features, and building a deep neural network model to forecast Alzheimer's disease. To improve predictive performance, feature engineering and extensive data integration were probably involved in the process. In multi-omics data integration, which can be difficult, it is necessary to address potential batch effects and platform differences in addition to requiring comprehensive and high-quality datasets (Park et al., 2020).

Wang et.al used approach in deep learning and knowledge graphs to predict drug-target interactions, with an emphasis on drug repositioning for Alzheimer's disease. To get accurate predictions, it probably involved building a knowledge graph, extracting features, and conditioning deep learning models. One possible limitation is the dependence on the completeness and quality of the knowledge graph data, which may affect the predictions of drug-target interactions and suggestions for drug repositioning in terms of their accuracy and applicability (Wang et al., 2022).

Grassi et.al suggested for gathering clinical data and creating a machine learning algorithm for predicting the conversion of Alzheimer's disease. In order to improve prediction capabilities, transfer learning—which uses knowledge from a related task or domain—was used to evaluate the algorithm's accuracy. The availability of pertinent and sufficiently large source datasets is critical to the success of transfer learning, but this is not always the case (Grassi et al., 2019).

Li,Habes et.al used in order to predict early Alzheimer's disease dementia, the employed methodology included preprocessing hippocampal MRI data, building a deep learning model, and training it using features from MRI scans. The effectiveness of the model was probably assessed using a variety of metrics and validation methods. A drawback of this method is that it is highly dependent on the availability and quality of MRI data, which may restrict its applicability and generalizability (Li et al., 2019).

Grueso et.al suggested as a means of forecasting the development of Alzheimer's disease dementia from mild cognitive impairment. The extraction of data, evaluation of quality, and synthesis of results were probably done to compile an overview of the field's current state. A limitation that makes it difficult to draw consistent conclusions and generalize findings is the variation in data sources and methodologies among the reviewed studies (Grueso & Viejo-Sobera, 2021).

Khan et.al used a method while carefully choosing training data to forecast Alzheimer's. This procedure probably involved finding pertinent source domains, extracting features, and fine-tuning the model. Selecting the most informative training data can be difficult and subjective, which could have an impact on the model's performance. Furthermore, transfer learning's applicability to different datasets is limited by how similar the source and target domains are to one another (Khan et al., 2019).

Sudharsan et.al suggest the principal component analysis was used to improve predictive models and reduce dimensionality, along with machine learning techniques and preprocessing data related to Alzheimer's disease. To increase the precision of the predictions, data features were converted. One possible disadvantage of principal component analysis is that it loses interpretability, which makes it difficult to comprehend the contributing factors to the prediction of Alzheimer's disease. Furthermore, the representativeness and quality of the input data have a major impact on the performance of the model (Sudharsan & Thailambal, 2021).

Chang et.al evaluating the potential of new biomarkers for Alzheimer's disease diagnosis. In order to increase the accuracy of the diagnosis, this procedure sought to find patterns and associations in the data. Lack of large and varied biomarker datasets, which can be difficult to find and could restrict how broadly the model can be applied. Furthermore, it might be more difficult to comprehend the biological mechanisms underlying the diagnosis due to the interpretability of machine learning models (Chang et al., 2021).

3. PROPOSED WORK

The severity of Alzheimer's disease worsens as it increases. Because of variations in the brain, specific proteins are deposited in the brain in this illness. Alzheimer's disease causes the brain to shrink and eventually die. Alzheimer's disease is not curable, but it does cause a person's memory, reasoning, conduct, and social skills to gradually degrade. These modifications have an effect on functioning. In the modern world, there are more cases of these illnesses. The primary cause of this condition is a prolonged period of improper blood flow to the brain. The early diagnosis of Alzheimer disease is the output of the Alzheimer disease prediction system, which uses data from the dataset that is thought to contain risk factors as inputs. The following highlights the primary contributions to this proposed research project:

- To select the most pertinent features using a feature selection method in order to prevent redundant data. The most significant k features are selected using the feature selection method, and the feature values are then scaled using a standard scaler.
- In this proposed method the Alzheimer disease is predicted with a feature emotion recognition.

In emotion recognition, the depression data is filtered and verified with oasis dataset.

- To use the oasis dataset, which has a large number of missing values, to train the model.
- We use Random Forest, XGBoost and Cross Validation algorithms are used for classifiers to predict Alzheimer Disease.

Dataset

The dataset used here is OASIS. The attribute in the dataset which is taken for the proposed algorithm is Age, M/F(Male/Female), MMSE(Mini mental State), CDR(Clinical Dementia Rating), SES(Social and Economic Status), eTiv(Total Incremental Value), nWBV(Normalized total brain volume), ASF(Atlas Scaling Factor). This attributes with emotion recognition details also combined to detect the early sign of Alzheimer disease.

Data Preprocessing

RE-based BiLSTM for missing data imputation This approach is vital for data analytics, where the quality of imputation holds significant importance. Given the era of big data, an immense amount of data is generated every second and is utilized for the analytics purpose for various domains like stakeholders, and several business decisions making applications. The occurrence of missing data makes the wrong decision making and degrades the performance. Therefore, achieving optimal performance requires precise data imputation. This research introduces a method for imputing missing data in large datasets using a BiLSTM model with a regression layer. The classifier, weights and biases are adjusted using the RE algorithm to minimize loss during the learning process. The incomplete input data is fed as input to the proposed system, in which the pre-processing based on normalization is performed to organize the data for easy execution further. Next, the normalized data is input into the BiLSTM model to impute missing data. To improve imputation accuracy and reduce training loss, the BiLSTM biases and weights are fine-tuned using the RE algorithm.

Figure 1 provides a visual representation of the proposed method.The following are the machine learning Algorithms used for prediction

- Random Forest
- XGBoost

This section discusses the contemporary classification algorithms which are implemented to decide the best algorithm to predict the Alzheimer disease accurately at the early stage.

The proposed architecture is discussed in Figure 2.

Proposed Algorithm

XGBOOST

XGBOOST Gradient boosting techniques are efficiently implemented with XGBoost. A mathematical breakthrough, however, has not been achieved. Gradient boosting is a well-built system that improves accuracy and optimizes performance. Tree learning algorithms are used along with linear models. Ensemble learning is enhanced with boosting. Boosting and Bagging are two ways to learn sequentially, e.g.: Random Forest. AI models can be displayed more effectively and accurately when assembled using the ensemble learning strategy. Consolidate the weak predictions from various weak learners into one, based on their standard number. Currently, their weak learners are created by applying basic Machine Learning algorithms to a variety of dataset distributions. The vast majority of the base AI computations

Figure 2. Architecture of proposed work

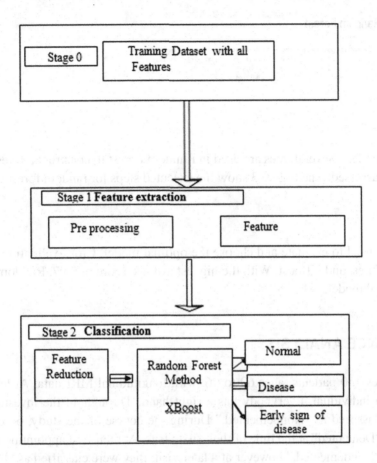

rely on decision trees. Consequently, with these base algorithms weak guidelines are produced with every iteration. So after many cycles, the weak learners are stabilized and the strong ones are formed so they can anticipate the result more precisely.

The most effective and fastest method it uses is gradient-boosted decision trees. In this case, D stands for the dataset, N for the quantity of training samples, and i is between 1 and n, {xi, yi} represents the ith training example.

Random Forest Algorithm

Random Forest Classification Unpruned classification-based trees comprise Random Forest. Due to its non-effectiveness against noise in the dataset and very low risk of overfitting, it gives astounding results in terms of solving a variety of real-life problems. This algorithm works faster than other tree-based algorithms and improves testing and validation data accuracy over many others. Individual decision trees are aggregated into random forests. When building a random tree, there are several ways to optimize its performance. Because it does not encounter the overfitting issue, a random forest model performs better than a decision tree model. Different decision trees, each entirely different from the others, make

Figure 3. Average score

Random Forest

```
In [71]:  score = cross_val_score(ensemble.RandomForestClassifier(random_state= 42),
                                   features, labels, cv= kf, scoring='accuracy')
          print(f'Scores for each fold are: {score}')
          print(f'Average score: {"{:.2f}".format(score.mean())}')
```

up random forest models. Several trees are used in Random Forest to construct a forest and each tree is then continuously assessed. The Figure 3 show the executed steps for random forest algorithm.

Cross Validation

Cross-validation is used to evaluate and choose the optimal model. Cross-validation is applied to two models: Random Forest and XBoost. With the highest average score of 0.97, Random Forest is chosen to construct the final model.

4. PERFORMANCE ANALYSIS

The dataset includes 150 patients, ages 60 to 96, with longitudinal MRI data. At least one scan was performed on each individual. Everybody has a right hand. Throughout the investigation, 72 of the individuals were classified as "Nondemented." During the course of the study, 64 of the individuals were classified as "Demented" at the time of their first visits. At their first appointment, 14 participants were classified as "Nondemented," however at a later visit, they were classified as "Demented." These are classified as "Converted."According to the figure 4 in the graph below, men are more likely than women to have dementia.

The following Figure 5 in graph indicates that the Nondemented group outperformed the Demented group on the Mini Mental State Examination (MMSE) by a significant margin. The most popular test for evaluating memory and other cognitive function issues is the MMSE. The MMSE has a range of values from 0 to The atlas scaling factor, the estimated total intracranial volume, the normalized whole brain volume, and the mini-mental state exam (MMSE) score are examples of clinical variables. 30, with scores of 25 or above often being regarded as normal. Severe impairment is typically indicated by a score of less than 10, and moderate dementia is indicated by a score between 10 and 20. Early-stage Alzheimer's patients typically have scores between 20 and 25. Figures 5-8 describe about ASF analysis, eTIV and nWBV analysis.

According to the chart, the brain volume ratio of the non-demented group is higher than that of the demented group. This is thought to be the result of diseases that cause the brain's tissue to shrink.

We have taken two approaches to addressing this problem. The first is to simply remove the rows that have null values. 'Imputation', or substituting the missing values with the corresponding values, is the other method. We believe that imputation would improve our model's performance because we only have 150 data points.

Figure 4. Gender and demented rate

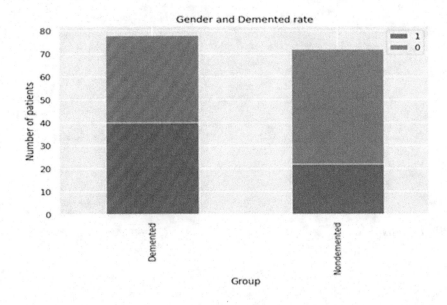

Figure 5. MMSE analysis

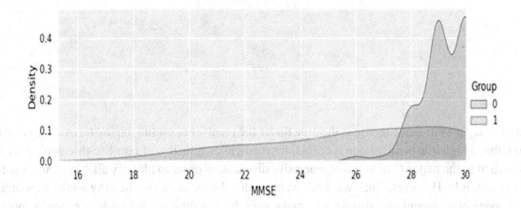

Figure 6. ASF analysis

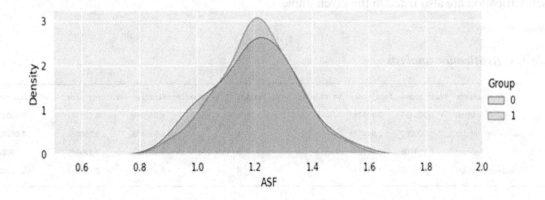

Figure 7. eTIV analysis

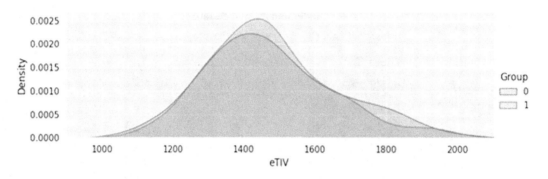

Figure 8. nWBV analysis

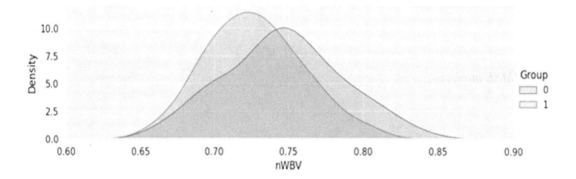

Our primary performance metric is the area under the receiver operating characteristic curve (AUC). We think that a high true positive rate is crucial for medical diagnostics of non-life-threatening terminal diseases, such as the majority of neurodegenerative diseases, in order to identify all Alzheimer's patients as soon as possible. However, since we don't want to mistakenly identify a healthy adult as mentally ill and start medical treatment, we also want to make sure that the false positive rate is as low as possible. Therefore, AUC appeared to be the perfect option for a performance metric. The following table 1 shows the different classifiers with training score and testing score. No of mis classification and percentage of misclassification are also listed in the given Table 1.

Table 1. Classification analysis

	Classifiers	Train score	Test score	No of Missclassification	% of Missclasification	Training time	Prediction time
0	Random forest	0.975410	0.910714	4	8.888889	0.025142	0.002500
1	Random forest with CV	1.000000	0.910714	4	8.888889	0.866884	0.062739
2	Xgboost	0.964406	0.872024	6	13.333333	0.123368	0.000881
3	Xgboost with CV	1.000000	0.910714	4	8.888889	0.420718	0.000897

Figure 9. Comparison analysis

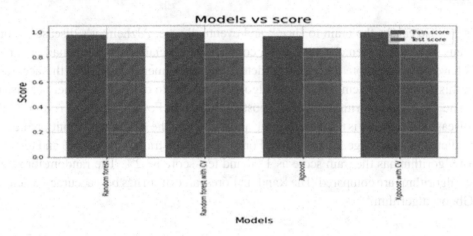

Figure 10. Confusion matrix

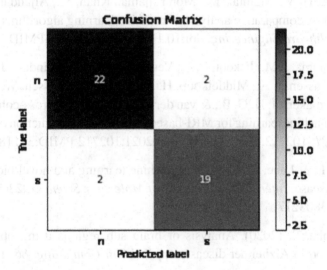

We suggested using a random forest approach to predict Alzheimer's disease in older adults early on. Next, a comparison is made between the random forest performance measures and those of XGBoost and XGBoost with CV. The comparative analysis shows that the proposed approach performs better than others approaches. Figure 9 shows comparison analysis of different algorithms.

Figure 9 shows the confusion matrix analysis for proposed work. In addition to offering scientific guidance (optimal subset) for clinical decision-making, the proposed interpretable framework helps achieve excellent performance in imbalanced AD multiclassification tasks, which facilitates disease management and generates new research ideas for optimizing AD prevention and treatment programs.

5. CONCLUSION

Alzheimer's disease causes the brain to shrink and eventually die. Alzheimer's disease is not curable, but it does cause a person's memory, reasoning, conduct, and social skills to gradually degrade. More researcher's have proposed more algorithm to detect the Alzheimer disease. But the accuracy rate is very less. In this proposed system an efficient algorithm is used to detect the Alzheimer disease in the early stage. The proposed algorithm uses XGBoost and Random Forest algorithm is used to detect the Alzheimer disease. The dataset is used for training and also using the emotion recognition the Alzheimer disease is predicted in early stage. The Random Forest Algorithm train score is 97% and test score 91%. The Xgboost algorithm has the train score as 1.00 and test score 87.2%. The random forest algorithm and XGboost algorithms are compared. The Random Forest algorithm has best accuracy when compared with the XGboost algorithm.

REFERENCES

Bari Antor, M., Jamil, A. H. M., Mamtaz, M., Monirujjaman Khan, M., Aljahdali, S., Kaur, M., Singh, P., & Masud, M. (2021). A comparative analysis of machine learning algorithms to predict alzheimer's disease. *Journal of Healthcare Engineering*. doi:10.1155/2021/9917919 PMID:34336171

Bron, E. E., Klein, S., Papma, J. M., Jiskoot, L. C., Venkatraghavan, V., Linders, J., Aalten, P., De Deyn, P. P., Biessels, G. J., Claassen, J. A., Middelkoop, H. A., Smits, M., Niessen, W. J., van Swieten, J. C., van der Flier, W. M., Ramakers, I. H. G. B., & van der Lugt, A. (2021). Cross-cohort generalizability of deep and conventional machine learning for MRI-based diagnosis and prediction of Alzheimer's disease. *NeuroImage. Clinical*, *31*, 102712. doi:10.1016/j.nicl.2021.102712 PMID:34118592

Chang, C. H., Lin, C. H., & Lane, H. Y. (2021). Machine learning and novel biomarkers for the diagnosis of Alzheimer's disease. *International Journal of Molecular Sciences*, *22*(5), 2761. doi:10.3390/ijms22052761 PMID:33803217

Chitradevi, D., & Prabha, S. (2020). Analysis of brain sub regions using optimization techniques and deep learning method in Alzheimer disease. *Applied Soft Computing*, *86*, 105857. doi:10.1016/j.asoc.2019.105857

Ding, Y., Sohn, J. H., Kawczynski, M. G., Trivedi, H., Harnish, R., Jenkins, N. W., Lituiev, D., Copeland, T. P., Aboian, M. S., Mari Aparici, C., Behr, S. C., Flavell, R. R., Huang, S.-Y., Zalocusky, K. A., Nardo, L., Seo, Y., Hawkins, R. A., Hernandez Pampaloni, M., Hadley, D., & Franc, B. L. (2019). A deep learning model to predict a diagnosis of Alzheimer disease by using 18F-FDG PET of the brain. *Radiology*, *290*(2), 456–464. doi:10.1148/radiol.2018180958 PMID:30398430

Fisher, C. K., Smith, A. M., Walsh, J. R., Simon, A. J., Edgar, C., Jack, C. R., Holtzman, D., Russell, D., Hill, D., Grosset, D., Wood, F., Vanderstichele, H., Morris, J., Blennow, K., Marek, K., Shaw, L. M., Albert, M., Weiner, M., Fox, N., ... Kubick, W. (2019). Machine learning for comprehensive forecasting of Alzheimer's Disease progression. *Scientific Reports*, *9*(1), 13622. doi:10.103841598-019-49656-2 PMID:31541187

Franzmeier, N., Koutsouleris, N., Benzinger, T., Goate, A., Karch, C. M., Fagan, A. M., McDade, E., Duering, M., Dichgans, M., Levin, J., Gordon, B. A., Lim, Y. Y., Masters, C. L., Rossor, M., Fox, N. C., O'Connor, A., Chhatwal, J., Salloway, S., Danek, A., ... Ewers, M. (2020). Predicting sporadic Alzheimer's disease progression via inherited Alzheimer's disease-informed machine-learning. *Alzheimer's & Dementia*, *16*(3), 501–511. doi:10.1002/alz.12032 PMID:32043733

Grassi, M., Loewenstein, D. A., Caldirola, D., Schruers, K., Duara, R., & Perna, G. (2019). A clinically-translatable machine learning algorithm for the prediction of Alzheimer's disease conversion: Further evidence of its accuracy via a transfer learning approach. *International Psychogeriatrics*, *31*(7), 937–945. doi:10.1017/S1041610218001618 PMID:30426918

Grueso, S., & Viejo-Sobera, R. (2021). Machine learning methods for predicting progression from mild cognitive impairment to Alzheimer's disease dementia: A systematic review. *Alzheimer's Research & Therapy*, *13*(1), 1–29. doi:10.118613195-021-00900-w PMID:34583745

Jain, R., Jain, N., Aggarwal, A., & Hemanth, D. J. (2019). Convolutional neural network based Alzheimer's disease classification from magnetic resonance brain images. *Cognitive Systems Research*, *57*, 147–159. doi:10.1016/j.cogsys.2018.12.015

Kavitha, C., Mani, V., Srividhya, S. R., Khalaf, O. I., & Tavera Romero, C. A. (2022). Early-stage Alzheimer's disease prediction using machine learning models. *Frontiers in Public Health*, *10*, 853294. doi:10.3389/fpubh.2022.853294 PMID:35309200

Khan, N. M., Abraham, N., & Hon, M. (2019). Transfer learning with intelligent training data selection for prediction of Alzheimer's disease. *IEEE Access : Practical Innovations, Open Solutions*, *7*, 72726–72735. doi:10.1109/ACCESS.2019.2920448

Kumari, R., Nigam, A., & Pushkar, S. (2020). Machine learning technique for early detection of Alzheimer's disease. *Microsystem Technologies*, *26*(12), 3935–3944. doi:10.100700542-020-04888-5

Kundaram, S. S., & Pathak, K. C. (2021). Deep learning-based Alzheimer disease detection. In *Proceedings of the Fourth International Conference on Microelectronics, Computing and Communication Systems: MCCS 2019* (pp. 587-597). Springer Singapore.

Lee, J., Meijer, E., Langa, K. M., Ganguli, M., Varghese, M., Banerjee, J., Khobragade, P., Angrisani, M., Kurup, R., Chakrabarti, S. S., Gambhir, I. S., Koul, P. A., Goswami, D., Talukdar, A., Mohanty, R. R., Yadati, R. S., Padmaja, M., Sankhe, L., Rajguru, C., ... Dey, A. B. (2023). Prevalence of dementia in India: National and state estimates from a nationwide study. *Alzheimer's & Dementia*, *19*(7), 2898–2912. doi:10.1002/alz.12928 PMID:36637034

Leong, L. K., & Abdullah, A. A. (2019, November). Prediction of Alzheimer's disease (AD) using machine learning techniques with Boruta algorithm as feature selection method. *Journal of Physics: Conference Series*, *1372*(1), 012065. doi:10.1088/1742-6596/1372/1/012065

Li, H., Habes, M., Wolk, D. A., & Fan, Y. (2019). A deep learning model for early prediction of Alzheimer's disease dementia based on hippocampal magnetic resonance imaging data. *Alzheimer's & Dementia*, *15*(8), 1059–1070. doi:10.1016/j.jalz.2019.02.007 PMID:31201098

Nawaz, H., Maqsood, M., Afzal, S., Aadil, F., Mehmood, I., & Rho, S. (2021). A deep feature-based real-time system for Alzheimer disease stage detection. *Multimedia Tools and Applications*, *80*(28-29), 35789–35807. doi:10.100711042-020-09087-y

Neelaveni, J., & Devasana, M. G. (2020, March). Alzheimer disease prediction using machine learning algorithms. In *2020 6th international conference on advanced computing and communication systems (ICACCS)* (pp. 101-104). IEEE. 10.1109/ICACCS48705.2020.9074248

Odusami, M., Maskeliūnas, R., Damaševičius, R., & Krilavičius, T. (2021). Analysis of features of Alzheimer's disease: Detection of early stage from functional brain changes in magnetic resonance images using a finetuned ResNet18 network. *Diagnostics (Basel)*, *11*(6), 1071. doi:10.3390/diagnostics11061071 PMID:34200832

Park, C., Ha, J., & Park, S. (2020). Prediction of Alzheimer's disease based on deep neural network by integrating gene expression and DNA methylation dataset. *Expert Systems with Applications*, *140*, 112873. doi:10.1016/j.eswa.2019.112873

Sudharsan, M., & Thailambal, G. (2021). Alzheimer's disease prediction using machine learning techniques and principal component analysis (PCA). *Materials Today: Proceedings*.

Venugopalan, J., Tong, L., Hassanzadeh, H. R., & Wang, M. D. (2021). Multimodal deep learning models for early detection of Alzheimer's disease stage. *Scientific Reports*, *11*(1), 3254. doi:10.103841598-020-74399-w PMID:33547343

Wang, S., Du, Z., Ding, M., Rodriguez-Paton, A., & Song, T. (2022). KG-DTI: A knowledge graph based deep learning method for drug-target interaction predictions and Alzheimer's disease drug repositions. *Applied Intelligence*, *52*(1), 846–857. doi:10.100710489-021-02454-8 PMID:34764597

Yang, Z., & Liu, Z. (2020). The risk prediction of Alzheimer's disease based on the deep learning model of brain 18F-FDG positron emission tomography. *Saudi Journal of Biological Sciences*, *27*(2), 659–665. doi:10.1016/j.sjbs.2019.12.004 PMID:32210685

Yiğit, A., & Işik, Z. (2020). Applying deep learning models to structural MRI for stage prediction of Alzheimer's disease. *Turkish Journal of Electrical Engineering and Computer Sciences*, *28*(1), 196–210. doi:10.3906/elk-1904-172

Chapter 10
Malware Analysis and Classification Using Machine Learning Models

Swadeep Swadeep
Vellore Institute of Technology, Chennai, India

Karmel Arockiasamy
Vellore Institute of Technology, Chennai, India

Karthika Perumal
Vellore Institute of Technology, Chennai, India

ABSTRACT

In modern times, it has become common practice for major corporations to utilize computers for storing data. Unfortunately, the frequency of malware attacks has increased, which facilitates unauthorized individuals' access to private information. Analyzing malware has become a critical task in safeguarding information systems against malicious attacks. Therefore, machine learning techniques have become an effective tool for automating investigations using static and dynamic analysis, combining malware with similar behavior into separate families based on proximity. Deep learning techniques improve the accuracy of malware variant detection and classification by building neural networks with more potentially different layers. This research aims to address this issue by training machine learning models using various algorithms on a dataset obtained by performing static and dynamic analysis on both malicious and benign samples. The resulting models were then combined to produce superior results compared to those obtained from a single model, which can be seen in the results.

1. INTRODUCTION

The current world heavily depends on computers and a microprocessor or a microcontroller can be found in all appliances today. This computing power is being used in all industries and is connected to the

DOI: 10.4018/978-1-6684-8531-6.ch010

Copyright © 2024, IGI Global. Copying or distributing in print or electronic forms without written permission of IGI Global is prohibited.

world with the help of the internet. People are becoming more dependent on these systems to increase their productivity. But these vast amounts of systems also produce vast amounts of data and use vast amounts of computing resources. To gain access to these resources and the vast amounts of data, people try to infect the host computer with malicious software, also known as malware, which can be used for financial gains. Malware is created to cause harm to systems or networks and gain access to these systems even when they're not authorized.

2. LITERATURE SURVEY

In Akbar et al. (2021), various machine learning models have been used to classify APTs by converting the APT traces into a graph. Their work mainly focuses on identifying different tactics of Advanced Persistent Threats based on logs from executing MITRE ATT&CK framework, which is then reduced to make it noise-free, which also yields limited attack traces for identification. It was seen that SetConv, A New Approach for Learning from Imbalanced Data, gave the best accuracy metrics.

The main study of Rath et al. (2022) is to find the current trends and applications to achieve organization-level cyber security with the help of AI. This paper also talks about the various cyber threats such as viruses, worms, rootkits, botnets, etc. It also talks about the drawbacks of AI systems in cyber security such as the accumulation of data. They also had to gather large amounts of malicious codes, non-malicious codes, and various abnormalities to create a model which can be used at an organizational level. Using hypothesis testing, they concluded that the use of up-to-date preventive antivirus and anti-cyber protection software is a nice remedy for updated cybercrime and control. Cybenko & Hallman (2021) studies the various advantages that machine learning, game theory, and secure distributed computing offer for current technology such as IoT, unmanned autonomous vehicles, etc. They also look at adaptive cyber defense where the cyber defense techniques adapt to the changes of the attacker and the operating environment (such as reconfiguration). Here, the problem of improving performance while interacting with the real environment is studied with the help of distributed upper-confidence bound algorithm. Byzantine Fault tolerance and blockchain technologies are used in a distributed adaptive cyber-defensive system to make the systems robust under untrusted agent operations.

In Hota & Hota (2022), the trend of open banking is studied in recent years, and the various threats to open banking are discussed. Security in open banking is an important aspect, especially with the rise of open banking since the covid outbreak. According to their studies, 48% of the customers want the banks to provide product information based on their actions. It can be seen that data breaches and human error are the two primary risks associated with open banking. This paper also studies the risks faced in digital transactions and open banking. The evolution of advanced persistent threats increases the difficulty of detecting cyber-attack campaigns and hence Zou et al. (2020) studies various approaches to help detect such attacks. The common characteristics of APT attack campaigns are analyzed by studying past campaigns and looking at the impact they caused. Current methods to detect APTs are studied. It was seen that existing approaches were based on unsupervised connecting the dots through provenance tracking across multiple events that look safe singularly but malicious when together and have a drawback of dependence-explosion. A top-down approach can take advantage of known APTs and solve the problem of dependence explosion and an approach to this was modeled.

In Costales et al. (2020), a live attack on deep learning systems was proposed which patches the parameters of the model to achieve pre-defined malicious behavior on a specific set of inputs. The feasibility of this attack was demonstrated on various deep learning models. It was seen that the desired Trojan behavior could be achieved with a few small patches and with limited access to training data. Details on how this attack can be carried out in real systems are provided and a technique to bypass the STRIP defense method is provided to showcase the devastating potential of patches. In Tiwari & Srivastava (2022), the current state of cybercrime in India and its impact on women and children is studied. Here, the trend of cybercrimes from 2017-19 in India is studied to understand the scenario of various cybercrimes such as cyber blackmailing, fake profiling, cyber stalking, etc. The research methodology employs a qualitative approach to compile comparable data on cybercrime and computer crime activities across the different states of India. The various threats against women and children were studied and the results showed which states had which problems. From the results, it was seen that in Maharashtra, the cybercrimes committed towards children were the maximum.

SDN is a new network paradigm that isolates the network control frame from the data plane. This allows network programmability but it also gives rise to various security threats. Cherukuri & Sinha (2022) gives a review of the various security threats of SDNs and their mitigation strategies. It was seen that SDNs are susceptible to implementation attacks, enforcement attacks, and policy attacks. It is also susceptible to various security threats such as Link Flooding attacks, DDoS, Packet Injection, Topology poisoning, and Wormhole attacks. The mitigation techniques for the above attacks are also studied. In Gao & Nepal (2020), an overview of backdoor attacks on deep neural networks is given and a methodology to prevent these background attacks is studied. It is seen that the backdoor models behave incorrectly when the input contains a trigger that fires the backdoor to hijack the model. Scenarios in which backdoor attacks can be used to compromise the system are studied to show that backdoor attacks are a real threat. In this paper, an easy-to-deploy defense is also studied and analyzed which works with various input types.

Garg & Baliyan (2020) presents various insights on the role of machine learning in handling cyberattacks and cyber threats. Their main focus is on the Android OS which is highly vulnerable according. It talks about the various ML techniques available in the market and it also studies various vulnerabilities, their trends, and their impact to segregate the most vulnerable attacks. The vulnerabilities were found through the CVE database. From the paper, it was seen that attacks such as DoS, code execution, overflow, etc. are the most severe attacks on android devices. In Dutta & Kant (2020), a new approach to integrating artificial intelligence and machine learning with cyber threat intelligence for the collection of actionable threat intelligence from various sources is studied. The importance of threat intelligence in the aspect of cyber security is also studied. A model for generating actionable threat intelligence implementing a supervised machine learning approach employing a Naïve Bayes classifier is also discussed.

In Sarabi et al. (2021), the drawbacks of currently used network scanning are studied, and seen that exhaustive scanning is time-consuming and out of a large number of IP addresses and ports scanned, the majority of them are unanswered as they are inactive. To solve the above drawback, a new framework has been studied which uses machine learning to predict if a host will respond to probes on different ports. From applying this technique on the ports, it was seen that bandwidth was saved from 26.7%-72% while achieving a 90%-99% true positive rate.

In Iyer & Rajagopal (2020), Subashini et al. (2020), and Thomas et al. (2020), a study on the implementation of intelligent algorithms such as machine learning techniques, and deep learning algorithms for solving cyber security problems such as network and information security, secure communication, intrusion detection, etc. are studied and analyzed. It was seen that the use of these intelligent algorithms helps in improving the performance of security, threat detection, throughput, and vulnerability detection.

Through the study, it was also seen that these algorithms are utilized in various places to solve a wide variety of cyber security problems. The various software vulnerabilities such as race conditions, SQL injection, etc., are discussed and their detection process is analyzed. The challenges in machine learning are also studied such as large data size, multi-dimensional data, skewed distribution of data, computing speed, and cost associated with it.

In Palša et al. (2022), malware and benign files are collected and analyzed using XGBoost and randomized tree algorithms. The malware files are downloaded from virus share and various benign files are taken from portable freeware. Static and dynamic analysis of the files were done using dependency walker and its output was processed into a dataset that had a list of imported and exported functions of various modules. Dynamic analysis was also performed to get the behavior of the files when executed, in a secure environment detached from the main network. This was done using Cuckoo sandbox and the output from this analysis was extracted as features for the dataset. Finally, both the static analysis and dynamic analysis results were taken to find if the file is malicious or not. The paper Gibert et al. (2020) is a survey paper that talks about various research papers in malware analysis and the methods used by them. The various tools that are available for static and dynamic analysis and what the tool can be used for are also studied and hence gives an insight into the various methods available to get data from the static and dynamic analysis, the various machine learning algorithms used for detection and classification of malware and most importantly it studies the recent trends in malware analysis and sees where there has been development in this field.

3. PROPOSED WORK

Malware is a growing threat to individuals, organizations and governments worldwide. With the increasing use of technology in our daily lives and the growing sophistication of cybercriminals, the threat of malware is becoming more prevalent. Malware can take many forms, including viruses, worms, Trojans, ransom ware and spyware. It can cause significant harm by stealing sensitive information, disrupting operations and causing financial loss. They are becoming increasingly sophisticated and difficult to detect. There were more than 2.8 billion malware attacks worldwide in the first half of 2022 and more than 2,70,000 malware variants were seen in the first half of 2022 alone which was an increase of 45% from last year. Since the dependency and usage of computers in increasing vastly, malicious users are also working hard to get unauthorized access to our systems and creating new malware at an alarming rate. Hence, it is very important to analyse these files before running them on a system, or else the system might be under the control of the malicious user. The existing malware is also being modified so that it can evade firewalls and antivirus software. Manual analysis of malware consumes a lot of time and the code is obfuscated which makes the analysis take a long time. The internet is filled with malicious content. The rise of torrents and other pirated sites have huge amounts of malicious files which vary a lot and many of the malware present on the sites are modified or new, hence evading the antivirus software.

By using various static and dynamic analysis methods and training various models using various parameters, such as using a binary image of the malicious file for a model, using the function calls as parameters for another model, etc., and creating a vast ensemble of these models can help in detecting malware easily. The lack of proper soft wares to avoid malicious files to run in a system can five rise to vast problems and thus urgent action has to be taken to address the problem of the spread of malware. The government has already taken action by spreading information about how malwares are spread and why everyone has to avoid fishy sites and mails, but still people are prone to these sites and mails. Corporations have also taken lots of action to avoid data breach and unauthorized access to their systems by placing various firewalls and keeping information sessions on avoiding phishing mails, but still it is seen that data breaches in corporations are very common, showing the improvements which can be done in this field.

The spread of malware threats has become a serious challenge to cyber security in recent years. With new malware samples emerging daily, it is crucial to develop effective malware analysis and classification techniques to identify, isolate, and mitigate these threats. In this proposed work, we aim to explore various techniques for malware analysis and classification, including both static and dynamic analysis methods (hybrid analysis), machine learning, and sandboxing. The primary objective of this proposed work is to develop robust and efficient strategies for identifying and mitigating the threat of malware, particularly in real-world scenarios. By combining various malware analysis techniques and leveraging machine learning to develop a more comprehensive understanding of the malware landscape, detect new and emerging threats more quickly, and develop effective mitigation strategies to protect against them. Overall, this proposed work aims to contribute to the advancement of the field of cyber security by improving the ability to detect and mitigate malware threats. The spread of malware files has increased many folds and it is very important to apply new techniques to protect the systems from this software with ill intentions. The main goal of this research is to come up with a model that will detect if the file is malicious or not. It is then classified into its family type based on the features of the file.

To get started, various malicious executable files (PE files) are downloaded with the help of VirusShare which is a repository of malicious files, and benign files are downloaded with the help of Executable binaries found online for downloads. This is a crucial step to create the dataset to be used for creating the machine learning models. After getting the binary files, the first step is to create a dataset to implement the machine learning models. The first dataset which will be created is the image dataset by reading the binary file and converting it into an image with respect to the binary input stream. This dataset can be labelled with the help of the hash values associated with the binary file and VirusTotal which gives insight about already reported malwares. A normal CNN and VGG are applied on this dataset to classify malwares into their families. It can be seen that the same families of malware have similar images which is helpful in sorting the malwares into their families.

Another dataset which can be generated is the static analysis data which is the imported functions in the PE extracted from Cuckoo Sandbox reports. This dataset can be generated from other tools such as PE file in python or PEstudio but since Cuckoo is going to be used for dynamic analysis results, the static analysis data can be taken from here itself. Here, the 1000 most imported functions are taken as columns and it is seen if the function is imported in the file or not. Another dataset to be generated is the PE Section Headers which can be extracted from Cuckoo Sandbox again. This gives us information about the entropy of the file, which is a measure of the randomness or uncertainty in the data. It is calculated by analysing the distribution of byte values in the file, and can be used as an indicator of whether the file is compressed, encrypted, or obfuscated in some way.

The last dataset to be generated is the API call sequence which is produced during the execution of the binary in a sandboxed environment. It is very important that the binary runs in a sandboxed environment as it is malicious in nature. This is done with the help of cuckoo sandbox which helps in running the binary executable in an isolated environment, keeping the host system safe. The proposed flow can be understood through the architecture diagram seen in Figure 1.

Figure 1. Architectural design of the malware analysis

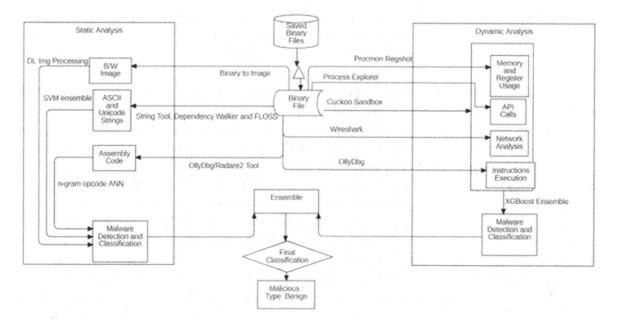

3.1 Static Analysis

Static malware analysis is a technique used to examine the code of malicious software without running it. This method is essential in identifying the behavior of a malware and understanding how it operates. Static analysis is performed using various tools that analyze the file structure, function calls, API interactions, and other relevant characteristics of a malware. Static malware analysis played a crucial role in this project by enabling the analysis of malware and the creation of a dataset for machine learning models. This method involves extracting various features from the header, optional header, and different sections of the Portable Executable (PE) format used by Microsoft Windows executable and Dynamic Link Libraries (DLLs). DLLs provide essential linkage and execution information of code when loaded into Windows and are also used to analyze imported libraries and the types of linkage used in the execution of executable files. PE files contain a header and sections, with the header including various feature groups such as DOS, PE, Optional, and Sections Table, while the sections contain features like Code, Imports, and Data.

3.2 Dynamic Analysis

Another important module of this project is the dynamic analysis of the binary files. For conducting dynamic analysis, Cuckoo sandbox was used. Cuckoo Sandbox is a dynamic analysis tool for malware, to extract behaviors during runtime execution. The primary purpose was to isolate the actual system from the testing environment and obtain necessary information about the malware execution. Cuckoo Sandbox generates a report that provides a summarized overview of the malware's execution. This report consists of several sections, each dealing with different information. Multiple features from the Cuckoo Sandbox report, including summary information, files, API calls during execution, registry keys, IP addresses and DNS queries, and access URLs can be extracted and used to create a dataset.

3.3 Machine Learning Models

KNN is a type of supervised learning algorithm that is used for classification and regression. In the context of malware analysis, KNN has been used to classify malware samples based on various features such as system calls, API calls, and binary code. The KNN algorithm works by calculating the distance between the input data point and all the data points in the training dataset. The KNN algorithm then selects the K-nearest neighbors to the input data point based on their distances and assigns the input data point to the class that has the majority of the K-nearest neighbors. One of the advantages of KNN is that it is a simple and intuitive algorithm that can be easily implemented. However, KNN can be sensitive to the choice of distance metric and the value of K, and may not work well with high-dimensional data.

MLP is a type of supervised learning algorithm that is used for classification and regression. In the context of malware analysis, MLP has been used to classify malware samples based on various features such as system calls, API calls, and binary code. The MLP algorithm works by creating a network of nodes, where each node is connected to other nodes in the network. The MLP algorithm consists of an input layer, one or more hidden layers, and an output layer. CNN is a type of neural network that is designed to handle and extract features from images or other types of data that have a spatial or temporal relationship. In the context of malware analysis, CNN can be used to extract features from the binary code of the malware samples and classify them based on these features. To apply CNN on the malware dataset, the first step is to convert the binary code of the malware samples into a format that can be used as input to the CNN model.

LSTM (Long Short-Term Memory) is a type of recurrent neural network that is widely used in natural language processing, speech recognition, and other sequence-based tasks. LSTM has also been applied to the field of malware analysis and classification, particularly in the analysis of dynamic behavior of malware samples. To use LSTM for malware classification, the system calls made by the malware sample are first preprocessed and converted into a numerical format.

3.4 Ensemble

Creating an ensemble of models is a powerful technique used in machine learning to improve the accuracy and reliability of predictions. The main idea behind an ensemble is to combine the predictions of multiple models, each with different strengths and weaknesses, to produce a more accurate and robust prediction. Ensemble methods are commonly used in machine learning and there are several ways to create an ensemble of models, each with its own advantages and disadvantages. One of the most popular techniques is bagging, which involves training multiple models on different subsets of the training data and then combining their predictions by taking the average or majority vote. This technique can help to reduce over fitting and improve the stability of predictions. Another popular ensemble method is boosting, which involves training multiple weak models in sequence, with each model focusing on the training examples that were misclassified by the previous models. The final prediction is then made by combining the predictions of all the models. Stacking can be particularly useful when the models have complementary strengths and weaknesses. The flow can be seen in Figure 3.

Figure 2. Final model architecture

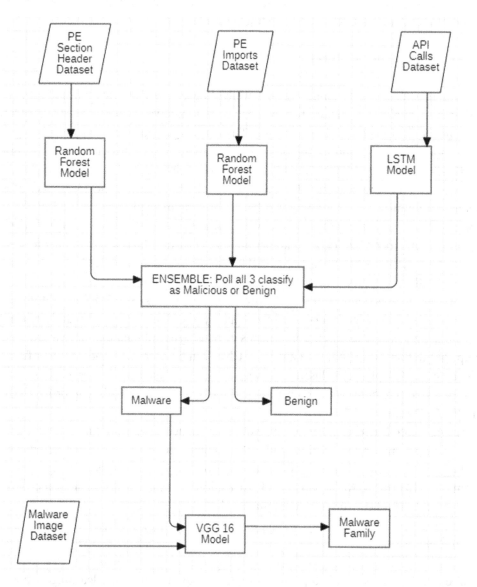

4. RESULTS AND DISCUSSIONS

4.1 Experimental setup

To protect the host system, first install VMWare and start a Virtual Machine which is isolated from the host system. Install Python and any required packages and libraries for the experiment in the VM. Prepare the dataset for the experiment and load it into memory. Split the dataset into training and testing sets using a suitable ratio. Train the various models on the training set and validate it on the testing set. Evaluate the performance of the model based on suitable metrics such as accuracy, precision, recall, and F1-score. Create the ensemble model by combining the prediction of all the various models.

4.2 Image Dataset

Figure 3. Confusion matrix for CNN [Accuracy: 1; F1 Score: 1]

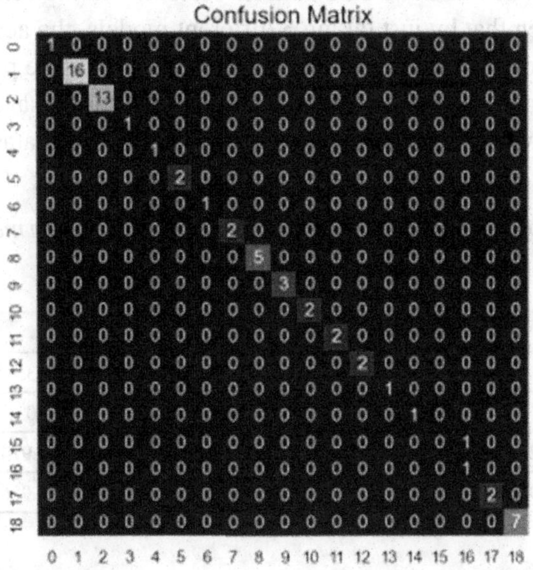

Figure 4. Confusion matrix for VGG16 [Accuracy: 0.96875; F1 Score: 0.933622]

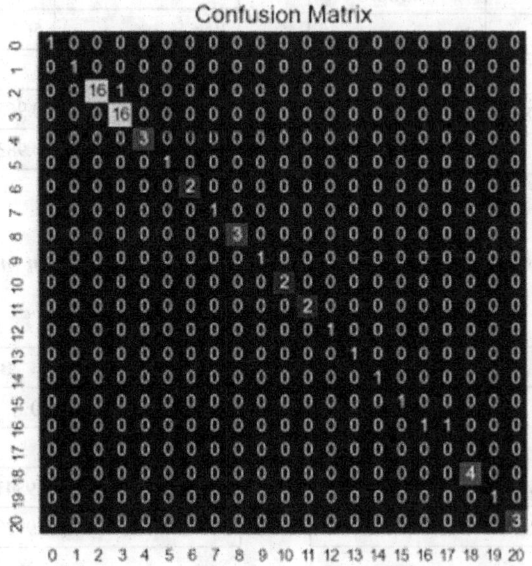

5. CONCLUSION AND FUTURE WORK

This research proposed a new method to classify malware by collecting various datasets of a malware with different properties each and using the best model for each dataset in the final dataset to create the best possible model. This work was done on a smaller scale due to the lack of resources. Even on the smaller scale, it could be seen that by just taking 3 different models, the accuracy and the f1 score was great for the combined model which will be a helpful start for the future projects. The model used for classifying the malwares also gave good results. In conclusion, it can be said that the mixture of various models on various datasets will give better results than just taking one dataset for malwares.

Table 1. Confusion matrix of random forest for PE function imports dataset

	Benign	Malware
Benign	89	64
Malware	20	4359
Accuracy	0.9823455233291298	
F1 Score	0.9908316961362148	

Table 2. Confusion matrix of KNN for PE function imports dataset

	Benign	Malware
Benign	135	64
Malware	20	4359
Accuracy	0.974989491382934	
F1 Score	0.9868783768883008	

Table 3. Confusion matrix of random forest for PE section header dataset

	Benign	Malware
Benign	77	78
Malware	31	4144
Accuracy	0.9748267898383371	
F1 Score	0.9870191735143503	

Table 4. Confusion matrix of KNN for PE section header dataset

	Benign	Malware
Benign	56	99
Malware	37	4138
Accuracy	0.9685912240184757	
F1 Score	0.9838326200665716	

Table 5. Confusion matrix of MLP for API calls dataset

	Benign	Malware
Benign	60	49
Malware	6	4273
Accuracy:	0.9874658158614403	
F1 Score:	0.993605394721544	

Table 6. Confusion matrix of LSTM for API calls dataset

	Benign	Malware
Benign	50	59
Malware	8	4271
Accuracy	0.9847310847766636	
F1 Score	0.9922174468579393	

Table 7. Confusion matrix of mixed model on complete dataset

	Benign	Malware
Benign	167	34
Malware	0	7794
Accuracy	0.9957473420888056	
F1 Score	0.9978235821277686	

Table 8. Summary of the research work done

Model (Dataset)	Accuracy	F1 Score
Random Forest (PE Function Imports)	0. 98234	0. 99083
KNN (PE Function Imports)	0.97498	0.98687
Random Forest (PE Section Header)	0.97482	0.98701
KNN (PE Section Header)	0.96859	0.98383
MLP (API Calls)	0.98746	0.99360
LSTM (API Calls)	0.98473	0.99221
Ensemble Model (Combined)	0.99574	0.99782
CNN (Image)	1	1
VGG16 (Image)	0.96875	0.93362

REFERENCES

Akbar, K. A., Wang, Y., Islam, M. S., Singhal, A., Khan, L., & Thuraisingham, B. (2021, December). Identifying Tactics of Advanced Persistent Threats with Limited Attack Traces. In *International Conference on Information Systems Security* (pp. 3-25). Springer. 10.1007/978-3-030-92571-0_1

Cherukuri, A. K. A., & Sinha, S. (2022). Analysis and Mitigation Strategies of Security Issues of Software-Defined Networks. *Cross-Industry Applications of Cyber Security Frameworks*, 36-70.

Costales, R., Mao, C., Norwitz, R., Kim, B., & Yang, J. (2020). Live trojan attacks on deep neural networks. In *Proceedings of the IEEE/CVF Conference on Computer Vision and Pattern Recognition Workshops* (pp. 796-797). 10.1109/CVPRW50498.2020.00406

Cybenko, G., & Hallman, R. (2021). Resilient Distributed Adaptive Cyber-Defense Using Blockchain. *Game Theory and Machine Learning for Cyber Security*, 485-498.

Dutta, A., & Kant, S. (2020, December). An overview of cyber threat intelligence platform and role of artificial intelligence and machine learning. In *International Conference on Information Systems Security* (pp. 81-86). Springer. 10.1007/978-3-030-65610-2_5

Gao, Y., & Nepal, S. (2020, December). A Defence Against Input-Agnostic Backdoor Attacks on Deep Neural Networks. In *International Conference on Information Systems Security* (pp. 69-80). Springer. 10.1007/978-3-030-65610-2_4

Garg, S., & Baliyan, N. (2020, December). Machine learning based android vulnerability detection: A roadmap. In *International Conference on Information Systems Security* (pp. 87-93). Springer. 10.1007/978-3-030-65610-2_6

Gibert, D., Mateu, C., & Planes, J. (2020). The rise of machine learning for detection and classification of malware: Research developments, trends and challenges. *Journal of Network and Computer Applications*, *153*, 102526. doi:10.1016/j.jnca.2019.102526

Hota, L., & Hota, D. C. (2022). Cyber Security at the Heart of Open Banking: An Existing and Futuristic Approach. In Cross-Industry Applications of Cyber Security Frameworks (pp. 182-201). IGI Global.

Iyer, S. S., & Rajagopal, S. (2020). Applications of machine learning in cyber security domain. In *Handbook of Research on Machine and Deep Learning Applications for Cyber Security* (pp. 64–82). IGI Global. doi:10.4018/978-1-5225-9611-0.ch004

Palša, J., Ádám, N., Hurtuk, J., Chovancová, E., Madoš, B., Chovanec, M., & Kocan, S. (2022). MLMD—A Malware-Detecting Antivirus Tool Based on the XGBoost Machine Learning Algorithm. *Applied Sciences (Basel, Switzerland)*, *12*(13), 6672. doi:10.3390/app12136672

Rath, R. C., Baral, S. K., & Goel, R. (2022). Role of Artificial Intelligence on Cybersecurity and Its Control. In *Cross-Industry Applications of Cyber Security Frameworks* (pp. 15–35). IGI Global. doi:10.4018/978-1-6684-3448-2.ch002

Sarabi, A., Jin, K., & Liu, M. (2021). Smart Internet Probing: Scanning Using Adaptive Machine Learning. *Game Theory and Machine Learning for Cyber Security*, 411-437.

Subashini, P., Krishnaveni, M., Dhivyaprabha, T. T., & Shanmugavalli, R. (2020). Review on intelligent algorithms for cyber security. In *Handbook of Research on Machine and Deep Learning Applications for Cyber Security* (pp. 1–22). IGI Global. doi:10.4018/978-1-5225-9611-0.ch001

Thomas, T. P., Vijayaraghavan, A., & Emmanuel, S. (2020). Machine learning and cybersecurity. In *Machine Learning Approaches in Cyber Security Analytics* (pp. 37–47). Springer. doi:10.1007/978-981-15-1706-8_3

Tiwari, S., & Srivastava, R. (2022). Cyber Security Trend Analysis: An Indian Perspective. In Cross-Industry Applications of Cyber Security Frameworks (pp. 1-14). IGI Global.

Zou, Q., Sun, X., Liu, P., & Singhal, A. (2020). An approach for detection of advanced persistent threat attacks. *Computer*, *53*(12), 92–96. doi:10.1109/MC.2020.3021548

Chapter 11
Improved Breast Cancer Detection in Mammography Images:
Integration of Convolutional Neural Network and Local Binary Pattern Approach

Olalekan Joel Awujoola
[iD] https://orcid.org/0000-0002-1842-021X
Nigerian Defence Academy, Nigeria

Theophilus Enem Aniemeka
Nigerian Airforce Institute of Technology, Nigeria

Francisca N. Ogwueleka
[iD] https://orcid.org/0000-0002-6021-8584
University of Abuja, Nigeria

Oluwasegun Abiodun Abioye
Nigerian Defence Academy, Nigeria

Abidemi Elizabeth Awujoola
Nigerian Defence Academy, Nigeria

Celestine Ozoemenam Uwa
Nigerian Defence Academy, Nigeria

ABSTRACT

Cancer, characterized by uncontrolled cell division, is an incurable ailment, with breast cancer being the most prevalent form globally. Early detection remains critical in reducing mortality rates. Medical imaging is vital for localizing and diagnosing breast cancer, providing key insights for identification. This study introduces an automatic hybrid feature recognition method for breast cancer diagnosis using images from two mammography datasets. The method employs a convolutional neural network (CNN) and local binary pattern (LBP) for feature extraction. Correlation-based feature selection techniques reduce dimensionality, enabling faster computation and improved accuracy. The proposed model's superiority is established through comparative analysis with cutting-edge deep models, achieving 96% accuracy across the MIAS and INbreast datasets. The hybrid method demonstrates high accuracy with minimal computational tasks.

DOI: 10.4018/978-1-6684-8531-6.ch011

Copyright © 2024, IGI Global. Copying or distributing in print or electronic forms without written permission of IGI Global is prohibited.

1. INTRODUCTION

Breast cancer stands as the most frequently diagnosed cancer across the globe. According to a World Health Organization (WHO) study, more than 2.26 million new cases of breast cancer were estimated in 2020 (Wilkinson & Gathani, 2022). Belgium and the Netherlands reported the highest age-standardized incidence rates of breast cancer, while developing nations like Somalia and Syria experienced the highest breast cancer-related mortality. In a more recent study, Siegel et al. (2023) underscore that breast cancer continues to be the most prevalent cancer diagnosed in women in 2023, constituting 31% of female cancer cases. Notably, female breast cancer incidence rates have exhibited a gradual increase of about 0.5% per year since the mid-2000s, with excess body weight being identified as a contributing factor (Pfei et al., 2018).

This disease is characterized by disruptions in the cell cycle, enabling uncontrolled cell division, often surpassing the healthy limits. The repercussions of this excessive cell division include the assault on neighboring tissues and the potential to spread to other body tissues via the bloodstream (Kaszak et al, 2022; Chow 2010). Among the various types of cancer, breast cancer predominantly afflicts women, with an estimated incidence of 8-9% among this demographic (Kuo et al., 2016). Currently, standard cancer treatments primarily involve surgical procedures and chemotherapy. However, when the severity reaches a certain threshold, often referred to as the final stage or the tau tolerance limit, these treatments yield less significant results. Consequently, early detection plays a pivotal role in minimizing the adverse outcomes (Schiffman et al., 2015).

Regrettably, many women remain unaware of their breast cancer status. A crucial step they can take is performing manual self-examinations to detect any abnormal lumps in the breast area. Should any such anomalies be identified, it is imperative to pursue further evaluation to determine if they indicate breast cancer. Consulting a medical professional for additional assessments is essential, yet this step is sometimes overlooked, leading to exacerbated conditions in the future.

Despite dedicated efforts by medical professionals and researchers, a definitive method for treating breast cancer remains elusive, and reliable evidence for its prevention has yet to be established (Al-Antari et al.,2020). Certain components within breast cancer tissues exhibit high malignancy, posing a severe threat to patients' lives as they can metastasize to vital organs (Punitha et al., 2021; Mao et al.,2022). The proliferation of mammary cells can give rise to tumors in women, which are classified as benign or malignant based on criteria such as their size, location, and Breast Imaging Reporting and Data System (BI-RADS) scores (Byra, 2021). While benign tumors are non-life-threatening and can be managed with medication to inhibit further growth, malignant tumors have the potential to spread to other parts of the body through the lymphatic system or blood, rendering them much more perilous (El Zarif & Haraty, 2020; Jansson et al., 2021). This uncontrolled cell proliferation in the breast results in the formation of malignant tumors, which can only be addressed through surgery or radiation therapy (Song, 2021).

Early detection of breast cancer is pivotal for precise diagnosis and analysis, prompting many researchers to turn to biomedical imaging to assist specialist radiologists. Various techniques such as Magnetic Resonance Imaging (MRI), mammography, and ultrasound are employed for breast carcinoma identification (Sadad et al., 2018; Jubeen et al., 2022). However, the extensive volume of images challenges radiologists in pinpointing potential cancerous areas. Therefore, an efficient automated method is necessary, with computer-aided diagnostic (CAD) systems now being utilized to aid radiologists in the detection of cancerous breast tumors (Zeebaree ET AL., 2021).

In developed countries, the application of machine learning and deep learning algorithms for breast cancer screening is becoming increasingly common (Torres et al., 2019). These algorithms are used to predict the presence of breast cancer-related anomalies within digitized images obtained from various diagnostic methods, including magnetic resonance imaging, ultrasounds, digital breast tomosynthesis, mammogram-derived breast density, tissue images, and cell nuclei from fine needle aspirates of breast masses (Debelee et al., 2020; Zhou et al., 2020; Yu et al., 2021). This study introduces the concept that deep learning algorithms can also be applied to breast cancer prognosis, further expanding their application in this critical field.

Deep learning has emerged as a significant technological breakthrough in recent years, demonstrating superior performance in various machine learning tasks, such as object detection and classification, surpassing conventional state-of-the-art methods. Unlike traditional machine learning approaches that rely on manual feature extraction, which can be challenging due to its dependence on domain knowledge, deep learning techniques dynamically learn the appropriate feature extraction process directly from the input data, tailored to the desired output. This obviates the need for laborious feature engineering and evaluation of feature discrimination, while facilitating the reproducibility of methodologies. With the rise of deep learning, numerous studies have explored deep architectures (Tsochatzidis et al., 2019). Among these, the convolutional neural network (CNN) has become the most prevalent type. In a study by Ha et al. (2019), various CNNs were tested and compared with two hand-crafted descriptors for mass diagnosis, utilizing the Breast Cancer Digital Repository Film Mammography (BCDR-FM) dataset. The authors observed performance enhancements with a combination of learned and hand-crafted representations.

In recent years, the fusion of multiple imaging modalities and feature extraction techniques has emerged as a promising approach to enhance the accuracy and reliability of breast cancer classification systems (Sajid et al., 2023). Notably, the combination of Convolutional Neural Networks (CNNs) and Local Binary Pattern (LBP) features has garnered significant attention due to their complementary strengths in capturing intricate patterns and textures present in mammography and histopathology images (Samee et al., 2022). CNNs have demonstrated remarkable capabilities in learning complex hierarchical representations from raw image data, enabling them to discern intricate spatial features and patterns (Touahri et al., 2019). On the other hand, LBP, a powerful texture descriptor, excels in capturing local micro-level patterns that are vital for characterizing specific tissue structures and anomalies in breast cancer images (Madduri et al., 2021).

This research aims to harness the synergistic benefits of CNNs and LBPs (Local Binary Patterns) through an automated hybrid feature recognition system for breast cancer images. By amalgamating the strengths of both techniques, this study seeks to develop a comprehensive and efficient approach for accurately classifying and diagnosing breast cancer, thereby enabling early detection and personalized treatment planning. It is believed that integrating low-level features with high-level features can enhance recognition accuracy.

The proposed automated hybrid recognition system is expected to make a significant contribution to the field of medical image analysis, providing enhanced precision and reliability in identifying malignant and benign tissues from mammography images. This work builds upon the findings of Sajid et al. (2023), where the authors combined all the features extracted from low-level features of HOG (Histogram of Oriented Gradients) and LBP with high-level CNN features.

This research holds the potential to pave the way for more effective and accessible diagnostic tools, ultimately leading to improved patient care and outcomes in the fight against breast cancer.

The structure of this paper is outlined as follows: Section 2 presents a comprehensive review of the relevant literature, covering the CNN and LBP methodologies. Section 3 introduces the novel approach centered on the integration of Hybrid feature extraction fusion. The findings of the experiments conducted are consolidated in Section 4. Lastly, Section 5 concludes this research, highlighting the key outcomes and contributions of the study.

2. REVIEW OF RELATED LITERATURE

The literature review for this study provides a critical examination and synthesis of existing research and scholarly works related to the application of Convolutional Neural Networks (CNNs) and Local Binary Pattern (LBP) in the domain of breast cancer classification.

The applications of AI/ML techniques transcend the healthcare sector, extending to various domains, such as network intrusion detection, image synthesis, optical character recognition, and facial expression recognition (Bohr & Memarzadeh, 2022). In healthcare, the integration of AI/ML methodologies has significantly impacted numerous aspects, including remote patient monitoring, virtual assistance, hospital management, and drug discovery, along with advancements in radiological imaging analysis for risk assessment, disease diagnosis, prognosis, and therapy response evaluation (Wen & Huang, 2022).

Breast cancer ranks as the second leading cause of death among women worldwide, affecting approximately 12.5 percent of women across diverse societies. Early detection plays a critical role, potentially reducing mortality rates by up to 40% (Miglioretti et al., 2016). Among the various diagnostic methods, medical imaging is highly effective, with digital mammography being essential for early detection (Hong et al., 2020). While techniques such as ultrasound and magnetic resonance imaging (MRI) are also utilized, digital mammography remains at the forefront.

Machine learning has significantly contributed to addressing several challenges associated with mammography, including false positive rates, subjective interpretations, and limitations in detecting cancer-induced changes (Hong et al., 2020). The development of accurate prediction models requires an extensive repository of normal and tumor samples. However, acquiring such data for training purposes is inherently complex, particularly in medical contexts like breast mammography (Adedigba et al., 2022).

Singh et al. (2020) conducted research using a conditional Generative Adversarial Network (cGAN) for breast tumor segmentation. The generative network was trained to identify tumor regions and produce a binary mask, while the adversarial network was tasked with discerning between real (ground truth) and synthetic segmentation. Subsequently, a CNN architecture was employed to classify the segmentation shape into four categories: irregular, lobular, oval, and round. The CNN architecture comprised three convolutional layers with kernel sizes of 9×9, 5×5, and 4×4, along with two fully connected (FC) layers. Their classification approach achieved an 80% accuracy rate when tested on the DDSM dataset.

Similarly, in the same year, Singh et al. introduced a conditional Generative Adversarial Network (cGAN) tailored for segmenting breast tumors within a specified region of interest (ROI) in a mammogram. The generative network was designed to learn tumor identification and generate binary masks outlining the identified area. Simultaneously, the adversarial network was trained to differentiate between real (ground truth) and synthetic segmentations, compelling the generative network to produce highly realistic binary masks. Notably, the proposed method demonstrated superior performance compared to various state-of-the-art approaches. This assertion was validated through diverse experiments conducted on two distinct datasets, namely the publicly available INbreast dataset and an in-house private dataset.

The segmentation model yielded impressive results, achieving a high Dice coefficient and Intersection over Union (IoU) of 94% and 87%, respectively.

Bonavita et al.(2020) suggested an approach to evaluate nodule malignancy utilizing 3D convolutional neural networks and incorporating it into an existing automated end-to-end pipeline for lung cancer detection. Independent subsets of the LIDC dataset were utilized for both the training and testing stages. By incorporating the probabilities of nodule malignancy into a basic lung cancer pipeline, the F1-weighted score was enhanced by 14.7%. Furthermore, integrating the malignancy model itself through transfer learning surpassed the baseline prediction by 11.8% of the F1-weighted score.

In 2021, the authors Hekal et al.(2021) introduced a novel computer-aided detection (CAD) and classification system designed to distinguish between two types of mammogram tumors (mass and calcification) by categorizing them as either benign or malignant. The CAD system employs an automated optimal Otsu thresholding method to identify tumor-like regions (TLRs). Subsequently, deep convolutional neural networks (CNNs) - specifically, the AlexNet and ResNet-50 architectures - are employed to process the extracted TLRs and extract pertinent features from the mammograms. The extracted CNN features are then normalized and fed into a support vector machine classifier to decode the classes of mammogram structures, including Benign Calcification, Benign Mass, Malignant Calcification, and Malignant Mass nodules. The experimental evaluation was conducted on 2800 mammogram images sourced from the Curated Breast Imaging Subset of the Digital Database of Screening Mammography, a publicly available dataset. The proposed CAD system exhibited an accuracy of 0.91 for classifying the regions of interest (ROIs) into the four specified classes, utilizing the AlexNet model, and 0.84 using the ResNet-50 model, employing a fivefold cross-validation approach.

In 2022, Hikmah et al. put forth an approach to enhance the detection process for craniocaudal (CC) view and mediolateral oblique (MLO) view angles separately, aiming to elevate the detection performance for breast cancer diagnosis with a focus on CC and MLO view analysis. The researchers implemented an image processing framework for multi-view screening, aiming to improve diagnostic outcomes compared to single-view analysis. Within this framework, the authors incorporated image enhancement, segmentation, and feature extraction stages. Enhancing image quality was crucial, given the relatively low contrast in mammographic images, which often leads to overlapping between cancerous and normal tissues. For segmentation, the authors employed a texture-based approach using first-order local entropy. Furthermore, they calculated the radius value and the region of probable cancer based on the findings of feature extraction. The study's outcomes revealed an 88.0% accuracy for breast cancer detection using the CC view and an 80.5% accuracy using the MLO view.

Abunasser et al. (2023) utilized a proposed Deep Learning model alongside five additional fine-tuned Deep Learning models, including Xception, InceptionV3, VGG16, MobileNet, and ResNet50, trained on the ImageNet database. They applied these models to classify Breast cancer MRI images into BA, BF, BPT, BTA, MDC, MLC, MMC, and MPC categories. The dataset was sourced from the Kaggle repository for breast cancer detection and classification, which was enhanced using the GAN technique. Notably, the dataset contained images with four magnifications (40X, 100X, 200X, 400X, and the Complete Dataset). The authors conducted a comprehensive evaluation of the proposed Deep Learning model and the five pre-trained models individually, conducting a total of 30 experiments. The assessment involved measuring the F1-score, recall, precision, and accuracy for all models. The classification F1-score accuracies for Xception, InceptionV3, ResNet50, VGG16, MobileNet, and the Proposed Model (BCCNN) were reported as 97.54%, 95.33%, 98.14%, 97.67%, 93.98%, and 98.28%, respectively. Furthermore, the authors emphasized the positive impact of Dataset Boosting, preprocessing, and balancing in improving the detection and classification of breast cancer for both the proposed model (BCCNN) and the fine-tuned pretrained models. They noted that the highest accuracies were achieved when using the 400X magnification of the MRI images, attributed to their superior image resolution.

Oluwasegun et al. (2023) revealed that the prevailing models designed for breast cancer classification lack universality. In response, the authors proposed a versatile model employing the EfficientNetB2 pretrained network. Only the feature extraction module of the network was utilized, and the fully connected layer was substituted with three distinct classifiers, namely MGSVM, CUBIC SVM, and XGBOOST, for the classification of the extracted features. The study employed eight evaluation metrics to gauge the effectiveness of the proposed models. Experimental findings demonstrated that the fusion of EfficientNetB2 and the MGSVM classifier proved to be more universal and effective for the diagnosis and classification of breast cancer. Notably, this hybrid model exhibited outstanding performance in classifying mammography breast images from both datasets, achieving impressive metrics including an overall accuracy of 99.47%, a sensitivity rate of 99.31%, precision of 99.44%, F1-score of 99.44%, AUC of 99.44%, a low FNR (False Negative Rate) of 0.007, a kappa score of 0.98, and a manageable time complexity of 231.44 seconds on the MIAS Dataset.

The authors, Sajid et al. (2023) proposed an innovative framework for classifying breast cancer using mammogram images. Their framework integrated robust features extracted from a novel Convolutional Neural Network (CNN) alongside handcrafted features, including HOG (Histogram of Oriented Gradients) and LBP (Local Binary Pattern). The classification task involved employing three machine learning classifiers: KNN, Random Forest, and XGBoost. Notably, XGBoost achieved the highest accuracy at 91.5%, while KNN and Random Forest yielded accuracies of 85% and 75%, respectively.

This study builds upon the work of Sajid et al. (2023) by eliminating HOG, which is known for its higher computational complexity compared to LBP. This computational difference arises from HOG's computation of gradient orientations and construction of histograms, whereas LBP, as a simpler operator, exhibits greater computational efficiency (Kortli et al., 2018). Additionally, Ruby & Chandran (2016) highlighted the widespread use of HOG in human and pedestrian detection tasks, while LBP finds application in face recognition, texture classification, and image retrieval.

Maleki & Niaki (2023) proposed research aimed at processing Computerized Tomography (CT) images of lung cancer patients for early disease diagnosis. The first approach involved processing the images using a Convolutional Neural Network (CNN) and employing an Artificial Neural Network (ANN) for image classification. In the second approach, the images underwent preprocessing and segmentation before being subjected to CNN and ANN. The third method entailed converting all preprocessed and segmented images into numerical data using specific feature extraction algorithms. Additionally, dimensional reduction and feature selection algorithms were utilized in conjunction with three machine learning techniques, namely Gradient Boosting (GB), Random Forest (RF), and Support Vector Machine (SVM), for classification. An extensive comparative analysis was conducted to determine the most effective technique. The methodologies were evaluated using a set of lung CT scan images collected from a medical center. The results demonstrated that employing either SVM or RF classification techniques led to a 95% accuracy rate in diagnosing lung cancer.

Zakareya et al. (2023) introduced an innovative approach aimed at enhancing breast cancer classification detection and addressing the challenge of limited data for deep learning applications. Drawing inspiration from two leading deep networks, namely GoogLeNet and the residual block, the authors incorporated granular computing, shortcut connections, two learnable activation functions in place of traditional ones, and an attention mechanism. These additions were anticipated to not only improve the accuracy of diagnosis but also alleviate the burden on healthcare professionals. The integration of granular computing was particularly instrumental in enhancing the accuracy of diagnosis by capturing intricate and nuanced details from cancer images. Through two detailed case studies, the proposed model's performance was thoroughly assessed and compared against various state-of-the-art deep models and existing methodologies. Notably, the proposed model achieved a commendable accuracy of 93% for ultrasound images and 95% for breast histopathology images, highlighting its significant superiority and potential impact in the field of breast cancer detection.

2.1 Locally Binary Patterns

Locally Binary Patterns (LBP) represent a widely used high texture descriptor approach in various applications. Initially developed for face recognition and texture classification, the LBP descriptor's robustness stems from its binary coding of threshold intensity values. Generally, the LBP descriptor operates within a 3x3 pixel matrix $(p_1....p_8)$ of an image.

Within this matrix, each pixel is compared to the value of the central pixel (p_0) to create a binary code. If a neighbor pixel's value is lower than the center pixel $i(p_0)$ value, it is assigned a zero; otherwise, it is assigned one. This binary code is then multiplied by powers of two and summed to derive the locally binary pattern descriptor value for the central pixel. The LBP is defined within a 3x3 matrix, as demonstrated by Equation (1) while Figure 1 described the LBP descriptor.

$$LBP = \sum_{p=1}^{8} 2^p S(i_0 - i_p), with\ S(x) = \{_1^0 {=}_{x\leq0}^{x\geq0} \tag{1}$$

Where i_c and i_p are the intensity value of the center pixel and neighborhood pixels, respectively.

The primary advantages of Local Binary Patterns (LBP) lie in its efficient computational requirements, its seamless adaptability to multi-scale applications, and its resilience to monotonic alterations in gray-scale. LBP descriptors encompass three distinct patterns, namely the rotation-invariant uniform pattern, rotation-invariant pattern, and uniform pattern (Huang et al., 2011). The essence of LBP is rooted in the comparison of binary commands derived from the contrasts in pixel intensities between the central pixel and its adjacent eight pixels within the image.

Therefore, LBP is a powerful texture descriptor that is computationally efficient, adaptable to multi-scale applications, and resilient to monotonic alterations in gray-scale. The LBP operator labels the pixels of an image with decimal numbers, called Local Binary Patterns or LBP codes, which encode the local

Figure 1. The LBP descriptor
Kortli et al. (2018)

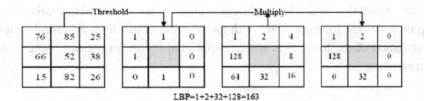

Figure 2. Typical convolutional neural network architecture

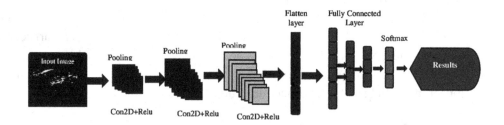

structure around each pixel. Uniform patterns are used in the computation of LBP labels, making them rotation and grayscale invariant.

2.2 Convolutional Neural Networks

Convolutional Neural Networks CNN's are a special form of multilayer perceptrons, which are designed specifically to recognize two-dimensional shapes with a high degree of invariance to translation, scaling, skewing, and other forms of distortion (Wagner, 2016). CNNs are a part of the deep learning field, but with the advantage that they can be trained by standard back propagation algorithms. CNN are extensively applied in pattern recognition systems, where the convolution kernel plays an important role in performance improvement (Chen et al., 2019). The field of deep learning in general relies on computational power and became popular with the use of graphical processor units for computation and the possibility to initialize the networks via a layer wise pre-training (Bengio et al., 2013).

Also CNNs can be described as supervised feed-forward networks that proved considerably significant performance on the large-scale object classification applications. The basic structure of the CNNs is stimulated by the key visual cortex of the human brain, which oversees the processing of visual information (Bautista et al., 2016). In the image classification, compared with the traditional handcrafted features extraction methods, the CNNs can automatically extract the learnable visual features from the large-scale dataset input images from the classes to perform the classification. One of the main superiorities of the CNNs over traditional classification methods is that, in CNNs, representation of the features and the classifier are employed in the same network to eliminate their dependencies. The typical architecture of the CNNs principally comprises three types of layers, (i) convolution layers, (ii) pooling layers, and (iii) the connecting layers, briefly discussed below and shown in Figure 2.

2.2.1 Convolutional Layers

Convolutional layers are considered as one of the most important layers in the CNNs, which consist of the defined set of learnable filters. The filters are spatially smaller than the input-size, which slides over the input image data during the forward pass to produce the two-dimensional activation map. The activation map indicates the location along with the strength of the detected visual features in an input image. The calculation of the features of the convolutional layers is obtained using (Butt, et al.,2022) as expressed in equation 2.

$$y_n^l = fl(\sum m - {}_n^l y_m^{l-1}) \qquad\qquad (2)$$

Where y_n^l is the nth term feature maps of 1-layer, $m \dashrightarrow \dfrac{n}{l}$ is the C-kernel, while feature extraction from layer-l, and y_m^{l-1} is the Characteristic patterns linked to layer-l.

2.2.2 Pooling Layers

Pooling layer is commonly used between consecutive convolution layers of the CNN structure to gradually minimize the spatial representation size to reduce computations while retaining useful information, which helps in controlling overfitting during the learning process. It is important to mention that there are two types of pooling layers being used in the existing state-of-the-art CNNs, i.e., a pooling layer having filter size = 2 along with stride = 3, which is called overlapping pooling; the other pooling layer with filter size = 2 is having stride of 2. Besides, some other types of pooling, i.e., L2-norm pooling and average-pooling functions, have also been used in the existing CNNs. The pooling function can be performed using equation 3 and is expressed as:

$$y_n^l = fl(z_n^{l-1} x w_n^l + b_n^l) \qquad\qquad (3)$$

Where z_n^{l-1} the value is extracted from l-1 convolution features, w_n^l is the map weight, and b_n^l is the offset value.

2.2.3 Drop-Out Layer

In CNNs, regularization is a common way to avoid the effects of overfitting by adding a significant amount of penalty to the utilized loss function. In this regard, drop-out layer is added at the bottom of proposed network, so that the system does not learn interdependent weights of features.

2.2.4 Fully Connected Layer.

In the final section of structure of CNNs, neurons of fully connected layer are linked with all the activations of the previous layer to minimalize the feature dimensions. -e final pooling layer of the CNNs flattens the convolutional layer, which is forwarded to fully connected nodes of the network. In the next step, the matrix multiplication is applied to compute these activations followed by a bias factor offset. Fully connected neurons can be computed using equation 4.

$$y_n^l = \left(\sum_{m=1}^{N_{l-1}} y_m^{l-1} w_{m,n}^l + b_n^l \right) \qquad\qquad (4)$$

Where N_l is the No of neutrons of output layer y_n^{l-1} is the m characteristics pattern of layer l-1, and $w_{m,n}^l$ is the connected weights.

3. PROPOSED METHODOLOGY

The model demonstrates the hybridization of a Convolutional Neural Network (CNN) model with Local Binary Pattern (LBP) features, an image feature extractor, for the recognition of cancer images. The process begins by importing necessary libraries, including TensorFlow and Scikit-learn, both of which play pivotal roles in various aspects of the model development process. Subsequently, the model loads and preprocesses images from a specified dataset directory containing mammography cancer images. These images undergo resizing and transformation into grayscale (input_shape: 128x128x1), a standard preprocessing step in image analysis tasks, to facilitate uniform processing.

Local Binary Pattern (LBP) features are first extracted from the preprocessed images, enabling the representation of texture information within the images. This feature extraction process aids in capturing subtle visual patterns that can indicate various characteristics of the cancerous tissues, facilitating more nuanced analysis and classification (radius: 3, n_points: 24).

The core of the model is established through a four-layer CNN architecture. This architecture comprises Conv2D layers with varying filters and kernel sizes (32 filters with 3x3 kernel size, 64 filters with 3x3 kernel size, 128 filters with 3x3 kernel size, and 256 filters with 3x3 kernel size). BatchNormalization layers are incorporated to enhance training stability, while MaxPooling2D layers with 2x2 pool sizes aid in downsampling and feature selection. Strategically positioned Dropout layers with a dropout rate of 0.25 mitigate overfitting and improve the model's generalizability. The rectified linear unit (ReLU) activation function is employed throughout the CNN layers, ensuring non-linearity and effective feature extraction.

To amalgamate the information obtained from the CNN model and the extracted LBP features, a combined model architecture seamlessly integrates the outputs from the CNN model and the LBP features. This integration creates a comprehensive representation of both structural and textural information from the cancer images. The final Dense layer, equipped with a sigmoid activation function, facilitates multi-label classification, enabling the model to effectively categorize and discern various attributes and characteristics of cancerous tissues within the images.

The model is compiled using the Adam optimizer with a learning rate of 0.001 and binary cross-entropy loss, with accuracy serving as the principal evaluation metric. The dataset is divided into training and testing sets, and the labels are encoded using LabelEncoder and one-hot encoding techniques. Additionally, the LBP features are standardized using the StandardScaler, promoting consistent and optimal model training. The model is trained for 100 epochs, with a batch size of 32, and a validation split of 0.2.

Following the training phase, the model's performance is thoroughly assessed on the test set. A comprehensive classification report, a confusion matrix, and a Receiver Operating Characteristic (ROC) curve are generated to evaluate the model's classification accuracy and visualize its predictive capabilities. The plotted training versus validation loss and accuracy provide insights into the model's learning dynamics and its ability to generalize to unseen data.

The implemented CNN model, enriched with LBP features, serves as a robust framework for the recognition of cancer images. Its intricate architecture, integration of essential techniques such as regularization and standardization, and comprehensive evaluation metrics contribute to its efficacy in accurately classifying and characterizing different attributes and features within cancerous tissues, highlighting its potential for real-world applications in the domain of cancer image analysis and diagnosis. The proposed visual representation of the framework for fusion of low-level features from the LBP and high-level features from the deep CNN is shown in Figure 3.

Figure 3. Proposed framework for fusion of low-level features from the LBP and high-level features from the deep CNN

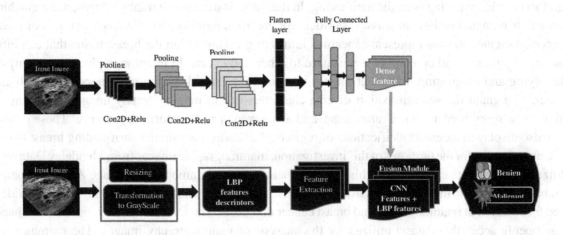

Finally, TensorFlow, a popular open-source machine learning framework, is leveraged for building and training the CNN model, utilizing its rich set of functionalities such as defining neural network layers, optimizing the model with specific loss functions and metrics, and facilitating model compilation, training, and evaluation. Throughout the developmental process, various TensorFlow components, including layers like Conv2D, MaxPooling2D, Dense, Dropout, and BatchNormalization, are intricately integrated to construct a sophisticated CNN architecture tailored for cancer recognition tasks.

Moreover, Scikit-learn, a comprehensive machine learning library, is employed for crucial data pre-processing operations and performance evaluations. Tasks such as data splitting into training and testing sets, label encoding, and standardization of LBP features are efficiently executed using Scikit-learn's diverse functionalities. The library's metrics and evaluation tools, such as classification reports, confusion matrices, and ROC curves, contribute significantly to assessing the model's classification accuracy and visualizing its predictive capabilities.

The combined efforts of both TensorFlow and Scikit-learn in the model ensure a comprehensive approach to model development, training, and evaluation, thereby enhancing the accuracy and robustness of the cancer recognition system. This integration of two powerful libraries underscores the significance of leveraging diverse tools and techniques to achieve optimal results in complex machine learning tasks, ultimately paving the way for advancements in the field of cancer recognition and analysis. To validate the proposed approach, accuracy, precision, recall, and F1-measure are calculated as a part of a controlled experiment.

3.1 Dataset

Within the realm of medical imaging and breast cancer investigation, a mammography dataset typically encompasses a compilation of medical images referred to as mammograms. These images are specifically obtained using mammography, a specialized imaging method employing low-dose X-rays to visualize the internal structures of the breast. The images consist of benign and malignant breast masses; benign masses constitute non-cancerous lumps or growths within the breast tissue, resulting from a variety of factors including hormonal fluctuations, inflammation, and fibrocystic changes in breast tissue. While benign masses are usually harmless and do not necessitate treatment, they can sometimes cause discomfort or pain, requiring periodic monitoring. In the analysis of mammography images, distinguishing between benign and malignant masses is critical for precise diagnosis and effective treatment of breast cancer. Malignant masses represent cancerous lumps or growths within the breast tissue that can infiltrate nearby tissues and potentially metastasize to other body parts. In mammography image analysis, identifying and diagnosing malignant masses is crucial for early detection and intervention in breast cancer. Malignant masses can exhibit diverse characteristics in mammography images, including an irregular or spiky border, an irregular shape, and an uneven or non-uniform appearance. These masses may also display associated calcifications or regions of distortion within the surrounding breast tissue.

Consequently, for the purposes of this investigation, mammographic images from Mendeley Data were utilized. The datasets employed for this research included the Mammographic Image Analysis Society database (MIAS) and the INbreast datasets. The MIAS database consists of digital mammograms widely used for research in mammography and breast cancer diagnosis. The INbreast dataset, on the other hand, is an openly accessible dataset utilized for the analysis of mammography images. The mammogram images from Mendeley Data underwent preprocessing using data augmentation and contrast-limited adaptive histogram equalization techniques. Subsequent to augmentation, the MIAS dataset contained 3816 images, while the INbreast dataset comprised 7632 images.

4. EXPERIMENTAL RESULTS AND DISCUSSION

In conducting this research, we employed the TensorFlow and Scikit-learn frameworks for data processing and in-depth analysis. The experimental setup involved utilizing an Hp Proliant DL380p Gen8 system configured with 20GB of RAM. This configuration was instrumental in executing the experiments aimed at evaluating the performance of the proposed hybrid model.

4.1 Experiment with MIAS Dataset

Results

Two experiments were conducted using two distinct datasets of Mammography breast cancer images, namely the MIAS and the INbreast datasets. The initial experiment focused on the evaluation of the MIAS dataset, while the second experiment focused on the INbreast dataset. Figure 4 displays samples of the original and LBP images from the MIAS experiment, and further results obtained are presented in Table 1, which provides the classification report, and Table 2, which shows the overall accuracy and other relevant metrics. Additionally, Figure 5 depicts the confusion matrix, while Figure 6 illustrates the Receiver Operating Characteristic (ROC) curve. Figures 7 and 8 depict the training versus validation loss and the training versus validation accuracy, respectively.

Figure 2 displays the original breast cancer images alongside their corresponding Local Binary Pattern (LBP) images. Local Binary Pattern is a texture descriptor used for feature extraction in image analysis. In this context, the LBP images represent a transformed version of the original images, where texture patterns are highlighted to aid in the analysis and classification of breast cancer. This transformation allows for enhanced feature recognition, facilitating the identification of key characteristics for the

Figure 4. Showing the original breast cancer images and the equivalent LBP images

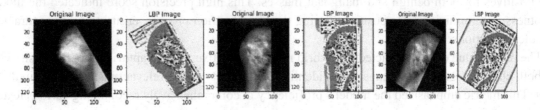

Table 1. Classification report on MIAS dataset

Class	Precision	Recall	F1-Score	Support
Benign Masses	0.97	0.98	0.97	495
Malignant Masses	0.95	0.94	0.95	269
Accuracy			0.96	764
macro avg	0.96	0.96	0.96	764
weighted avg	0.96	0.96	0.96	764

classification and diagnosis of breast cancer. The comparison between the original and LBP images in Figure 2 provides valuable insights into the effectiveness of LBP in enhancing the discriminative features necessary for accurate classification and diagnosis in the context of breast cancer detection.

The results presented in Table 1 exhibit precision values of 0.97 for Benign Masses and 0.95 for Malignant Masses. Similarly, the recall values were 0.98 and 0.94 for Benign and Malignant Masses, respectively. These high precision and recall scores are indicative of the model's strong performance in classifying the two classes within the MIAS dataset. Moreover, the f1-scores for both classes were 0.97 and 0.95, demonstrating the model's robustness in capturing the balance between precision and recall.

The overall accuracy achieved was 0.96, underscoring the model's ability to effectively classify both Benign and Malignant Masses within the MIAS dataset.

The evaluation of the hybrid model on the MIAS dataset, as revealed in Table 2, shows an impressive set of performance metrics, showcasing the model's efficacy in accurately classifying both benign and malignant masses within breast cancer images. The metrics indicated the model's overall proficiency in capturing and categorizing various instances within the dataset.

The accuracy metric, which stood at 0.96, demonstrated that the hybrid model correctly classified approximately 96% of the images in the dataset. This high accuracy score emphasized the model's ability to make precise classifications, showcasing its reliability in real-world applications.

Table 2. Performance matrices evaluation

Accuracy	Precision	Recall	F1-Score	Kappa	FNR	Sensitivity
0.96	0.96	0.96	0.96	0.9105	0.0706	0.9526

Furthermore, the precision score of 0.96 underlined the model's capability to accurately identify true positives for both benign and malignant masses. This high precision score indicated the model's adeptness in minimizing false positives during the classification process, ensuring more accurate and reliable predictions.

The recall value of 0.96 depicted the hybrid model's effectiveness in capturing the true positive rate for both classes, signifying its capacity to identify the majority of the relevant instances within the dataset. This metric emphasized the model's proficiency in comprehensively recognizing various features and characteristics associated with benign and malignant masses.

The F1-score, serving as the harmonic mean of precision and recall, also stood at 0.96, highlighting the hybrid model's balanced performance in achieving accurate and reliable classifications. This robust F1-score emphasized the model's ability to maintain a fine equilibrium between precision and recall, enhancing its credibility in making precise and dependable predictions.

The Kappa coefficient, which measured at 0.9105, indicated a strong agreement between the predicted classifications and the actual classes in the dataset. This high Kappa score underscored the model's reliability and consistency in its predictions, bolstering its credibility in practical applications.

The False Negative Rate (FNR) of 0.0706 demonstrated the model's proficiency in minimizing the number of false negatives during classification, illustrating its capability to accurately identify actual positive instances within the dataset.

Moreover, the sensitivity score, also known as the true positive rate, registered at 0.9526, further emphasized the model's accuracy in detecting actual positive cases within the dataset, highlighting its competence in recognizing critical features associated with both benign and malignant masses.

Lastly, the evaluation of the hybrid model on the MIAS dataset showcased its robust performance in accurately classifying benign and malignant masses within breast cancer images. The high accuracy, precision, recall, F1-score, Kappa coefficient, and low False Negative Rate and high sensitivity collectively demonstrated the model's potential for reliable integration into real-world applications for breast cancer diagnosis and analysis.

The confusion matrix obtained from the experiment, as depicted in Figure 5, provides valuable insights into the performance of the hybrid model in classifying benign and malignant masses within the MIAS dataset. The matrix indicates the number of instances correctly and incorrectly classified by the model for each class.

In the confusion matrix, the diagonal elements represent the number of instances that were correctly classified. In this case, the top-left element (483) signifies the number of instances of benign masses that were correctly classified, while the bottom-right element (252) represents the number of instances of malignant masses that were accurately identified by the model.

On the other hand, the off-diagonal elements of the matrix represent the misclassifications made by the model. The top-right element (12) indicates the number of instances of benign masses that were wrongly classified as malignant, and the bottom-left element (17) denotes the number of instances of malignant masses that were incorrectly classified as benign.

Analyzing the confusion matrix provides a comprehensive understanding of the model's performance, enabling the identification of specific areas where the model might be struggling or excelling. The relatively low numbers in the off-diagonal elements indicate that the model generally performs well in accurately distinguishing between benign and malignant masses. However, the presence of misclassifications highlights potential areas for improvement, indicating the necessity for further fine-tuning or adjustments in the model's training and classification processes.

Figure 5. Confusion matrix obtained from the evaluation of the proposed model on MIAS dataset

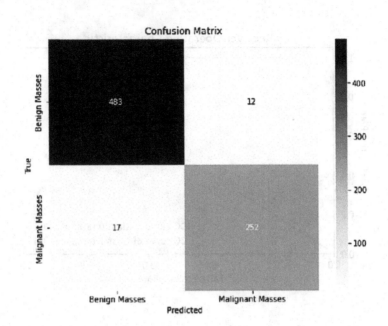

Additionally, the confusion matrix aids in the assessment of the model's sensitivity and specificity, essential factors in evaluating its performance. The values in the matrix contribute to the calculation of these metrics, providing a deeper understanding of the model's ability to correctly identify true positives and true negatives, as well as false positives and false negatives.

Overall, the analysis of the confusion matrix offers valuable insights into the strengths and weaknesses of the hybrid model, allowing for informed decision-making in refining the model's architecture and training process to enhance its performance and reliability in accurately classifying benign and malignant masses within breast cancer images.

The Receiver Operating Characteristic (ROC) curve as visualized in Figure 6, is a significant evaluation metric that provides insights into the performance of a classification model, particularly in distinguishing between different classes. The ROC curve is particularly useful in assessing the trade-off between true positive rate and false positive rate at various classification thresholds. The areas under the ROC curves are indicative of the model's ability to differentiate between the classes effectively.

The results obtained from the evaluation of the ROC curves for the classes "Benign masses" and "Malignant masses" demonstrated remarkable performance, as evidenced by the area under the curves, which both registered at 0.99. These high values suggest that the hybrid model effectively differentiated between benign and malignant masses with a high degree of accuracy. A value of 0.99 for the area under the ROC curve signifies that the model's true positive rate is exceptionally high, with a low corresponding false positive rate, emphasizing the model's strong capability in accurately identifying instances of both benign and malignant masses. The proximity of the area under the ROC curve to 1 indicates that the model achieved a high level of discrimination ability, making it adept at correctly classifying instances from the two classes, thereby bolstering its credibility and reliability in practical applications.

Furthermore, the consistent area under the ROC curves for both classes underscore the model's robust performance in handling instances from different categories, indicating its general effectiveness in

Figure 6. ROC obtained from the evaluation of the MIAS dataset

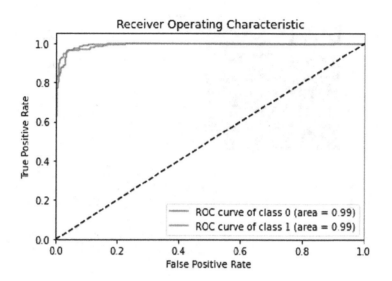

Figure 7. Train versus validation loss

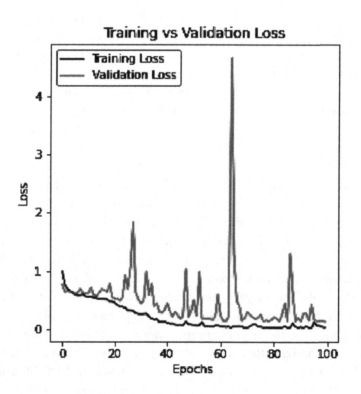

classifying various types of masses within the dataset. The convergence of the ROC curves to the upper left corner of the plot signifies the model's strong sensitivity and specificity, highlighting its proficiency in achieving a balance between true positive and false positive rates. The impressive ROC curve results emphasize the hybrid model's efficacy in accurately differentiating between benign and malignant masses within breast cancer images. The high area under the curves signifies the model's strong discriminatory power and reliability, further reinforcing its potential for real-world applications in the field of breast cancer diagnosis and analysis.

Figure 7 and Figure 8 provide the training results, which illustrate the progression of the model's performance throughout the training process. They focus on the training and validation loss, as well as the training and validation accuracy across multiple epochs. Moreover, the analysis of the training versus validation loss and the training versus validation accuracy provides crucial insights into the model's learning process and generalization capabilities.

The training versus validation loss graph in Figure 7 indicates the model's ability to minimize its error during the training process while avoiding overfitting. Over the course of the 100 epochs, it can be observed that the training loss consistently decreased, signifying the models improved capability in minimizing errors on the training data. On the other hand, the validation loss initially decreased, indicating effective generalization to the validation set. However, around epoch 25, the validation loss began to fluctuate, which could be an early sign of overfitting. Towards the end of the training, the validation loss remained relatively stable, indicating the model's ability to generalize well to unseen data.

Figure 8. Train versus validation accuracy

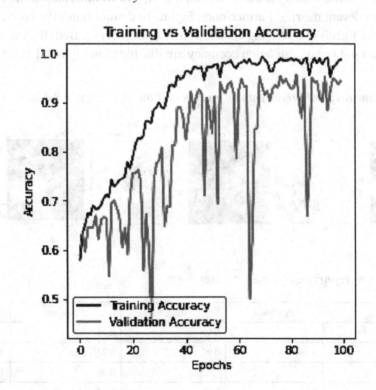

Furthermore, the training versus validation accuracy graph as shown in Figure 8 illustrates the model's learning progress in correctly predicting the labels of the training and validation datasets. Throughout the training, both the training and validation accuracy increased, highlighting the model's learning capability and its capacity to make accurate predictions on both the training and validation sets. The fluctuations in the validation accuracy during the mid-epochs could be indicative of the model's struggle to generalize to unseen data. However, the consistency in the increasing trend of both training and validation accuracy overall suggests that the model effectively learned from the training data and could generalize well to the validation set, albeit with slight fluctuations.

Therefore, the analysis of the training versus validation loss and the training versus validation accuracy demonstrates that the model achieved impressive performance in learning from the training data. Although some signs of overfitting were observed in the validation loss and accuracy during the mid-epochs, the model exhibited strong potential in generalizing to the validation set. The stability and convergence of both the training and validation metrics towards the later epochs indicate the model's ability to maintain a balance between learning from the training data and generalizing to unseen data, emphasizing its overall effectiveness and robustness

4.2 Experiment With INbreast Dataset

This study also implemented the proposed model to evaluate another dataset of breast mammography images. This assessment primarily focuses on the INbreast Dataset. Figure 9 illustrates examples of both the original and LBP images obtained from the INbreast experiment. The corresponding results are delineated in Table 3, which includes the classification report, and Table 4, presenting the comprehensive accuracy and other relevant metrics. Furthermore, Figure 10 demonstrates the confusion matrix, while Figure 11 depicts the Receiver Operating Characteristic (ROC) curve. Both the training versus validation loss and the training versus validation accuracy are illustrated in Figures 12 and 13, respectively.

Figure 9. Showing the original breast cancer images and the equivalent LBP images

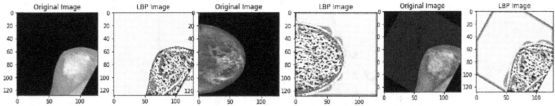

Table 3. Classification report on INbreast dataset

Class	Precision	Recall	F1-Score	Support
Benign	0.95	0.93	0.94	539
Malignant	0.96	0.97	0.97	988
Accuracy			0.96	1527
macro avg	0.96	0.95	0.95	1527
weighted avg	0.96	0.96	0.96	1527

Table 4. Performance matrices evaluation

Accuracy	Precision	Recall	F1-Score	Kappa	FNR	Sensitivity
0.96	0.96	0.95	0.95	0.9078	0.0263	0.9516

Table 3 is the classification report resulting from the evaluation of a model's performance in classifying breast cancer images from the INbreast dataset. It provides valuable insights into the model's ability to correctly identify both the "benign" and "malignant" classes.

For the "benign" class, the model demonstrates a high precision of 0.95, indicating that when it predicts an image as "benign," it is correct 95% of the time. The recall value of 0.93 implies that the model successfully identifies 93% of the actual "benign" cases. The F1-score, which considers both precision and recall, is 0.94, suggesting a good balance between precision and recall for this class.

For the "malignant" class, the model achieves even higher precision (0.96) and recall (0.97), indicating its strong ability to accurately identify "malignant" cases. The F1-score of 0.97 suggests excellent performance in terms of the model's accuracy in classifying the "malignant" cases.

Overall, the high accuracy of 0.96 for the entire dataset implies that the model performs well in distinguishing between "benign" and "malignant" breast cancer images. The macro-average F1-score of 0.95 indicates that the model is effective in achieving a balance between precision and recall for both classes, ensuring reliable performance across the board.

The evaluation results presented in Table 4 offer a comprehensive overview of the performance metrics obtained from the classification of breast cancer using the INbreast dataset. These metrics provide valuable insights into the model's effectiveness in accurately identifying instances of breast cancer.

The accuracy achieved by the model was 0.96, indicating a high level of precision in correctly classifying 96% of the breast cancer cases. This implies that the model's predictions were largely reliable and aligned with the actual outcomes.

The precision value of 0.96 suggests that when the model made a positive prediction, it was accurate 96% of the time. This demonstrates the model's ability to minimize false positives and make precise identifications of actual positive cases.

In terms of recall, the model exhibited a value of 0.95, implying that it successfully identified 95% of the actual positive cases. This suggests that the model had a strong capability to capture the majority of the positive instances within the dataset.

The F1-score, which is the harmonic mean of precision and recall, was 0.95, indicating a balanced performance between precision and recall. This underscores the model's ability to strike a favorable balance between accurately identifying positive cases and minimizing false positives.

The Kappa value of 0.9078 represents the model's agreement with the ground truth, considering the possibility of chance agreement. This value suggests a substantial level of agreement beyond what could be expected by chance alone, further emphasizing the model's robust performance.

The False Negative Rate (FNR) was 0.0263, indicating that only 2.63% of the actual positive instances were incorrectly predicted as negative by the model. This showcases the model's efficiency in minimizing the instances of false negatives, which is crucial in the context of breast cancer classification.

The sensitivity value of 0.9516 signifies the proportion of actual positive cases correctly identified by the model, emphasizing the model's ability to accurately detect instances of breast cancer.

Figure 10. Confusion matrix obtained from INbreast evaluation

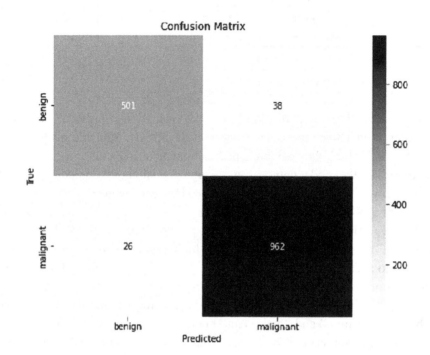

Therefore, these performance metrics collectively highlight the model's high accuracy, precision, and robustness in effectively classifying breast cancer instances within the INbreast dataset.

This confusion matrix in Figure 10, provides a detailed breakdown of the model's performance in predicting the classes of benign and malignant cases. The matrix demonstrates that out of the total instances of benign cases, 501 were correctly classified as benign, while 38 were incorrectly classified as malignant. Similarly, out of the total instances of malignant cases, 962 were correctly classified as malignant, whereas 26 were incorrectly classified as benign.

The confusion matrix serves as a crucial tool for understanding the performance of the model, especially in terms of its ability to correctly predict the different classes. It provides a clear overview of the distribution of correct and incorrect classifications, aiding in the assessment of the model's overall effectiveness in classifying benign and malignant instances within the INbreast dataset.

The ROC curve in Figure 11 illustrates the diagnostic ability of a binary classifier system as its discrimination threshold is varied. In the experiment conducted, the ROC curve analysis for both the Benign and Malignant classes yielded significant results.

The ROC curve for the class Benign demonstrated an impressive area under the curve (AUC) value of 0.99, indicating a high level of accuracy and effectiveness in the model's ability to distinguish between true positive and false positive rates for the benign class. The proximity of the curve to the upper left corner of the plot signifies the excellent performance of the model in correctly identifying benign cases while minimizing false positives.

Similarly, the ROC curve for the class Malignant also exhibited an AUC value of 0.99, highlighting the model's strong discriminatory power in correctly identifying instances of malignancy. The curve's

Figure 11. ROC

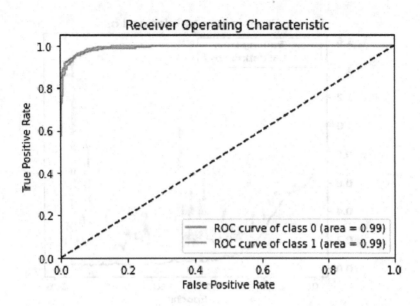

proximity to the upper left corner of the graph indicates the model's high sensitivity and specificity in accurately classifying malignant cases while minimizing false positives.

In summary, the ROC analysis underscores the robust performance of the model in effectively distinguishing between benign and malignant instances within the dataset. The high AUC values obtained for both classes serve as a testament to the model's accuracy and reliability in differentiating between the two classes, indicating its potential for precise and reliable classification of breast cancer cases.

The training and validation phases are vital for evaluating the proficiency and adaptability of deep learning models. Monitoring the training versus validation loss and training versus validation accuracy is crucial in understanding the learning dynamics and generalization capability of the model during the training period.

Throughout the 100 epochs of training, a noticeable pattern emerged. Initially, at Epoch 1, the model encountered a relatively high loss of 0.7742 and exhibited moderate accuracy of 0.5832, demonstrating that the model was still in the early stages of learning. However, as the training progressed, the loss steadily decreased, reaching 0.0295 at Epoch 75, signifying that the model was able to minimize errors effectively and converge towards optimal performance. Simultaneously, the training accuracy exhibited a consistent upward trend, climbing from 0.5832 at Epoch 1 to a remarkable 0.9885 at Epoch 75, suggesting that the model progressively assimilated the intricate patterns embedded in the dataset.

Analogously, the validation results mirrored this positive trend, indicating that the model was adept at generalizing to unseen data. The validation loss decreased from 0.6162 at Epoch 1 to 0.1343 at Epoch 75, while the validation accuracy climbed from 0.6945 at Epoch 1 to an impressive 0.9607 at Epoch 75. Ultimately, the final reported training accuracy of 0.9934 and validation accuracy of 0.9599 as shown in Figure 11 underscored the model's capability to achieve high accuracy on both the training and validation datasets. Correspondingly, the final training loss of 0.0211 and validation loss of 0.1743

Figure 12. Train versus validation loss

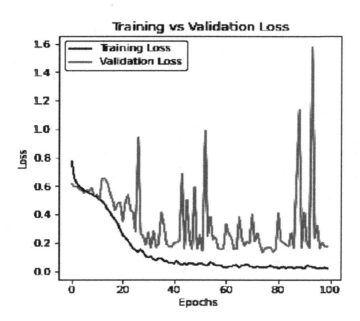

Figure 13. Train versus validation accuracy

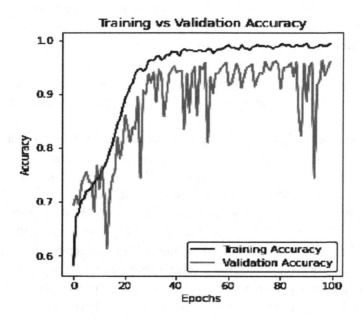

as shown in Figure 12 highlighted the model's effectiveness in minimizing errors and optimizing its overall performance.

These findings collectively emphasize the model's capacity to learn intricate patterns effectively, thus showcasing its potential for accurate predictions and dependable performance on unseen data.

4.3 Comparison With Other Existing Models

The creation of the hybrid model, which merges low-level features obtained from Local Binary Pattern (LBP) and high-level features extracted through deep Convolutional Neural Networks (CNN) for mammography breast cancer images, represents a substantial breakthrough in the field. To ensure a comprehensive evaluation of the proposed hybrid model, a comparative analysis has been conducted with other works in the field. This comparison illuminates the strengths and advantages of the developed model over its counterparts, emphasizing its effectiveness and underscoring its potential to advance the state-of-the-art in mammography-based breast cancer detection. Table 5 highlights the comparative results of the models.

Table 5. Results comparison

Author	Model	Accuracy
Zakareya et al, (2023)	DNN R3_R5_R35 Model	95%
Sajid et al., (2023)	Deep Learned Features Boosted with Handcrafted Features	91.5%
Developed Model	Hybridization of Lbp and CNN	96%

In Table 5, it is evident that Zakareya et al., (2023), proposed the DNN Model, which achieved an accuracy of 95%. Their model integrated a deep neural network architecture to enhance breast cancer classification, demonstrating a notable level of accuracy in their predictions. This highlights the effectiveness of their approach in accurately identifying breast cancer from mammography images.

In the study by Sajid et al. (2023), the authors employed a combination of deep learned features and handcrafted features (CNN, LBP and HOG), resulting in an accuracy of 91.5%. While their approach showed promising results, the achieved accuracy was slightly lower compared to other models. This indicates the potential of integrating deep learned features with manually engineered features but also emphasizes the challenges in achieving optimal accuracy through this approach.

The developed model in this research involved the hybridization of Local Binary Pattern (LBP) and Convolutional Neural Networks (CNN), resulting in a remarkable accuracy of 96%. The successful fusion of LBP and CNN illustrates the effectiveness of this hybrid approach in accurately detecting and classifying breast cancer from mammography images. This superior accuracy highlights the robustness and efficacy of the hybrid model, suggesting its potential for advancing the state-of-the-art in mammography-based breast cancer detection.

The comparison in Table 5 underscores the importance of innovative model design and feature integration in achieving high accuracy in the detection and classification of breast cancer from mammography images. It demonstrates the potential for leveraging deep learning techniques and a combination of features to enhance the overall accuracy and reliability of breast cancer detection, contributing to improved healthcare outcomes and patient care.

5. CONCLUSION AND RECOMMENDATION

The examination of existing literature has yielded valuable insights into a variety of machine learning methods and algorithms employed for predicting breast cancer and other ailments. Many of these methods have gained popularity and acknowledgment through studies published on various platforms.

Consequently, automating the diagnostic process enables healthcare professionals to focus on developing tailored treatment plans for patients. This not only improves patient outcomes but also reduces healthcare costs by minimizing unnecessary procedures and tests. The utilization of machine learning and deep learning techniques in the detection of breast cancer has the potential to revolutionize the diagnosis and management of this disease. Incorporating these tools into healthcare systems has the potential to decrease cancer-related mortality rates and enhance the overall management of breast cancer.

This study presents an effective and efficient framework designed to accurately detect breast cancer from mammography images. The research demonstrates that combining low-level features with high-level features can enhance the accuracy of identification, and the results obtained indicate superiority over the discoveries made by Sajid et al. (2023). Moreover, the model underwent evaluation using two mammography datasets to assess its ability to generalize

For future improvements to the present study, there is a plan to advance this system by developing an attention mechanism-guided model for the selection of pertinent extracted features. The aim is to achieve improved and precise recognition of breast cancer images.

REFERENCES

Abunasser, B. S., Al-Hiealy, M. R. J., Zaqout, I. S., & Abu-Naser, S. S. (2023). Convolution Neural Network for Breast Cancer Detection and Classification Using Deep Learning. *Asian Pacific Journal of Cancer Prevention*, 24(2), 531. PMID:36853302

Adedigba, A. P., Adeshina, S. A., & Aibinu, A. M. (2022). Performance Evaluation of Deep Learning Models on Mammogram Classification Using Small Dataset. *Bioengineering (Basel, Switzerland)*, 2022(9), 161. doi:10.3390/bioengineering9040161 PMID:35447721

Al-Antari, M. A., Han, S. M., & Kim, T. S. (2020). Evaluation of deep learning detection and classification towards computer-aided diagnosis of breast lesions in digital X-ray mammograms. *Computer Methods and Programs in Biomedicine*, 196, 105584. doi:10.1016/j.cmpb.2020.105584 PMID:32554139

Bautista, M. A., Sanakoyeu, A., Tikhoncheva, E., & Ommer, B. (2016). Cliquecnn: Deep unsupervised exemplar learning. *Advances in Neural Information Processing Systems*, 29.

Bengio, Y., Courville, A., & Vincent, P. (2013). Representation Learning: A Review and New Perspectives. *IEEE Transactions on Pattern Analysis and Machine Intelligence*, 35(8), 1798–1828. doi:10.1109/TPAMI.2013.50 PMID:23787338

Bohr, A., & Memarzadeh, K. (2020). The rise of artificial intelligence in healthcare applications. In *Artificial Intelligence in healthcare* (pp. 25–60). Academic Press. doi:10.1016/B978-0-12-818438-7.00002-2

Bonavita, I., Rafael-Palou, X., Ceresa, M., Piella, G., Ribas, V., & Ballester, M. A. G. (2020). Integration of convolutional neural networks for pulmonary nodule malignancy assessment in a lung cancer classification pipeline. *Computer Methods and Programs in Biomedicine*, *185*, 105172. doi:10.1016/j.cmpb.2019.105172 PMID:31710985

Butt, F. M., Hussain, L., Jafri, S. H. M., Lone, K. J., Alajmi, M., Abunadi, I., Al-Wesabi, F. N., & Hamza, M. A. (2022, May). Optimizing parameters of artificial intelligence deep convolutional neural networks (CNN) to improve prediction performance of load forecasting system. *IOP Conference Series. Earth and Environmental Science*, *1026*(1), 012028. doi:10.1088/1755-1315/1026/1/012028

Byra, M. (2021). Breast mass classification with transfer learning based on scaling of deep representations. *Biomedical Signal Processing and Control*, *69*, 102828. doi:10.1016/j.bspc.2021.102828

Chen, J., Du, L., He, H., & Guo, Y. (2019). Convolutional factor analysis model with application to radar automatic target recognition. *Pattern Recognition*, *87*, 140–156. doi:10.1016/j.patcog.2018.10.014

Chow, A. Y. (2010). Cell Cycle Control by Oncogenes and Tumor Suppressors: Driving the Transformation of Normal Cells into Cancerous Cells. *Nature Education*, *3*(9), 7.

El Zarif, O., & Haraty, R. A. (2020). Toward information preservation in healthcare systems. In *Innovation in Health Informatics* (pp. 163–185). Academic Press. doi:10.1016/B978-0-12-819043-2.00007-1

Girma, D. T., Friedhelm, S., Achim, I., & Dereje, Y. (2020). Survey of deep learning in breast cancer image analysis. *Evolving Systems*, *11*(1), 143–163. doi:10.100712530-019-09297-2

Ha, R., Chang, P., Mutasa, S., Karcich, J., Goodman, S., Blum, E., Kalinsky, K., Liu, M. Z., & Jambawalikar, S. (2019). Convolutional neural network using a breast MRI tumor dataset can predict oncotype Dx recurrence score. *Journal of Magnetic Resonance Imaging*, *49*(2), 518–524. doi:10.1002/jmri.26244 PMID:30129697

Hekal, A. A., Elnakib, A., & Moustafa, H. E. D. (2021). Automated early breast cancer detection and classification system. *Signal, Image and Video Processing*, *15*(7), 1497–1505. doi:10.100711760-021-01882-w

Hikmah, N. F., Sardjono, T. A., Mertiana, W. D., Firdi, N. P., & Purwitasari, D. (2022). An Image Processing Framework for Breast Cancer Detection Using Multi-View Mammographic Images. *EMITTER International Journal of Engineering Technology*, 136-152.

Hong, S., Song, S. Y., Park, B., Suh, M., Choi, K. S., Jung, S. E., Kim, M. J., Lee, E. H., Lee, C. W., & Jun, J. K. (2020). Effect of digital mammography for breast cancer screening: A comparative study of more than 8 million Korean women. *Radiology*, *294*(2), 247–255. doi:10.1148/radiol.2019190951 PMID:31793847

Huang, D., Shan, C., Ardabilian, M., Wang, Y., & Chen, L. (2011). Local binary patterns and its application to facial image analysis: A survey. *IEEE Transactions on Systems, Man, and Cybernetics. Part C, Applications and Reviews*, *41*(6), 765–781. doi:10.1109/TSMCC.2011.2118750

Jansson, D., Dieriks, V. B., Rustenhoven, J., Smyth, L. C., Scotter, E., Aalderink, M., & Dragunow, M. (2021, February). Cardiac glycosides target barrier inflammation of the vasculature, meninges and choroid plexus. *Communications Biology*, *4*(1), 260. doi:10.103842003-021-01787-x PMID:33637884

Jubeen, M., Rahman, H., Rahman, A. U., Wahid, S. A., Imran, A., Yasin, A., & Ihsan, I. (2022). An automatic breast cancer diagnostic system based on mammographic images using convolutional neural network classifier. *Journal of Computing & Biomedical Informatics*, *4*(01), 77–86.

Kaszak, I., Witkowska-Piłaszewicz, O., Domrazek, K., & Jurka, P. (2022). The novel diagnostic techniques and biomarkers of canine mammary tumors. *Veterinary Sciences*, *9*(10), 526. doi:10.3390/vetsci9100526 PMID:36288138

Kortli, Y., Jridi, M., Al Falou, A., & Atri, M. (2018). A comparative study of cfs, lbp, hog, sift, surf, and brief for security and face recognition. In *Advanced Secure Optical Image Processing for Communications* (pp. 13–1). IOP Publishing. doi:10.1088/978-0-7503-1457-2ch13

Kuo, J. H., Chabot, J. A., & Lee, J. A. (2016). Breast cancer in thyroid cancer survivors: An analysis of the Surveillance, Epidemiology, and End Results-9 database. *Surgery*, *159*(1), 23–30. doi:10.1016/j.surg.2015.10.009 PMID:26522696

Louise, W., & Toral, G. (2022). Understanding breast cancer as a global health concern. *The British Journal of Radiology*, *95*(1130), 20211033. doi:10.1259/bjr.20211033 PMID:34905391

Madduri, A., Adusumalli, S. S., Katragadda, H. S., Dontireddy, M. K. R., & Suhasini, P. S. (2021, August). Classification of Breast Cancer Histopathological Images using Convolutional Neural Networks. In *2021 8th International Conference on Signal Processing and Integrated Networks (SPIN)* (pp. 755-759). IEEE 10.1109/SPIN52536.2021.9566015

Maleki, N., & Niaki, S. T. A. (2023). An intelligent algorithm for lung cancer diagnosis using extracted features from Computerized Tomography images. *Healthcare Analytics*, *3*, 100150. doi:10.1016/j.health.2023.100150

Mao, Y. J., Lim, H. J., Ni, M., Yan, W. H., Wong, D. W. C., & Cheung, J. C. W. (2022). Breast tumour classification using ultrasound elastography with machine learning: A systematic scoping review. *Cancers (Basel)*, *14*(2), 367. doi:10.3390/cancers14020367 PMID:35053531

Miglioretti, D. L., Lange, J., Van Den Broek, J. J., Lee, C. I., Van Ravesteyn, N. T., Ritley, D., Kerlikowske, K., Fenton, J. J., Melnikow, J., de Koning, H. J., & Hubbard, R. A. (2016). Radiation-induced breast cancer incidence and mortality from digital mammography screening: A modeling study. *Annals of Internal Medicine*, *164*(4), 205–214. doi:10.7326/M15-1241 PMID:26756460

Oluwasegun, A. A., Sadiq, T., Odimba, C. R., & Olalekan, J. (n.d.). Generic Hybrid Model for Breast Cancer Mammography Image Classification Using EfficientNetB2. *DUJOPAS, 9*(3b), 281-289.

Pfeiffer, R. M., Webb-Vargas, Y., Wheeler, W., & Gail, M. H. (2018). Proportion of us trends in breast cancer incidence attributable to long-term changes in risk factor distributions. *Cancer Epidemiology, Biomarkers & Prevention*, *27*(10), 1214–1222. doi:10.1158/1055-9965.EPI-18-0098

Punitha, S., Al-Turjman, F., & Stephan, T. (2021). An automated breast cancer diagnosis using feature selection and parameter optimization in ANN. *Computers & Electrical Engineering*, *90*, 106958. doi:10.1016/j.compeleceng.2020.106958

Ruby, A. U., & Chandran, J. G. C. (2016). A Theoretical Approach on Face Recognition with Single Sample per Class using CS-LBP and Gabor Magnitude and Phase. *Indian Journal of Science and Technology*, *9*, 31.

Sadad, T., Munir, A., Saba, T., & Hussain, A. (2018). Fuzzy C-means and region growing based classification of tumor from mammograms using hybrid texture feature. *Journal of Computational Science*, *29*, 34–45. doi:10.1016/j.jocs.2018.09.015

Sajid, U., Khan, R. A., Shah, S. M., & Arif, S. (2023). Breast cancer classification using deep learned features boosted with handcrafted features. *Biomedical Signal Processing and Control*, *86*, 105353. doi:10.1016/j.bspc.2023.105353

Samee, N. A., Atteia, G., Meshoul, S., Al-antari, M. A., & Kadah, Y. M. (2022). Deep learning cascaded feature selection framework for breast cancer classification: Hybrid CNN with univariate-based approach. *Mathematics*, *10*(19), 3631. doi:10.3390/math10193631

Schiffman, J. D., Fisher, P. G., & Gibbs, P. (2015). Early detection of cancer: Past, present, and future. *American Society of Clinical Oncology Educational Book*, *35*(1), 57–65. doi:10.14694/EdBook_AM.2015.35.57 PMID:25993143

Siegel, R. L., Miller, K. D., Wagle, N. S., & Jemal, A. (2023). Cancer statistics, 2023. *Ca Cancer J Clin*, *73*(1), 17-48. https://acsjournals.onlinelibrary.wiley.com/doi/abs/ doi:10.3322/caac.21763

Singh, V. K., Rashwan, H. A., Romani, S., Akram, F., Pandey, N., Sarker, M. M. K., & Torrents-Barrena, J. (2020). Breast tumor segmentation and shape classification in mammograms using generative adversarial and convolutional neural network. *Expert Systems with Applications*, *139*, 112855. doi:10.1016/j.eswa.2019.112855

Song, B. I. (2021). A machine learning-based radiomics model for the prediction of axillary lymph-node metastasis in breast cancer. *Breast Cancer (Tokyo, Japan)*, *28*(3), 664–671. doi:10.100712282-020-01202-z PMID:33454875

Torres-Galván, J. C., Guevara, E., & González, F. J. (2019, May). *Comparison of deep learning architectures for pre-screening of breast cancer thermograms. In 2019 Photonics North (PN)*. IEEE.

Touahri, R., Aziz, I. N., Hammami, N. E., Aldwairi, M., & Benaida, F. (2019, April). Automated breast tumor diagnosis using local binary patterns (LBP) based on deep learning classification. In *2019 International Conference on Computer and Information Sciences (ICCIS)* (pp. 1-5). IEEE. 10.1109/ICCISci.2019.8716428

Tsochatzidis, L., Costaridou, L., & Pratikakis, I. (2019). Deep learning for breast cancer diagnosis from mammograms—A comparative study. *Journal of Imaging*, *5*(3), 37. doi:10.3390/jimaging5030037 PMID:34460465

Wagner, S. A. (2016). SAR ATR by a combination of convolutional neural network and support vector machines. *IEEE Transactions on Aerospace and Electronic Systems*, *52*(6), 2861–2872. doi:10.1109/TAES.2016.160061

Wang, Z., Dong, N., Dai, W., Rosario, S. D., & Xing, E. P. (2018). Classification of breast cancer histopathological images using convolutional neural networks with hierarchical loss and global pooling. In *International conference image analysis and recognition* (pp. 745-753). Cham: Springer International Publishing. 10.1007/978-3-319-93000-8_84

Wen, Z., & Huang, H. (2022). The potential for artificial intelligence in healthcare. *Journal of Commercial Biotechnology*, *27*(4).

Yu, K., Tan, L., Lin, L., Cheng, X., Yi, Z., & Sato, T. (2021). Deep-learning-empowered breast cancer auxiliary diagnosis for 5GB remote E-health. *IEEE Wireless Communications*, *28*(3), 54–61. doi:10.1109/MWC.001.2000374

Zakareya, S., Izadkhah, H., & Karimpour, J. (2023). A New Deep-Learning-Based Model for Breast Cancer Diagnosis from Medical Images. *Diagnostics (Basel)*, *13*(11), 1944. doi:10.3390/diagnostics13111944 PMID:37296796

Zeebaree, D. Q., Abdulazeez, A., Zebari, D. A., Haron, H., & Hamed, H. N. A. (2021). Multi-Level Fusion in Ultrasound for Cancer Detection Based on Uniform LBP Features. *Computers, Materials & Continua*, *66*(3).

Zhou, L.-Q., Wu, X.-L., Huang, S.-Y., Wu, G.-G., Ye, H.-R., Wei, Q., Bao, L.-Y., Deng, Y.-B., Li, X.-R., Cui, X.-W., & Dietrich, C. F. (2020). Lymph node metastasis prediction from primary breast cancer us images using deep learning. *Radiology*, *294*(1), 19–28. doi:10.1148/radiol.2019190372 PMID:31746687

Chapter 12
Predicting Depression From Social Media Users by Using Lexicons and Machine Learning Algorithms

Santhi Selvaraj

(iD) https://orcid.org/0000-0002-3252-4728

Mepco Schlenk Engineering College, India

S. Selva Nidhyananthan

(iD) https://orcid.org/0000-0001-9131-8409

Mepco Schlenk Engineering College, India

ABSTRACT

Depression is one of the most common health issues among individuals. The rate of psychotic treatments is increasing day by day. Depression is created in many ways among the people, especially through work stress, financial burden, unemployment among the adults. Today, the emergence of social media into people's lives makes them expose their feelings and emotions on the social media platforms. The aim of this work is to predict the depressive features from social media users' comments by using machine learning techniques. Multinomial naïve bayes, non-linear support vector machine, and artificial neural network methods are used for classifying the features and comparing it using performance evaluation metrics and get the best classifier. This system includes data pre-processing, feature extraction, data splitting, classification, and performance evaluation. The results show that the proposed system has gradually improved performance accuracy. According to the results, ANN gives 99.19%, the best accuracy compared to other machine learning classifiers.

DOI: 10.4018/978-1-6684-8531-6.ch012

Copyright © 2024, IGI Global. Copying or distributing in print or electronic forms without written permission of IGI Global is prohibited.

INTRODUCTION

Web 2.0, which is the conceptual and technological framework that allows users to share their ideas, opinions, and thoughts through virtual or social networks and communities, was made possible by the Web 2.0 collection of web-based applications known as social media (Kaplan, 2010). Various social media platforms, such as social networks, media sharing platforms, discussion forums, networks for user reviews, blogs and microblogs, and social commerce platforms are used based on data and applications (Sara Gancho, 2017). Based on Global Statistics (India Social Media Statistics, 2022) report, YouTube, Facebook, Instagram, and Twitter have the largest percentage of users and access rate. These social media platforms are used by millions of people to share information, photographs, news, live audio, and videos (Waseem Akram, 2018).

Trillions bytes of data are shared every second on social media, which can be in structured or unstructured data formats (Stefan Stieglitza et al., 2018) so Big data in social media could be analyzed (Prashant Sahatiya, 2018). Currently, social media is more important in health care applications than in other commercial ones. Health care organizations and medical management have looked into how social media may be used to connect different health informatics systems and develop interactions between patients and clinicians (How to Use Social Media in Healthcare, 2022). The majority of academics are now focusing on social networks analysis, which entails capturing relational or structured data in the form of social entities like people, groups, and organizations with some connections between them (Shazia Tabassum, 2018).

Depression is an extreme mental health problem among the people world-wide relevance of their ages, gender and religion. In this modern world of communication and technology, people feel more comfortable in sharing their thoughts and emotions on social media platforms / social networking sites on a daily basis. Anybody can view a person's mood through their comments, posts, videos and depression level is sensed easily by their comments and posts. This creates an environment that provides additional information regarding the depression disorder among the people. Social Media websites such as twitter and Facebook have become to express peoples' activity and thoughts by creating and posting the chats among the people.

In general, psychologists diagnose depressed humans through face-to-face counselling sessions followed by clinical depression criteria. But in modern world, most of the machine learning, deep learning and text mining methods have been improved to detect latent depression in initial stage itself. In day-to-day life the number of users in social media is increasing so social media platforms act as a reflecting mirror of people's mood. It is also more convenient to find a depressed user based on their comments, posts etc.

Currently, most of the researchers using social media platforms like Reddit, Twitter, Facebook to identify the depression among the people. Numerous research on depression detection has been done by identifying crucial depressive disorder of the social media users with the help of tweets posted by users. The aim of this work, to predict depressed feature through leveraging social media data. In order to find the depression using the user comments on social media, this work tend to use a Lexicon related model (Genghao, 2020).

The comments from the collected dataset contain both depressed and non-depressed words even neutral words, but our work tends to separate those words and train the machine with the correct labels then classify the comments and predict the depressed feature. Hence the overall objective of this work is to propose the model that predicts the depressive, non-depressive and neutral features. Text has been taken as input data for this model. This creates an awareness among the people to know the depressed user using their words. We have to predict the depression from social media text by applying the various process such as label assigning, depressed word extraction and model construction using machine and deep learning algorithms.

The problem of examining depressed people in social media using their comments. It is not an easy task to identify depressed people as early as possible. Since social media users post their comments in different emotions. A small initiative in this work is extracting the depressive words from the social media user comments. For this process, many methodologies have been used. This initiative can help people to identify depressed users through depressive features present in their comments.

The main objectives of this work are to assign Class Labels to the Dataset and to predict depressed and non-depressed features using Machine Learning and Deep Learning algorithms. Finally, the best classifiers according to their accuracy are found. Adult care physicians who are there ready to detect depression in adults can identify the depressive users by the depressive words identified by this work. Then generate reports of their depressive levels and give counselling by contacting them manually. The platforms that can be used for this work are social networking sites like Facebook, Twitter, Reddit, etc.

The remaining sections of this chapter are out-lined as follows: Section 2 describes the related works for the current system. Section 3 describes the overall architecture and methodologies of proposed system, while Section 4 describes the Experiments and Results of the proposed system. Section 5 concludes the proposed work.

BACKGROUND AND LITERATURE REVIEW

This section focuses on reviewing the various methods for predicting and detecting the depression from text. Ashtik Mahapatra (2020) proposed a Co-training based classification method for predicting the eating disorders, depression, anxiety and mental diseases. In this model, the patients were classified and associated with chronic mental illness diseases. Co-training is one of the semi-supervised learning methods, which is incorporated with various classifiers such as Naive Bayes, Support Vector Machine, and Random Forest. They have used the Reddit platform to download depression posts and top 5 comments to construct feature space. The results of co-training techniques are effective compared to the traditional classifiers.

Fiza Azam M et al (2021) developed a depression identification system using sentiment analysis. This model fully focused on developing a machine learning model involved in analyzing linguistic patterns obtained from the Twitter dataset and determining whether the user has depressive symptoms or not. Random Forest and Support Vector Machine models are trained and concluded that the Random Forest model has more efficiency. Finally, the accuracy is achieved by both Machine Learning models, it is near to 80%.

Kuhaneswaran et al (2021) proposed the detection of depression for social media users. The data is given into two dissimilar types of classifiers such as Naive Bayes and NB Tree. These two classifiers are compared based on their accuracies to find out the best algorithm for detecting depression. This work starts with sentiment analysis to recognize the sentiment label and score. The labeled data are given into the Machine Learning algorithm that allow the classifier to check if the data is classified into correct classes. The model has been realized into two contrasting sizes of tweet datasets to get the accuracy in classifying depressive and non-depressive tweets. Both the classifiers, Naive Bayes and NBTree got equivalent accuracy of 92.34% and hence concluded that both the classifiers are equally efficient.

Keshu Malviya et al (2021) developed certain standard models such as SVM and Linear Model. The Transformers model with Reddit data was achieved a high accuracy for determining depression in social media users. Transformer model is nothing but a deep learning technique that does the mechanism of self-attention which allows the input to communicate with each other and identify where there should be more attention. The dataset used in this model have given a balanced and smooth implementation so obtained the higher accuracy of 98%.

Sudha et al (2020) developed a depression detection system, that detects depression from the social media user, through machine learning technique. In this work, the depression was detected by using Naïve Bayes, Decision Tree, Random Forest algorithms and K-Nearest Neighbors. Further, continuous analyzing of previous readings of the user to detect the changes in the depression level. And also, the user is immediately warned about their depression level and they are urged to seek the help of the professionals. Data was obtained from the patients or users on the regular basis in the form of text. Finally, accuracy of the model was calculated through evaluation metrics.

Akshi et al (2019) proposed an Anxious Depression (AD) prediction system for social media tweets. The feature set of the model was described by using a 5-attributes vector-like word, timing, frequency, sentiment, and contrast based on the user posting pattern. This lexicon is constructed to identify the existence of anxiety indicators. Time and frequency of tweets are studied for lack of symmetry and opinion polarity analytics was done to find out inconsistencies in behavioral posts. The model was trained using three classifiers like Random Forest, multinomial Naive Bayes, Gradient Boosting and take major voting using an ensemble voting classifier. The classification accuracy of 85.09% was achieved in this model for 100 users' tweets from social media.

Zhang et al (2019) developed a system for constructing a sentiment lexicon of each topic. It was an important basement for analysing sentiment in social networks. Though, in social media need a sentiment lexicon and it was constructed based on filtering text model, Sentiment relationship graph, CRM Model, Spectral clustering model. By using this system, it was solved the sentiment words of topics and increase the performance and accuracy of the sentiment lexicon.

Giuntini et al (2021) proposed TROAD (Tracing the Roadmap of Depressive Users) framework for identifying consecutive patterns and long-time mental state depressed user in social network sites. This algorithm monitors the frequent activity of the user's post on the Reddit dataset and it maintains the user's silence for generating patterns. It takes psychological and contextual information from user's comment. It was hard in governing negative emotions common among users with depression and readability was poor due to consecutive patterns.

Hatoon AlSagri et al (2020) proposed a system for detecting depressed Twitter Tweets based on user's tweets and network behavior by applying Machine learning algorithms. Classifiers are trained and tested based on users' activities features from the network and check whether the person is depressed or not. The classifiers used for this system was Naive Bayes, Linear SVM, Decision Tree. Evaluation metrics like accuracy, F1-score was found for evaluating the system.

Anu Priya et al (2020) offered a system for forecasting depression, stress level and anxiety by using machine learning algorithms. Data collection was done through hired and unhired people throughout diverse cultures and communities through DASS 21(Depression, Anxiety, Stress Scale questionnaire). In this work, F1-score was found for identifying the high-quality accuracy framework among the five algorithms like Naive Bayes, K-NN classifier, Decision Tree classifier, Random Forest classifier and Support Vector Machine. The accuracy of Naive Bayes became observed to be the highest, even though Random Forest recognized as the high-quality model. Due to this problem, this model produced imbalanced classes so the selection of high-quality model was made on the premise of the f1 score and solve the imbalanced partitioning.

Suyash Dabhane et al (2020) proposed work on detection of depression using ML techniques have been functioned out. Here Ensemble learning approach and various machine learning methods were used to detect depression. Machine Learning algorithms along with the ensemble method is helped to build an efficient and high accurate model for detecting depression on social media.

G. Geetha et al (2020) developed a work to help patients suffering from depression by earlier identification of the signs and symptoms of depression which was more useful to them. This Method has taken the writing pattern of textual contents and linguistic clues of tweets for identification of depression users. Naive Bayes, Support Vector Machine, Logistic Regression and Random Forest classifiers were used for classifying textual and linguistic tweets. The accuracy of Bayes theorem as 88.5%, Random Forest as 95.1%, Support Vector Machine as 96.1% and Logistic Regression was 96.2%. The result has been concluded that Logistic Regression have given the better performance among the classifiers.

MAIN FOCUS OF THE CHAPTER

The idea of this work is to predict the depression from social media users' tweets by using the depressive and non-depressive lexicons and machine learning algorithms. This work uses the various machine learning classifier algorithms like SVM, Naïve Bayes, ANN and compare the performance of these algorithms using Accuracy, Precision, Recall and F1-Score.

PROPOSED METHODOLOGY

The proposed work involves different Machine Learning approaches to classify and predict the depressive features (Depressed and Non-Depressed) from the dataset. The dataset consists of comments of users from social media. The proposed system made up of five steps:

1. Data Pre-Processing
2. Feature Extraction
3. Data Splitting
4. Classification
5. Performance Evaluation

1. Dataset Description

The dataset considered for this work is Kaggle which carries 50997 records and which are Twitter comments of the user in social media. Initially, the dataset doesn't have class labels so converting it into supervised data is the part of this work after structuring the comments are labeled as depressive, non-depressive and neutral.

Figure 1 presents the flow of predicting depressive features using two aspects training and testing. It encompasses Machine Learning Classifiers like Naive Bayes, Non-linear Support vector Machine and

Figure 1. The overall architecture of proposed system

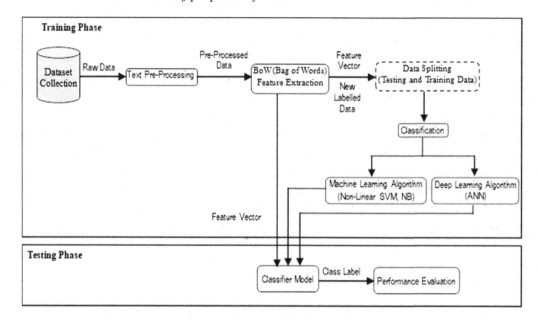

Artificial Neural Network. It includes sub methods such as text pre-processing, feature extraction and labelling. Finally classified labels are evaluated through performance evaluation.

2. Data Pre-Processing

Text preprocessing is a way to remove the unwanted information from the text data before send into the model. The unwanted information from the raw data in various representation like stop words, punctuations, emotions, etc. Pre-processing is common for both training and testing of the model. This step contains four processes which are explained below:

i) Remove Stop Words

Stop words are words, they don't have any semantic information for the whole online comments. It includes pronouns, auxiliary verbs, determinant, interjections, etc. The elimination of stop words and elimination of special symbols support the sequence of sentiment classification framework for achieving better performance and accuracy.

ii) Tokenization

Tokenization is used for separating each sentence into tokens. Each tokens are considered as words in the sentence.

iii) Lemmatization

In this process, words are lemmatized to root or lemmas. It looks through the provided dictionary to extract the base form of the word. Along with word reduction, it also considers the complete language vocabulary for doing morphological analysis of the word.

iv) IT ALSO REMOVES the URLs, Numbers, HTML Tags, Special Characters, and Hashtags From the User Comments

This data pre-processing is done by using python language with Natural Language Toolkit (NLTK) and it takes forty seven lines of code including the function as word_tokenize(), WordNetLemmatizer() and stopwords.words().

3. Feature Extraction and Labelling

In this work Count-Vectorizer method is used to extract the feature from the user data. It is used to transform the texts into vectors according to frequency of each word present in the entire documents. Count-Vectorizer converts the text documents to token counts and construct the sparse matrix. This incorporation produces a sparse representation of the count. The collection of depressive words within the index of 90 and above 90 it has neutral words, totally the collected lexicon has 130 words (Genghao et al., n.d.; Akshi Kumar et al., n.d.).

Count-vectorizer forms the sparse matrix or feature vector based on the frequency count of the user comments. The initial un-labeled dataset is labeled by extracting the depressive words of the particular user comment based on the results of the feature vector. If the depressive words are found in the user comment it is labeled as Depressed or Neutral based on the index otherwise it is labeled as non-depressed. This step takes one hundred and thirty lines of codes including the functions as CountVectorizer(), fit(), get_feature_names(), transform().

The collected words are considered as the feature for depressive users. Count-vectorizer forms the sparse matrix or feature vector based on the frequency count of the user comments. The initial un-labeled dataset is labeled by extracting the depressive words of the particular user comment based on the results of the feature vector. If the depressive words are found in the user comment it is labeled as Depressed or Neutral based on the index otherwise it is labeled as non-depressed.

Feature Extraction Algorithms includes two main steps BOW (Bag- Of- Words) and Label Encoding. The steps of each algorithm are listed below in Algorithm 1 and Algorithm 2:

Algorithm1 Bag of words()

```
// Input                  : tweet:Each tweet of user
// Output                 : bow_feature: Feature Vector of each tweet
{
        Initialize feature_vectors bow_feature = [0,0,...,0]
        for words in tweet do
                if words in dictionary then
```

Table 1. Lexicon for depression prediction

Depressive Words (90 Words)			Neutral Words (40 Words)	
1. restless	31. edge	61. sad		
2. sick	32. hurt	62. low		
3. sorrow	33. fear	63. fat		
4. unhappy	34. illusion	64. desperate		
5. abandon	35. afraid	65. panic		
6. upset	36. danger	66. never	91. Stability	111. strong
7. sensitive	37. jump	67. helpless	92. comfort	112. perfect
8. bored	38. melancholy	68. forget	93. happy	113. praise
9. crap	39. collapse	69. loser	94. happiness	114. precious
10. apastia	40. Close	70. bad	95. successful	115. progress
11. weak	41. rubbish	71. give up	96. confidence	116. congratulate
12. empty	42. worthless	72. tired	97. sunshine	117. love
13. ugly	43. goodbye	73. guilt	98. struggle	118. welcome
14. shatter	44. shadow	74. torture	99. positive	119. kindness
15. suicide	45. haze	75. disappoint	100. brave	120. robust
16. suicidal	46. destroy	76. dark	101. enjoy	121. earnest
17. cry	47. meaningless	77. lonely	102. peace	122. agree
18. death	48. sleepless	78. suffer	103. enthusiasm	123. support
19. anxious	49. regret	79. awful	104. healthy	124. award
20. Shit	50. stress	80. Broke	105. satisfied	125. advantage
21. escape	51. suspect	81. problem	106. active	126. good deal
22. insomnia	52. frustration	82. die	107. grow up	127. develop
23. depressed	53. unsuccessful	83. reject	108. pride	128. warm
24. negative	54. blame	84. useless	109. good	129. bright colored
25. fail	55. lost	85. leave	110. admire	130. understand
26. ruin	56. damaged	86. depression		
27. antidepressant	57. pathetic	87. nervous		
28. dissatisfied	58. kill	88. cut wrist		
29. painful	59. crash	89. Hate		
30. fuck	60. nobody	90. frustrated		

```
                                    token_index = getIndex(dictionary,
words)

                                    bow_feature[token_index]++
                        end if
                        else
                                    continue
                        end else
            end for
return bow_feature
}
```

These words are indicated in Table 1.

Algorithm2 Label encoding()


```
// Input: tweet: Each tweet of user, bow_feature: Feature Vector of all tweets
// Output: Tweet: Class Labels assigned to each tweet
```

```
{
for each word in tweet do
                depressed_wordCount =0
                neutral_wordCount =0
                if the bow_feature.index(word) < 90 then
                                depressed_wordCount ++
                end if
                else if the bow_feature.index(word) > =90 then
                                neutral_wordCount ++
                end
end for
if depressed_wordCount > neutral_wordCount then
                class label = Depressed
end if
else if depressed_wordCount<neutral_wordCount then
                class label = Neutral
end if
else if depressed_wordCount==neutral_wordCount and depressed_wordCount!=0 then
                class label = Depressed
end if
else
                class label=Non-Depressed
end
}
```

4. Data Splitting

Data splitting is the act of separating available dataset into two parts for training and validation. One part of the dataset is used to increase a prediction rate of the model and the other is used to assess the performance of the models. In machine and deep learning classification model, maximum amount of dataset is used for training and lesser quantity of the dataset is used for testing. Similarly in our work, 80% of data is passed to training and 20% of data is passed to testing.

5. Classification

In classification, it involves both Machine learning and deep learning classifier. Non-linear Support Vector Machine, Multinomial Naive Bayes is used as a classifier in the machine learning techniques. In deep learning Artificial Neural Network is used as a classifier. The model construction takes 180 lines of code includes the MultinomialNB(), SVC() and sequential() functions which are presented in the sklearn package.

i) Non-Linear Support Vector Machine (SVM)

SVM is used to solve both categorical and numerical type of data by using decision boundaries and margins. Decision boundaries helps to divide the data points using hyperplanes. If we used two input attributes then the hyperplane is a straight line otherwise two-dimensional plane is constructed if more than two attributes. Kernelized SVM has maintained kernels, which changes the input data space into a higher-dimensional space. SVM kernel function is written as k(x,x'). In this work Radial Basis Function kernel is used for multiple class classification.

$$K\left(x_i, x_j\right) = e^{-\gamma\left(x_i, x_j\right)^2}$$

(1)

Most of the time SVM are used for binary classification, assign the data points either in 1 or 0. In multiclass problem, the classes are splitting into more than one binary classification cases, which is known as one-vs-rest. It separates the statistics factor into class x and the rest. The one-vs-rest approach uses m SVM's for classifying m classes.

ii) Multinomial Naïve Bayes

Multinomial Naive Bayes algorithm comes under supervised algorithm which is based on Bayes theorem and is used for fixing classification problems. A naive Bayes classifier is a set of many algorithms in which all of the algorithms stake a one common principle that means every feature being associated with one class and remaining features are associated with other classes. The presence or absence of each feature doesn't affect the other features because of using alpha function, it avoids probability zero problem. Naive Bayes has contained effective set of rules for textual content analysis and solve the problem with more than one classes.

$$P\left(A|B\right) = \frac{P\left(B|A\right) * P\left(A\right)}{P\left(B\right)}$$

(2)

Where,
   P(B) = Class B's Prior Probability
   P(A) = Class A's Prior Probability
   P(B|A) = Probability of the occurrence of predictor B given class A

iii) Artificial Neural Network

The Artificial neural network has 3 layers entry layer, hidden layer and output layer. The entry layer takes the input data and passes them to the hidden layer and the output layer produces the predicted value and those neural networks need to be learnt with few training data. Activation Function is an essential part of the neural networks which activates each node in feature extraction and at last output is calculated. In this work, ReLu activation function is used in input layer and hidden layer then Sigmoid function is used in output layer. ANN has the capacity to learn the non-linear model for maintaining many complicated relationships between non-linear input and output layer.

6. Performance Evaluation

Standard overall performance assessment is completed to estimate our proposed ANN, Naïve Bayes, SVM model. We consider the following main evaluation metrics for assessing our models.

i) Accuracy

The accuracy of a model is a measure of its correctness. It indicates how well the model can anticipate the incoming data's target value or class. The higher accuracy says that the model is more comfortable with prediction and actual values.

$$Accuracy = \frac{True\ Positive + True\ Negative}{Total\ Number\ of\ instances} \tag{3}$$

ii) Recall

The true positive rate of the model is defined as recall or sensitivity. It indicates how many right predictions the classifier makes for a given class in relation to the actual count for that class.

$$Recall = \frac{True\ Positive}{True\ Positive + False\ Negative} \tag{4}$$

iii) Precision

The number of true positives divided with the overall number of positive predictions is called precision.

$$Precision = \frac{True\ Positive}{True\ Positive + False\ Positive} \tag{5}$$

iv) F1 Score

F1 score is an average of the prediction Method's accuracy and true positive rate. Its values range from 0 to 1 and the value zero being the lowest score and one denoting the highest.

$$\textbf{F1 Score} = 2 * \frac{\textbf{Precision*Recall}}{\textbf{Precision + Recall}} \tag{6}$$

EXPERIMENTAL RESULTS

In this study, we have Labeled the Dataset as Depressed, Neutral, Non-Depressed by using lexicons and examined the execution of various classifiers for depression prediction.

1. Data Preprocessing Results

The following result represents the data preprocessing and label assignments for sample tweets collected from the social media users. The same following process is done for all 50997 tweets.

Tweet 1	Tweet 2	Tweet 3
is upset that he can't update his Facebook by texting it... and might cry as a result School today also. Blah!	@Kenichan I dived many times for the ball. Managed to save 50% The rest go out of bounds	@LettyA ahh ive always wanted to see rent love the soundtrack!!
↓ Convert to Lower Case		
is upset that he can't update his facebook by texting it... and might cry as a result school today also. blah!	@kenichan i dived many times for the ball. managed to save 50% the rest go out of bounds	@lettya ahh ive always wanted to see rent love the soundtrack!!
↓ Remove digits		
is upset that he can't update his facebook by texting it... and might cry as a result school today also. blah!	@kenichan i dived many times for the ball. managed to save % the rest go out of bounds	@lettya ahh ive always wanted to see rent love the soundtrack!!
↓ Remove mentions		
is upset that he can't update his facebook by texting it... and might cry as a result school today also. blah!	i dived many times for the ball. managed to save % the rest go out of bounds	ahh ive always wanted to see rent love the soundtrack!!
↓ Remove Special character		
is upset that he cant update his facebook by texting it and might cry as a result school today also blah	i dived many times for the ball managed to save the rest go out of bounds	ahh ive always wanted to see rent love the soundtrack
↓ Remove Stop Words		
upset update facebook texting might cry result school today also blah	dived many times ball managed save rest go bounds	ahh ive always wanted see rent love soundtrack
↓ Tokenization		
['upset', 'update', 'facebook', 'texting', 'might',' cry',' result', 'school', 'today', 'also',' blah']	['dived', 'many', 'times', ' ball' 'managed', 'save',' rest',' go', 'bounds']	['ahh', 'ive', 'always', 'wanted', 'see',' rent', 'love', 'soundtrack']
↓ Lemmatization		
['upset', 'update', 'facebook', 'texting', 'might',' cry',' result', 'school', 'today', 'also',' blah']	['dived', 'many', 'times', ' ball' 'managed', 'save',' rest',' go', 'bound']	['ahh', 'ive', 'always', 'wanted', 'see',' rent', 'love', 'soundtrack']
↓ Label Assigning		
['**upset**', 'update', 'facebook', 'texting', 'might',' **cry**',' result', 'school', 'today', 'also',' blah']	['dived', 'many', 'times', ' ball' 'managed', 'save',' rest',' go', 'bound']	['ahh', 'ive', 'always', 'wanted', 'see',' rent', '**love**', 'soundtrack']
↓ Depressed and Neutral Word Counting Using Lexicons		
Depressed: 2 Neutral:0	Depressed: 0 Neutral:0	Depressed: 0 Neutral:1
↓ Assign Labels		
Depressed	**Non-Depressed**	**Neutral**

2. Label Assignment Results

Initially raw dataset contains nearly fifty-one thousand data, after assigning class labels nearly ten thousand data is labeled as depressed, thirty-six thousand data is labeled as non-depressed and five thousand data is labeled as neutral. Figure 2 presents the count of each class after assigning class labels for the unstructured dataset.

Figure 2. Histogram of labels assignment

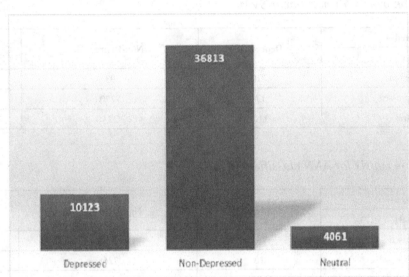

3. Classification Results

These results show the confusion matrix of each classifier and compare the predicted and actual values of each classifier. In this matrix, Diagonal elements represent the True Positive values, the sum of corresponding column excluding TP value is called False Positive, the sum of corresponding row exclude the TP value is called False Negative and rest diagonal elements are considered as True Negative.

The confusion matrix of multinomial Naive Bayes classifier is indicated in Table 2.

The confusion matrix of SVM Classifier is indicated in Table 3.

The confusion matrix of ANN classifier is indicated in Table 4.

Figure 3 presents the Precision, Recall and F1 score of classifiers like NB, SVM, ANN these values are obtained from the confusion matrix of corresponding classifiers.

The accuracy obtained by each classifier algorithm is indicated in Table 5.

Table 2. Confusion matrix for multinomial naïve bayes

Predicted→ Actual↓	Depressed	Non-Depressed	Neutral
Depressed	149	649	1
Non-Depressed	1	7306	11
Neutral	0	1625	458

Table 3. Confusion matrix for non-linear SVM

Predicted→ Actual↓	Depressed	Non-Depressed	Neutral
Depressed	701	93	5
Non-Depressed	17	7270	31
Neutral	115	225	1743

Table 4. Confusion matrix for ANN classifier

Predicted→ Actual↓	Depressed	Non-Depressed	Neutral
Depressed	782	2	15
Non-Depressed	16	7268	34
Neutral	9	7	2067

Figure 3. Comparison of NB, SVM, ANN

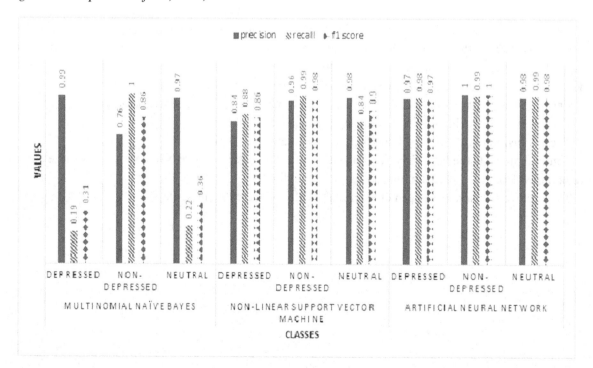

Table 5. Accuracy of the classifiers

Classifier Model	Accuracy
Multi-nominal Naïve Bayes	77.57%
Non-Linear Support Vector Machine	95.23%
Artificial Neural Network	99.19%

CONCLUSION

In this work, we tend to identify the depressive features using Twitter and social media. We tried to create a closer connection between depression and language usage by applying Natural Language Processing and Text Classification techniques. We collected the dataset from Kaggle and convert the unsupervised dataset into supervised dataset by using Bag of Words and label encoding technique. The extracted features are sent to classifiers for training the model and classify the test data by using multinomial Naive Bayes classifier, Non-linear SVM and ANN classifier. Among all these classifiers, ANN gets the highest performance for classifying the text by reaching an accuracy of 99.19%. We got this result by evaluating through evaluation metrics rather than accuracy. We believe this experiment is beneficial in environments like healthcare to extract the depressive words from social media and keep track the mental state of the user in social media.

REFERENCES

Akram, W. (2018). A Study on Positive and Negative Effects of Social Media on Society. *International Journal on Computer Science and Engineering*, 5(10), 347–354.

AlSagri & Ykhlef. (2020). Machine Learning-based Approach for Depression Detection in Twitter Using Content and Activity Features. *IEICE Transactions on Information and Systems, E103.D*(8), 1-16.

Azam, F., & Agro, M. (2021). Identifying Depression Among Twitter Users using Sentiment Analysis. *International Conference on Artificial Intelligence*, 44-49. 10.1109/ICAI52203.2021.9445271

Dabhane & Chawan. (2020). Depression Detection on Social Media using Machine Learning Techniques. *International Research Journal of Engineering and Technology*, 7(11), 97–100.

Gancho. (2017). Social Media: A literature review. *e-Revista LOGO*. 6(2), 59–68.

Geetha, Saranya, Chakrapani, Ponsam, Safa, & Karpagaselvi. (2020). Early Detection of Depression from Social Media Data Using Machine Learning Algorithms. *International Conference on Power, Energy, Control and Transmission Systems*, 1-6. 10.1109/ICPECTS49113.2020.9336974

Giuntini, F. T., de Moraes, K. L. P., Cazzolato, M. T., Kirchner, L. F., Dos Reis, M. J. D., Traina, A. J. M., Campbell, A. T., & Ueyama, J. (2021). Tracing the Emotional Roadmap of Depressive Users on social media Through Sequential Pattern Mining. *IEEE Access : Practical Innovations, Open Solutions*, 9, 9762–97635. doi:10.1109/ACCESS.2021.3095759

How to Use Social Media in Healthcare: A Guide for Health Professionals. (2022). Available: https://blog.hootsuite.com/social-media-health-care

India Social Media Statistics 2022. (2022). Available: https://www.theglobalstatistics.com/india-social-media-statistics/

Kaplan, A. M., & Haenlein, M. (2010). Users of the world, unite! the challenges and opportunities of social media. *Business Horizons*, *53*(1), 59–68. doi:10.1016/j.bushor.2009.09.003

Kuhaneswaran & Govindasamy. (2021). Depression Detection Using Machine Learning Techniques on Twitter Data. *2021 5th International Conference on Intelligent Computing and Control Systems*, 960-966.

Kumar, A., Sharma, A., & Arora, A. (2019). Anxious Depression Prediction in Real-time Social Data. *Proceeding of International Conference on Advanced Engineering, Science, Management and Technology*, 1-7. 10.2139srn.3383359

Li, G., Li, B., Huang, L., & Hou, S. (2020). Automatic Construction of a Depression-Domain Lexicon Based on Microblogs: Text Mining Study. *JMIR Medical Informatics*, *8*(6), 1–17. doi:10.2196/17650 PMID:32574151

Mahapatra, A. (2020). A Novel Approach for Identifying Social Media Posts Indicative of Depression. *IEEE International Symposium on Sustainable Energy, Signal Processing and Cyber Security*, 1-6. 10.1109/iSSSC50941.2020.9358866

Malviya, K., & Roy, B. (2021). A Transformers Approach to Detect Depression in social media. *International Conference on Artificial Intelligence and Smart Systems*, 718-723. 10.1109/ICAIS50930.2021.9395943

Priya, A., Garga, S., & Tigga, N. P. (2020). Predicting Anxiety, Depression, and Stress in Modern Life using Machine Learning Algorithms. *International Conference on Computational Intelligence and Data Science,* 1258-1267. 10.1016/j.procs.2020.03.442

Sahatiya, P. (2018). Big Data Analytics on Social Media Data: A Literature Review. *Int. Res. J. of Engg and Tech.*, *5*(2), 189–192.

Stieglitza, S., Mirbabaiea, M., Rossa, B., & Chris-toph, N. (2018). Social media analytics – Challenges in topic discovery, data collection, and data preparation, Int. J. of In-fo. *Manag.*, *39*, 156–168.

Sudha, Sreemathi, Nathiya, & RahiniPriya. (2020). Depression Detection using Machine Learning. *International Journal of Research and Advanced Development*, 1-6.

Tabassum, S., Pereira, F. S. F., Fernandes, S., & Gama, J. (2018). Social Network Analysis: An Overview. *Wiley In-terdisciplinary Reviews Data Mining and Know.*, *8*(5), 1–30.

Zhang, B., Xu, D., Zhang, H., & Li, M. (2019). STCS Lexicon: Spectral-Clustering-Based Topic-Specific Chinese Sentiment Lexicon Construction for social Networks. *IEEE Transactions on Computational Social Systems*, *6*(6), 2–10. doi:10.1109/TCSS.2019.2941344

KEY TERMS AND DEFINITIONS

Bag of Words: In order to process natural language, machine learning algorithms can use the bag-of-words technique, which gives a feature representation of free-form text and count of the total occurrences of most frequently used words.

Depression: Depression is a mood illness that results in a constant sense of melancholy and boredom. It may be detected with mild, moderate, and severe.

Sentiment Lexicons: A sentiment lexicon is a list of words classified according to whether they are good or negative or neutral.

Social Media: Social media is a group of web-based programmes that provide the conceptual and technical underpinnings for users to communicate their ideas, opinions, and thoughts through online communities and social networks.

Chapter 13
Mental Stress Detection Using Bidirectional Encoder Representations From Transformers

A. Vennila
Kongu Engineering College, India

S. Balambigai
Kongu Engineering College, India

A. S. Renugadevi
iD https://orcid.org/0000-0003-0619-3088
Kongu Engineering College, India

J. Charanya
iD https://orcid.org/0009-0003-8880-9639
Kongu Engineering College, India

ABSTRACT

It seems as if people start losing control as they become easily upset, frustrated, and overwhelmed, having problems in resting and quieting their mind, and also feeling bad about themselves, lonely, worthless, and depressed, and avoiding others. If they have experienced the above symptoms, then there is a chance that they are suffering from mental stress. They have to take proper care of their mental health. Stress can be taken care of if it is properly handled and for that detection of stress or the mental state is necessary to provide proper care. The first step in stress detection is sentiment analysis of the users' daily conversations. The authors have proposed an NLP model and have trained it to produce a score for the input ranging between 0 and 1 where 0 is the negative end and 1 is the positive end. The trained model can predict the scores with an accuracy of above 92% on Twitter.

DOI: 10.4018/978-1-6684-8531-6.ch013

Copyright © 2024, IGI Global. Copying or distributing in print or electronic forms without written permission of IGI Global is prohibited.

1. INTRODUCTION

Over the most recent twenty years, analysts have understood that there is a significant connection between the actual soundness of every person's enthusiastic state. This has prompted expanding interest in emotional registering (AC) which utilizes innovation to perceive the full of feeling condition of an individual. Dr. Rosalind Picard of the Massachusetts Institute of Technology (MIT) distributed the primary book on full of feeling processing. Since that, In the domain of human- computer interaction, it has become a major branch. It detects an individual's present emotion by analyzing their physiological and bodily expressions. Joy, anger, surprise, contempt, sorrow, and fear are some of the most common fundamental emotional states inferred by affective computing. It is a creating issue and it has transformed into an inevitable piece of our standard schedules. The early acknowledgment will lessen the mischief it expenses and hold it back from being progressing. The harms of weight on human well-being have been known by scientists and a critical number of endeavors have made as of late to foster a programmed pressure estimating framework by utilizing shrewd gadgets and progressed AC algorithms. The construction of the input vector space from the existing document vector space is a part of the Sentiment Analysis process. Vector space mapping can be achieved in one of two ways. Because feature extraction is done by applying statistical measures directly, machine learning- based or statistical-based feature extraction methods are widely used. The most usually utilized philosophy for identifying Feelings from text is Naive Bayes and LSTMs. These techniques relatively have exceptionally high precision than another strategy. However, these techniques have higher exactness which will more often than non- fizzle sometimes like mocking comments as the custom customary Long transient memory produced for the first is an experimentation practice and it is difficult to tune the hyper boundaries to get the higher precision, accuracy, affectability, and explicitness. The generally utilized many AI calculations like Help Vector Machines require colossal computational time for learning. The more words that are available altogether in each sentence or expression, the more equivocal the word in the center becomes. BERT represents the expanded significance by perusing bidirectionally, representing the impact of any remaining words in a sentence on the center word, and taking out the left-to-right force that predispositions words towards specific importance as the sentence progress.

2. RELATED WORK

L. Zhao et al., (2021) In his study a model named Augmented Education (N = 156) is led, which totals multisource social information spreading over on the web and disconnected learning as well as exercises inside and outside the homeroom. Metrics assessing linear and nonlinear behavioural changes, in particular, can be used to acquire a deeper understanding of the characteristics that lead to outstanding or poor performance. of campus lifestyles are assessed; also, characteristics that characterise dynamic Long short-term memory is used to extract changes in temporal lifestyle patterns (LSTM). Next, a classification technique based onmachine learning is being developed to predict academic success. Finally, visible feedback is being developed to help students (particularly at-risk students) improve their relationships with the university and achieve a better accuracy. Experiments show that the Augment ED model may accurately predict students' academic records.

A. R. Subhani et al. (2017) states that mental stress has been a major social issue and it has the ability to create functional incapacity at work. Chronic stress may also be linked to a number of psychophysiological illnesses. Stress, for example, can lead to depression, stroke, heart attack, and cardiac arrest. According to current neuroscience, the human brain is the likely target of mental stress since the human brain's perception defines a hazardous and stressful situation. In this context, an objective metric for assessing stress levels that takes the human brain into account might significantly decrease the negative effects. As a result, this study proposes a machine learning approach that provides EEG data analysis of stressed individuals. Individuals were subjected to stress in the lab, which was induced using a well-known experimental paradigm based on the Montreal imaging stress task. The stress induction is justified by task performance and subjective feedback. According to the data, the suggested framework has 94.6 percent accuracy for two- level stress detection and 83.4 percent accuracy for multiple level identification. Finally, the suggested EEG-based ML system can objectively assess stress levels at different levels. The proposed architecture could facilitate the creation of a computer-aided design.

Ding et al. (2020) said that the aging population, survival demands, and learning pressures all increase the intensity of human competitiveness. Anxiety and panic have been plaguing some college students for some time, and mental health issues are on the rise. The rise of social media social networks like Weibo, QQ, and WeChat has given college students not just more convenient way to connect, but also a new emotional outlet. They may use social media to capture their daily lives in real time and manage with family or friends to express feelings and reduce anger. Simultaneously, the rise of social media has provided a new outlet for spotting traumatised visitors. A user's social network data is examined by current computer technology to detect whether or not he or she is sad. This study employs text-level mining of Sina Weibo data from students to identify depression among college students. To begin, gather text data from a variety of sources. To begin, collect text data from college students on Sina Weibo and turn it into machine learning input data. To extract features, deep neural networks are deployed. To classify the input data and, finally, to recognise depression, a deep integrated support vector machine (DISVM) approach is used. The DISVM increases the accuracy of depression diagnosis by making the recognition model more stable. The suggested depression detection approach, according to simulated testing, can identify future depression patients among college students. A population was built using data from Sina Weibo. The aim of this study Adnan, Nadia, et al. (2012) is to examine the stress level and brainwave balancing index (BBI) of university students at the beginning and end of a study semester. Sheldon Cohen's Perceived Stress Scale (PSS) questionnaire is used to measure stress levels, while Guger Technologies' g-Mobilab was used to record the brainwave signals. The framework's main goal is to give conceptually disparate word and document embeddings a straightforward, uniform interface. This effectively hides all engineering complexity specific to embeddings, enabling researchers to "mix and match" different embeddings with minimal effort (Alan Akbik et al., 2019). Three terms make up the proposed model's description of SC: the phasic component, the tonic component, and an additive white Gaussian noise term that includes measurement errors, artefacts, and model prediction errors. With a rigorous methodology based on sparsity, mathematical convex optimisation, and Bayesian statistics, this physiologically inspired model fully explains EDA (Alberto Greco et al., 2016).

3. PROPOSED METHOD

3.1 Bert Sentimental Analysis

BERT (Bidirectional Encoder Representations from Transformers). It is a Google-developed transformer-based machine learning approach for pre-training in natural language processing (NLP). When compared to frequently used heuristics, the design seeks to integrate numerous hidden layers of BERT in a way that enhances the accuracy of the Twitter sentiment analysis job. The average of the past four layers, which corresponds to a linear combination, is a common heuristic. Because tweets employ such a diverse range of languages, a fixed technique of layer combination, such as a linear combination, may not fully exploit BERT's capabilities. For instance, tweets including extraordinary words may help more from data which is available in the prior layers of BERT's character-based embeddings while more proper tweets may profit from the other layers. First chance to conquer this project is to consider the successive data stream between resulting layers through a repetitive unit. The gathering of various levels together could be helpful on the grounds that one biGRU's capacity might restrict its capacity to catch all of the data from the 12 layers. Thus, the isolated the work by utilizing various bi-GRUs and distributing gathered embeddings to them. To distinguish the best harmony between joining data across layers and the capacity of a solitary bi- GRU, the trial with various quantities of bi-GRUs. An illustration of the model engineering utilized. Figure 1 shows the flowchart of Bert Sentimental Analysis.

4. EXPERIMENTAL SETUP

First, we have downloaded the dataset IMDb dataset from Kaggle. Hugging Face's transformers library includes pre-trained BERT models and tokenizers. Glorot initialization is used to initialise dense layers, and a dropout rate of 0.5 is utilised. After every epoch, the Adam optimizer is multiplied by 0.9 with a starting learning rate of 1 to 5. Do fine-tuning on the whole BERT model in each iteration to balance the embeddings with the dataset. For all preliminaries, utilize a group size of 64 and train for an aggregate of 15 ages. A coarse grid search is used to choose the hyperparameters, although it is not comprehensive owing to computing resource constraints. The models are trained on a node with an NVIDIA GeForce GTX 1060 and an Intel Core i7 7th generation CPU using a single GPU. We have to follow the steps below:

- We have to import the downloaded dataset from my drive to google colab.
- Then tokenize the input into sub-tokens, then embed those sub-tokens
- After preprocessing the dataset have to split the dataset into training data (70%) and testing data (30%).
- BERT Sentimental Analysis is built to train and test the preprocessed dataset.
- We compared the output of our model by varying epoch values.
- Also, by altering the number of layers hidden we have compared the output of our model.
- For prediction and evaluating the model we compared the results of activation functions by varying layers and epochs.

Figure 1. Flow chart of BERT sentimental analysis

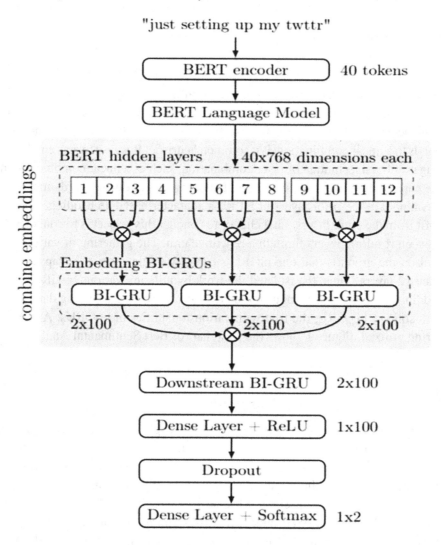

5. RESULTS AND DISCUSSIONS

The IMDb reviews dataset was used in this thesis. There are a whole total of 50,000 reviews in all. The model's hyper parameters, such as batch size, were set at 128 with 5 epochs and a dropout of 0.25. Transformers picked ADAM as the optimizer for Bidirectional Encoder Representation. After multiple trials and comparisons of model accuracy, the hyper parameters were chosen. The model was also chosen after a series of experiments with diverse dropout rates. The accuracy of the model's predictions was used as a criterion to compare model performance. As the dataset grew larger, the models' accuracy improved. The training picture for training the model is shown below . The model's accuracy is 92.4 percent after this final training.

5.1 Prediction of Negative Sentiment

Figure 2 shows the prediction score of the negative sentence.

Figure 2. Prediction of negative sentiment

```
1
2
3
4 predict_sentiment(model, tokenizer, "This film is terrible")
5
6
7

0.0073115453124046633
```

5.2 Prediction of Positive Sentiment

The Figure 3 shows the prediction score of positive sentences.

Figure 3. Prediction of positive sentiment

```
[39]  1
      2
      3
      4 predict_sentiment(model, tokenizer, "This film is great")
      5
      6
      7

      0.927232027053833
```

5.3 Prediction of Negative Sentiment in Sarcastic Comment

Figure 4 shows the Prediction of negative sentiment in sarcastic sentence.

Figure 4. Prediction of negative sentiment in sarcastic comment

```
1
2
3
4 predict_sentiment(model, tokenizer, "grr .. ready for school .. i hate uniforms ! ! ugh we need our real clothes !"
5
6
7

0.11376281827688217
```

5.4 Prediction of Positive Sentiment in Sarcastic Comment

Figure 5 shows the Prediction of positive sentiment in sarcastic comment.

Figure 5. Prediction of positive sentiment in sarcastic comment

```
[42]  1
      2
      3
      4 predict_sentiment(model, tokenizer, "When people ask me stupid questions, it is my legal obligation to give a sarcastic remark.")
      5
      6
      7

   0.7934311032295227
```

Figure 6 shows the training accuracy and prediction accuracy in predicting the positive and negative sentences. The training result is given in Figure 7.

Figure 6. Training graph

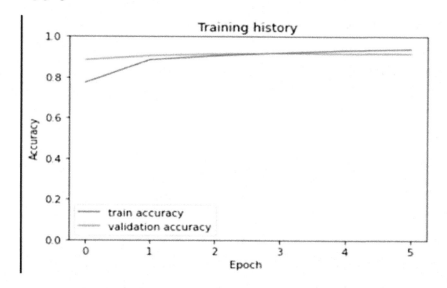

Table 1 provides the observation of the result obtained with the proposed model and Table 2 provides the comparison of the models with the other models.

Figure 7. Training result

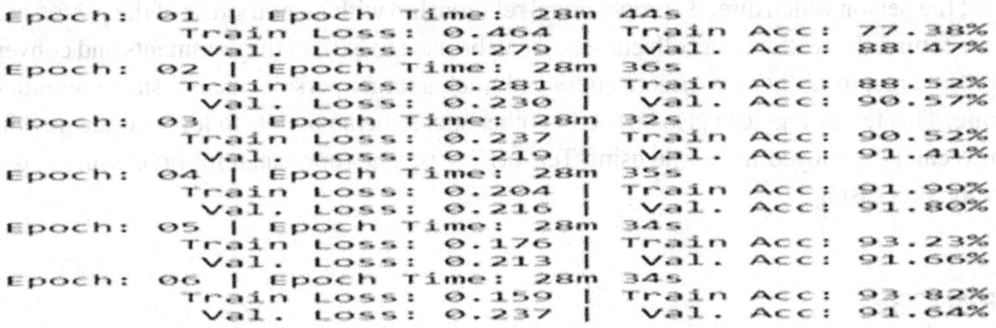

```
Epoch: 01 | Epoch Time: 28m 44s
         Train Loss: 0.464 | Train Acc: 77.38%
         Val. Loss: 0.279 | Val. Acc: 88.47%
Epoch: 02 | Epoch Time: 28m 36s
         Train Loss: 0.281 | Train Acc: 88.52%
         Val. Loss: 0.230 | Val. Acc: 90.57%
Epoch: 03 | Epoch Time: 28m 32s
         Train Loss: 0.237 | Train Acc: 90.52%
         Val. Loss: 0.219 | Val. Acc: 91.41%
Epoch: 04 | Epoch Time: 28m 35s
         Train Loss: 0.204 | Train Acc: 91.99%
         Val. Loss: 0.216 | Val. Acc: 91.80%
Epoch: 05 | Epoch Time: 28m 34s
         Train Loss: 0.176 | Train Acc: 93.23%
         Val. Loss: 0.213 | Val. Acc: 91.66%
Epoch: 06 | Epoch Time: 28m 34s
         Train Loss: 0.159 | Train Acc: 93.82%
         Val. Loss: 0.237 | Val. Acc: 91.64%
```

Table 1. Observation of the result

Input	Predicted Range [0-1]	Inference
This film is terrible	0.007	NEGATIVE
This film is great	0.9272	POSITIVE
Get ready for school .. I hate uniform !! ugh we need our real clothes	0.1137	NEGATIVE
When people ask me stupid questions, it is my legal obligation to give a sarcastic remark	0.7934	POSITIVE

Table 2. Comparison of results with other models

	Method	Acc	Author
Cross- lingual	Ensemble	81.00%	Wan,X
	Co-Train	81.30%	Wan,X
	CLMM	83.02%	Mengi
Lexical Based	Corpus	74.00%	Turkey
Cross- Domain	Active Learning	80.00%(avg)	Li, S
	Thesaurus	80.00%(avg)	Bollegala
	SFA	80.00%(avg)	Pan S J
Machine Learning	SVM	86.40%	Pang,Lee
	Co-Training SVM	82.52%	Liu
	Deep learning (LSTM)	85.29%	Richard
	Proposed Architecture	**91.64%**	

6. CONCLUSION AND FUTURE SCOPE

A sentiment analysis by using Bidirectional Encoder Representation from Transformers is proposed. The proposed methodology is having very low computational time which makes it a lightweight algorithm. The proposed fine-tuning framework can be generalized to solve transfer learning problems. The achieved accuracy is 91.64% with a training set consisting of 50.000 reviews. From this, the positive or negative emotion of the person which directly proportional relationship with mental stress of the person are identified. In the future, the twitter data collection tool can be used to extract the comments and conversations by a specific target to further the effectiveness and track a target persons mental state continuously for monitoring. This technology can also be used in other social media outlets to for accurate tracking. This model also can be deployed in mobile using Tensorflow js. The time taken for processing was suitable for real time processing.

REFERENCES

Adnan, N. (2012). University students stress level and brainwave balancing index: Comparison between early and end of study semester. In *Research and Development (SCOReD) 2012 IEEE Student Conference on*. IEEE.

Akbik, A., Bergmann, T., Blythe, D., Rasul, K., Schweter, S., & Vollgraf, R. (2019). An easy-to-use framework for state-of-the heart NLP. Academic Press.

Ding, Y., Chen, X., Fu, Q., & Zhong, S. (2020). A Depression Recognition Method for College Students Using Deep Integrated Support Vector Algorithm. *IEEE Access : Practical Innovations, Open Solutions*, *8*, 75616–75629. doi:10.1109/ACCESS.2020.2987523

Greco, A., Valenza, G., Lanata, A., Scilingo, E. P., & Citi, L. (2016). A Convex Optimization Approach to Electrodermal Activity Processing. *IEEE Transactions on Biomedical Engineering*, *63*(4), 1. doi:10.1109/TBME.2015.2474131 PMID:26336110

Jawahar, G., Sagot, B., & Seddah, D. (2019).. What does BERT learn about the structure of language. *Proceedings of the 57th Annual Meeting of the Association for Computational Linguistics*, 3651–3657. 10.18653/v1/P19-1356

Kharde, V., & Sonawane, S. (2016). Sentiment Analysis of Twitter Data: A Survey of Techniques. *International Journal of Computer Applications*, *139*(11), 5–15. doi:10.5120/ijca2016908625

Meng, X. (2012). Cross-lingual mixture model for sentiment classification. *Proceedings of the 50th Annual Meeting of the Association for Computational Linguistics: Long Papers-Volume 1*.

Subhani, A. R., Mumtaz, W., Saad, M. N. B. M., Kamel, N., & Malik, A. S. (2017). Machine Learning Framework for the Detection of Mental Stress at Multiple Levels. *IEEE Access : Practical Innovations, Open Solutions*, *5*, 13545–13556. doi:10.1109/ACCESS.2017.2723622

Talaat, A. S. (2023). Sentiment analysis classification system using hybrid BERT models. *Journal of Big Data*, *10*(1), 110. doi:10.118640537-023-00781-w

Wan, X. (2012). A Comparative Study of Cross-Lingual Sentiment Classification. In *Proceedings of the IEEE/WIC/ACM International Joint Conferences on Web Intelligence and Intelligent Agent Technology-Volume 1* (pp. 24-31). 10.1109/WI-IAT.2012.54

Zhao, L., Chen, K., Song, J., Zhu, X., Sun, J., Caulfield, B., & Namee, B. M. (2021). Academic Performance Prediction Based on Multisource, Multifeature Behavioral Data. *IEEE Access : Practical Innovations, Open Solutions, 9*, 5453–5465. doi:10.1109/ACCESS.2020.3002791

Chapter 14
SCRNN:
A Deep Model for Colorectal Cancer Classification From Histological Images – Implementation Using TensorFlow

K. G. Suma
VIT-AP University, India

Gurram Sunitha
Mohan Babu University, India

Mohammad Gouse Galety
ⓘ https://orcid.org/0000-0003-1666-2001
Samarkand International University of Technology, Uzbekistan

ABSTRACT

Colorectal cancer holds a prominent place on the global health landscape. Its early detection is crucial for successful patient outcomes. Histological analysis of tissue samples plays an indispensable role in diagnosing and classifying colorectal cancer. Accurate classification is paramount, as it influences the choice of treatment and patient prognosis. This chapter investigates the statistics surrounding colorectal cancer, its vital role in the healthcare sector, and the transformative potential of artificial intelligence in automating its diagnosis. This chapter proposes a ShuffleNetV2-CRNN (SCRNN), a novel deep learning architecture designed for colorectal cancer classification from histological images. SCRNN combines the efficiency of ShuffleNetV2 for feature extraction with the context-awareness of a convolutional-recurrent neural network for precise classification. SCRNN is evaluated against chosen deep models – Simple CNN, vGG16, ResNet-18, and MobileNet. Experimental results demonstrate appreciable performance of SCRNN across a diverse range of tissue types.

DOI: 10.4018/978-1-6684-8531-6.ch014

Copyright © 2024, IGI Global. Copying or distributing in print or electronic forms without written permission of IGI Global is prohibited.

INTRODUCTION

Colorectal cancer is a significant global health concern, characterized by the uncontrolled growth of abnormal cells in the colon or rectum (Mármol et al. 2017). This chapter probes into the statistics surrounding colorectal cancer, its vital role in the healthcare sector. Also, the transformative potential of artificial intelligence in automating its diagnosis is highlighted.

Colorectal cancer ranks as the most common forms of cancer worldwide, and its impact on healthcare cannot be overstated (Patil et al. 2017). It accounts for a substantial portion of global cancer cases (Raj et al. 2023). According to statistics, it is the third most common cancer in the world, with over 1.9 million diagnosed cases and nearly 1 million deaths in 2020 (Siegel et al. 2020). In 2023, it is estimated that there will be 153,020 cases in USA and approximately 35% death cases will be there (Siegel et al. 2023). This high incidence places colorectal cancer at the forefront of healthcare concerns, emphasizing the need for effective diagnosis and treatment strategies.

Early detection of colorectal cancer is critical for successful treatment. Timely diagnosis increases the chances of survival and reduces the burden on healthcare systems (Castelo et al. 2022). Furthermore, colorectal cancer profoundly impacts the lifestyle and quality of life of patients (Bouter et al. 2022). Also, their families get affected as well. This underscores the importance of accurate and efficient diagnostic tools.

Covid-19 pandemic significantly disrupted healthcare services worldwide. Elective surgeries and diagnostic procedures, including cancer screenings and treatments, were either canceled or postponed. This contributed to the adverse effects of the covid-19 pandemic on potential cancer care. The global healthcare system has to continue to be flexible and responsive as people struggle with the pandemic's aftereffects (Kajiwara Saito et al. 2022). To ensure that cancer patients receive the care they need. Understanding these dynamics is vital to develop strategies that minimize the impact of future healthcare disruptions.

The emergence of artificial intelligence has opened new avenues for improving colorectal cancer diagnosis (Yu et al. 2022). These technologies enable the development of automated systems. Such systems can analyze histological images with precision, speed, and consistency, thereby enhancing the diagnostic process .

Colorectal cancer detection and classification represent a pivotal application of machine learning and deep learning for healthcare (Waljee et al. 2022). These techniques provide the means to extract intricate patterns and features from histological images. Thus, allowing for accurate differentiation between healthy and cancerous tissues. The context and significance lie in the potential to reduce human error, improve diagnostic accuracy, and expedite the decision-making process in clinical settings.

The proposed ShuffleNetV2-CRNN (SCRNN) model represents a novel approach to the classification of colorectal cancer from histological images. Its core strength lies in its efficient feature extraction capabilities, enabled by ShuffleNetV2 (Ma et al. 2018). Also, by its ability to analyze and interpret these features using the Convolutional-Recurrent Neural Network (CRNN) (Shi et al. 2016). By implementing SCRNN with TensorFlow, it leverages a versatile and robust deep learning framework, ensuring scalability and practicality in real-world healthcare applications. The experimental results showcase SCRNN's ability to accurately classify colorectal tissue types.

This chapter aligns with the book's theme by showcasing the practical application of deep learning within the healthcare domain. The proposed SCRNN architecture represents a novel approach that illustrates how deep learning techniques can be harnessed to address challenges in medical field.

The subsequent sections provide a detailed design of the SCRNN deep model, dataset used, implementation using TensorFlow. A comprehensive overview of preprocessing the dataset, SCRNN's training and fine-tuning processes is presented. The experimental results achieved through SCRNN architecture are compared with other deep models in the context of colorectal cancer classification from histological images.

LITERATURE REVIEW

Histopathology plays a critical role in the diagnosis of colorectal cancer and many other medical conditions. Histological images offer a microscopic view of tissue samples, revealing intricate details of cellular structures and tissue morphology (Ayyad et al. 2021). In the case of colorectal cancer, histological images provide essential visual information about the presence of abnormal cells. These images represent growth patterns of abnormal cells and the overall tissue architecture (Gurcan et al. 2009). Pathologists and healthcare professionals rely on these images to identify and differentiate between healthy and cancerous tissues. Further to classify cancer types, determine the stage of cancer progression, and make critical decisions regarding treatment strategies. The rich visual data contained within histological images serves as the foundation for accurate and reliable diagnoses. Thus, making them an indispensable resource in the field of medical pathology and a critical component in the development of advanced deep learning models for automated cancer classification.

The context of colorectal cancer classification lies in the urgent need for accurate and timely diagnosis of this prevalent form of cancer (Rompianesi et al. 2022). Early detection is pivotal in improving patient outcomes and reducing healthcare burdens. Accurate classification and staging of the disease are essential for treatment planning and patient care. In this context, development of advanced techniques, offer the potential to revolutionize the classification process by automating the analysis of histological images. This not only expedites the diagnostic process but also enhances its precision. Ultimately leading to better patient care.

Manual diagnosis of colorectal cancer presents several challenges (Liang et al. 2022). It is a time-consuming process, demanding hours of meticulous examination by skilled pathologists. This can lead to delays in diagnosis and treatment planning. Human error and inter-observer variability are inherent risks, as interpretations can vary among pathologists. Histological images contain subtle features and patterns. Such complexity can often challenge accurate classification. Moreover, the growing volume of patients makes it more challenging. These challenges highlight the critical need for automated solutions. Such solutions are expected to provide more accurate and efficient cancer classification by significantly reducing diagnostic time, enhance consistency.

Cancer diagnosis and classification are complex tasks in the field of medical pathology. Machine learning has emerged as a powerful tool for improving the accuracy and efficiency of cancer classification (Kennion et al. 2022). Deep learning has been extensively applied to image-based cancer classification, leveraging the capabilities of CNNs(Davri et al. 2022). For colorectal cancer, histological images play a crucial role. Deep CNN architectures have demonstrated remarkable performance in extracting features and detecting cancerous tissues from these images (Tamang et al. 2021).

Many studies have explored the integration of multiple data modalities for enhanced cancer classification (Ho et al. 2021). Beyond histological images, researchers have considered genetic and clinical data. This multi-modal approach improves the accuracy of colorectal cancer diagnosis and better informs treatment decisions.

Data augmentation techniques have been employed to mitigate the challenges of limited medical data. These techniques artificially increase the size of the dataset, improving the model's generalization capabilities (Wei et al. 2019). Proper data preprocessing, including normalization and noise reduction, is also critical for reliable results.

Transfer learning, where pretrained models are fine-tuned for specific tasks, has gained popularity (Kassani et al. 2022). Researchers have adapted models pretrained on large image datasets for cancer analysis. This approach accelerates model convergence and enhances classification accuracy.

Some researchers have explored ensemble learning techniques and hybrid models that combine the strengths of various deep learning architectures (Talukder et al. 2022). Combining CNNs, RNNs and other models has led to improved classification performance for various cancer types.

While the focus is on model performance, several studies emphasize the clinical relevance of deep learning in real-world healthcare settings (Brockmoeller et al. 2022). Successful integration of deep learning models into clinical practice requires addressing interpretability, ethics, and regulatory concerns.

Challenges include the need for larger, more diverse datasets, addressing class imbalances, and ensuring model explainability (Alboaneen et al. 2023). Future research should continue to improve the robustness and generalization of deep learning models for colorectal cancer classification, making them even more clinically applicable.

These findings reinforce the significance of precise colorectal cancer classification and the suitability of deep learning as a robust tool for healthcare professionals (Mansur et al. 2023). In a healthcare landscape where early diagnosis is paramount, deep learning systems reliability and accuracy make it a significant leap forward.

SCRNN DEEP MODEL FOR COLORECTAL CANCER CLASSIFICATION FROM HISTOLOGICAL IMAGES

Deep learning architectures take a strong stand in automating the detection and classification of colorectal cancers. Their ability to learn hierarchical features and recognize subtle patterns in images is crucial for achieving high accuracy in cancer diagnosis.

This book chapter proposes a novel ShuffleNetV2-CRNN (SCRNN) model for classification of colorectal cancer histological images (Figure 1). SCRNN is a two-stage deep learning model.

1) Stage-1 performs feature extraction from histological images. ShuffleNetV2 is employed as the feature extraction component. It efficiently extracts relevant features from colorectal cancer histological images. Features extracted by stage-1 acts as input for stage-2.

2) Stage-2 receives input from stage-1. It analyzes and interprets image features extracted by stage-1. CRNN is used in this stage to perform classification. It does so by learning from image features extracted in stage-1. CRNN combines convolutional and recurrent layers to efficiently analyze the input. Convolutional layers are inherently capable of recognizing features from images. Recurrent layers are inherently capable of performing sequential analysis and understand the image context.

Figure 1. SCRNN deep model

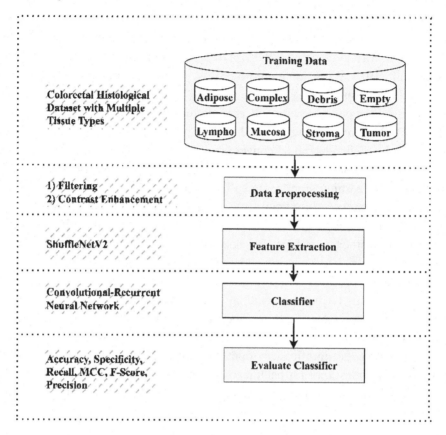

Stage-1: Feature Extraction From Histological Images

ShuffleNetV2 is chosen as feature extraction component for SCRNN. ShuffleNetV2 is a deep learning architecture designed exclusively for image feature extraction. It is a lightweight model. It is distinguished by two distinct operations: channel shuffling and group convolutions. These techniques enable it to extract important visual characteristics, patterns, and structures from histological images. They also minimise the deep model's computational complexity and size. As a result, it is ideal for resource-constrained settings and applications. The architecture of ShuffleNetV2 is aimed to strike a balance between accuracy and computing efficiency. Because of this, it is an excellent candidate for the feature extraction phase of the SCRNN model.

The basic ShuffleNetV2 architecture is presented in Figure 2. It starts with a series of convolutional layers to capture low-level features from histological images. It introduces "shuffle units", which include group convolution operations. These units enable information exchange between channels and reduce computational load. They consist of several key components –

a) Pointwise Group Convolution operation applies 1x1 convolutions to the input channels, partitioned into groups. It helps mix information between different channel groups.

b) Channel Shuffle: This step reorders the feature maps, promoting cross-group information flow.

Figure 2. ShuffleNetV2 architecture
Source: Ma et al. (2018)

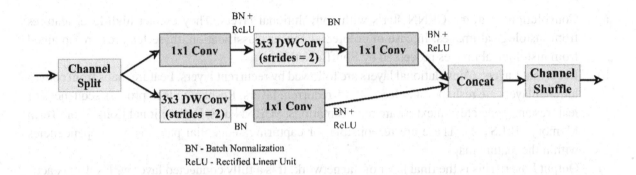

BN - Batch Normalization
ReLU - Rectified Linear Unit

c)   Depthwise Separable Convolution: Depthwise separable convolutions further reduce computational cost by applying spatial and pointwise convolutions separately.

ShuffleNetV2 employs bottleneck blocks that reduce the number of channels. These blocks consist of a combination of pointwise and depthwise separable convolutions. Downsample and transition layers are used to reduce spatial dimensions of feature maps. While increasing the number of channels. This helps capture higher-level features. The network ends with max pooling. It aggregates feature maps and reduces them to a fixed-size representation.

The mathematical model for Stage-1 is as follows. Let I represent histological image dimensions. A convolution operation is defined as

$$I^{cl+1} = \sigma \left(LW^{cl} \times I^{cl} + b^{cl} \right) \tag{1}$$

where cl is current convolution layer, σ is activation function, LW is learnable weights, b is bias value.
The channel shuffling operation is defined as

$$I^{cl+1} = Shuffle\left(I^{cl} \right) \tag{2}$$

This operation rearranges the channels in the feature maps to promote cross-group information flow.
The process is applied recursively through the layers of the ShuffleNetV2 architecture, leading to a set of feature maps that capture hierarchical features and abstractions.

Stage-2: Classification of Histological Images

CRNN is a hybrid deep learning architecture. CRNN combines harnesses the power of both convolutional and recurrent neural networks. It is primarily designed for sequence data. It is well-suited for classification of sequential data in the context of ShuffleNetV2 and colorectal cancer classification. The features obtained from ShuffleNetV2 are preprocessed and reshaped to create sequences of feature maps. These sequences are treated as input data for the subsequent CRNN component. Key Components of CRNN are as follows (Figure 3).

a) Convolutional Layers: CRNN starts with convolutional layers. They extract high-level features from histological images. In case of colorectal cancer classification, these features are obtained from histological images processed by ShuffleNetV2.
b) Recurrent Layers: Convolutional layers are followed by recurrent layers. Feature maps from convolutional layers are reshaped and fed into the recurrent layers. Reshaping is to process sequences of features and generate context-aware representations. SCRNN uses Bidirectional Long Short-Term Memory (BiLSTM). These are responsible for capturing sequential patterns and dependencies within the feature maps.
c) Output Layer: This is the final layer of the network. It is a fully connected layer with softmax activation for classification tasks. This layer assigns class labels to the processed sequences. It allows SCRNN to classify histological images into different colorectal cancer categories.

The combination of ShuffleNetV2 with CRNN leverages the strengths of both architectures. ShuffleNetV2 efficiently extracts image features, while CRNN processes these features as sequences, capturing the temporal relationships among them. This approach is particularly relevant in histological image classification where the order and context of features are essential for colorectal cancer diagnosis.

The mathematical model for Stage-2 is as follows. Let T represent number of time steps. Let S represent input sequence characterized by T and F where F represents number of features at each time step t.

A convolutional layer extracts local features from S at each time step t. A CNN operation at t is defined as

$$C^t = \sigma\left(LW^c \times S^t + b^c\right) \tag{3}$$

where C is output feature map, LW is learnable weights, c is convolution, b is bias value, σ is activation function.

C^t is fed into recurrent layer. Hidden state H of recurrent layer at t is defined as

$$H^t = RNN\left(C^t, H^{t-1}\right) \tag{4}$$

where RNN is recurrent operation.

The output of the recurrent layer can be used for various purposes, such as classification or sequence generation. The output Y of output layer at t is defined as

$$Y^t = OutputLayer\left(H^t\right) \tag{5}$$

Figure 3. CRNN model

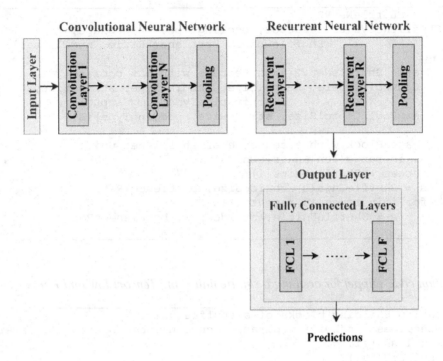

IMPLEMENTATION USING TENSORFLOW

The entire SCRNN architecture is implemented using TensorFlow deep learning framework. Keras is used for ease of programming. Keras is a high-level API for TensorFlow. TensorFlow and Keras provide a flexible and robust platform for developing, training, and deploying deep neural networks.

The Python code snippet for implementing ShuffleNetV2 using TensorFlow and Keras is shown in Figure 4. The ShuffleNetV2() function specifies the ShuffleNetV2 architecture as a whole. To construct the model, numerous parameters such as scaling factor, bottleneck ratio, and number of shuffle units at each step are required. Layer by layer, the model is built, using convolutional layers, shuffle units, and a final output layer. Channel splitting, channel shuffling, and max pooling are all part of the design.

Figure 5 shows a snippet of Python code for implementing a shuffle unit with TensorFlow and Keras. The ShuffleUnit() method defines a basic ShuffleNetV2 building block. Depthwise separable convolutions, bottleneck layers, and channel shuffling are all part of it. When necessary, it also supports strided convolutions for downsampling.

Figure 6 presents Python code snippet for implementation of CRNN using TensorFlow and Keras. It defines the function CRNN() that takes an input shape as an argument. The input layer is defined with the shape specified by the shape argument. A 1D convolutional layer (CNN) is applied to the input data. Output of CNN layers pass through a BiLSTM layer. A dense layer (outputs) is added for classification. CRNN model is compiled using a custom optimizer. The loss function and performance metrics are set.

Figure 7 presents Python code snippet for implementation of SCRNN using TensorFlow and Keras. The TrainSCRNN() function starts by creating an SCRNN model using the CRNN function. The model's

Figure 4. Python code snippet for creating ShuffleNetV2 using TensorFlow and Keras

```
1    # Create ShuffleNetV2
2    def ShuffleNetV2(scaleFactor, poolingType, inputShape,
                       ShuffleUnits, bottleneckRatio, numClasses):
3
4        # Create ShuffleNetV2 architecture with max pooling
5        s = Conv2D(filters, kernelSize, paddingType, strideSize,
6                              activationType)(img_input)
         s = MaxPool2D(poolSize, strideSize, paddingType)(s)
7
8        # Create Block with a sequence of shufflenet units
9        for i in range(len(ShuffleUnits)):
10           repeat = ShuffleUnits[i]
11           s = ShuffleUnit(s, strideSize, bottleneckRatio)
12           for i in range(1, repeat+1):
13               s = ShuffleUnit(s, strideSize, bottleneckRatio)
```

Figure 5. Python code snippet for creating a shuffle unit using TensorFlow and Keras

```
1    # Creating building blocks of a shuffle unit
2    # It includes depthwise separable convolutions, bottleneck layers, and
3    # channel shuffling.
4    def ShuffleUnit():
5        # Creating left channel split
6        # Creating 3x3 DWConv with Batch Normalization
7        s1 = DepthwiseConv2D(kernelSize, strideSize, paddingType)(inputs)
8        s1 = BatchNormalization(axis=bn_axis)(s1)
9        # Creating 1x1 Conv with Batch Normalization and ReLU
10       s1 = Conv2D(bottleneckChannels, kernelSize, strideSize,
11                                       paddingType)(s1)
12       s1 = BatchNormalization(axis=bn_axis)(s1)
13       s1 = Activation('relu')(s1)
14       # Creating right channel split
15       # Creating 1x1 Conv with Batch Normalization and ReLU
16       s2 = Conv2D(bottleneckChannels, kernelSize, strideSize,
17                                       paddingType)(inputs)
18       s2 = BatchNormalization(axis=bn_axis)(s2)
19       s2 = Activation('relu')(s2)
20       # Creating 3x3 DWConv with Batch Normalization
21       s2 = DepthwiseConv2D(kernelSize, strideSize, paddingType)(s2)
22       s2 = BatchNormalization(axis=bn_axis)(s2)
23       # Creating 1x1 Conv with Batch Normalization and ReLU
24       s2 = Conv2D(bottleneckChannels, kernelSize, strideSize,
25                                       paddingType)(s2)
26       s2 = BatchNormalization(axis=bn_axis)(s2)
27       s2 = Activation('relu')(s2)
28       # Concat channels
29       ret = Concatenate(axis=bn_axis)([s1, s2])
30       # Shuffle Channels
31       ret = Lambda(channel_shuffle)(ret)
```

Figure 6. Python code snippet for creating CRNN using TensorFlow and Keras

```
1   # Create CRNN model
2   def CRNN(shape):
3      # Define the input layer with the specified shape
4      inputs = Input(shape=shape)
5      # Apply a 1D convolutional layer
6      CNN = Conv1D(filters, kernelSize, paddingType,
7                                   activationType)(inputs)
8      # Apply a bidirectional LSTM layer, returning sequences
9      CRNN = Bidirectional(LSTM(size, return_sequences=True)(CNN)
10     # Apply a dense layer
11     outputs = Dense(len(CLASSES), activationType)(CRNN)
12     # Create the model with the specified inputs and outputs
13     CRNNModel = Model(inputs, outputs)
14     # Compile the model using the custom optimizer
15     CRNNModel.compile(optimizerType, lossType, metricsList)
16     # Display the model summary
17     CRNNModel.summary()
18     # return CRNN model
19     return CRNNModel
```

Figure 7. Python code snippet for training SCRNN using TensorFlow and Keras

```
1   # Train SCRNN model
2   def TrainSCRNN():
3      # Create SCRNN model by calling CRNN() function with
4      # 'shape' argument.
5      SCRNN = CRNN(shape)
6
7      # Load pre-trained weights from the specified 'path.'
8      SCRNN.load_weights(path)
9      # Train SCRNN model using the training data and perform
10     # validation.
11
12     _ = SCRNN.fit(trainingData, validationData, numEpochs,
13                   batchSize)
14     # Use trained SCRNN model to make predictions on training data
15     trainingPerformance = SCRNN.predict(trainingDatax)
16
17     # Use trained SCRNN model to make predictions on test data
18     testPerformance = SCRNN.predict(testDataX)
```

architecture and layers are specified based on the provided shape argument. The SCRNN model loads pre-trained weights. SCRNN model is trained using fit() method. The trained SCRNN model is used to make predictions on training and test data.

Table 1. Details of dataset

Item	Description
Type	Dataset containing textures in colorectal cancer histology
Domain	Medical Histology
# Images	5000
# Classes	8 (Lympho, Stroma, Complex, Adipose, Tumor, Debris, Mucosa, Empty)
# Images per Class	625
Image Dimensions	150 pixels x 150 pixels (74μm x 74μm)
Balanced Greyscale Intensity	Yes
Staining Intensity Variation	Present

EXPERIMENTAL RESULTS

This section presents details of colorectal dataset used to evaluate performance of SCRNN. An outline of hyperparameter setup is described. The performance of SCRNN against other chosen deep models is discussed.

Dataset

The dataset used consists of histological images of colorectal cancer tissue (Kather et al. 2016). It includes low-grade tumor images and high-grade tumor images. Contiguous tissue areas within the digitized slides were manually annotated and tessellated. This process involved creating non-overlapping tissue tiles, each measuring 150 pixels by 150 pixels. The dimensions of these tiles correspond to approximately 74 micrometers by 74 micrometers. It includes tissue tiles of various scales, capturing features ranging from individual cells (approximately 10 micrometers) to larger structures like mucosal glands (greater than 50 micrometers). This diversity in scales allows for analysis of various textural features of histological images. Dataset comprises eight distinct types of tissue. Each of these tissue types represents a different aspect of the colorectal cancer histology (Table 1). The dataset consists of 625 non-overlapping tissue tiles for each cancer type which capture various tissue types and textures.

Data Preprocessing

Data preprocessing is performed to enhance the quality and relevance of the input data. Gaussian filter is applied to reduce noise and detail in colorectal cancer histological images. It removes small-scale details and sharp transitions, which can make an image appear smoother. Kernel size is set to 5x5 pixels. The size of kernel determines the extent of smoothing or blurring applied to the image. Standard deviation determines the spread of the Gaussian kernel. A smaller value results in a narrower kernel, preserving more image details. While a larger value results in a wider kernel, leading to more smoothing or blurring. Its value is set to 1. This value provides a balanced approach to noise reduction and detail preservation. It helps reduce noise while still retaining important details.

Further, contrast of images is enhanced by applying CLAHE technique. The input image image is first converted from BGR to LAB color space. LAB color space consists of three channels: *L* (lightness), *A* (color component along the green-magenta axis), and *B* (color component along the blue-yellow axis). LAB image is split into its individual channels, resulting in a list of LAB planes. The *L* channel, which represents the image's lightness, will be enhanced to improve contrast. CLAHE is a variant of histogram equalization that enhances contrast while limiting amplification of noise. It is adaptive, to the local image content. Clip limit is taken as two. The grid size of tiles is taken to be five-by-five pixels. CLAHE operation is applied to L channel, enhancing the contrast of *L* in LAB image. This step aims to improve the overall contrast of the image while preserving local variations. An enhanced LAB image is created by merging enhanced *L* channel with original *A* and *B* channels. BGR color space image is created by converting the enhanced LAB image. This image is contrast-enhanced image.

Hyperparameter Setup

Fine-tuning techniques are applied to optimize the model's performance for colorectal cancer classification. Experimentation has been repeated through the hyperparameter search space to investigate the best model. The optimal parameter setup is detailed in Table 2.

SCRNN is trained using RMSProp optimizer. For training deep models, RMSprop can provide faster convergence compared to standard gradient descent. The adaptive learning rate feature of RMSprop can

Table 2. Hyperparameter setup

Layer	Description
Model = Data Preprocessing *kernelSize - ks, strideSize - ss, activationType - at, filters = f, poolSize = ps, poolingType - pt, BatchNormalization - bn*	
Image Filter	Guassian, KernelSize = (5, 5), sigma_x = 1
Contrast Enhancement	CLAHE
Model = ShuffleNetV2 *scaleFactor = 1.0, inputShape = (32, 32, 3), ShuffleUnits = [3, 7, 3], paddingType = 'same' bottleneckRatio = 1, bottleneckChannels = [0.0, 0.0, 116.0, 464.0]*	
Conv2D	f = 24, ks = (3, 3), ss = (2, 2), pt = ReLU
MaxPool2D	ps = (3, 3), s = (2, 2)
Shuffle Unit-s1-Conv2D	ks = (1, 1), s = 1, bn = yes, at = ReLU
Shuffle Unit-s1-DepthwiseConv2D	ks = 3, s = 2, bn = yes
Shuffle Unit-s1-Conv2D	ks = 1, s = 1, bn = yes, at = ReLU
Shuffle Unit-s2-DepthwiseConv2D	ks = 3, s = 2, bn = yes
Shuffle Unit-s2-Conv2D	ks =1, s = 1, bn = yes
Conv2D	f = 1024, ks = 1, s = 1, at = ReLU
Pooling	max
Model = CRNN	
CNN	f = 512, ks = 3, pt = 'same', at = ReLU
BiLSTM	size = 256
Dense Layer	Size = 8, at = softmax, optimizer = RMSprop, loss = categorical_crossentropy

reduce the need for manual tuning of the learning rate. This saves time and effort in the hyperparameter tuning process. RMSprop is a versatile optimizer that works well in image classification.

Experimental Results

The SCRNN model operates on a dataset comprising histological images of colorectal tissue. SCRNN model is trained on the preprocessed dataset to learn the patterns associated with different types of colorectal tissue. Figure 8 shows the sample "Mucosa" type image at various stages of SCRNN.

Experimental setup involved training and testing the models using a dataset of histological images. The dataset is divided into training and validation datasets to ensure robust evaluation. RMSprop optimizer is used for training as it offered adaptive learning rates and contributed to stable and efficient convergence during the training process. Early stopping with a patience of 5 epochs is employed to prevent overfitting. The models were trained using a batch size of 128 and a maximum of 50 epochs. SCRNN's performance is evaluated using metrics including MCC to provide a comprehensive understanding of SCRNN's effectiveness in colon cancer classification.

The performance of SCRNN is evaluated against other deep models. Experimental results demonstrate the model's capability to classify colorectal tissue accurately (Table 3). A comparative analysis of proposed SCRNN model with other deep learning architectures is performed. Other deep models include Simple CNN, VGG16, ResNet-18, and MobileNet. The primary objective is to evaluate SCRNN's performance in context of colon cancer classification based on histological images.

Figures 9,10, 11, 12 shows the confusion matrix, accuracy & loss curves, P-R curve, ROC curve of SCRNN training and validation respectively. The confusion matrix indicates that SCRNN has achieved a high degree of accuracy in classifying different tissue types within the colon cancer histological images. The diagonal from top-left to bottom-right represents the true positives (correctly classified samples) for each tissue type. Strong values along this diagonal for all classes suggest that SCRNN is proficient at classifying most samples correctly. Some misclassifications can be observed in the matrix, indicated by non-zero values outside the diagonal. These misclassifications are not extensive, reflecting the robustness of SCRNN. 'Complex' and 'Mucosa' classes exhibit some confusion. SCRNN seems to occasionally confuse these two tissue types. However, the misclassifications between 'Tumor' and 'Debris' are relatively minor.

The baseline model, a simple CNN, achieved a commendable accuracy of 95.47%. While it demonstrated high specificity (96.53%), and MCC (0.9110) indicated room for improvement. However, its recall (88.57%) indicates some difficulty in recognizing cancerous regions, potentially leading to missed cases. The VGG16 model exhibited an accuracy of 96.73% and notably high specificity (97.22%). These results imply a robust ability to classify non-cancerous tissue accurately. It also showed improved recall (91.24%) and an MCC of 0.9013, indicating a strong performance compared to Simple CNN, enhancing its ability to detect cancerous regions. ResNet-18 demonstrated accuracy (98.99%) and high specificity (98.36%). These results suggest a strong capability to correctly classify non-cancerous tissue. Its recall (93.19%) and MCC (0.9247) surpasses that of VGG16, underlining an enhanced ability to identify cancerous regions. MobileNet delivered an accuracy of 99.12%, with a high specificity of 98.73%. It achieved an impressive recall (93.87%) and MCC (0.9256), showcasing its capabilities detecting cancerous regions.

SCRNN model performed better than other chosen architectures with an accuracy of 99.53%. It exhibited an appreciable specificity of 99.16%. These results signify the model's proficiency in classifying non-cancerous tissue. With a recall of 94.50%, SCRNN excels at cancerous region identification.

The MCC value of 0.9344 indicated the model's robust performance. SCRNN achieved an F-Score of 0.9412 and precision of 0.9464.

While MobileNet and ResNet-18 demonstrate remarkable performance, it is noteworthy that SCRNN's marginally higher recall and MCC values set it apart. These metrics are critical in medical image analysis, where correctly identifying cancerous regions is paramount.

SCRNN achieved the highest accuracy among all models, indicating its ability to correctly classify histological images into eight classes. The impressive specificity, recall, MCC, F-Score, and precision values further emphasize the model's excellence in distinguishing different classes of colon cancer.

The observations from the P-R curve of SCRNN are as follows. The high accuracy and precision values for all classes indicate SCRNN's ability to make correct predictions for each tissue type. SCRNN demonstrate robustness in classifying various tissue types within colon cancer histological images. The

Figure 8. Sample histological image at various stages of SCRNN

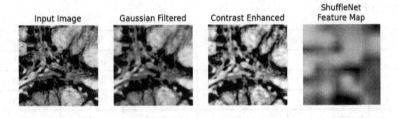

Figure 9. Confusion matrix of SCRNN

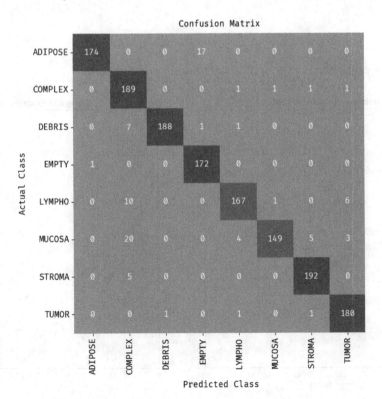

almost identical accuracy and precision values for each class suggest that SCRNN consistently classifies tissue types without significant bias towards false positives or false negatives. It not only achieves high accuracy but also maintains high precision. Thus, ensuring that the majority of positive predictions are true positives, minimizing the risk of false alarms.

The observations from the ROC curve of SCRNN are as follows. The high ROC AUC values for all classes suggest that SCRNN has exceptional discriminative power. It is proficient at distinguishing between positive and negative cases for each tissue type. These results indicate SCRNN's robustness in classifying different tissue types within colon cancer histological images. It maintained a low false positive rate while demonstrating a high true positive rate. High ROC AUC values are indicative of minimized misclassifications. The consistently high ROC AUC values for all classes demonstrate SCRNN's stability in its ability to classify tissue types accurately. Thus, ensuring that SCRNN is adept at making correct predictions.

Table 3. Evaluation of SCRNN

Model	Accuracy	Specificity	Recall	MCC	F-Score	Precision
Simple CNN	0.9547	0.9653	0.8857	0.9110	0.8901	0.9012
VGG16	0.9673	0.9722	0.9124	0.9013	0.9126	0.9178
ResNet-18	0.9899	0.9836	0.9319	0.9247	0.9220	0.9263
MobileNet	0.9912	0.9873	0.9387	0.9256	0.9298	0.9379
SCRNN	**0.9953**	**0.9916**	**0.9450**	**0.9344**	**0.9412**	**0.9464**

Figure 10. Accuracy and loss curves of SCRNN training and validation

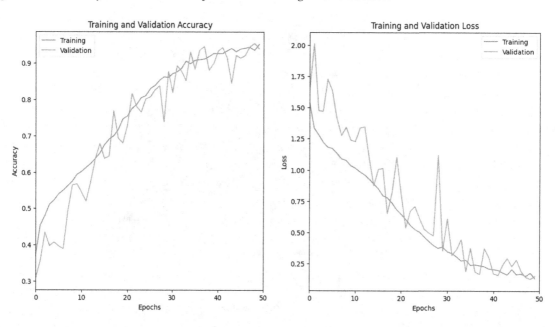

Figure 11. P-R curve of SCRNN

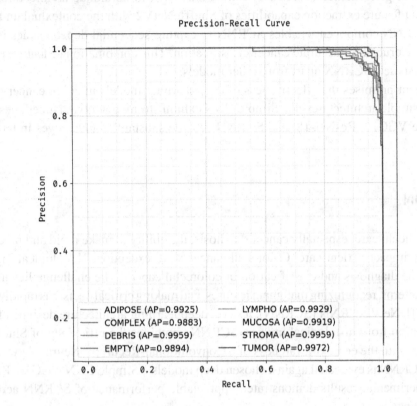

Figure 12. ROC curve of SCRNN

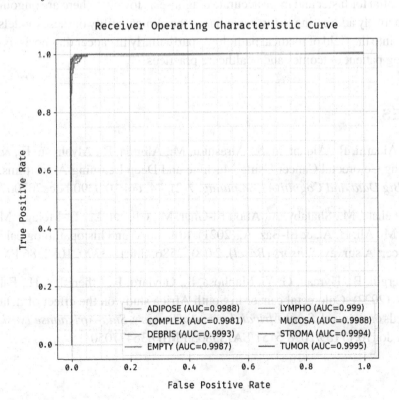

The remarkable performance of SCRNN can be attributed to its unique architecture, which combines the efficient feature extraction capabilities of ShuffleNetV2 with the contextual understanding of a CRNN. The CRNN component enables SCRNN to capture sequential dependencies in histological images, which are crucial for accurate cancer classification. This combination of feature extraction and contextual analysis sets SCRNN apart from other models.

The experiment promises the effectiveness of deep learning models in colon cancer classification. Even relatively simple architectures like Simple CNN exhibit strong potential. Nonetheless, more complex models like VGG16, ResNet-18, and SCRNN provide substantial advantages in terms of overall performance.

CONCLUSION

In the context of healthcare, especially cancer diagnosis, the ability to make rapid and precise decisions can significantly impact patient care. Colorectal cancer is no exception. Histological images play an integral role in the diagnosis and classification of colorectal cancer. The challenge lies in deciphering intricate tissue patterns, recognizing malignant features, and making critical decisions rapidly. This chapter proposed a ShuffleNetV2-CRNN (SCRNN), a novel deep learning architecture designed for colorectal cancer classification from histological images. SCRNN combines the efficiency of ShuffleNetV2 for feature extraction with the context-awareness of a Convolutional-Recurrent Neural Network for precise classification. SCRNN is evaluated against chosen deep models – Simple CNN, vGG16, ResNet-18 and MobileNet. Experimental results demonstrated appreciable performance of SCRNN across a diverse range of tissue types.

Deep learning has shown tremendous promise in advancing the classification of colorectal cancer, offering the potential for faster and more accurate diagnoses. However, there are ongoing challenges that researchers are actively addressing to further enhance the clinical utility of these models. The integration of deep learning into the field of medical pathology, particularly in cancer diagnosis, is a significant step toward improving patient outcomes and healthcare practices.

REFERENCES

Alboaneen, D., Alqarni, R., Alqahtani, S., Alrashidi, M., Alhuda, R., Alyahyan, E., & Alshammari, T. (2023). Predicting Colorectal Cancer Using Machine and Deep Learning Algorithms: Challenges and Opportunities. *Big Data and Cognitive Computing*, 7(2), 74. doi:10.3390/bdcc7020074

Ayyad, S. M., Shehata, M., Shalaby, A., Abou El-Ghar, M., Ghazal, M., El-Melegy, M., Abdel-Hamid, N. B., Labib, L. M., Ali, H. A., & El-Baz, A. (2021). Role of AI and histopathological images in detecting prostate cancer: A survey. *Sensors (Basel)*, 21(8), 2586. doi:10.339021082586 PMID:33917035

Bouter, C., Puttergill, B., Hyman, G. Y., Maphosa, S., Gaylard, P., Etheredge, H., Fabian, J., Ruff, P., & Bebington, B. (2022). Colorectal cancer in South Africa study on the effect of delayed diagnosis to treatment intervals on survival. *South African Journal of Surgery. Suid-Afrikaanse Tydskrif vir Chirurgie*, 60(4), 229–234. doi:10.17159/2078-5151/SAJS3803 PMID:36477050

Brockmoeller, S., Echle, A., Ghaffari Laleh, N., Eiholm, S., Malmstrøm, M. L., Plato Kuhlmann, T., Levic, K., Grabsch, H. I., West, N. P., Saldanha, O. L., Kouvidi, K., Bono, A., Heij, L. R., Brinker, T. J., Gögenür, I., Quirke, P., & Kather, J. N. (2022). Deep learning identifies inflamed fat as a risk factor for lymph node metastasis in early colorectal cancer. *The Journal of Pathology*, *256*(3), 269–281. doi:10.1002/path.5831 PMID:34738636

Castelo, M., Sue-Chue-Lam, C., Paszat, L., Kishibe, T., Scheer, A. S., Hansen, B. E., & Baxter, N. N. (2022). Time to diagnosis and treatment in younger adults with colorectal cancer: A systematic review. *PLoS One*, *17*(9), e0273396. doi:10.1371/journal.pone.0273396 PMID:36094913

Davri, A., Birbas, E., Kanavos, T., Ntritsos, G., Giannakeas, N., Tzallas, A. T., & Batistatou, A. (2022). Deep learning on histopathological images for colorectal cancer diagnosis: A systematic review. *Diagnostics (Basel)*, *12*(4), 837. doi:10.3390/diagnostics12040837 PMID:35453885

Gurcan, M. N., Boucheron, L. E., Can, A., Madabhushi, A., Rajpoot, N. M., & Yener, B. (2009). Histopathological image analysis: A review. *IEEE Reviews in Biomedical Engineering*, *2*, 147–171. doi:10.1109/RBME.2009.2034865 PMID:20671804

Ho, D., Tan, I. B. H., & Motani, M. (2021, April). Predictive models for colorectal cancer recurrence using multi-modal healthcare data. In *Proceedings of the Conference on Health, Inference, and Learning* (pp. 204-213). 10.1145/3450439.3451868

Kajiwara Saito, M., Morishima, T., Ma, C., Koyama, S., & Miyashiro, I. (2022). Diagnosis and treatment of digestive cancers during COVID-19 in Japan: A Cancer Registry-based Study on the Impact of COVID-19 on Cancer Care in Osaka (CanReCO). *PLoS One*, *17*(9), e0274918. doi:10.1371/journal.pone.0274918 PMID:36126088

Kassani, S. H., Kassani, P. H., Wesolowski, M. J., Schneider, K. A., & Deters, R. (2022). Deep transfer learning based model for colorectal cancer histopathology segmentation: A comparative study of deep pre-trained models. *International Journal of Medical Informatics*, *159*, 104669. doi:10.1016/j.ijmedinf.2021.104669 PMID:34979435

Kather, J. N., Weis, C. A., Bianconi, F., Melchers, S. M., Schad, L. R., Gaiser, T., Marx, A., & Zollner, F. (in press). Multi-class texture analysis in colorectal cancer histology (2016). *Scientific Reports*.

Kennion, O., Maitland, S., & Brady, R. (2022). Machine learning as a new horizon for colorectal cancer risk prediction? A systematic review. *Health Sciences Review (Oxford, England)*, *4*, 100041. doi:10.1016/j.hsr.2022.100041

Liang, F., Wang, S., Zhang, K., Liu, T. J., & Li, J. N. (2022). Development of artificial intelligence technology in diagnosis, treatment, and prognosis of colorectal cancer. *World Journal of Gastrointestinal Oncology*, *14*(1), 124–152. doi:10.4251/wjgo.v14.i1.124 PMID:35116107

Ma, N., Zhang, X., Zheng, H. T., & Sun, J. (2018). Shufflenet v2: Practical guidelines for efficient cnn architecture design. In *Proceedings of the European conference on computer vision (ECCV)* (pp. 116-131). 10.1007/978-3-030-01264-9_8

Mansur, A., Saleem, Z., Elhakim, T., & Daye, D. (2023). Role of artificial intelligence in risk prediction, prognostication, and therapy response assessment in colorectal cancer: Current state and future directions. *Frontiers in Oncology*, *13*, 1065402. doi:10.3389/fonc.2023.1065402 PMID:36761957

Mármol, I., Sánchez-de-Diego, C., Pradilla Dieste, A., Cerrada, E., & Rodriguez Yoldi, M. J. (2017). Colorectal carcinoma: A general overview and future perspectives in colorectal cancer. *International Journal of Molecular Sciences*, *18*(1), 197. doi:10.3390/ijms18010197 PMID:28106826

Patil, P. S., Saklani, A., Gambhire, P., Mehta, S., Engineer, R., De'Souza, A., Chopra, S., & Bal, M. (2017). Colorectal cancer in India: An audit from a tertiary center in a low prevalence area. *Indian Journal of Surgical Oncology*, *8*(4), 484–490. doi:10.100713193-017-0655-0 PMID:29203978

Raj, S., Kishor, K., Devi, S., Sinha, D. K., Madhawi, R., Singh, R. K., Prakash, P., & Kumar, S. (2023). Epidemiological trends of colorectal cancer cases in young population of Eastern India: A retrospective observational study. *Journal of Cancer Research and Therapeutics*.

Rompianesi, G., Pegoraro, F., Ceresa, C. D., Montalti, R., & Troisi, R. I. (2022). Artificial intelligence in the diagnosis and management of colorectal cancer liver metastases. *World Journal of Gastroenterology*, *28*(1), 108–122. doi:10.3748/wjg.v28.i1.108 PMID:35125822

Shi, B., Bai, X., & Yao, C. (2016). An end-to-end trainable neural network for image-based sequence recognition and its application to scene text recognition. *IEEE Transactions on Pattern Analysis and Machine Intelligence*, *39*(11), 2298–2304. doi:10.1109/TPAMI.2016.2646371 PMID:28055850

Siegel, R. L., Miller, K. D., Goding Sauer, A., Fedewa, S. A., Butterly, L. F., Anderson, J. C., Cercek, A., Smith, R. A., & Jemal, A. (2020). Colorectal cancer statistics, 2020. *CA: a Cancer Journal for Clinicians*, *70*(3), 145–164. doi:10.3322/caac.21601 PMID:32133645

Siegel, R. L., Wagle, N. S., Cercek, A., Smith, R. A., & Jemal, A. (2023). Colorectal cancer statistics, 2023. *CA: a Cancer Journal for Clinicians*, *73*(3), 233–254. doi:10.3322/caac.21772 PMID:36856579

Talukder, M. A., Islam, M. M., Uddin, M. A., Akhter, A., Hasan, K. F., & Moni, M. A. (2022). Machine learning-based lung and colon cancer detection using deep feature extraction and ensemble learning. *Expert Systems with Applications*, *205*, 117695. doi:10.1016/j.eswa.2022.117695

Tamang, L. D., & Kim, B. W. (2021). Deep learning approaches to colorectal cancer diagnosis: A review. *Applied Sciences (Basel, Switzerland)*, *11*(22), 10982. doi:10.3390/app112210982

Waljee, A. K., Weinheimer-Haus, E. M., Abubakar, A., Ngugi, A. K., Siwo, G. H., Kwakye, G., Singal, A. G., Rao, A., Saini, S. D., Read, A. J., Baker, J. A., Balis, U., Opio, C. K., Zhu, J., & Saleh, M. N. (2022). Artificial intelligence and machine learning for early detection and diagnosis of colorectal cancer in sub-Saharan Africa. *Gut*, *71*(7), 1259–1265. doi:10.1136/gutjnl-2022-327211 PMID:35418482

Wei, J., Suriawinata, A., Vaickus, L., Ren, B., Liu, X., Wei, J., & Hassanpour, S. (2019). Generative image translation for data augmentation in colorectal histopathology images. *Proceedings of Machine Learning Research*, *116*, 10. PMID:33912842

Yu, C., & Helwig, E. J. (2022). The role of AI technology in prediction, diagnosis and treatment of colorectal cancer. *Artificial Intelligence Review*, *55*(1), 1–21. doi:10.100710462-021-10034-y PMID:34248245

Chapter 15
SRAM Memory Testing Methods and Analysis:
An Approach for Traditional Test Algorithms to ML Models

M. Parvathi

BVRIT HYDERABAD College of Engineering for Women, India

ABSTRACT

In the scenario of growing technologies towards single digit nanometer range, the existing algorithmic contemporary test methods have become inadequate in detecting all the faults within the static random access memory. To address the issues related to contemporary test methods, machine learning-based test analysis is proposed, which elevates the method of dataset preparation using various process parameters that are drawn from functional fault models (FFMs). The outcome of this proposed work is modeling of FFMs using ML regression, classification, and further prediction with accuracy analysis. The experiments resulted that logistic regression is best suited model that resulting with high accuracy in the range of 95% to 97%, compared to the linear regression model that results in accuracy levels in the range of 26.58% to 63%.

1. INTRODUCTION

Generally, IC testing comprises two ways: one is at the wafer level, and the other is at the package level. The wafer level test is a die or probe test that involves measurement of resistance and capacitance at the test location. If the observations differ from what was expected, this leads to fault identification. Similarly, the final test, which is the wafer test, will be done after packaging. This requires a probe, probe card, and test socket as a setup that decides whether the packaged chip has any faults or not. Deploying AI and machine learning (ML) algorithmic techniques in the VLSI domain at the design and manufacturing levels will reduce the test time. Most importantly, using automated learning algorithms will result in less effort in understanding and processing data at various abstraction levels. As a result, it reduces

DOI: 10.4018/978-1-6684-8531-6.ch015

Copyright © 2024, IGI Global. Copying or distributing in print or electronic forms without written permission of IGI Global is prohibited.

the manufacturing turnaround time, cost and further leads to an improvement in the IC yield. In general, defects in the IC layout will cause an effective fault in the circuit at the functional level. Machine learning helps while working with EDA tools in obtaining fault-free VLSI designs by predicting the defects on the chip and using that result to find better solutions during production.

A fault in embedded SRAM is an abstraction of a physical defect at various levels. Memory test algorithms are essential tools for detecting memory failures. Various test methods are used to detect and locate the fault (Shibaji Banerjee,Dipanwita Roy Chowdhury and Bhargab B.Bhattacharya (2005), TM Mak, Debika Bhattacharya, Cheryl Prunty, Bob Roeder, Nermine Ramadan, Joel Ferguson, Jianlin Yu.(1998), J. van de Goor. (1998), J.F.Li, K.L.Cheng, C.T.Huang, and C.W.Wu. (2001), Verilog Digital System Desigh. (2008)). March tests are one of the most efficient approaches for ensuring the correctness of SRAM functionality Balwinder Singh, Sukhleen Bindra Narang, and Arun Khosla.(2010). March tests are examples of algorithmic implementation that often target a definite fault model (Aiman Zakwan Jidin, Razaidi Hussin, Lee Weng Fook, Mohd Syafiq Mispan.(2021), Muddapu Parvathi, N. Vasantha, K. Satya Parasad (2012), Nor Azura Zakaria, W.Z.W. Hasan, I.A. Halin, R.M Sidek, Xiaoqing Wen. (2012)). Faults in SRAM may be single or multiple. Single faults are simple in nature, appear with the cell itself, and are easily captured by applying their corresponding fault models. However, multiple faults are not that simple to extract. Multiple faults are of two types: linked and unlinked. In linked faults, a fault in one cell will change the behavior of the other cell, whereas in unlinked faults, a change in the behavior of one cell does not affect the behavior of the other cell (Said Hamdioui, Ad J. van de Goor, Mike Rodgers.(2002), Rob Dekker, Frans Beenker, And Loek Thijssen.(1990)). There are many March algorithm models that can be observed in the literature that address single-stick and transition faults (G. Harutunyan And V. A. Vardanian, Y. Zorian.(2007), TM Mak, Debika Bhattacharya, Cheryl Prunty, Bob Roeder, Nermine Ramadan, Joel Ferguson, Jianlin Yu.(1998), M. I. Masnita, W. H. W. Zuha, R. M. Sidek, and A.H. Izhal (n.d)). However, as the process technology has grown to nanometer design techniques, SRAMs are brought to the level of sub-threshold operation, and the occurrence of multiple faults has grown in a similar manner, leading to the identification of a new type of March test to detect multiple faults (Chen-Wei Lin, Hung-Hsin Chen, Hao-Yu Yang, Chin-Yuan Huang, Mango C.-T. Chao, and Rei-Fu Huang.(2013). The other way of differentiating types of faults lies in its operation while detecting them. This gives the category of two types: static and dynamic faults. If the faults are sensitized by performing a single operation, they are called static faults, whereas if more than two operations are required, they are called dynamic faults (G. Harutunyan And V. A. Vardanian, Y. Zorian (2007). In this scenario, March primitives have become an essential measure of test models, in which faults can be observed by selecting appropriate sensitizing input and reading the corresponding output from the cell. Numerous March algorithms can be explored in the literature (Said Hamdioui, Zaid Al-Ars Ad J. van de Goor Mike Rodgers.(2003), A. Benso, A. Bosio, S. Di Carlo, G. Di Natale, P. Prinetto. (2006), Bosio A., Di Carlo S., Di Natale G., Prinetto P. (2007), Alberto Bosio, Giorgio Di Natale. (2008), Aiman Zakwan Jidin, Razaidi Hussin, Lee Weng Fook, Mohd Syafiq Mispan, Nor Azura Zakaria, Loh Wan Ying, and Norshuhani Zamin (2022), Aiman Zakwan Jidin, Razaidi Hussin, Mohd Syafiq Mispan, Lee Weng Fook, Loh Wan Ying (2022), G. Nguyen et al.(2019), C. Shorten and T. M. Khoshgoftaar (2019), R. Vinayakumar, M. Alazab, K. P. Soman, P. Poornachandran, A. Al-Nemrat, and S. Venkatraman (2019), K. Sivaraman, R. M. V. Krishnan, B. Sundarraj, and S. Sri Gowthem (2019), A. D. Dwivedi, G. Srivastava, S. Dhar, and R. Singh (2019), F. Al-Turjman, H. Zahmatkesh, and L. Mostarda (2019), S. Kumar and M. Singh (2019), L. M. Ang, K. P. Seng, G. K. Ijemaru, and A. M. Zungeru (2019), B. P. L. Lau et al.(2019), S. Martirosyan and G. Harutyunyan (2019), A. J. Van De Goor (1993), N. A. Zakaria (2013), I.S. Irobi, Z.

Al-Ars, and M. Renovell (2010), Z. Al-Ars, S. Hamdioui, A.J. van der Goor, and G. Mueller(2008), N. A. Zakaria, W. Z. W. Hassan, I. A. Halin, R. M. Sidek, and X. Wen (2013),....) and are delved into to address the critical issue of high fault coverage. To name a few, March SL with the complexity of 41n for detecting simple linked faults, March AB in the similar line developed for detecting linked faults as in March SL, but with less complexity, i.e., 19n, March AB1 of length 11N, and March AB2 of length 22N, respectively, can be observed. A March test algorithm with the highest length of 100N (M. H. Tehranipour, Z. Navabi, S. M. Fakhraie (2001) can also be observed for the detection of all two-cell dynamic faults with two fault-sensitizing operations in word-oriented memory architectures. However, the use of built-in self-test (BIST), an essential part of embedded systems in addition to the core logic that provides speed testing, makes possible the use of a course of algorithms in order to reach the target assigned high fault coverage. BIST provides both online and offline testing facilities with ease, making it one of the more cost-effective solutions compared to the external automatic test equipment (Dongkyu Youn: Taehyung Kim and Sungju Park(2001), M. H. Tehranipour, Z. Navabi, S. M. Fakhraie (2001), Tin Quang Bui, Lam Dang Pham, Hieu Minh Nguyen, Viet Thai Nguyen, Thong Chi Le, Trang Hoang (2016), Zhikuang Cai, Ying Wang, ShihuanLiu, Kai Lv, Zixuan Wang (2019), Robert Aitken (2007). It uses a sequence generator for various algorithm selections, through which test sequences will be given as inputs to the circuit under test (CUT). The comparator compares the normal output with the existing values to decide whether a particular cell is at fault. The test sequences are becoming larger as the memory sizes become more complex with advancements in VLSI embedded core designs. This has led to an increase in test length, which causes test latency problems in large, complex memory architectures.

Due to scale-down technologies, large memory architectures have been dominated compared to their core logic area that influences parasitic parameters like capacitance and resistance (Chen-Wei Lin, Hung-Hsin Chen, Hao-Yu Yang, Chin-Yuan Huang, Mango C.-T. Chao, and Rei-Fu Huang (2013), Aiman Zakwan Jidin, Razaidi Hussin, Mohd Syafiq Mispan, Lee Weng Fook, Loh Wan Ying (2022)). This parasitic effect causes additional faults that are not detected by the existing test methods. The initial approach was inductive fault analysis, through which realistic fault models were developed for a given process technology. This process is a mere mapping of defect to failure that results in the required functional fault model. These, however, are handled by resistive-opens and short-falls (S.Manoj and J.Pineda de Gyvez (2007), S.Borri, M.H.Hassan, P.Girard, S.Pravossoudovitch, and A.Virazel (2003), D.Niggemeyer, M.Redeker, and J.Otterstedt (1998)) which are timing-dependent fault models. In addition to that, while mapping the failure models with test cases, some of the fault models may perfectly map with defect models. But some may remain unknown, leading to an undetectable fault or faults. This makes the test inadequate during the process variation under sub-micron memory models. Authors in (M.Venkatesham, S.K.Sinha and M Parvathi (2021), M.Venkatesham, S.K.Sinha and M Parvathi (July, 2021), M.Venkatesham, S. K.Sinha and M. Parvathi. (Dec, 2021), S.Irobi,Z.Al-Ars and S.Hamdioui (2010), M.Parvathi, K.Satya Prasad, N.Vasantha (2017), V. Maddela, S. K. Sinha, M. Parvathi and V. Sharma (2022), M.Parvathi, N. Vasantha, and K. Satya Prasad (2013), M.Parvathi, N. Vasantha, and K. Satya Prasad (2015), V. Maddela, S. K. Sinha and M. Parvathi (2021), M. Parvathi, N.Vasantha, K.Satya Prasad (2017)) have proposed a new test method, called the parasitic extraction method that uses parasitic resistance and capacitance for fault estimation or detection as well as fault occurrence location. This method is also used to address the issues of limited fault coverage, test latency, and undetectable faults. In the parasitic extraction method, each fault model is built into an electrical circuit environment model, and the corresponding layout can be extracted using EDA tools. Further, these layouts were used for the extraction of parasitic R and C. A fault model dictionary was the outcome of the approach that helps the test engineers estimates their design parameters in a fault-free environment.

However, due to advancements in technology, it is essential to figure out the new models that are used for testing VLSI embedded cores with ease and accuracy. The proposed test method of machine learning-based analysis not only explains the use of ML but also focuses on how to overcome issues such as test latency, fault coverage problems, and test length. These issues are addressed in this chapter. The initial process of the proposed method of ML-based fault modeling uses an electrical circuit model of fault-free SRAM, from which the layout is to be extracted and through which the necessary electrical parameters such as parasitic resistances, capacitances, power dissipation, critical path delay, and maximum current are to be extracted. Further, these parameters are used to list out various fault models, and the resulting list will be used as a dataset to apply to the chosen ML algorithm. Section 2 will discuss fault models, defect models, and defect to fault model mapping. Section 3 will discuss a review of March test method approaches, and their limitations, as well as the parasitic extraction method. Section 4 continues with the proposed ML-based test method using the Scikit and Tensor Flow environments in terms of the experimental procedures that are required to be carried out. Further, section 5 deals with results and comparisons, and section 6 gives the conclusions.

2. REVIEW ON MEMORY TECHNOLOGIES AND FAULT MODEL ANALYSIS

Memory that is used for embedded applications and used along with the logic core can be treated as embedded memory. On the other hand, external or standalone memories such as such as hard disks and RAM that are not integrated on the chip, used as an external component within the system. As a result, testing embedded memory is more difficult than testing standalone, which is done similarly to standard IC testing. Currently, SRAMs (Static Random Access Memory) are used with most embedded systems due to their advantages of speed and reliability in data retention. Traditional SRAM as shown in Figure.1, comprises a 6T (6 transistors) cell architecture with two bit lines (BL and BLB) for reading or writing the data and two internal cell nodes (Q and QB) to represent the stored value. In order to access the cell during a write or read operation, access line WL is necessary. In addition, supply and ground lines VDD and VSS support the cell's working condition. A single cell is capable of storing either '0' or '1' based on the written value; otherwise, the cell is at fault. The proposed work explained in this chapter is done on the 120nm (0.12 um) technology. The same process can be extended to any other technology level too.

2.1. Fault Models: An Insight

Faults are unwanted observations that differ from the expected outcomes. In SRAM, faults may occur due to unwanted node-to-node shorting or opening. This leads to the possibility that the cell may stick at a particular value instead of responding normally to the inputs given. In general, the faults that are caused by the presence of a defect in the chip can be mapped using the Functional Fault Model (FFM). The faults that occur in single-cell SRAMs are classified into simple and linked faults based on their behavior in a multi-cell environment. The difference between simple and linked faults depends on the number of cells that are actively participating in creating a fault in a particular cell. Single (or simple) faults that will exist within the observation cell itself and may not be influenced by the faulty behavior of other cells. Single faults are easily detectable. However, linked faults involve more than one cell; a cell

Figure 1. Single cell 6T SRAM

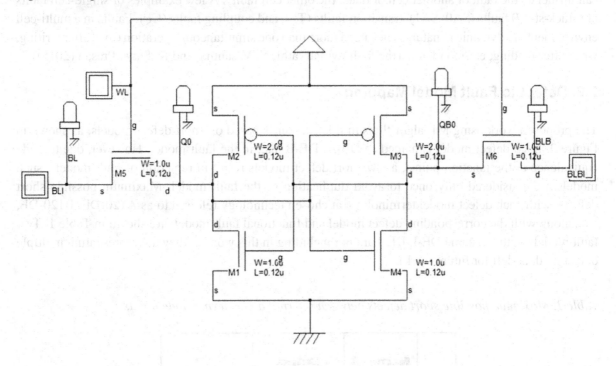

Figure 2. Fault models under consideration with defect injection at node to node points

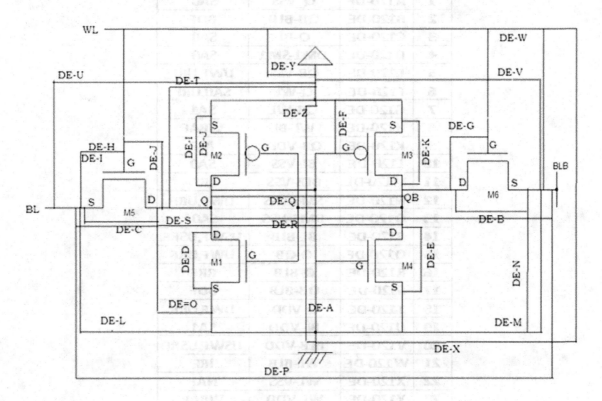

can influence the fault of another cell or make the other cell faulty. A few examples of single-cell faults are stuck-st-1/0 faults (SA0, SA1), transition faults (TF), and coupling faults (CF). Faults in a multi-cell environment are dynamic in nature. They need more than one simultaneous operation (read after writing, write after reading, etc.) to identify the fault (M.Parvathi, N. Vasantha, and K. Satya Prasad (2015)).

2.2. Defect to Fault Model Mapping

The proposed work using ML algorithms in this chapter is based on short defect models, as shown in Figure 2. Each defect model is named as DE-A, DE-B, etc. in the fault model. However, due to node equivalence at the junction points, a few short defect models result in repletion of fault models; such models are considered only once to avoid duplication of the fault model. Maximum possible short defects, with each defect model terminology at chosen technology referred to as A120-DE, B120-DE, etc., along with the corresponding defect model and functional fault model, are shown in Table 1. Two fault models with the name DE-I, DE-J are not including in this work as they are representing multiple defect models (left for future work).

Table 1. Maximum possible short defects between internal and external node points

S.No	Name of theDefect	Defect Model	FFM
1	A120-DE	Q_VSS	SA0
2	B120-DE	QB-BLB	BDF
3	C120-DE	Q-BL	SA0
4	D120-DE	DM1-SM1	SA0
5	E120-DE	QB-VSS	UWF,URF
6	F120-DE	Q-WL	SA0,URF
7	G120-DE	QB-WL	SA1
8	H120-DE	WL-BL	WBAF
9	K120-DE	QB-VDD	IOF
10	L120-DE	BL-VSS	SA0
11	M120-DE	BLB-VSS	IRF
12	N120-DE	SM6-VSS	UWF,URF
13	O120-DE	DM5-VSS	SA0
14	P120-DE	BL-BLB	USWF,USRF
15	Q120-DE	Q-QB	UWF,URF
16	R120-DE	Q-BLB	RRF
17	S120-DE	QB-BLB	BDF
18	T120-DE	Q-VDD	UWF,URF
19	U120-DE	BL-VDD	SA1
20	V120-DE	BLB-VDD	USWF,USRF
21	W120-DE	WL-BLB	IRF
22	X120-DE	WL-VSS	NAF
23	Y120-DE	WL-VDD	WBAF
24	Z120-DE	VDD-VSS	UWF,URF

The worth noting point from Table 1 is, few faults are repetitive in behavior but their fault models are different. As an example, stuck-at-0 (SA0) appears in S.No.1, 3, 4, 10 and 13. Though fault wise they are similar in behavior but the defect model for occurrence of this fault is different.

3. REVIEW ON MARCH ALGORITHMS AND TEST COMPLEXITIES

Fault model is the basic requirement prior to the application of any algorithm, through which the behavior of particular fault can be studied well. Functional fault model is the basis of reduced fault model through which the deviation of actual memory to faulty memory will be analyzed. The basic functional fault model is defined with single cell SRAM architecture in which sensitizing, write and read are the basic operations required for fault analysis. March algorithms are applied to a particular fault model in terms of primitives, such that the difference between an expected (fault-free) and the observed (faulty) memory behavior. A primitive can be denoted by:

$$< S / F / R >$$

Where S denotes sensitizing operation, F denotes the faulty output observed from the cell and R denotes the expected actual read value from the cell. In the case of multiple cell or two cell scenario, the primitive will be represented as

$$< S_a ; S_v / F / R >$$

Where S_a and S_v are the Sequence of Sensitizing Operations and/or Conditions respectively applied to a-cell and v-cell, needed to sensitize the given fault. Using the ease in representation of primitives, the March algorithms have reached the complexity beyond 100n that makes the test more complex and delayed simulation results. Various fault models and their corresponding primitive notations are observed in Table 2.

3.1. Need of BIST Models and Test Algorithms: Review Perspective

Built-in Self-Test (BIST) is an essential technique usually used for embedded memory testing because of its ease of use, efficiency in speed testing, especially shorter test time, and cost effectiveness. BIST for memory testing comprises memory as a "circuit under test (CUT) and a "test pattern generator (TPG) as essential components. The additional parts that make the testing complete are the comparator and controller. On the other hand, BIST can also be used for logic testing under the name LBIST, which uses random logic with additional components like a signature analyzer and a scan chain.

BIST testing can be done in two modes: online mode and offline mode. Online mode of testing involves the real-time running operation of the core logic, whereas offline mode of testing involves the test running for a specific duration during which the test circuit is away from its normal operation. In either of the modes, the test involves a test pattern through which the expected output will be analyzed to decide whether the CUT is faulty or not. The test patterns are the crucial deciding factors in identifying the fault within the CUT. The test patterns will be generated by a test pattern generator. The selection of test patterns is based on the cut under consideration. For example, if CUT is memory-affected with a

Table 2. Fault models and their corresponding primitive notations

S. No	Fault Model	Definition	Primitive Notation
1.	SF	A cell has a state fault if its logic value flips before it is accessed, even if no operation is performed on it.	$< 1/0/->, < 0/1/->$
2.	TF	A cell has a transition fault if it fails to undergo a transition in a write operation	$< 0w1/0/->, < 1w0/1/->$
3.	WDF	A cell suffers from a write destructive fault if a non-transition write operation causes a transition in the cell.	$< 0w0/\uparrow/->, < 1w1/\downarrow/->$
4.	RDF	A cell is said to have a read destructive fault if a read operation performed on the cell changes the data in the cell, and returns an incorrect value on the output.	$< r0/\uparrow/1 >, < r1/\downarrow/0 >$
5.	DRDF	A cell suffers from a deceptive read destructive fault if a read operation performed on the cell changes the logic value of the cell, while returning the correct value as the output.	$< r0/\uparrow/0 >, < r1/\downarrow/1 >$
6.	RRDF	A cell has a random read destructive fault if a read operation performed on the cell, changes the logic value of the cell and returns a random value.	$< r0/\uparrow/? >, < r1/\downarrow/? >$
7.	IRF	A cell is said to have an incorrect read fault if a read operation performed on the cell returns the incorrect logic value while keeping the correct value in the cell.	$< r0/0/1 >, < r1/1/0 >$
8.	RRF	A cell suffers from a random read fault if a read operation returns a random value while keeping the correct value in the cell.	$< r0/0/? >, < r1/1/? >$
9.	USF	A cell has an undefined state fault if the logic value of the cell flips to an undefined state before the cell is accessed, even if no operation is performed on it	$< 1/?/->, < 0/?/->$
10.	UWF	A cell is said to have an undefined write fault if the cell is brought in an undefined state by a write operation.	$< 0w0/?/->, < 0w1/?/->, < 1w0/?/->, < 1w1/?/->$
11.	URF	A cell is said to have an undefined read fault if the cell is brought in an undefined state by a read operation	$< rx/?/0 >, < rx/?/1 >, < rx/?/? >$
12.	SAF	A cell is said to have a stuck-at fault if it remains always stuck at a given value for all performed operations	$< V/0/->, < V/1/->$
13.	NAF	A cell suffers from a no access fault if the cell is not accessible.	$\{< 0w1/0/->, < 1w0/1/->, < x/x/? >\}$
14.	DRF	A cell is said to have a data retention fault if the state of the cell changes after a certain time T, and without accessing the cell.	$< 1T/\downarrow/->, < 0T/\uparrow/->, < xT/?/->$

stuck fault, the algorithms and test patterns are to be selected accordingly to detect the underlying stuck fault; if the algorithm is not able to detect the fault, it is required to discard the chosen algorithm and incorporate another suitable algorithm or test pattern. Hence, while designing the BIST architecture, it is essential to decide on the test pattern generator and corresponding test patterns or algorithms. Various test methodologies have been implemented to identify memory defects. Traditional test methods are zero/one, checkerboard, GALPAT, walking 1/0, and sliding diagonal to name a few. Initially, investigations were carried out based on fault and fault modeling. The majority of the test methodologies are based on the type of fault that occurs in the memory. For ensuring the SRAM operating correctly different testing methods are used. March tests are efficient for ensuring the correct functionality of SRAMs (D.Niggemeyer, M.Redeker, and J.Otterstedt(1998), A.J.V. De Goor (1993)). March tests as an example of algorithmic implementation, often target a definite fault model (M.Parvathi, N.Vasantha, K. Satya Parasad (2012). However, most of the algorithms are strict to apply to the functional fault models, which lead to issues in detecting some of the escaped faults from the test.

Table 3. Fault models observed from parasitic extraction method

S.No	Short Defect	Fault Model	Node Q Fault Free C=4.15fF R=7550Ω		Node QB Fault Free C=4.64 fF R=6489Ω		Node WL Fault Free C=1.98 fF R=369Ω		Node BL Fault Free C=1 fF R=1158Ω		Node BLB Fault Free C=0.95 fF R=2094Ω	
			C,fF	R,Ω	C,fF	R,Ω	C,fF	R,Ω	C,fF	R,Ω	C,fF	R,Ω
1	WL-BL	WBA	6.47	12919	4.64	6489	NA	NA	1.74	1341	0.95	2094
2	QB-VDD	IOF	4.49	7550	6.68	11858	1.98	369	1	1158	0.95	2094
3	QB-BLB	BDF	5.53	9860	4.64	6489	1.98	369	0.98	1158	NA	NA
4	QB-BL	USWF & USRF	4.5	7550	6.27	9954	1.99	369	NA	NA	0.95	2094

3.2. Problem of MARCH Notation for Undetectable Faults

Undetectable faults are the faults that are not detectable using existing March algorithms since their application is restricted to use in functional fault models. The faults that easily escape the test fall into this category. Table 3 represents list of undetectable faults results out of parasitic extraction method.

These undetectable faults can be found using the parasitic extraction method of fault detection (M.Venkatesham, S.K.Sinha and M Parvathi (2021), M.Venkatesham, S.K.Sinha and M Parvathi (July, 2021), M.Venkatesham, S. K.Sinha and M. Parvathi. (Dec, 2021), S.Irobi,Z.Al-Ars and S.Hamdioui (2010), M.Parvathi, K.Satya Prasad, N.Vasantha (2017), V. Maddela, S. K. Sinha, M. Parvathi and V. Sharma (2022), M.Parvathi, N. Vasantha, and K. Satya Prasad (2013), M.Parvathi, N. Vasantha, and K. Satya Prasad (2015), V. Maddela, S. K. Sinha and M. Parvathi (2021), M. Parvathi, N.Vasantha, K.Satya Prasad (2017)) that extracts faults within the SRAM cell from any corner. Based on their behavior, these undetectable faults are named Write Before Access Fault (WBA), Incorrect Order Fault (IOF), Bit Line Delay Fault (BDF), and Unstabilized Write or Read Fault (USWF/USRF).

3.3. Parasitic Extraction Method of Testing- An approach for Dataset Creation

Parasitic extraction method is exact reversible method of Inductive Fault model Analysis (IFA). In IFA faults model are extracted from defect injection at layout level. Though the resulting fault models are realistic in nature, but many undefined fault models were left unrealized.

This problem is addressed in parasitic extraction method, in which, initially the fault model will be considered in its electrical circuit model, the corresponding defect model would be extracted from its layout (M.Parvathi, N. Vasantha, and K. Satya Prasad (2015), V. Maddela, S. K. Sinha and M. Parvathi (2021)). This further helped in analyzing the faulty behavior in terms of extracted parasitic values of resistance (R), and capacitance(C). Not only RC, the other related parameters are critical path delay (CPD, ns), power dissipation (Pd, m/uW), maximum current (Imax, mA) are also considered for the proposed ML based analysis. List of all these parameters are used as dataset in the proposed work. Table 4 shows the simulation parameters CPD, PD and IDD observed for chosen fault models under short defect analysis, are used as first dataset.

Table 4. Simulation parameters CPD, PD, and IDD observed for chosen fault models

S.No	FFM	CPD,ns	W1(BL=1,BLB=0,WL=1)		W0(BL=0,BLB=1,WL=1)		R1(Q=1,QB=0,WL=1)		R0(Q=0,QB=1,WL=1)	
			PD	IDD	PD	IDD	PD	IDD	PD	IDD
1	FF(Fault Free S	1.9	1.962µ	0	7.509µ	1.058	1.48m	2.208	1.48m	2.208
2	SA0	3.12	0.317m	1.062	2.457µ	0.38	1.786m	2.208	1.48m	2.208
3	BDF	3.12	1.961µ	0.019	2.549µ	0.363	1.781m	2.208	1.48m	2.208
4	SA0	3.12	0.319m	1.153	1.852µ	0	1.781m	2.208	1.48m	2.208
5	SA0	3.12	0.592m	1.215	1.64µ	0	2.57m	2.208	0.987m	1.472
6	UWF,URF	2.91	1.657µ	0	0.592m	1.215	0.99m	1.472	2.57m	2.208
7	SA0,URF	3.08	0	0	6.818µ	0.014	1n	0	0.357m	0.736
8	SA1	4.7	0	0	0	0	1n	0	0.357m	0.736
9	WRAF	1.9	0	0	0	0	1n	0	0.357m	0.736
10	IOF	2.9	3.348µ	0.014	0	0	0.357m	0.736	1n	0
11	SA0	2.07	28.645µ	0.06	6n	0	0.568m	1.177	1n	0
12	IRF	3.04	0	0	0	0	0.607m	1.255	0.249m	0.519
13	UWF,URF	2.91	1.657µ	0	0.592m	1.215	0.99m	1.472	2.57m	2.208
14	SA0	3.12	0.502m	1.034	0.502m	1.034	3.426m	2.944	0.98m	1.472
15	USWF,USRF	3.12	0.592m	1.215	0.592m	1.215	1.69m	2.208	1.992m	2.208
16	UWF,URF	4.17	0.504m	1.033	0.503m	1.033	3.426m	2.944	0.974m	1.472
17	RRF	2.13	2.523µ	0.046	0.471m	1.09	1.781m	2.208	2.081m	2.208
18	BDF	2.3	0.419m	0.859	2.136µ	0.063	1.781m	2.208	2.081m	2.208
19	UWF,URF	3.08	5n	0.001	16.567µ	0.107	3n	0	0.658m	1.353
20	SA1	2.07	0.187µ	0.095	17µ	0.097	0.188µ	0.011	0.595m	1.223
21	USWF,USRF	3.04	9.202µ	0.018	0.156m	0.341	0.295m	0.606	0.301m	0.617
22	IRF	2.28	0	0	0.156m	0.341	0.209m	0.46	0.301m	0.617
23	NAF	2.07	30.51µ	0.063	0.21m	0.467	0.595m	1.223	0.301m	0.617
24	WRAF	2.07	0.21m	0.47	0.21m	0.467	0.301m	0.617	0.301m	0.617
25	UWF,URF	1.9	0	0	0	0	0	0	0	0

Table 5. Simulation parameters of parasitic extracted C, R, L, observed at nodes Q, QB, BL, and BLB for chosen fault models

S.No	Defect Type	Defect Mode	FFM	CQ	RQ	LQ	CQB	RQB	LQB	CWL	RWL	CBL	RBL	LBL	CBLB	RBLB	LBLB
1	FF120-DE	NOFAULT	NOFAULT	4.15E-15	7550	6.70E-05	4.64E-15	6489	6.70E-05	1.94E-15	329	2.86E-05	1.86E-15	1158	2.16E-05	9.58E-16	2894	2.86E-05
2	A120-DE	Q_VSS	SA0	5.53E-15	9860	8.20E-05	4.64E-15	6489	6.70E-05	1.94E-15	329	2.86E-05	1.86E-15	1158	2.16E-05	9.58E-16	2894	2.86E-05
3	B120-DE	QB-BLB	BDF	5.53E-15	9860	8.20E-05	4.64E-15	6489	6.70E-05	1.94E-15	329	2.86E-05	9.58E-16	1158	2.86E-05	NA	NA	NA
4	C120-DE	Q-BL	SA0	5.53E-15	8921	8.20E-05	4.64E-15	6489	6.70E-05	1.94E-15	329	2.86E-05	NA	NA	NA	9.58E-16	2894	2.86E-05
5	D120-DE	DM1-SM1	SA0	NA	NA	NA	4.48E-15	6489	6.38E-05	1.94E-15	329	2.78E-05	9.58E-16	1158	2.86E-05	9.38E-16	2894	1.94E-05
6	E120-DE	QB-VSS	UWF,URF	NA	NA	NA	NA	NA	NA	1.94E-15	329	2.78E-05	9.58E-16	1158	2.86E-05	9.38E-16	2894	1.94E-05
7	F120-DE	Q-WL	SA0,URF	6.47E-15	12919	9.80E-05	4.64E-15	6489	6.70E-05	1.94E-15	329	2.86E-05	1.86E-15	1158	2.16E-05	9.58E-16	2894	2.86E-05
8	G120-DE	QB-WL	SA1	6.47E-15	12919	9.80E-05	6.22E-15	6955	8.50E-05	NA	NA	NA	9.58E-16	1158	2.16E-05	9.38E-16	2894	1.94E-05
9	H120-DE	WL-BL	WRAF	6.47E-15	12919	9.80E-05	4.64E-15	6489	6.70E-05	NA	NA	NA	1.74E-15	1341	2.86E-05	9.58E-16	2894	2.86E-05
10	K120-DE	QB-VDD	IOF	4.49E-15	7550	6.70E-05	6.09E-15	11859	1.06E-04	1.94E-15	329	2.86E-05	1.86E-15	1158	2.16E-05	9.58E-16	2894	2.86E-05
11	L120-DE	BL-VSS	SA0	4.48E-15	7534	6.70E-05	6.09E-15	11859	1.06E-04	2.04E-15	329	2.96E-05	2.65E-15	3467	3.76E-05	9.70E-16	2895	2.86E-05
12	M120-DE	BLB-VSS	IRF	4.48E-15	7534	6.70E-05	6.87E-15	11859	1.65E-04	2.04E-15	329	2.96E-05	2.59E-15	5590	4.66E-05	NA	NA	NA
13	N120-DE	SM6-VSS	UWF,URF	4.54E-15	7572	6.70E-05	NA	NA	NA	1.94E-15	329	2.78E-05	9.58E-16	1158	2.86E-05	9.38E-16	2894	1.94E-05
14	O120-DE	DM6-VSS	SA0	NA	NA	NA	9.70E-15	16345	1.35E-04	1.94E-15	329	2.78E-05	9.58E-16	1158	2.86E-05	9.38E-16	2894	1.94E-05
15	P120-DE	BL-BLB	USWF,USRF	4.49E-15	7550	5.09E-15	8798	1.30E-05	1.94E-15	329	2.86E-05	NA	NA	NA	1.54	3251	2.96E-05
16	Q120-DE	Q-QB	UWF,URF	NA	NA	NA	9.70E-15	16345	1.35E-04	1.94E-15	329	2.78E-05	9.58E-16	1158	2.86E-05	9.38E-16	2894	1.94E-05
17	R120-DE	Q-BLB	IRF	5.00E-15	9642	7.50E-05	5.09E-15	8798	1.30E-05	1.94E-15	329	2.86E-05	9.58E-16	1158	2.86E-05	NA	NA	NA
18	S120-DE	QB-BLB	BDF	4.50E-15	7550	6.70E-05	6.27E-15	9954	9.30E-05	1.94E-15	329	2.86E-05	NA	NA	NA	9.58E-16	2894	2.86E-05
19	T120-DE	Q-VDD	UWF,URF	6.45E-15	12903	9.80E-05	5.09E-15	8798	1.30E-05	1.94E-15	329	2.86E-05	1.86E-15	1158	2.16E-05	9.58E-16	2894	2.86E-05
20	U120-DE	BL-VDD	SA1	4.48E-15	7534	6.70E-05	5.09E-15	8798	1.30E-05	2.03E-15	329	2.96E-05	3.65E-15	6527	55	9.70E-16	2895	2.86E-05
21	V120-DE	BLB-VDD	USWF,USRF	4.48E-15	7534	6.70E-05	5.09E-15	8798	1.30E-05	2.03E-15	329	2.96E-05	1.86E-15	1158	2.16E-05	3.82E-15	7464	5.59E-05
22	W120-DE	WL-BLB	IRF	4.48E-15	7534	6.70E-05	5.09E-15	8798	1.30E-05	NA	NA	NA	9.58E-16	1158	2.86E-05	4.64E-15	7830	7.38E-05
23	X120-DE	WL-VSS	NAF	4.48E-15	7534	6.70E-05	4.61E-15	6489	3.86E-05	3.86E-15	329	4.66E-05	1158	2.86E-05	3.16E-15	7464	5.74E-05
24	Y120-DE	WL-VDD	WRAF	4.48E-15	7534	6.70E-05	4.61E-15	6489	6.70E-05	5.21E-15	848	8.26E-05	1.86E-15	1158	2.16E-05	9.58E-16	2894	2.86E-05
25	Z120-DE	VDD-VSS	UWF,URF	4.55E-15	7664	6.80E-05	4.61E-15	6472	6.70E-05	1.94E-15	329	2.86E-05	1.86E-15	1158	2.16E-05	9.58E-16	2894	2.86E-05

Table 5 shows the simulation parameters for parasitic resistance, length, and capacitance (RLC) that are used as a second dataset in the proposed work. 'NA' refers to the absence of a corresponding node that resulted from fault imposition in the name of a short defect at that node. The first line in the series is fault-free (FF120-DE) SRAM, considered for fault-free parasitic values, to be compared with each fault model's parasitic RLC values. It is observed that wherever a short defect is injected (or two nodes are shorted), the corresponding R, L, and C are affected, and hence the fault gets elevated from that node. For such kind of huge number of sample observations ML algorithmic based test methods are must to consider.

4. PROPOSED ML-BASED TEST METHOD USING SCIKIT AND TENSOR FLOW ENVIRONMENTS

The approach for testing of SRAM faults using ML algorithms is done in experimental way. Initially the parameters of CPD, IDD, and PD are considered as one set, to formulate the dataset. Then ML algorithms are deployed to model, to predict and to find accuracy analysis.

4.1. Experiment-1: Linear Regression Model for FFM Analysis Using CPD, IDD, and PD

In this approach the all sort of short defect fault models are recaptured into corresponding layout defect models, from which the corresponding CPD, IDD, and PD values for each fault model are tabulated, as shown in Table 6.

Table 6. Simulation parameters as features and labels for linear regression model

PD_UW	IDD_mA	CPD_nS	OP	FFM_map
317	1.062	3.12	1	35
319	1.153	3.12	1	31
529	1.215	3.12	1	35
502	1.034	3.12	1	35
419	0.859	2.3	1	42
504	1.033	4.17	1	34
210	0.47	2.07	1	76
592	1.215	3.12	1	12
502	1.034	3.12	2	35
592	1.215	2.91	2	45
592	1.215	2.91	2	45
503	1.033	4.17	2	34
17	0.097	2.07	2	16
210	0.467	2.07	2	76
156	0.341	2.28	2	72
592	1.215	3.12	2	12
156	0.341	3.04	2	26
471	1.09	2.13	2	32
210	0.467	2.07	2	75
1786	2.208	3.12	3	35
1781	2.208	3.12	3	31
2570	2.208	3.12	3	35
568	1.177	2.07	3	15

Total number of samples observed is 58, in which the first 23 are depicted in the Table 6. The dataset comprises features and labels, in which features CPD, IDD, OP and PD are considered as independent parameters and label 'FFM_map' is considered as dependent variable. CPD is critical path delay in nano sec, IDD is observed maximum operating current in milli Amp, OP is operation of SRAM whether is write-0, write-1 or read-0, or read-1. Finally, PD is power dissipation observed against to each operation. For all the fault models under consideration each parameter is observed from the simulation models (Table 5). Each FFM from Table 5 is mapped according to node-node for short defect mapping, as shown in Table 7. For example if BL is shorted to BLB as short defect, it is mapped as '12' in the dataset and corresponding fault model is USWF, USRF (Table 5). Similarly if BL is shorted to VSS, it is mapped as '15' in the dataset and the corresponding fault model is SA0 (Table 5).

Table 7. Node-node for short defect mapping used in linear regression table

Node Values	NODES	1 BL	2 BLB	3 Q	4 QB	5 VSS	6 VDD	7 WL
1	BL	11	12	13	14	15	16	17
2	BLB	21	22	23	24	25	26	27
3	Q	31	32	33	34	35	36	37
4	QB	41	42	43	44	45	46	47
5	VSS	51	52	53	54	55	56	57
6	VDD	61	62	63	64	65	66	67
7	WL	71	72	73	74	75	76	77

The model accuracy is observed from linear regression algorithm, and is 26.58%, corresponding mapping is shown in Figure 3. The mean squared error observed in this case is '0' indicates the model fitting is appropriate, but the distance between simulated parameters are not fit to the model of linear regression.

Figure 3. Linear regression FFM mapping, based on actual and predicted values of CPD, IDD, OP, and PD

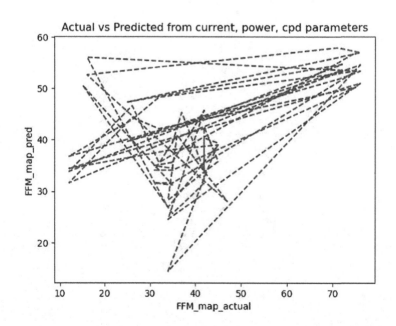

4.2. Experiment-2: Logistic Regression Model for FFM Analysis Using CPD, IDD, and PD

Dataset Table 6 is used as with deployment of logistic regression model, in which label FFM_map is chosen for either True or False category, as shown in Table 7.

Table 8. Simulation parameters as features and labels for logistic regression model

PD_UW	IDD_mA	CPD_nS	OP	FFM_map
1.96	0	1.9	1	0
3.17	1.062	3.12	1	1
3.19	1.153	3.12	1	1
5.29	1.215	3.12	1	1
5.02	1.034	3.12	1	1
4.19	0.859	2.3	1	1
5.04	1.033	4.17	1	1
2.10	0.47	2.07	1	1
5.92	1.215	3.12	1	1
7.509	1.058	1.9	2	0
5.02	1.034	3.12	2	1
5.92	1.215	2.91	2	1
5.92	1.215	2.91	2	1
5.03	1.033	4.17	2	1
1.7	0.097	2.07	2	1
2.10	0.467	2.07	2	1
1.56	0.341	2.28	2	1
5.92	1.215	3.12	2	1
1.56	0.341	3.04	2	1
4.71	1.09	2.13	2	1
2.10	0.467	2.07	2	1
14.80	2.208	1.9	3	0
17.86	2.208	3.12	3	1

In this case, the least valued fault models are also included (in previous table for linear regression they were removed due to variation problem), hence the total samples observed are 62, and first 23 are shown in Table 7. During this process, observed the frequency of fault occurrence with respect to each model parameter chosen independently. Corresponding variation of fault frequency with respect to PD is shown in Figure 4. Similarly with other parameters IDD and CPDs also observed, as shown in Figures 5&6 respectively.

From these observations, one can notice that the frequency of fault occurrence is more influenced by power dissipation parameters (Figure 4). The accuracy observed is improved in this model, as shown in Figure 7. Test accuracy observed is 97%, and train accuracy observed is 84%. It was identified that, compared to linear regression, the logistic regression model is best suited for improving the model's fit with better prediction accuracies.

Figure 4. Frequency of fault occurrence with respect to model parameter PD, microWatt

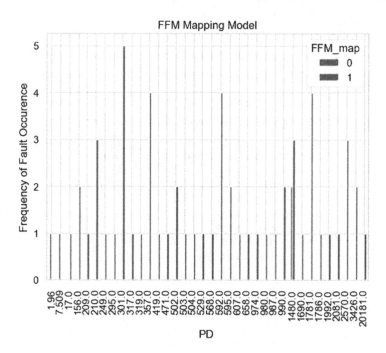

Figure 5. Frequency of fault occurrence with respect to model parameter IDD, mA

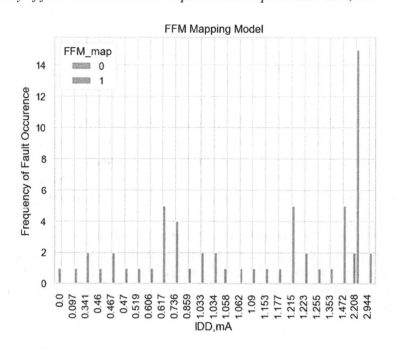

Figure 6. Frequency of fault occurrence with respect to model parameter CPD, nS

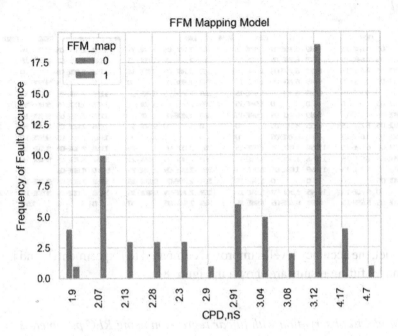

Figure 7. Test and train accuracy using logistic regression model

```
Number of Observations ::  62
      PD_UW  IDD_mA  CPD_nS  OP  FFM_map
0      1.96   0.000    1.90   1      0
1    317.00   1.062    3.12   1      1
2    319.00   1.153    3.12   1      1
3    529.00   1.215    3.12   1      1
4    502.00   1.034    3.12   1      1
Data set headers :: ['PD_UW', 'IDD_mA', 'CPD_nS', 'OP', 'FFM_map']
train_x size ::  (43, 4)
train_y size ::  (43,)
test_x size ::  (19, 4)
test_y size ::  (19,)
edu_target_frequencies=  {1: {0: 1, 1: 8}, 2: {0: 1, 1: 11}, 3: {0: 1, 1: 1
8}, 4: {0: 1, 1: 21}}
Train Accuracy ::  0.9767441860465116
Test Accuracy ::  0.8421052631578947
```

4.3. Experiment-3: Linear Regression Model for FFM Analysis Using RLC Parameters as Dataset

In this case, the dataset is considered with observed parasitic capacitance, resistance and lengths at each node, that are taken as features (CQ, RQ, LQ, CQB, etc.). The mapped FFM is considered as label, dependent parameter, corresponding dataset is shown in Table 8. Both column and row wise total number of samples is 416, in which first 256 are shown in Table 8.

Table 9. Dataset with observed simulations of parasitic capacitance, resistance, and lengths for linear regression model

CQ	RQ	LQ	CQB	RQB	LQB	CWL	RWL	LWL	CBL	RBL	LBL	CBLB	RBLB	LBLB	FFM
4.15E-15	7550	6.70E-05	4.64E-15	6489	6.70E-05	1.98E-15	369	2.80E-05	1.00E-15	1158	2.10E-05	9.50E-16	2094	2.00E-05	0
5.53E-15	9860	8.20E-05	4.64E-15	6489	6.70E-05	1.98E-15	369	2.80E-05	1.00E-15	1158	2.10E-05	9.50E-16	2094	2.00E-05	35
5.53E-15	9860	8.20E-05	4.64E-15	6489	6.70E-05	1.98E-15	369	2.80E-05	9.80E-16	1158	2.00E-05	0	0	0	42
5.53E-15	8921	8.20E-05	4.64E-15	6489	6.70E-05	1.98E-15	369	2.80E-05	0	0	0	9.50E-16	2094	2.00E-05	31
0	0	0	4.49E-15	6489	6.30E-05	1.94E-15	369	2.70E-05	9.80E-16	1158	2.00E-05	9.30E-16	2094	1.90E-05	35
4.54E-15	7572	6.70E-05	0	0	0	1.94E-15	369	2.70E-05	9.80E-16	1158	2.00E-05	9.30E-16	2094	1.90E-05	45
6.47E-15	12919	9.80E-05	4.64E-15	6489	6.70E-05	1.98E-15	369	2.80E-05	1.00E-15	1158	2.10E-05	9.50E-16	2094	2.00E-05	37
6.47E-15	12919	9.80E-05	6.22E-15	6855	8.50E-05	0	0	0	9.80E-16	1158	2.00E-05	9.30E-16	2094	1.90E-05	47
6.47E-15	12919	9.80E-05	4.64E-15	6489	6.70E-05	0	0	0	1.74E-15	1341	2.80E-05	9.50E-16	2094	2.00E-05	71
4.49E-15	7550	6.70E-05	6.68E-15	11858	1.00E-04	1.98E-15	369	2.80E-05	1.00E-15	1158	2.10E-05	9.50E-16	2094	2.00E-05	46
4.48E-15	7534	6.70E-05	6.68E-15	11858	1.00E-04	2.04E-15	369	2.90E-05	2.05E-15	3467	3.70E-05	9.70E-16	2095	2.00E-05	15
4.48E-15	7534	6.70E-05	6.87E-15	11859	1.05E-04	2.04E-15	369	2.90E-05	2.59E-15	5560	4.60E-05	0	0	0	25
4.54E-15	7572	6.70E-05	0	0	0	1.94E-15	369	2.70E-05	9.80E-16	1158	2.00E-05	9.30E-16	2094	1.90E-05	45
0	0	0	9.70E-15	16345	1.36E-04	1.94E-15	369	2.70E-05	9.80E-16	1158	2.00E-05	9.30E-16	2094	1.90E-05	35
4.49E-15	7550	6.70E-05	5.69E-15	8798	8.30E-05	1.98E-15	369	2.80E-05	0	0	0	154	3251	2.90E-05	12

Using this model, the accuracy level is improved compared to Experiment-1, and is observed as 63%, corresponding model fitting results are shown in Figure 8.

Figure 8. FFM Model fit observation with linear regression using RLC parameters

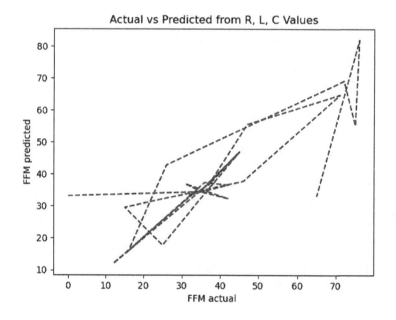

4.4. Experiment-4: Logistic Regression Model for FFM Analysis Using RLC Parameters as Dataset

In this case, the label for model fitting FFM is considered as either true or false value based on fault occurrence, corresponding dataset is shown in Table 9.

Table 10. Dataset with observed simulations of parasitic RLC for logistic regression model

CQ	RQ	LQ	CQB	RQB	LQB	CWL	RWL	LWL	CBL	RBL	LBL	CBLB	RBLB	LBLB	FFM
4.15E-15	7550	6.70E-05	4.64E-15	6489	6.70E-05	1.98E-15	369	2.80E-05	1.00E-15	1158	2.10E-05	9.50E-16	2094	2.00E-05	0
5.53E-15	9860	8.20E-05	4.64E-15	6489	6.70E-05	1.98E-15	369	2.80E-05	1.00E-15	1158	2.10E-05	9.50E-16	2094	2.00E-05	1
5.53E-15	9860	8.20E-05	4.64E-15	6489	6.70E-05	1.98E-15	369	2.80E-05	9.80E-16	1158	2.00E-05	0	0	0	1
5.53E-15	8921	8.20E-05	4.64E-15	6489	6.70E-05	1.98E-15	369	2.80E-05	0	0	0	9.50E-16	2094	2.00E-05	1
0	0	0	4.49E-15	6489	6.30E-05	1.94E-15	369	2.70E-05	9.80E-16	1158	2.00E-05	9.30E-16	2094	1.90E-05	1
4.54E-15	7572	6.70E-05	0	0	0	1.94E-15	369	2.70E-05	9.80E-16	1158	2.00E-05	9.30E-16	2094	1.90E-05	1
6.47E-15	12919	9.80E-05	4.64E-15	6489	6.70E-05	1.98E-15	369	2.80E-05	1.00E-15	1158	2.10E-05	9.50E-16	2094	2.00E-05	1
6.47E-15	12919	9.80E-05	6.22E-15	6855	8.50E-05	0	0	0	9.80E-16	1158	2.00E-05	9.30E-16	2094	1.90E-05	1
4.15E-15	7550	6.70E-05	4.64E-15	6489	6.70E-05	1.98E-15	369	2.80E-05	1.00E-15	1158	2.10E-05	9.50E-16	2094	2.00E-05	0
4.49E-15	7550	6.70E-05	6.68E-15	11858	1.00E-04	1.98E-15	369	2.80E-05	1.00E-15	1158	2.10E-05	9.50E-16	2094	2.00E-05	1
4.48E-15	7534	6.70E-05	6.68E-15	11858	1.00E-04	2.04E-15	369	2.90E-05	2.05E-15	3467	3.70E-05	9.70E-16	2095	2.00E-05	1
4.48E-15	7534	6.70E-05	6.87E-15	11859	1.05E-04	2.04E-15	369	2.90E-05	2.58E-15	5560	4.60E-05	0	0	0	1
4.15E-15	7550	6.70E-05	4.64E-15	6489	6.70E-05	1.98E-15	369	2.80E-05	1.00E-15	1158	2.10E-05	9.50E-16	2094	2.00E-05	0
0	0	0	9.70E-15	16345	1.36E-04	1.94E-15	369	2.70E-05	9.80E-16	1158	2.00E-05	9.30E-16	2094	1.90E-05	1
4.49E-15	7550	6.70E-05	5.69E-15	8798	8.30E-05	1.98E-15	369	2.80E-05	0	0	0	1.54	3251	2.90E-05	1
0	0	0	9.70E-15	16345	1.36E-04	1.94E-15	369	2.70E-05	9.80E-16	1158	2.00E-05	9.30E-16	2094	1.90E-05	1
5.00E-15	9642	7.50E-05	5.69E-15	8798	8.30E-05	1.99E-15	369	2.80E-05	9.80E-16	1158	2.00E-05	0	0	0	1

Figure 9. Accuracy observation in parasitic RLC for logistic regression model

```
        FFM
0        0
1       35
2       42
3       31
4       35
train_x size ::  (20, 15)
train_y size ::  (20,)
test_x size ::  (5, 15)
test_y size ::  (5,)
edu_target_frequencies= {2e-05: {0: 1, 35: 1}, 0.0: {0: 0, 35: 0}, 1.9e-05:
{0: 0, 35: 2}, 2.9e-05: {0: 0, 35: 0}, 5.5e-05: {0: 0, 35: 0}, 7.3e-05: {0:
0, 35: 0}, 5.7e-05: {0: 0, 35: 0}}
Train Accuracy ::  0.95
Test Accuracy ::  0.2
```

In this model, the accuracy levels are further improved compared to experiment-3, and is 95%.

5. RESULTS AND COMPARISONS

The proposed method of ML based test analysis is for function fault model mapping using chosen fault models is comparably outperformed as observed in experiment 1 to 4. The accuracy observations are shown in Table 11.

Table 11. Comparison of accuracies on chosen ML model deployed and parameters consideration

S.No	Experiment-No	ML Model Deployed	Parameters Under Consideration	Number of samples in the Model Dataset (X &Y together)	% Accuracy Observed
1	1	Linear Regression	CPD, PD, IDD, OP	290	26.58
2	2	Logistic Regression	CPD, PD, IDD, OP	310	97.67
3	3	Linear Regression	R,L,C at each node	416	63%
4	4	Logistic Regression	R,L,C at each node	480	95%

In this method, one can observe that the logistic regression is best suited for modeling the functional fault mapping while taking parametric variations under consideration. The accuracy level is high in both the experiments of 2 & 4 which are logistic models. Another advantage observed in this is raise number of samples compared to linear models.

6. CONCLUSION

For detection of undetectable faults, existing primitive based algorithms are not sufficient to use in higher end technologies. Hence taking the advantage of parasitic extraction method, undetectable faults are observed in addition to few existing fault models. All these fault model's simulation parameters from that are extracted from corresponding layouts are considered as inputs to the dataset. As an experimental base, linear and logistic regression models are implemented. Functional fault model mapping is done in two ways, by considering parameters like power dissipation, maximum required current, critical path delay as one set and the other simulation parameters like parasitic R, L and C together as another set, deployed into regression models. Observed the corresponding model fitting and prediction accuracies from the simulation results, in which logistic regression is best suited model resulting with high accuracy in the range of 95% to 97%, compared to linear regression model that results in accuracy levels in the range of 26.58% to 63%. The number of samples in the datasets is considerably achieved from parasitic extraction outcomes. If the samples are increased, better the accuracy can be observed. With the advance of process technology in VLSI, new fault model and test methods are essential to identify. The results of this proposed ML based test method proven to be one such approach that results in improvement in fault model mapping with easiness. These kinds of ML models and test analyses are essential in testing of VLSI circuits in order to improve the test efficiency with better accuracy.

REFERENCES

Aitken, R. (2007). Defect or Variation? Characterizing Standard Cell Behaviour at 90nm and Below. *Proceedings of the 8th International Symposium on Quality Electronic Design (ISQED'07).*

Al-Ars, Z., Hamdioui, S., van der Goor, A. J., & Mueller, G. (2008). Defect Oriented Testing of the Strap Problem Under Process Variations in DRAMs. *Proceedings of the IEEE International Test Conference (ITC).* 10.1109/TEST.2008.4700631

Al-Turjman, F., Zahmatkesh, H., & Mostarda, L. (2019). Quantifying uncertainty in internet of medical things and big-data services using intelligence and deep learning. *IEEE Access : Practical Innovations, Open Solutions, 7*, 115749–115759. doi:10.1109/ACCESS.2019.2931637

Ang, L. M., Seng, K. P., Ijemaru, G. K., & Zungeru, A. M. (2019). Deployment of IoV for Smart Cities: Applications, Architecture, and Challenges. *IEEE Access : Practical Innovations, Open Solutions, 7*, 6473–6492. doi:10.1109/ACCESS.2018.2887076

Banerjee, S., Chowdhury, D. R., & Bhattacharya, B. B. (2005). *Proceedings of the 2005 IEEE International Workshop on Memory Technology, Design and Testing(MTDT'05).* IEEE.

Benso, A., Bosio, A., Di Carlo, S., Di Natale, G., & Prinetto, P. (2006). A 22n March Test for Realistic Static Linked Faults in SRAMs. *IEEE 11th European Test Symposium (ETS).*

Borri, S., Hage-Hassan, M., Girard, P., Pravossoudovitch, S., & Virazel, A. (2003). Defect Oriented Dynamic Faults Models for Embedded SRAMs. *Proceedings of the 8th IEEE European Test Workshop.* 10.1109/ETW.2003.1231664

Bosio, A., Di Carlo, S., Di Natale, G., & Prinetto, P. (2007). March AB, a State-of-the-Art March Test for Realistic Static Linked Faults and Dynamic Faults in SRAMs. *IET Computers & Digital Techniques, 1*(3), 237-245.

Bosio, A., & Di Natale, G. (2008). March Test BDN: A New March Test For Dynamic Faults. Control Engineering And Applied Informatics. *CEAI, 10*(2), 3–9.

Bui, Pham, Nguyen, Nguyen, Le, & Hoang. (2016). An Effective Architecture of Memory Built-In Self-Test for Wide Range of SRAM. *2016 International Conference on Advanced Computing and Applications*, 121-124. 10.1109/ACOMP.2016.026

Cai, Wang, Liu, Lv, & Wang. (2019). A Novel BIST Algorithm for Low-voltage SRAM. *2019 IEEE International Test Conference in Asia (ITC-Asia).* 10.1109/ITC-Asia.2019.00036

Chen, T.-J., Li, J.-F., & Tseng, T.-W. (2012, June). Cost-Efficient Built-In Redundancy Analysis with Optimal Repair Rate for Word-Oriented RAMs. *IEEE Transactions on Computer-Aided Design of Integrated Circuits and Systems, 31*(6), 930–940. Advance online publication. doi:10.1109/TCAD.2011.2181510

Dekker, R., Beenker, F., & Thijssen, A. L. (1990, June). A Realistic Fault Model and Test Algorithms for Static Random Access Memories. *IEEE Transactions on Computer-Aided Design of Integrated Circuits and Systems, 9*(6), 567–572. doi:10.1109/43.55188

Dwivedi, A. D., Srivastava, G., Dhar, S., & Singh, R. (2019). A decentralized privacy-preserving health-care blockchain for IoT. *Sensors (Basel)*, *19*(2), 1–17. doi:10.339019020326 PMID:30650612

Hamdioui, van de Goor, & Rodgers. (2003). March SL: A Test For All Static Linked Memory Faults in the v-cell. *Proceedings of the 12th Asian Test Symposium (ATS'03)*.

Hamdioui, S., Al-ars, Z., van de Goor, A. J., & Rodgers, M. (2003). Dynamic Faults in Random Access Memories: Concept, Fault Models and Tests. *Journal of Electronic Testing*, *19*(2), 195–205. doi:10.1023/A:1022802010738

Hamdioui, S., van de Goor, A. J., & Rodgers, M. (2002). March SS: A Test for All Static Simple RAM Faults. *Proceedings of the 2002 IEEE International Workshop on Memory Technology, Design and Testing (MTDT 2002)*, 1-6. 10.1109/MTDT.2002.1029769

Harutunyan, G., Vardanian, V. A., & Zorian, Y. (2007). Minimal March Tests for Detection of Dynamic Faults in Random Access Memories. *Journal of Electronic Testing*, *23*(1), 55–74. doi:10.100710836-006-9504-8

Irobi, I. S., Al-Ars, Z., & Renovell, M. (2010). Parasitic Memory Effect in CMOS SRAMs. *Proceedings of the IEEE International Design and Test Workshop (IDT)*.

Irobi, S., Al-Ars, Z., & Hamdioui, S. (2010). Detecting Memory Faults in the Presence of Bit Line Coupling in SRAM Devices. *IEEE International Test Conference*. 10.1109/TEST.2010.5699246

Jidin, Hussin, Mispan, Fook, & Ying. (2022). Reduced March SR Algorithm for Deep-Submicron SRAM Testing. *2022 IEEE International Conference on Semiconductor Electronics (ICSE)*.

Jidin, Hussin, Fook, Mispan, Zakaria, Ying, & Zamin. (2022). Generation of New Low-Complexity March Algorithms for Optimum Faults Detection in SRAM. *2022 IEEE*. doi:10.1109/TCAD.2022.3229281

Jidin, A. Z., Hussin, R., Fook, L. W., & Mispan, M. S. (2021). An Automation Program for March Algorithm Fault Detection Analysis. *Proceedings of 2021 IEEE Asia Pacific Conference on Circuit and Systems (APCCAS)*, 149–152. 10.1109/APCCAS51387.2021.9687806

Jidin, A. Z., Hussin, R., Fook, L. W., & Mispan, M. S. (2021) A review paper on memory fault models and test algorithms. *Bulletin of Electrical Engineering and Informatics, 10*(6), 3083-3093. doi:10.11591/eei.v10i6.3048

Jidin, A. Z., Hussin, R., Mispan, M. S., & Fook, L. W. (2021). Novel March Test Algorithm Optimization Strategy for Improving Unlinked Faults Detection. *Proceedings of 2021 IEEE Asia Pacific Conference on Circuit and Systems (APCCAS)*, 117–120. 10.1109/APCCAS51387.2021.9687791

Lau, B. P. L., Marakkalage, S. H., Zhou, Y., Hassan, N. U., Yuen, C., Zhang, M., & Tan, U.-X. (2019). A survey of data fusion in smart city applications. *Information Fusion, 52*(January), 357–374. doi:10.1016/j.inffus.2019.05.004

Li, J. F., Cheng, K. L., Huang, C. T., & Wu, C. W. (2001). March based RAM diagnostic algorithms for stuck-at and coupling faults. *Proc, IEEE ITC*, 758-767.

Lin, C.-W., Chen, H.-H., Yang, H.-Y., Huang, C.-Y., Chao, M. C.-T., & Huang, R.-F. (2013, March). Fault Models and Test Methods for Subthreshold SRAMs. *IEEE Transactions on Computers*, *62*(3), 468–481. doi:10.1109/TC.2011.252

Maddela, V., Sinha, S. K., & Parvathi, M. (2021). Extraction of Undetectable Faults in 6T- SRAM Cell. 2021 *Proceedings of International Conference on Communication, Control and Information Sciences (ICCISc)*, 1-5. 10.1109/ICCISc52257.2021.9484987

Maddela, V., Sinha, S. K., Parvathi, M., & Sharma, V. (2022). Fault Detection and Analysis in embedded SRAM for sub nanometer technology. *Proceedings of International Conference on Applied Artificial Intelligence and Computing (ICAAIC)*, 1784-1788. 10.1109/ICAAIC53929.2022.9793265

Mak, Bhattacharya, Prunty, Roeder, Ramadan, Ferguson, & Yu. (1998). Cache Ram Inductive Faulta Nalysiws Ith Fabd Efect Modeling. *International Test Conference*, *32*(2), 862-871.

Manoj & Pineda de Gyvez. (2007). Defect-Oriented Testing for Nano-Metric CMOS VLSI Circuits. In *Frontiers in Electronic Testing* (vol. 34). Springer.

Martirosyan & Harutyunyan. (2019). An Efficient Fault Detection and Diagnosis Methodology for Volatile and Non-Volatile Memories. *Proceedings of 2019 Computer Science and Information Technologies (CSIT)*, 47–51. . doi:10.1109/CSITechnol.2019.8895189

Muddapu Parvathi, Vasantha, & Satya Parasad. (2012). Modified March C - Algorithm for Embedded Memory Testing. *International Journal of Electrical and Computer Engineering, 2*(5), 571-576.

Nguyen, G., Dlugolinsky, S., Bobák, M., Tran, V., López García, Á., Heredia, I., Malík, P., & Hluchý, L. (2019). Machine Learning and Deep Learning frameworks and libraries for large-scale data mining: A survey. *Artificial Intelligence Review*, *52*(1), 77–124. doi:10.100710462-018-09679-z

Niggemeyer, D., Redeker, M., & Otterstedt, J. (1998). Integration of Non-classical Faults in Standard March Tests. *Proceedings. International Workshop on Memory Technology, Design and Testing*. 10.1109/MTDT.1998.705953

Nor Azura Zakaria, Hasan, Halin, Sidek, & Wen. (2012). Fault Detection with Optimum March Test Algorithm. *3rd International Conference on Intelligent Systems, Modelling and Simulation, ISMS-2012, 47*. 10.1109/ISMS.2012.88

Parvathi, Vasantha, & Satya Prasad. (2013). Fault Model Analysis by Parasitic Extraction Method for Embedded SRAM. *International Journal of Research in Engineering and Technology, 2*(12).

Parvathi, M. (2018). New March Elements for Faults due to Open Defects in eSRAM. *Proceedings of First International Conference on Digital Contents and Applications (DCA 2018)*.

Parvathi, M., Satya Prasad, K., & Vasantha, N. (2017). Testing of Embedded SRAMs using Parasitic Extraction Method. In H. Ibrahim, S. Iqbal, S. S. Teoh, & M. T. Mustaffa (Eds.), *Proceedings of Robotic, Vision, Signal Processing and Power Applications (ROVISP), Empowering Research and Innovation* (pp. 47–61). Springer LNEE. doi:10.1007/978-981-10-1721-6_6

Parvathi, M., Vasantha, N., & Satya Parasad, K. (2012, October). Modified March C - Algorithm for Embedded Memory Testing. *Iranian Journal of Electrical and Computer Engineering*, 2(5), 571–576. doi:10.11591/ijece.v2i5.1587

Parvathi, M., Vasantha, N., & Satya Prasad, K. (2015). New Fault Model Analysis for Embedded SRAM Cell for Deep Submicron Technologies using Parasitic Extraction Method. *Proceedings of IEEE conference on VLSI Systems, Architecture, Technology and Applications (VLSI-SATA),* 1-6. 10.1109/VLSI-SATA.2015.7050471

Parvathi, M., Vasantha, N., & Satya Prasad, K. (2017). Testing of e-SRAM Using MMC- Algorithm and Parasitic Extraction Method. *LAP Lambert Academic Publishing, ISBN-13,* 9786202095464.

Reddy, S., Pomeranz, I., Huaxing, T., Kajihara, S., & Kinoshita, S. (2002). On Testing of Interconnect Open Defects in Combinational Logic Circuits with Stems of Large Fanout. *Proceedings of IEEE International Test Conference (ITC),* 83–89. 10.1109/TEST.2002.1041748

Rodriguez-Montanes, R., Volf, P., & de Gyvez, J. P. (2002). Resistance Characterization for Weak Open Defects. *IEEE Design & Test of Computers,* 19(5), 18–26. doi:10.1109/MDT.2002.1033788

Shorten, C., & Khoshgoftaar, T. M. (2019). A survey on Image Data Augmentation for Deep Learning. *Journal of Big Data,* 6(1), 2019. doi:10.118640537-019-0197-0

Singh, B., Narang, S. B., & Khosla, A. (2010). Modeling and Simulation of Efficient March Algorithm for Memory Testing. IC3 2010, Part II, CCIS 95, 96–107.

Sivaraman, Krishnan, Sundarraj, & Sri Gowthem. (2019). Network failure detection and diagnosis by analyzing syslog and SNS data: Applying big data analysis to network operations. *Int. J. Innov. Technol. Explor. Eng.,* 8(9), 883–887. . doi:10.35940/ijitee.I3187.0789S319

Stratigopoulos. (2018). Machine Learning Applications in IC Testing. *2018 23rd IEEE European Test Symposium (ETS).*

Tehranipour, M. H., Navabi, Z., & Fakhraie, S. M. (2001). An Efficient BIST Method For Testing of Embedded SRAMs. *IEICE Electronics Express,* 6(15), 1091–1097.

van de Goor. (1998). *Testing Semiconductor Memories: Theory and Practice.* Academic Press.

Van De Goor, A. J. (1993). Using March tests to test SRAMs. *IEEE Design & Test of Computers,* 10(1), 8–14. doi:10.1109/54.199799

van de Goor, A. J., & Al-Ars, Z. (2000). Functional Memory Faults: A Formal Notation and a Taxonomy. *Proceedings of VLSI Test Symposium (VTS),* 281–289. 10.1109/VTEST.2000.843856

Venkatesham, M., Sinha, S. K., & Parvathi, M. (2021a). Analysis of Open Defect Faults in Single 6T SRAM Cell Using R and C Parasitic Extraction Method. *Proceedings of IEEE International Conference on Disruptive Technologies for Multi-Disciplinary Research and Applications (CENTCON-2021),* 213-217. 10.1109/CENTCON52345.2021.9687916

Venkatesham, M., Sinha, S. K., & Parvathi, M. (2021b). Extraction of Undetectable Faults in 6T-SRAM Cell. *Proceedings of IEEE International Conference on Communication, Control and information Sciences(ICCISc),* 13-17.

Venkatesham, M., Sinha, S. K., & Parvathi, M. (2021c). Study on Paradigm of Variable Length SRAM Embedded Memory Testing. *Proceedings of the Fifth International Conference on Electronics, Communication and Aerospace Technology (ICECA) 2021.*

Verilog Digital System Design. (2008). *Zainalabedin Navabi* (2nd ed.). McGraw Hill.

Vinayakumar, R., Alazab, M., Soman, K. P., Poornachandran, P., Al-Nemrat, A., & Venkatraman, S. (2019). Deep Learning Approach for Intelligent Intrusion Detection System. *IEEE Access : Practical Innovations, Open Solutions, 7,* 41525–41550. doi:10.1109/ACCESS.2019.2895334

Youn, Kim, & Park. (2001). *A Microcode-based Memory BIST Implementing Modified March Algorithm.* IEEE.

Zakaria. (2013). *Multiple and solid data background scheme for testing static single cell faults on SRAM memories.* Universiti Putra Malaysia.

Zakaria, N. A., Hassan, W. Z. W., Halin, I. A., Sidek, R. M., & Wen, X. (2013). Fault detection with optimum March test algorithm. *Journal of Theoretical and Applied Information Technology, 47*(1), 18–27.

Zhao, W., & Cao, Y. (2006). New Generation of Predictive Technology Model for Sub-45nm Early Design Exploration. *IEEE Transactions on Electron Devices, 53*(11), 2816–2823. doi:10.1109/TED.2006.884077

Chapter 16
Imagining the Sustainable Future With Industry 6.0:
A Smarter Pathway for Modern Society and Manufacturing Industries

Richa Singh
BIT Mesra, India

Amit Kumar Tyagi
ⓘ https://orcid.org/0000-0003-2657-8700
National Institute of Fashion Technology, New Delhi, India

Senthil Kumar Arumugam
ⓘ https://orcid.org/0000-0002-5081-9183
Christ University, Bangalore, India

ABSTRACT

Industry is defined as the production of goods and services through the transformation of raw materials and resources into valuable products. It involves the creation of finished products or services through various stages of production that may include manufacturing, processing, assembly, packaging, and distribution. Industries have played a significant role in the economic growth and development of nations throughout history. They have contributed to the creation of employment opportunities, the development of new technologies, and the improvement of living standards. Over the years, the industrial sector has gone through numerous changes, and each of these changes has been termed as an "Industry Revolution."

1. INTRODUCTION

Modern, cutting-edge digital technologies are proliferating at the speed of light. Businesses and industries, however, have a difficult time accepting new technologies to adapt to their shifting behaviour. For industries to gain momentum and succeed with these cutting-edge high-speed technologies, they must

DOI: 10.4018/978-1-6684-8531-6.ch016

Copyright © 2024, IGI Global. Copying or distributing in print or electronic forms without written permission of IGI Global is prohibited.

work at the speed of light. By modifying or adopting an agile mentality, industries can quickly absorb these changes. Technology's digitalization is a journey, not a destination; it supports business models, the healthcare system, industrial industries, etc. for their expansion, shapes businesses, and benefits consumers. The transition from mechanisation to electrification to electronification to computation to mass customization to mass personalisation to virtualization to digitization to intelligence has reached its pivot point. Researchers are already beginning to consider industry 6.0, a futuristic concept, as a step beyond industry 5.0. The concept of Industry 6.0 changes depending on the demands of various sectors. It can also be omnipresent, customer-driven, human-centred, anti-fragile manufacturing, virtualized, human co-robot centric, and homogeneous assets, among other things. According to future predictions for industry 6.0, there will be a hyper-connection between industries, a high degree of mass customization and mass personalization of services and goods, as well as a dynamic supply chain management concept and a high degree of class one lot size thinking, which will allow information to travel freely between nations (Business Finland, 2015).

About every ten years, wireless communication networks undergo an iterative process of evolution. Many nations and standardisation bodies throughout the world have stated their ambitions for 6G research currently, which is still in the early stages of study. The first significant 6G research initiative in the world was started by the Finnish government in 2018. In March 2019, the Federal Communications Commission (FCC) in the US recommended building 6G based on "mmWave + THz + satellite" and opened the terahertz (THz) spectrum for 6G research. The NextG Alliance, a trade association with a focus on the administration of 6G development in North America, was established in October 2020 under the leadership of the Alliance for Telecommunications Industry Solutions (ATIS) (Iscan & No, 2021).

The Japan 6G Strategic Plan was published in April 2020 by Japan's Ministry of Internal Affairs and Communications. The 6G timetable was made public in South Korea in January 2020, and its commercial launch was projected for 2028. Germany announced an investment in 6G research in April 2021, including a 6G Platform and a 6G Research Hub. For next-generation networks and services, the 6G Smart Networks and Services Industry Association (6G-IA) has been established in Europe. The International Telecommunications Union (ITU), a global organisation for standardisation, published the inaugural 6G research timetable in February 2020. By 2023, it's anticipated that research on the 6G vision and related technical ideas would be finished (Martynov et al., 2019).

In contemporary civilizations, consumerism is becoming increasingly significant. A consumption model that considers consumers' growing importance is required to inform consumer-oriented policy. The dominant consumption model in market economy theory and consumer policy has typically been founded on the idea of consumer sovereignty. This paradigm serves as the market economy's explanation and moral framework (Hansen & Schrader, 1997). To establish regulated, controlled functionality within the confines of legality, current technical advancements must work hand in hand with the administrative sector. Enterprise architecture should be created to make sure that the human input component is never cut off from a completely automated process chain. The new framework might provide flexible work hours, which, as appealing as they may sound to the workers, might turn out to be a blessing with two curses. The average salary of the workers will undoubtedly be negatively impacted by a flexible schedule. Second, the revenue might not be consistent, resulting in unanticipated hiccups along the route that could financially upset modern society.

The paper is organized as the next section discusses about Industry 6.0 and its Key features and technologies. The next section discusses about the Sustainability Challenges in Manufacturing followed by the Industry 6.0 aligns with sustainability goals. Later on, the Benefits of Industry 6.0 for Modern Society has been discussed. The challenges, discussion and vision has been discussed in the next section.

2. UNDERSTANDING INDUSTRY 6.0

Defining Industry 6.0 and Its Evolution

The next stage of industrialization, known as Industry 6.0, is concerned with developing fully integrated, intelligent production systems that can function with little assistance from humans. It blends human intellect with artificial intelligence, cloud computing power, large data processing, and human-robot collaboration.

Industry 1.0: The Birth of the Industrial Revolution

Industry 1.0, also known as the first industrial revolution, began during the late 18th century and lasted until the mid-19th century. It was characterized by the widespread use of mechanized production, the utilization of energy sources such as coal and steam-power, and the emergence of the first factories. This revolution allowed for mass production to become possible and saw the emergence of the first industrial giants such as the cotton mills and ironworks.

Industry 2.0: The Era of Mass Production

Industry 2.0 was marked by the introduction of electricity and the invention of new technologies such as the assembly line. This revolution led to increased productivity, efficiency, and quality in the production of goods, as well as the emergence of new industries such as the automobile industry.

Industry 3.0: The Rise of Automation

Industry 3.0, also known as the digital revolution, saw the use of electronic technologies to create computer-based systems, robotic production lines, and automated factories. This revolution allowed for the emergence of the internet, as well as the development of new technologies such as 3D printing, big data, and cloud computing.

Industry 4.0: Automation and Digitization

Industry 4.0, also known as the fourth industrial revolution, began in the early 21st century and is characterized using automation and data exchange. This revolution has allowed for the development of the internet of things (IoT), artificial intelligence, and machine learning. It has also enabled the use of 3D printing, big data, and cloud computing (Yang & Gu, 2021).

The growth of Industry 4.0 is driven by several factors, including the need to increase productivity and efficiency, the emergence of new technologies such as artificial intelligence and machine learning, and the increasing use of the internet of things (IoT). The use of automation and data exchange allows for faster and more accurate data processing, as well as increased efficiency in the production of goods.

Additionally, the development of new technologies such as artificial intelligence and machine learning allow for more efficient decision-making and problem-solving capabilities. Finally, the use of the internet of things (IoT) allows for improved communication and data-sharing between connected devices.

The Evolution of Industry 5.0: Humans and Machines Working Together

Industry 5.0, also known as the Human-Tech partnership, aims to bring together the benefits of Industry 4.0 with the human touch. It emphasizes the importance of human creativity, innovation, and problem-solving skills, while also utilizing advanced technologies such as AI, robotics, and IoT. Industry 5.0 aims to create a work environment where machines and humans work in collaboration, with machines performing repetitive and dangerous tasks while humans focus on more complex and creative work. This approach is expected to lead to increased efficiency, productivity, and job satisfaction, while also promoting social responsibility and sustainability (Raja Santhi & Muthuswamy, 2023). The need for Industry 5.0 is driven by the need to remain competitive in the global market, as well as the increasing demand for increased efficiency, productivity, and quality. Additionally, the use of advanced technologies such as cognitive computing, artificial intelligence and machine learning allow for improved decision-making and problem-solving capabilities, as well as the potential for new business models.

Industry 5.0 is a revolutionary advancement in the industrial sector (Figure 1), with the potential to drastically improve productivity, efficiency, and quality across various industries. This revolution is characterized by using advanced technologies such as artificial intelligence, machine learning, and the internet of things (IoT). The prospects of Industry 5.0 are promising, as the use of advanced technologies and automation will continue to improve productivity and efficiency across various industries. Additionally, the development of new technologies such as blockchain, quantum computing, and advanced robotics will allow for the potential for new business models and the development of new products. Overall, Industry 5.0 is focused on creating a more sustainable, collaborative, and customer-centric manufacturing environment that leverages the strengths of both humans and machines.

Industry 6.0

Industry 6.0(Future Concept), also known as the sixth industrial revolution, is characterized by using advanced technologies such as quantum computing, and nanotechnology over the pre-built Industry 5.0 architecture. These technologies will enable more efficient and effective solutions to solve complex problems, as well as the potential for new business models. The use of Industry 6.0 technologies will also provide the potential for advanced robotics, and increased safety and security in production and manufacturing processes. Additionally, the use of blockchain technology will enable secure and reliable data-sharing and communication between connected devices, as well as the potential for new economic models. Ultimately, the use of Industry 6.0 will continue to revolutionize the way we produce, manage, and consume goods, services, and information but as with any technological advancement, Industry 6.0 may also have some potential drawbacks or negative impacts.

Figure 1. Evolution from Industry 1.0 to 5.0

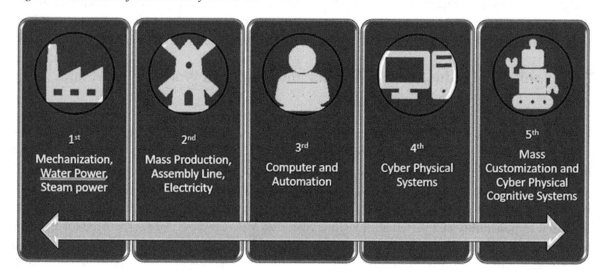

Addressing the Drawbacks of Industry 6.0: Strategies and Solutions

The advent of Industry 6.0 presents a multitude of challenges that require substantial investment in the development of technological, social, and economic infrastructures to ensure their smooth integration into society. The development of new technologies and automation is likely to have a profound impact on employment, with many jobs being rendered obsolete or transformed. This may exacerbate existing inequalities in society and result in job displacement for many people, particularly those with lower levels of education or training. Additionally, the widespread adoption of Industry 6.0 technologies may also result in increased environmental degradation, resource depletion, and pollution, which could have serious consequences for future generations. To address these challenges, policymakers must take a proactive approach to ensure that Industry 6.0 is implemented in a socially and environmentally responsible manner. This may involve the implementation of new regulations and policies aimed at mitigating the negative impacts of automation and ensuring that the benefits of technological progress are shared equitably across society.

3. SUSTAINABILITY CHALLENGES IN MANUFACTURING

Modern construction processes have been made more durable and effective thanks to AEC Industry 6.0's cutting-edge technology, cutting-edge digitalization, and environmentally conscious practises. The many advantages of AEC Industry 5.0 have been thoroughly analysed by the academic community. Increased stakeholder involvement, automation, robots for optimisation, data-driven decision-making processes, and cautious resource management are a few examples. However, this study reveals the challenges associated with putting AEC Industry 6.0 concepts into practise. It necessitates the coordination of the technical skills of numerous stakeholders, the orchestration of interoperable standards, and the strengthening of cybersecurity protocols (Almusaed, Yitmen, & Almssad, 2023).

3.1 Exploring Sustainability Issues in Traditional Manufacturing

Industry 6.0's main objective is to seize new technologies that can be used on a global scale, provide wealth and prosperity away from the workplace, and support national development across all planetary boundaries. This revolution would support the idea of sustainability, encourage living in harmony with nature, and advance the concept of the human virtual digital twin, which would allow everyone to view both real-world items and virtual product information concurrently.

3.2 The Environmental and Social Impacts of Industrial Processes

Communication and information have made the game more accessible. Organisations in the public sector must deliver essential services while utilising innovative strategies like artificial intelligence analytics that other sectors have adopted (Baragde, 2023). They picture a "Society 5.0." In this kind society, technology and economic achievement solve social problems. Society 5.0 will help with issues like ageing populations, environmental sustainability, healthcare, transportation, and more with the use of AI, IoT, and robotics. Technology may benefit society as well. According to Society 6.0, economic development and social issues will be balanced in the future via real-world and digital solutions (Žižek et al., 2021).

3.3 The Need for a Paradigm Shift in Manufacturing

The interaction between humans and machines was determined by human needs and the state of technology at the time. The numerous industrial revolutions as well as shifts in manufacturing philosophies are examples of how this connection has changed throughout time. The connection changed because of technological advancements. With each passing century, machines have acquired new features, prowess, and even aptitudes that are exclusively human—like classification, inference, or vision. Thus, the connection between humans and machines is changing.

3.4 The Role of Industry 6.0 in Sustainability

Remote regions and unique circumstances continue to be communication blind zones, with services mostly restricted to terrestrial mobile communications. 6G will integrate satellite communications (Shen et al., 2022; Wang et al., 2023), unmanned aerial vehicle (UAV) communications (Mozaffari et al., 2019), terrestrial ultra-dense communication networks, maritime communications (Yu et al., 2020), underwater communications (Jouhari et al., 2019), and underground communications (Saeed et al., 2019) to transition from terrestrial communications to space-air-ground-sea communications and provide ubiquitous global coverage. 6G will accomplish seamless three-dimensional (3D) ubiquitous coverage and connection by fusing together numerous communication networks, offering a variety of communication services.

- **Full application:** Massive amounts of data will be produced by 6G due to the variety of services and ongoing development of communication infrastructure. To completely explore the intelligent potential of 6G networks and realise several intelligent applications, new technologies like AI and big data will be fully utilised.
- **All digital:** The virtual world is more than just a computerised replica of the real world. The digital world can draw conclusions and generating forecasts that are comparable to those made in

the physical world (6G Promotion Group, 2021) and can serve as a guide for making decisions in the physical world by accurately reflecting and forecasting the physical world in real time. As the physical and digital worlds are connected by 6G, applications such as digital twin cities and the intelligent linkage of "human-machine-things environments," including the "environment" of the virtual world, will be made possible (CCID, 2020).

- **All spectra:** The need for wireless mobile traffic is rising dramatically as new high-data rate communication services and applications continue to develop. Radio frequency (RF) band spectrum congestion, which prevents existing communication systems from providing higher rate services, is a problem.

- **All senses:** Users will be able to access holographic communications and storage, immersive XR, tactile Internet, and other applications in 6G with the help of several communication technologies. Through a variety of sensory organs, people's perspective of reality is obtained. 6G communication networks support reliable communications with large bandwidth and low latency.

- **Strong security:** Security has grown in importance as communication networks continue to improve. With the development of new application scenarios, new technologies, and a massive user information explosion, 6G will face several new security threats in addition to more common ones like viruses and distributed denial of service (DDoS) attacks, such as large-scale data breaches and learning-powered attacks.

4. HOW INDUSTRY 6.0 ALIGNS WITH SUSTAINABILITY GOALS

Industry 6.0 is taking on the appearance of a futuristic sector with a far greater scope than the existing industrial revolutions that have existed up to this point. With the use of human beings' noble creativity combined with machines and modern production systems in the highly advanced digital technology environment, this revolution will seek to influence industries 6.0 towards transforming the work culture of people. In this setting, human beings may control machines directly with their minds thanks to digital technology, which are also seen as providing more resource-efficient and user-friendly production solutions than previous industrial revolutions. Future industry 6.0 emphasises co-working with technology (digital twins), economy, homogeneous assets, safety, resilience, Antifragility, and harmony with nature (Almusaed, Yitmen, & Almssad, 2023).

4.1 Leveraging IoT, AI, and Automation for Sustainable Manufacturing

IoT plays a significant role in encouraging sustainable manufacturing practises in the manufacturing sector. When IoT devices are used in manufacturing processes, businesses can increase productivity, resource efficiency, and environmental impact. Real-time data gathering, analysis, and control are made possible by IoT, which enables connection and communication between physical devices, equipment, and systems. IoT can improve resource efficiency, lessen environmental impact, and promote operational sustainability when used in sustainable manufacturing practises. With the introduction of artificial intelligence (AI), the manufacturing sector has undergone a profound change that allows businesses to optimise costs while streamlining operations. Manufacturers may significantly reduce costs by identifying inefficiencies, automating procedures, and making data-driven choices by utilising the potential of AI.

4.2 Key Features and Technologies Associated With Industry 6.0

"Ubiquitous, customer-driven, virtualized, antifragile manufacturing" is what industry 6.0 is referred to as. It is characterised by hyper-connected factories with dynamic supply chains where data flows across domains, on the one hand, and customer-centric, highly customised lot-size-1 thinking, on the other. Due to their integration into a networked environment and the requirement to manage digital, optimised manufacturing, these also alter the role of humans as production workers. We have significant weaknesses in addition to our strengths that position us to lead the next industrial revolution. All industries in Europe need to have a higher level of ICT knowledge. We also need multidisciplinary research, development, and innovation, as well as a long-term public commitment strategy and considerable financial commitments (Chourasia et al., 2022).

4.3 How Industry 6.0 Differs From Previous Industrial Revolutions

Industrialization brought about several historical inventions and firsts while also changing the economy, transportation, health, and medical fields. From a critical standpoint, the first four industrial revolutions as they have historically developed are reviewed. Each one's primary technological advancement is briefly covered. The TECIS vision is of a society where all of humanity is served by our technology, systems, and procedures. This is known as "human-machine symbiosis" and is a theory of how control and automation technologies and systems might be used to the advantage of all life. For the meta CO-VID-19 phase, a fresh, sustainable economic model is required. The INDUSTRY 6.0, a novel idea for the humanised revolution, is put forth. The expansion of the technological base ignited the industrial

Figure 2. 6G vision

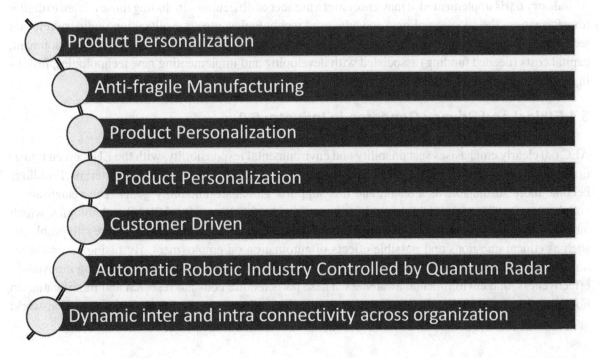

revolution. Unadulterated emancipation is predicted to be achieved by innovation within a few decades. It is risky to predict the insurgency and how it will evolve. One thing is certain, though: it will be an interdisciplinary world organised by all participants in the global political system, from industry and government to academia and daily people. We shall examine the contemporary changes made between IR 1.0 and IR 6.0 (Duggal et al., 2022). (Figure 2)

Few other technological revolutions (with emerging technologies) in different useful applications have bene explained in (Deekshetha & Tyagi, 2023; Gomathi et al., 2023; Nair & Tyagi, 2023; Nair et al., 2021; Rekha et al., 2019; Rekha et al., 2020; Tyagi, 2020a; Tyagi, 2020b; Tyagi, 2023; Abraham et al., 2021).

4.4 Benefits of Industry 6.0 for Modern Society

Industry 6.0 would support globally interconnected industries and offer dynamic value networks, dynamic supply chains, and information flow transparency between all internal and external administrations. Maintaining the proper balance or mastering the learning economy would be a way of life. It encourages the concept of the virtual human digital twin, which allows anybody to simultaneously view real items and virtual product information, connecting manufacturing businesses around the globe and facilitating greater technical support, comprehension, and decision-making. The anticipated concept for this revolution will be antifragile manufacturing, where anti-brittleness can be attained through flexible system design. The non-functional requirements, which evaluate software systems based on openness, usability, security, mobility, and other traits, will determine this.

5. CHALLENGES AND CONSIDERATIONS

As industry 6.0 is implemented, it may encounter a number of difficulties, including those related to digital transformation, the adoption of new and advanced technologies, resource allocation, industry-relevant technology, internationalisation, industry collaboration, freedom to conduct research in development, capital costs (needed funding) associated with developing and implementing new technologies, reskilling costs, and adoption of 5G and 6G technologies.

5.1 Ethical and Privacy Concerns in Industry 6.0

AEC 6.0 clearly emphasises sustainability and environmental responsibility, with the EU's green transitions emphasising artificial intelligence (AI), renewable energy, and energy-efficient materials. Buildings become more sustainable as a result, and this supports global sustainability goals. The visualisation, collaboration, and immersion of design have been considerably boosted by VR/AR technologies, which have also improved planning and decreased errors. Despite these developments, there are still problems, such as ethical questions and possible effects of automation on employment. By fusing several technologies and ideas, AEC 6.0 hopes to revolutionise intelligent construction by encouraging innovation, effectiveness, and environmental awareness. These parts require constant research and modification in both theoretical and practical areas due to their complexity. Future studies ought to focus on real-world applications, moral dilemmas, and the development of uniform frameworks.

5.2 Security Challenges in a Connected Manufacturing Ecosystem

IoT device security is becoming increasingly important for providers of industrial IoT solutions as more and more IoT devices are introduced into the globe every day. In addition, there are many difficulties with the security of IoT devices.

- Safety of data and some privacy issues like cloud, web, and mobile
- IoT software damages authorized access to a computer system
- Inadequate testing and upgradation is also an IoT security challenge
- Problems in the network is also a security hurdle
- Adequate consolidation of data
- Converting data into a code
- Strong password usage
- Problems in the IoT hardware

6. A VISION FOR THE SUSTAINABLE FUTURE

A development paradigm that assures the long-term wellbeing of all people is known as sustainable development. The definition of sustainable development is "development that satisfies the needs of the present without compromising the capacity of future generations to meet their own needs." (WCED 1987). The sustainable development paradigm emphasises the suffering of future generations while outlining future scenarios that come from unchecked growth to put moral pressure on the current generation.

- **Sustainable Energy:** India's strategy for sustainable development includes the transition to clean and renewable energy sources. The youth may help by promoting the use of renewable energy, encouraging energy efficiency, and looking into creative ways to solve energy-related problems.
- **Environmental conservation:** Ensuring the environment's preservation and protection is essential for a sustainable future. Youth can actively participate in programmes like tree-planting drives, waste-management efforts, and awareness-raising campaigns on the value of conserving biodiversity.
- **Digital Empowerment:** Using technology to make a positive social impact is a key strategy for sustainable growth. The youth can significantly contribute to closing the digital divide, fostering digital literacy, and using digital platforms for civic involvement, education, and business.
- **Social Inclusion and Equality:** Promoting social inclusion and equality is essential for sustainable development. Youth may stand out for underrepresented groups, advance gender equality, encourage diversity in the workplace and in school, and campaign to alleviate hunger and poverty.
- **Education and Skill Development**: Access to high-quality educational and career-development opportunities is crucial for empowering young people and promoting sustainable development. Young people can acquire the skills necessary for a sustainable and prosperous future by actively participating in educational initiatives, mentoring programmes, and vocational training.
- **Responsible Consumption and Production**: Promotion of ethical consumption and production practises is essential for achieving sustainable development. The younger generation can adopt sustainable lifestyles, support locally produced goods, and promote recycling and waste reduction.

- **Entrepreneurship and Innovation**: Innovation and entrepreneurship among young people are essential for both economic expansion and long-term development. Young people can drive innovation, build sustainable company models, and come up with solutions to urgent social and environmental problems by encouraging an entrepreneurial mindset.

- **Civic Engagement and Policy Advocacy**: The youth may support India's 2030 vision by being involved in civic activities, contributing to policy discussions, and lobbying for sustainable development policies. They can influence decision-making procedures and promote change by actively sharing their ideas.

- **Collaboration and Partnerships**: Sustainable development requires partnerships between corporations, government agencies, educational institutions, and youth organisations. To jointly advance India's 2030 vision, the youth can cultivate alliances, engage in cross-sectoral collaborations, and take part in multi-stakeholder initiatives.

- **Responsible Digital Citizenship:** Digital citizenship has never been more important, especially in light of the growing power of digital platforms. The youth can convey encouraging words, fight cyberbullying, advocate for online safety, and use social media to create awareness of issues related to sustainable development.

- **Envisioning the impact of Industry 6.0 on modern society:** Coexisting robots will be the industrial norm by the time of the next industrial revolution, according to the regressive route leading to it. The likely outcome of earlier revolutions that concentrated on technical automation and customised manufacturing would be monolithic production facilities, where the machines are connected to numerous task-specific AI algorithms that work together to produce in accordance with customer requirements. The sixth revolution will make use of the following technologies to improve many facets of productivity and quality of life in general printing in multiple dimensions, robo-medics, helpful home robots, and deep dive alternative energy.

7. THE POTENTIAL FOR INDUSTRY 6.0 TO ADDRESS GLOBAL CHALLENGES

Industry 6.0 is an ideology movement that embraces improvements and changes in almost every field. These developments have been divided into four main categories, including intelligent manufacturing, robotic automation, society and policy, and. Numerous areas of study should be undertaken, including, but not limited to, quantum control, interplanetary resource collecting and manufacture, renewable energy, complete machine independence, and airborne manufacturing platforms. Technological developments in these areas may enable us to research and create brand-new manufacturing and resource-gathering processes. Hence in anticipation of Industry 6.0, it is crucial to set up legal frameworks and make sure that societal preparations are taken to be ready for its technological breakthroughs. Collaboration between corporations, governments, and society will be essential in creating the infrastructure required to achieve the new standards. AMT will be involved in the procedure. Additionally, these developments will alter how we view the economy and the job market. The demography will be affected by personalised manufacturing and adaptive automation, which will lead to a change in the job structure.

8. CONCLUSION

Theoretically speaking, Industry 6.0 will completely alter how the manufacturing industry operates if it becomes a reality. Due to widespread fears that their jobs will be lost due to complete industry automation, it is imperative that there be more jobs created than lost when implementing any new industrial revolution. Otherwise, social dissatisfaction and unfavorable perceptions could develop. The provision of virtualized antifragile manufacturing and antifragile services is the main goal of this revolution. The emphasis would be on customer-centric, customer-focused business practices, highly interconnected sectors with dynamic supply chains, automated flexibility, and internal value networks where appropriate connections within the organization or outside across the many nations and its administrative territories might occur.

REFERENCES

6G Promotion Group. (2021). *White Paper on 6G Overall Vision and Potential Key Technologies*. Available: http://www.caict.ac.cn/kxyj/qwfb/ztbg/202106/ P020210604552573543918.pdf

Almusaed, A., Yitmen, I., & Almssad, A. (2023). Reviewing and Integrating AEC Practices into Industry 6.0: Strategies for Smart and Sustainable Future-Built Environments. *Sustainability (Basel)*, *15*(18), 13464. doi:10.3390u151813464

Baragde. (2023). Information Technology for Enhancing Public Sector Sustainability. In *Leadership and Governance for Sustainability* (pp. 204–221). IGI Global. doi:10.4018/978-1-6684-9711-1.ch011

Business Finland. (2015). *From Industry X to Industry 6.0, Ant fragile manufacturing for people, planet, and profit with passion*. AIF, White paper. Retrieved from https://www.alliedict.fi/wpcontent/uploads/2021/08/Industry-X-White-Paper3.5.2021_Final.pdf

CCID. (2020). *6G Concepts and Vision*. White Paper. Available: http://www.ccidwise.com/uploads/soft/200311/1-200311133959.pdf

Chourasia, S., Tyagi, A., Pandey, S. M., Walia, R. S., & Murtaza, Q. (2022). Sustainability of Industry 6.0 in global perspective: Benefits and challenges. *MPAN. Journal of Metrology Society of India*, *37*(2), 443–452. doi:10.100712647-022-00541-w

Deekshetha & Tyagi. (2023). Automated and intelligent systems for next-generation-based smart applications. In Data Science for Genomics. Academic Press. doi:10.1016/B978-0-323-98352-5.00019-7

Duggal, A. S., Malik, P. K., Gehlot, A., Singh, R., Gaba, G. S., Masud, M., & Al-Amri, J. F. (2022). A sequential roadmap to Industry 6.0: Exploring future manufacturing trends. *IET Communications*, *16*(5), 521–531. doi:10.1049/cmu2.12284

Gomathi, L., Mishra, A. K., & Tyagi, A. K. (2023). Industry 5.0 for Healthcare 5.0: Opportunities, Challenges and Future Research Possibilities. *2023 7th International Conference on Trends in Electronics and Informatics (ICOEI)*, 204-213. 10.1109/ICOEI56765.2023.10125660

Hansen, U., & Schrader, U. (1997). A modern model of consumption for a sustainable society. *Journal of Consumer Policy, 20*(4), 443–468. doi:10.1023/A:1006842517219

Iscan & No. (2021). *An Old Problem in the New Era: Effects of Artificial Intelligence to Unemployment on the Way to Industry 5.0* [Yeni Çagda ˇ Eski Bir Sorun: Endüstri 5 . 0 Yolunda Yapay Zekanın ˙ Issizlige Etkileri]. Academic Press.

Jouhari, M., Ibrahimi, K., Tembine, H., & Ben-Othman, J. (2019, July). Underwater wireless sensor networks: A survey on enabling technologies, localiza tion protocols, and Internet of underwater things. *IEEE Access : Practical Innovations, Open Solutions, 7*, 96879–96899. doi:10.1109/ACCESS.2019.2928876

Martynov, V. V., Shavaleeva, D. N., & Zaytseva, A. A. (2019). Information technology as the basis for transformation into a digital society and Industry 5.0. *Proceedings of the 2019 IEEE International Conference Quality Management, Transport and Information Security, Information Technologies IT and QM and IS 2019.* 10.1109/ITQMIS.2019.8928305

Mozaffari, Saad, Bennis, Nam, & Debbah. (2019). A tutorial on UAVs for wireless networks: Applications, challenges, and open problems. *IEEE Commun. Surveys Tuts., 21*(3), 2334-2360.

Nair, M. M., & Tyagi, A. K. (2023). AI, IoT, blockchain, and cloud computing: The necessity of the future. In Distributed Computing to Blockchain. Academic Press. doi:10.1016/B978-0-323-96146-2.00001-2

Nair, M. M., Tyagi, A. K., & Sreenath, N. (2021). The Future with Industry 4.0 at the Core of Society 5.0: Open Issues, Future Opportunities and Challenges. *2021 International Conference on Computer Communication and Informatics (ICCCI),* 1-7. 10.1109/ICCCI50826.2021.9402498

Raja Santhi, A., & Muthuswamy, P. (2023). Industry 5.0 or industry 4.0S? Introduction to industry 4.0 and a peek into the prospective industry 5.0 technologies. *Int J Interact Des Manuf, 17*(2), 947–979. doi:10.100712008-023-01217-8

Rekha, Tyagi, & Krishna Reddy. (2019). A Wide Scale Classification of Class Imbalance Problem and its Solutions: A Systematic Literature Review. *Journal of Computer Science, 15*(7), 886-929.

Rekha, G., Malik, S., Tyagi, A. K., & Nair, M. M. (2020). Intrusion Detection in Cyber Security: Role of Machine Learning and Data Mining in Cyber Security. *Advances in Science, Technology and Engineering Systems Journal, 5*(3), 72–81. doi:10.25046/aj050310

Saeed, N., Alouini, M.-S., & Al-Naffouri, T. Y. (2019). Toward the Internet of underground things: A systematic survey. IEEE Commun. Surveys Tuts., 21(4), 3443–3466.

Shen, X., Gao, J., Wu, W., Li, M., Zhou, C., & Zhuang, W. (2022). Holistic network virtualization and pervasive network intelligence for 6G. IEEE Commun. Surveys Tuts., 24(1), 1–30. doi:10.1109/COMST.2021.3135829

Tyagi. (2020a). *Artificial Intelligence and Machine Learning Algorithms. In Challenges and Applications for Implementing Machine Learning in Computer Vision.* IGI Global. doi:10.4018/978-1-7998-0182-5.ch008

Tyagi, . (2020b). *Challenges of Applying Deep Learning in Real-World Applications. In Challenges and Applications for Implementing Machine Learning in Computer Vision.* IGI Global. doi:10.4018/978-1-7998-0182-5.ch004

Tyagi. (2023). Decentralized everything: Practical use of blockchain technology in future applications. In Distributed Computing to Blockchain. Academic Press. doi:10.1016/B978-0-323-96146-2.00010-3

Tyagi, A. K., Fernandez, T. F., Mishra, S., & Kumari, S. (2021). Intelligent Automation Systems at the Core of Industry 4.0. In A. Abraham, V. Piuri, N. Gandhi, P. Siarry, A. Kaklauskas, & A. Madureira (Eds.), *Intelligent Systems Design and Applications. ISDA 2020. Advances in Intelligent Systems and Computing* (Vol. 1351). Springer. doi:10.1007/978-3-030-71187-0_1

Wang, C.-X., You, X., Gao, X., Zhu, X., Li, Z., Zhang, C., Wang, H., Huang, Y., Chen, Y., Haas, H., Thompson, J. S., Larsson, E. G., Renzo, M. D., Tong, W., Zhu, P., Shen, X., Poor, H. V., & Hanzo, L. (2023). On the road to 6G: Visions, requirements, key technologies and testbeds. *IEEE Communications Surveys and Tutorials*, 25(2), 905–974. doi:10.1109/COMST.2023.3249835

Yang, F., & Gu, S. (2021). Industry 4.0, a revolution that requires technology and national strategies. *Complex & Intelligent Systems*, 7(3), 1311–1325. doi:10.100740747-020-00267-9

Yu, C., Li, J., Zhang, C., Li, H., He, R., & Lin, B. (2020). Maritime broadband communications: Applications, challenges and an offshore 5G-virtual MIMO paradigm. *Proc. IEEE ISPA/BDCloud/SocialCom/SustainCom'20*, 1286–1291. 10.1109/ISPA-BDCloud-SocialCom-SustainCom51426.2020.00190

Žižek, S. Š., Mulej, M., & Potočnik, A. (2021). The Sustainable Socially Responsible Society: Well-Being Society 6.0. *Sustainability (Basel)*, 13(16), 9186. doi:10.3390u13169186

Chapter 17
Dew Computing:
State of the Art, Opportunities, and Research Challenges

Amit Kumar Tyagi

iD https://orcid.org/0000-0003-2657-8700

National Institute of Fashion Technology, New Delhi, India

ABSTRACT

Dew computing is an emerging paradigm that extends the edge computing concept by leveraging the resources available in the surrounding environment. This chapter presents a state-of-the-art review of dew computing, including its definition, characteristics, and architecture. The authors also discuss the opportunities and challenges of dew computing and provide a comprehensive survey of recent research efforts in this area. Specifically, they highlight the potential of dew computing to address the challenges of resource-constrained devices, increase data privacy and security, and improve network efficiency. However, several research challenges need to be addressed, including resource management, security, privacy, and interoperability. They discuss the future research directions and potential applications of dew computing in various domains, such as healthcare, smart cities, and the internet of things (IoT). In summary, dew computing has the potential to revolutionize the way we perceive and utilize computing resources and opens up a new research frontier for computer science and engineering.

1. INTRODUCTION

Dew computing is an emerging paradigm that extends the concept of edge computing, which is about processing data as close to the source as possible, by leveraging the resources available in the surrounding environment. Dew computing takes this a step further by utilizing the resources that are not directly connected to the internet, such as sensors, mobile devices, and other smart objects. These resources, which are often overlooked, can be used to create a distributed computing infrastructure that can be accessed and utilized by various applications and services. Note that the term "dew computing" was first introduced in 2015 by Dr. Hong Zhu, a professor at Oxford Brookes University, to describe a new com-

DOI: 10.4018/978-1-6684-8531-6.ch017

Copyright © 2024, IGI Global. Copying or distributing in print or electronic forms without written permission of IGI Global is prohibited.

puting paradigm that takes advantage of the resources available in the physical environment. The term "dew" is used to describe the phenomenon of water droplets that form on surfaces in the early morning when the temperature drops, which is similar to the concept of collecting resources from the surrounding environment. Dew computing has several characteristics that distinguish it from other computing paradigms. First, it is a distributed computing paradigm that utilizes resources from multiple sources, including sensors, mobile devices, and other smart objects. Second, it is a dynamic computing paradigm that can adapt to changing environments and resource availability. Third, it is a context-aware computing paradigm that considers the context in which the computing resources are available. In summary, dew computing has the potential to revolutionize the way we utilize computing resources and create a more efficient and sustainable computing infrastructure.

2. BACKGROUND OF CLOUD, FOG, EDGE, AND GRID COMPUTING

In this section, we will discuss background related to cloud, fog, edge, and grid computing as:

A. Cloud Computing

The supply of computing services, such as servers, storage, databases, networking, software, analytics, and intelligence, over the internet is known as cloud computing (i.e., the "cloud"). This eliminates the need for enterprises to purchase and maintain their own infrastructure by enabling access to and use of a variety of computer resources.

Three basic categories of cloud computing services are available as follows:

- Infrastructure as a Service (IaaS): It is a basic building blocks of computing infrastructure, including servers, storage, and networking, which organizations can use to build and run their own applications.
- Platform as a Service (PaaS): This enables businesses to create, test, and deploy applications without having to maintain the underlying infrastructure by providing a full-featured cloud development and deployment environment, including operating systems, programming languages, and tools.
- Software as a Service (SaaS): This gives users online access to programs and software, such as email, customer relationship management (CRM), and productivity tools.

Some benefits of cloud computing include increased scalability, flexibility, reliability, and cost-effectiveness. However, there are also potential drawbacks, such as security concerns and the need to rely on internet connectivity.

B. Fog Computing

Fog computing is a distributed computing concept that aims to provide services closer to end-users by using computing resources in edge devices such as routers, switches, and gateways. In this way, it reduces the latency and bandwidth requirements of cloud-based applications. Fog computing is particularly useful in scenarios where there is a large volume of data generated by IoT (Internet of Things) devices that need to be processed in real-time. By bringing the computing closer to the source, fog computing can reduce the latency and processing time needed to analyze and act on the data. This can lead to faster decision-making, improved operational efficiency, and reduced bandwidth costs. Fog computing also provides better security and privacy by keeping sensitive data local to the devices that generate it. It reduces the risk of data breaches and unauthorized access to sensitive information. Some use cases of fog computing include smart cities, industrial IoT, healthcare, and autonomous vehicles, among others. Fog computing is seen as complementary to cloud computing, with both technologies working together to provide a more robust and efficient computing infrastructure.

C. Edge Computing

Edge computing, a distributed computing paradigm, reduces the amount of data that must be transferred to a central data center or cloud by bringing computation and data storage closer to the point of need. In edge computing, processing is performed at the "edge" of the network, typically in the form of devices and sensors located in the physical world, such as IoT devices, mobile phones, and autonomous vehicles. Edge computing is becoming increasingly popular due to the growth of IoT devices and the need for real-time processing of data generated by these devices. By processing data at the edge of the network, it is possible to reduce latency, improve reliability, and reduce the amount of data that needs to be transmitted to a centralized location. Edge computing is typically implemented using a combination of hardware and software technologies, such as edge servers, gateways, and edge analytics platforms. These technologies enable the processing of data at the edge of the network, and the aggregation and transfer of data to centralized locations for further processing and analysis. In summary, edge computing is an emerging technology that has the potential to transform the way we process and analyze data, particularly in applications where real-time processing is critical.

D. Grid Computing

Grid computing is a distributed computing paradigm that enables the sharing of computing resources across multiple organizations or institutions.

- In grid computing, a large number of geographically distributed computers are connected together to form a virtual supercomputer that can be used to solve complex problems that cannot be handled by a single computer or server.
- Grid computing involves the use of middleware software that enables the transparent sharing of resources, including processing power, storage capacity, and network bandwidth. This middleware software enables applications to be distributed across the grid, with each node in the grid contributing a portion of its computing resources to the application.
- Grid computing is used in a wide range of applications, including scientific research, weather forecasting, and financial modeling. It enables researchers to access computing resources that are not available at their own institution, and to collaborate with other researchers around the world.
- One of the main benefits of grid computing is that it enables organizations to make more efficient use of their computing resources. By sharing resources across multiple organizations, it is possible to reduce the cost of computing and to improve the scalability and availability of computing resources.

In summary, grid computing is a powerful computing paradigm that enables organizations to share resources and collaborate on complex problems. It has the potential to transform the way we approach scientific research, engineering, and other fields that require large-scale computing resources.

E. Security Issues in Grid, Cloud, Fog, and Edge Computing

Each of these computing paradigms has its own unique security issues that need to be addressed.

- Grid Computing: In grid computing, security threats can arise from unauthorized access to the grid resources, attacks on the middleware or grid services, and denial-of-service attacks. Access control methods, firewalls, intrusion detection systems, and encrypted communication protocols can all be used to counter these risks.
- Cloud Computing: cloud computing include data breaches, data loss, and data theft. Access control procedures, firewall and intrusion detection systems, secure communication protocols, and encryption techniques can all be used to secure data while it is in use and in transit.
- Fog Computing: Fog computing introduces security challenges related to the distributed nature of the infrastructure and the large number of connected devices. Security threats can arise from attacks on the fog nodes, data breaches, and denial-of-service attacks. Access control techniques, firewalls, intrusion detection systems, and secure communication protocols can all be used to combat these issues.
- Edge Computing: Edge computing introduces security challenges related to the distribution of data processing and storage across multiple devices. Security threats can arise from unauthorized access to the devices, attacks on the communication channels, and data breaches. By putting in place access control mechanisms, installing firewalls and intrusion detection systems, and utilizing secure communication protocols, these issues can be resolved.

In general, securing distributed computing systems requires a multi-layered approach that involves securing the infrastructure, the communication channels, and the data. This can be achieved by implementing appropriate security mechanisms at each layer of the architecture, including access control, encryption, firewalls, intrusion detection, and secure communication protocols. Additionally, regular security audits and vulnerability assessments should be conducted to identify and address any potential security threats.

3. PRIVACY ISSUES IN GRID, CLOUD, FOG, AND EDGE COMPUTING

Grid computing, cloud computing, fog computing, and edge computing are all different paradigms of distributed computing that involve the processing and storage of data across multiple devices and infrastructure. As a result, these paradigms introduce various privacy issues that need to be addressed.

- Grid Computing: In grid computing, privacy threats can arise from the sharing of data across multiple organizations or users. These threats can be addressed by implementing privacy-preserving mechanisms, such as data anonymization and encryption, to protect sensitive data from unauthorized access.

- Cloud Computing: Privacy threats in cloud computing include the collection and use of personal data by cloud service providers without user consent. These threats can be addressed by implementing data privacy policies and agreements, providing users with transparency and control over their data, and using encryption techniques to secure data at rest and in transit.
- Fog Computing: In fog computing, privacy threats can arise from the collection and processing of data at the edge of the network, which may involve sensitive information such as location and health data. These threats can be addressed by implementing privacy-preserving mechanisms, such as data anonymization and encryption, to protect sensitive data from unauthorized access.
- Edge Computing: Privacy threats in edge computing include the collection and processing of personal data by devices at the edge of the network without user consent. These threats can be addressed by implementing data privacy policies and agreements, providing users with transparency and control over their data, and using encryption techniques to secure data at rest and in transit.

In general, protecting privacy in distributed computing systems requires a multi-layered approach that involves protecting the data, the devices, and the communication channels. This can be achieved by implementing appropriate privacy-preserving mechanisms, such as data anonymization, encryption, and access control, and by providing users with transparency and control over their data. Additionally, regular privacy audits and assessments should be conducted to identify and address any potential privacy threats.

4. IMPORTANCE OF DEW COMPUTING OVER CLOUD, FOG, EDGE, AND GRID COMPUTING

Dew computing is a relatively new concept in the field of distributed computing that focuses on enabling data processing and storage, typically on devices such as sensors, smartphones, and other IoT devices. Dew computing offers several advantages over other forms of distributed computing. Here are some of the key advantages of dew computing:

- Low latency: By processing and storing data at the edge of the network, dew computing can reduce the latency involved in transferring data to a centralized cloud or data center. This is particularly important in applications where real-time processing is critical, such as in industrial automation or autonomous vehicles.
- Increased privacy and security: Since data is processed and stored locally on devices, dew computing can offer increased privacy and security compared to cloud computing, where data is stored in remote data centers that are potentially vulnerable to cyber-attacks.
- Reduced bandwidth requirements: Dew computing can cut down on the amount of data transmission required by processing data locally on edge devices to centralized data centers, thus reducing bandwidth requirements and associated costs.
- Improved scalability: Dew computing can be more scalable than cloud computing since it allows for distributed processing across a large number of edge devices, rather than relying on a centralized data center.
- Reduced energy consumption: By processing data locally on edge devices, dew computing can reduce the energy consumption associated with transmitting data to centralized data centers, thus making it a more energy-efficient solution.

In summary, dew computing offers several advantages over other forms of distributed computing, particularly in applications where low latency, privacy, security, and energy efficiency are critical considerations. However, it is worth noting that dew computing is still an emerging technology and its adoption is likely to be driven by specific use cases and applications.

5. LITERATURE REVIEW

The client-server architecture, which positions two servers at either end of a communication link, provided the foundation for the dew-cloud design at first. By using a dew server, a user can access their personal information more freely and autonomously without requiring an Internet connection (Ray, 2017). The data are mostly kept at the dew server as a local copy to synchronize the Internet with the master copy at the cloud side. The combination of the dew domain naming system and dew domain name redirection has made it possible to map across several local dew sites. New services including infrastructure-as-a-dew, software-as-a-dew-service, and software-as-a-dew-product are now introduced with the DC (Ray, 2017). The following are the paper's main contributions: DC must be defined with clarity and specificity, its concept and working principle must be thoroughly discussed, potential application situations must be considered, and technological challenges must be overcome. The goal of this article is to conceptualize how the ICT user base would be empowered soon with virtually internet-free browsing. Dew computing is a rapidly developing field of study with lots of application potential (Wang, 2016). They suggest a new definition of dew computing in this work. The updated description is: In the context of cloud computing, "dew computing" refers to an on-premises computer software-hardware organization paradigm in which the on-premises computer offers capability both independent of cloud services and collaborative with them. Realizing the maximum potential of on-premises computers and cloud services is the aim of dew computing. The independent and collaborative aspects of dew computing are highlighted in this definition. We also suggest a set of dew computing categories. New applications might be inspired by these categories.

Cloud computing, fog computing, and dew computing are three scalable distributed computing paradigms that link in a vertical hierarchical manner—is taken into consideration in the study given by Skala et al. (2015). The existing distributed computing architecture's new structural layer of Dew Computing is described and acknowledged in this work. Both high-end and low-end computing needs are met by the vertical, complementary, hierarchical division of Cloud to Dew Computing in both daily life and business. Particularly for ideas and initiatives like the Internet of Things (IoT) and the Internet of Everything (IoE), these new computing paradigms are less expensive and perform better. Rindos & Wang (2016) has examine the fundamentals of dew computing and talk about its advantages and disadvantages. Dew computing advances on-premises software to the point where cloud services are continuously used to support it. Dew computing is the route that on-premise software will go in the future. We suggest a new class of computers called dew computers, which are based on the characteristics and needs of dew computing. Even if we can now picture several aspects of dew computers, more research is still required to pinpoint all their specific qualities. Cloud computing and dew computing are closely related.

The main focus of the study by Gushev (2020) is the dew computing architecture, which expands on this concept with a specific design out of the edge. This work seeks to provide a dew computing architecture for use in cyber-physical systems, explain the new features and functions, and contrast it with other dew computing designs. In Gusev (2017), we describe the dew server's organizational structure, linkages to IoT devices, and IoT solutions using the dew computing architectural paradigm in the context of all available cloud-based solutions. We outline the objectives and specifications of dew servers, an extra computational layer in the architecture of a cloud based IoT solution. The fog computing and cloudlet solutions, in comparison, offer a summary of the entire advancements in computing. From an architectural and organizational perspective, the dew servers are systems that communicate with higher-level cloud servers as well as gather, process, and offload streaming data from IoT sensors and devices.

In Wang et al. (2017), the authors have focused on the history of dew computing, including its inception, current state of research, level of progress, and effects on the evolution of Internet computing paradigms. After compiling and analyzing every research paper on del computing that are aware of, they discovered that papers is divided into three categories: early explorations of del computing, feature research on del computing, and application research on del computing. Recently, there has been a rapid advancement in commercial development in the dew computing industry, leading to the creation and introduction of numerous dew computing products. They examine the evolution of Internet computing paradigms from information location to dew computing in order to identify it from other Internet computing paradigms and to highlight its key characteristics. Singh et al. (2020) offer an intelligent intrusion detection DaaS for EoT ecosystems. An intelligent warning filtration system in DaaS is designed using a deep learning-based classifier. By utilizing deep belief networks, the filtration accuracy in this mechanism is increased (or maintained). When EoT tasks were previously offloaded utilizing cloud-based solutions, the burden on the middle layer and the communication delay grew. The research, "Internet of things-based real-time model study on e-healthcare: Device, message service and dew computing," examines three potential solutions: multitask of popular microprocessor modules; (ii) IoT streams produced by processor sensors that are centered on the cloud; (iii) context-aware local computing built on dew computing.

In the article provided by Hirsch et al. (2021) they research about several useful heuristics for job scheduling, including cases involving cutting-edge smartphones. We corroborate prior findings and gain a better understanding of the problem's baseline methods using the outcomes of fresh simulated situations. In order to perform real-time stream processing utilizing In the research that is being presented, a dew-cloud aided cyber-physical system (CPS) is suggested to examine the relationship between meteorological and personal health characteristics (Manocha et al., 2021). The main goal of the effort is to identify the health risks brought on by the unpredictability of climatic elements in real time. Smart sensors with IoT support are used to collect constant data from indoor environments that directly or indirectly have a significant impact on an individual's health. The data is evaluated online to assess the likelihood of unusual health occurrences using the Weighted-Nave Bayes modelling technique, which has a high data classification efficiency. To hasten the study of resource management strategies in Dynamic settings, Hirsch et al. (2020) suggest a trace-based toolbox built on modular software artefacts. The adoption of a trace-driven technique ensures the applicability of the simulated scenarios. The Dew-Cloud-based Internet of Things-based music crowdsourcing methodology is described in Roy et al. (2021). In this effort, we have also talked about the system performance metrics for energy use, service latency, and information transfer speed. The proposed paradigm and the traditional cloud computing schema have also been contrasted about the amount of time required for data transfer and the total system's energy consumption. The hierarchical cloud-fog-dew architecture is presented in Javadzadeh et al. (2022) to overcome the drawbacks of cloud computing in real-time applications, such as latency and resource management. It tries to cut down on both Internet traffic and electricity usage. Moreover, Non-dominated Sorting Genetic Algorithm II supports the suggested paradigm to achieve scalability. In the study presented by Singh et al. (2022), a model based on Dew-Cloud is created to provide hierarchical federated learning

(HFL). The suggested Dew-Cloud paradigm offers enhanced IoMT essential application availability along with a higher level of data privacy (s). With distributed Dew servers, the hierarchical long-term memory (HLSTM) concept is implemented with cloud computing as the backend.

6. STATE OF THE ART FOR DEW COMPUTING

Dew computing is a relatively new concept, and as such, it is still an emerging field of research and development. Nonetheless, there have been some recent advances in dew computing that are worth noting:

- Development of dew computing platforms: Several companies and research organizations have developed dew computing platforms that enable data processing and storage at the edge of the network. These platforms typically consist of a suite of software tools and frameworks that allow developers to build and deploy dew computing applications on edge devices.
- Standardization efforts: The OpenFog Consortium, a group of companies and academic institutions focused on advancing fog computing, has recently expanded its scope to include dew computing. This group is working on developing standards and best practices for dew computing, which could help accelerate its adoption.
- Integration with machine learning and AI: There is growing interest in using machine learning and artificial intelligence (AI) in dew computing applications, particularly in areas such as image and speech recognition. Some researchers have proposed using deep learning algorithms on edge devices to enable real-time processing of large volumes of data.
- Use in IoT applications: Dew computing is particularly well-suited for IoT applications, where a large number of devices generate data that needs to be processed and acted upon in real-time. Some companies are exploring the use of dew computing in smart cities, autonomous vehicles, and other IoT applications.
- Security and privacy considerations: As with any form of distributed computing, security and privacy are critical considerations for dew computing. Some researchers are exploring ways to ensure the security and privacy of data processed on edge devices, such as using encryption and secure enclaves.

In summary, dew computing is still an emerging field, but there are several promising developments that could help accelerate its adoption in the coming years.

7. RESEARCH GAPS IN DEW COMPUTING

Dew computing is a new paradigm in computing that seeks to leverage the capabilities of edge computing, cloud computing, and other technologies to provide computing services to resource-constrained devices and users. While research in this area has been ongoing, there are still some gaps that need to be addressed. Here are some of the research gaps in dew computing (Tefera et al., 2019; Wang, 2017; Wang & Skala, 2018):

- Security and privacy: One of the major research gaps in dew computing is the issue of security and privacy. Dew computing requires the sharing of resources and data across multiple devices and networks, which increases the risk of cyber-attacks and data breaches. More research is needed to develop secure and privacy-preserving dew computing systems.
- Resource allocation: Another research gap is how to allocate resources effectively in dew computing systems. Resource allocation in dew computing is challenging due to the dynamic nature of the environment and the limited resources available on edge devices. More research is needed to develop efficient resource allocation algorithms and techniques for dew computing.
- Fault tolerance: Dew computing systems are susceptible to hardware and software failures, which can result in service disruptions and downtime. More research is needed to develop fault-tolerant dew computing systems that can ensure service availability and reliability.
- Energy efficiency: Energy efficiency is another important research gap in dew computing. Edge devices are typically resource-constrained and have limited battery life. Therefore, it is important to develop energy-efficient dew computing systems that can prolong the battery life of edge devices.
- Interoperability: Interoperability is a challenge in dew computing due to the heterogeneity of devices and networks involved. More research is needed to develop interoperability standards and protocols that can enable seamless communication and resource sharing across dew computing systems.

In summary, the research gaps in dew computing present significant challenges that need to be addressed to enable the development of efficient, secure, and reliable dew computing systems.

8. THEORY AND CONCEPT BEHIND USING DEW COMPUTING IN SMART ERA

Dew computing is a relatively new computing paradigm that involves leveraging the computing resources available at the edge of a network, rather than relying solely on centralized cloud computing infrastructure. In the context of the smart era, which is characterized by the proliferation of connected devices and the Internet of Things (IoT), dew computing has emerged as an important approach for managing the vast amounts of data generated by these devices and enabling real-time processing and decision-making. The concept behind dew computing is to distribute computing resources closer to the source of data generation, such as sensors, mobile devices, or other IoT endpoints, rather than relying on centralized data centers or cloud servers. This allows for faster processing, reduced latency, and improved reliability and resilience of the overall system. Additionally, by processing data at the edge, can save on network bandwidth and reduce costs. In all cases, the goal is to move computation closer to the data source, either by deploying computing resources directly on the device or by leveraging nearby edge servers or gateways. In the smart era, dew computing is particularly important for enabling real-time applications such as autonomous vehicles, industrial automation, and smart cities, where decisions need to be made quickly based on real-time data. By processing data at the edge, dew computing can help ensure that these applications are able to operate with low latency and high reliability, even in the face of network disruptions or failures.

In summary, dew computing represents a promising approach for addressing the challenges of managing and processing the massive amounts of data generated by the smart era, and enabling a new generation of real-time, intelligent applications.

9. APPLICATIONS POTENTIALS OF DEW COMPUTING

Dew computing has a wide range of potential applications across various industries and domains, including:

- Smart cities: Dew computing can be used to support a range of smart city applications, such as intelligent transportation systems, smart grids, and public safety. By processing data at the edge, dew computing can enable faster decision-making and improve the overall performance and reliability of these systems.
- Industrial automation: Dew computing can be used in manufacturing and other industrial settings to support real-time monitoring, control, and optimization of production processes. By leveraging edge computing resources, dew computing can enable more efficient and responsive operations, reduce downtime, and improve quality control.
- Healthcare: Dew computing can be used to support remote patient monitoring, telemedicine, and other healthcare applications that require real-time processing of data. By processing data at the edge, dew computing can enable faster diagnosis and treatment, reduce the need for hospitalization, and improve patient outcomes.
- Agriculture: Dew computing can be used to support precision agriculture, where data from sensors and other sources can be used to optimize crop yields and reduce waste. By processing data at the edge, dew computing can enable real-time monitoring and control of irrigation, fertilization, and other agricultural processes.
- Retail: Dew computing can be used to support personalized marketing, inventory management, and other retail applications. By processing data at the edge, dew computing can enable real-time analysis of customer behavior and preferences, and enable more efficient and responsive operations.

In summary, dew computing has the potential to enable a wide range of real-time, intelligent applications across various industries and domains, and help organizations unlock the full potential of the smart era.

10. POSSIBLE CHALLENGES TOWARDS IMPLEMENTATION OF DEW COMPUTING IN REAL WORLD'S APPLICATIONS

Dew computing, also relatively new computing paradigm called "fog computing" intends to bring cloud computing closer to the network's edge, where data is produced and consumed. While dew computing has the potential to enhance privacy and security, decrease latency, and improve speed, there are a number of issues that must be resolved before it can be extensively used in practical applications (Wang, 2017). Some of these challenges include:

- Security: One of the primary concerns with dew computing is security. Data transmitted and stored in the dew computing environment is more vulnerable to attacks due to its distributed nature, making it more challenging to secure. Developers need to ensure that security measures are in place to protect data and systems.
- Interoperability: The dew computing ecosystem is still in its early stages, and there is currently no standardization on how dew computing systems should be designed or deployed. This makes it challenging to integrate different dew computing systems and devices from different vendors.
- Scalability: As the number of dew computing devices increases, the system's scalability becomes a significant concern. Developers need to ensure that the system can handle the increased workload and traffic without sacrificing performance.
- Connectivity: Dew computing requires reliable connectivity between devices, and this can be challenging in areas with poor network coverage. Developers need to ensure that the dew computing environment is designed to handle connectivity issues.
- Data Management: With data generated and stored at the edge of the network, data management becomes more complex. Developers need to ensure that the data is correctly managed, stored, and transmitted between devices, while still maintaining its integrity.
- Power Management: Dew computing devices are often small and have limited power. Developers need to ensure that the devices are designed to conserve power while still providing the necessary processing power and storage capacity.
- Cost: Dew computing requires additional hardware and software infrastructure, which can increase the overall cost of deploying and maintaining a system. Developers need to ensure that the cost of dew computing is reasonable and justifiable for the intended application.

In summary, dew computing has the potential to revolutionize computing by extending cloud computing to the edge of the network. However, addressing these challenges is crucial to ensure that dew computing can be widely adopted and integrated into real-world applications.

11. OPPORTUNITIES FOR FUTURE TOWARDS DEW COMPUTING

Dew computing, also known as fog computing, presents several opportunities for the future of computing (Tefera et al., 2019). Some of these opportunities include:

- Improved Performance: Dew computing can improve application performance by reducing latency and improving response times. By bringing computing closer to the source of data, it can eliminate the need for data to be sent to a remote server, processed, and then sent back to the device.
- Enhanced Security: Dew computing can improve security by reducing the number of points in the system where data is vulnerable to attacks. By processing data locally, dew computing can reduce the risk of data breaches and cyber-attacks.
- Greater Flexibility: Dew computing enables greater flexibility by allowing for the deployment of computing resources closer to the edge of the network. This means that applications can be designed to be more distributed, and resources can be allocated more efficiently.

- Improved Resource Utilization: Dew computing can improve resource utilization by distributing computing resources across multiple devices. By doing so, it can reduce the need for dedicated computing hardware, which can save costs and improve energy efficiency.
- Increased Availability: Dew computing can improve availability by providing redundant resources at the edge of the network. By doing so, it can reduce the risk of system downtime and provide a more reliable service to end-users.
- New Applications: Dew computing opens up new possibilities for applications that were previously not possible or were too expensive to develop. For example, dew computing can enable real-time analysis of data in IoT applications, which can improve decision-making and reduce the need for manual intervention.
- Better User Experience: Dew computing can improve the user experience by providing faster response times and reducing latency. By doing so, it can provide a more responsive and interactive user experience for applications that require real-time feedback.

In summary, dew computing presents several opportunities for the future of computing. As dew computing continues to evolve and mature, we can expect to see more applications and use cases that leverage this technology to improve performance, security, flexibility, and resource utilization.

12. CONCLUSION

In conclusion and discussed above, dew computing represents a new paradigm for computing that extends cloud computing to the edge of the network. It offers several benefits, including improved performance, enhanced security, greater flexibility, and improved resource utilization. Dew computing also presents opportunities for new applications and use cases that were previously not possible or too expensive to develop. However, dew computing also presents several research challenges that need to be addressed, including security, interoperability, scalability, connectivity, data management, power management, and cost. Addressing these challenges is crucial to ensure that dew computing can be widely adopted and integrated into real-world applications. Current state-of-the-art research in dew computing is focused on addressing these challenges and developing new technologies and architectures that can support the unique requirements of dew computing environments. Some of the key areas of research in dew computing include security, networking, data management, power management, and application development. In summary, dew computing is a promising technology that has the potential to revolutionize computing by bringing computation and storage closer to where data is generated and consumed. While there are still challenges to be addressed, dew computing presents several opportunities for the future of computing and has the potential to enable new applications and use cases that were previously not possible.

REFERENCES

Gusev, M. (2017). A dew computing solution for IoT streaming devices. In *2017 40th International Convention on Information and Communication Technology, Electronics and Microelectronics (MIPRO)* (pp. 387-392). IEEE. 10.23919/MIPRO.2017.7973454

Gushev, M. (2020). Dew computing architecture for cyber-physical systems and IoT. *Internet of Things : Engineering Cyber Physical Human Systems*, *11*, 100186. doi:10.1016/j.iot.2020.100186

Hirsch, M., Mateos, C., Rodriguez, J. M., & Zunino, A. (2020). DewSim: A trace-driven toolkit for simulating mobile device clusters in Dew computing environments. *Software, Practice & Experience*, *50*(5), 688–718. doi:10.1002pe.2696

Hirsch, M., Mateos, C., Zunino, A., Majchrzak, T. A., Grønli, T.-M., & Kaindl, H. (2021). A task execution scheme for dew computing with state-of-the-art smartphones. *Electronics (Basel)*, *10*(16), 2006. doi:10.3390/electronics10162006

Javadzadeh, G., Rahmani, A. M., & Kamarposhti, M. S. (2022). Mathematical model for the scheduling of real-time applications in IoT using Dew computing. *The Journal of Supercomputing*, *78*(5), 1–25. doi:10.100711227-021-04170-z

Manocha, A., Bhatia, M., & Kumar, G. (2021). Dew computing-inspired health-meteorological factor analysis for early prediction of bronchial asthma. *Journal of Network and Computer Applications*, *179*, 102995. doi:10.1016/j.jnca.2021.102995

Ray, P. P. (2017). An introduction to dew computing: Definition, concept and implications. *IEEE Access : Practical Innovations, Open Solutions*, *6*, 723–737. doi:10.1109/ACCESS.2017.2775042

Rindos, A., & Wang, Y. (2016). Dew computing: The complementary piece of cloud computing. In *2016 IEEE International Conferences on Big Data and Cloud Computing (BDCloud), Social Computing and Networking (SocialCom), Sustainable Computing and Communications (SustainCom)(BDCloud-SocialCom-SustainCom)* (pp. 15-20). IEEE. 10.1109/BDCloud-SocialCom-SustainCom.2016.14

Roy, S., Sarkar, D., & De, D. (2021). DewMusic: Crowdsourcing-based internet of music things in dew computing paradigm. *Journal of Ambient Intelligence and Humanized Computing*, *12*(2), 2103–2119. doi:10.100712652-020-02309-z

Singh, P., Gaba, G. S., Kaur, A., Hedabou, M., & Gurtov, A. (2022). Dew-cloud-based hierarchical federated learning for intrusion detection in IoMT. *IEEE Journal of Biomedical and Health Informatics*. PMID:35816521

Singh, P., Kaur, A., Aujla, G. S., Batth, R. S., & Kanhere, S. (2020). Daas: Dew computing as a service for intelligent intrusion detection in edge-of-things ecosystem. *IEEE Internet of Things Journal*, *8*(16), 12569–12577. doi:10.1109/JIOT.2020.3029248

Skala, K., Davidovic, D., Afgan, E., Sovic, I., & Sojat, Z. (2015). Scalable distributed computing hierarchy: Cloud, fog and dew computing. *Open Journal of Cloud Computing*, *2*(1), 16–24.

Tefera, G., She, K., & Deeba, F. (2019). Decentralized adaptive latency-aware cloud-edge-dew architecture for unreliable network. *Proceedings of the 2019 11th International conference on machine learning and computing*, 142-146. 10.1145/3318299.3318380

Wang, Y. (2016). Definition and categorization of dew computing. *Open Journal of Cloud Computing*, *3*(1), 1–7.

Wang, Y. (2017). The theory and applications of dew computing. *Proceedings of the 27th Annual International Conference on Computer Science and Software Engineering*, 317-317.

Wang, Y., & Skala, K. (2018). The 3rd international workshop on dew computing. *Proceedings of the 28th Annual International Conference on Computer Science and Software Engineering*, 357-358.

Wang, Y., Skala, K., Rindos, A., Gusev, M., Yang, S., & Pan, Y. (2017). Dew computing and transition of internet computing paradigms. *ZTE Communications*, *15*(4), 30–37.

Chapter 18
The Future of Artificial Intelligence in Blockchain Applications

Amit Kumar Tyagi
 https://orcid.org/0000-0003-2657-8700
National Institute of Fashion Technology, New Delhi, India

Shrikant Tiwari
 https://orcid.org/0000-0001-6947-2362
Galgotias University, Greater Noida, India

ABSTRACT

The integration of artificial intelligence (AI) and blockchain technologies represents a powerful synergy with the potential to revolutionize various industries. This chapter explores the promising future of AI in blockchain applications, shedding light on the significant impacts, challenges, and opportunities it offers. AI's capabilities in data analysis, pattern recognition, and automation find natural alignment with blockchain's immutable, transparent, and decentralized ledger technology. The chapter examines several key use cases where AI and blockchain intersect, including supply chain management, healthcare, finance, and smart contracts. It also discusses the challenges of scalability, data privacy, and regulatory compliance, and how AI can address or mitigate these issues. Furthermore, the chapter highlights the opportunities for innovation and disruption in emerging AI-powered blockchain applications, such as self-executing smart contracts, fraud detection, and identity verification.

1. INTRODUCTION TO BLOCKCHAIN TECHNOLOGY, FEATURES AND USE CASES

1.1 Evolution, Features, and Challenges of Blockchain Technology

Blockchain technology is a decentralized and distributed ledger system (Gomathi et al., 2023; Sk et al.,

DOI: 10.4018/978-1-6684-8531-6.ch018

Copyright © 2024, IGI Global. Copying or distributing in print or electronic forms without written permission of IGI Global is prohibited.

2022) that underlies cryptocurrencies like Bitcoin, but its applications extend far beyond digital currencies. Here, we will discuss the evolution, features, and challenges of blockchain technology. Here, the evolution of Blockchain Technology can be discussed as:

- Pre-Bitcoin Era (2008): The concept of blockchain technology was first introduced in a whitepaper published by an anonymous person or group known as Satoshi Nakamoto in 2008. It was designed to serve as the underlying technology for the digital currency Bitcoin.
- Bitcoin (2009): The first blockchain network was implemented with the launch of Bitcoin in 2009. Bitcoin's blockchain is a public ledger that records all Bitcoin transactions in a transparent and immutable way.
- Altcoins (2011-present): Following Bitcoin's success, alternative cryptocurrencies (altcoins) were created, each with its own blockchain. These introduced variations in consensus mechanisms, block generation times, and other features.
- Ethereum (2015): Ethereum introduced the concept of smart contracts, enabling programmable and self-executing contracts on the blockchain. This expanded the potential use cases of blockchain beyond simple transactions.
- Enterprise Adoption (2016-present): Blockchain technology gained the attention of businesses and governments for its potential in various industries, including finance, supply chain management, healthcare, and more.
- Features of Blockchain Technology:
- Decentralization: Blockchain operates on a decentralized network of nodes (computers). This decentralization enhances security, as there is no central point of control.
- Immutable Ledger: Once data is recorded on the blockchain, it is extremely difficult to alter or delete, ensuring data integrity.
- Transparency: Transactions on a public blockchain are visible to anyone, promoting transparency and trust.
- Security: Cryptographic techniques and consensus mechanisms, like proof of work (PoW) or proof of stake (PoS), ensure the security of the network.
- Smart Contracts: Ethereum popularized smart contracts, enabling automated, self-executing agreements without intermediaries.
- Permissioned Blockchains: Some blockchains are permissioned, meaning only authorized entities can participate, making them suitable for business applications.

Challenges of Blockchain Technology:

- Scalability: Blockchains can become slow and costly as more users join the network. Improving scalability is a major challenge.
- Energy Consumption: Proof of work blockchains, like Bitcoin, require significant computational power and energy, leading to environmental issues.
- Interoperability: Different blockchain networks often have limited interoperability, making it challenging to exchange data and assets between them.
- Regulatory and Legal Issues: The regulatory landscape for blockchain and cryptocurrencies is evolving and can be uncertain, creating challenges for adoption.

- Privacy: Public blockchains are transparent, which can be a disadvantage when it comes to protecting sensitive data. Privacy solutions are being developed.
- Security Issues: While blockchain technology is considered secure, there are still vulnerabilities in smart contracts, consensus algorithms, and wallet security.
- Adoption Barriers: Integrating blockchain into existing systems and processes can be complex and costly, deterring adoption in some industries.
- User-Friendly Interfaces: The technology can be complex for non-technical users, making user-friendly interfaces and wallets important for widespread adoption.

Blockchain technology continues to evolve, and its impact is felt across various sectors, despite the challenges it faces. As the technology matures, it is likely that solutions to these challenges will be developed, further expanding its utility and relevance

1.2 Features, Characteristics, and Challenges of AI

Artificial Intelligence (AI) is a broad field of computer science that focuses on creating systems or machines capable of performing tasks that would typically require human intelligence (Tyagi, Abraham, Kaklauskas et al, 2022; Pal et al., 2022; Srivastava et al., 2023). AI exhibits several features and characteristics while also facing certain challenges:

Features and Characteristics of AI:

- Learning and Adaptation: AI systems can learn from data and adapt their behavior. Machine learning, a subset of AI, involves algorithms that improve their performance as they process more data.
- Problem-Solving: AI can tackle complex problems by processing large volumes of data and making decisions or providing solutions based on patterns and information.
- Automation: AI can automate tasks that are repetitive, time-consuming, or dangerous for humans, improving efficiency and safety.
- Natural Language Processing (NLP): AI can understand and generate human language, enabling applications like chatbots, language translation, and voice assistants.
- Computer Vision: AI systems can interpret and process visual data, making it useful for tasks like image and video analysis, facial recognition, and object detection.
- Pattern Recognition: AI excels at identifying patterns and anomalies in data, which is valuable for applications in fraud detection, medical diagnosis, and more.
- Decision-Making: AI can make decisions based on data and predefined rules, and some AI systems can adapt their decisions based on changing conditions.
- Recommendation Systems: AI is used for building recommendation engines, which provide personalized recommendations for products, content, and services.
- Predictive Analytics: AI can predict future events or trends by analyzing historical data, which is used in applications like financial forecasting, weather prediction, and demand forecasting.
- Robotics: AI plays a key role in robotics, enabling robots to perform tasks, interact with their environment, and even exhibit some degree of autonomy.

Challenges of AI:

- Data Quality and Quantity: AI systems heavily rely on data, and the quality and quantity of data available can significantly impact their performance. Biased or incomplete data can lead to biased models.
- Bias and Fairness: AI models can inherit biases present in the training data, leading to unfair and discriminatory outcomes. Ensuring fairness and mitigating bias is a significant challenge.
- Interpretability: Many AI models are complex, and understanding how they make decisions can be challenging. Interpretability is important in fields like healthcare and law.
- Ethical and Legal Issues: AI can raise ethical and legal issues, such as privacy violations, liability, and responsibility for AI-generated decisions.
- Scalability: Developing AI models that work well with large datasets and real-time processing is a challenge. Scaling AI solutions to handle increased demands can be difficult.
- Energy Efficiency: Some AI models, especially deep learning models, are computationally intensive and require substantial energy resources. Improving energy efficiency is essential.
- Security: AI systems can be vulnerable to adversarial attacks, where attackers manipulate input data to deceive the model or compromise its functionality.
- Regulation and Standards: The regulatory landscape for AI is still evolving, and creating standards and regulations for AI technologies is a complex process.
- Lack of Common Sense: AI systems lack common-sense reasoning and human-like understanding of the world, which can limit their performance in certain tasks.
- Human-AI Collaboration: Integrating AI into various industries and ensuring seamless collaboration with human workers is a challenge, as it requires rethinking job roles and training.

Hence, AI is a rapidly advancing field, and addressing these challenges is essential to realize its potential while ensuring responsible and ethical use. Researchers, policymakers, and industry stakeholders are actively working to overcome these obstacles and create AI systems that are safe, fair, and beneficial to society.

1.3 Significance of AI-Blockchain Integration in This Smart Era

The integration of Artificial Intelligence (AI) and Blockchain technology (Pal et al., 2022; Tyagi et al., 2020) holds significant promise in this smart era, offering a range of benefits and opportunities across various industries. Here are some key reasons why the integration of AI and Blockchain is significant:

- Enhanced Security: Blockchain's decentralized and immutable ledger makes it a secure platform for data storage and transactions. When combined with AI, which can analyze patterns and detect anomalies, this integration can provide advanced security solutions. For instance, AI can be used to monitor blockchain transactions for suspicious activities, enhancing fraud detection and prevention.
- Data Privacy and Control: Blockchain can empower individuals to have greater control over their data. AI can help users manage and share their data securely. Smart contracts, a feature of blockchain, can enable users to grant access to their data for specific AI applications, ensuring data privacy and consent.

- Supply Chain Optimization: Integrating AI and blockchain can lead to more transparent and efficient supply chains. AI can help analyze data from IoT devices and other sources, while blockchain can provide a secure and immutable record of the supply chain's history. This combination enhances traceability, reduces fraud, and improves overall supply chain management.

- Decentralized AI: Traditional AI systems often rely on centralized data storage and processing. Blockchain allows for decentralized AI models where data remains with the users. This can encourage the development of AI applications that respect user privacy and control, without relying on a single centralized authority.

- Quality Data for AI: AI's performance depends on the quality and quantity of data. Blockchain's ability to validate and secure data can ensure that AI models are trained on reliable and trustworthy data, reducing the risk of biased or unreliable models.

- Smart Contracts and AI Oracles: Smart contracts can execute automatically when predefined conditions are met. AI oracles can provide external data to smart contracts. This combination can enable a wide range of automated, self-executing agreements and applications, from insurance policies to financial services.

- Tokenization and Digital Assets: The integration of blockchain and AI can enable the creation and management of digital assets, such as non-fungible tokens (NFTs) and cryptocurrencies. AI can help manage these assets, analyze their market performance, and personalize user experiences related to these assets.

- AI-Powered Identity Management: Blockchain can provide a secure foundation for identity management systems. AI can be used for biometric recognition and identity verification, creating a robust, decentralized solution for identity and access control.

- Medical and Healthcare Applications: The combination of AI and blockchain can improve healthcare data management. Patients can securely share their medical records with AI-powered diagnostic and treatment systems, while maintaining control over their data privacy.

- Energy and Sustainability: AI and blockchain can be used for optimizing energy grids and managing renewable energy resources. AI can predict energy demand, while blockchain can facilitate peer-to-peer energy trading and ensure the transparent and fair allocation of resources.

The integration of AI and blockchain has the potential to transform numerous industries, offering innovative solutions to long-standing challenges. However, it's important to consider the technical and regulatory challenges, as well as the ethical implications of this integration. Proper governance, privacy protection, and compliance with relevant regulations are critical to realizing the full potential of AI-Blockchain integration in the smart era.

1.4 AI Role for Smart Contracts

Artificial Intelligence (AI) plays a significant role in enhancing the capabilities and functionalities of smart contracts, making them smarter, more versatile, and better equipped to handle complex real-world scenarios. Here are some of the key roles that AI can play in smart contracts:

- Dynamic Contract Execution: AI can enable smart contracts to adapt and make real-time decisions based on external data and changing conditions. For example, in an insurance contract, AI can assess damage claims using images or IoT data and automatically determine the payout amount.

- Advanced Monitoring and Triggers: AI can continuously monitor external data sources for specific triggers or events that should activate a smart contract. For instance, an AI-powered smart contract could automatically execute a supply chain payment when a shipment reaches its destination as verified by GPS data.

- Predictive Analytics: AI can use historical data and predictive modeling to forecast future events. Smart contracts can use these predictions to make decisions, such as automatically adjusting pricing or triggering actions when certain conditions are likely to occur.

- Natural Language Processing (NLP): AI-driven NLP can enable more user-friendly interaction with smart contracts. Users can interact with smart contracts in plain language, and the AI can translate these instructions into code for contract execution.

- Automated Dispute Resolution: AI can be used to automate the resolution of disputes in smart contracts. By analyzing data and predefined contract terms, AI can determine whether contract conditions have been met and execute the appropriate actions.

- Fraud Detection and Prevention: AI can identify anomalies and fraudulent activities by analyzing transaction data. Smart contracts can be programmed to take preventive or corrective actions when AI detects potential fraud.

- Risk Assessment: AI can assess the risks associated with smart contract terms and conditions. This information can be used to optimize contract terms, pricing, and actions to mitigate potential risks.

- Scalability: AI can help manage and optimize the performance of smart contract networks. This is particularly important in networks with a high volume of transactions, where AI can ensure efficient processing and resource allocation.

- Personalization: AI can personalize smart contracts based on user preferences and historical data. For instance, a subscription service smart contract could automatically adjust its terms and offerings based on individual user behavior and preferences.

- Data Integration: AI can facilitate the integration of external data sources, such as social media or weather data, to make smart contracts more context-aware and responsive to changing conditions.

- Proactive Maintenance: In the case of smart contracts governing IoT devices, AI can predict maintenance needs and schedule repairs or replacements when AI algorithms detect a potential issue.

- Supply Chain Optimization: AI-powered smart contracts can optimize supply chain processes by dynamically adjusting orders, logistics, and inventory management based on demand and market conditions.

The integration of AI with smart contracts can make them more adaptable, efficient, and capable of handling complex, real-world scenarios. It enables a wide range of applications across various industries, from finance and insurance to supply chain management and healthcare. However, it's essential to ensure that AI-driven smart contracts are designed with privacy, security, and ethical issues in mind to realize their full potential.

1.5 AI Role in Identity Verification and Other Uses

Artificial Intelligence (AI) plays a important role in identity verification and has a wide range of other applications across various industries. Here are some of the key uses of AI in identity verification and other domains:

AI in Identity Verification:

- Biometric Identification: AI enables the use of biometric data, such as facial recognition, fingerprint scans, and voice recognition, for identity verification. It compares the provided biometric data with stored records to confirm the user's identity.
- Document Verification: AI-powered systems can analyze official documents like passports, driver's licenses, and ID cards to verify their authenticity. These systems can detect forgeries and tampering.
- Behavioral Biometrics: AI can analyze user behavior patterns, such as typing speed, mouse movement, and touchscreen gestures, to verify identity. This is particularly useful for continuous authentication.
- Multi-Factor Authentication (MFA): AI can enhance MFA systems by analyzing multiple factors like something the user knows (e.g., password), something the user has (e.g., mobile device), and something the user is (e.g., biometric data).
- Risk-Based Authentication: AI assesses the risk associated with a particular login or transaction based on various factors, including user behavior and historical data. It can then adjust authentication requirements accordingly.
- User Behavior Analysis: AI can monitor and analyze user behavior in real-time to detect unusual or suspicious activity, providing an additional layer of security in identity verification.

AI in Other Applications:

- Healthcare: AI is used for medical image analysis, disease diagnosis, drug discovery, and personal health monitoring. It can help improve patient care, reduce medical errors, and enhance healthcare efficiency.
- Finance and Fraud Detection: AI is employed in fraud detection and prevention in banking and financial services. It analyzes transaction data to identify unusual patterns or potential fraud.
- Customer Service: Chatbots and virtual assistants use AI to provide automated customer support, answer queries, and assist with various tasks, enhancing customer service.
- Natural Language Processing (NLP): AI-driven NLP is used for language translation, sentiment analysis, chatbots, and content generation.
- Recommendation Systems: AI algorithms are used by platforms like Amazon, Netflix, and social media to suggest products, movies, and content based on user preferences and behavior.
- Autonomous Vehicles: AI powers self-driving cars, enabling them to navigate, make decisions, and react to the environment without human intervention.
- Manufacturing and Industry: AI is employed for predictive maintenance, quality control, and process optimization in manufacturing and industrial settings.
- Agriculture: AI-driven precision agriculture uses sensors and data analysis to optimize crop management, reduce resource use, and improve yields.
- Education: AI is used for personalized learning, automating administrative tasks, and providing educational content tailored to individual students.
- Security and Surveillance: AI is used for video analytics, facial recognition, and object detection to enhance security and surveillance systems.

- Environmental Monitoring: AI assists in environmental monitoring and conservation efforts, analyzing data from sensors and satellites to track climate changes and protect ecosystems.
- Content Creation: AI can generate content, such as text, images, and music, for various applications, from journalism and marketing to creative arts.

Hence, AI's versatility and ability to process and analyze large amount of data make it a powerful tool in identity verification and a wide range of other domains, enabling automation, efficiency, and improved decision-making. However, it's essential to consider ethical and privacy issues when implementing AI in these applications.

1.6 Organization of the Work

This work is summarized in seven sections.

2. MACHINE LEARNING AND PREDICTIVE ANALYTICS

2.1 ML for Anomaly Detection in This Smart Era

Machine learning (ML) for anomaly detection is a critical application in the smart era (A. K. V. et al., 2022; Gomathi et al., 2023; Nair & Tyagi, 2022; Varsha, 2020), where large amount of data are generated from various sources, such as IoT devices, sensors, and networks. Anomaly detection using ML techniques helps identify unusual patterns or deviations in data, which can be indicative of security breaches, equipment failures, fraud, or other important events. Here's how ML is used for anomaly detection in this context:

- Data Preprocessing: ML for anomaly detection often begins with data preprocessing. This step involves data cleaning, normalization, and transformation to prepare the data for analysis. It's essential to ensure the data is of high quality and consistency.
- Feature Engineering: Relevant features are selected or engineered to help the model identify anomalies effectively. This step may involve dimensionality reduction techniques to reduce the complexity of the dataset.
- Supervised vs. Unsupervised Learning: Anomaly detection can be performed using both supervised and unsupervised learning approaches.
- Unsupervised Learning: Unsupervised techniques, like clustering and density estimation, are commonly used for anomaly detection. These methods identify anomalies by detecting data points that deviate significantly from the norm, without requiring labeled data.
- Supervised Learning: In some cases, supervised ML models are trained on labeled data where anomalies are known. Once the model is trained, it can classify new data points as normal or anomalous.

Algorithms and Models: Various ML algorithms are used for anomaly detection, including:

- Clustering Algorithms: Such as k-means, DBSCAN, and hierarchical clustering, can group similar data points and identify anomalies as data points that don't fit well into any cluster.
- Isolation Forests: A tree-based algorithm that isolates anomalies by splitting the data into smaller subsets.
- Autoencoders: A type of neural network that learns to encode and decode data, with anomalies producing higher reconstruction errors.
- One-Class SVM: A support vector machine that separates normal data from anomalies in high-dimensional space.
- Time Series Analysis: Techniques like Seasonal Decomposition of Time Series (STL) and Prophet are used for anomaly detection in time series data.
- Model Training: Models are trained on historical data to learn the characteristics of normal data patterns. The goal is to create a baseline model of normal behavior.
- Thresholding: After model training, a threshold is set to determine when a data point should be classified as an anomaly. Data points with scores above this threshold are considered anomalies.
- Continuous Monitoring: In the smart era, real-time or near-real-time monitoring is important. Anomaly detection models need to continuously process incoming data and identify anomalies as they occur.
- Alerts and Actions: When an anomaly is detected, systems can generate alerts, notifications, or even take automated actions to address the anomaly, such as shutting down machine or alerting security personnel.
- Feedback Loop: A feedback loop is established to improve the model's performance over time. Anomaly detection models are updated and retrained as new data becomes available, allowing them to adapt to changing conditions and new anomalies.

Note that ML for anomaly detection is applied in various domains, including cybersecurity, fraud detection, predictive maintenance, quality control, and healthcare. It helps organizations proactively address issues, improve security, reduce downtime, and enhance operational efficiency in the smart era. However, it's essential to fine-tune models and continually update them to maintain their accuracy and effectiveness as data patterns evolve.

2.2 Predictive Analytics for Fraud Prevention

Predictive analytics is a powerful tool for fraud prevention, as it allows organizations to proactively identify and mitigate fraudulent activities by analyzing historical data and identifying patterns and anomalies. Here are the key steps and issues in using predictive analytics for fraud prevention:

A. Data Collection and Preparation:
  - Gather and centralize data from various sources, such as transaction logs, customer information, and access logs.
  - Ensure data is clean, accurate, and consistent, as the quality of input data significantly impacts the effectiveness of predictive models.
B. Feature Engineering:
  - Identify relevant features or variables that can help detect fraud. These features might include transaction amount, location, time, user behavior, and more.

    ◦   Create new features or transform existing ones to extract meaningful information, such as calculating transaction frequency or identifying user patterns.

C.   Data Labeling:
    ◦   Annotate historical data to distinguish between genuine transactions and fraudulent ones. This labeled dataset is used for model training and evaluation.

D.   Model Selection:
    ◦   Choose appropriate machine learning algorithms for predictive analytics. Common algorithms include logistic regression, decision trees, random forests, support vector machines, and neural networks.
    ◦   Ensemble methods, such as gradient boosting and stacking, can improve predictive accuracy.

E.   Model Training:
    ◦   Train the selected model(s) on the labeled dataset. The model learns to recognize patterns and correlations in the data.

F.   Model Validation and Evaluation:
    ◦   Use techniques like cross-validation to assess the model's performance. Common evaluation metrics include accuracy, precision, recall, F1-score, and the receiver operating characteristic (ROC) curve.
    ◦   Adjust the model's hyperparameters to optimize its performance.

G.   Real-Time Monitoring:
    ◦   Implement real-time monitoring of transactions and activities. The predictive model is applied to incoming data, and it scores transactions or events for potential fraud.
    ◦   Set a threshold for fraud scores; transactions exceeding this threshold are flagged as potentially fraudulent.

H.   Alerts and Interventions:
    ◦   When the model identifies a transaction as potentially fraudulent, the system can generate alerts or take preventive actions. Actions may include blocking the transaction, requesting additional verification, or notifying security personnel.

I.   Continuous Model Improvement:
    ◦   Regularly update and retrain the predictive model using fresh data. As fraudsters adapt their tactics, the model should adapt too.
    ◦   Leverage feedback loops to improve the model's accuracy and efficiency.

J.   User Behavior Analysis:
    ◦   Consider analyzing user behavior and identifying anomalies. For example, if a user typically makes small transactions but suddenly makes a large one, it could be a sign of fraudulent activity.

K.   Integration with Other Security Measures:
    ◦   Integrate predictive analytics for fraud prevention with other security measures, such as two-factor authentication, CAPTCHA, and biometric verification.

L.   Regulatory Compliance:
    ◦   Ensure that the predictive analytics system complies with relevant laws and regulations, such as data privacy laws like GDPR or industry-specific regulations.

M.   Education and Training:
    ◦   Train staff to interpret and respond to alerts and to understand the limitations of predictive analytics. Human expertise is important for effective fraud prevention.

Predictive analytics for fraud prevention is an ongoing process that requires continuous improvement and adaptation to evolving fraud tactics. By leveraging historical data, machine learning, and real-time monitoring, organizations can effectively identify and mitigate fraudulent activities, reducing financial losses and maintaining trust with customers.

2.3 AI and ML in Supply Chain Management

Artificial Intelligence (AI) and Machine Learning (ML) are revolutionizing supply chain management by providing tools and techniques to optimize operations, enhance visibility, and improve decision-making. Here are some of the ways AI and ML are being used in supply chain management:

- Demand Forecasting: AI and ML algorithms analyze historical sales data, seasonality, and various external factors to make accurate demand forecasts. This helps companies optimize inventory levels, reduce carrying costs, and prevent stockouts or overstock situations.
- Inventory Management: AI-powered systems continuously monitor inventory levels and automatically reorder stock when it's running low. ML can optimize reorder points and quantities, reducing excess inventory and minimizing holding costs.
- Supply Chain Planning: ML models optimize the allocation of resources, such as transportation, warehousing, and labor, to meet customer demand efficiently. They can suggest the most cost-effective routes, carrier selections, and production schedules.
- Route Optimization: AI algorithms optimize transportation routes, taking into account factors like traffic, weather, and delivery time windows. This reduces fuel consumption and transportation costs while ensuring on-time deliveries.
- Warehouse Management: ML is used for dynamic slotting, which optimizes the placement of products within warehouses to reduce picking times and improve efficiency. AI-powered robots can assist in automated picking and packing processes.
- Supplier Selection and Management: AI can assess potential suppliers and provide recommendations based on historical performance, reliability, and cost factors. It helps in vendor risk assessment and supplier relationship management.
- Quality Control: Machine learning models can analyze data from sensors and cameras to detect product defects, ensuring that only high-quality products reach the market.
- Predictive Maintenance: AI monitors equipment and machinery to predict maintenance needs, reducing unplanned downtime and preventing disruptions in the supply chain.
- Real-time Visibility: AI and IoT (Internet of Things) devices provide real-time visibility into the location and condition of goods throughout the supply chain. This enables better tracking, monitoring, and response to disruptions.
- Order Fulfillment: ML models optimize order picking and packing, reducing errors and improving order accuracy. They can also suggest cross-selling and upselling opportunities based on customer behavior.
- Risk Management: AI analyzes various risks, such as geopolitical, weather-related, and market risks, to proactively manage and mitigate potential disruptions to the supply chain.
- Sustainability and Green Logistics: AI can optimize logistics to reduce carbon emissions and support sustainability initiatives. It identifies eco-friendly transportation options and routes.

- Demand Shaping: AI and ML can influence demand by tailoring marketing and pricing strategies to optimize supply chain efficiency. This can reduce peak demand pressures and improve order fulfillment.
- Customs and Compliance: AI helps with trade compliance by ensuring that shipments meet regulatory requirements, reducing the risk of delays or fines.
- Blockchain Integration: Combining AI with blockchain technology enhances transparency, traceability, and security within the supply chain, particularly for product authenticity and tracking.

Hence, the adoption of AI and ML in supply chain management leads to cost reductions, increased efficiency, improved customer service, and the ability to adapt to rapidly changing market conditions. It also empowers organizations to make data-driven decisions and respond to disruptions effectively, ultimately creating a more agile and competitive supply chain.

3. DECENTRALIZED AUTONOMOUS ORGANIZATIONS (DAOs)

3.1 AI-Driven Decision-Making for Next Generation Society

AI-driven decision-making plays an important role in shaping the next generation of society by enhancing efficiency, innovation, and the overall quality of life. Here are some key aspects of AI-driven decision-making for the next generation society:

- Efficient Resource Allocation: AI can optimize the allocation of resources, including energy, transportation, and healthcare, to reduce waste and environmental impact. For instance, AI can help create smart grids for energy distribution and manage traffic flow to reduce congestion and emissions.
- Personalized Healthcare: AI-driven decision-making in healthcare enables personalized treatment plans, drug discovery, and early disease detection. It allows healthcare providers to tailor medical interventions to an individual's unique genetic and health profile, improving patient outcomes.
- Education and Lifelong Learning: AI-powered adaptive learning systems provide personalized educational content and feedback. These systems help students of all ages acquire knowledge and skills more efficiently, making lifelong learning more accessible.
- Sustainable Urban Planning: AI can optimize city planning by analyzing data on traffic patterns, pollution levels, and energy consumption. It helps create smart cities with efficient transportation, reduced pollution, and improved living conditions.
- Environmental Conservation: AI assists in monitoring and preserving the environment by analyzing satellite imagery and sensor data. It enables the early detection of deforestation, wildlife poaching, and climate change impacts.
- Enhanced Transportation: AI-driven autonomous vehicles and smart traffic management systems improve transportation safety, reduce accidents, and alleviate traffic congestion. This technology can make transportation more convenient and accessible for people of all ages.
- Financial Inclusion: AI-driven credit scoring and risk assessment models expand access to financial services for underserved populations. These models help extend microloans and other financial products to those who were previously excluded from the formal financial system.

- Crisis Response and Management: AI analyzes real-time data during crises, such as natural disasters and disease outbreaks. It supports rapid decision-making and resource allocation to mitigate the impact of these events.
- Content Creation and Entertainment: AI-generated content, including music, art, and writing, adds to the creative landscape. AI-driven recommendation systems personalize entertainment and content consumption, making it more engaging.
- Cybersecurity: AI enhances threat detection and response in the digital realm. It identifies and mitigates cyber threats in real-time, protecting individuals and organizations from data breaches and cyberattacks.
- Ethical Decision-Making: AI can be used to help individuals and organizations make more ethical decisions by analyzing and flagging potential ethical dilemmas, biases, or conflicts of interest.
- Agricultural Efficiency: AI-driven precision agriculture optimizes crop management and resource usage, increasing yields while reducing environmental impact. It helps ensure food security for a growing global population.
- Inclusive Technologies: AI is employed to create inclusive technologies that enable people with disabilities to access and interact with digital systems, improving their quality of life.
- Energy Efficiency: AI-driven smart grids, energy management systems, and predictive maintenance reduce energy consumption and carbon emissions, contributing to a more sustainable society.
- Global Collaboration: AI-driven translation and communication tools break down language barriers, fostering global collaboration and understanding across borders.

While AI-driven decision-making holds immense potential for improving society, it also raises important ethical and privacy issues. It is important to establish responsible AI practices, transparency, and regulatory frameworks to ensure that AI benefits society as a whole and respects individual rights and values.

3.2 Smart Governance in DAOs

Smart governance in Decentralized Autonomous Organizations (DAOs) is a critical aspect of their functioning. DAOs are blockchain-based entities (Nair & Tyagi, 2023) that aim to provide a transparent, decentralized, and autonomous way to manage and make decisions about shared resources, such as cryptocurrency funds or assets. Smart governance mechanisms help facilitate decision-making and ensure the organization operates effectively. Here are key elements of smart governance in DAOs:

- Token-based Voting: Many DAOs use token-based voting, where participants hold tokens that represent their stake in the organization. The number of tokens a participant holds often correlates with their voting power. This ensures that individuals with larger stakes have a proportionate say in governance.
- Proposal Submission: DAO participants can submit proposals for various actions, such as changing the organization's rules, allocating resources, or making investments. Proposals are typically recorded on the blockchain for transparency.

- Quorums and Thresholds: DAOs often require a minimum number of votes, known as a quorum, and a minimum percentage of affirmative votes, known as a threshold, for a proposal to be accepted. These mechanisms ensure that important decisions have a sufficient level of support.
- Delegation: Participants can delegate their voting power to others, allowing for more granular governance. This can enhance participation by enabling experts or representatives to make decisions on behalf of token holders.
- Vote Weighting: Some DAOs allow for vote weighting based on factors other than token holdings. For example, reputation-based systems may give more weight to participants who have consistently made informed decisions.
- Multisignature Wallets: In the context of smart governance, multisignature wallets are often used for additional security. They require multiple private key signatures to execute transactions or proposals, reducing the risk of unauthorized actions.
- Time-Locked Proposals: Some DAOs implement time-locked proposals, allowing participants to schedule future decisions. This can help with long-term planning and governance continuity.
- Dispute Resolution: In the event of conflicts or disputes, DAOs can use smart contracts to implement dispute resolution mechanisms, often involving arbitration by trusted third parties.
- Governance Tokens: Some DAOs issue separate governance tokens, which are distinct from the tokens used for other transactions within the organization. These tokens give participants the right to vote on governance matters.
- Off-Chain Governance: While many governance actions occur on-chain (recorded on the blockchain), some decisions may require off-chain discussions and deliberation. Off-chain governance platforms and forums can facilitate discussions before proposals are made on-chain.
- Transparency and Auditability: Smart governance in DAOs is underpinned by transparency and auditability. Participants can track proposals, voting results, and transaction history on the blockchain.
- Open Participation: DAOs often aim to promote open and inclusive participation, allowing anyone with tokens to contribute to governance. This helps prevent centralization and promotes a decentralized decision-making process.

Smart governance in DAOs is still evolving, and different DAOs may implement variations of these mechanisms to suit their specific goals and community preferences. It's important to ensure that smart governance is designed with security, fairness, and transparency in mind and to continuously adapt and improve the governance processes as the DAO grows and faces new challenges.

3.3 Challenges and Governance Models in This Smart Era

In the smart era, AI technology and Big data play a major role in our lives and societies (Deshmukh et al., 2022; Tyagi, 2023; Tyagi, Chandrasekaran, & Sreenath, 2022), there are various challenges and governance models that need to be considered. Here are some key challenges and governance approaches:

Challenges:

- Privacy and Data Protection: The collection, storage, and use of personal data by smart technologies raise significant privacy issues. Governance must ensure that individuals' data is protected and used responsibly.

- Cybersecurity: As smart technologies become more prevalent, they become attractive targets for cyberattacks. Effective governance involves robust cybersecurity measures and rapid incident response.
- Ethical AI and Automation: The ethical use of AI and automation technologies is a challenge. Governance should address issues like algorithmic bias, job displacement, and the responsible use of autonomous systems.
- Digital Inclusion: Not everyone has equal access to smart technologies, leading to digital divides. Governance models should aim for digital inclusion and equitable access to technology.
- Regulatory Frameworks: The fast pace of technological advancement often outpaces regulatory frameworks. Effective governance involves adapting existing regulations and creating new ones to address emerging challenges.
- Data Ownership and Sovereignty: Determining data ownership and sovereignty in a global context can be complex. Governance models must address these issues and consider national and international regulations.
- Environmental Impact: Smart technologies can have significant energy and resource consumption. Governance should encourage eco-friendly and sustainable technologies and practices.
- Information Manipulation: The spread of misinformation and the potential for deepfakes are growing issues. Governance models need to address the spread of false or misleading information while protecting free speech.
- AI and Autonomous Systems Liability: As AI and autonomous systems make decisions, liability issues arise. Governance models must establish clear accountability and liability frameworks.

Governance Models:

- Self-Regulation: Industries can develop self-regulatory standards and codes of conduct to ensure responsible use of technology. This approach can be proactive and adaptable.
- Government Regulation: Governments can pass laws and regulations to govern smart technologies, protecting citizens and addressing societal issues. These regulations may vary by region and application.
- Multi-Stakeholder Approaches: Collaborative governance models involve multiple stakeholders, including governments, industry, academia, and civil society, working together to address challenges and create standards.
- Decentralized Autonomous Organizations (DAOs): In some contexts, DAOs can self-govern through smart contracts and token-based voting. This model can provide transparency and decentralization.
- Public-Private Partnerships: Governments and private entities can work together to develop governance models. These partnerships leverage public resources and private sector innovation.
- Blockchain-Based Governance: Blockchain technology can be used for transparent and decentralized governance, particularly in cases involving data ownership and decentralized decision-making.
- AI Ethics Frameworks: Organizations and governments are developing AI ethics frameworks to guide the development and use of AI technologies, emphasizing transparency, fairness, and accountability.
- International Agreements: For global challenges, international agreements and organizations play a important role in setting standards and promoting cooperation among nations.

- Continuous Adaptation: Governance models need to be adaptable and continuously updated to keep pace with rapidly evolving technologies and challenges.

Effective governance in the smart era requires a combination of regulatory measures, ethical issues, transparency, and collaboration among stakeholders. It should balance innovation with the protection of individual rights and societal interests while promoting responsible and sustainable technological advancement.

4. PRIVACY AND SECURITY

4.1 Privacy-Preserving Blockchains Mechanism in This Smart Era

Privacy-preserving mechanisms (Abraham et al., 2022; Sheth & Tyagi, 2022) in blockchains have become increasingly important in the smart era, where data and transactions are shared across decentralized networks. These mechanisms aim to protect the confidentiality and anonymity of users while still providing the benefits of blockchain technology. Here are some of the key privacy-preserving mechanisms used in blockchain systems:

- Confidential Transactions: Confidential transactions use cryptographic techniques like Pedersen commitments or zero-knowledge proofs to hide the transaction amount while still ensuring the validity of the transaction. This prevents outsiders from knowing the specific amounts being transacted.
- Ring Signatures: Ring signatures enable anonymous transactions by mixing the spender's input with a group of other possible signers. This makes it challenging to determine the actual source of a transaction.
- Zero-Knowledge Proofs: Zero-knowledge proofs, such as zk-SNARKs (Zero-Knowledge Succinct Non-Interactive Arguments of Knowledge), allow a party to prove knowledge of certain information without revealing that information. This is used to verify transactions without exposing transaction details.
- Confidential Assets: Some blockchain platforms enable the creation of confidential assets, where the identity and nature of the asset being transferred are kept private. This is important for financial and asset management applications.
- Homomorphic Encryption: Homomorphic encryption allows computations to be performed on encrypted data without the need to decrypt it first. This can be used for private data processing in blockchain applications.
- Ring Confidential Transactions (RingCT): RingCT combines ring signatures with confidential transactions, allowing for both confidential amounts and transaction origins in privacy-preserving blockchain systems.
- Differential Privacy: Differential privacy mechanisms add noise to data to protect individual privacy while still enabling data analysis and aggregation on the blockchain.
- State Channels: State channels allow participants to conduct off-chain transactions that are only settled on-chain when needed. This minimizes on-chain data exposure and provides privacy for participants.

- Privacy Coins: Some blockchain projects, such as Monero and Zcash, are designed from the ground up to provide enhanced privacy features, making it difficult to trace transactions or identify participants.
- Consortium Blockchains: In consortium blockchains, where a limited set of known participants is involved, privacy-preserving mechanisms can be implemented more effectively because of the controlled environment.
- Privacy Policies and Governance: Some blockchains implement governance mechanisms that allow users to define privacy policies, specifying who can access their data and under what conditions.
- Multi-Signature Wallets: Multi-signature wallets can be used to enhance privacy by requiring multiple parties to sign off on a transaction, making it more challenging to trace the source.
- Decentralized Identity Solutions: Privacy-preserving blockchains can incorporate decentralized identity systems that allow users to control their identity and personal data, sharing only what's necessary for specific transactions.

These privacy-preserving mechanisms are essential to address the privacy issues associated with blockchain technology. They are especially important in financial, healthcare, and identity management applications where sensitive information must be protected while still benefiting from the transparency, security, and immutability of blockchain systems.

4.2 AI for Security and Threat Detection

Artificial Intelligence (AI) is a powerful tool for enhancing security and threat detection across various domains. AI-driven security solutions can analyze large amount of data, identify patterns, and respond to potential threats in real-time. Here are some key applications of AI in security and threat detection:

- Anomaly Detection: AI systems can learn normal behavior patterns in a network, system, or environment. When they detect deviations from these patterns, they raise alerts, which can indicate potential security threats or breaches.
- Intrusion Detection Systems (IDS): AI-based IDS use machine learning to identify unauthorized access, data breaches, or other suspicious activities in computer networks. They can detect and respond to both known and unknown threats.
- Malware Detection: AI-powered malware detection systems can identify and quarantine malicious software, even if it's a new, previously unseen variant. These systems use behavioral analysis and signature-based techniques.
- Phishing Detection: AI algorithms can analyze emails and websites for signs of phishing attacks. They check for suspicious URLs, email headers, and content to prevent users from falling victim to phishing schemes.
- Endpoint Security: AI-driven endpoint security solutions protect individual devices (endpoints) by continuously monitoring and analyzing behavior. They can block suspicious activities and quarantine infected devices.
- User and Entity Behavior Analytics (UEBA): AI analyzes user and entity behavior to identify abnormal actions or access patterns that may indicate insider threats or compromised accounts.

- Network Traffic Analysis: AI-based network traffic analysis tools monitor data flows, detect unusual network activities, and identify potential security threats or breaches in real-time.
- Vulnerability Management: AI can scan and assess an organization's network, systems, and applications to identify vulnerabilities and recommend patches or fixes, reducing the attack surface.
- Threat Intelligence: AI is used to collect, analyze, and disseminate threat intelligence data. It helps organizations stay informed about emerging threats and vulnerabilities.
- Security Chatbots: AI-powered chatbots can provide real-time support for security-related queries, assist in incident response, and guide users through security protocols.
- Video Surveillance and Facial Recognition: AI-driven video analysis systems can recognize faces, objects, and behaviors, allowing for advanced surveillance and threat detection in public spaces and critical infrastructure.
- Predictive Threat Analysis: AI can analyze historical data to predict potential security threats and vulnerabilities, enabling organizations to proactively address security risks.
- Fraud Detection: In financial and e-commerce sectors, AI is used to detect fraudulent transactions and activities by analyzing transaction patterns, user behavior, and other data.
- Physical Security: AI-powered systems enhance physical security through video analytics, access control, and threat detection in public spaces and buildings.
- IoT Security: AI can monitor and secure IoT devices, which are often vulnerable to attacks, by identifying and responding to suspicious behavior.
- Cloud Security: AI-based cloud security solutions protect cloud-based assets and data by continuously monitoring for unauthorized access and data breaches.

AI-driven security and threat detection solutions are valuable for organizations seeking to protect their assets, data, and reputation in an ever-evolving threat landscape. They can improve the accuracy and speed of threat detection while reducing the burden on human security analysts. However, it's important to continually update and adapt these systems to address new and evolving threats.

4.3 Ethical Use of AI in Blockchain in This Smart Era

The ethical use of AI in blockchain in the smart era is of utmost importance to ensure that technology benefits individuals and society as a whole while respecting individual rights and values. Here are key issues for the ethical use of AI in blockchain:

- Transparency: Ensure that the operation of AI systems within the blockchain is transparent and understandable. Users and stakeholders should have insight into how AI makes decisions, especially in decentralized autonomous organizations (DAOs) and smart contracts.
- Accountability: Establish mechanisms to assign responsibility and accountability for AI-driven decisions. In blockchain, this may include clear lines of accountability for smart contracts and DAOs.
- Data Privacy: Protect user data and privacy when implementing AI in blockchain applications. Anonymize data where necessary and comply with data protection regulations, such as GDPR.
- Bias and Fairness: Be aware of and address biases in AI algorithms that may discriminate against certain groups. Ensure that blockchain-based AI systems are designed and trained with fairness in mind.

- Security: Implement strong security measures to safeguard AI models and data in blockchain. This includes measures to prevent tampering with models and to protect sensitive data.

- Consent: Seek informed consent when collecting and processing personal data in blockchain-based AI applications. Users should understand how their data will be used and have the option to opt in or out.

- Open Source and Collaboration: Encourage open-source development and collaboration within the blockchain and AI communities to foster ethical practices and collective oversight.

- Regulatory Compliance: Comply with relevant laws and regulations in the jurisdictions where the blockchain-based AI application operates. Stay informed about evolving regulatory landscapes.

- Human Oversight: Ensure there is a human oversight component in AI-driven decisions. In some cases, human intervention may be necessary, particularly when the AI system's decisions have significant real-world impact.

- Community Governance: In DAOs, smart contracts, and blockchain networks, involve the community in governance and decision-making. Ensure that all stakeholders have a voice in shaping policies related to AI use.

- Fair Distribution of Benefits: Consider how the benefits of AI in blockchain are distributed among participants and stakeholders. Ensure that no single group disproportionately benefits from AI technology.

- Education and Awareness: Promote awareness and education about the ethical issues related to AI in blockchain. This includes educating developers, users, and stakeholders.

- Periodic Audits: Conduct periodic audits and assessments of AI systems and their ethical implications, especially in complex blockchain environments.

- Third-Party Audits: Consider involving third-party auditors and experts to assess the ethical implications and practices of AI within the blockchain system.

Hence, ethical issues in AI and blockchain go beyond technology and involve social, legal, and regulatory dimensions. As these technologies continue to evolve, it's important to maintain a strong commitment to ethical use, public trust, and the broader ethical principles that guide responsible innovation.

5. TOKENIZATION AND DIGITAL ASSETS

5.1 Tokenization of Real-World Assets

Tokenization of real-world assets is a process that involves converting physical or tangible assets into digital tokens on a blockchain or distributed ledger technology (DLT) platform. This process allows these assets to be traded and transferred more easily and efficiently. Tokenization has the potential to revolutionize the way we own, buy, and sell various types of assets. Here are the key aspects and benefits of tokenizing real-world assets:

- Types of Assets: Virtually any tangible or intangible asset can be tokenized, including real estate, art, stocks, bonds, commodities, private equity, and more.

Benefits of Tokenization:

- Liquidity: Tokenized assets can be traded 24/7 on secondary markets, enhancing liquidity compared to traditional markets with limited trading hours.
- Fractional Ownership: Tokenization enables fractional ownership, allowing multiple investors to own a portion of an asset, making it more accessible.
- Efficiency: Digital tokens streamline asset transfer and reduce the administrative and intermediation costs associated with asset ownership.
- Accessibility: Investors from around the world can access a broader range of assets, including those previously reserved for accredited or institutional investors.
- Transparency: Transactions and ownership are recorded on a blockchain, providing transparency and reducing fraud.
- Security: Blockchain technology enhances the security of asset ownership and transactions.
- Dividend Distribution: Tokenization simplifies the distribution of dividends, interest payments, or rental income to asset owners.
- Automated Compliance: Smart contracts can be used to automatically enforce compliance with relevant regulations, such as Know Your Customer (KYC) and Anti-Money Laundering (AML) rules.
- Token Standards: Tokens can be issued as security tokens, utility tokens, or other types, depending on the rights and utilities they confer. Compliance with regulatory requirements is essential, particularly for security tokens.
- Regulatory Issues: Different jurisdictions have varying regulations issueing the tokenization of assets. It's important to navigate these regulations to ensure compliance. Regulatory compliance may include registration with securities authorities, reporting requirements, and investor accreditation rules.
- Tokenization Platforms: There are various blockchain platforms and protocols that support asset tokenization, including Ethereum, Tezos, and Stellar. Each has its own characteristics and features, and the choice depends on the specific use case and regulatory environment.
- Custody and Security: Storing and securing tokenized assets are important. Solutions like digital asset custodians and multisignature wallets are often used to protect these assets.
- Marketplaces and Exchanges: Digital asset marketplaces and exchanges facilitate the trading of tokenized assets, providing liquidity and price discovery.
- Legal Agreements: Clear legal agreements, including smart contracts, are essential to define the terms and conditions of tokenized asset ownership, transfer, and trading.
- Fractionalization: Tokenization can divide an asset into multiple tokens, each representing a specific portion. This makes it easier for multiple investors to hold shares in the same asset.
- Real-World Use Cases: Tokenization has been applied to various assets, including real estate, art, venture capital, and even fine wine.

Tokenization of real-world assets has the potential to democratize investing and open up new opportunities for individuals and institutions to diversify their portfolios. However, it also presents regulatory and legal challenges that must be addressed for widespread adoption. As the technology matures and regulatory frameworks evolve, tokenization is likely to become an integral part of the financial landscape.

5.2 AI-Enhanced Asset Management

AI-enhanced asset management is the application of artificial intelligence (AI) and machine learning (ML) techniques to improve the management and optimization of various assets, including financial portfolios, real estate, infrastructure, and more. AI-driven asset management leverages data analytics, predictive modeling, and automation to make more informed decisions and enhance asset performance. Here are key aspects and benefits of AI-enhanced asset management:

Key Aspects:

- Data Analytics: AI-driven asset management relies on large amount of historical and real-time data to make informed decisions. Data sources can include market data, economic indicators, news, social sentiment, and asset-specific data.
- Predictive Modeling: AI models use historical data to make predictions about asset performance. These models can forecast market trends, asset prices, and risk factors, enabling better decision-making.
- Risk Management: AI algorithms can assess risk and provide risk profiles for individual assets or portfolios. This helps in developing strategies to mitigate risk and optimize asset allocation.
- Portfolio Optimization: AI can recommend optimal asset allocations and trading strategies to maximize returns while managing risk within a portfolio.
- Algorithmic Trading: AI-driven trading algorithms can execute buy and sell orders based on pre-defined criteria, often in real-time. These algorithms can capture opportunities and respond to market fluctuations faster than human traders.
- Alternative Data: AI-enhanced asset management can incorporate alternative data sources, such as satellite imagery, social media sentiment analysis, and supply chain data, to gain insights into asset performance.
- Customized Solutions: AI can tailor asset management strategies to the specific goals, risk tolerance, and preferences of individual investors or institutional clients.
- Continuous Learning: Machine learning models continuously learn from new data, adapting to changing market conditions and refining their predictions and strategies over time.

Benefits:

- Improved Decision-Making: AI's ability to process large amount of data and identify patterns and trends enables more informed asset management decisions.
- Risk Mitigation: AI can help identify and manage risks more effectively, reducing the likelihood of large losses in portfolios.
- Enhanced Efficiency: Automation of routine tasks and real-time analysis improves the efficiency of asset management processes.
- Diversification: AI can recommend diversified portfolios, reducing concentration risk and enhancing overall returns.
- Personalization: AI allows for tailored asset management solutions that align with individual client objectives and risk tolerance.
- Reduced Human Bias: AI-driven decisions are less influenced by human bias, leading to more objective and data-driven asset management.

- Alpha Generation: AI models can discover alpha (excess returns) in the market by identifying opportunities that might be overlooked by traditional methods.
- Cost Reduction: Automation and efficiency improvements can reduce the cost of asset management, benefiting both clients and asset managers.

AI-enhanced asset management is becoming increasingly prevalent in the financial industry, with many asset management firms and financial institutions adopting these technologies to gain a competitive edge. While AI offers significant benefits, it's essential to ensure that these systems are transparent, explainable, and compliant with relevant regulations to maintain trust and confidence in the asset management process

5.3 Future of Digital Finance

The future of digital finance promises to be transformative, driven by technological advancements, changing consumer preferences, and evolving regulatory frameworks. Here are some key trends and potential developments that may shape the future of digital finance:

- Central Bank Digital Currencies (CBDCs): Many central banks are exploring or piloting CBDCs, which are digital representations of national currencies. CBDCs have the potential to revolutionize the payment system, enhance financial inclusion, and provide central banks with more control over monetary policy.
- Blockchain and Cryptocurrencies: Blockchain technology and cryptocurrencies like Bitcoin and Ethereum continue to disrupt traditional financial systems. They offer decentralized, secure, and efficient methods for transferring value and assets. As regulatory clarity improves, they are likely to play a more significant role in finance.
- Decentralized Finance (DeFi): DeFi platforms are creating open and permissionless financial ecosystems. They enable lending, borrowing, trading, and other financial services without the need for traditional intermediaries. DeFi has the potential to democratize access to financial services globally.
- NFTs (Non-Fungible Tokens): NFTs represent ownership of unique digital assets and are becoming popular for digital collectibles, art, and other unique items. They have the potential to revolutionize ownership and provenance in various industries.
- AI and Big Data: Artificial intelligence and big data analytics are transforming financial services. They enable better risk assessment, personalization, fraud detection, and predictive analytics for investment and lending.
- Regulatory Evolution: As digital finance matures, regulators are developing frameworks to address risks and ensure consumer protection. Regulatory clarity and consistency are important for fostering innovation while maintaining stability and security.
- Cross-Border Payments: Digital finance can simplify cross-border payments, reducing transaction costs and time delays. Solutions like stablecoins and blockchain-based networks aim to improve international remittances.
- Open Banking: Open banking initiatives and APIs enable consumers to share their financial data securely with third-party applications and services. This fosters competition and innovation in the financial sector.

- Financial Inclusion: Digital finance can extend financial services to unbanked and underbanked populations, improving their access to credit, savings, and insurance.
- Sustainable Finance: Digital finance can play a pivotal role in advancing sustainable and responsible investing. ESG (Environmental, Social, and Governance) issues are increasingly integrated into investment decisions.
- Fintech Partnerships: Traditional financial institutions are partnering with fintech companies to leverage their technology and innovation. These collaborations enhance customer experience and drive digital transformation.
- Cybersecurity and Data Privacy: As digital finance grows, the importance of robust cybersecurity and data privacy measures increases to protect sensitive financial information and prevent fraud.
- Quantum Computing: In the long term, quantum computing may have a significant impact on financial services, enabling faster and more complex computations for risk analysis, cryptography, and optimization.
- Decentralized Identity: Digital identity solutions are evolving, allowing individuals to have more control over their personal data and privacy. Decentralized identity systems can enhance security and reduce the risk of data breaches.
- Smart Contracts and Automation: Smart contracts on blockchain platforms automate financial agreements and processes, reducing the need for intermediaries and the potential for errors.

The future of digital finance is likely to be dynamic and increasingly interconnected with other emerging technologies. However, challenges related to regulation, security, and adoption remain, and addressing these challenges will be critical to realizing the full potential of digital finance in the years ahead.

6. FUTURE CHALLENGES AND RESEARCH OPPORTUNITIES TOWARDS AI-BLOCKCHAIN INTEGRATION

The integration of AI and blockchain presents exciting possibilities but also comes with its set of challenges and research opportunities. Here are some of the future challenges and research areas related to AI-Blockchain integration, as mentioned in Table 1.

Hence, the convergence of AI and blockchain technologies holds significant promise, and addressing these challenges and pursuing these research opportunities will be important for unlocking the full potential of this integration in various domains, including finance, healthcare, supply chain, and more. Researchers and innovators should work collaboratively to drive advancements and address these critical issues.

6.1 New Trends in Blockchain Applications

Blockchain technology continues to evolve, leading to new trends and applications in various industries. Here are some of the new and emerging trends in blockchain applications:

- Decentralized Finance (DeFi): DeFi continues to be a hot trend in blockchain. It involves the use of blockchain and cryptocurrency to recreate traditional financial services such as lending, borrowing, and trading without intermediaries.

Table 1. Issues, challenges and research opportunities towards AI-blockchain integration

Issues	Challenges	Research Opportunity
Scalability:	Blockchains often have scalability limitations, especially in public networks, which may hinder AI processing.	Developing scalable blockchain consensus mechanisms, sidechains, or layer-2 solutions that can handle the computational demands of AI workloads.
Privacy and Security:	Privacy and security issues are heightened when AI models and data are integrated into a transparent and immutable blockchain.	Designing privacy-preserving techniques (like zero-knowledge proofs) and secure, verifiable computation methods for AI on the blockchain.
Interoperability:	Different blockchains and AI systems may not seamlessly work together, making data sharing and integration complex.	Exploring interoperability standards and protocols to facilitate cross-blockchain communication and data exchange.
Energy Efficiency:	Proof-of-work (PoW) blockchains, like Bitcoin and Ethereum, consume substantial energy, which is not sustainable for AI computations.	Developing energy-efficient consensus mechanisms (e.g., proof-of-stake) and optimizing AI algorithms for blockchain environments to reduce energy consumption.
Decentralized AI Oracles:	Blockchain-based AI applications often require external data (e.g., real-world events) that are difficult to verify on-chain.	Designing decentralized AI oracles to securely and reliably feed external data into smart contracts or AI models on the blockchain.
Governance and Decision-Making	Governance models in decentralized systems, like DAOs, often lack clear mechanisms for AI-driven decision-making.	Developing transparent and decentralized governance models that incorporate AI-driven decision support.
Smart Contract Security:	Vulnerabilities in smart contracts can lead to disastrous financial losses in DeFi and other applications.	Enhancing the security of smart contracts, using AI for automated code auditing and vulnerability detection.
Data Availability and Quality	Reliable and high-quality data is important for AI training and inference on the blockchain.	Researching methods for incentivizing data providers to contribute accurate and valuable data to blockchain-based AI models.
User Experience:	Complex interfaces and usability issues may deter widespread adoption of AI-Blockchain applications.	Studying user experience and human-computer interaction to make AI-Blockchain applications more accessible and user-friendly.
Hybrid Models:	Integrating AI models that partially reside off-chain and on-chain, maintaining efficiency and trust.	Developing hybrid models and architectures for AI-Blockchain integration to optimize the balance between trust and performance.

- **Non-Fungible Tokens (NFTs):** NFTs have gained immense popularity for representing ownership and provenance of unique digital assets like art, collectibles, virtual real estate, and more. The NFT market has witnessed significant growth.
- **Blockchain in Supply Chain:** Blockchain is being increasingly used to enhance supply chain management, enabling transparent and efficient tracking of products from manufacturer to consumer. This is particularly valuable in ensuring the authenticity of products and food safety.
- **Central Bank Digital Currencies (CBDCs):** Many central banks are exploring and piloting CBDCs, which are digital versions of national currencies. CBDCs have the potential to revolutionize payment systems and monetary policies.
- **Blockchain for Sustainability:** Blockchain is being used to track and verify sustainable and ethical practices in industries like agriculture, fashion, and mining, allowing consumers to make more informed choices.

- Cross-Chain Integration: Solutions are emerging to facilitate interoperability between different blockchains, allowing assets and data to move seamlessly across multiple networks.
- Decentralized Autonomous Organizations (DAOs): DAOs are gaining popularity, providing decentralized governance models for making decisions and managing shared resources, often using blockchain-based tokens.
- Blockchain for Healthcare: Blockchain is used to secure and manage healthcare data, ensuring patient privacy, interoperability of medical records, and the authentication of pharmaceuticals.
- Blockchain in Gaming: Blockchain technology is transforming the gaming industry by enabling true ownership of in-game assets and provably scarce digital collectibles.
- Blockchain Voting: Some regions are exploring blockchain-based voting systems to enhance transparency, security, and accessibility in elections and referendums.
- Blockchain in Intellectual Property: Blockchain can be used to register and protect intellectual property rights, such as patents, copyrights, and trademarks.
- Blockchain for Identity Management: Blockchain-based identity solutions are emerging, offering individuals control over their personal data and privacy.
- Blockchain and IoT Integration: Combining blockchain with the Internet of Things (IoT) for secure and transparent data sharing and device management.
- Blockchain for Legal and Smart Contracts: Blockchain is being used for secure, transparent, and automated smart contracts in legal applications.
- Blockchain in Energy and Carbon Trading: Blockchain applications are being developed for tracking energy production and carbon emissions, facilitating sustainable energy management.
- Blockchain in Education: Some educational institutions are exploring the use of blockchain to verify and secure academic credentials.
- Blockchain in Government: Governments are exploring blockchain for various use cases, including land registry, public records, and taxation.
- Blockchain and AI Integration: Combining blockchain and artificial intelligence for secure, transparent data management and AI model training.

Note that these trends demonstrate the versatility and potential of blockchain technology in addressing a wide range of challenges and opportunities across multiple sectors. As blockchain continues to evolve, it's important to consider the specific use cases and industries where it can make the most impact and drive innovation.

6.2 Role of Emerging Technologies in Blockchain Applications

Emerging technologies are playing a significant role in enhancing the capabilities and expanding the applications of blockchain technology. Here's how several emerging technologies are being integrated into blockchain applications:

- Artificial Intelligence (AI) and Machine Learning (ML): AI and ML are used to improve data analytics, predict market trends, enhance smart contract functionality, and provide insights for risk management in blockchain applications. These technologies enable automation, pattern recognition, and the development of more sophisticated algorithms for blockchain-based systems.

- Internet of Things (IoT): IoT devices generate large amount of data. Blockchain can provide a secure and transparent way to manage and verify this data, improving supply chain visibility, automated smart contracts, and data integrity in IoT applications.
- Quantum Computing: While still emerging, quantum computing has the potential to break current encryption schemes, including those used in blockchain. Research is ongoing to develop quantum-resistant blockchain solutions to ensure long-term security.
- 5G Connectivity: High-speed, low-latency 5G networks enhance the scalability and real-time capabilities of blockchain applications. This is particularly valuable for IoT, supply chain management, and decentralized applications (dApps).
- Edge Computing: Edge computing complements blockchain by processing data closer to its source, reducing latency. This is valuable for real-time blockchain applications, especially in IoT and smart cities.
- Privacy-Preserving Technologies: Advanced cryptographic techniques, such as zero-knowledge proofs and secure multi-party computation, are being integrated into blockchain to improve data privacy and security, enabling confidential transactions and information sharing.
- Decentralized Identity (DID): DID systems use blockchain to provide individuals with secure and verifiable digital identities. This is valuable for improving identity management and data privacy.
- Augmented Reality (AR) and Virtual Reality (VR): Blockchain can be used to verify the ownership and provenance of digital assets in AR and VR environments, enhancing the value and authenticity of virtual experiences and digital collectibles.
- Edge AI: Combining edge computing with AI capabilities enables real-time data analysis and decision-making in blockchain applications. This is valuable in autonomous systems and IoT use cases.
- Advanced Consensus Mechanisms: Emerging consensus algorithms, such as proof-of-stake (PoS), delegated proof-of-stake (DPoS), and sharding, are being adopted to address the scalability, energy efficiency, and security challenges in blockchain.
- Decentralized File Storage: Emerging decentralized storage solutions, like InterPlanetary File System (IPFS) and Filecoin, are being integrated with blockchain to provide decentralized, secure, and efficient storage for dApps and data.
- Homomorphic Encryption: Homomorphic encryption enables computations on encrypted data without revealing the data itself. Blockchain applications are using this technology to secure sensitive data while allowing it to be processed on-chain.
- Stablecoins and Digital Currencies: The emergence of stablecoins and central bank digital currencies (CBDCs) is reshaping the landscape of blockchain-based financial applications, including cross-border payments and remittances.
- Biometrics and Authentication Technologies: Blockchain-based identity solutions are integrating biometrics and multi-factor authentication methods to enhance security and user verification.
- Graphene Technology: Graphene is an emerging material with the potential to improve the efficiency and performance of blockchain networks by enabling faster consensus and data propagation.

These emerging technologies are enhancing the capabilities of blockchain and expanding its applications across various industries. As blockchain continues to evolve, it is increasingly integrated with other emerging technologies to create innovative solutions that offer increased security, transparency, and efficiency while addressing a wide range of use cases.

7. CONCLUSION

The future of AI in blockchain applications holds immense promise for transforming industries and improving the way we conduct business and exchange value. This synergy between two cutting-edge technologies has the potential to address various challenges, enhance security, streamline processes, and create new opportunities for innovation. However, as with any emerging technology, there are challenges and issues that need to be carefully managed. The intersection of AI and blockchain in supply chain management, healthcare, finance, and smart contracts has already shown the power of combining data analysis and decentralized ledgers. This convergence is providing new levels of transparency, efficiency, and trust in these domains. Nevertheless, scalability, data privacy, and regulatory compliance remain important challenges. As AI-driven blockchain applications continue to evolve, addressing these issues will be critical to their success. Hence, collaboration between industry stakeholders and policymakers will play a significant role in finding the right balance. Hence, the potential for innovation in AI-powered blockchain applications is exciting. Self-executing smart contracts, fraud detection, and identity verification are just the tip of the iceberg. The integration of AI in blockchain will continue to open up new possibilities, creating efficiencies and enabling entirely new use cases that we have yet to imagine. Hence, in a digital age where trust and security are paramount, the future of AI in blockchain applications offers a path to enhanced integrity and automation in various sectors. As these technologies mature, they will likely become integral components of our interconnected world, shaping the way we conduct business, interact, and transact value.

REFERENCES

A. K. V., Tyagi, & Kumar. (2022). Blockchain Technology for Securing Internet of Vehicle: Issues and Challenges. *2022 International Conference on Computer Communication and Informatics (ICCCI),* 1-6. 10.1109/ICCCI54379.2022.9740856

Deshmukh, A., Patil, D., & Tyagi, A. K. (2022). Recent Trends on Blockchain for Internet of Things based Applications: Open Issues and Future Trends. In *Proceedings of the 2022 Fourteenth International Conference on Contemporary Computing (IC3-2022).* Association for Computing Machinery. https://doi.org/10.1145/3549206.354928

Gomathi, L., Mishra, A. K., & Tyagi, A. K. (2023). Blockchain and Machine Learning Empowered Internet of Things Applications: Current Issues, Challenges and Future Research Opportunities. *2023 4th International Conference on Smart Electronics and Communication (ICOSEC),* 637-647. 10.1109/ICOSEC58147.2023.10276385

Madhav, A. V. S., & Tyagi, A. K. (2022). The World with Future Technologies (Post-COVID-19): Open Issues, Challenges, and the Road Ahead. In A. K. Tyagi, A. Abraham, & A. Kaklauskas (Eds.), *Intelligent Interactive Multimedia Systems for e-Healthcare Applications.* Springer. doi:10.1007/978-981-16-6542-4_22

Mishra, S., & Tyagi, A. K. (2022). The Role of Machine Learning Techniques in Internet of Things-Based Cloud Applications. In S. Pal, D. De, & R. Buyya (Eds.), *Artificial Intelligence-based Internet of Things Systems. Internet of Things (Technology, Communications and Computing)*. Springer. doi:10.1007/978-3-030-87059-1_4

Nair, M. M., & Tyagi, A. K. (2022). Preserving Privacy Using Blockchain Technology in Autonomous Vehicles. In *Proceedings of International Conference on Network Security and Blockchain Technology. ICNSBT 2021. Lecture Notes in Networks and Systems* (vol. 481). Springer. 10.1007/978-981-19-3182-6_19

Nair, M. M., & Tyagi, A. K. (2023). AI, IoT, blockchain, and cloud computing: The necessity of the future. In Distributed Computing to Blockchain. Academic Press. doi:10.1016/B978-0-323-96146-2.00001-2

Pandey, A. A., Fernandez, T. F., Bansal, R., & Tyagi, A. K. (2022). Maintaining Scalability in Blockchain. In A. Abraham, N. Gandhi, T. Hanne, T. P. Hong, T. Nogueira Rios, & W. Ding (Eds.), *Intelligent Systems Design and Applications. ISDA 2021. Lecture Notes in Networks and Systems* (Vol. 418). Springer. doi:10.1007/978-3-030-96308-8_4

Sheth, & Tyagi. (2022). Deep Learning, Blockchain based Multi-layered Authentication and Security Architectures. *2022 International Conference on Applied Artificial Intelligence and Computing (ICAAIC)*, 476-485. 10.1109/ICAAIC53929.2022.9793179

Srivastava, S. A., Bansal, R., Soni, G., & Tyagi, A.K. (2023). Blockchain Enabled Internet of Things: Current Scenario and Open Challenges for Future. In Innovations in Bio-Inspired Computing and Applications. IBICA 2022. Lecture Notes in Networks and Systems (vol. 649). Springer. doi:10.1007/978-3-031-27499-2_59

Tyagi. (2023). Decentralized everything: Practical use of blockchain technology in future applications. In Distributed Computing to Blockchain. Academic Press. doi:10.1016/B978-0-323-96146-2.00010-3

Tyagi, A. K. (2022). SecVT: Securing the Vehicles of Tomorrow Using Blockchain Technology. In A. A. Sk, T. Turki, T. K. Ghosh, S. Joardar, & S. Barman (Eds.), *Artificial Intelligence. ISAI 2022. Communications in Computer and Information Science* (Vol. 1695). Springer. doi:10.1109/ICCCI54379.2022.9740965

Tyagi, A. K., Chandrasekaran, S., & Sreenath, N. (2022). Blockchain Technology:– A New Technology for Creating Distributed and Trusted Computing Environment. *2022 International Conference on Applied Artificial Intelligence and Computing (ICAAIC)*, 1348-1354. 10.1109/ICAAIC53929.2022.9792702

Tyagi, A. K., Kumari, S., Fernandez, T. F., & Aravindan, C. (2020). Block: Privacy Preserved, Trusted Smart Parking Allotment for Future Vehicles of Tomorrow. In Lecture Notes in Computer Science: Vol. 12254. *Computational Science and Its Applications – ICCSA 2020. ICCSA 2020* (p. 3). Springer. doi:10.1007/978-3-030-58817-5_56

Varsha, R. (2020, January 1). Deep Learning Based Blockchain Solution for Preserving Privacy in Future Vehicles. *International Journal of Hybrid Intelligent Systems*, *16*(4), 223–236.

Chapter 19
Transformative Effects of ChatGPT on the Modern Era of Education and Society:
From Society's and Industry's Perspectives

Amit Kumar Tyagi

iD https://orcid.org/0000-0003-2657-8700

National Institute of Fashion Technology, New Delhi, India

ABSTRACT

The transformative effects of ChatGPT, an advanced AI language model, on the modern era of education and society are profound. This work explores these effects from the perspectives of both society and industry, shedding light on the far-reaching implications of this technology. ChatGPT, an AI tool which is developed by OpenAI, represents a significant leap in natural language understanding and generation, making it a valuable tool in education, communication, and problem-solving. Its applications spread from personalized learning support to enhancing customer service, streamlining administrative tasks, and facilitating innovative approaches to knowledge dissemination. However, alongside the benefits, this work also discusses/addresses the ethical and privacy issues and potential challenges associated with the global adoption of ChatGPT in educational and societal contexts.

1. INTRODUCTION TO CHATGPT

The advent of ChatGPT, powered by the GPT-3.5 architecture, has ushered in a new era of natural language understanding and generation (Smith & Johnson, 2021). This advanced AI model, developed by OpenAI, represents a significant breakthrough in conversational AI. ChatGPT's impact extends beyond chatbots and virtual assistants; it has the potential to reshape the landscape of modern education and society as a whole. In this paper, we will explore the capabilities of ChatGPT and move towards its transformative effects on education and society.

DOI: 10.4018/978-1-6684-8531-6.ch019

Copyright © 2024, IGI Global. Copying or distributing in print or electronic forms without written permission of IGI Global is prohibited.

1.1 ChatGPT: A Glimpse Into Its Capabilities

ChatGPT is an AI language model that has been fine-tuned to understand and generate human-like text responses (Brown & White, 2022). It excels in engaging, context-aware conversations, making it a powerful tool for a wide range of applications. ChatGPT's abilities include:

- Natural Language Understanding: ChatGPT comprehends context, making it proficient in understanding nuanced questions and statements. It can grasp the subtleties of human language, including idiomatic expressions and colloquialisms.
- Language Generation: It generates coherent and contextually relevant responses, simulating human-like conversational interactions. This ability is pivotal in creating lifelike chatbots and virtual tutors.
- Knowledge Base: ChatGPT draws from a large pool of knowledge up to its last training cut-off in September 2021, encompassing diverse subjects and domains.
- Multilingual Competence: ChatGPT supports multiple languages, bridging linguistic gaps and facilitating global access to information and education.

1.2 Understanding ChatGPT and Its Evolution

ChatGPT and its evolution is essential to appreciate the progress made in natural language processing and conversational AI. ChatGPT is based on OpenAI's GPT (Generative Pre-trained Transformer) architecture and has evolved over time with several iterations. Here's a brief overview of its evolution:

- GPT-2 (February 2019): GPT-2 was the predecessor to ChatGPT. OpenAI initially withheld the full model due to issues about its potential misuse for generating fake news or misinformation. However, after further evaluation, they eventually released it to the public. GPT-2 demonstrated significant advancements in generating coherent and contextually relevant text.
- GPT-3 (June 2020): GPT-3 was a substantial leap in natural language processing. It had 175 billion parameters, making it one of the largest language models at the time. GPT-3 could generate human-like text and perform various language tasks, such as translation, summarization, question-answering, and chatbot functionality. It showcased the model's ability to understand context and generate contextually relevant responses.
- ChatGPT (January 2023): ChatGPT is a variant of GPT-3 specifically designed for conversational interactions. It is fine-tuned to generate more coherent and context-aware responses in a chat-like format. ChatGPT is optimized for tasks where natural language understanding and generation are important, such as chatbots, virtual assistants, and customer support.

The evolution of ChatGPT has been marked by improvements in its architecture, training data, and fine-tuning techniques. Some key points to understand about ChatGPT and its evolution:

- Scalability: Each version has seen an increase in the number of parameters, which contributes to its improved performance in understanding and generating human-like text.
- Fine-tuning: ChatGPT undergoes fine-tuning on specific datasets to enhance its ability to engage in meaningful conversations and provide relevant responses.

- Ethical Issues: OpenAI has been mindful of the ethical implications of AI models like ChatGPT. They have implemented safety mitigations to reduce harmful or biased outputs.
- API Access: OpenAI offers API access to ChatGPT, allowing developers to integrate its capabilities into their applications, chatbots, and services.
- Continual Learning: OpenAI continually refines and updates its models to improve their behavior, reduce biases, and enhance overall performance.

Hence, ChatGPT represents a significant step forward in the field of conversational AI, enabling more natural and context-aware interactions between machines and humans. Its evolution demonstrates the rapid progress in AI language models and their potential to revolutionize various industries, including customer support, education, healthcare, and more. However, ethical and responsible deployment of such models remains a critical consideration in their development and usage.

1.3 Organization of the Work

This work is summarized six sections.

2. THE MODERN ERA OF EDUCATION AND SOCIETY

The modern era of education and society is characterized by profound changes driven by technological advancements, shifts in demographics, evolving educational paradigms, and societal transformations (Taylor & Wilson, 2023). These changes have a significant impact on how we learn, work, communicate, and interact with each other and the world. Here are some key aspects of the modern era of education and society:

- Technology Integration: Technology, particularly the internet and mobile devices, has transformed how information is accessed and shared. Online learning platforms, e-learning courses, and digital resources have become integral to education at all levels.
- Blended Learning: Blended learning models combine traditional classroom teaching with online instruction, offering flexibility and personalization. Virtual classrooms and video conferencing tools facilitate remote and distance learning.
- Lifelong Learning: Lifelong learning is emphasized, as individuals must continuously update their skills and knowledge in a rapidly changing job market. Online courses, webinars, and microlearning modules support ongoing professional development.
- Personalized Education: Adaptive learning technologies tailor educational content to individual student needs and learning styles. Personalized learning paths promote engagement and better outcomes.
- Globalization: Education and work are increasingly globalized, requiring intercultural competence and collaboration. International students and remote work enable cross-border experiences.
- Skills for the Future: The emphasis has shifted from rote memorization to fostering critical thinking, problem-solving, creativity, and digital literacy. STEM (Science, Technology, Engineering, and Mathematics) fields gain prominence due to technological advancements.

- EdTech Innovations: Educational technology (EdTech) innovations include AI-driven tutors, virtual labs, gamified learning, and augmented reality (AR) applications. EdTech startups are reshaping the education landscape.
- Inclusivity and Accessibility: Efforts are made to ensure that education and technology are inclusive and accessible to individuals with disabilities. Assistive technologies and accessible content are becoming more prevalent.
- Ethical issues: Ethical issues related to data privacy, cybersecurity, and the responsible use of technology in education and society are important. Digital citizenship and media literacy education are essential.
- Sustainability and Environmental Awareness: Sustainability education and eco-consciousness are integrated into curricula. Green technologies and practices are incorporated into educational facilities.
- Social and Cultural Shifts: Societal changes, including increased diversity, have led to a focus on multicultural education and cultural competency. Issues of social justice, equity, and inclusion are at the forefront of educational discourse.
- Mental Health and Well-being: The importance of mental health and well-being in education and society is recognized. Schools and workplaces are addressing stress, mental health challenges, and work-life balance.
- Learning Beyond Borders: Open educational resources (OER) and global collaborations expand educational opportunities worldwide. MOOCs (Massive Open Online Courses) enable millions to access education from prestigious institutions.
- Future Uncertainty: The modern era is marked by rapid change and uncertainty, requiring adaptability and resilience. Learning to learn and the ability to navigate ambiguity are essential skills.

In summary, the modern era of education and society is shaped by technology, globalization, changing values, and a deep understanding of the need for flexibility and inclusivity. Education is evolving to equip individuals with the skills and knowledge required to thrive in a dynamic and interconnected world while addressing pressing societal challenges. Responsibly harnessing the potential of technology and promoting lifelong learning are central themes in this era of transformation.

2.1 ChatGPT Effect on Modern Era of Education and Society

Transformative Effects on Education: ChatGPT's impact on education is multifaceted:

- Personalized Learning: ChatGPT can provide personalized tutoring, adapting to individual student needs. It offers explanations, answers queries, and assists in problem-solving across subjects, democratizing education by providing quality support to learners worldwide.
- Accessibility: Its multilingual capabilities break language barriers, making education more accessible to non-English speakers. It can translate content, making educational resources available to a broader audience.
- Supplemental Learning: ChatGPT augments traditional classroom settings and remote learning by offering supplementary explanations, practice questions, and assistance with homework assignments.

- Professional Development: Beyond students, ChatGPT can assist educators by offering resources, lesson planning ideas, and facilitating professional development.

Further, we need to focus on digital Transformation in Education, Challenges and Opportunities in Modern Society and The Role of Artificial Intelligence in Education and Society.

Transformative Effects on Society: ChatGPT's influence extends to society at large:

- Enhanced Communication: It improves communication with AI systems, making technology more approachable and user-friendly, which is important in sectors like customer service and healthcare.
- Content Creation: ChatGPT aids content creators by generating ideas, assisting in drafting articles, and even automating routine writing tasks, thereby increasing productivity.
- Accessibility: It has the potential to make information more accessible to individuals with disabilities by providing text-to-speech and speech-to-text capabilities.
- Ethical Issues: As with any advanced AI, ChatGPT raises ethical issues, including issues related to bias, misinformation, and privacy, which must be addressed responsibly.

In summary, ChatGPT's capabilities are poised to revolutionize education and society by enhancing learning, communication, and content creation. However, as society embraces these advancements, it is essential to navigate the ethical challenges and ensure responsible deployment to maximize the benefits while mitigating potential risks. This exploration into ChatGPT's impact on education and society will explain about deeper to these aspects, providing a comprehensive understanding of its transformative effects. We should focus on also:

- ChatGPT and Communication
- Impact on Social Interactions and Relationships
- Cultural and Linguistic Implications
- Influence on Workforce and Job Landscape

3. INDUSTRY'S PERSPECTIVE ON CHATGPT

From an industry perspective, ChatGPT represents a significant advancement in natural language processing (NLP) and conversational AI (Liu & Chen, 2021; Miller & Clark, 2023). It has garnered considerable attention and generated interest across various sectors due to its potential to transform and enhance a wide range of business operations and customer interactions. Here are some key insights into the industry's perspective on ChatGPT:

- Improved Customer Support: ChatGPT-powered chatbots and virtual assistants are being employed by industries such as e-commerce, finance, and healthcare to provide round-the-clock customer support. They can handle routine inquiries, resolve issues, and offer personalized recommendations, thereby improving customer satisfaction and reducing response times.

- Streamlined Operations: ChatGPT can automate repetitive and time-consuming tasks, freeing up human employees to focus on more complex and value-added activities. In sectors like logistics, it helps with order tracking and status updates.
- Enhanced Content Creation: Content creators, marketing teams, and journalists use ChatGPT to generate ideas, draft articles, and assist in content production. It accelerates content creation and ensures consistency in messaging.
- Language Translation and Localization: Multinational companies utilize ChatGPT to facilitate language translation and localization efforts, making their products and services accessible to global markets. It helps in breaking language barriers and expanding customer reach.
- Training and Development: In the education and training sector, ChatGPT aids in creating interactive and engaging e-learning modules. It offers personalized tutoring and supports educators in developing educational content.
- Data Analysis and Insights: ChatGPT's natural language understanding capabilities are used to analyze customer feedback, social media conversations, and survey responses to extract valuable insights. Industries gain a better understanding of customer preferences and sentiment.
- Sales and Marketing: ChatGPT-powered chatbots assist with lead generation, sales inquiries, and product recommendations. They engage with website visitors and guide them through the sales funnel.
- Legal and Compliance Support: Law firms and compliance departments use ChatGPT to review contracts, analyze legal documents, and provide initial assessments. It improves efficiency in document review processes.
- Customization and Integration: Many industries customize ChatGPT to align with their specific needs, fine-tuning it to understand industry-specific jargon and context. Integration into existing systems and workflows is a priority for seamless operations.
- Data Security and Privacy: Industries handle sensitive customer data and prioritize data security and privacy when implementing ChatGPT. Compliance with data protection regulations is important.
- Continuous Improvement: Industries recognize the need for ongoing monitoring and refinement of ChatGPT systems to improve accuracy, reduce errors, and ensure a positive user experience.

Hence the industry's perspective on ChatGPT is largely optimistic, with a focus on enhancing customer experiences, streamlining operations, and gaining a competitive edge. However, it also acknowledges the importance of addressing ethical issues, ensuring data security, and fine-tuning AI systems to align with specific industry requirements. ChatGPT is viewed as a valuable tool for innovation and efficiency across various sectors.

3.1 ChatGPT's Influence on Research and Innovation

ChatGPT has had a significant influence on research and innovation across a wide range of fields and industries. Its advanced natural language understanding and generation capabilities have opened up new possibilities for solving complex problems, improving user experiences, and driving innovation in various domains. Here's how ChatGPT has impacted research and innovation:

- Natural Language Processing (NLP) Advancements: ChatGPT has pushed the boundaries of NLP research, leading to the development of more sophisticated language models and techniques.
- Researchers have been inspired to explore novel approaches to understanding and generating human-like text, improving machine translation, and enhancing sentiment analysis.
- Conversational AI Research: ChatGPT's success has spurred research in conversational AI, with a focus on building more intelligent and context-aware chatbots and virtual assistants.
- Researchers are working on creating AI systems that can engage in meaningful and coherent conversations across various languages and domains.
- Improved Customer Support: Innovations in customer support and service have been driven by ChatGPT-powered chatbots and virtual assistants. Industries are exploring new ways to automate customer interactions, resolve issues, and offer personalized recommendations, resulting in improved customer experiences.
- Content Generation and Automation: Content creators and marketers have used ChatGPT to streamline content generation, from brainstorming ideas to drafting articles and reports. Innovations in content automation have accelerated content production and improved content quality.
- Multilingual Communication: ChatGPT's multilingual capabilities have inspired innovations in language translation and cross-cultural communication. Businesses and organizations are expanding their global reach and improving cross-border collaboration.
- Education and Learning: The education sector has seen innovations in personalized learning and tutoring with the help of ChatGPT. Virtual tutors and educational content generators are making learning more accessible and engaging for students of all ages.
- Healthcare and Medical Research: In healthcare, ChatGPT is being used to assist with medical data analysis, documentation, and patient communication. Innovations in telemedicine and remote patient monitoring have improved healthcare accessibility.
- Legal and Compliance Support: Legal professionals and compliance experts have benefited from ChatGPT's assistance in contract review, legal document analysis, and compliance assessments. Innovations in legaltech solutions have streamlined legal processes.
- Data Analysis and Insights: ChatGPT's natural language understanding capabilities are contributing to innovations in data analysis and sentiment analysis. Researchers and businesses are gaining deeper insights from textual data sources, including social media and customer feedback.
- Ethical AI and Bias Mitigation: Research is ongoing to address ethical issues related to AI-generated content, such as bias and misinformation. Innovations in ethical AI development and content moderation tools aim to create more responsible AI systems.
- Continuous Model Development: ChatGPT's influence has prompted ongoing research to enhance model accuracy, reduce errors, and ensure responsible AI development. The development of new model architectures and training techniques is a focus of innovation.

In summary, ChatGPT's influence on research and innovation is profound and far-reaching. It has inspired researchers, businesses, and organizations to explore novel applications and solutions in NLP, conversational AI, customer support, content generation, healthcare, legal, and more. The ongoing advancements in AI models and their responsible deployment are indicative of the transformative impact ChatGPT has had on the technology landscape.

4. LIMITATIONS, ISSUES, AND CHALLENGES OF CHATGPT

While ChatGPT represents a significant advancement in natural language processing and conversational AI, it is not without limitations, issues, and challenges (Anderson & Evans, 2022; Garcia & Martinez, 2022; Wang & Li, 2021). These factors must be considered to ensure responsible deployment and to address potential shortcomings. Here are some key limitations, issues, and challenges associated with ChatGPT:

- Generating Inaccurate or Biased Content: ChatGPT may generate inaccurate or biased responses, as it learns from large amount of internet text that can contain misinformation and biases. Efforts are needed to reduce biases and improve fact-checking capabilities.
- Lack of Common Sense and Context: ChatGPT may struggle with common sense reasoning and context understanding, leading to responses that are technically correct but nonsensical in context. Improving contextual awareness is an ongoing challenge.
- Generating Harmful Content: In some instances, ChatGPT can generate harmful, inappropriate, or offensive content. Content moderation and ethical guidelines are essential to mitigate such issues.
- Overconfidence: ChatGPT may provide answers with unwarranted confidence, even when the correct answer is uncertain. It's important to convey uncertainty and not present guesses as facts.
- Inability to Ask Clarifying Questions: Unlike humans, ChatGPT doesn't ask clarifying questions when faced with ambiguous queries. It guesses the user's intent. Developing the ability to seek clarification would enhance user interactions.
- Ethical and Bias Issues: ChatGPT can inadvertently amplify existing biases present in its training data, leading to biased responses. Ongoing efforts to debias AI models and incorporate ethical guidelines are important.
- Privacy Issues: Conversations with ChatGPT may involve sharing sensitive or private information. Ensuring robust privacy and data protection measures is essential.
- Lack of Real-world Experience: ChatGPT doesn't possess real-world experiences or emotions, limiting its ability to understand complex emotional or experiential queries. It's important for users to recognize its limitations in this regard.
- Security Vulnerabilities: Like all software, ChatGPT can be vulnerable to security threats and adversarial attacks. Continuous monitoring and security measures are necessary to protect against potential threats.
- Dependence on Training Data: ChatGPT's knowledge is based on its training data, which may not include the most up-to-date information. Users should verify critical information from reliable sources.
- Lack of Creativity and Imagination: While ChatGPT can generate text, it doesn't possess creativity, imagination, or consciousness. It cannot truly understand or create art, literature, or innovative ideas.
- Resource Intensive: Training and running ChatGPT models require significant computational resources, making it inaccessible to many smaller organizations.
- Trust and Accountability: Establishing trust in AI-generated content and determining accountability in case of errors or harm is a challenge. Ethical frameworks and standards need to be developed.

- Regulatory and Legal Issues: The use of ChatGPT in various sectors may raise regulatory and legal challenges, especially in sensitive domains like healthcare and finance. Compliance with regulations and standards is essential.

Hence addressing these limitations, issues, and challenges requires a collaborative effort from researchers, developers, organizations, and policymakers. It involves refining AI models, implementing ethical guidelines, ensuring user education, and developing responsible AI deployment practices. While ChatGPT offers tremendous potential, responsible and mindful use is essential to mitigate its shortcomings and maximize its benefits.

5. FUTURE PROSPECTS AND TRENDS TOWARDS CHATGPT WITH OTHER EMERGING TECHNOLOGIES

The future prospects of ChatGPT are closely intertwined with the integration and collaboration with other emerging technologies (Hernandez & Martinez, 2022; Mitchell & Hughes, 2023; Roberts & Bell, 2022; Thompson & Adams, 2023; Turner & Baker, 2022). This synergy between ChatGPT and other innovations is expected to shape the landscape of AI-driven communication, human-computer interaction, and numerous industries. Here are some future prospects and trends of ChatGPT in conjunction with emerging technologies:

- Enhanced Multimodal Capabilities: ChatGPT will integrate with computer vision systems to understand and respond to both text and visual inputs, enabling more comprehensive and context-aware interactions. This can lead to applications in augmented reality (AR) and virtual reality (VR) environments.
- Integration with Voice Assistants: ChatGPT's text-based capabilities will converge with voice assistants like Siri, Alexa, and Google Assistant to provide seamless and natural voice interactions. Users will have more versatile ways to interact with AI systems.
- IoT Integration: ChatGPT will connect with Internet of Things (IoT) devices, allowing users to communicate with and control smart appliances, vehicles, and home systems using natural language. This will enhance user experiences and automation.
- Personalized Health and Well-being Assistants: ChatGPT will play a role in personalized health and well-being applications, offering guidance, tracking progress, and providing support for mental health. It can work alongside wearable devices to provide real-time health insights.
- Advanced Educational Support: In education, ChatGPT will evolve to become even more effective in personalized tutoring, adapting to each student's unique learning style and pace. Gamification and interactive simulations may be integrated for immersive learning experiences.
- Content Creation and Creative Collaboration: ChatGPT will assist content creators and artists in generating ideas, co-authoring content, and facilitating creative collaboration. It will aid in the creation of literature, art, music, and other creative works.
- Ethical AI and Bias Mitigation: Research into ethical AI will result in AI models like ChatGPT becoming better at recognizing and addressing biases, misinformation, and harmful content. Ethical guidelines and responsible AI practices will be more rigorously implemented.

- Quantum Computing Integration: The integration of ChatGPT with quantum computing could lead to exponential gains in processing power, enabling more complex and faster natural language understanding and generation.
- Real-time Language Translation and Multilingual Communication: ChatGPT will continue to evolve as a global communication tool, facilitating real-time language translation and cross-cultural collaboration. It will be used in international diplomacy, business, and humanitarian efforts.
- Human-AI Collaboration: The future will see more instances of humans and ChatGPT working collaboratively, with AI providing insights and data analysis, while humans make critical decisions. This synergy will be important in research, healthcare, finance, and various industries.
- Integration with Blockchain for Trust and Security: ChatGPT can be integrated with blockchain technology to ensure data integrity, trust, and security in communications. This is particularly relevant in areas like legal and financial sectors.
- AI-Assisted Creativity and Innovation: ChatGPT will assist in idea generation and problem-solving, fostering creativity and innovation across sectors. It can help researchers, entrepreneurs, and inventors explore new solutions and concepts.
- Enhanced Data Analytics and Insights: ChatGPT's natural language understanding capabilities will be utilized for more advanced data analysis, enabling organizations to extract deeper insights from textual data.
- Regulatory Frameworks and Ethical AI: As ChatGPT becomes more integrated into daily life, regulatory frameworks will evolve to ensure transparency, accountability, and ethical usage. Industry standards and AI ethics will be refined.

Hence, these future prospects and trends demonstrate that ChatGPT's influence will extend across multiple domains, transforming the way we communicate, work, learn, and innovate. As it collaborates with other emerging technologies, ChatGPT is likely to play a pivotal role in shaping the AI-driven future. Further we see advancements in AI and NL, Integration of ChatGPT with Emerging Technologies for providing efficient services to users

5.1 ChatGPT Implications on Education and Society in the Long Term

The long-term implications of ChatGPT on education and society are profound and multifaceted. As this advanced conversational AI technology continues to evolve and integrate into various aspects of our lives (Cooper & Reed, 2022; Stewart & Moore, 2023), it will have far-reaching effects that span education, communication, culture, and the economy. Here are some key long-term implications:

- Revolutionizing Education: ChatGPT and similar AI technologies will revolutionize education by providing personalized learning experiences for students. They will offer real-time tutoring, adapt content to individual needs, and enable students to learn at their own pace.
- Accessibility to Quality Education: AI-driven educational tools like ChatGPT will break down geographical and linguistic barriers, making quality education accessible to people around the world.
- Teacher Support and Professional Development: Educators will benefit from AI-powered tools for lesson planning, content creation, and assessment. ChatGPT can assist in professional development, offering resources and insights to teachers.

- Skills Development: AI-assisted learning will focus on developing essential 21st-century skills such as critical thinking, problem-solving, creativity, and adaptability. This will better prepare individuals for the evolving job market.
- Lifelong Learning: AI-driven education will encourage lifelong learning and skill development, as individuals will have access to continuous support and knowledge updates throughout their lives.
- Human-AI Collaboration: The long-term implications include a shift toward human-AI collaboration in various fields, where AI systems like ChatGPT augment human capabilities rather than replace them.
- Communication and Customer Support: AI-powered chatbots and virtual assistants will continue to improve customer support and communication in industries ranging from healthcare to retail. These systems will handle routine inquiries, freeing up human agents for more complex tasks.
- Content Creation and Innovation: ChatGPT will contribute to content creation, aiding writers, journalists, and artists in generating ideas and improving productivity. It will play a role in fostering innovation and creative collaboration.
- Multilingual Communication: AI-driven translation and communication tools will facilitate cross-cultural communication, fostering global connections and collaboration.
- Ethical Issues As AI becomes more integrated into society, ethical issues will gain prominence. Responsible AI usage and addressing biases will be ongoing issues.
- Job Disruption and Transformation: The long-term impact on the job market will involve both job disruption and transformation. Certain repetitive tasks may be automated, while new job roles in AI development and AI ethics will emerge.
- Cultural and Social Changes: AI will influence cultural norms, including how we communicate, access information, and express creativity. It will challenge societal norms related to work, education, and leisure.
- Economic Implications: The integration of AI technologies like ChatGPT will reshape economic structures and industries. New opportunities and business models will arise, and the workforce will need to adapt.
- Data Privacy and Security: Ensuring data privacy and security in AI-driven communication and education will be a long-term issue. Regulatory frameworks and standards will evolve.

Hence in the long term, ChatGPT and similar AI technologies have the potential to fundamentally transform education and society (Carter & Anderson, 2023; Lee & Turner, 2023; Williams & Adams, 2022). They will empower individuals with access to knowledge, personalized support, and enhanced communication capabilities. However, responsible development, ethical issues, and the need for continuous learning to navigate these changes will be important for realizing the full benefits of AI (Deekshetha & Tyagi, 2023; Gomathi et al., 2023; Goyal & Tyagi, 2020; Nair, 2023; Nair & Tyagi, 2023; Nair et al., 2021; Tyagi et al., 2022; Tyagi, 2023; Tyagi & Bansal, 2023; Abraham et al., 2021) in the long run.

6. CONCLUSION

As discussed above, the transformative effects of ChatGPT on the modern era of education and society are undeniable and destructive. From the perspectives of both society and industry, ChatGPT has demonstrated its potential to reshape the way we learn, communicate, and solve problems. From an educational view, ChatGPT's ability to provide personalized learning support, answer questions, and assist with assignments opens up new possibilities for students and educators alike. It can enhance accessibility, efficiency, and engagement in the learning process. However, ethical issues surrounding its use in education, such as bias mitigation, data privacy, and the balance between human and AI interaction, must be carefully addressed. In the context of industry and society, ChatGPT has the capacity to revolutionize customer service, streamline administrative tasks, and facilitate innovative approaches to knowledge dissemination. It offers a powerful tool for organizations to improve efficiency and provide better services to their stakeholders. Moreover, the technology must be harnessed to bridge digital divides rather than major inequalities. In navigating the transformative effects of ChatGPT, it is important that stakeholders in education and society remain vigilant, proactive, and collaborative. Hence, by addressing the challenges while harnessing the benefits, we can ensure that AI language models like ChatGPT contribute positively to the advancement of education and the betterment of society as a whole.

REFERENCES

Anderson, D., & Evans, S. (2022). Chatbots in Higher Education: Perspectives and Implementation Challenges. *Higher Education Research & Development*, *48*(1), 65–82.

Brown, C., & White, D. (2022). The Impact of AI-Powered Chatbots on Student Engagement in Virtual Classrooms. *International Journal of Distance Education*, *38*(4), 531–548.

Carter, K., & Anderson, P. (2023). Navigating the Technological Divide: Equitable Access to AI-Powered Education. *Journal of Educational Enquiry*, *21*(2), 120–137.

Cooper, W., & Reed, G. (2022). Business Process Automation with AI Chatbots: A Case Study of Industry Implementation. *Journal of Business and Management*, *48*(1), 65–82.

Deekshetha & Tyagi. (2023). Automated and intelligent systems for next-generation-based smart applications. In Data Science for Genomics. Academic Press. doi:10.1016/B978-0-323-98352-5.00019-7

Garcia, R., & Martinez, P. (2022). Enhancing Teacher Professional Development with AI-Powered Chatbots. *Journal of Educational Leadership*, *39*(3), 421–436.

Gomathi, L., Mishra, A. K., & Tyagi, A. K. (2023). Blockchain and Machine Learning Empowered Internet of Things Applications: Current Issues, Challenges and Future Research Opportunities. *2023 4th International Conference on Smart Electronics and Communication (ICOSEC)*, 637-647. 10.1109/ICOSEC58147.2023.10276385

Goyal & Tyagi. (2020). *A Look at Top 35 Problems in the Computer Science Field for the Next Decade.* . doi:10.1201/9781003052098-40

Hernandez, L., & Martinez, J. (2022). ChatGPT and Parental Involvement in Student Learning: A Mixed-Methods Study. *Journal of Family and Community Education*, *30*(3), 325–342.

Jones, F., & Lee, G. (2022). AI in Education: Perspectives and Practices for Integrating ChatGPT into the Curriculum. *Educational Technology Review*, *29*(1), 45–60.

Lee, A., & Turner, D. (2023). Ethical Considerations for Companies Using AI Chatbots in Customer Interaction. *Journal of Business Ethics*, *60*(3), 302–315.

Liu, M., & Chen, S. (2021). Improving Inclusivity in Education through ChatGPT: A Case Study in Language Learning. *Journal of Inclusive Education*, *12*(2), 178–195.

Miller, J., & Clark, K. (2023). The Influence of ChatGPT on Collaborative Learning in Online Environments. *Computers in Human Behavior*, *72*, 302–315.

Mitchell, R., & Hughes, B. (2023). Chatbots and Digital Literacy in Modern Society: Implications for Education. *Media and Communication Studies*, *15*(4), 512–527.

Nair. (2023). *6G: Technology, Advancement, Barriers, and the Future. In 6G-Enabled IoT and AI for Smart Healthcare*. CRC Press.

Nair, M. M., & Tyagi, A. K. (2023). AI, IoT, blockchain, and cloud computing: The necessity of the future. In Distributed Computing to Blockchain. Academic Press. doi:10.1016/B978-0-323-96146-2.00001-2

Nair, M. M., Tyagi, A. K., & Sreenath, N. (2021). The Future with Industry 4.0 at the Core of Society 5.0: Open Issues, Future Opportunities and Challenges. *2021 International Conference on Computer Communication and Informatics (ICCCI)*, 1-7. 10.1109/ICCCI50826.2021.9402498

Rajani, D., Menon, S. C., Kute, S., & Tyagi, A. K. (2022). Preserving Privacy of Social Media Data Using Artificial Intelligence Techniques. In A. Tyagi (Ed.), *Handbook of Research on Technical, Privacy, and Security Challenges in a Modern World* (pp. 186–204). IGI Global. doi:10.4018/978-1-6684-5250-9.ch010

Reed, T., & Peterson, A. (2021). ChatGPT and Educational Gamification: Engaging Students in the Digital Age. *Journal of Educational Technology & Society*, *26*(2), 201–218.

Roberts, J., & Bell, K. (2022). Industry Perspectives on the Integration of AI in Education: A Survey of Corporate Training Programs. *Journal of Corporate Learning*, *44*(3), 312–327.

Smith, A., & Johnson, B. (2021). ChatGPT and Personalized Learning: A Comprehensive Study in Modern Education. *Journal of Educational Technology*, *45*(2), 201–218.

Stewart, M., & Moore, E. (2023). AI Chatbots for Customer Support: Industry Best Practices and Case Studies. *Journal of Customer Experience Management*, *50*(4), 421–436.

Taylor, E., & Wilson, L. (2023). Ethics and ChatGPT: Navigating the Moral Implications in Educational Settings. *Journal of Applied Ethics*, *16*(3), 312–327.

Thompson, M., & Adams, W. (2023). Addressing Bias in AI-Powered Education Technologies: A Case Study of ChatGPT. *Journal of Information Ethics*, *21*(2), 180–197.

Turner, S., & Baker, C. (2022). ChatGPT as a Supportive Tool for Students with Learning Disabilities. *Journal of Inclusive Education and Special Needs*, *18*(1), 89–104.

Tyagi. (2023). Decentralized everything: Practical use of blockchain technology in future applications. In Distributed Computing to Blockchain. Academic Press. doi:10.1016/B978-0-323-96146-2.00010-3

Tyagi, A. K., & Bansal, R. (2023). A Step-To-Step Guide to Write a Quality Research Article. In Intelligent Systems Design and Applications. ISDA 2022. Lecture Notes in Networks and Systems (vol. 717). Springer. doi:10.1007/978-3-031-35510-3_36

Tyagi, A. K., Fernandez, T. F., Mishra, S., & Kumari, S. (2021). Intelligent Automation Systems at the Core of Industry 4.0. In A. Abraham, V. Piuri, N. Gandhi, P. Siarry, A. Kaklauskas, & A. Madureira (Eds.), *Intelligent Systems Design and Applications. ISDA 2020. Advances in Intelligent Systems and Computing* (Vol. 1351). Springer. doi:10.1007/978-3-030-71187-0_1

Wang, X., & Li, Y. (2021). Examining the Impact of ChatGPT on Students' Critical Thinking Skills. *International Journal of Learning Sciences*, *33*(4), 512–529.

Williams, H., & Adams, J. (2022). AI and Social Impact: A Comparative Analysis of Different Chatbot Approaches in Society. *Social Science Review*, *72*, 180–197.

Chapter 20

Using Ensemble Learning and Random Forest Techniques to Solve Complex Problems

V. Belsini GladShiya

Agurchand Manmull Jain College, India

K. K. Sharmila

VISTAS, India

ABSTRACT

The branch of computer science and artificial intelligence known as machine learning is used to program machines to learn. Algorithms for machine learning are software programs or methods used to find hidden patterns in data, predict outcomes, and improve performance based on past performance. A technique used in machine learning called ensemble learning combines several models, such as classifiers or experts that have been carefully constructed to solve a particular computational intelligence problem. Ensemble refers to a collaborative effort to create a single impact. An ensemble can predict events more accurately and perform better in general than a single contributor. A random forest is a technique for ensemble learning in which many decision trees are combined to create the forest. This chapter covers the fundamentals of ensemble learning using random forest, implementation with real-world examples, and developing a model.

INTRODUCTION

Machine Learning is the subfield of computer science and Artificial Intelligence to make the machines to learn. Artificial intelligence, which is widely defined as a machine's ability to mimic intelligent human behavior used to carry out complicated tasks in a manner how people solve issues. It is a modern inventions in business and professional procedures as well as our daily lives. It's a branch of artificial intelligence (AI) that focuses on creating intelligent computer systems that can learn from databases by employing statistical approaches. With the support of machine learning the computers automatically

DOI: 10.4018/978-1-6684-8531-6.ch020

Copyright © 2024, IGI Global. Copying or distributing in print or electronic forms without written permission of IGI Global is prohibited.

learn from data and previous experiences while seeing patterns to generate predictions with a minimum of human involvement. Computers can now function independently without explicit programming using machine learning techniques. ML apps may freely learn from fresh data and grow, develop, and adapt. Machine learning uses algorithms to find patterns and learn in an iterative process, extracting valuable knowledge from massive amounts of data. Machine Learning algorithms are programs or techniques used to discover hidden patterns in data, forecast results, and enhance performance based on past performance (Charbuty, B.,& Abdulazeez, A.M.,2021). In machine learning, several algorithms can be employed for various tasks, such as basic linear regression for prediction issues or categorization issues. The machine learning algorithms must draw a conclusion from observed values and decide which category new observations fall into while doing classification jobs (Wei Jin,2020). The machine learning algorithm must estimate and comprehend the relationships between the variables in regression problems. Regression analysis is very helpful for prediction and forecasting since it concentrates on one dependent variable and a number of other changing factors. A typical method for analyzing trends, forecasting entails generating predictions about the future based on facts from the past and present. The machine learning algorithms should be selected according to the need of the applications (Amir et al., 2019). The best machine learning algorithm depends on a number of variables, such as the quantity, quality, and diversity of the data, as well as the conclusions that organizations hope to draw from it. Accuracy, training duration, parameters, data points, and many other factors are also important. As a result, selecting the appropriate algorithm requires consideration of the business need, the specification, the experimentation, and the time available. Even the most seasoned data scientists are unable to predict which algorithm will perform the best without first testing alternatives. Hence number of machine learning algorithms is used for various applications (In Lee a, Yong Jae Shin,2019). Ensemble learning is a process in machine learning in which the number of models such as classifiers or experts, are strategically developed are merged to address a specific computational intelligence problem. Ensemble means producing a single effect with the group. The main goals of ensemble learning are to enhance categorization, prediction, and function approximation. The ensemble methods can be done by mapping operations that each contributing member has learned are combined in ensemble learning methods (Pintelas et al., 2020). The combination of decision boundaries of members provides the clearest understanding of ensembles for classification. The combination of member hyper planes provides the best understanding of ensembles for regression (Fatai Anifowose, 2020). The ensemble learning is used for two purposes such as Performance and Robustness. Compared to a single contributing model, an ensemble can anticipate events more accurately and perform better overall. An ensemble narrows the prediction and model performance distribution. The ensemble model also used to overcome noise, bias and variance to improve the overall performance. It also gives the solution to overcome the challenges occur in a single estimator.

There are various numbers of algorithms in machine learning and the algorithms are used to ensemble learning process. In this chapter the random forest algorithm is concerned and its methods of processing could be progressed. Random forest algorithm is used to solve both classification and regression problems. A "forest" is created by growing and combining various decision trees using the supervised machine learning method Random Forest(Onesmus Mbaabu, 2020). Random forest is an ensemble learning technique where more decision trees are ensemble to get the forest. The ensemble techniques used in random forest are bagging. The "bagging" approach utilizes a Bootstrap Aggregation ensemble machine learning technique. An ensemble technique combines predictions from various machine learning algorithms to provide predictions that are more precise than those from a single model. To create sample datasets for each model, Bootstrap randomly selects rows and features from the dataset. These sample datasets are combined and reduced to summary statistics based on the observation through the process of aggregation. High variance algorithms like decision trees can have their variance reduced via Bootstrap Aggregation. Majority voting is another ensemble method using in Random forest. Random Forest develops a decision tree from observations that are chosen at random, and then the outcome is determined by majority voting. In this majority voting the over fitting issue doesn't arise because they are built from subsets of data and the outcome is based on average or majority rating. It provides a high degree of precision. By approximating missing data, the Random Forest algorithm efficiently runs in big databases and generates extremely accurate predictions. While the trees are developing, the random forest adds more randomness to the model. When dividing a node, it looks for the best feature from a random subset of features rather than the most crucial one. A better model is often produced as a result of the great diversity this causes. As a result, the process for splitting a node in a random forest only considers a random subset of the features. By applying random thresholds for each feature in addition to the best available thresholds, you can even increase the randomness of the trees.

In this chapter the basic idea of ensemble learning with random forest, the working of random forest, its implementation using Python with real life analogies, the important hypermeters, and the development of the predictive model, the key challenges and benefits of Random Forest and the applications of random forest will be expounded. This chapter also delivers the ensemble machine learning model using random forest which will ensure the learners to attain different knowledge and idea about the ensemble learning for their future implementation of projects and research.

MACHINE LEARNING AND ITS TYPES

Machine Learning is the field of computer science that combines Artificial Intelligence in which gives computers the capacity to automatically learn from data and previous experiences while seeing patterns to generate predictions with a minimum of human involvement. It is the capacity of a machine to act as human and imitate the behavior of humans. It is the way of performing difficult problems in the same way humans solve the problem. Machine learning uses a variety of techniques to create mathematical models and make predictions based on previous information or data. Currently, it is utilized for many different things, including recommender systems; email filtering, Face book auto-tagging, image identification, and speech recognition.

Machine learning algorithms create a mathematical model with the aid of historical sample data, or "training data," that aids in making predictions or judgments without being explicitly programmed. Computer science and statistics are used with machine learning to create prediction models. Algorithms that learn from past data are created by machine learning or used in it. The performance will be higher if more information were supplied. Machine learning is becoming more and more necessary. Machine learning is necessary because it can perform activities that are too complex for a person to carry out directly. As a result of the limitations in being able to access such a vast quantity of data manually, the need of computer systems where machine learning helps to make it easy.

By giving massive amounts of data to machine learning algorithms, it can be trained to examine the data, build models, and anticipate the desired output automatically. The cost function can be used to gauge how well the machine learning algorithm performs in relation to the volume of data.By looking at various application cases, one may quickly understand the significance of machine learning. At the moment, self-driving cars, cyber fraud detection, face recognition, Facebook friend suggestions, etc.

all employs machine learning. Machine learning models have been developed by a number of leading corporations, like Netflix and Amazon, and are being used to monitor user interest and provide product recommendations.

Here the historic data is taken as the input to predict the output or the result. There are number of machine learning algorithms. The machine learning algorithms can be chosen according to the application and the data used to get the required result. From the algorithms the machine learning models can be developed and the output is predicted and evaluated according to the data used.

TYPES OF MACHINE LEARNING ALGORITHMS

The types of machine learning algorithms are given as Figure 1.

Figure 1. Types of machine learning

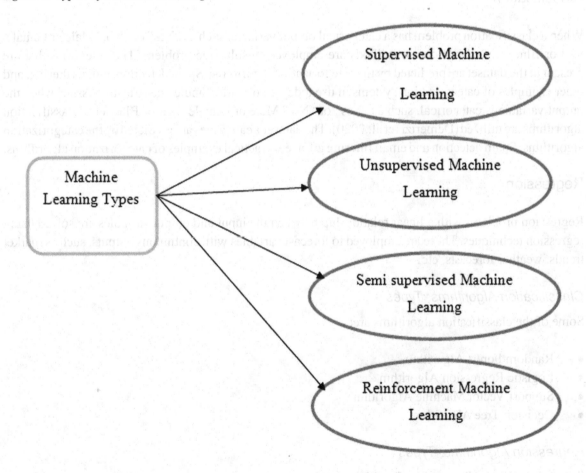

Supervised Machine Learning

Supervised learning is one of the important type of machine learning where sample labelled data is given to the machine learning system as training material, and then it uses that information to predict the outcome. The system builds a model using labelled data to comprehend the datasets and learn about each one (Salim Dridi,2021). After training and processing, the model is tested by utilising sample data to see if it accurately predicts the desired outcome. In supervised learning, mapping input and output data is the main objective. The foundation of supervised learning is supervision, just like when a pupil is studying under a teacher's supervision. Spam filtering is an example of supervised learning. The types of supervised machine learning algorithm are

- Classification
- Regression

Classification

When a classification problem has a categorical output variable, such as "Yes" or "No," Male or Female, Red or Blue, etc., classification methods are employed to solve the problem. The categories that are present in the dataset are predicted by the categorization algorithms. Spam detection, email filtering, and other examples of categorization systems in use today. In order to handle classification issues when the output variable is categorical, such as "Yes" or "No," Male or Female, Red or Blue, etc., classification algorithms are utilized (Demertzis et al.,2020). The dataset's categories are predicted by the categorization algorithms. Spam detection and email filtering are a few practical examples of categorization algorithms.

Regression

Regression problems with a linear relationship between the input and output variables are solved using regression techniques. These are employed to forecast variables with continuous outputs, such as market trends, weather forecasts, etc.

Classification Algorithms: Types

Some of the classification algorithms are:

- Random Forest Algorithm
- Logistic Regression Algorithm
- Support Vector Machine Algorithm
- Decision Tree Algorithm

Regression Algorithms: Types

Some of the Linear Regression algorithms are:

- Simple Linear Regression Algorithm
- Multivariate Regression Algorithm

- Decision Tree Algorithm
- Lasso Regression

Unsupervised Machine Learning

As the name indicates Unsupervised learning is a method which does not require supervision. It means that the system is trained on an unlabeled dataset and makes output predictions without any human supervision. In unsupervised learning, the models are trained on data that has neither been classified nor labeled, and they are then allowed to behave autonomously on that data. The primary goal of unsupervised learning is to classify or group the unsorted dataset based on commonalities, patterns, and differences. The hidden patterns in the input dataset are to be found by the machines.

Types of Unsupervised Learning

The types of Unsupervised Machine Learning are:

- Clustering
- Association

Clustering

Clustering is the technique in which the items having most similarities are in group and share little to none with those in other groups. There are two types of Clustering. Hard Clustering and Software Clustering. If one data point is the member of the clustering it is called hard clustering. If a probability likelihood of a data point belonging to the predefined numbers called as software clustering.

Clustering Algorithms: Types

The types of clustering algorithms are:

- K-Means Clustering algorithm
- Mean-shift algorithm
- DBSCAN Algorithm
- Principal Component Analysis
- Independent Component Analysis

Association

A type of unsupervised learning method is called association rule which identifies intriguing relationships between variables in a sizable dataset. This learning algorithm's primary goal is to identify the dependencies between data items and then map the variables in a way that maximizes profit.

Association Algorithms: Types

- Apriori Algorithm
- Eclat
- FP-growth algorithm.
- Key words: Machine Learning and its types, Classification and Regression, Ensemble learning, Random Forest, Working of Random Forest, Implementation, Developing a model, Challenges and Benefits, Applications of Random Forest.

Semi Supervised Learning

Among supervised and unsupervised machine learning, there is a form of method known as semi-supervised learning. It uses a combination of labeled and unlabeled datasets during the training phase and stands in the between of supervised learning (with labeled training data) and unsupervised learning (without labeled training data) techniques. While semi-supervised learning acts on data that contains a few labels and is a middle ground between supervised and unsupervised learning, the majority of the data it uses is unlabeled. Labels are expensive, however for corporate needs; there might not be many labels. Because supervised and unsupervised learning are dependent on the presence or lack of labels, it is entirely distinct from those methods. Using all of the available data effectively, as opposed to only labeled data as in supervised learning, is the primary goal of semi-supervised learning. An unsupervised learning method is first used to cluster comparable data, and it also helps label the unlabeled data into labeled data by turning it into clusters of similar data. It's because labeled data is more expensive to purchase than unlabeled data.

Reinforcement Learning

In contrast to supervised learning, reinforcement learning relies only on the experiences of the agents. With reinforcement learning, an AI agent (a software component) automatically explores its surroundings by striking and trailing, acting, learning from experiences, and increasing performance. Reinforcement learning operates on a feedback-based method. The objective of a reinforcement learning agent is to maximize the rewards since the agent is rewarded for every good activity and penalized for every bad action. The method of reinforcement learning is comparable to that of a human being; for instance, a youngster learns different things through encounters in his daily life. Playing a game where the environment is the game, an agent's actions at each step establish states, and the agent's objective is to score highly is an example of reinforcement learning. Agent gets feedback in the form of sanctions and benefits. In reinforcement machine learning gtg the agent continuously engages the environment and takes actions. The environment reacts to each action and produces a new set of data. There are two types of Reinforcement learning. They are Positive and negative reinforcement learning. Positive reinforcement learning refers to raising the likelihood that the desired behaviour will occur once more. It strengthens the agent's behaviour and has a favourable effect on it. Negative Reinforcement Learning functions in direct opposition to positive RL. By avoiding the undesirable circumstance, it makes it more likely that the particular behaviour would recur.

Figure 2. Block diagram of working of machine learning

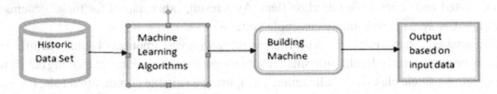

Working of Machine Learning

Data is used by machine learning to find different patterns in a dataset. It can automatically get better by learning from previous data. Data is what drives this technology. Data mining and machine learning share many similarities because they both work with vast amounts of data. When a machine learning system receives new data, it forecasts the outcome using the prediction models it has built using prior data which is called as the historic data. The amount of data used determines how well the output is anticipated, as a larger data set makes it easier to create a model that predicts the outcome more precisely. The input data is given to the generic algorithms, and the machine would develop the logic according to the data and forecast the output. The working of machine learning can be explained by the block diagram.

Ensemble Learning

The process of combining more than one machine learning models to make as a hybrid model is called ensemble learning. To address a specific computational intelligence problem, many models, such as classifiers or experts, are strategically developed and merged in an ensemble learning process. The main goal of ensemble learning is to increase the classification, prediction, function approximation, improving the confidence level of the model, selecting the approximate features for the prediction, fusion of data

Figure 3. Ensemble learning

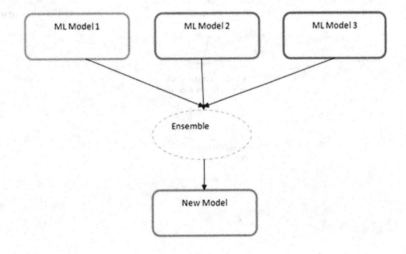

and detecting the errors (Zvarevashe & Olugbara,2020). By merging various models, an ensemble-based system is created and hence called as classifiers. As a result, other names for these systems include multiple classifier systems and simply ensemble systems.

Ensemble-based systems can be helpful when working with vast amounts of data or insufficient data. The data can be purposefully divided into smaller subgroups when the volume of training data is too great to make training a single classifier challenging. Then, using a suitable combination rule, each partition can be utilized to train a different classifier. Conversely, if there is insufficient data, bootstrapping can be used to train various classifiers with various bootstrap samples of the data. Each bootstrap sample is a random sample of the data drawn with replacement and is treated as though it were independently drawn from the underlying distribution.

Random Forest

In machine learning, one of the popular machine learning algorithms is Random Forest which is a part of the supervised learning methodology. It can be applied to ML issues involving both classification and regression. It is built on the idea of ensemble learning, which is a method of integrating various classifiers to address difficult issues and enhance model performance (Sai Nikhilesh Kasturi,2019). Random Forest, as the name implies, is a classifier that uses a number of decision trees on different subsets of the provided dataset and averages them to increase the dataset's predictive accuracy. Instead than depending on a single decision tree, the random forest uses forecasts from each tree and predicts the result based on the votes of the majority of predictions. Higher accuracy and overfitting are prevented by the larger number of trees in the forest.

Figure 4. Ensemble random forest

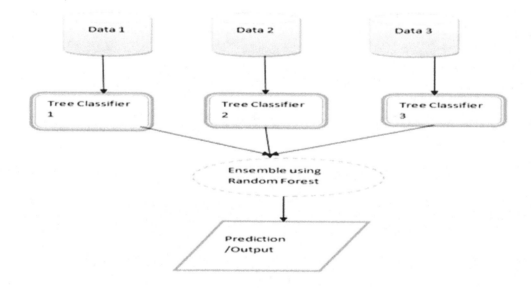

Working of Random Forest

Random forest works under two phases. In the first phase N decision trees are combined to generate the random forest, and in the second phase predictions are made for each tree that was produced in the first phase. The steps involved in this process are given below:

Step 1: From the training data set select K data points.

Step 2: From the chosen data points the decision tree could be constructed.

Step 3: For the constructed trees select N for the size

Step 4: Steps 1 and 2 are repeated.

Step 5: Find each decision tree's forecasts for any new data points, then place them in the category that receives the most votes.

Machine Learning: Process

The Steps involved in developing a machine learning model are:

- Data Collection
- Data Preprocessing
- Feature Selection
- Training the data with the machine learning model
- Testing the data
- Prediction result
- Evaluation result
  - The data can be collected from any data repository or data source from online sources or it can be collected from any organizations or individuals according to the need of the applications.
  - The data should be preprocessed in the way that it should be cleaned and it should not have null values or missing values. If the data has the null values or missing values the accuracy of the model will be affected.
  - The data should be formatted and the additional attributes or the needed attributes are removed or added according to the need and this also will increase the accuracy of the model.
  - In the preprocessed data the features should be selected or the target variable should be set and the prediction is according to the feature selected.
  - The machine learning model is selected and the data is manipulated with the model and its results are calculated. In the machine learning model the data set is trained and with the trained set the set of data is tested and the result is predicted.
  - The accuracy and other metrics can also be calculated to evaluate how the model performs and the prediction is also done. The process of the machine learning model has been given in the below figure.

Figure 5. Process of machine learning model

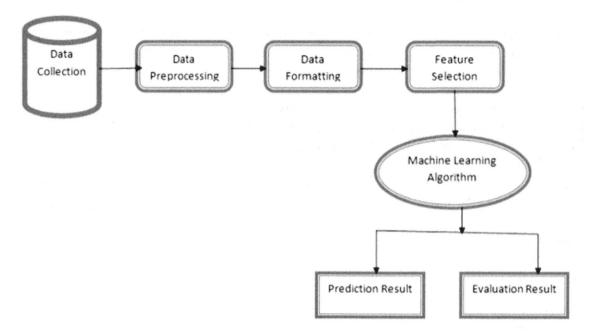

Random Forest Implementation

The random forest is used to predict the type of shopping of the customer according to the rating given to the purchase. The target value is set and if the rating the target the shopping is good and if it is below the shopping is average. The decision tree or classification tree is used to classify the types of customers and the types of product in a super market. The data set is taken from Kaggle.com. The data set contain 1000 rows and 17 columns.

The implementation can be done by using any types of machine learning tools or programming languages. This implementation is done by using Orange tool. Orange tool is an Open access machine learning tool to predict the future occurrences as true or false using the target variable. The orange tool contains widgets which is very easy to perform the analytics of data to give the results.

The dataset is given to the file widget and it is connected with the table and suitable algorithms are taken from the menu and the connection is done to predict the result. The work flow of orange tool is given by

The data set is taken from kaggle.com and converted into CSV (Comma-Separated Values))file format. The file is loaded in the file widget and it is connected with the table. The classification of attributes is given using the sieve diagram. The sieve diagram indicates the classification analysis of each attributes. It indicates the female customers are 53% and the male customers are 47%.Hence it is predicted female customers are mostly doing the shopping than male customers. The work flow and the sieve diagram are shown in Figure 7.

The data is given to the classification or decision tree where the classification is done through this. The classification is done by gender type, customer type and also with the rating. The result of classification tree is shown as Figure 8.

Figure 6. Work flow of random forest using orange tool

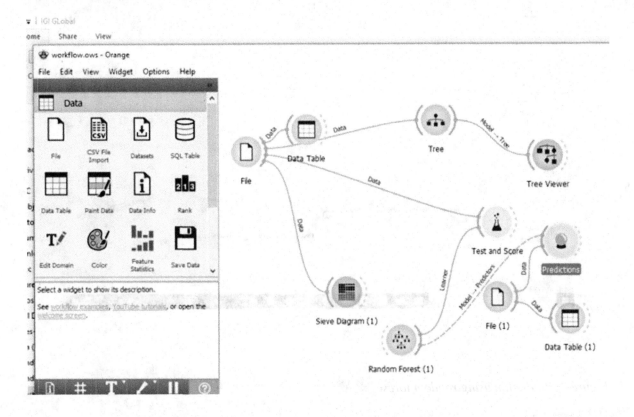

Figure 7. Work flow with sieve diagram

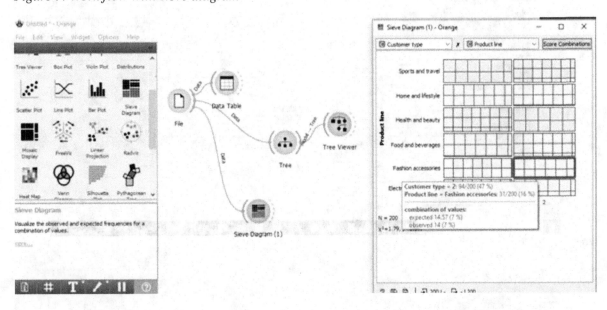

Figure 8. Classification tree

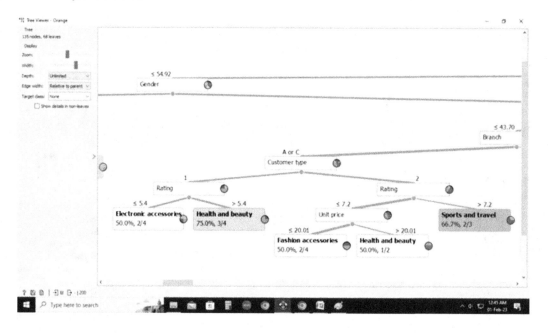

Figure 9. Prediction using random forest

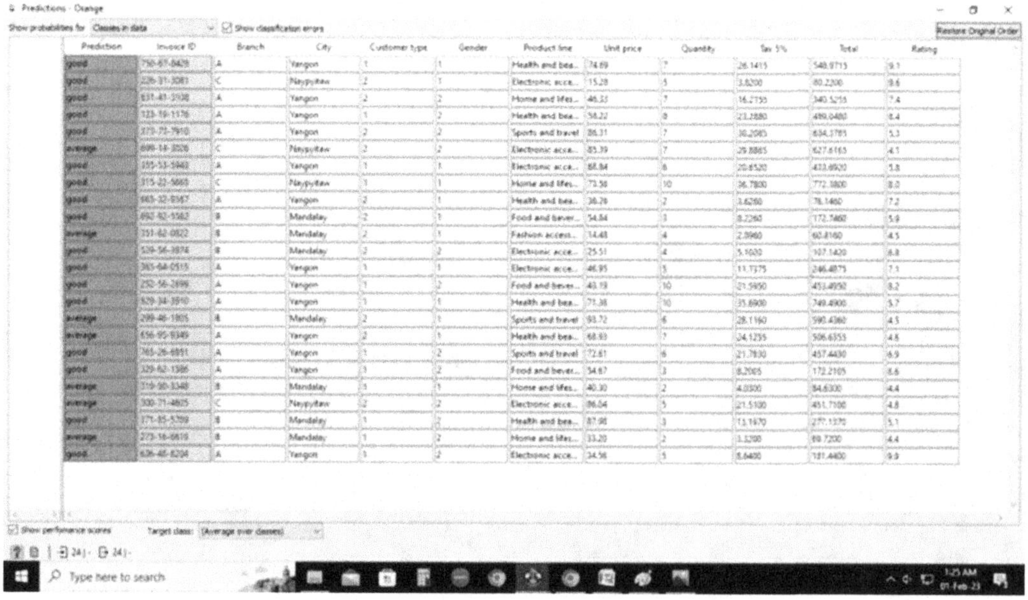

The data set is given to the random forest algorithm and its prediction and evaluation results are found. The rating is given as the target variable and according to that the prediction is done. If the rating is above 5% the shopping is a good shopping if the rating is below 5% the average shopping is done. The prediction result of random forest is shown as Figure 9.

The evaluation result of random forest is done by finding its accuracy and some other metrics. The metrics used to evaluate the performance of random forest are:

- Classification Accuracy
- Precision
- Recall
- F1 Score

Classification Accuracy

Classification is a metrics to evaluate the machine learning algorithm which usually means it to be accurate. It measures the proportion of accurate predictions to all input samples. It is given as the ratio of the true or correct predictions to the total number of samples. It is given as:

Classification accuracy = Number of correct predictions / Total number of samples

Precision

Precision is the metric which defines the ratio of number of correct positive results to the number of predicted positive results which is predicted by the classifier. The precision value can be found using the relation:

Precision = True Positives / True Positives +False Positives

Recall

Recall is also a metric which supports the machine learning algorithms to identify the ratio of the correct positive results to all the relevant values. The recall relation is given as:

Recall = True Positives / True Positives +False Negatives

F1 Score

The harmonic mean between precision and recall is the F1 score measure. F1 score value can be found using the formula:

F1 score= 2 x Precision x Recall / Precision +Recall

Where

- True Positives (TP) is the number of correctly predicted samples termed as positive.
- False Positives (FP) is the number of wrongly predicted samples as positive.
- True Negatives (TN) is the number of correctly predicted as negative.
- False Negatives (TN) is the number of wrongly predicted samples as negative.

The above metrics and the performance of the random forest algorithm can be noted. The classification accuracy of random forest is given as 92%, the accuracy or the performance of the algorithm is 83%, the precision value is 89%, Recall value is 92% and F1 score is 89%. The threshold value of these metrics are 1. (100%). The evaluation result is shown in Figure 10.

Figure 10. Evaluation result of random forest

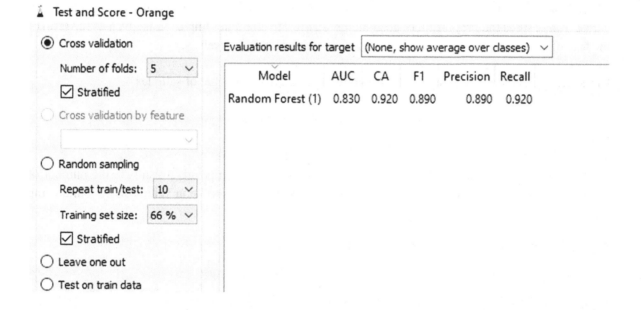

Advantages of Random Forest

- Random forest reduces over fitting and improves the accuracy.
- It is adaptable to problems involving classification and regression.
- Both categorical and continuous values can be used with it.
- It automates filling in data's missing values.
- Data normalization is not necessary because a rule-based methodology is used.
- A random forest generates accurate predictions that are simple to comprehend.
- Large datasets can be handled effectively.
- In comparison to the decision tree method, the random forest algorithm offers a higher level of accuracy in outcome prediction.
- The Random Forest model will be less prone to overfitting and provide a more generic answer.

- Random Forest can be used to address problems involving classification and regression.
- Random Forest is effective with both continuous and categorical variables.
- . Missing values can be handled easily by Random Forest.
- No feature scaling is necessary: Because Random Forest uses a rule-based approach rather than distance calculation, there is no need for feature scaling (standardization and normalization).
- . Effectively manages non-linear parameters: Non-linear characteristics have no impact on the outcome.
- Missing values can be handled easily by Random Forest.
- Random Forest often handles outliers automatically and is robust to them.
- Random Forest is a fairly stable algorithm. Even if a new data point is added to the dataset, the algorithm's overall performance is not significantly impacted because, while the new data may have an effect on one tree, it is exceedingly unlikely to have an effect on all the trees.
- Noise has a lower relative impact on Random Forest.

Disadvantages of Random Forest

- Complexity: Random Forest generates numerous trees (as opposed to the decision tree's one tree) and then aggregates the results of each tree. This algorithm needs a lot more resources and computing power to accomplish this.
- Longer Training Period: Because Random Forest generates several trees (instead of just one tree, as in decision trees), and bases decisions on the majority of votes, it requires significantly longer training than decision trees.
- Sometimes they have biases towards particular qualities.
- Sluggish- The random forest approach can become quite slow and inefficient for real-time forecasts due to the presence of a huge number of trees, which is one of its main drawbacks.
- Random forest is not suitable for use with linear algorithms.
- Random forest might not perform well with little or low-dimensional data (data with few features). Because there is a significant decrease in randomness.
- For data with a lot of noise, random forest might overfit. Random forest minimizes the degree of overfitting by voting, but its prediction is still overfitted compared to linear model, which is defined by strong matching of existing data (Karlos et al.,2020).
- The accuracy of prediction can be improved by increasing the number of trees. However, because there are more trees involved in random forest, it frequently takes more time and space to train the model.
- When compared to other algorithms, its computations may be considerably more complex. Additionally, it is difficult to understand since, while it indicates the relevance of a feature, it does not offer full visibility into the coefficients of a linear regression.

Applications of Random Forest

Some of the application areas of Random forest are:

- Banking Sector
  - Detection of credit card fraud

- ○ Segmentation of Customers
- ○ Loan Default Prediction
- Medical Care and Healthcare
  - ○ Prediction of Cardiovascular Disease
  - ○ Diabetes Prognosis
  - ○ Prediction of Breast Cancer
- Market Prediction for the Stock
  - ○ Analysis of Stock Market Sentiment
  - ○ Price detection for bitcoin
  - ○ Product Recommendation for customers
- E-Commerce
  - ○ Search Ranking
  - ○ Price Optimization
  - ○ Product Recommendation

The provision of financial facilities is crucial economically. Because a growing economy and an increase in capital are caused by each other. The banking industry makes up the majority of consumers. There are many devoted customers, including those who engage in fraud. In order to determine whether the client is trustworthy or dishonest, random forest analysis is used. Using a random forest machine learning system, we can quickly determine whether the client is trustworthy or not. A framework uses a diverse set of random algorithms to categorize fraudulent transactions according to a number of patterns.

Credit card firms must identify fraudulent credit card purchases in order to prevent consumers from being charged for goods they have not ordered. However, it is a very challenging task because there may only be 1000 fraud incidents in a million or more transactions, or just 0.1 percent of the dataset, leading to very unbalanced datasets. The ML algorithms such as Random forest are particularly likely to produce erroneous classifiers when trained on imbalanced datasets because they appear to demonstrate a preference for the majority class, perceiving the minority class as noise in the dataset. The algorithm might anticipate almost all situations belonging to the majority class, which would result in a high accuracy score. The Random Forest Classifier is still applicable in this situation.

During Customer Segmentation the data on internal structure based on annual expenditure amounts of various consumers across a range of product categories. This serves a number of purposes, one of which is to more clearly illustrate the heterogeneity of the many categories of customers that a wholesale dealer deals with. The distributor will gain knowledge on how to better tailor their distribution programme to each client's demands by doing this.

In Healthcare and medicine a complicated blend of specific chemicals is required for medicines. Random forest can therefore be utilized to identify the excellent blend in medicines. With the help of a machine learning system, it is now simpler to identify and anticipate the drug sensitivity of a medication. Reviewing the patient's medical file also helps in determining the patient's condition. The growing number of machine learning applications in medicine gives us a glimpse of a time in the future when innovation, analysis, and data-gathering will work together to benefit numerous patients unknowingly. Soon, ML-based applications utilizing real-time patient data from various healthcare systems will be relatively prevalent in many different nations, enhancing the effectiveness of innovative treatments.

Diabetes is a type of metabolic disease brought on by the pancreas not producing enough insulin. Diabetes can cause coma, cardiovascular dysfunction, renal and retinal failure, joint failure, sexual dysfunction, pathogenic effects on immunity, weight loss, and peripheral vascular illnesses. It can also cause the pathological destruction of pancreatic beta cells. As a result, a solid framework for the early diagnosis of diabetes was put forth, complete with outlier rejection, missing values, data standardization, K-fold validation, and several Machine Learning (ML) classifiers. In this, Random Forest outperforms all other classifiers.

The Random Forest algorithm can be used to study the stock market's activity. It is also possible to depict the potential loss or gain associated with buying a specific stock. One technique to project future inventory costs is through stock market forecasting. The ideal timing to buy and sell stocks is difficult to predict because stock values change daily. Since its creation, it has been a fascinating subject for researchers and investors. Machine learning produces a wide range of algorithms, with Random Forest reportedly being one of the best at forecasting future stock prices. Data mining has been utilized to estimate stock market prices for the NSE stock market using Random Forest algorithms.

Stock Market Analysis and Prediction uses Google Finance data for technical analysis, visualization, and prediction. by examining stock market information, especially a few massive technology stocks and others. In order to analyze a stock's risk based on its prior performance history, Pandas are employed to gather stock details, conceive of various parts of it, and look at a few different assessment methods. Because of the financial industry's fundamentals and in part as a result of the interaction between known variables (such as the previous day's closing price, the P/E ratio, etc.) and unknowable ones (such as election results, rumors, etc.), stock prices are thought to be extremely competitive and subject to sudden changes. An astute investor will predict the price of a stock, buying or selling it before the price increases. An effective prediction algorithm will directly result in high profits for investment firms, implying a direct correlation between the accuracy of the prediction algorithm and the profit generated from the algorithm's use. This is true even though it is very difficult to replace the knowledge acquired by an experienced trader.

Digital currencies known as cryptocurrencies have generated a lot of investor interest in the financial markets. This project aims to forecast daily prices, in particular the daily closing price of the cryptocurrency Bitcoin. This is quite important while making trading selections. The price of Bitcoin is influenced by a number of factors, making price forecasting a dynamic and technically difficult Endeavour. The historical time sequence, which includes Bitcoin's historical price history over many years, was used to train the random forest model to make predictions. Features including the beginning price, highest price, lowest price, closing price, Bitcoin value, currency volume, and weighted price of the following day were taken into consideration in order to estimate the closing price.

It can be challenging to advise or suggest what the consumer should see. Here, a forest-based random algorithm can be applied. Selling similar products to your clients by following a predetermined pattern and paying attention to their level of interest in the product. Amazon has demonstrated that product reviews are effective. The Recommendation Engine accounts for 35% of their sales. But it takes a lot of computer power to find the relevant trends in product sales and shopping behaviour. Machine learning can be used to accomplish that. Smart employees can create "if this, then that" rules, however this limits the scope of the guidelines to simply demonstrating the employee's competence. Machine learning is able to continuously quantify consumer behaviour while also uncovering new trends. It's effective to suggest things that your clients weren't even aware they desired. A framework for recommendations has been built using Random Forest. The main presumption is that a consumer's review will be more likely to be suggested for the job if their review score is greater. This will prevent us from recommending to our customers lovely but outdated products. This technique is also useful for people who don't have any records in the database because we can only recommend trendy goods to them.

Pricing optimization is important. Pricing online is crucially important. It can't be merely rely on a fixed markup percentage or even the local market price to close the purchase. With only a few clicks, prices are compared amongst competitors more easily than before. And consumers don't worry about getting a fantastic deal. Machine learning technology can change prices in order to simultaneously take into account several variables. The price may be impacted by the competitors' rates, demand, time of day, and clientele. Machine learning technology enables price changes in accordance with demand.

CONCLUSION

The linearity of the data is assumed in linear regression. While this presumption makes the model simple to understand, it frequently limits its ability to forecast. As a result, Random forest makes it a success, they tend to predict more accurately than linear regression. Random forest will adapt to nonlinearities detected in the data. More precisely, medium to big datasets are highly suited for ensemble learning methods like random forests. The methods for logistic regression and linear regression will not operate when the number of independent variables is greater than the number of observations because there are too many estimated parameters. Because not all predictor variables are used at once, random forest works. As an ensemble tree-based learning system, the random forest model averages predictions from numerous individual trees. The random forest algorithm more precisely predicts the error rate. More particular, it has been demonstrated analytically that the error rate will always converge as the number of trees rises.

Hence this chapter exposes the idea about the ensemble machine learning and random forest and their implementation, advantages, disadvantages, applications which gives the overview of the machine learning algorithm to promote the research scholars, students to perform more researches and more analytics of data in future.

REFERENCES

Charbuty, B., & Abdulazeez, A.M. (2021). Classification Based on Decision Tree Algorithm for Machine Learning. *Journal of Applied Sciences and Technology Trends*.

Demertzis, K., & Iliadis, L. (2020). *GeoAI: A Model-Agnostic Meta-Ensemble Zero- Shot Learning Method for Hyperspectral Image Analysis and Classification*. Academic Press.

Dridi. (2021). *Supervised Learning - A Systematic Literature Review*. Research Gate.

Jin, W. (2020, February 6). Research on Machine Learning and Its Algorithms and Development. *Journal of Physics*.

Karlos, S., Kostopoulos, G., & Kotsiantis, S. (2020). *A Soft-Voting Ensemble Based Co-Training Scheme Using Static Selection for Binary Classification Problems*. Academic Press.

Mosavi, Salimi, Ardabili, Rabczuk, Shamshirband, & Varkonyi-Koczy. (2019). *State of the Art of Machine Learning Models in Energy Systems, a Systematic Review*. Academic Press.

Pintelas, E., Livieris, I.E., & Pintelas, P. (2020). *A Grey-Box Ensemble Model Exploiting Black-Box Accuracy and White-Box Intrinsic Interpretability*. Academic Press.

Zvarevashe, K., & Olugbara, O. (2020). *Ensemble Learning of Hybrid Acoustic Features for Speech Emotion Recognition*. Academic Press.

Compilation of References

6G Promotion Group. (2021). *White Paper on 6G Overall Vision and Potential Key Technologies.* Available: http://www. caict.ac.cn/kxyj/qwfb/ztbg/202106/ P020210604552573543918.pdf

A. K. V., Tyagi, & Kumar. (2022). Blockchain Technology for Securing Internet of Vehicle: Issues and Challenges. *2022 International Conference on Computer Communication and Informatics (ICCCI),* 1-6. 10.1109/ICCCI54379.2022.9740856

Abadi, M., Barham, P., Chen, J., Chen, Z., Davis, A., Dean, J., Devin, M., Ghemawat, S., Irving, G., Isard, M., Kudlur, M., Levenberg, J., Monga, R., Moore, S., Murray, D. G., Steiner, B., Tucker, P., Vasudevan, V., Warden, P., … Zheng, X. (n.d.). *TensorFlow: A system for large-scale machine learning.* Academic Press.

AbadiM.AgarwalA.BarhamP.BrevdoE.ChenZ.CitroC.CorradoG. S.DavisA.DeanJ.DevinM.GhemawatS.GoodfellowI. HarpA.IrvingG.IsardM.JiaY.JozefowiczR.KaiserL.KudlurM.ZhengX. (2016). TensorFlow: Large-Scale Machine Learning on Heterogeneous Distributed Systems. https://arxiv.org/abs/1603.04467

Abdallah, M., Sharbaji, S., Sharbaji, M., Daher, Z., Faour, T., Mansour, Z., & Hneino, M. (2020). Diagnostic accuracy of the Finnish Diabetes Risk Score for the prediction of undiagnosed type 2 diabetes, prediabetes, and metabolic syndrome in the Lebanese University. *Diabetology & Metabolic Syndrome, 12*(1), 84. doi:10.118613098-020-00590-8 PMID:33014142

Abdelbaki, H., Gelenbe, E., & Kocak, T. (1999). Matched neural filters for EMI based mine detection. *IJCNN'99. International Joint Conference on Neural Networks. Proceedings, 5,* 3236–3240. 10.1109/IJCNN.1999.836174

Aberathne, I., Kulasiri, D., & Samarasinghe, S. (2023). Detection of Alzheimer's disease onset using MRI and PET neuroimaging: Longitudinal data analysis and machine learning. *Neural Regeneration Research, 18*(10), 2134–2140. doi:10.4103/1673-5374.367840 PMID:37056120

Abunasser, B. S., Al-Hiealy, M. R. J., Zaqout, I. S., & Abu-Naser, S. S. (2023). Convolution Neural Network for Breast Cancer Detection and Classification Using Deep Learning. *Asian Pacific Journal of Cancer Prevention, 24*(2), 531. PMID:36853302

Adadi, A., & Berrada, M. (2018). Peeking inside the black-box: A survey on explainable artificial intelligence (XAI). *IEEE Access : Practical Innovations, Open Solutions, 6,* 52138–52160. doi:10.1109/ACCESS.2018.2870052

Adankon, M. M., & Cheriet, M. (2009). Model selection for the LS-SVM. Application to handwriting recognition. *Pattern Recognition, 42*(12), 3264–3270. doi:10.1016/j.patcog.2008.10.023

Adedigba, A. P., Adeshina, S. A., & Aibinu, A. M. (2022). Performance Evaluation of Deep Learning Models on Mammogram Classification Using Small Dataset. *Bioengineering (Basel, Switzerland), 2022*(9), 161. doi:10.3390/bioengineering9040161 PMID:35447721

Adek, R. T., & Ula, M. (2020). A Survey on The Accuracy of Machine Learning Techniques for Intrusion and Anomaly Detection on Public Data Sets. *2020 International Conference on Data Science, Artificial Intelligence, and Business Analytics (DATABIA)*. 10.1109/DATABIA50434.2020.9190436

Adnan, N. (2012). University students stress level and brainwave balancing index: Comparison between early and end of study semester. In *Research and Development (SCOReD) 2012 IEEE Student Conference on*. IEEE.

Aerts, H. J. W. L., Velazquez, E. R., Leijenaar, R. T. H., Parmar, C., Grossmann, P., Carvalho, S., Bussink, J., Monshouwer, R., Haibe-Kains, B., Rietveld, D., Hoebers, F., Rietbergen, M. M., Leemans, C. R., Dekker, A., Quackenbush, J., Gillies, R. J., & Lambin, P. (2014). Decoding tumour phenotype by noninvasive imaging using a quantitative radiomics approach. *Nature Communications*, *5*(1), 1. Advance online publication. doi:10.1038/ncomms5006 PMID:24892406

Ahmad, A. M., Eckert, C., Teredesai, A., & McKelvey, G. (2018). Interpretable Machine Learning in Healthcare. In *IEEE Intelligent Informatics Bulletin* (pp. 1–7). IEEE.

Ahmad, A. S., Hassan, M. Y., Abdullah, M. P., Rahman, H. A., Hussin, F., Abdullah, H., & Saidur, R. (2014). A review on applications of ANN and SVM for building electrical energy consumption forecasting. *Renewable & Sustainable Energy Reviews*, *33*, 102–109. doi:10.1016/j.rser.2014.01.069

Ahmed, W. S., & Karim, A. A. (2020). The Impact of Filter Size and Number of Filters on Classification Accuracy in CNN. *2020 International Conference on Computer Science and Software Engineering (CSASE)*, 88–93. 10.1109/CSASE48920.2020.9142089

Ahmed, Z., Mohamed, K., Zeeshan, S., & Dong, X. (2020). Artificial intelligence with multi-functional machine learning platform development for better healthcare and precision medicine. *Database (Oxford)*, *2020*, baaa010. doi:10.1093/database/baaa010 PMID:32185396

Ahsan, M. M., Luna, S. A., & Siddique, Z. (2022). Machine-learning-based disease diagnosis: A comprehensive review. *Healthcare (Basel)*, *10*(3), 541. doi:10.3390/healthcare10030541 PMID:35327018

Aitken, R. (2007). Defect or Variation? Characterizing Standard Cell Behaviour at 90nm and Below. *Proceedings of the 8th International Symposium on Quality Electronic Design (ISQED'07)*.

Akakuru, O. C., Adakwa, C. B., Ikoro, D. O., Eyankware, M. O., Opara, A. I., Njoku, A. O., Iheme, K. O., & Usman, A. (2023). Application of artificial neural network and multi-linear regression techniques in groundwater quality and health risk assessment around Egbema, Southeastern Nigeria. *Environmental Earth Sciences*, *82*(3), 77. doi:10.100712665-023-10753-1

Akbar, K. A., Wang, Y., Islam, M. S., Singhal, A., Khan, L., & Thuraisingham, B. (2021, December). Identifying Tactics of Advanced Persistent Threats with Limited Attack Traces. In *International Conference on Information Systems Security* (pp. 3-25). Springer. 10.1007/978-3-030-92571-0_1

Akbik, A., Bergmann, T., Blythe, D., Rasul, K., Schweter, S., & Vollgraf, R. (2019). An easy-to-use framework for state-of-the heart NLP. Academic Press.

Akram, W. (2018). A Study on Positive and Negative Effects of Social Media on Society. *International Journal on Computer Science and Engineering*, *5*(10), 347–354.

Al-Antari, M. A., Han, S. M., & Kim, T. S. (2020). Evaluation of deep learning detection and classification towards computer-aided diagnosis of breast lesions in digital X-ray mammograms. *Computer Methods and Programs in Biomedicine*, *196*, 105584. doi:10.1016/j.cmpb.2020.105584 PMID:32554139

Al-Ars, Z., Hamdioui, S., van der Goor, A. J., & Mueller, G. (2008). Defect Oriented Testing of the Strap Problem Under Process Variations in DRAMs. *Proceedings of the IEEE International Test Conference (ITC).* 10.1109/TEST.2008.4700631

Albawi, S., Mohammed, T. A., & Al-Zawi, S. (2017). Understanding of a convolutional neural network. *2017 International Conference on Engineering and Technology (ICET)*, 1–6. 10.1109/ICEngTechnol.2017.8308186

Alboaneen, D., Alqarni, R., Alqahtani, S., Alrashidi, M., Alhuda, R., Alyahyan, E., & Alshammari, T. (2023). Predicting Colorectal Cancer Using Machine and Deep Learning Algorithms: Challenges and Opportunities. *Big Data and Cognitive Computing, 7*(2), 74. doi:10.3390/bdcc7020074

Alcala-Fdez, J. (2006). Hybrid learning models to get the interpretability – accuracy trade-off in fuzzy modeling. *Soft Computing, 10*(9), 717–734. doi:10.100700500-005-0002-1

Alemu, K., Adugna, G., Lemessa, F., & Muleta, D. (2016). Current status of coffee berry disease (colletotrichum kahawae waller & bridge) in Ethiopia. *Archiv für Phytopathologie und Pflanzenschutz, 49*(17-18), 421–433. doi:10.1080/03235408.2016.1228736

Alharbi, W. S., & Rashid, M. (2022). A review of deep learning applications in human genomics using next-generation sequencing data. *Human Genomics, 16*(1), 26. doi:10.118640246-022-00396-x PMID:35879805

Al-Hiary, H., Bani-Ahmad, S., Reyalat, M., Braik, M., & Alrahamneh, Z. (2011). Fast and accurate detection and classification of plant diseases. *International Journal of Computer Applications, 17*(1), 31–38. doi:10.5120/2183-2754

Almusaed, A., Yitmen, I., & Almssad, A. (2023). Reviewing and Integrating AEC Practices into Industry 6.0: Strategies for Smart and Sustainable Future-Built Environments. *Sustainability (Basel), 15*(18), 13464. doi:10.3390u151813464

Alpsoy, A., Yavuz, A., & Elpek, G. O. (2021). Artificial intelligence in pathological evaluation of gastrointestinal cancers. *Artif Intell Gastroenterol, 2*(6), 141-156.

AlSagri & Ykhlef. (2020). Machine Learning-based Approach for Depression Detection in Twitter Using Content and Activity Features. *IEICE Transactions on Information and Systems, E103.D*(8), 1-16.

Altmann, A., Tolosi, L., Sander, O., & Lengauer, T. (2010). Permutation importance: A corrected feature importance measure. *Bioinformatics (Oxford, England), 26*(10), 1340–1347. doi:10.1093/bioinformatics/btq134 PMID:20385727

Al-Turjman, F., Zahmatkesh, H., & Mostarda, L. (2019). Quantifying uncertainty in internet of medical things and big-data services using intelligence and deep learning. *IEEE Access : Practical Innovations, Open Solutions, 7*, 115749–115759. doi:10.1109/ACCESS.2019.2931637

Amann, J., Blasimme, A., Vayena, E., Frey, D., & Madai, V. I. (2020). Explainability for artificial intelligence in healthcare: A multidisciplinary perspective. *BMC Medical Informatics and Decision Making, 20*(1), 1–9. doi:10.118612911-020-01332-6 PMID:33256715

Anderson, D., & Evans, S. (2022). Chatbots in Higher Education: Perspectives and Implementation Challenges. *Higher Education Research & Development, 48*(1), 65–82.

Ang, L. M., Seng, K. P., Ijemaru, G. K., & Zungeru, A. M. (2019). Deployment of IoV for Smart Cities: Applications, Architecture, and Challenges. *IEEE Access : Practical Innovations, Open Solutions, 7*, 6473–6492. doi:10.1109/ACCESS.2018.2887076

Aritonang, M., & Sihombing, D. J. C. (2019, November). An Application of Backpropagation Neural Network for Sales Forecasting Rice Miling Unit. In *2019 International Conference of Computer Science and Information Technology (ICoSNIKOM)* (pp. 1-4). IEEE. 10.1109/ICoSNIKOM48755.2019.9111612

Atalay, V., Gelenbe, E., & Yalabik, N. (1992). The random neural network model for texture generation. *International Journal of Pattern Recognition and Artificial Intelligence*, *06*(01), 131–141. doi:10.1142/S0218001492000072

Auckland. (n.d.). https://www.cs.auckland.ac.nz/courss/compsci373s1c/PatricesLectures/Image%20Filtering.pdf

Ayyad, S. M., Shehata, M., Shalaby, A., Abou El-Ghar, M., Ghazal, M., El-Melegy, M., Abdel-Hamid, N. B., Labib, L. M., Ali, H. A., & El-Baz, A. (2021). Role of AI and histopathological images in detecting prostate cancer: A survey. *Sensors (Basel)*, *21*(8), 2586. doi:10.339021082586 PMID:33917035

Azam, F., & Agro, M. (2021). Identifying Depression Among Twitter Users using Sentiment Analysis. *International Conference on Artificial Intelligence*, 44-49. 10.1109/ICAI52203.2021.9445271

Bakircioğlu, H., Gelenbe, E., & Carin, L. (1997). Random neural network recognition of shaped objects in strong clutter. In W. Gerstner, A. Germond, M. Hasler, & J.-D. Nicoud (Eds.), *Artificial Neural Networks—ICANN'97* (pp. 961–966). Springer. doi:10.1007/BFb0020277

Bakırcıoğlu, H., & Koçak, T. (2000). Survey of random neural network applications. *European Journal of Operational Research*, *126*(2), 319–330. doi:10.1016/S0377-2217(99)00481-6

Banegas-Luna, A. J., Pena-Garcia, J., Iftene, A., Guadagni, F., Ferroni, P., Scarpato, N., Zanzotto, F. M., Bueno-Crespo, A., & Perez-Sanchez, H. (2021). Towards the interpretability of machine learning predictions for medical applications targeting personalised therapies: A cancer case survey. *International Journal of Molecular Sciences*, *22*(9), 4394. doi:10.3390/ijms22094394 PMID:33922356

Banerjee, A., Chakraborty, C., Kumar, A., & Biswas, D. (2020). Emerging trends in IoT and big data analytics for biomedical and health care technologies. Handbook of data science approaches for biomedical engineering, 121-152. doi:10.1016/B978-0-12-818318-2.00005-2

Banerjee, S., Chowdhury, D. R., & Bhattacharya, B. B. (2005). *Proceedings of the 2005 IEEE International Workshop on Memory Technology, Design and Testing(MTDT'05)*. IEEE.

Baragde. (2023). Information Technology for Enhancing Public Sector Sustainability. In *Leadership and Governance for Sustainability* (pp. 204–221). IGI Global. doi:10.4018/978-1-6684-9711-1.ch011

Bari Antor, M., Jamil, A. H. M., Mamtaz, M., Monirujjaman Khan, M., Aljahdali, S., Kaur, M., Singh, P., & Masud, M. (2021). A comparative analysis of machine learning algorithms to predict alzheimer's disease. *Journal of Healthcare Engineering*. doi:10.1155/2021/9917919 PMID:34336171

Bashir, S., & Sharma, N. (2012). Remote area plant disease detection using image processing. *IOSR Journal of Electronics and Communication Engineering*, *2*(6), 31–34. doi:10.9790/2834-0263134

Bautista, M. A., Sanakoyeu, A., Tikhoncheva, E., & Ommer, B. (2016). Cliquecnn: Deep unsupervised exemplar learning. *Advances in Neural Information Processing Systems*, 29.

Belenguer, L. (2022). AI bias: Exploring discriminatory algorithmic decision-making models and the application of possible machine-centric solutions adapted from the pharmaceutical industry. *AI and Ethics*, *2*(4), 771–787. doi:10.100743681-022-00138-8 PMID:35194591

Bener, A., Barisik, C. C., Acar, A., & Ozdenkaya, Y. (2019). Assessment of the Gail Model in estimating the risk of breast cancer: Effect of cancer worry and risk in healthy women. *Asian Pacific Journal of Cancer Prevention*, *20*(6), 1765–1771. doi:10.31557/APJCP.2019.20.6.1765 PMID:31244298

Bengio, Y., Courville, A., & Vincent, P. (2013). Representation Learning: A Review and New Perspectives. *IEEE Transactions on Pattern Analysis and Machine Intelligence*, *35*(8), 1798–1828. doi:10.1109/TPAMI.2013.50 PMID:23787338

Benmalek, E., Elmhamdi, J., & Jilbab, A. (2021). Comparing CT scan and chest X-ray imaging for COVID-19 diagnosis. *Biomedical Engineering Advances*, *1*, 100003. doi:10.1016/j.bea.2021.100003 PMID:34786568

Benso, A., Bosio, A., Di Carlo, S., Di Natale, G., & Prinetto, P. (2006). A 22n March Test for Realistic Static Linked Faults in SRAMs. *IEEE 11th European Test Symposium (ETS)*.

Bera, K., Schalper, K. A., Rimm, D. L., Velcheti, V., & Madabhushi, A. (2019). Artificial intelligence in digital pathology – new tools for diagnosis and precision oncology. *Nature Reviews. Clinical Oncology*, *16*(11), 703–715. doi:10.103841571-019-0252-y PMID:31399699

Bernabe-Ortiz, A., Perel, P., Miranda, J. J., & Smeeth, L. (2018). Diagnostic accuracy of the Finnish Diabetes Risk Score (FINDRISC) for undiagnosed T2DM in Peruvian population. *Primary Care Diabetes*, *12*(6), 517–525. doi:10.1016/j.pcd.2018.07.015 PMID:30131300

Bernal, J., & Mazo, C. (2022). Transparency of artificial intelligence in healthcare: Insights from professionals in computing and healthcare worldwide. *Applied Sciences (Basel, Switzerland)*, *12*(20), 10228. doi:10.3390/app122010228

Bitton, A., & Gaziano, T. (2010). The Framingham Heart Study's impact on global risk assessment. *Progress in Cardiovascular Diseases*, *53*(1), 68–78. doi:10.1016/j.pcad.2010.04.001 PMID:20620429

Bogdanovic, B., Eftimov, T., & Simjanoska, M. (2022). In-depth insights into Alzheimer's disease by using explainable machine learning approach. *Scientific Reports*, *12*(1), 6508. doi:10.103841598-022-10202-2 PMID:35444165

Bohr, A., & Memarzadeh, K. (2020). The rise of artificial intelligence in healthcare applications. *Artifical Intelligence in Healthcare*, 25-60.

Bohr, A., & Memarzadeh, K. (2020). The rise of artificial intelligence in healthcare applications. In *Artificial Intelligence in healthcare* (pp. 25–60). Academic Press. doi:10.1016/B978-0-12-818438-7.00002-2

Bonavita, I., Rafael-Palou, X., Ceresa, M., Piella, G., Ribas, V., & Ballester, M. A. G. (2020). Integration of convolutional neural networks for pulmonary nodule malignancy assessment in a lung cancer classification pipeline. *Computer Methods and Programs in Biomedicine*, *185*, 105172. doi:10.1016/j.cmpb.2019.105172 PMID:31710985

Borrellas, P., & Unceta, I. (2021). The challenges of machine learning and their economic implications. *Entropy (Basel, Switzerland)*, *23*(3), 275. doi:10.3390/e23030275 PMID:33668772

Borri, S., Hage-Hassan, M., Girard, P., Pravossoudovitch, S., & Virazel, A. (2003). Defect Oriented Dynamic Faults Models for Embedded SRAMs. *Proceedings of the 8th IEEE European Test Workshop*. 10.1109/ETW.2003.1231664

Bosio, A., Di Carlo, S., Di Natale, G., & Prinetto, P. (2007). March AB, a State-of-the-Art March Test for Realistic Static Linked Faults and Dynamic Faults in SRAMs. *IET Computers & Digital Techniques*, *1*(3), 237-245.

Bosio, A., & Di Natale, G. (2008). March Test BDN: A New March Test For Dynamic Faults. Control Engineering And Applied Informatics. *CEAI*, *10*(2), 3–9.

Bouter, C., Puttergill, B., Hyman, G. Y., Maphosa, S., Gaylard, P., Etheredge, H., Fabian, J., Ruff, P., & Bebington, B. (2022). Colorectal cancer in South Africa study on the effect of delayed diagnosis to treatment intervals on survival. *South African Journal of Surgery. Suid-Afrikaanse Tydskrif vir Chirurgie*, *60*(4), 229–234. doi:10.17159/2078-5151/SAJS3803 PMID:36477050

Bratko, I. (1997). Machine Learning: Between Accuracy and Interpretability. In *Learning, networks and statistics* (pp. 163–177). Springer. doi:10.1007/978-3-7091-2668-4_10

Brockmoeller, S., Echle, A., Ghaffari Laleh, N., Eiholm, S., Malmstrøm, M. L., Plato Kuhlmann, T., Levic, K., Grabsch, H. I., West, N. P., Saldanha, O. L., Kouvidi, K., Bono, A., Heij, L. R., Brinker, T. J., Gögenür, I., Quirke, P., & Kather, J. N. (2022). Deep learning identifies inflamed fat as a risk factor for lymph node metastasis in early colorectal cancer. *The Journal of Pathology, 256*(3), 269–281. doi:10.1002/path.5831 PMID:34738636

Bron, E. E., Klein, S., Papma, J. M., Jiskoot, L. C., Venkatraghavan, V., Linders, J., Aalten, P., De Deyn, P. P., Biessels, G. J., Claassen, J. A., Middelkoop, H. A., Smits, M., Niessen, W. J., van Swieten, J. C., van der Flier, W. M., Ramakers, I. H. G. B., & van der Lugt, A. (2021). Cross-cohort generalizability of deep and conventional machine learning for MRI-based diagnosis and prediction of Alzheimer's disease. *NeuroImage. Clinical, 31*, 102712. doi:10.1016/j.nicl.2021.102712 PMID:34118592

Brown, C., & White, D. (2022). The Impact of AI-Powered Chatbots on Student Engagement in Virtual Classrooms. *International Journal of Distance Education, 38*(4), 531–548.

Bui, Pham, Nguyen, Nguyen, Le, & Hoang. (2016). An Effective Architecture of Memory Built-In Self-Test for Wide Range of SRAM. *2016 International Conference on Advanced Computing and Applications*, 121-124. 10.1109/ACOMP.2016.026

Burges, C. J. C., Platt, J. C., & Jana, S. (2003). Distortion discriminant analysis for audio fingerprinting. *IEEE Transactions on Speech and Audio Processing, 11*(3), 165–174. doi:10.1109/TSA.2003.811538

Business Finland. (2015). *From Industry X to Industry 6.0, Ant fragile manufacturing for people, planet, and profit with passion.* AIF, White paper. Retrieved from https://www.alliedict.fi/wpcontent/uploads/2021/08/Industry-X-White-Paper3.5.2021_Final.pdf

Butt, F. M., Hussain, L., Jafri, S. H. M., Lone, K. J., Alajmi, M., Abunadi, I., Al-Wesabi, F. N., & Hamza, M. A. (2022, May). Optimizing parameters of artificial intelligence deep convolutional neural networks (CNN) to improve prediction performance of load forecasting system. *IOP Conference Series. Earth and Environmental Science, 1026*(1), 012028. doi:10.1088/1755-1315/1026/1/012028

Byra, M. (2021). Breast mass classification with transfer learning based on scaling of deep representations. *Biomedical Signal Processing and Control, 69*, 102828. doi:10.1016/j.bspc.2021.102828

Byvatov, E., & Schneider, G. (2003). Support vector machine applications in bioinformatics. *Applied Bioinformatics, 2*(2), 67–77. PMID:15130823

Cai, Wang, Liu, Lv, & Wang. (2019). A Novel BIST Algorithm for Low-voltage SRAM. *2019 IEEE International Test Conference in Asia (ITC-Asia)*. 10.1109/ITC-Asia.2019.00036

Carremans, B. (2019, January 8). *Handling overfitting in deep learning models.* Medium. https://towardsdatascience.com/handling-overfitting-in-deep-learning-models-c760ee047c6e

Carter, K., & Anderson, P. (2023). Navigating the Technological Divide: Equitable Access to AI-Powered Education. *Journal of Educational Enquiry, 21*(2), 120–137.

Carvalho, D. V., Pereira, E. M., & Cardoso, J. S. (2019). Machine learning interpretability: A survey on methods and metrics. *Electronics (Basel), 8*(8), 832. doi:10.3390/electronics8080832

Castelo, M., Sue-Chue-Lam, C., Paszat, L., Kishibe, T., Scheer, A. S., Hansen, B. E., & Baxter, N. N. (2022). Time to diagnosis and treatment in younger adults with colorectal cancer: A systematic review. *PLoS One, 17*(9), e0273396. doi:10.1371/journal.pone.0273396 PMID:36094913

CCID. (2020). *6G Concepts and Vision.* White Paper. Available: http://www.ccidwise.com/uploads/sof t/200311/1-200311133959.pdf

Chang, C. H., Lin, C. H., & Lane, H. Y. (2021). Machine learning and novel biomarkers for the diagnosis of Alzheimer's disease. *International Journal of Molecular Sciences*, 22(5), 2761. doi:10.3390/ijms22052761 PMID:33803217

Chan, T.-H., Jia, K., Gao, S., Lu, J., Zeng, Z., & Ma, Y. (2015). PCANet: A Simple Deep Learning Baseline for Image Classification? *IEEE Transactions on Image Processing*, 24(12), 5017–5032. doi:10.1109/TIP.2015.2475625 PMID:26340772

Charbuty, B., & Abdulazeez, A.M. (2021). Classification Based on Decision Tree Algorithm for Machine Learning. *Journal of Applied Sciences and Technology Trends*.

Chen, J., Du, L., He, H., & Guo, Y. (2019). Convolutional factor analysis model with application to radar automatic target recognition. *Pattern Recognition*, 87, 140–156. doi:10.1016/j.patcog.2018.10.014

Chen, K., Fu, K., Yan, M., Gao, X., Sun, X., & Wei, X. (2018). Semantic Segmentation of Aerial Images With Shuffling Convolutional Neural Networks. *IEEE Geoscience and Remote Sensing Letters*, 15(2), 173–177. doi:10.1109/LGRS.2017.2778181

Chen, T.-J., Li, J.-F., & Tseng, T.-W. (2012, June). Cost-Efficient Built-In Redundancy Analysis with Optimal Repair Rate for Word-Oriented RAMs. *IEEE Transactions on Computer-Aided Design of Integrated Circuits and Systems*, 31(6), 930–940. Advance online publication. doi:10.1109/TCAD.2011.2181510

Cherukuri, A. K. A., & Sinha, S. (2022). Analysis and Mitigation Strategies of Security Issues of Software-Defined Networks. *Cross-Industry Applications of Cyber Security Frameworks*, 36-70.

Chitradevi, D., & Prabha, S. (2020). Analysis of brain sub regions using optimization techniques and deep learning method in Alzheimer disease. *Applied Soft Computing*, 86, 105857. doi:10.1016/j.asoc.2019.105857

Chourasia, S., Tyagi, A., Pandey, S. M., Walia, R. S., & Murtaza, Q. (2022). Sustainability of Industry 6.0 in global perspective: Benefits and challenges. *MPAN. Journal of Metrology Society of India*, 37(2), 443–452. doi:10.100712647-022-00541-w

Chow, A. Y. (2010). Cell Cycle Control by Oncogenes and Tumor Suppressors: Driving the Transformation of Normal Cells into Cancerous Cells. *Nature Education*, 3(9), 7.

Chowdhury, S., Joel-Edgar, S., Dey, P. K., Bhattacharya, S., & Kharlamov, A. (2023). Embedding transparency in artificial intelligence machine learning models: Managerial implications on predicting and explaining employee turnover. *International Journal of Human Resource Management*, 34(14), 2732–2764. doi:10.1080/09585192.2022.2066981

Cocanour, C. S. (2017). Informed consent—It's more than a signature on a piece of paper. *American Journal of Surgery*, 214(6), 993–997. doi:10.1016/j.amjsurg.2017.09.015 PMID:28974311

Cohen, J., & Ezer, T. (2013). Human rights in patient care: A theoretical and practice framework. *Health & Hum. Rts.*, 15, 7. PMID:24421170

Colonna, L. (2019). Privacy, risk, anonymization, and data sharing in the internet of health things. *Pitt. J. Tech. L. & Pol'y*, 20, 148.

Confalonieri, R., Coba, L., Wagner, B., & Besold, T. R. (2021). A historical perspective of explainable Artificial Intelligence. *Wiley Interdisciplinary Reviews. Data Mining and Knowledge Discovery*, 11(1), e1391. doi:10.1002/widm.1391

Cooper, W., & Reed, G. (2022). Business Process Automation with AI Chatbots: A Case Study of Industry Implementation. *Journal of Business and Management*, 48(1), 65–82.

Costales, R., Mao, C., Norwitz, R., Kim, B., & Yang, J. (2020). Live trojan attacks on deep neural networks. In *Proceedings of the IEEE/CVF Conference on Computer Vision and Pattern Recognition Workshops* (pp. 796-797). 10.1109/CVPRW50498.2020.00406

Cramer, C., Gelenbe, E., & Gelenbe, P. (1998). Image and video compression. *IEEE Potentials*, *17*(1), 29–33. doi:10.1109/45.652854

Cybenko, G., & Hallman, R. (2021). Resilient Distributed Adaptive Cyber-Defense Using Blockchain. *Game Theory and Machine Learning for Cyber Security*, 485-498.

Dabhane & Chawan. (2020). Depression Detection on Social Media using Machine Learning Techniques. *International Research Journal of Engineering and Technology*, *7*(11), 97–100.

Dada, E. G., Bassi, J. S., Chiroma, H., Shafi'i, M. A., Adetunmbi, A. O., & Ajibuwa, O. E. (2019). Machine learning for email spam filtering: Review, approaches and open research problems. *Heliyon, 5*(6). doi:10.1016/j.heliyon.2019.e01802

Dahlin, E. (2021). Mind the gap! On the future of AI research. *Humanities & Social Sciences Communications*, *8*(1), 71. doi:10.105741599-021-00750-9

Daniel, C., Cenggoro, T. W., & Pardamean, B. (2023). A systematic literature review of machine learning application in COVID-19 medical image classification. *Procedia Computer Science*, *216*, 749–756. doi:10.1016/j.procs.2022.12.192 PMID:36643182

Datacamp. (n.d.-a). https://www.datacamp.com/tutorial/decision-tree-classification-python

Datacamp. (n.d.-b). https://www.datacamp.com/tutorial/random-forests-classifier-python

Datacamp. (n.d.-c). https://www.datacamp.com/tutorial/k-means-clustering-python

Davenport, T., & Kalakota, R. (2019). The potential for artificial intelligence in healthcare. *Future Healthcare Journal*, *6*(2), 94–98. doi:10.7861/futurehosp.6-2-94 PMID:31363513

Davri, A., Birbas, E., Kanavos, T., Ntritsos, G., Giannakeas, N., Tzallas, A. T., & Batistatou, A. (2022). Deep learning on histopathological images for colorectal cancer diagnosis: A systematic review. *Diagnostics (Basel)*, *12*(4), 837. doi:10.3390/diagnostics12040837 PMID:35453885

De Backer, G. (2022). New insights in cardiovascular risk estimation and stratification. *e-Journal of Cardiology Practice, 22*, 16.

De La Vega, F. M., Chowdhury, S., Moore, B., Frise, E., McCarthy, J., Hernandez, E. J., Wong, T., James, K., Guidugli, L., Agrawal, P. B., Genetti, C. A., Brownstein, C. A., Beggs, A. H., Löscher, B.-S., Franke, A., Boone, B., Levy, S. E., Õunap, K., Pajusalu, S., ... Kingsmore, S. F. (2021). Artificial intelligence enables comprehensive genome interpretation and nomination of candidate diagnoses for rare genetic diseases. *Genome Medicine*, *13*(1), 153. doi:10.118613073-021-00965-0 PMID:34645491

de Melo, G., Macedo, S. O., Vieira, S. L., & Leandro Oliveira, L. G. (2018). Classification of images and enhancement of performance using parallel algorithm to detection of pneumonia. *2018 IEEE International Conference on Automation/XXIII Congress of the Chilean Association of Automatic Control (ICA-ACCA)*, 1–5. 10.1109/ICA-ACCA.2018.8609734

Deekshetha & Tyagi. (2023). Automated and intelligent systems for next-generation-based smart applications. In Data Science for Genomics. Academic Press. doi:10.1016/B978-0-323-98352-5.00019-7

Deka, P. C. (2014). Support vector machine applications in the field of hydrology: A review. *Applied Soft Computing*, *19*, 372–386. doi:10.1016/j.asoc.2014.02.002

Dekker, R., Beenker, F., & Thijssen, A. L. (1990, June). A Realistic Fault Model and Test Algorithms for Static Random Access Memories. *IEEE Transactions on Computer-Aided Design of Integrated Circuits and Systems*, *9*(6), 567–572. doi:10.1109/43.55188

Demertzis, K., & Iliadis, L. (2020). *GeoAI: A Model-Agnostic Meta-Ensemble Zero- Shot Learning Method for Hyperspectral Image Analysis and Classification*. Academic Press.

Deng, J., Dong, W., Socher, R., Li, L.-J., Li, K., & Fei-Fei, L. (2009). ImageNet: A large-scale hierarchical image database. *2009 IEEE Conference on Computer Vision and Pattern Recognition*, 248–255. 10.1109/CVPR.2009.5206848

Deshmukh, A., Patil, D., & Tyagi, A. K. (2022). Recent Trends on Blockchain for Internet of Things based Applications: Open Issues and Future Trends. In *Proceedings of the 2022 Fourteenth International Conference on Contemporary Computing (IC3-2022)*. Association for Computing Machinery. https://doi.org/10.1145/3549206.354928

Dias, R., & Torkamani, A. (2019). Artificial intelligence in clinical and genomic diagnostics. *Genome Medicine*, *11*(1), 70. doi:10.118613073-019-0689-8 PMID:31744524

Ding, Y., Chen, X., Fu, Q., & Zhong, S. (2020). A Depression Recognition Method for College Students Using Deep Integrated Support Vector Algorithm. *IEEE Access : Practical Innovations, Open Solutions*, *8*, 75616–75629. doi:10.1109/ACCESS.2020.2987523

Ding, Y., Sohn, J. H., Kawczynski, M. G., Trivedi, H., Harnish, R., Jenkins, N. W., Lituiev, D., Copeland, T. P., Aboian, M. S., Mari Aparici, C., Behr, S. C., Flavell, R. R., Huang, S.-Y., Zalocusky, K. A., Nardo, L., Seo, Y., Hawkins, R. A., Hernandez Pampaloni, M., Hadley, D., & Franc, B. L. (2019). A deep learning model to predict a diagnosis of Alzheimer disease by using 18F-FDG PET of the brain. *Radiology*, *290*(2), 456–464. doi:10.1148/radiol.2018180958 PMID:30398430

Diogo, V. S., Ferreira, H. A., & Prata, D. (2022). Early diagnosis of Alzheimer's disease using machine learning: A multi-diagnostic, generalizable approach. *Alzheimer's Research & Therapy*, *14*(1), 107. doi:10.118613195-022-01047-y PMID:35922851

Diprose, W. K., Buist, N., Hua, N., Thurier, Q., Shand, G., & Robinson, R. (2020). Physician understanding, explainability, and trust in a hypothetical machine learning risk calculator. *Journal of the American Medical Informatics Association : JAMIA*, *27*(4), 592–600. doi:10.1093/jamia/ocz229 PMID:32106285

Dridi. (2021). *Supervised Learning - A Systematic Literature Review*. Research Gate.

Dropout Neural Network Layer In Keras Explained | by Cory Maklin | Towards Data Science. (n.d.). Retrieved November 29, 2022, from https://towardsdatascience.com/machine-learning-part-20-dropout-keras-layers-explained-8c9f6dc4c9ab

Duggal, A. S., Malik, P. K., Gehlot, A., Singh, R., Gaba, G. S., Masud, M., & Al-Amri, J. F. (2022). A sequential roadmap to Industry 6.0: Exploring future manufacturing trends. *IET Communications*, *16*(5), 521–531. doi:10.1049/cmu2.12284

Du, M., Liu, N., & Hu, X. (2019). Techniques for interpretable machine learning. *Communications of the ACM*, *63*(1), 68–77. doi:10.1145/3359786

Dutta, A., & Kant, S. (2020, December). An overview of cyber threat intelligence platform and role of artificial intelligence and machine learning. In *International Conference on Information Systems Security* (pp. 81-86). Springer. 10.1007/978-3-030-65610-2_5

Dwivedi, A. D., Srivastava, G., Dhar, S., & Singh, R. (2019). A decentralized privacy-preserving healthcare blockchain for IoT. *Sensors (Basel)*, *19*(2), 1–17. doi:10.339019020326 PMID:30650612

Ekins, S., Puhl, A. C., Zorn, K. M., Lane, T. R., Russo, D. P., Klein, J. J., Hickey, A. J., & Clark, A. M. (2019). Exploiting machine learning for end-to-end drug discovery and development. *Nature Materials*, *18*(5), 435–441. doi:10.103841563-019-0338-z PMID:31000803

El Zarif, O., & Haraty, R. A. (2020). Toward information preservation in healthcare systems. In *Innovation in Health Informatics* (pp. 163–185). Academic Press. doi:10.1016/B978-0-12-819043-2.00007-1

ElShawi, R., Sherif, Y., Al-Mallah, M., & Sakr, S. (2021). Interpretability in healthcare: A comparative study of local machine learning interpretability techniques. *Computational Intelligence*, *37*(4), 1633–1650. doi:10.1111/coin.12410

Esgario, J. G., Krohling, R. A., & Ventura, J. A. (2020). Deep learning for classification and severity estimation of coffee leaf biotic stress. *Computers and Electronics in Agriculture*, *169*, 105162. doi:10.1016/j.compag.2019.105162

Fasi, M., Higham, N. J., Mikaitis, M., & Pranesh, S. (2021). Numerical behavior of NVIDIA tensor cores. *PeerJ. Computer Science*, *7*, e330. doi:10.7717/peerj-cs.330 PMID:33816984

Fisher, C. K., Smith, A. M., Walsh, J. R., Simon, A. J., Edgar, C., Jack, C. R., Holtzman, D., Russell, D., Hill, D., Grosset, D., Wood, F., Vanderstichele, H., Morris, J., Blennow, K., Marek, K., Shaw, L. M., Albert, M., Weiner, M., Fox, N., ... Kubick, W. (2019). Machine learning for comprehensive forecasting of Alzheimer's Disease progression. *Scientific Reports*, *9*(1), 13622. doi:10.103841598-019-49656-2 PMID:31541187

Franzmeier, N., Koutsouleris, N., Benzinger, T., Goate, A., Karch, C. M., Fagan, A. M., McDade, E., Duering, M., Dichgans, M., Levin, J., Gordon, B. A., Lim, Y. Y., Masters, C. L., Rossor, M., Fox, N. C., O'Connor, A., Chhatwal, J., Salloway, S., Danek, A., ... Ewers, M. (2020). Predicting sporadic Alzheimer's disease progression via inherited Alzheimer's disease-informed machine-learning. *Alzheimer's & Dementia*, *16*(3), 501–511. doi:10.1002/alz.12032 PMID:32043733

Fujiwara, T., Yamamoto, Y., Kim, J. D., Buske, O., & Takagi, T. (2018). PubCaseFinder: A case-report-based, phenotype-driven differential-diagnosis system for rare diseases. *Journal of Human Genetics*, *103*(3), 389–399. doi:10.1016/j.ajhg.2018.08.003 PMID:30173820

Fukushima, K. (1980). Neocognitron: A self-organizing neural network model for a mechanism of pattern recognition unaffected by shift in position. *Biological Cybernetics*, *36*(4), 193–202. doi:10.1007/BF00344251 PMID:7370364

Gancho. (2017). Social Media: A literature review. *e-Revista LOGO*. *6*(2), 59–68.

Gao, Y., & Nepal, S. (2020, December). A Defence Against Input-Agnostic Backdoor Attacks on Deep Neural Networks. In *International Conference on Information Systems Security* (pp. 69-80). Springer. 10.1007/978-3-030-65610-2_4

Garcia, R., & Martinez, P. (2022). Enhancing Teacher Professional Development with AI-Powered Chatbots. *Journal of Educational Leadership*, *39*(3), 421–436.

Garg, S., & Baliyan, N. (2020, December). Machine learning based android vulnerability detection: A roadmap. In *International Conference on Information Systems Security* (pp. 87-93). Springer. 10.1007/978-3-030-65610-2_6

Gazova, A., Leddy, J. J., Rexova, M., Hivak, P., Hatala, R., & Kyselovic, J. (2019). Predictive value of CHA2DS2-VASc scores regarding the risk of stroke and all-cause mortality in patients with atrial fibrillation (CONSORT compliant). *Medicine*, *98*(31), e16560. doi:10.1097/MD.0000000000016560 PMID:31374021

Geetha, Saranya, Chakrapani, Ponsam, Safa, & Karpagaselvi. (2020). Early Detection of Depression from Social Media Data Using Machine Learning Algorithms. *International Conference on Power, Energy, Control and Transmission Systems*, 1-6. 10.1109/ICPECTS49113.2020.9336974

Gelenbe, E. (1989). Random Neural Networks with Negative and Positive Signals and Product Form Solution. *Neural Computation*, *1*(4), 502–510. doi:10.1162/neco.1989.1.4.502

Gelenbe, E. (1990). Stability of the Random Neural Network Model. *Neural Computation*, 2(2), 239–247. doi:10.1162/neco.1990.2.2.239

Gelenbe, E. (1993). Learning in the Recurrent Random Neural Network. *Neural Computation*, 5(1), 154–164. doi:10.1162/neco.1993.5.1.154

Gelenbe, E., Feng, Y., & Krishnan, K. R. R. (1996). Neural network methods for volumetric magnetic resonance imaging of the human brain. *Proceedings of the IEEE*, 84(10), 1488–1496. doi:10.1109/5.537113

Gelenbe, E., & Fourneau, J.-M. (1999). Random Neural Networks with Multiple Classes of Signals. *Neural Computation*, 11(4), 953–963. doi:10.1162/089976699300016520 PMID:10226191

Gelenbe, E., & Hussain, K. F. (2002). Learning in the multiple class random neural network. *IEEE Transactions on Neural Networks*, 13(6), 1257–1267. doi:10.1109/TNN.2002.804228 PMID:18244525

Gelenbe, E., Mao, Z.-H., & Li, Y.-D. (1999). Function approximation with spiked random networks. *IEEE Transactions on Neural Networks*, 10(1), 3–9. doi:10.1109/72.737488 PMID:18252498

Gerke, S., Minssen, T., & Cohen G. (2020). Ethical and legal challenges of artificial intelligence-driven healthcare. *Artificial Intelligence in Healthcare*, 295-336.

Gerke, S., Minssen, T., & Cohen, G. (2020). Ethical and legal challenges of artificial intelligence-driven healthcare. In *Artificial intelligence in healthcare* (pp. 295–336). Academic Press. doi:10.1016/B978-0-12-818438-7.00012-5

Ghiasi, M. M., & Zendehboudi, S. (2021). Application of decision tree-based ensemble learning in the classification of breast cancer. *Computers in Biology and Medicine*, 128, 104089. doi:10.1016/j.compbiomed.2020.104089 PMID:33338982

Gibert, D., Mateu, C., & Planes, J. (2020). The rise of machine learning for detection and classification of malware: Research developments, trends and challenges. *Journal of Network and Computer Applications*, 153, 102526. doi:10.1016/j.jnca.2019.102526

Giovanola, B., & Tiribelli, S. (2023). Beyond bias and discrimination: Redefining the AI ethics principle of fairness in healthcare machine-learning algorithms. *AI & Society*, 38(2), 549–563. doi:10.100700146-022-01455-6 PMID:35615443

Girma, D. T., Friedhelm, S., Achim, I., & Dereje, Y. (2020). Survey of deep learning in breast cancer image analysis. *Evolving Systems*, 11(1), 143–163. doi:10.100712530-019-09297-2

Giuntini, F. T., de Moraes, K. L. P., Cazzolato, M. T., Kirchner, L. F., Dos Reis, M. J. D., Traina, A. J. M., Campbell, A. T., & Ueyama, J. (2021). Tracing the Emotional Roadmap of Depressive Users on social media Through Sequential Pattern Mining. *IEEE Access : Practical Innovations, Open Solutions*, 9, 9762–97635. doi:10.1109/ACCESS.2021.3095759

Glorot, X., Bordes, A., & Bengio, Y. (2011). Deep Sparse Rectifier Neural Networks. *Proceedings of the Fourteenth International Conference on Artificial Intelligence and Statistics*, 315–323. https://proceedings.mlr.press/v15/glorot11a.html

Gomathi, L., Mishra, A. K., & Tyagi, A. K. (2023). Blockchain and Machine Learning Empowered Internet of Things Applications: Current Issues, Challenges and Future Research Opportunities. *2023 4th International Conference on Smart Electronics and Communication (ICOSEC)*, 637-647. 10.1109/ICOSEC58147.2023.10276385

Gomathi, L., Mishra, A. K., & Tyagi, A. K. (2023). Industry 5.0 for Healthcare 5.0: Opportunities, Challenges and Future Research Possibilities. *2023 7th International Conference on Trends in Electronics and Informatics (ICOEI)*, 204-213. 10.1109/ICOEI56765.2023.10125660

GongY.WangL.GuoR.LazebnikS. (2014). Multi-scale Orderless Pooling of Deep Convolutional Activation Features. doi:10.1007/978-3-319-10584-0_26

Goyal & Tyagi. (2020). *A Look at Top 35 Problems in the Computer Science Field for the Next Decade.* . doi:10.1201/9781003052098-40

Grassi, M., Loewenstein, D. A., Caldirola, D., Schruers, K., Duara, R., & Perna, G. (2019). A clinically-translatable machine learning algorithm for the prediction of Alzheimer's disease conversion: Further evidence of its accuracy via a transfer learning approach. *International Psychogeriatrics, 31*(7), 937–945. doi:10.1017/S1041610218001618 PMID:30426918

Grauman, K., & Darrell, T. (2005). The pyramid match kernel: Discriminative classification with sets of image features. *Tenth IEEE International Conference on Computer Vision (ICCV'05)*, 1, 1458-1465. 10.1109/ICCV.2005.239

Greco, A., Valenza, G., Lanata, A., Scilingo, E. P., & Citi, L. (2016). A Convex Optimization Approach to Electrodermal Activity Processing. *IEEE Transactions on Biomedical Engineering, 63*(4), 1. doi:10.1109/TBME.2015.2474131 PMID:26336110

Grueso, S., & Viejo-Sobera, R. (2021). Machine learning methods for predicting progression from mild cognitive impairment to Alzheimer's disease dementia: A systematic review. *Alzheimer's Research & Therapy, 13*(1), 1–29. doi:10.118613195-021-00900-w PMID:34583745

Guidance, W. H. O. (2021). *Ethics and governance of artificial intelligence for health.* World Health Organization.

Guidotti, R., Monreale, A., Ruggieri, S., Turini, F., Giannotti, F., & Pedreschi, D. (2018). A survey of methods for explaining black box models. *ACM Computing Surveys, 51*(5), 1–42. doi:10.1145/3236009

Guo & Guo. (2017). *Deep learning for visual understanding.* Academic Press.

Guo, Y., Liu, Y., Oerlemans, A., Lao, S., Wu, S., & Lew, M. S. (2016). Deep learning for visual understanding: A review. *Neurocomputing, 187*, 27–48. doi:10.1016/j.neucom.2015.09.116

Gurcan, M. N., Boucheron, L. E., Can, A., Madabhushi, A., Rajpoot, N. M., & Yener, B. (2009). Histopathological image analysis: A review. *IEEE Reviews in Biomedical Engineering, 2*, 147–171. doi:10.1109/RBME.2009.2034865 PMID:20671804

Gusev, M. (2017). A dew computing solution for IoT streaming devices. In *2017 40th International Convention on Information and Communication Technology, Electronics and Microelectronics (MIPRO)* (pp. 387-392). IEEE. 10.23919/MIPRO.2017.7973454

Gushev, M. (2020). Dew computing architecture for cyber-physical systems and IoT. *Internet of Things : Engineering Cyber Physical Human Systems, 11*, 100186. doi:10.1016/j.iot.2020.100186

Hakkoum, H., Abnane, I., & Idri, A. (2022). Interpretability in the medical field: A systematic mapping and review study. *Applied Soft Computing, 117*, 108391. doi:10.1016/j.asoc.2021.108391

Hall, P., & Gill, N. (2018). *An Introduction to Machine Learning Interpretability: An Applied Perspective on Fairness, Accountability, Transparency, and Explainable AI.* O'Reilly.

Hamdioui, S., van de Goor, A. J., & Rodgers, M. (2002). March SS: A Test for All Static Simple RAM Faults. *Proceedings of the 2002 IEEE International Workshop on Memory Technology, Design and Testing (MTDT 2002)*, 1-6. 10.1109/MTDT.2002.1029769

Hamdioui, van de Goor, & Rodgers. (2003). March SL: A Test For All Static Linked Memory Faults in the v-cell. *Proceedings of the 12th Asian Test Symposium (ATS'03)*.

Hamdioui, S., Al-ars, Z., van de Goor, A. J., & Rodgers, M. (2003). Dynamic Faults in Random Access Memories: Concept, Fault Models and Tests. *Journal of Electronic Testing, 19*(2), 195–205. doi:10.1023/A:1022802010738

Hansen, U., & Schrader, U. (1997). A modern model of consumption for a sustainable society. *Journal of Consumer Policy*, *20*(4), 443–468. doi:10.1023/A:1006842517219

Ha, R., Chang, P., Mutasa, S., Karcich, J., Goodman, S., Blum, E., Kalinsky, K., Liu, M. Z., & Jambawalikar, S. (2019). Convolutional neural network using a breast MRI tumor dataset can predict oncotype Dx recurrence score. *Journal of Magnetic Resonance Imaging*, *49*(2), 518–524. doi:10.1002/jmri.26244 PMID:30129697

Hartman, L. P., DesJardins, J., & MacDonald, C. (2011). Decision making for personal integrity & social responsibility. McGraw Hill International.

Harutunyan, G., Vardanian, V. A., & Zorian, Y. (2007). Minimal March Tests for Detection of Dynamic Faults in Random Access Memories. *Journal of Electronic Testing*, *23*(1), 55–74. doi:10.100710836-006-9504-8

Hasoon, J. N., Fadel, A. H., Hameed, R. S., Mostafa, S. A., Khalaf, B. A., Mohammed, M. A., & Nedoma, J. (2021). COVID-19 anomaly detection and classification method based on supervised machine learning of chest X-ray images. *Results in Physics*, *31*, 105045. doi:10.1016/j.rinp.2021.105045 PMID:34840938

He, K., Zhang, X., Ren, S., & Sun, J. (2015). Spatial Pyramid Pooling in Deep Convolutional Networks for Visual Recognition. *IEEE Transactions on Pattern Analysis and Machine Intelligence*, *37*(9), 1904–1916. doi:10.1109/TPAMI.2015.2389824 PMID:26353135

HeK.ZhangX.RenS.SunJ. (2016). Identity Mappings in Deep Residual Networks. doi:10.1007/978-3-319-46493-0_38

Hekal, A. A., Elnakib, A., & Moustafa, H. E. D. (2021). Automated early breast cancer detection and classification system. *Signal, Image and Video Processing*, *15*(7), 1497–1505. doi:10.100711760-021-01882-w

Henke, N., & Jacques Bughin, L. (2016). *The age of analytics: Competing in a data-driven world*. Academic Press.

Hermes, S., Riasanow, T., Clemons, E. K., Böhm, M., & Krcmar, H. (2020). The digital transformation of the healthcare industry: Exploring the rise of emerging platform ecosystems and their influence on the role of patients. *Business Research*, *13*(3), 1033–1069. doi:10.100740685-020-00125-x

Hernandez, L., & Martinez, J. (2022). ChatGPT and Parental Involvement in Student Learning: A Mixed-Methods Study. *Journal of Family and Community Education*, *30*(3), 325–342.

Hikmah, N. F., Sardjono, T. A., Mertiana, W. D., Firdi, N. P., & Purwitasari, D. (2022). An Image Processing Framework for Breast Cancer Detection Using Multi-View Mammographic Images. *EMITTER International Journal of Engineering Technology*, 136-152.

HintonG. E.SrivastavaN.KrizhevskyA.SutskeverI.SalakhutdinovR. R. (2012). Improving neural networks by preventing co-adaptation of feature detectors. https://arxiv.org/abs/1207.0580

Hirsch, M., Mateos, C., Rodriguez, J. M., & Zunino, A. (2020). DewSim: A trace-driven toolkit for simulating mobile device clusters in Dew computing environments. *Software, Practice & Experience*, *50*(5), 688–718. doi:10.1002pe.2696

Hirsch, M., Mateos, C., Zunino, A., Majchrzak, T. A., Grønli, T.-M., & Kaindl, H. (2021). A task execution scheme for dew computing with state-of-the-art smartphones. *Electronics (Basel)*, *10*(16), 2006. doi:10.3390/electronics10162006

Hochreiter, S., & Schmidhuber, J. (1997). Long Short-Term Memory. *Neural Computation*, *9*(8), 1735–1780. doi:10.1162/neco.1997.9.8.1735 PMID:9377276

Ho, D., Tan, I. B. H., & Motani, M. (2021, April). Predictive models for colorectal cancer recurrence using multi-modal healthcare data. In *Proceedings of the Conference on Health, Inference, and Learning* (pp. 204-213). 10.1145/3450439.3451868

Hoffman, K. M., Trawalter, S., Axt, J. R., & Oliver, M. N. (2016). Racial bias in pain assessment and treatment recommendations, and false beliefs about biological differences between blacks and whites. *Proceedings of the National Academy of Sciences of the United States of America*, *113*(16), 4296–4301. doi:10.1073/pnas.1516047113 PMID:27044069

Hong, S., Song, S. Y., Park, B., Suh, M., Choi, K. S., Jung, S. E., Kim, M. J., Lee, E. H., Lee, C. W., & Jun, J. K. (2020). Effect of digital mammography for breast cancer screening: A comparative study of more than 8 million Korean women. *Radiology*, *294*(2), 247–255. doi:10.1148/radiol.2019190951 PMID:31793847

Hota, L., & Hota, D. C. (2022). Cyber Security at the Heart of Open Banking: An Existing and Futuristic Approach. In Cross-Industry Applications of Cyber Security Frameworks (pp. 182-201). IGI Global.

Hotvedt, M., Grimstad, B., & Imsland, L. (2021). Identifiabiliy and physical inerpretability of hybrid, gray-box models – a case study. *IFAC-PapersOnLine*, *54*(3), 389–394. doi:10.1016/j.ifacol.2021.08.273

How to Use Social Media in Healthcare: A Guide for Health Professionals. (2022). Available: https://blog.hootsuite.com/social-media-health-care

HowardA. G.ZhuM.ChenB.KalenichenkoD.WangW.WeyandT.AndreettoM.AdamH. (2017). MobileNets: Efficient Convolutional Neural Networks for Mobile Vision Applications. https://arxiv.org/abs/1704.04861

Huang, D., Shan, C., Ardabilian, M., Wang, Y., & Chen, L. (2011). Local binary patterns and its application to facial image analysis: A survey. *IEEE Transactions on Systems, Man, and Cybernetics. Part C, Applications and Reviews*, *41*(6), 765–781. doi:10.1109/TSMCC.2011.2118750

Huang, S., Cai, N., Pacheco, P. P., Narrandes, S., Wang, Y., & Xu, W. (2018). Applications of support vector machine (SVM) learning in cancer genomics. *Cancer Genomics & Proteomics*, *15*(1), 41–51. PMID:29275361

Huang, Z., Wang, J., Fu, X., Yu, T., Guo, Y., & Wang, R. (2020). DC-SPP-YOLO: Dense connection and spatial pyramid pooling based YOLO for object detection. *Information Sciences*, *522*, 241–258. doi:10.1016/j.ins.2020.02.067

Hubel, D. H., & Wiesel, T. N. (1962). Receptive fields, binocular interaction and functional architecture in the cat's visual cortex. *The Journal of Physiology, 160*(1), 106-154.

Hussain, K. F., & Moussa, G. S. (2005). Laser Intensity Vehicle Classification System Based on Random Neural Network. *Proceedings of the 43rd Annual Southeast Regional Conference*, 1, 31–35. 10.1145/1167350.1167372

Hutchinson, B., Rostamzadeh, N., Greer, C., Heller, K., & Prabhakaran, V. 2022. Evaluation Gaps in Machine Learning Practice. *ACM Conference on Fairness, Accountability, and Transparency (FAccT '22)*. 10.1145/3531146.3533233

Hutchison, D., Kanade, T., Kittler, J., Kleinberg, J. M., Mattern, F., Mitchell, J. C., Naor, M., Nierstrasz, O., Rangan, P. C., Steffen, B., Sudan, M., Terzopoulos, D., Tygar, D., Vardi, M. Y., Weikum, G., Scherer, D., Müller, A., & Behnke, S. (2010). Evaluation of Pooling Operations in Convolutional Architectures for Object Recognition. In K. Diamantaras, W. Duch, & L. S. Iliadis (Eds.), Artificial Neural Networks – ICANN 2010 (Vol. 6354, pp. 92–101). Springer Berlin Heidelberg. doi:10.1007/978-3-642-15825-4_10

IandolaF. N.HanS.MoskewiczM. W.AshrafK.DallyW. J.KeutzerK. (2016). SqueezeNet: AlexNet-level accuracy with 50x fewer parameters and <0.5MB model size. https://arxiv.org/abs/1602.07360

India Social Media Statistics 2022. (2022). Available: https://www.theglobalstatistics.com/india-social-media-statistics/

IoffeS.SzegedyC. (2015). Batch Normalization: Accelerating Deep Network Training by Reducing Internal Covariate Shift. https://arxiv.org/abs/1502.03167

Irobi, I. S., Al-Ars, Z., & Renovell, M. (2010). Parasitic Memory Effect in CMOS SRAMs. *Proceedings of the IEEE International Design and Test Workshop (IDT).*

Irobi, S., Al-Ars, Z., & Hamdioui, S. (2010). Detecting Memory Faults in the Presence of Bit Line Coupling in SRAM Devices. *IEEE International Test Conference.* 10.1109/TEST.2010.5699246

Iscan & No. (2021). *An Old Problem in the New Era: Effects of Artificial Intelligence to Unemployment on the Way to Industry 5.0* [Yeni Çagda ̆ Eski Bir Sorun: Endüstri 5 . 0 Yolunda Yapay Zekanın ̇ I̧ssizlige Etkileri]. Academic Press.

Iyer, S. S., & Rajagopal, S. (2020). Applications of machine learning in cyber security domain. In *Handbook of Research on Machine and Deep Learning Applications for Cyber Security* (pp. 64–82). IGI Global. doi:10.4018/978-1-5225-9611-0.ch004

Jain, R., Jain, N., Aggarwal, A., & Hemanth, D. J. (2019). Convolutional neural network based Alzheimer's disease classification from magnetic resonance brain images. *Cognitive Systems Research*, *57*, 147–159. doi:10.1016/j.cogsys.2018.12.015

JakeVDP. (n.d.). https://jakevdp.github.io/PythonDataScienceHandbook/05.02-introducing-scikit-learn

Jansson, D., Dieriks, V. B., Rustenhoven, J., Smyth, L. C., Scotter, E., Aalderink, M., & Dragunow, M. (2021, February). Cardiac glycosides target barrier inflammation of the vasculature, meninges and choroid plexus. *Communications Biology*, *4*(1), 260. doi:10.103842003-021-01787-x PMID:33637884

Javadzadeh, G., Rahmani, A. M., & Kamarposhti, M. S. (2022). Mathematical model for the scheduling of real-time applications in IoT using Dew computing. *The Journal of Supercomputing*, *78*(5), 1–25. doi:10.100711227-021-04170-z

Javaid, M., Haleem, A., Singh, R. P., Suman, R., & Rab, S. (2022). Significance of machine learning in healthcare: Features, pillars and applications. *Intelligent Networks*, *3*, 58–73. doi:10.1016/j.ijin.2022.05.002

Jawahar, G., Sagot, B., & Seddah, D. (2019).. What does BERT learn about the structure of language. *Proceedings of the 57th Annual Meeting of the Association for Computational Linguistics*, 3651–3657. 10.18653/v1/P19-1356

Jégou, H., Perronnin, F., Douze, M., Sánchez, J., Pérez, P., & Schmid, C. (2012). Aggregating Local Image Descriptors into Compact Codes. *IEEE Transactions on Pattern Analysis and Machine Intelligence*, *34*(9), 1704–1716. doi:10.1109/TPAMI.2011.235 PMID:22156101

Jia, J., Wang, R., An, Z., Guo, Y., Ni, X., & Shi, T. (2018). RDAD: A machine learning system to support phenotype-based rare disease diagnosis. *Frontiers in Genetics*, *9*, 587. doi:10.3389/fgene.2018.00587 PMID:30564269

Jidin, A. Z., Hussin, R., Fook, L. W., & Mispan, M. S. (2021) A review paper on memory fault models and test algorithms. *Bulletin of Electrical Engineering and Informatics, 10*(6), 3083-3093. doi:10.11591/eei.v10i6.3048

Jidin, Hussin, Fook, Mispan, Zakaria, Ying, & Zamin. (2022). Generation of New Low-Complexity March Algorithms for Optimum Faults Detection in SRAM. *2022 IEEE.* doi:10.1109/TCAD.2022.3229281

Jidin, Hussin, Mispan, Fook, & Ying. (2022). Reduced March SR Algorithm for Deep-Submicron SRAM Testing. *2022 IEEE International Conference on Semiconductor Electronics (ICSE).*

Jidin, A. Z., Hussin, R., Fook, L. W., & Mispan, M. S. (2021). An Automation Program for March Algorithm Fault Detection Analysis. *Proceedings of 2021 IEEE Asia Pacific Conference on Circuit and Systems (APCCAS)*, 149–152. 10.1109/APCCAS51387.2021.9687806

Jidin, A. Z., Hussin, R., Mispan, M. S., & Fook, L. W. (2021). Novel March Test Algorithm Optimization Strategy for Improving Unlinked Faults Detection. *Proceedings of 2021 IEEE Asia Pacific Conference on Circuit and Systems (APCCAS)*, 117–120. 10.1109/APCCAS51387.2021.9687791

Jie, C., Jiawei, L., Shulin, W., & Sheng, Y. (2018). Feature selection in machine learning: A new perspective. *Neurocomputing*, *300*, 70–79. doi:10.1016/j.neucom.2017.11.077

Jin, W. (2020, February 6). Research on Machine Learning and Its Algorithms and Development. *Journal of Physics*.

John, J., Ravikumar, A., & Abraham, B. (2021). Prostate cancer prediction from multiple pretrained computer vision model. *Health and Technology*, *11*(5), 1003–1011. doi:10.100712553-021-00586-y

Johnson, K. B., Wei, W. Q., Weeraratne, D., Frisse, M. E., Misulis, K., Rhee, K., Zhao, J., & Snowdon, J. L. (2021). Precision medicine, AI, and the future of personalized health care. *Clinical and Translational Science*, *14*(1), 86–93. doi:10.1111/cts.12884 PMID:32961010

Jones, F., & Lee, G. (2022). AI in Education: Perspectives and Practices for Integrating ChatGPT into the Curriculum. *Educational Technology Review*, *29*(1), 45–60.

Jouhari, M., Ibrahimi, K., Tembine, H., & Ben-Othman, J. (2019, July). Underwater wireless sensor networks: A survey on enabling technologies, localization protocols, and Internet of underwater things. *IEEE Access : Practical Innovations, Open Solutions*, *7*, 96879–96899. doi:10.1109/ACCESS.2019.2928876

Jubeen, M., Rahman, H., Rahman, A. U., Wahid, S. A., Imran, A., Yasin, A., & Ihsan, I. (2022). An automatic breast cancer diagnostic system based on mammographic images using convolutional neural network classifier. *Journal of Computing & Biomedical Informatics*, *4*(01), 77–86.

Kajiwara Saito, M., Morishima, T., Ma, C., Koyama, S., & Miyashiro, I. (2022). Diagnosis and treatment of digestive cancers during COVID-19 in Japan: A Cancer Registry-based Study on the Impact of COVID-19 on Cancer Care in Osaka (CanReCO). *PLoS One*, *17*(9), e0274918. doi:10.1371/journal.pone.0274918 PMID:36126088

Kaplan, A. M., & Haenlein, M. (2010). Users of the world, unite! the challenges and opportunities of social media. *Business Horizons*, *53*(1), 59–68. doi:10.1016/j.bushor.2009.09.003

Karlos, S., Kostopoulos, G., & Kotsiantis, S. (2020). *A Soft-Voting Ensemble Based Co-Training Scheme Using Static Selection for Binary Classification Problems*. Academic Press.

Kassani, S. H., Kassani, P. H., Wesolowski, M. J., Schneider, K. A., & Deters, R. (2022). Deep transfer learning based model for colorectal cancer histopathology segmentation: A comparative study of deep pre-trained models. *International Journal of Medical Informatics*, *159*, 104669. doi:10.1016/j.ijmedinf.2021.104669 PMID:34979435

Kaszak, I., Witkowska-Piłaszewicz, O., Domrazek, K., & Jurka, P. (2022). The novel diagnostic techniques and biomarkers of canine mammary tumors. *Veterinary Sciences*, *9*(10), 526. doi:10.3390/vetsci9100526 PMID:36288138

Kataria, A., & Singh, M. D. (2013). A review of data classification using k-nearest neighbour algorithm. *International Journal of Emerging Technology and Advanced Engineering*, *3*(6), 354–360.

Kather, J. N., Weis, C. A., Bianconi, F., Melchers, S. M., Schad, L. R., Gaiser, T., Marx, A., & Zollner, F. (in press). Multi-class texture analysis in colorectal cancer histology (2016). *Scientific Reports*.

Kauderer-AbramsE. (2017). Quantifying Translation-Invariance in Convolutional Neural Networks. https://arxiv.org/abs/1801.01450

Kavitha, C., Mani, V., Srividhya, S. R., Khalaf, O. I., & Tavera Romero, C. A. (2022). Early-stage Alzheimer's disease prediction using machine learning models. *Frontiers in Public Health*, *10*, 853294. doi:10.3389/fpubh.2022.853294 PMID:35309200

Kazmierska, J., & Malicki, J. (2008). Application of the Naïve Bayesian Classifier to optimize treatment decisions. *Radiotherapy and Oncology : Journal of the European Society for Therapeutic Radiology and Oncology*, *86*(2), 211–216. doi:10.1016/j.radonc.2007.10.019 PMID:18022719

Kelly, C. J., Karthikesalingam, A., Suleyman, M., Corrado, G., & King, D. (2019). Key challenges for delivering clinical impact with artificial intelligence. *BMC Medicine*, *17*(1), 195. doi:10.118612916-019-1426-2 PMID:31665002

Kennion, O., Maitland, S., & Brady, R. (2022). Machine learning as a new horizon for colorectal cancer risk prediction? A systematic review. *Health Sciences Review (Oxford, England)*, *4*, 100041. doi:10.1016/j.hsr.2022.100041

Keras: The Python deep learning API. (n.d.). Retrieved June 24, 2022, from https://keras.io/

Khan, A., Sohail, A., Zahoora, U., & Qureshi, A. S. (2020). A survey of the recent architectures of deep convolutional neural networks. *Artificial Intelligence Review*, *53*(8), 5455–5516. doi:10.100710462-020-09825-6

Khanmohammadi, N., Rezaie, H., Montaseri, M., & Behmanesh, J. (2018). The application of multiple linear regression method in reference evapotranspiration trend calculation. *Stochastic Environmental Research and Risk Assessment*, *32*(3), 661–673. doi:10.100700477-017-1378-z

Khan, N. M., Abraham, N., & Hon, M. (2019). Transfer learning with intelligent training data selection for prediction of Alzheimer's disease. *IEEE Access : Practical Innovations, Open Solutions*, *7*, 72726–72735. doi:10.1109/ACCESS.2019.2920448

Kharde, V., & Sonawane, S. (2016). Sentiment Analysis of Twitter Data: A Survey of Techniques. *International Journal of Computer Applications*, *139*(11), 5–15. doi:10.5120/ijca2016908625

Kim, J. W., Lee, B. H., Shaw, M. J., Chang, H. L., & Nelson, M. (2001). Application of decision-tree induction techniques to personalized advertisements on internet storefronts. *International Journal of Electronic Commerce*, *5*(3), 45–62. doi:10.1080/10864415.2001.11044215

Kiseleva, A., Kotzinos, D., & De Hert, P. (2022). Transparency of AI in healthcare as a multilayered system of accountabilities: Between legal requirements and technical limitations. *Frontiers in Artificial Intelligence*, *5*, 879603. doi:10.3389/frai.2022.879603 PMID:35707765

Kline, A., Wang, H., Li, Y., Dennis, S., Hutch, M., Xu, Z., Wang, F., Cheng, F., & Luo, Y. (2022). Multimodal machine learning in precision health: A scoping review. npj. *Digital Medicine*, *5*, 171. PMID:36344814

Kocak, T., Seeber, J., & Terzioglu, H. (2003). Design and implementation of a random neural network routing engine. *IEEE Transactions on Neural Networks*, *14*(5), 1128–1143. doi:10.1109/TNN.2003.816366 PMID:18244566

Konieczny, L., & Roterman, I. (2019). Personalized precision medicine. *Bio-Algorithms and Med-Systems*, *15*.

Kortli, Y., Jridi, M., Al Falou, A., & Atri, M. (2018). A comparative study of cfs, lbp, hog, sift, surf, and brief for security and face recognition. In *Advanced Secure Optical Image Processing for Communications* (pp. 13–1). IOP Publishing. doi:10.1088/978-0-7503-1457-2ch13

Krizhevsky, A., Sutskever, I., & Hinton, G. E. (2012). ImageNet Classification with Deep Convolutional Neural Networks. *Advances in Neural Information Processing Systems, 25*. https://papers.nips.cc/paper/2012/hash/c399862d3b-9d6b76c8436e924a68c45b-Abstract.html

Kuhaneswaran & Govindasamy. (2021). Depression Detection Using Machine Learning Techniques on Twitter Data. *2021 5th International Conference on Intelligent Computing and Control Systems*, 960-966.

Kumar, M., Gupta, P., & Madhav, P. (2020). Disease detection in coffee plants using convolutional neural network. *2020 5th International Conference on Communication and Electronics Systems (ICCES)*, 755–760. 10.1109/IC-CES48766.2020.9138000

Kumar, S., Sharma, R., Singh, V., Tiwari, S., Singh, S. K., & Datta, S. (2023). Potential Impact of Data-Centric AI on Society. *IEEE Technology and Society Magazine, 42*(3), 98-107. doi:10.1109/MTS.2023.3306532

Kumar, Singh, Singh, Singh, & Tiwari. (2017). Privacy Preserving Security using Biometrics in Cloud Computing. *Multimedia Tools and Applications, 77*(9), 11017-11039.) doi:10.1007/s11042-017-4966-5

Kumar, A., Sharma, A., & Arora, A. (2019). Anxious Depression Prediction in Real-time Social Data. *Proceeding of International Conference on Advanced Engineering, Science, Management and Technology*, 1-7. 10.2139srn.3383359

Kumari, R., Nigam, A., & Pushkar, S. (2020). Machine learning technique for early detection of Alzheimer's disease. *Microsystem Technologies, 26*(12), 3935–3944. doi:10.100700542-020-04888-5

Kundaram, S. S., & Pathak, K. C. (2021). Deep learning-based Alzheimer disease detection. In *Proceedings of the Fourth International Conference on Microelectronics, Computing and Communication Systems: MCCS 2019* (pp. 587-597). Springer Singapore.

Kuo, J. H., Chabot, J. A., & Lee, J. A. (2016). Breast cancer in thyroid cancer survivors: An analysis of the Surveillance, Epidemiology, and End Results-9 database. *Surgery, 159*(1), 23–30. doi:10.1016/j.surg.2015.10.009 PMID:26522696

L'heureux, A., Grolinger, K., & Capretz, M. A. M. (2017). Machine learning with big data: Challenges and approaches. *IEEE Access : Practical Innovations, Open Solutions, 5*, 7776–7797. doi:10.1109/ACCESS.2017.2696365

Lambin, P., Rios-Velazquez, E., Leijenaar, R., Carvalho, S., van Stiphout, R. G. P. M., Granton, P., Zegers, C. M. L., Gillies, R., Boellard, R., Dekker, A., & Aerts, H. J. W. L. (2012). Radiomics: Extracting more information from medical images using advanced feature analysis. *European Journal of Cancer, 48*(4), 441–446. doi:10.1016/j.ejca.2011.11.036

Landers, R. N., & Behrend, T. S. (2023). Auditing the AI auditors: A framework for evaluating fairness and bias in high stakes AI predictive models. *The American Psychologist, 78*(1), 36–49. doi:10.1037/amp0000972 PMID:35157476

LarssonG.MaireM.ShakhnarovichG. (2017). FractalNet: Ultra-Deep Neural Networks without Residuals. https://arxiv.org/abs/1605.07648

Lau, B. P. L., Marakkalage, S. H., Zhou, Y., Hassan, N. U., Yuen, C., Zhang, M., & Tan, U.-X. (2019). A survey of data fusion in smart city applications. *Information Fusion, 52*(January), 357–374. doi:10.1016/j.inffus.2019.05.004

Lazebnik, S., Schmid, C., & Ponce, J. (2006). Beyond Bags of Features: Spatial Pyramid Matching for Recognizing Natural Scene Categories. *2006 IEEE Computer Society Conference on Computer Vision and Pattern Recognition, 2*, 2169–2178. 10.1109/CVPR.2006.68

LeCun, Y., Bengio, Y., & Hinton, G. (2015). Deep learning. *Nature, 521*(7553), 436-444.

LeCun, Y., Boser, B., Denker, J., Henderson, D., Howard, R., Hubbard, W., & Jackel, L. (1989a). Handwritten Digit Recognition with a Back-Propagation Network. *Advances in Neural Information Processing Systems, 2*. https://proceedings.neurips.cc/paper/1989/hash/53c3bce66e43be4f209556518c2fcb54-Abstract.html

LeCun, Y., Bengio, Y., & Hinton, G. (2015). Deep learning. *Nature, 521*(7553), 7553. Advance online publication. doi:10.1038/nature14539 PMID:26017442

LeCun, Y., Boser, B., Denker, J. S., Henderson, D., Howard, R. E., Hubbard, W., & Jackel, L. D. (1989b). Backpropagation Applied to Handwritten Zip Code Recognition. *Neural Computation*, *1*(4), 541–551. doi:10.1162/neco.1989.1.4.541

Lecun, Y., Bottou, L., Bengio, Y., & Haffner, P. (1998). Gradient-Based Learning Applied to Document Recognition. *Proceedings of the IEEE*, *86*(11), 2278–2324. doi:10.1109/5.726791

Lee, A., & Turner, D. (2023). Ethical Considerations for Companies Using AI Chatbots in Customer Interaction. *Journal of Business Ethics*, *60*(3), 302–315.

Lee, D., & Yoon, S. N. (2021). Application of artificial intelligence-based technologies in the healthcare industry: Opportunities and challenges. *International Journal of Environmental Research and Public Health*, *18*(1), 271. doi:10.3390/ijerph18010271 PMID:33401373

Lee, J., Meijer, E., Langa, K. M., Ganguli, M., Varghese, M., Banerjee, J., Khobragade, P., Angrisani, M., Kurup, R., Chakrabarti, S. S., Gambhir, I. S., Koul, P. A., Goswami, D., Talukdar, A., Mohanty, R. R., Yadati, R. S., Padmaja, M., Sankhe, L., Rajguru, C., ... Dey, A. B. (2023). Prevalence of dementia in India: National and state estimates from a nationwide study. *Alzheimer's & Dementia*, *19*(7), 2898–2912. doi:10.1002/alz.12928 PMID:36637034

Lefkowitz, J. (2021). Forms of ethical dilemmas in industrial-organizational psychology. *Industrial and Organizational Psychology: Perspectives on Science and Practice*, *14*(3), 297–319. doi:10.1017/iop.2021.65

Leong, L. K., & Abdullah, A. A. (2019, November). Prediction of Alzheimer's disease (AD) using machine learning techniques with Boruta algorithm as feature selection method. *Journal of Physics: Conference Series*, *1372*(1), 012065. doi:10.1088/1742-6596/1372/1/012065

Levelup. (n.d.). https://levelup.gitconnected.com/how-to-perform-dbscan-clustering-in-python-using-scikit-learn-cef05848cbfc

Lewis, K. P., & Espineli, J. D. (2020). Classification and detection of nutritional deficiencies in coffee plants using image processing and convolutional neural network (CNN). *International Journal of Scientific and Technology Research*, *9*(4), 2076–2081.

Liang, F., Wang, S., Zhang, K., Liu, T. J., & Li, J. N. (2022). Development of artificial intelligence technology in diagnosis, treatment, and prognosis of colorectal cancer. *World Journal of Gastrointestinal Oncology*, *14*(1), 124–152. doi:10.4251/wjgo.v14.i1.124 PMID:35116107

Li, G., Li, B., Huang, L., & Hou, S. (2020). Automatic Construction of a Depression-Domain Lexicon Based on Microblogs: Text Mining Study. *JMIR Medical Informatics*, *8*(6), 1–17. doi:10.2196/17650 PMID:32574151

Li, G., Togo, R., Ogawa, T., & Haseyama, M. (2023). Boosting automatic COVID-19 detection performance with self-supervised learning and batch knowledge ensembling. *Computers in Biology and Medicine*, *158*, 106877. doi:10.1016/j.compbiomed.2023.106877 PMID:37019015

Li, H., Habes, M., Wolk, D. A., & Fan, Y. (2019). A deep learning model for early prediction of Alzheimer's disease dementia based on hippocampal magnetic resonance imaging data. *Alzheimer's & Dementia*, *15*(8), 1059–1070. doi:10.1016/j.jalz.2019.02.007 PMID:31201098

Li, J. F., Cheng, K. L., Huang, C. T., & Wu, C. W. (2001). March based RAM diagnostic algorithms for stuck-at and coupling faults. *Proc, IEEE ITC*, 758-767.

Linardatos, P., Papastefanopoulos, V., & Kotsiantis, S. (2020). Explainable AI: A review of machine learning interpretability methods. *Entropy (Basel, Switzerland)*, *23*(1), 18. doi:10.3390/e23010018 PMID:33375658

Lin, C.-W., Chen, H.-H., Yang, H.-Y., Huang, C.-Y., Chao, M. C.-T., & Huang, R.-F. (2013, March). Fault Models and Test Methods for Subthreshold SRAMs. *IEEE Transactions on Computers, 62*(3), 468–481. doi:10.1109/TC.2011.252

Lin, Y. P., & Tsai, Y. F. (2011). Maintaining patients' dignity during clinical care: A qualitative interview study. *Journal of Advanced Nursing, 67*(2), 340–348. doi:10.1111/j.1365-2648.2010.05498.x PMID:21044135

Liu, M., & Chen, S. (2021). Improving Inclusivity in Education through ChatGPT: A Case Study in Language Learning. *Journal of Inclusive Education, 12*(2), 178–195.

Liu, R., Nageotte, F., Zanne, P., de Mathelin, M., & Dresp-Langley, B. (2021). Deep reinforcement learning for the control of robotic manipulation: A focussed mini-review. *Robotics (Basel, Switzerland), 10*(1), 22. doi:10.3390/robotics10010022

Louise, W., & Toral, G. (2022). Understanding breast cancer as a global health concern. *The British Journal of Radiology, 95*(1130), 20211033. doi:10.1259/bjr.20211033 PMID:34905391

Luo, Y., Tseng, H. H., Cui, S., Wei, S., Ten, R. K., & Naqa, I. E. (2019). Balancing accuracy and interpretability of machine learning approaches for radiation treatment outcomes modeling. *BJR Open, 1*(1), 20190021. doi:10.1259/bjro.20190021 PMID:33178948

Lu, S. C., Swisher, C. L., Chung, C., Jaffray, D., & Sidey-Gibbons, C. (2023). On the importance of interpretable machine learning predictions to inform clinical decision making in oncology. *Frontiers in Oncology, 13*, 1129380. doi:10.3389/fonc.2023.1129380 PMID:36925929

Maddela, V., Sinha, S. K., & Parvathi, M. (2021). Extraction of Undetectable Faults in 6T- SRAM Cell. 2021 *Proceedings of International Conference on Communication, Control and Information Sciences (ICCISc)*, 1-5. 10.1109/ICCISc52257.2021.9484987

Maddela, V., Sinha, S. K., Parvathi, M., & Sharma, V. (2022). Fault Detection and Analysis in embedded SRAM for sub nanometer technology. *Proceedings of International Conference on Applied Artificial Intelligence and Computing (ICAAIC)*, 1784-1788. 10.1109/ICAAIC53929.2022.9793265

Madduri, A., Adusumalli, S. S., Katragadda, H. S., Dontireddy, M. K. R., & Suhasini, P. S. (2021, August). Classification of Breast Cancer Histopathological Images using Convolutional Neural Networks. In *2021 8th International Conference on Signal Processing and Integrated Networks (SPIN)* (pp. 755-759). IEEE 10.1109/SPIN52536.2021.9566015

Madhav, A. V. S., & Tyagi, A. K. (2022). The World with Future Technologies (Post-COVID-19): Open Issues, Challenges, and the Road Ahead. In A. K. Tyagi, A. Abraham, & A. Kaklauskas (Eds.), *Intelligent Interactive Multimedia Systems for e-Healthcare Applications*. Springer. doi:10.1007/978-981-16-6542-4_22

Maeo, J., Rius-Peris, J. M., Marana-Perez, A. I., Valiente-Armero, A., & Torres, A. M. (2021). Extreme gradient boosting machine learning method for predicting medical treatment in patients with acute bronchiolitis. *Biocybernetics and Biomedical Engineering, 41*(2), 792–801. doi:10.1016/j.bbe.2021.04.015

Magesh, G., Muthuswamy, P., & Singh, B. (2015). Use of Information Technology among school students in the State of Tamil Nadu, India. *International Journal of Applied Engineering Research: IJAER, 10*(1), 2201–2209.

Mahapatra, A. (2020). A Novel Approach for Identifying Social Media Posts Indicative of Depression. *IEEE International Symposium on Sustainable Energy, Signal Processing and Cyber Security*, 1-6. 10.1109/iSSSC50941.2020.9358866

Mahesh, B. (2020). Machine learning algorithms-a review. *International Journal of Science and Research, 9*, 381-386.

Mak, Bhattacharya, Prunty, Roeder, Ramadan, Ferguson, & Yu. (1998). Cache Ram Inductive Faulta Nalysiws Ith Fabd Efect Modeling. *International Test Conference, 32*(2), 862-871.

Maleki, N., & Niaki, S. T. A. (2023). An intelligent algorithm for lung cancer diagnosis using extracted features from Computerized Tomography images. *Healthcare Analytics*, *3*, 100150. doi:10.1016/j.health.2023.100150

Malviya, K., & Roy, B. (2021). A Transformers Approach to Detect Depression in social media. *International Conference on Artificial Intelligence and Smart Systems*, 718-723. 10.1109/ICAIS50930.2021.9395943

Ma, N., Zhang, X., Zheng, H. T., & Sun, J. (2018). Shufflenet v2: Practical guidelines for efficient cnn architecture design. In *Proceedings of the European conference on computer vision (ECCV)* (pp. 116-131). 10.1007/978-3-030-01264-9_8

Manley, K., Nyelele, C., & Egoh, B. N. (2022). A review of machine learning and big data applications in addressing ecosystem service research gaps. *Ecosystem Services*, *57*, 1010478. doi:10.1016/j.ecoser.2022.101478

Manocha, A., Bhatia, M., & Kumar, G. (2021). Dew computing-inspired health-meteorological factor analysis for early prediction of bronchial asthma. *Journal of Network and Computer Applications*, *179*, 102995. doi:10.1016/j.jnca.2021.102995

Manoj & Pineda de Gyvez. (2007). Defect-Oriented Testing for Nano-Metric CMOS VLSI Circuits. In *Frontiers in Electronic Testing* (vol. 34). Springer.

Manso, G. L., Knidel, H., Krohling, R. A., & Ventura, J. A. (2019). *A smartphone application to detection and classification of coffee leaf miner and coffee leaf rust.* arXiv preprint arXiv:1904.00742.

Mansur, A., Saleem, Z., Elhakim, T., & Daye, D. (2023). Role of artificial intelligence in risk prediction, prognostication, and therapy response assessment in colorectal cancer: Current state and future directions. *Frontiers in Oncology*, *13*, 1065402. doi:10.3389/fonc.2023.1065402 PMID:36761957

Mao, Y. J., Lim, H. J., Ni, M., Yan, W. H., Wong, D. W. C., & Cheung, J. C. W. (2022). Breast tumour classification using ultrasound elastography with machine learning: A systematic scoping review. *Cancers (Basel)*, *14*(2), 367. doi:10.3390/cancers14020367 PMID:35053531

Marcos, A. P., Rodovalho, N. L. S., & Backes, A. R. (2019). Coffee leaf rust detection using convolutional neural network. *2019 XV Workshop de Visão Computacional (WVC)*, 38–42. 10.1109/WVC.2019.8876931

Marelli, L., Lievevrouw, E., & Van Hoyweghen, I. (2020). Fit for purpose? The GDPR and the governance of European digital health. *Policy Studies*, *41*(5), 447–467. doi:10.1080/01442872.2020.1724929

Mármol, I., Sánchez-de-Diego, C., Pradilla Dieste, A., Cerrada, E., & Rodriguez Yoldi, M. J. (2017). Colorectal carcinoma: A general overview and future perspectives in colorectal cancer. *International Journal of Molecular Sciences*, *18*(1), 197. doi:10.3390/ijms18010197 PMID:28106826

Marr, B. (2018). How is AI used in healthcare – 5 powerful real-world examples that show the latest advances. *Forbes*.

Martirosyan & Harutyunyan. (2019). An Efficient Fault Detection and Diagnosis Methodology for Volatile and Non-Volatile Memories. *Proceedings of 2019 Computer Science and Information Technologies (CSIT)*, 47–51. . doi:10.1109/CSITechnol.2019.8895189

Martynov, V. V., Shavaleeva, D. N., & Zaytseva, A. A. (2019). Information technology as the basis for transformation into a digital society and Industry 5.0. *Proceedings of the 2019 IEEE International Conference Quality Management, Transport and Information Security, Information Technologies IT and QM and IS 2019*. 10.1109/ITQMIS.2019.8928305

McQueen, R. J., Garner, S. R., Nevill-Manning, C. G., & Witten, I. H. (1995). Applying machine learning to agricultural data. *Computers and Electronics in Agriculture*, *12*(4), 275–293. doi:10.1016/0168-1699(95)98601-9

Meng, X. (2012). Cross-lingual mixture model for sentiment classification. *Proceedings of the 50th Annual Meeting of the Association for Computational Linguistics: Long Papers-Volume 1*.

Mengistu, A. D., Mengistu, S. G., & Alemayehu, D. M. (2016). Image analysis for ethiopian coffee plant diseases identification. IJBB, 10(1).

Miglioretti, D. L., Lange, J., Van Den Broek, J. J., Lee, C. I., Van Ravesteyn, N. T., Ritley, D., Kerlikowske, K., Fenton, J. J., Melnikow, J., de Koning, H. J., & Hubbard, R. A. (2016). Radiation-induced breast cancer incidence and mortality from digital mammography screening: A modeling study. *Annals of Internal Medicine*, *164*(4), 205–214. doi:10.7326/M15-1241 PMID:26756460

Miller, D. D., & Brown, E. W. (2018). Artificial intelligence in medical practice: The question to the answer? *The American Journal of Medicine*, *131*(2), 129–133. doi:10.1016/j.amjmed.2017.10.035 PMID:29126825

Miller, J., & Clark, K. (2023). The Influence of ChatGPT on Collaborative Learning in Online Environments. *Computers in Human Behavior*, *72*, 302–315.

Mishra, S., & Tyagi, A. K. (2022). The Role of Machine Learning Techniques in Internet of Things-Based Cloud Applications. In S. Pal, D. De, & R. Buyya (Eds.), *Artificial Intelligence-based Internet of Things Systems. Internet of Things (Technology, Communications and Computing)*. Springer. doi:10.1007/978-3-030-87059-1_4

Mitchell, R., & Hughes, B. (2023). Chatbots and Digital Literacy in Modern Society: Implications for Education. *Media and Communication Studies*, *15*(4), 512–527.

Moat, Williams, Baena, Wilkinson, Demissew, Challa, Gole, & Davis. (2017). *Coffee farming and climate change in ethiopia: impacts, forecasts, resilience and opportunities-summary*. Academic Press.

Mohammad Amini, M., Jesus, M., Fanaei Sheikholeslami, D., Alves, P., Hassanzadeh Benam, A., & Hariri, F. (2023). Artificial Intelligence Ethics and Challenges in Healthcare Applications: A Comprehensive Review in the Context of the European GDPR Mandate. *Machine Learning and Knowledge Extraction*, *5*(3), 1023–1035. doi:10.3390/make5030053

Mohapatra, Prasad, & Nayak. (2021). Wheat Rust Disease Detection Using Deep Learning. *Data Science and Data Analytics: Opportunities and Challenges*, 191.

Molnar, C., Konig, G., Herbinger, J., Freiesleben, T., Dandl, S., & Scholbeck, C. A. (2022). General pitfalls of model-agnostic interpretation methods for machine learning models. AI - Beyond Explainable AI, Science, 13200, 39-68.

Moraffah, R., Karami, M., Guo, R., Raglin, A., & Liu, H. (2020). Causal interpretability for machine learning – problems, methods and evaluation. *SIGKDD Explorations*, *22*(1), 18–33. doi:10.1145/3400051.3400058

Mosavi, Salimi, Ardabili, Rabczuk, Shamshirband, & Varkonyi-Koczy. (2019). *State of the Art of Machine Learning Models in Energy Systems, a Systematic Review*. Academic Press.

Mou, J., & Li, J. (2020). Effects of Number of Filters of Convolutional Layers on Speech Recognition Model Accuracy. *2020 19th IEEE International Conference on Machine Learning and Applications (ICMLA)*, 971–978. 10.1109/ICMLA51294.2020.00158

Mozaffari, Saad, Bennis, Nam, & Debbah. (2019). A tutorial on UAVs for wireless networks: Applications, challenges, and open problems. *IEEE Commun. Surveys Tuts.*, *21*(3), 2334-2360.

Muddapu Parvathi, Vasantha, & Satya Parasad. (2012). Modified March C - Algorithm for Embedded Memory Testing. *International Journal of Electrical and Computer Engineering, 2*(5), 571-576.

Mukhamediev, R., Yakunin, K., Iskakov, S., Sainova, S., Abdilmanova, A., & Kuchin, Y. (2015). *Comparative analysis of classification algorithms.* . doi:10.1109/ICAICT.2015.7338525

Murdoch, B. (2021). Privacy and artificial intelligence: Challenges for protecting health information in a new era. *BMC Medical Ethics*, 22(1), 122. doi:10.118612910-021-00687-3 PMID:34525993

Murdoch, W. J., Singh, C., Kumbier, K., Abbasi-Asl, R., & Yu, B. (2018). Interpretable machine learning: Definitions, methods, and applications. *Proceedings of the National Academy of Sciences of the United States of America*, 116(44), 22071–22080. doi:10.1073/pnas.1900654116 PMID:31619572

Nair, M. M., & Tyagi, A. K. (2022). Preserving Privacy Using Blockchain Technology in Autonomous Vehicles. In *Proceedings of International Conference on Network Security and Blockchain Technology. ICNSBT 2021. Lecture Notes in Networks and Systems* (vol. 481). Springer. 10.1007/978-981-19-3182-6_19

Nair, M. M., & Tyagi, A. K. (2023). AI, IoT, blockchain, and cloud computing: The necessity of the future. In Distributed Computing to Blockchain. Academic Press. doi:10.1016/B978-0-323-96146-2.00001-2

Nair. (2023). *6G: Technology, Advancement, Barriers, and the Future. In 6G-Enabled IoT and AI for Smart Healthcare.* CRC Press.

Nair, M. M., Tyagi, A. K., & Sreenath, N. (2021). The Future with Industry 4.0 at the Core of Society 5.0: Open Issues, Future Opportunities and Challenges. *2021 International Conference on Computer Communication and Informatics (ICCCI)*, 1-7. 10.1109/ICCCI50826.2021.9402498

Nanda, Mohapatra, & Satpathy. (2023). Wheat Rust Disease Detection Using Convolutional Neural Network. *Journal of Harbin Engineering University, 44*(6), 253-259.

Nawaz, H., Maqsood, M., Afzal, S., Aadil, F., Mehmood, I., & Rho, S. (2021). A deep feature-based real-time system for Alzheimer disease stage detection. *Multimedia Tools and Applications*, 80(28-29), 35789–35807. doi:10.100711042-020-09087-y

Neelaveni, J., & Devasana, M. G. (2020, March). Alzheimer disease prediction using machine learning algorithms. In *2020 6th international conference on advanced computing and communication systems (ICACCS)* (pp. 101-104). IEEE. 10.1109/ICACCS48705.2020.9074248

Nguyen, G., Dlugolinsky, S., Bobák, M., Tran, V., López García, Á., Heredia, I., Malík, P., & Hluchý, L. (2019). Machine Learning and Deep Learning frameworks and libraries for large-scale data mining: A survey. *Artificial Intelligence Review*, 52(1), 77–124. doi:10.100710462-018-09679-z

Nicholson Price, W. II, & Glenn Cohen, I. (2019). Privacy in the age of medical big data. *Nature Medicine*, 25(1), 37–43. doi:10.103841591-018-0272-7 PMID:30617331

Nieto-Martinez, R., Barengo, N. C., Restrepo, M., Grinspan, A., Assefi, A., & Mechanick, J. I. (2023). *Large scale application of the Finnish diabetes risk score in Latin American and Caribbean populations: A descriptive study.* Academic Press.

Niggemeyer, D., Redeker, M., & Otterstedt, J. (1998). Integration of Non-classical Faults in Standard March Tests. *Proceedings. International Workshop on Memory Technology, Design and Testing.* 10.1109/MTDT.1998.705953

Nor Azura Zakaria, Hasan, Halin, Sidek, & Wen. (2012). Fault Detection with Optimum March Test Algorithm. *3rd International Conference on Intelligent Systems, Modelling and Simulation, ISMS-2012, 47.* 10.1109/ISMS.2012.88

Nweke, H. F., Teh, Y. W., Al-garadi, M. A., & Alo, U. R. (2018). Deep learning algorithms for human activity recognition using mobile and wearable sensor networks: State of the art and research challenges. *Expert Systems with Applications*, 105, 233–261. doi:10.1016/j.eswa.2018.03.056

O'neill, O. (2002). *Autonomy and trust in bioethics.* Cambridge University Press. doi:10.1017/CBO9780511606250

Odusami, M., Maskeliūnas, R., Damaševičius, R., & Krilavičius, T. (2021). Analysis of features of Alzheimer's disease: Detection of early stage from functional brain changes in magnetic resonance images using a finetuned ResNet18 network. *Diagnostics (Basel), 11*(6), 1071. doi:10.3390/diagnostics11061071 PMID:34200832

Olesen, J. B., Torp-Pedersen, C., Hansen, M. L., & Lip, G. Y. H. (2012). The value of the CHA2DS2-VASc score for refining stroke risk stratification in patients with atrial fibrillation with a CHADS2 score 0-1: A nationwide cohort study. *Thrombosis and Haemostasis, 107*(6), 1172–1179. doi:10.1160/TH12-03-0175 PMID:22473219

Oluwasegun, A. A., Sadiq, T., Odimba, C. R., & Olalekan, J. (n.d.). Generic Hybrid Model for Breast Cancer Mammography Image Classification Using EfficientNetB2. *DUJOPAS, 9*(3b), 281-289.

Palša, J., Ádám, N., Hurtuk, J., Chovancová, E., Madoš, B., Chovanec, M., & Kocan, S. (2022). MLMD—A Malware-Detecting Antivirus Tool Based on the XGBoost Machine Learning Algorithm. *Applied Sciences (Basel, Switzerland), 12*(13), 6672. doi:10.3390/app12136672

Pandey, A. A., Fernandez, T. F., Bansal, R., & Tyagi, A. K. (2022). Maintaining Scalability in Blockchain. In A. Abraham, N. Gandhi, T. Hanne, T. P. Hong, T. Nogueira Rios, & W. Ding (Eds.), *Intelligent Systems Design and Applications. ISDA 2021. Lecture Notes in Networks and Systems* (Vol. 418). Springer. doi:10.1007/978-3-030-96308-8_4

Park, C., Ha, J., & Park, S. (2020). Prediction of Alzheimer's disease based on deep neural network by integrating gene expression and DNA methylation dataset. *Expert Systems with Applications, 140*, 112873. doi:10.1016/j.eswa.2019.112873

Park, D. J., Park, M. W., Lee, H., Kim, Y. J., Kim, Y., & Park, Y. H. (2021). Development of machine learning model for diagnostic disease prediction based on laboratory tests. *Scientific Reports, 11*(1), 7567. doi:10.103841598-021-87171-5 PMID:33828178

Parvathi, M., Vasantha, N., & Satya Prasad, K. (2015). New Fault Model Analysis for Embedded SRAM Cell for Deep Submicron Technologies using Parasitic Extraction Method. *Proceedings of IEEE conference on VLSI Systems, Architecture, Technology and Applications (VLSI-SATA)*, 1-6. 10.1109/VLSI-SATA.2015.7050471

Parvathi, Vasantha, & Satya Prasad. (2013). Fault Model Analysis by Parasitic Extraction Method for Embedded SRAM. *International Journal of Research in Engineering and Technology, 2*(12).

Parvathi, M. (2018). New March Elements for Faults due to Open Defects in eSRAM. *Proceedings of First International Conference on Digital Contents and Applications (DCA 2018).*

Parvathi, M., Satya Prasad, K., & Vasantha, N. (2017). Testing of Embedded SRAMs using Parasitic Extraction Method. In H. Ibrahim, S. Iqbal, S. S. Teoh, & M. T. Mustaffa (Eds.), *Proceedings of Robotic, Vision, Signal Processing and Power Applications (ROVISP), Empowering Research and Innovation* (pp. 47–61). Springer LNEE. doi:10.1007/978-981-10-1721-6_6

Parvathi, M., Vasantha, N., & Satya Parasad, K. (2012, October). Modified March C - Algorithm for Embedded Memory Testing. *Iranian Journal of Electrical and Computer Engineering, 2*(5), 571–576. doi:10.11591/ijece.v2i5.1587

Parvathi, M., Vasantha, N., & Satya Prasad, K. (2017). Testing of e-SRAM Using MMC- Algorithm and Parasitic Extraction Method. *LAP Lambert Academic Publishing, ISBN-13*, 9786202095464.

PascanuR.GulcehreC.ChoK.BengioY. (2014). How to Construct Deep Recurrent Neural Networks. https://arxiv.org/abs/1312.6026

Patil, P. S., Saklani, A., Gambhire, P., Mehta, S., Engineer, R., De'Souza, A., Chopra, S., & Bal, M. (2017). Colorectal cancer in India: An audit from a tertiary center in a low prevalence area. *Indian Journal of Surgical Oncology*, 8(4), 484–490. doi:10.100713193-017-0655-0 PMID:29203978

Pedregosa, Varoquaux, Gramfort, Michel, Thirion, & Grisel. (2011). Scikit-learn: Machine learning in Python. *Journal of Machine Learning Research*, 12(Oct), 2825–2830.

Pfeiffer, R. M., Webb-Vargas, Y., Wheeler, W., & Gail, M. H. (2018). Proportion of us trends in breast cancer incidence attributable to long-term changes in risk factor distributions. *Cancer Epidemiology, Biomarkers & Prevention*, 27(10), 1214–1222. doi:10.1158/1055-9965.EPI-18-0098

Pfob, A., Lu, S. C., & Sidey-Gibbons, C. (2022). Machine learning in medicine: A practical introduction to techniques for data pre-processing, hyperparameter tuning, and model comparison. *BMC Medical Research Methodology*, 22(1), 1–15. doi:10.118612874-022-01758-8 PMID:36319956

Pintelas, E., Livieris, I.E., & Pintelas, P. (2020). *A Grey-Box Ensemble Model Exploiting Black-Box Accuracy and White-Box Intrinsic Interpretability*. Academic Press.

Pinto, C., Furukawa, J., Fukai, H., & Tamura, S. (2017). Classification of green coffee bean images basec on defect types using convolutional neural network (CNN). *2017 International Conference on Advanced Informatics, Concepts, Theory, and Applications (ICAICTA)*, 1–5. 10.1109/ICAICTA.2017.8090980

Prakash, R. M., Saraswathy, G., Ramalakshmi, G., Mangaleswari, K., & Kaviya, T. (2017). *Detection of leaf diseases and classification using digital image processing. In 2017 international conference on innovations in information, embedded and communication systems (ICIIECS)*. IEEE.

Priya, A., Garga, S., & Tigga, N. P. (2020). Predicting Anxiety, Depression, and Stress in Modern Life using Machine Learning Algorithms. *International Conference on Computational Intelligence and Data Science*, 1258-1267. 10.1016/j.procs.2020.03.442

Pudjihartono, N., Fadason, T., Kempa-Liehr, A. W., & O'Sullivan, J. M. (2022). A review of feature selection methods for machine learning-based disease risk prediction. *Frontiers in Bioinformatics*, 2, 927312. doi:10.3389/fbinf.2022.927312 PMID:36304293

Punitha, S., Al-Turjman, F., & Stephan, T. (2021). An automated breast cancer diagnosis using feature selection and parameter optimization in ANN. *Computers & Electrical Engineering*, 90, 106958. doi:10.1016/j.compeleceng.2020.106958

Raja Santhi, A., & Muthuswamy, P. (2023). Industry 5.0 or industry 4.0S? Introduction to industry 4.0 and a peek into the prospective industry 5.0 technologies. *Int J Interact Des Manuf*, 17(2), 947–979. doi:10.100712008-023-01217-8

Rajani, D., Menon, S. C., Kute, S., & Tyagi, A. K. (2022). Preserving Privacy of Social Media Data Using Artificial Intelligence Techniques. In A. Tyagi (Ed.), *Handbook of Research on Technical, Privacy, and Security Challenges in a Modern World* (pp. 186–204). IGI Global. doi:10.4018/978-1-6684-5250-9.ch010

Rajkomar, A., Hardt, M., Howell, M. D., Corrado, G., & Chin, M. H. (2018). Ensuring fairness in machine learning to advance health equity. *Annals of Internal Medicine*, 169(12), 866–872. doi:10.7326/M18-1990 PMID:30508424

Raj, S., Kishor, K., Devi, S., Sinha, D. K., Madhawi, R., Singh, R. K., Prakash, P., & Kumar, S. (2023). Epidemiological trends of colorectal cancer cases in young population of Eastern India: A retrospective observational study. *Journal of Cancer Research and Therapeutics*.

Ranzato, M., Boureau, Y.-L., & LeCun, Y. (n.d.). *Sparse Feature Learning for Deep Belief Networks*. Academic Press.

Ra, P. K., Nathawat, M. S., & Onagh, M. (2012). Application of multiple linear regression model through GIS and remote sensing for malaria mapping in Varanasi District, India. *Health Science Journal*, *6*(4), 731.

Rasheed, K., Qayyum, A., Ghaly, M., Al-Fuqaha, A., Razi, A., & Qadir, J. (2022). Explainable, trustworthy, and ethical machine learning for healthcare: A survey. *Computers in Biology and Medicine*, *149*, 106043. doi:10.1016/j.compbiomed.2022.106043 PMID:36115302

Rath, R. C., Baral, S. K., & Goel, R. (2022). Role of Artificial Intelligence on Cybersecurity and Its Control. In *Cross-Industry Applications of Cyber Security Frameworks* (pp. 15–35). IGI Global. doi:10.4018/978-1-6684-3448-2.ch002

Ravikumar, A., & Sriraman, H. (2023). Acceleration of Image Processing and Computer Vision Algorithms. In Handbook of Research on Computer Vision and Image Processing in the Deep Learning Era. IGI Global. doi:10.4018/978-1-7998-8892-5.ch001

Ravikumar, A. (2021). Non-relational multi-level caching for mitigation of staleness & stragglers in distributed deep learning. *Proceedings of the 22nd International Middleware Conference: Doctoral Symposium*, 15–16. 10.1145/3491087.3493678

Ravikumar, A., Sriraman, H., Saketh, P. M. S., Lokesh, S., & Karanam, A. (2022). Effect of neural network structure in accelerating performance and accuracy of a convolutional neural network with GPU/TPU for image analytics. *PeerJ. Computer Science*, *8*, e909. doi:10.7717/peerj-cs.909 PMID:35494877

Ray, P. P. (2017). An introduction to dew computing: Definition, concept and implications. *IEEE Access : Practical Innovations, Open Solutions*, *6*, 723–737. doi:10.1109/ACCESS.2017.2775042

Reddy, S., Allan, S., Coghlan, S., & Cooper, P. (2020). A governance model for the application of AI in health care. *Journal of the American Medical Informatics Association : JAMIA*, *27*(3), 491–497. doi:10.1093/jamia/ocz192 PMID:31682262

Reddy, S., Pomeranz, I., Huaxing, T., Kajihara, S., & Kinoshita, S. (2002). On Testing of Interconnect Open Defects in Combinational Logic Circuits with Stems of Large Fanout. *Proceedings of IEEE International Test Conference (ITC)*, 83–89. 10.1109/TEST.2002.1041748

Reed, T., & Peterson, A. (2021). ChatGPT and Educational Gamification: Engaging Students in the Digital Age. *Journal of Educational Technology & Society*, *26*(2), 201–218.

Rekha, Tyagi, & Krishna Reddy. (2019). A Wide Scale Classification of Class Imbalance Problem and its Solutions: A Systematic Literature Review. *Journal of Computer Science, 15*(7), 886-929.

Rekha, G., Malik, S., Tyagi, A. K., & Nair, M. M. (2020). Intrusion Detection in Cyber Security: Role of Machine Learning and Data Mining in Cyber Security. *Advances in Science, Technology and Engineering Systems Journal, 5*(3), 72–81. doi:10.25046/aj050310

Ren & Malik. (2003). Learning a classification model for segmentation. *Proceedings Ninth IEEE International Conference on Computer Vision*, 10–17. 10.1109/ICCV.2003.1238308

Rindos, A., & Wang, Y. (2016). Dew computing: The complementary piece of cloud computing. In *2016 IEEE International Conferences on Big Data and Cloud Computing (BDCloud), Social Computing and Networking (SocialCom), Sustainable Computing and Communications (SustainCom)(BDCloud-SocialCom-SustainCom)* (pp. 15-20). IEEE. 10.1109/BDCloud-SocialCom-SustainCom.2016.14

Roberts, J., & Bell, K. (2022). Industry Perspectives on the Integration of AI in Education: A Survey of Corporate Training Programs. *Journal of Corporate Learning*, *44*(3), 312–327.

Robin, M., John, J., & Ravikumar, A. (2021). Breast Tumor Segmentation using U-NET. *2021 5th International Conference on Computing Methodologies and Communication (ICCMC)*, 1164–1167. 10.1109/ICCMC51019.2021.9418447

Robin, M., Ravikumar, A., & John, J. (2022). Classification of Histopathological Breast Cancer Images using Pretrained Models and Transfer Learning. In M. Saraswat, H. Sharma, K. Balachandran, J. H. Kim, & J. C. Bansal (Eds.), *Congress on Intelligent Systems* (pp. 587–597). Springer Nature Singapore. doi:10.1007/978-981-16-9113-3_43

Rockhill, B., Spiegelman, D., Byrne, C., Hunter, D. J., & Colditz, G. A. (2001). Validation of the Gail et al. Model of Breast Cancer Risk Prediction and Implications for Chemoprevention. *Journal of the National Cancer Institute*, *93*(5), 353–366. doi:10.1093/jnci/93.5.358 PMID:11238697

Rodriguez-Montanes, R., Volf, P., & de Gyvez, J. P. (2002). Resistance Characterization for Weak Open Defects. *IEEE Design & Test of Computers*, *19*(5), 18–26. doi:10.1109/MDT.2002.1033788

Rompianesi, G., Pegoraro, F., Ceresa, C. D., Montalti, R., & Troisi, R. I. (2022). Artificial intelligence in the diagnosis and management of colorectal cancer liver metastases. *World Journal of Gastroenterology*, *28*(1), 108–122. doi:10.3748/wjg.v28.i1.108 PMID:35125822

Roy, S., Sarkar, D., & De, D. (2021). DewMusic: Crowdsourcing-based internet of music things in dew computing paradigm. *Journal of Ambient Intelligence and Humanized Computing*, *12*(2), 2103–2119. doi:10.100712652-020-02309-z

Rrmoku, K., Selimi, B., & Ahmedi, L. (2022). Application of trust in recommender systems—Utilizing naive Bayes classifier. *Computation (Basel, Switzerland)*, *10*(1), 6. doi:10.3390/computation10010006

Ruby, A. U., & Chandran, J. G. C. (2016). A Theoretical Approach on Face Recognition with Single Sample per Class using CS-LBP and Gabor Magnitude and Phase. *Indian Journal of Science and Technology*, *9*, 31.

Rudin, C., Chen, C., Chen, Z., Huang, H., Semenova, L., & Zhong, C. (2022). Interpretable machine learning: Fundamental principles and 10 grand challenges. *Statistics Surveys*, *16*(none), 1–85. doi:10.1214/21-SS133

Sadad, T., Munir, A., Saba, T., & Hussain, A. (2018). Fuzzy C-means and region growing based classification of tumor from mammograms using hybrid texture feature. *Journal of Computational Science*, *29*, 34–45. doi:10.1016/j.jocs.2018.09.015

Saeed, N., Alouini, M.-S., & Al-Naffouri, T. Y. (2019). Toward the Internet of underground things: A systematic survey. IEEE Commun. Surveys Tuts., 21(4), 3443–3466.

Sahatiya, P. (2018). Big Data Analytics on Social Media Data: A Literature Review. *Int. Res. J. of Engg and Tech.*, *5*(2), 189–192.

Sajid, U., Khan, R. A., Shah, S. M., & Arif, S. (2023). Breast cancer classification using deep learned features boosted with handcrafted features. *Biomedical Signal Processing and Control*, *86*, 105353. doi:10.1016/j.bspc.2023.105353

Samee, N. A., Atteia, G., Meshoul, S., Al-antari, M. A., & Kadah, Y. M. (2022). Deep learning cascaded feature selection framework for breast cancer classification: Hybrid CNN with univariate-based approach. *Mathematics*, *10*(19), 3631. doi:10.3390/math10193631

Sarabi, A., Jin, K., & Liu, M. (2021). Smart Internet Probing: Scanning Using Adaptive Machine Learning. *Game Theory and Machine Learning for Cyber Security*, 411-437.

Saritas, M. M., & Yasar, A. (2019). Performance analysis of ANN and Naive Bayes classification algorithm for data classification. *International Journal of Intelligent Systems and Applications in Engineering*, *7*(2), 88-91.

Sarker, I. (2021). Machine Learning: Algorithms, Real-World Applications and Research Directions. *SN Computer Science*. doi:10.1007/s42979-021-00592-x

Schiffman, J. D., Fisher, P. G., & Gibbs, P. (2015). Early detection of cancer: Past, present, and future. *American Society of Clinical Oncology Educational Book*, *35*(1), 57–65. doi:10.14694/EdBook_AM.2015.35.57 PMID:25993143

Schwartz, M. S. (2016). Ethical decision-making theory: An integrated approach. *Journal of Business Ethics, 139*(4), 755–776. doi:10.100710551-015-2886-8

SciKit-Learn. (n.d.-a). https://scikit-learn.org/stable/

SciKit-Learn. (n.d.-b). https://scikit-learn.org/stable/modules/svm.html

SciKit-Learn. (n.d.-c). https://scikit-learn.org/stable/modules/naive_bayes.html

SCORE2 working group and ESC Cardiovascular risk collaboration. (2021). SCORE2 risk prediction algorithms: new models to estimate 10-year risk of cardiovascular disease in Europe. *Eur Heart J, 42*(25), 2439-2454.

Scott, P. A., Vlimki, M., Leino-Kilpi, H., Dassen, T., Gasull, M., Lemonidou, C., & Arndt, M. (2003). Autonomy, privacy and informed consent 1: Concepts and definitions. *British Journal of Nursing (Mark Allen Publishing), 12*(1), 43–47. doi:10.12968/bjon.2003.12.1.10999 PMID:12574725

Shah, F. M., Joy, S. K. S., Ahmed, F., Hossain, T., Humaira, M., Ami, A. S., Paul, S., Jim, M. A. R. K., & Ahmed, S. (2021). A Comprehensive Survey of COVID-19 Detection Using Medical Images. *SN Computer Science, 2*(6), 434. doi:10.100742979-021-00823-1 PMID:34485924

Shahin, O. R., Alshammari, H. H., Taloba, A. I., & El-Aziz, R. M. A. (2022). Machine Learning Approach for Autonomous Detection and Classification of COVID-19 Virus. *Computers & Electrical Engineering: An International Journal, 101*, 108055. doi:10.1016/j.compeleceng.2022.108055

Sharifani, K., & Amini, M. (2023). Machine Learning and Deep Learning: A Review of Methods and Applications. *World Information Technology and Engineering Journal, 10*(07), 3897–3904.

Shen, X., Gao, J., Wu, W., Li, M., Zhou, C., & Zhuang, W. (2022). Holistic network virtualization and pervasive network intelligence for 6G. IEEE Commun. Surveys Tuts., 24(1), 1–30. doi:10.1109/COMST.2021.3135829

Sheth, & Tyagi. (2022). Deep Learning, Blockchain based Multi-layered Authentication and Security Architectures. *2022 International Conference on Applied Artificial Intelligence and Computing (ICAAIC),* 476-485. 10.1109/ICAAIC53929.2022.9793179

Shi, B., Bai, X., & Yao, C. (2016). An end-to-end trainable neural network for image-based sequence recognition and its application to scene text recognition. *IEEE Transactions on Pattern Analysis and Machine Intelligence, 39*(11), 2298–2304. doi:10.1109/TPAMI.2016.2646371 PMID:28055850

Shorten, C., & Khoshgoftaar, T. M. (2019). A survey on Image Data Augmentation for Deep Learning. *Journal of Big Data, 6*(1), 2019. doi:10.118640537-019-0197-0

Shultz, M. M. (1985). From informed consent to patient choice: A new protected interest. *The Yale Law Journal, 95*(2), 219. doi:10.2307/796352 PMID:11658859

Siala, H., & Wang, Y. (2022). SHIFTing artificial intelligence to be responsible in healthcare: A systematic review. *Social Science & Medicine, 296*, 114782. doi:10.1016/j.socscimed.2022.114782 PMID:35152047

Siegel, R. L., Miller, K. D., Wagle, N. S., & Jemal, A. (2023). Cancer statistics, 2023. *Ca Cancer J Clin, 73*(1), 17-48. https://acsjournals.onlinelibrary.wiley.com/doi/abs/ doi:10.3322/caac.21763

Siegel, R. L., Miller, K. D., Goding Sauer, A., Fedewa, S. A., Butterly, L. F., Anderson, J. C., Cercek, A., Smith, R. A., & Jemal, A. (2020). Colorectal cancer statistics, 2020. *CA: a Cancer Journal for Clinicians, 70*(3), 145–164. doi:10.3322/caac.21601 PMID:32133645

Siegel, R. L., Wagle, N. S., Cercek, A., Smith, R. A., & Jemal, A. (2023). Colorectal cancer statistics, 2023. *CA: a Cancer Journal for Clinicians, 73*(3), 233–254. doi:10.3322/caac.21772 PMID:36856579

SimonyanK.ZissermanA. (2015). Very Deep Convolutional Networks for Large-Scale Image Recognition. https://arxiv.org/abs/1409.1556

Simplilearn. (n.d.). https://www.simplilearn.com/tutorials/scikit-learn-tutorial/sklearn-linear-regression-with-examples

Singh, B., Narang, S. B., & Khosla, A. (2010). Modeling and Simulation of Efficient March Algorithm for Memory Testing. IC3 2010, Part II, CCIS 95, 96–107.

Singh, B., & Acharjya, D. P. (2020). Computational intelligence techniques for efficient delivery of healthcare. *Health and Technology, 10*, 167–185.

Singh, P., Gaba, G. S., Kaur, A., Hedabou, M., & Gurtov, A. (2022). Dew-cloud-based hierarchical federated learning for intrusion detection in IoMT. *IEEE Journal of Biomedical and Health Informatics.* PMID:35816521

Singh, P., Kaur, A., Aujla, G. S., Batth, R. S., & Kanhere, S. (2020). Daas: Dew computing as a service for intelligent intrusion detection in edge-of-things ecosystem. *IEEE Internet of Things Journal, 8*(16), 12569–12577. doi:10.1109/JIOT.2020.3029248

Singh, V. K., Rashwan, H. A., Romani, S., Akram, F., Pandey, N., Sarker, M. M. K., & Torrents-Barrena, J. (2020). Breast tumor segmentation and shape classification in mammograms using generative adversarial and convolutional neural network. *Expert Systems with Applications, 139*, 112855. doi:10.1016/j.eswa.2019.112855

Sinshaw, N. T., Assefa, B. G., & Mohapatra, S. K. (2021). Transfer Learning and Data Augmentation Based CNN Model for Potato Late Blight Disease Detection. *2021 International Conference on Information and Communication Technology for Development for Africa (ICT4DA),* 30-35. 10.1109/ICT4DA53266.2021.9672243

Sinshaw, N. T., Assefa, B. G., Mohapatra, S. K., & Beyene, A. M. (2022). Applications of Computer Vision on Automatic Potato Plant Disease Detection: A Systematic Literature Review. *Computational Intelligence and Neuroscience, 2022*, 7186687. doi:10.1155/2022/7186687 PMID:36419507

Sivaraman, Krishnan, Sundarraj, & Sri Gowthem. (2019). Network failure detection and diagnosis by analyzing syslog and SNS data: Applying big data analysis to network operations. *Int. J. Innov. Technol. Explor. Eng., 8*(9), 883–887. . doi:10.35940/ijitee.I3187.0789S319

Sivic & Zisserman. (2003). Video Google: A text retrieval approach to object matching in videos. *Proceedings Ninth IEEE International Conference on Computer Vision,* 1470–1477. 10.1109/ICCV.2003.1238663

Skala, K., Davidovic, D., Afgan, E., Sovic, I., & Sojat, Z. (2015). Scalable distributed computing hierarchy: Cloud, fog and dew computing. *Open Journal of Cloud Computing, 2*(1), 16–24.

Smith, A., & Johnson, B. (2021). ChatGPT and Personalized Learning: A Comprehensive Study in Modern Education. *Journal of Educational Technology, 45*(2), 201–218.

Song, B. I. (2021). A machine learning-based radiomics model for the prediction of axillary lymph-node metastasis in breast cancer. *Breast Cancer (Tokyo, Japan), 28*(3), 664–671. doi:10.100712282-020-01202-z PMID:33454875

Sorte, L. X. B., Ferraz, C. T., Fambrini, F., dos Reis Goulart, R., & Saito, J. H. (2019). Coffee leaf disease recognition based on deep learning and texture attributes. *Procedia Computer Science, 159*, 135–144. doi:10.1016/j.procs.2019.09.168

SpringenbergJ. T.DosovitskiyA.BroxT.RiedmillerM. (2015). Striving for Simplicity: The All Convolutional Net. https://arxiv.org/abs/1412.6806

Srivastava, N., Hinton, G., Krizhevsky, A., Sutskever, I., & Salakhutdinov, R. (n.d.). *Dropout: A Simple Way to Prevent Neural Networks from Overfitting.* Academic Press.

Srivastava, R. K., Greff, K., & Schmidhuber, J. (2015). Training Very Deep Networks. *Advances in Neural Information Processing Systems, 28.* https://proceedings.neurips.cc/paper/2015/hash/215a71a12769b056c3c32e7299f1c5ed-Abstract.html

Srivastava, S. A., Bansal, R., Soni, G., & Tyagi, A.K. (2023). Blockchain Enabled Internet of Things: Current Scenario and Open Challenges for Future. In Innovations in Bio-Inspired Computing and Applications. IBICA 2022. Lecture Notes in Networks and Systems (vol. 649). Springer. doi:10.1007/978-3-031-27499-2_59

Stewart, M., & Moore, E. (2023). AI Chatbots for Customer Support: Industry Best Practices and Case Studies. *Journal of Customer Experience Management, 50*(4), 421–436.

Stieglitza, S., Mirbabaiea, M., Rossa, B., & Chris-toph, N. (2018). Social media analytics – Challenges in topic discovery, data collection, and data preparation, Int. J. of In-fo. *Manag., 39,* 156–168.

Stiglic, G., Kocbek, P., Fijacko, N., Zitnik, M., Verbert, K., & Cilar, L. (2020). Interpretability of machine learning-based prediction models in healthcare. *Wiley Interdisciplinary Reviews. Data Mining and Knowledge Discovery, 10*(5), e1379. doi:10.1002/widm.1379

Stratigopoulos. (2018). Machine Learning Applications in IC Testing. *2018 23rd IEEE European Test Symposium (ETS).*

Subashini, P., Krishnaveni, M., Dhivyaprabha, T. T., & Shanmugavalli, R. (2020). Review on intelligent algorithms for cyber security. In *Handbook of Research on Machine and Deep Learning Applications for Cyber Security* (pp. 1–22). IGI Global. doi:10.4018/978-1-5225-9611-0.ch001

Subhani, A. R., Mumtaz, W., Saad, M. N. B. M., Kamel, N., & Malik, A. S. (2017). Machine Learning Framework for the Detection of Mental Stress at Multiple Levels. *IEEE Access : Practical Innovations, Open Solutions, 5,* 13545–13556. doi:10.1109/ACCESS.2017.2723622

Sudha, Sreemathi, Nathiya, & RahiniPriya. (2020). Depression Detection using Machine Learning. *International Journal of Research and Advanced Development,* 1-6.

Sudharsan, M., & Thailambal, G. (2021). Alzheimer's disease prediction using machine learning techniques and principal component analysis (PCA). *Materials Today: Proceedings.*

Suhartono. (2013). Expert system in detecting coffee plant diseases. *Int. J. Electr. Energy, 1*(3), 156–162.

Szegedy, C., Liu, W., Jia, Y., Sermanet, P., Reed, S., Anguelov, D., Erhan, D., Vanhoucke, V., & Rabinovich, A. (2015). Going deeper with convolutions. *2015 IEEE Conference on Computer Vision and Pattern Recognition (CVPR),* 1–9. 10.1109/CVPR.2015.7298594

Tabassum, S., Pereira, F. S. F., Fernandes, S., & Gama, J. (2018). Social Network Analysis: An Overview. *Wiley Interdisciplinary Reviews Data Mining and Know., 8*(5), 1–30.

Talaat, A. S. (2023). Sentiment analysis classification system using hybrid BERT models. *Journal of Big Data, 10*(1), 110. doi:10.118640537-023-00781-w

Talukder, M. A., Islam, M. M., Uddin, M. A., Akhter, A., Hasan, K. F., & Moni, M. A. (2022). Machine learning-based lung and colon cancer detection using deep feature extraction and ensemble learning. *Expert Systems with Applications, 205,* 117695. doi:10.1016/j.eswa.2022.117695

Tamang, L. D., & Kim, B. W. (2021). Deep learning approaches to colorectal cancer diagnosis: A review. *Applied Sciences (Basel, Switzerland)*, *11*(22), 10982. doi:10.3390/app112210982

Taylor, E., & Wilson, L. (2023). Ethics and ChatGPT: Navigating the Moral Implications in Educational Settings. *Journal of Applied Ethics*, *16*(3), 312–327.

Tefera, G., She, K., & Deeba, F. (2019). Decentralized adaptive latency-aware cloud-edge-dew architecture for unreliable network. *Proceedings of the 2019 11th International conference on machine learning and computing*, 142-146. 10.1145/3318299.3318380

Tehranipour, M. H., Navabi, Z., & Fakhraie, S. M. (2001). An Efficient BIST Method For Testing of Embedded SRAMs. *IEICE Electronics Express*, *6*(15), 1091–1097.

Thomas, T. P., Vijayaraghavan, A., & Emmanuel, S. (2020). Machine learning and cybersecurity. In *Machine Learning Approaches in Cyber Security Analytics* (pp. 37–47). Springer. doi:10.1007/978-981-15-1706-8_3

Thompson, M., & Adams, W. (2023). Addressing Bias in AI-Powered Education Technologies: A Case Study of ChatGPT. *Journal of Information Ethics*, *21*(2), 180–197.

Timotheou, S. (2010). The Random Neural Network: A Survey. *The Computer Journal*, *53*(3), 251–267. doi:10.1093/comjnl/bxp032

Tiwari, S., & Srivastava, R. (2022). Cyber Security Trend Analysis: An Indian Perspective. In Cross-Industry Applications of Cyber Security Frameworks (pp. 1-14). IGI Global.

Tiwari, P., Colborn, K. L., Smith, D. E., Xing, F., Ghosh, D., & Rosenberg, M. A. (2020). Assessment of a machine learning model applied to harmonized electronic health record data for the prediction of incident atrial fibrillation. *JAMA Network Open*, *3*(1), e1919396–e1919396. doi:10.1001/jamanetworkopen.2019.19396 PMID:31951272

Torres-Galván, J. C., Guevara, E., & González, F. J. (2019, May). *Comparison of deep learning architectures for pre-screening of breast cancer thermograms. In 2019 Photonics North (PN)*. IEEE.

Touahri, R., Aziz, I. N., Hammami, N. E., Aldwairi, M., & Benaida, F. (2019, April). Automated breast tumor diagnosis using local binary patterns (LBP) based on deep learning classification. In *2019 International Conference on Computer and Information Sciences (ICCIS)* (pp. 1-5). IEEE. 10.1109/ICCISci.2019.8716428

Towardsdatascience. (n.d.-a). https://towardsdatascience.com/logistic-regression-using-python-sklearn-numpy-mnist-handwriting-recognition-matplotlib-a6b31e2b166a

Towardsdatascience. (n.d.-b). https://towardsdatascience.com/building-a-k-nearest-neighbors-k-nn-model-with-scikit-learn-51209555453a

Tsochatzidis, L., Costaridou, L., & Pratikakis, I. (2019). Deep learning for breast cancer diagnosis from mammograms—A comparative study. *Journal of Imaging*, *5*(3), 37. doi:10.3390/jimaging5030037 PMID:34460465

Turner, S., & Baker, C. (2022). ChatGPT as a Supportive Tool for Students with Learning Disabilities. *Journal of Inclusive Education and Special Needs*, *18*(1), 89–104.

Tyagi, A. K., & Bansal, R. (2023). A Step-To-Step Guide to Write a Quality Research Article. In Intelligent Systems Design and Applications. ISDA 2022. Lecture Notes in Networks and Systems (vol. 717). Springer. doi:10.1007/978-3-031-35510-3_36

Tyagi. (2020a). *Artificial Intelligence and Machine Learning Algorithms. In Challenges and Applications for Implementing Machine Learning in Computer Vision*. IGI Global. doi:10.4018/978-1-7998-0182-5.ch008

Tyagi, . (2020b). *Challenges of Applying Deep Learning in Real-World Applications. In Challenges and Applications for Implementing Machine Learning in Computer Vision.* IGI Global. doi:10.4018/978-1-7998-0182-5.ch004

Tyagi. (2023). Decentralized everything: Practical use of blockchain technology in future applications. In Distributed Computing to Blockchain. Academic Press. doi:10.1016/B978-0-323-96146-2.00010-3

Tyagi, A. K. (2022). SecVT: Securing the Vehicles of Tomorrow Using Blockchain Technology. In A. A. Sk, T. Turki, T. K. Ghosh, S. Joardar, & S. Barman (Eds.), *Artificial Intelligence. ISAI 2022. Communications in Computer and Information Science* (Vol. 1695). Springer. doi:10.1109/ICCCI54379.2022.9740965

Tyagi, A. K., Chandrasekaran, S., & Sreenath, N. (2022). Blockchain Technology:– A New Technology for Creating Distributed and Trusted Computing Environment. *2022 International Conference on Applied Artificial Intelligence and Computing (ICAAIC)*, 1348-1354. 10.1109/ICAAIC53929.2022.9792702

Tyagi, A. K., Fernandez, T. F., Mishra, S., & Kumari, S. (2021). Intelligent Automation Systems at the Core of Industry 4.0. In A. Abraham, V. Piuri, N. Gandhi, P. Siarry, A. Kaklauskas, & A. Madureira (Eds.), *Intelligent Systems Design and Applications. ISDA 2020. Advances in Intelligent Systems and Computing* (Vol. 1351). Springer. doi:10.1007/978-3-030-71187-0_1

Tyagi, A. K., Kumari, S., Fernandez, T. F., & Aravindan, C. (2020). Block: Privacy Preserved, Trusted Smart Parking Allotment for Future Vehicles of Tomorrow. In Lecture Notes in Computer Science: Vol. 12254. *Computational Science and Its Applications – ICCSA 2020. ICCSA 2020* (p. 3). Springer. doi:10.1007/978-3-030-58817-5_56

U., J., Olesnikova, A., Song, C. H., & Lee, W. D. (2009, January). The development and application of decision tree for agriculture data. In *2009 Second International Symposium on Intelligent Information Technology and Security Informatics* (pp. 16-20). IEEE.

Valsamis, E. M., Husband, H., & Chan, G. K. W. (2019). Segmented linear regression modelling of time-series of binary variables in healthcare. *Computational and Mathematical Methods in Medicine.* doi:10.1155/2019/3478598 PMID:31885678

van de Goor. (1998). *Testing Semiconductor Memories: Theory and Practice.* Academic Press.

Van De Goor, A. J. (1993). Using March tests to test SRAMs. *IEEE Design & Test of Computers, 10*(1), 8–14. doi:10.1109/54.199799

van de Goor, A. J., & Al-Ars, Z. (2000). Functional Memory Faults: A Formal Notation and a Taxonomy. *Proceedings of VLSI Test Symposium (VTS)*, 281–289. 10.1109/VTEST.2000.843856

Varsha, R. (2020, January 1). Deep Learning Based Blockchain Solution for Preserving Privacy in Future Vehicles. *International Journal of Hybrid Intelligent Systems, 16*(4), 223–236.

Varshney, S., & Dalal, T. (2016). Plant disease prediction using image processing techniques-a review. *International Journal of Computer Science and Mobile Computing, 5*(5), 394–398.

Venkatesham, M., Sinha, S. K., & Parvathi, M. (2021c). Study on Paradigm of Variable Length SRAM Embedded Memory Testing. *Proceedings of the Fifth International Conference on Electronics, Communication and Aerospace Technology (ICECA) 2021.*

Venkatesham, M., Sinha, S. K., & Parvathi, M. (2021a). Analysis of Open Defect Faults in Single 6T SRAM Cell Using R and C Parasitic Extraction Method. *Proceedings of IEEE International Conference on Disruptive Technologies for Multi-Disciplinary Research and Applications (CENTCON-2021)*, 213-217. 10.1109/CENTCON52345.2021.9687916

Venkatesham, M., Sinha, S. K., & Parvathi, M. (2021b). Extraction of Undetectable Faults in 6T-SRAM Cell. *Proceedings of IEEE International Conference on Communication, Control and information Sciences(ICCISc),* 13-17.

Venugopalan, J., Tong, L., Hassanzadeh, H. R., & Wang, M. D. (2021). Multimodal deep learning models for early detection of Alzheimer's disease stage. *Scientific Reports, 11*(1), 3254. doi:10.103841598-020-74399-w PMID:33547343

Verilog Digital System Design. (2008). *Zainalabedin Navabi* (2nd ed.). McGraw Hill.

Vinayakumar, R., Alazab, M., Soman, K. P., Poornachandran, P., Al-Nemrat, A., & Venkatraman, S. (2019). Deep Learning Approach for Intelligent Intrusion Detection System. *IEEE Access : Practical Innovations, Open Solutions, 7,* 41525–41550. doi:10.1109/ACCESS.2019.2895334

Vinuesa, R., Azizpour, H., Leite, I., Balaam, M., Dignum, V., Domisch, S., Felländer, A., Langhans, S. D., Tegmark, M., & Fuso Nerini, F. (2020). The role of artificial intelligence in achieving the sustainable development goals. *Nature Communications, 11*(1), 1–10. doi:10.103841467-019-14108-y PMID:31932590

Vujovic, Z. (2021). Classification Model Evaluation Metrics. *International Journal of Advanced Computer Science and Applications, 12*(6), 599–606. doi:10.14569/IJACSA.2021.0120670

Wagner, S. A. (2016). SAR ATR by a combination of convolutional neural network and support vector machines. *IEEE Transactions on Aerospace and Electronic Systems, 52*(6), 2861–2872. doi:10.1109/TAES.2016.160061

Waljee, A. K., Weinheimer-Haus, E. M., Abubakar, A., Ngugi, A. K., Siwo, G. H., Kwakye, G., Singal, A. G., Rao, A., Saini, S. D., Read, A. J., Baker, J. A., Balis, U., Opio, C. K., Zhu, J., & Saleh, M. N. (2022). Artificial intelligence and machine learning for early detection and diagnosis of colorectal cancer in sub-Saharan Africa. *Gut, 71*(7), 1259–1265. doi:10.1136/gutjnl-2022-327211 PMID:35418482

Wan, L., Zeiler, M., Zhang, S., LeCun, Y., & Fergus, R. (n.d.). *Regularization of Neural Networks using DropConnect.* Academic Press.

Wan, X. (2012). A Comparative Study of Cross-Lingual Sentiment Classification. In *Proceedings of the IEEE/WIC/ACM International Joint Conferences on Web Intelligence and Intelligent Agent Technology-Volume 1* (pp. 24-31). 10.1109/WI-IAT.2012.54

Wang, T. (2019). Gaining free or low-cost transparency with interpretable partial substitute. *Proceedings of the 36th International Conference on Machine Learning, Long Beach, California, PMLR 97.*

Wang, C.-X., You, X., Gao, X., Zhu, X., Li, Z., Zhang, C., Wang, H., Huang, Y., Chen, Y., Haas, H., Thompson, J. S., Larsson, E. G., Renzo, M. D., Tong, W., Zhu, P., Shen, X., Poor, H. V., & Hanzo, L. (2023). On the road to 6G: Visions, requirements, key technologies and testbeds. *IEEE Communications Surveys and Tutorials, 25*(2), 905–974. doi:10.1109/COMST.2023.3249835

Wang, S., Du, Z., Ding, M., Rodriguez-Paton, A., & Song, T. (2022). KG-DTI: A knowledge graph based deep learning method for drug-target interaction predictions and Alzheimer's disease drug repositions. *Applied Intelligence, 52*(1), 846–857. doi:10.100710489-021-02454-8 PMID:34764597

Wang, X., & Li, Y. (2021). Examining the Impact of ChatGPT on Students' Critical Thinking Skills. *International Journal of Learning Sciences, 33*(4), 512–529.

Wang, Y. (2016). Definition and categorization of dew computing. *Open Journal of Cloud Computing, 3*(1), 1–7.

Wang, Y. (2017). The theory and applications of dew computing. *Proceedings of the 27th Annual International Conference on Computer Science and Software Engineering,* 317-317.

Wang, Y., & Skala, K. (2018). The 3rd international workshop on dew computing. *Proceedings of the 28th Annual International Conference on Computer Science and Software Engineering*, 357-358.

Wang, Y., Skala, K., Rindos, A., Gusev, M., Yang, S., & Pan, Y. (2017). Dew computing and transition of internet computing paradigms. *ZTE Communications*, *15*(4), 30–37.

Wang, Z., Dong, N., Dai, W., Rosario, S. D., & Xing, E. P. (2018). Classification of breast cancer histopathological images using convolutional neural networks with hierarchical loss and global pooling. In *International conference image analysis and recognition* (pp. 745-753). Cham: Springer International Publishing. 10.1007/978-3-319-93000-8_84

Watson, D. S. (2022). Conceptual challenges for interpretable machine learning. *Synthese*, *200*(2), 65. doi:10.100711229-022-03485-5

Wei, J., Suriawinata, A., Vaickus, L., Ren, B., Liu, X., Wei, J., & Hassanpour, S. (2019). Generative image translation for data augmentation in colorectal histopathology images. *Proceedings of Machine Learning Research*, *116*, 10. PMID:33912842

Weissler, E. H., Naumann, T., Andersson, T., Ranganath, R., Elemento, O., Luo, Y., Freitag, D. F., Benoit, J., Hughes, M. C., Khan, F., Slater, P., Shameer, K., Roe, M., Hutchison, E., Kollins, S. H., Broedl, U., Meng, Z., Wong, J. L., Curtis, L., ... Ghassemi, M. (2021). The role of machine learning in clinical research: Transforming the future of evidence generation. *Trials*, *22*(1), 537. doi:10.118613063-021-05489-x PMID:34399832

Welteji, D. (2018). A critical review of rural development policy of ethiopia: Access, utilization and coverage. *Agriculture & Food Security*, *7*(1), 1–6. doi:10.118640066-018-0208-y

Wen, Z., & Huang, H. (2022). The potential for artificial intelligence in healthcare. *Journal of Commercial Biotechnology*, *27*(4).

Wiggins, M., Saad, A., Litt, B., & Vachtsevanos, G. (2008). Evolving a Bayesian classifier for ECG-based age classification in medical applications. *Applied Soft Computing*, *8*(1), 599–608. doi:10.1016/j.asoc.2007.03.009 PMID:22010038

Williams, H., & Adams, J. (2022). AI and Social Impact: A Comparative Analysis of Different Chatbot Approaches in Society. *Social Science Review*, *72*, 180 197.

Wu, M. C., Lin, S. Y., & Lin, C. H. (2006). An effective application of decision tree to stock trading. *Expert Systems with Applications*, *31*(2), 270–274. doi:10.1016/j.eswa.2005.09.026

Wu, Y., Zhang, L., Bhatti, U. A., & Huang, M. (2023). Interpretable machine learning for personalized medical recommendations: A LIME-based approach. *Diagnostics (Basel)*, *13*(16), 2681. doi:10.3390/diagnostics13162681 PMID:37627940

Xu, C., Yang, J., Lai, H., Gao, J., Shen, L., & Yan, S. (2019). UP-CNN: Un-pooling augmented convolutional neural network. *Pattern Recognition Letters*, *119*, 34–40. doi:10.1016/j.patrec.2017.08.007

Xu, L., Yan, S., Chen, X., & Wang, P. (2019). Motion Recognition Algorithm Based on Deep Edge-Aware Pyramid Pooling Network in Human–Computer Interaction. *IEEE Access : Practical Innovations, Open Solutions*, *7*, 163806–163813. doi:10.1109/ACCESS.2019.2952432

Xu, X., Jiang, X., Ma, C., Du, P., Li, X., Lv, S., Yu, L., Ni, Q., Chen, Y., Su, J., Lang, G., Li, Y., Zhao, H., Liu, J., Xu, K., Ruan, L., Sheng, J., Qiu, Y., Wu, W., ... Li, L. (2020). A Deep Learning System to Screen Novel Coronavirus Disease 2019 Pneumonia. *Engineering (Beijing)*, *6*(10), 1122–1129. doi:10.1016/j.eng.2020.04.010 PMID:32837749

Yadessa, A., Burkhardt, J., Bekele, E., Hundera, K., & Goldbach, H. (2020). The major factors influencing coffee quality in ethiopia: The case of wild arabica coffee (coffea arabica l.) from its natural habitat of southwest and southeast afromontane rainforests. *African Journal of Plant Science*, *14*(6), 213–230. doi:10.5897/AJPS2020.1976

Yang, F., & Gu, S. (2021). Industry 4.0, a revolution that requires technology and national strategies. *Complex & Intelligent Systems*, 7(3), 1311–1325. doi:10.100740747-020-00267-9

Yang, Y., Li, H. T., Han, Y. S., & Gu, H. Y. (2015). High resolution remote sensing image segmentation based on graph theory and fractal net evolution approach. *The International Archives of the Photogrammetry, Remote Sensing and Spatial Information Sciences*, *XL-7*(W4), 197–201. doi:10.5194/isprsarchives-XL-7-W4-197-2015

Yang, Z., & Liu, Z. (2020). The risk prediction of Alzheimer's disease based on the deep learning model of brain 18F-FDG positron emission tomography. *Saudi Journal of Biological Sciences*, 27(2), 659–665. doi:10.1016/j.sjbs.2019.12.004 PMID:32210685

Yiğit, A., & Işik, Z. (2020). Applying deep learning models to structural MRI for stage prediction of Alzheimer's disease. *Turkish Journal of Electrical Engineering and Computer Sciences*, 28(1), 196–210. doi:10.3906/elk-1904-172

Yoon, C. H., Torrance, R., & Scheinerman, N. (2022). Machine learning in medicine: Should the pursuit of enhanced interpretability be abandoned? *Journal of Medical Ethics*, *48*(9), 581–585. doi:10.1136/medethics-2020-107102 PMID:34006600

Youn, Kim, & Park. (2001). *A Microcode-based Memory BIST Implementing Modified March Algorithm.* IEEE.

Yu, C., & Helwig, E. J. (2022). The role of AI technology in prediction, diagnosis and treatment of colorectal cancer. *Artificial Intelligence Review*, 55(1), 1–21. doi:10.100710462-021-10034-y PMID:34248245

Yu, C., Li, J., Zhang, C., Li, H., He, R., & Lin, B. (2020). Maritime broadband communications: Applications, challenges and an offshore 5G-virtual MIMO paradigm. *Proc. IEEE ISPA/BDCloud/SocialCom/SustainCom'20*, 1286–1291. 10.1109/ISPA-BDCloud-SocialCom-SustainCom51426.2020.00190

Yu, K., Tan, L., Lin, L., Cheng, X., Yi, Z., & Sato, T. (2021). Deep-learning-empowered breast cancer auxiliary diagnosis for 5GB remote E-health. *IEEE Wireless Communications*, 28(3), 54–61. doi:10.1109/MWC.001.2000374

Zakareya, S., Izadkhah, H., & Karimpour, J. (2023). A New Deep-Learning-Based Model for Breast Cancer Diagnosis from Medical Images. *Diagnostics (Basel)*, *13*(11), 1944. doi:10.3390/diagnostics13111944 PMID:37296796

Zakaria. (2013). *Multiple and solid data background scheme for testing static single cell faults on SRAM memories.* Universiti Putra Malaysia.

Zakaria, N. A., Hassan, W. Z. W., Halin, I. A., Sidek, R. M., & Wen, X. (2013). Fault detection with optimum March test algorithm. *Journal of Theoretical and Applied Information Technology*, 47(1), 18–27.

Zeebaree, D. Q., Abdulazeez, A., Zebari, D. A., Haron, H., & Hamed, H. N. A. (2021). Multi-Level Fusion in Ultrasound for Cancer Detection Based on Uniform LBP Features. *Computers, Materials & Continua*, 66(3).

ZeilerM. D.FergusR. (2013). Stochastic Pooling for Regularization of Deep Convolutional Neural Networks. https://arxiv.org/abs/1301.3557

Zeru, A. (2006). *Diversity of arabica coffee populations in afromontane rainforests of Ethiopia in relation to colletotrichum kahawae and gibberella xylarioides* [Ph.D. dissertation]. Addis Ababa University.

Zhang, B., Xu, D., Zhang, H., & Li, M. (2019). STCS Lexicon: Spectral-Clustering-Based Topic-Specific Chinese Sentiment Lexicon Construction for social Networks. *IEEE Transactions on Computational Social Systems*, 6(6), 2–10. doi:10.1109/TCSS.2019.2941344

Zhang, Q., Yang, L. T., Chen, Z., & Li, P. (2018). A survey on deep learning for big data. *Information Fusion*, *42*, 146–157. doi:10.1016/j.inffus.2017.10.006

ZhangX.ZhouX.LinM.SunJ. (2017). ShuffleNet: An Extremely Efficient Convolutional Neural Network for Mobile Devices. https://arxiv.org/abs/1707.01083

Zhao, L., Chen, K., Song, J., Zhu, X., Sun, J., Caulfield, B., & Namee, B. M. (2021). Academic Performance Prediction Based on Multisource, Multifeature Behavioral Data. *IEEE Access : Practical Innovations, Open Solutions*, *9*, 5453–5465. doi:10.1109/ACCESS.2020.3002791

Zhao, L., Chen, Y., & Schaffner, D. W. (2001). Comparison of logistic regression and linear regression in modeling percentage data. *Applied and Environmental Microbiology*, *67*(5), 2129–2135. doi:10.1128/AEM.67.5.2129-2135.2001 PMID:11319091

Zhao, W., & Cao, Y. (2006). New Generation of Predictive Technology Model for Sub-45nm Early Design Exploration. *IEEE Transactions on Electron Devices*, *53*(11), 2816–2823. doi:10.1109/TED.2006.884077

Zhao, W., Zhong, Z., Xie, X., Yu, Q., & Liu, J. (2020). Relation Between Chest CT Findings and Clinical Conditions of Coronavirus Disease (COVID-19) Pneumonia: A Multicenter Study. *AJR. American Journal of Roentgenology*, *214*(5), 1072–1077. doi:10.2214/AJR.20.22976 PMID:32125873

Zhou, L.-Q., Wu, X.-L., Huang, S.-Y., Wu, G.-G., Ye, H.-R., Wei, Q., Bao, L.-Y., Deng, Y.-B., Li, X.-R., Cui, X.-W., & Dietrich, C. F. (2020). Lymph node metastasis prediction from primary breast cancer us images using deep learning. *Radiology*, *294*(1), 19–28. doi:10.1148/radiol.2019190372 PMID:31746687

Zhou, S. K., Le, H. N., Luu, K., Nguyen, H. V., & Ayache, N. (2021). Deep reinforcement learning in medical imaging: A literature review. *Medical Image Analysis*, *73*, 102193. doi:10.1016/j.media.2021.102193 PMID:34371440

Zhuang, X. D., Tian, T., Liao, L. Z., Dong, Y. H., Zhou, H. J., Zhang, S. Z., Chen, W. Y., Du, Z. M., Wang, X. Q., & Liao, X. X. (2022). Deep phenotyping and prediction of long-term cardiovascular disease: Optimized by machine learning. *The Canadian Journal of Cardiology*, *38*(6), 774–782. doi:10.1016/j.cjca.2022.02.008 PMID:35157988

Žižek, S. Š., Mulej, M., & Potočnik, A. (2021). The Sustainable Socially Responsible Society: Well-Being Society 6.0. *Sustainability (Basel)*, *13*(16), 9186. doi:10.3390u13169186

Zou, Q., Sun, X., Liu, P., & Singhal, A. (2020). An approach for detection of advanced persistent threat attacks. *Computer*, *53*(12), 92–96. doi:10.1109/MC.2020.3021548

Zvarevashe, K., & Olugbara, O. (2020). *Ensemble Learning of Hybrid Acoustic Features for Speech Emotion Recognition*. Academic Press.

About the Contributors

Puvvadi Baby Maruthi received Master of Computer Applications degree from JNTU Ananthapur in 2010, and the Ph.D degree from Sri Padmavati Mahila VisvaVidyalayam, Tirupati, in 2019. She is currently working as an Assistant Professor in Sri Venkateswara College of Engineering, Tirupati. She got gold medal in R programming in NPTEL. Her research interests include soft computing, information security, digital image processing and Machine Learning.

Amit Kumar Tyagi is working as Assistant Professor, at National Institute of Fashion Technology, 110016, New Delhi, India. Previously he has worked as Assistant Professor (Senior Grade 2), and Senior Researcher at Vellore Institute of Technology (VIT), Chennai Campus, 600127, Chennai, Tamilandu, India for the period of 2019-2022. He received his Ph.D. Degree (Full-Time) in 2018 from Pondicherry Central University, 605014, Puducherry, India. About his academic experience, he joined the Lord Krishna College of Engineering, Ghaziabad (LKCE) for the periods of 2009-2010, and 2012-2013. He was an Assistant Professor and Head- Research, Lingaya's Vidyapeeth (formerly known as Lingaya's University), Faridabad, Haryana, India for the period of 2018-2019. His supervision experience includes more than 10 Masters' dissertations and one PhD thesis. He has contributed to several projects such as "AARIN" and "P3- Block" to address some of the open issues related to the privacy breaches in Vehicular Applications (such as Parking) and Medical Cyber Physical Systems (MCPS). He has published over 150 papers in refereed high impact journals, conferences and books.

* * *

Senthil Kumar Arumugam is an Associate Professor of the Professional Studies department, CHRIST (Deemed to be University), Bangalore. His areas of specialisation are Accounting, Human Resource Management, E-Commerce, and Finance. He secured a PhD degree in Commerce from Bharathiar University, India, in 2014. He also qualified for UGC-NET in 2012. He completed his M.Phil in Commerce from Madurai Kamaraj University in 2003 and his M.Phil in Computer Science from Periyar University in 2007. He has 23 years of teaching, research, and admin experience in the Commerce and Computer Application fields. He is the author of 65 research articles, including one edited book and 9 book chapters. He is an Executive editorial member in six peer-reviewed journals. He has guided more than 100 students' research projects in UG/PG/M.Phil Programmes and currently guiding four PhD research scholars.

Abidemi Elizabeth Awujoola is a highly regarded Biology Teacher with more than fifteen years of experience teaching in the classroom. She holds a National Certificate in Education (NCE) in Biology/Chemistry from the Federal College of Education in Zaria, achieving an Upper Credit. Additionally, she completed her B.Tech in Biology Education with a Chemistry option at the Federal University of Technology in Minna, Nigeria, graduating with a second-class Upper Division. Currently, she is awaiting the External Assessment of her Master's defense in Biotechnology from the Nigerian Defence Academy's Postgraduate School.

Olalekan Awujoola is a seasoned Chief System Analyst Programmer for Nigerian Defence academy with over two decades of experience. His expertise encompasses a broad spectrum of skills acquired through dedicated work in the field. His passion for academics has no limit, has he acquired the following degrees. National certificate in Education (NCE) Mathematics/Physics from Institute of Education Ahmadu Bello University. Zaria, Bachelor of Technology (B.Tech) Mathematics with Computer science from Federal University of Technology, Masters of Science (M.sc) Computer Science from Ahmadu Bello University Zaria, Master of Science (Msc) Nuclear and Radiation Physics from Nigerian Defence Academy, Master of Science (M.sc) Information Technology from National Open University of Nigeria. He is currently on the verge of completing his PhD in Computer Science, eagerly anticipating the final stages of external assessment. He is deeply rooted in the pragmatic application of machine learning, Deep Learning, Artificial Intelligence, Internet of Things and Computer Vision an enthusiasm reflected in specializing in Python-based machine learning. This commitment is further evidenced by his contributions to an array of research papers and book chapters. In terms of technical proficiency, he excel in developing and implementing machine learning models to tackle real-world challenges and his favourable toolkit includes proficiency in Python, R, and Java, along with hands-on experience with TensorFlow, PyTorch, and scikit-learn frameworks.

Aryan Chopra is currently an undergraduate student at the Vellore Institite of Technology Vellore, where he is studying Information Technology. Prior to attending university, he completed his high school education at Delhi Public School, Gurugram. During his time at high school, Aryan has taken advantage of every opportunity to learn more about his chosen field and he was also a part of the school editorial board, being responsible for publishing the school year book. He is fond of reading and also published a fiction fantasy book on Kindle store in the year 2019. As an undergraduate student, his research interests include Machine Learning and Artificial Intelligence. In his spare time, he enjoys playing badminton and spending time with family and friends.

Theophilus Enem earned his Ph.D. from Babcock University, Ilisan Remo, Ogun State, Nigeria. With extensive experience teaching computer science at the university level, he holds the position of Senior Lecturer and currently serves as the head of the Department of Cyber at the Air Force Institute of Technology, located at the Nigerian Air Force Base in Kaduna, Nigeria.

Mohammad Gouse Galety has been working in CS since 1999. He is now a Professor in the CS department of Samarkand International University of Technology, Samarkand, Uzbekistan. He holds two PhDs in web mining and image processing of CS and two master's degrees in computers. The first master's degree in computer applications and the second in computer science. His research interests span computer and information science, mainly web mining, IoT, and AI. He (co)author of more than 50 journal papers and international conference proceedings indexed by Springer, Scopus, four patents, and five books. He is a Fellow of the IEEE. As of 2022, Google Scholar reports over 280 citations to his work. Since 1999, he has served in different national and international organizations like Sree Vidyanikethan Degree College, India; Emeralds Degree College, Tirupati, India; Brindavan College of Engineering, India; Kuwait Educational Center, Kuwait, Ambo University, Ethiopia; Debre Berhan University, Ethiopia, Lebanese French University, Erbil, Iraq, CUE, Erbil, Iraq. He teaches undergraduate and postgraduate students several courses on computer science and information technology/science engineering.

Belsini GladShiya V. is an Assistant Professor, Agurchand Manmull Jain College. She has received her Ph.D. from VISTAS, Chennai. Her research include Machine Learning, Predictive analytics and Big data. She has published two books, book chapters and Scopus indexed papers and presented papers in national and international conferences.

Ali Hussen is from Werabe University, Institute of Technology, Department of Information Systems.

Suma K. G. is working as an Associate Professor in the Department of Computer Science and Engineering, VIT-AP, India. She has received her Ph.D. degree from Anna University Chennai, INDIA in 2017. Her research areas include Image Processing, Medical Imaging, Machine Learning and Soft Computing. She carried several administrative roles in academics. She has won Young Women Engineer from IET in the year of 2020. She has published several Scopus and SCI indexed Journal publications, Book chapters, and attended national and international conferences and won prizes. She has 2 national/international patents.

Aditya Modi was born in Gorakhpur, Uttar Pradesh and attended high school at Little Flower School. He is currently an undergraduate student in information technology at Vellore Institute of Technology . Aditya 's research interests include natural language processing and machine learning. In his spare time, Aditya enjoys reading, playing cricket, and watching sci-fy movies.

Seid Mohammed received his diploma degree from the Informatics faculty of the Hawassa University, Sidama, Ethiopia in 2015. From 2015 to 20216 he was a Graduate Assistant II in the Mizan-Tepi University at south western Ethiopia. From 2017 to 2019 he was learn Master degree in the Jimma Institute of Technology at Jimma University and return back to Mizan Tepi university serves until 2021 with entitle lecturer. Since 2021 he is with Werabe University as instructor and researcher. His research interest includes technology and applications, Information retrieval, opinion mining, language and with technology, Security and optical telecommunication.

Sudhir Kumar Mohapatra received his PhD degree in Computer Science and Engineering with a specialization in Machine Learning for Software Testing. His research interest includes Application of Machine Learning in Software Testing and in Medical Image Diagnosis. He published research papers on testing, machine learning and cloud computing in reputable journals. He worked in different research projects from AASTU and AICTE. He is a regular reviewer of journal published by IEEE, Springer, Elsevier, Willy, Taylor and Francis, Hindawi.

Kanchan Naithani received her Ph.D. in the department of Computer Science & Engineering (CSE) from H.N.B. Garhwal University (A Central University) Srinagar Garhwal, Uttarakhand, India in Year 2023. She completed M.Tech in Computer Science and Engineering from G. B. Pant Engineering Institute of Technology, Ghurdauri, Pauri, Uttarakhand, India (2018) and B. Tech in Computer Science and Engineering from Graphic Era Hill University, Dehradun India (2016). Currently, she is working as an Assistant Professor in the School of Computing Science and Engineering (SCSE), Galgotias University, Greater Noida, Gautam Budha Nagar, Uttar Pradesh-203201 (India). She has authored and co-author more than 10 national and international journal publications, book chapters, and conference articles. Her research interests focus on Artificial Intelligence, Machine Learning, Sentiment Analysis, and Natural Language Processing. Dr. Kanchan is a member of ACM, CSI, ISTE. She is also a guest editorial board member and a reviewer for many international journals.

S. Selva Nidhyananthan received his Ph.D Degree from Anna University, Chennai, Tamil Nadu, India. He is currently working as Associate Professor, Senior Grade with the Department of Electronics and Communication Engineering. His current research interest includes Signal and Speech Processing, Image Processing, Internet of Things.

Francisca Nonyelum Ogwueleka is a Professor of Computer Science in the Faculty of Science, Nigerian Defence Academy, Kaduna. She holds a Ph.D from Nnamdi Azikiwe University,(2008). She was the Head of Department of Computer Science (2012-2015) and Director of ICT (2012-2014). She is the Dean of Military Science and Interdisciplinary Studies (2017 to date). She is a member of Computer Professionals Registration Council of Nigeria (CPN), Nigerian Computer Society (NCS), and Association for Computing Machinery (ACM). Her current research is on Big Data and Cyber Security.

Srinivas Prasad is Professor in the Department of Computer Science and Engineering, GITAM University, Visakhapatnam A.P., INDIA .He has 31 years of industry, teaching and research experience in India and USA. Dr Prasad has more than 40 publications in refereed journals, four patents, three books published and several more books were edited to his credit. His research interests span both Software engineering and Data Science.

Aswathy Ravikumar is a Research Associate at the Vellore Institute of Technology. A passionate AI/ ML Associate consultant with both industry and nine years of teaching experience at graduate and postgraduate levels. An enthusiast in the domains of artificial intelligence and data science, with numerous publications and projects and an excellent academic track record. Her research interest includes Distributed Deep Learning, Big Data and Accelerating Deep Learning performance using an HPC environment.

Santhi Selvaraj received her Post Graduate from Anna University, Chennai, Tamil Nadu, India. She is currently working as Assistant Professor, Senior Grade with the Department of Computer Science and Engineering. Her current research interest includes Text Mining, Sentiment Analysis, Recommendation Systems.

Brijendra Singh received Ph.D from VIT, Vellore, Tamilnadu, India. He is an Assistant Professor (Senior) in the School of Information Technology and Engineering at VIT University Vellore, Tamilnadu,

India. His research interests includes Health Informatics, Soft Computing Techniques, Artificial Intelligence, Rough Set and Knowledge Representations.

Harini Sriraman is an Associate Professor with Vellore Institute of Technology. She has more than 13 years of teaching experience. Her research interest includes Distributed and Parallel computing, Accelerating Deep Learning performance using HPC environment, Hardware based Domain Specific Acceleration and Energy efficient and sustainable computing. OrCID: Web of Science ResearcherID: AAB-4513-2019.

Gurram Sunitha is a professor of AI & ML, School of Computing, Mohan Babu University, Tirupati, India. Her research interests include Data Mining, Spatio-Temporal Analytics, Internet of Things and Artificial Intelligence. She has 9 patents and 3 books published to her credit. She has published around 30 papers in reputed journals and conferences. She has been serving as reviewer for several journals; and has served on the program committees and co-chaired for various international conferences.

Shrikant Tiwari (Senior Member, IEEE) was born in Karuwa Village, Maihar, Madhya Pradesh, India in 15th Aug. 1983. He received his Ph.D. in the Department of Computer Science & Engineering (CSE) from the Indian Institute of Technology (Banaras Hindu University), Varanasi (India) in 2012 and M. Tech. in Computer Science and Technology from the University of Mysore (India) in 2009. Currently, he is working as an Associate Professor in the School of Computing Science and Engineering (SCSE), Galgotias University, Greater Noida, Gautam Budha Nagar, Uttar Pradesh-203201 (India). He has authored and co-author more than 50 national and international journal publications, book chapters, and conference articles. He has five patents filed to his credit. His research interests include machine learning, deep learning, computer vision, medical image analysis, pattern recognition, and biometrics. Dr. Tiwari is a FIETE and member of ACM, IET, CSI, ISTE, IAENG, SCIEI. He is also a guest editorial board member and a reviewer for many international journals of repute.

Rati Kailash Prasad Tripathi is currently working as an Assistant Professor at Assam Central University, Silchar, Assam, India. She received her M. Pharm. (2011) and Ph.D. (2016) degrees from the Indian Institute of Technology, Banaras Hindu University, Varanasi (India); where she specialized in Pharmaceutical Chemistry with peculiar interest in synthetic medicinal chemistry, computational chemistry and molecular modelling. She has to her credit many scientific publications in journals of international repute. She has also authored 02 books and several book chapters. She is also a recipient of several research grants and prestigious awards like Senior Research Fellowship from the Indian Council of Medical Research, Government of India and Shri C. Subramaniam Award for Excellence in Character from Bhartiya Vidya Bhavan, Mumbai. She is an active member of many scientific Indian associations viz. Indian Pharmacy Graduates' Association (IPGA) and The Association of Pharmaceutical Teachers of India (APTI). She has also mentored several graduate, post graduate and PhD students. She also serves as an editorial board member and reviewer for many international journals of repute.

Celestine Ozoemenam Uwa is a faculty member in the Department of Computer Science at the Nigerian Defence Academy. He earned a BSc in Computer Science, an MSc in Computer Science, and an MSc in Mathematics. Currently, he is a dedicated research student specializing in the fields of AI and IoT.

Kishor Sonti V. J. K. is a professor with over 19 years of teaching, administrative and research experience. An outstanding performer awardee and received twice the best faculty award for professional excellence and commitment. International exposure with expertise in video content creation and a recipient of Erasmus plus grant. Active researcher with 42 publications in peer-reviewed journals, 2 patents published and one filed, supervising 5 research scholars (1 received Doctorate), authored 9 book chapters, a book and a monograph. A successful record in administrative abilities as a student development coordinator actively involved in steering, planning and in the implementation of student development activities and in student affairs. A motivational speaker, innovation ambassador, institution innovation council convener and serving as Mentor of Change as selected by NITI Aayog, Govt. of India for schools towards educational and societal transformation.

Index

U

Underfitting 73

V

Vanishing Gradient Problem 74, 85, 87-88
View of Society and Industry 374

X

X-Rays 112-113, 119, 177, 231

Recommended Reference Books

IGI Global's reference books are available in three unique pricing formats:
Print Only, E-Book Only, or Print + E-Book.

Order direct through IGI Global's Online Bookstore at
www.igi-global.com or through your preferred provider.

ISBN: 9781799884552
EISBN: 9781799884576
© 2022; 394 pp.
List Price: US$ **270**

ISBN: 9781799897101
EISBN: 9781799897125
© 2022; 335 pp.
List Price: US$ **250**

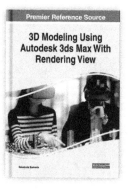

ISBN: 9781668441398
EISBN: 9781668441411
© 2022; 291 pp.
List Price: US$ **270**

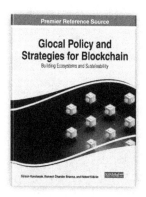

ISBN: 9781668441534
EISBN: 9781668441558
© 2023; 335 pp.
List Price: US$ **270**

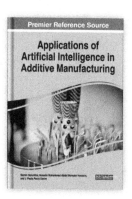

ISBN: 9781799885160
EISBN: 9781799885184
© 2022; 240 pp.
List Price: US$ **270**

ISBN: 9781799887638
EISBN: 9781799887652
© 2022; 306 pp.
List Price: US$ **270**

Do you want to stay current on the latest research trends, product announcements, news, and special offers?
Join IGI Global's mailing list to receive customized recommendations, exclusive discounts, and more.
Sign up at: **www.igi-global.com/newsletters.**

Publisher of Timely, Peer-Reviewed Inclusive Research Since 1988

www.igi-global.com   Sign up at www.igi-global.com/newsletters   f facebook.com/igiglobal   t twitter.com/igiglobal   in linkedin.com/igiglobal

Ensure Quality Research is Introduced to the Academic Community

Become an Evaluator for IGI Global Authored Book Projects

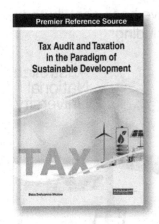

Premier Reference Source

Tax Audit and Taxation in the Paradigm of Sustainable Development

Premier Reference Source

Controlling Epidemics With Mathematical and Machine Learning Models

Premier Reference Source

School-Museum Relationships and Teaching Social Sciences in Formal Education

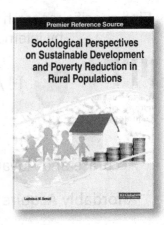

Premier Reference Source

Sociological Perspectives on Sustainable Development and Poverty Reduction in Rural Populations

The overall success of an authored book project is dependent on quality and timely manuscript evaluations.

Applications and Inquiries may be sent to:
development@igi-global.com

Applicants must have a doctorate (or equivalent degree) as well as publishing, research, and reviewing experience. Authored Book Evaluators are appointed for one-year terms and are expected to complete at least three evaluations per term. Upon successful completion of this term, evaluators can be considered for an additional term.

If you have a colleague that may be interested in this opportunity, we encourage you to share this information with them.

Easily Identify, Acquire, and Utilize Published Peer-Reviewed Findings in Support of Your Current Research

IGI Global OnDemand

Purchase Individual IGI Global OnDemand Book Chapters and Journal Articles

For More Information:
www.igi-global.com/e-resources/ondemand/

Browse through 150,000+ Articles and Chapters!

Find specific research related to your current studies and projects that have been contributed by international researchers from prestigious institutions, including:

- Accurate and Advanced Search
- Affordably Acquire Research
- Instantly Access Your Content
- Benefit from the InfoSci Platform Features

"*It really provides* **an excellent entry into the research literature of the field.** *It presents a manageable number of* **highly relevant sources** *on topics of interest to a wide range of researchers. The sources are* **scholarly, but also accessible** *to 'practitioners'.*"

- Ms. Lisa Stimatz, MLS, University of North Carolina at Chapel Hill, USA

Interested in Additional Savings?

Subscribe to

IGI Global OnDemand *Plus*

Learn More

Acquire content from over 128,000+ research-focused book chapters and 33,000+ scholarly journal articles for as low as US$ 5 per article/chapter (original retail price for an article/chapter: US$ 37.50).

7,300+ E-BOOKS.
ADVANCED RESEARCH.
INCLUSIVE & AFFORDABLE.

IGI Global
PUBLISHER of TIMELY KNOWLEDGE

IGI Global e-Book Collection

- **Flexible Purchasing Options** (Perpetual, Subscription, EBA, etc.)
- Multi-Year Agreements with **No Price Increases** Guaranteed
- **No Additional Charge** for Multi-User Licensing
- No Maintenance, Hosting, or Archiving Fees
- Continually Enhanced & Innovated **Accessibility Compliance Features** (WCAG)

Handbook of Research on Digital Transformation, Industry Use Cases, and the Impact of Disruptive Technologies
ISBN: 9781799877127
EISBN: 9781799877141

Handbook of Research on New Investigations in Artificial Life, AI, and Machine Learning
ISBN: 9781799886860
EISBN: 9781799886877

Handbook of Research on Future of Work and Education
ISBN: 9781799882756
EISBN: 9781799882770

Research Anthology on Physical and Intellectual Disabilities in an Inclusive Society (4 Vols.)
ISBN: 9781668435427
EISBN: 9781668435434

Innovative Economic, Social, and Environmental Practices for Progressing Future Sustainability
ISBN: 9781799895909
EISBN: 9781799895923

Applied Guide for Event Study Research in Supply Chain Management
ISBN: 9781799889694
EISBN: 9781799889717

Mental Health and Wellness in Healthcare Workers
ISBN: 9781799888130
EISBN: 9781799888147

Clean Technologies and Sustainable Development in Civil Engineering
ISBN: 9781799898108
EISBN: 9781799898122

Request More Information, or Recommend the IGI Global e-Book Collection to Your Institution's Librarian

For More Information or to Request a Free Trial, Contact IGI Global's e-Collections Team: eresources@igi-global.com | 1-866-342-6657 ext. 100 | 717-533-8845 ext. 100

Are You Ready to
Publish Your Research ?

IGI Global offers book authorship and editorship opportunities across 11 subject areas, including business, computer science, education, science and engineering, social sciences, and more!

Benefits of Publishing with IGI Global:

- Free one-on-one editorial and promotional support.

- Expedited publishing timelines that can take your book from start to finish in less than one (1) year.

- Choose from a variety of formats, including Edited and Authored References, Handbooks of Research, Encyclopedias, and Research Insights.

- Utilize IGI Global's eEditorial Discovery® submission system in support of conducting the submission and double-blind peer review process.

- IGI Global maintains a strict adherence to ethical practices due in part to our full membership with the Committee on Publication Ethics (COPE).

- Indexing potential in prestigious indices such as Scopus®, Web of Science™, PsycINFO®, and ERIC – Education Resources Information Center.

- Ability to connect your ORCID iD to your IGI Global publications.

- Earn honorariums and royalties on your full book publications as well as complimentary content and exclusive discounts.

Join Your Colleagues from Prestigious Institutions, Including:

Learn More at: www.igi-global.com/publish

or Contact IGI Global's Aquisitions Team at: acquisition@igi-global.com

Individual Article & Chapter Downloads
US$ 29.50/each

Easily Identify, Acquire, and Utilize Published Peer-Reviewed Findings in Support of Your Current Research

- Browse Over *170,000+ Articles & Chapters*
- *Accurate & Advanced* Search
- Affordably Acquire *International Research*
- *Instantly Access* Your Content
- Benefit from the *InfoSci® Platform Features*

THE UNIVERSITY
of NORTH CAROLINA
at CHAPEL HILL

" *It really provides an excellent entry into the research literature of the field. It presents a manageable number of highly relevant sources on topics of interest to a wide range of researchers. The sources are scholarly, but also accessible to 'practitioners'.* "

- Ms. Lisa Stimatz, MLS, University of North Carolina at Chapel Hill, USA

Interested in Additional Savings?

Subscribe to

IGI Global OnDemand *Plus*

Learn More

Acquire content from over 137,000+ research-focused book chapters and 33,000+ scholarly journal articles for as low as US$ 5 per article/chapter (original retail price for an article/chapter: US$ 29.50).

Printed in the United States
by Baker & Taylor Publisher Services

Printed in the United States
by Baker & Taylor Publisher Services